Categorical Data Analysis

Using the
SAS® System

Maura E. Stokes
Charles S. Davis
Gary G. Koch

Comments or Questions?

The authors assume complete responsibility for the technical accuracy of the content of this book. If you have any questions about the material in this book, please write to the authors at this address:

SAS Institute Inc.
Books by Users
Attn: Maura E. Stokes, Charles S. Davis, and Gary G. Koch
SAS Campus Drive
Cary, NC 27513

If you prefer, you can send e-mail to sasbbu@sas.com with "comments for Maura E. Stokes, Charles S. Davis, and Gary G. Koch" as the subject line, or you can fax the Books by Users program at (919) 677-4444.

The correct bibliographic citation for this manual is as follows: Stokes, Maura E., Davis, Charles S., Koch, Gary G., *Categorical Data Analysis Using the SAS® System*, Cary, NC: SAS Institute Inc., 1995. 499 pp.

Categorical Data Analysis Using the SAS® System

Copyright © 1995 by SAS Institute Inc., Cary, NC, USA.

ISBN 1-55544-219-6

1st printing, July 1995
2nd printing, July 1996
3rd printing, October 1997

Note that text corrections may have been made at each printing.

Table of Contents

Acknowledgements

We are grateful to David DeLong for his encouragement and support in the development of this project.

We are very appreciative of numerous colleagues who reviewed these chapters. Their comments and suggestions have greatly improved the book. We thank Sonia Davis, William Duckworth II, Suzanne Edwards, Stuart Gansky, Greg Goodwin, Wendy Greene, Duane Hayes, Allison Kinkead, Lisa LaVange, Antonio Pedroso-de-Lima, Annette Sanders, David Schlotzhauer, Catherine Tangen, Lisa Tomasko, and Greg Weier.

Donna Sawyer and Hanna Schoenrock edited this book. Valerie Woodrow and William Duckworth II assisted in its indexing.

Ginny Matsey designed the cover.

Chapter 1
Introduction

Chapter Table of Contents

Chapter 1
Introduction

1.1   Overview

Data analysts often encounter response measures that are categorical in nature; their outcomes reflect categories of information rather than the usual interval scale. Frequently, categorical data are presented in tabular form, known as contingency tables. Categorical data analysis is concerned with the analysis of categorical response measures, regardless of whether any accompanying explanatory variables are also categorical or are continuous. This book discusses hypothesis testing strategies for the assessment of association in contingency tables and sets of contingency tables. It also discusses various modeling strategies available for describing the nature of the association between a categorical outcome measure and a set of explanatory variables.

An important consideration in determining the appropriate analysis of categorical variables is their scale of measurement. Section 1.2 describes the various scales and illustrates them with data sets used in later chapters. Another important consideration is the sampling framework that produced the data; it determines the possible analyses and the possible inferences. Section 1.3 describes the typical sampling frameworks and their ramifications. Section 1.4 introduces the various analysis strategies discussed in this book and describes how they relate to one another. It also discusses the target populations generally assumed for each type of analysis and what types of inferences you are able to make to them. Section 1.5 reviews how the SAS System handles contingency tables and other forms of categorical data. Finally, Section 1.6 provides a guide to the material in the book for various types of readers, including indications of the difficulty level of the chapters.

1.2   Scale of Measurement

The scale of measurement of a categorical response variable is a key element in choosing an appropriate analysis strategy. By taking advantage of the methodologies available for the particular scale of measurement, you can choose a well-targeted strategy. If you do not take the scale of measurement into account, you may choose an inappropriate strategy that could lead to erroneous conclusions. Recognizing the scale of measurement and using it properly are very important in categorical data analysis.

Categorical response variables can be

- dichotomous
- discrete counts
- nominal
- ordinal
- grouped survival times

Dichotomous responses are those that have two possible outcomes—most often they are yes and no. Did the subject develop the disease ? Did the voter cast a ballot for the Democratic or Republican candidate ? Did the student pass the exam ? For example, the objective of a clinical trial for a new medication for colds is whether patients obtained relief from their pain-producing ailment. Consider Table 1.1, which is analyzed in Chapter 2, "The 2 × 2 Table."

Table 1.1   Respiratory Outcomes

Treatment	Favorable	Unfavorable	Total
Placebo	16	48	64
Test	40	20	60

The placebo group contains 64 patients, and the test medication group contains 60 patients. The columns contain the information concerning the categorical response measure: 40 patients in the Test group had a favorable response to the medication, and 20 subjects did not. The outcome in this example is thus dichotomous, and the analysis investigates the relationship between the response and the treatment.

Frequently, categorical data responses represent more than two possible outcomes, and often these possible outcomes take on some inherent ordering. Such response variables have an *ordinal* scale of measurement. Did the new school curriculum produce little, some, or high enthusiasm among the students ? Does the water exhibit low, medium, or high hardness ? In the former case, the order of the response levels is clear, but there is no clue as to the relative distances between the levels. In the latter case, there is a possible distance between the levels: medium might be twice the hardness of low, and high might be three times the hardness of low. Sometimes the distance is even clearer: a 50% potency dose versus a 100% potency dose versus a 200% potency dose. All three cases are examples of ordinal data.

An example of an ordinal measure occurs in data displayed in Table 1.2, which is analyzed in Chapter 8, "Logistic Regression I: Dichotomous Response." A clinical trial investigated a treatment for rheumatoid arthritis. Male and female patients were given either the active treatment or a placebo; the outcome measured was whether they showed marked, some, or no improvement at the end of the clinical trial. The analysis uses a modeling technique called the proportional odds model to assess the relationship between the response variable and gender and treatment.

Table 1.2 Arthritis Data

Sex	Treatment	Improvement			Total
		Marked	Some	None	
Female	Active	16	5	6	27
Female	Placebo	6	7	19	32
Male	Active	5	2	7	14
Male	Placebo	1	0	10	11

Note that categorical response variables can often be managed in different ways. You could combine the Marked and Some columns in Table 1.2 to produce a dichotomous outcome: No Improvement versus Improvement. Grouping categories is often done during an analysis if the resulting dichotomous response is also of interest.

Categorical response variables sometimes contain *discrete counts*. Instead of falling into categories that are labeled (yes, no) or (low, medium, high), the outcomes are numbers themselves. Was the litter size 1, 2, 3, 4, or 5 members ? Did the house contain 1, 2, 3, or 4 air conditioners ? While the usual strategy would be to analyze the mean count, the assumptions required for the standard linear model are often not met with discrete counts that have small range; the counts may not be distributed normally.

For example, researchers examining respiratory disease in children visited children in different regions two times and determined whether they showed symptoms of respiratory illness. The response measure was whether the children exhibited symptoms in 0, 1, or 2 periods. Table 1.3 contains these data, which are analyzed in Chapter 12, "Weighted Least Squares."

Table 1.3 Colds in Children

Sex	Residence	Periods with Colds			Total
		0	1	2	
Female	Rural	45	64	71	180
Female	Urban	80	104	116	300
Male	Rural	84	124	82	290
Male	Urban	106	117	87	310

The table represents a crossclassification of gender, residence, and number of periods with colds. The analysis is concerned with modeling mean colds as a function of gender and residence.

If you have more than two outcome categories, and there is no inherent ordering to the categories, you have a nominal measurement scale. Which of four candidates did you vote for in the town council election ? Do you prefer the beach, mountains, or lake for a vacation ? There is no underlying scale for such outcomes and no apparent way in which to order them.

Consider Table 1.4, which is analyzed in Chapter 5, "The $s \times r$ Table." Residents in one town were asked their political party affiliation and their neighborhood. Researchers were interested in whether political affiliation could predict neighborhood. Unlike ordinal response levels, the classifications Bayside, Highland, Longview, and Sheffeld lie on no conceivable underlying scale. However, you can still assess whether there is association in the table, which is done in Chapter 5.

Table 1.4   Distribution of Parties in Neighborhoods

Party	Neighborhood			
	Bayside	Highland	Longview	Sheffeld
Democrat	221	160	360	140
Independent	200	291	160	311
Republican	208	106	316	97

Finally, another type of response variable in categorical data analysis is one that represents *grouped survival times*. With survival data, you are tracking the number of patients with certain outcomes (possibly death) over time. Often, the times of the condition are grouped together so that the response variable represents the number of patients who fail during a specific time interval. Such data are called *grouped survival times*. For example, the data displayed in Table 1.5 are from Chapter 15, ''Categorized Time-to-Event Data.'' A clinical condition is treated with an active drug for some patients and with a placebo for others. The response categories are whether there are recurrences, no recurrences, or whether the patients left the study. The entries correspond to the time intervals 0–1 years, 1–2 years, and 2–3 years, which make up the rows of the table.

Table 1.5   Life Table Format for Clinical Condition Data

Controls				
Interval	No Recurrences	Recurrences	Withdrawals	At Risk
0–1 Years	50	15	9	74
1–2 Years	30	13	7	50
2–3 Years	17	7	6	30
Active				
Interval	No Recurrences	Recurrences	Withdrawals	At Risk
0–1 Years	69	12	9	90
1–2 Years	59	7	3	69
2–3 Years	45	10	4	59

1.3   Sampling Frameworks

Categorical data arise from different sampling frameworks. The nature of the sampling framework determines the assumptions that can be made for the statistical analyses and in turn influences the type of analysis that can be applied. The sampling framework also determines the type of inference that is possible. Study populations are limited to target populations, those populations to which inferences can be made, by assumptions justified by the sampling framework.

Generally, data fall into one of three sampling frameworks: historical data, experimental data, and sample survey data. Historical data are observational data, which means that the study population has a geographic or circumstantial definition. These may include all the occurrences of an infectious disease in a multicounty area, the children attending a particular elementary school, or those persons appearing in court during a specified time period. Highway safety data concerning injuries in motor vehicles is another example of historical data.

Experimental data are drawn from studies that involve the random allocation of subjects to different treatments of one sort or another. Examples include studies where types of fertilizer are applied to agricultural plots and studies where subjects are administered different dosages of drug therapies. In the health sciences, experimental data may include patients randomly administered a placebo or treatment for their medical condition.

In sample survey studies, subjects are randomly chosen from a larger study population. Investigators may randomly choose students from their school IDs and survey them about social behavior; national health care studies may randomly sample Medicare users and investigate physician utilization patterns. In addition, some sampling designs may be a combination of sample survey and experimental data processes. Researchers may randomly select a study population and then randomly assign treatments to the resulting study subjects.

The major difference in the three sampling frameworks described in this section is the use of randomization to obtain them. Historical data involve no randomization, and so it is often difficult to assume that they are representative of a convenient population. Experimental data have good coverage of the possibilities of alternative treatments for the restricted protocol population, and sample survey data have very good coverage of some larger population.

Note that the unit of randomization can be a single subject or a cluster of subjects. In addition, randomization may be applied to subsets, called strata or blocks, with equal or unequal probabilities. In sample surveys, this can lead to more complicated designs, such as stratified random samples, or even multistage cluster random samples. In experimental design studies, such considerations lead to repeated measurements (or split-plot) studies.

1.4   Overview of Analysis Strategies

Categorical data analysis strategies can be classified into those that are concerned with hypothesis testing and those that are concerned with modeling. Many questions about a categorical data set can be answered by addressing a specific hypothesis concerning association. Such hypotheses are often investigated with randomization methods. In addition to making statements about association, you also may want to describe the nature of the association in the data set. Statistical modeling techniques using maximum likelihood estimation or weighted least squares estimation are employed to describe this variation in terms of a parsimonious statistical model.

Most often the hypothesis of interest is whether association exists between the rows of a contingency table and its columns. The only assumption that is required is randomized allocation of subjects, either through the study design (experimental design) or through the hypothesis itself (necessary for historical data). In addition, particularly for the use of historical data, you often want to control for other explanatory variables that may have influenced the observed outcomes.

1.4.1 Randomization Methods

Table 1.1, the respiratory outcomes data, contains information obtained as part of a randomized allocation process. The hypothesis of interest is whether there is an association between treatment and outcome. For these data, the randomization is accomplished by the study design.

Table 1.6 contains data from a similar study. The main difference is that the study was conducted in two medical centers. The hypothesis of association is whether there is an association between treatment and outcome, controlling for any effect of center.

Table 1.6   Respiratory Improvement

Center	Treatment	Yes	No	Total
1	Test	29	16	45
1	Placebo	14	31	45
Total		43	47	90
2	Test	37	8	45
2	Placebo	24	21	45
Total		61	29	90

Chapter 2, "The 2×2 Table," is primarily concerned with the association in 2×2 tables; in addition, it discusses measures of association, that is, statistics designed to evaluate the strength of the association. Chapter 3, "Sets of 2×2 Tables," discusses the investigation of association in sets of 2×2 tables. When the table of interest has more than two rows and two columns, the analysis is further complicated by the consideration of scale of measurement. Chapter 4, "Sets of $2 \times r$ and $s \times 2$ Tables," considers the assessment of association in sets of tables where the rows (columns) have more than two levels.

Chapter 5 describes the assessment of association in the general $s \times r$ table, and Chapter 6, "Sets of $s \times r$ Tables," describes the assessment of association in sets of $s \times r$ tables. The investigation of association in tables and sets of tables is further discussed in Chapter 7, "Nonparametric Methods," which discusses traditional nonparametric tests that have counterparts among the strategies for analyzing contingency tables.

1.4.2 Modeling Strategies

Often, you are interested in describing the variation in your data with a statistical model. In the continuous data setting, you frequently fit a model to the expected mean response. However, with categorical outcomes, there are a variety of response functions that you can model. Depending on the response function that you choose, you may use weighted least squares or maximum likelihood methods to estimate the model parameters.

Perhaps the most common response function modeled for categorical data is the logit. If you have a dichotomous response and represent the proportion of those subjects with an event (versus no event) outcome as p, then the logit can be written

$$\log\left(\frac{p}{1-p}\right)$$

Logistic regression is a modeling strategy that relates the logit for a set of explanatory variables to a linear model. One of its benefits is that estimates of odds ratios, important measures of association, can be obtained from the parameter estimates. Maximum likelihood estimation is used to provide those estimates.

Chapter 8, "Logistic Regression I: Dichotomous Response," discusses logistic regression for a dichotomous outcome variable. Chapter 9, "Logistic Regression II: Polytomous Response," discusses logistic regression for the situation where there are more than two outcomes for the response variable. Logits called generalized logits can be analyzed when the outcomes are nominal. And logits called cumulative logits can be analyzed when the outcomes are ordinal. Chapter 10, "Conditional Logistic Regression," describes a specialized form of logistic regression that is appropriate when the data are highly stratified or arise from matched case-control studies.

In logistic regression, the objective is to predict a response outcome from a set of explanatory variables. However, sometimes you simply want to describe the structure of variation in a set of variables for which there are no obvious outcome or predictor variables. This occurs frequently for sociological studies. The loglinear model is a traditional modeling strategy for categorical data and is appropriate for describing the variation in such a set of variables. It is closely related to logistic regression, and the parameters in a loglinear model are also estimated with maximum likelihood estimation. Chapter 14, "Loglinear Models," discusses the loglinear model, including several typical applications.

Some application areas have features that lead to special statistical techniques being developed for them. One of these areas for categorical data is bioassay analysis. Bioassay is the process of determining the potency or strength of a reagent or stimuli based on the response it elicits in biological organisms. Logistic regression is a technique often applied in bioassay analysis, where its parameters take on specific meaning. Chapter 11, "Quantal Bioassay Analysis," discusses the use of categorical data methods for quantal bioassay.

Besides the logit, other useful response functions that can be modeled include proportions, means, and measures of association. Weighted least squares estimation is a method of analyzing response functions such as these, based on large sample theory. These methods are appropriate when you have sufficient sample size and when you have a randomly selected sample, either implicitly through study design or explicitly via assumptions concerning the representativeness of the data. Not only can you model a variety of useful functions, but weighted least squares estimation also provides a useful framework for the analysis of repeated categorical measurements, particularly those limited to a small number of repeated values.

Chapter 12, "Weighted Least Squares," addresses modeling categorical data with weighted least squares methods, and Chapter 13, "Modeling Repeated Measurements Data," discusses these techniques as applied to the analysis of repeated measurements data. Also described in Chapter 13 is the use of generalized estimating equations in the analysis of repeated measurements.

Finally, another special application area for categorical data analysis is the analysis of grouped survival data. Chapter 15 discusses some features of survival analysis that are pertinent to grouped survival data, including how to model them using a model called the piecewise exponential model. Since the Poisson regression model is employed to fit this model, the chapter also provides an overview of Poisson regression.

1.5   Working with Tables in the SAS System

This section discusses some considerations of managing tables with the SAS System. If you are already familiar with the FREQ procedure, you may want to skip this section.

Many times, categorical data are presented to the researcher in the form of tables, and other times, they are presented in the form of case record data. SAS procedures can handle either type of data. In addition, many categorical data are ordinal, so that the order of the levels of the rows and columns takes on special meaning. There are numerous ways that you can specify a particular order to SAS procedures.

Consider the following SAS DATA step that inputs the data displayed in Table 1.1.

```
data respire;
   input treat $ outcome $ count ;
   cards;
   placebo f 16
   placebo u 48
   test    f 40
   test    u 20
   ;
proc freq;
   weight count;
   tables treat*outcome;
run;
```

The data set RESPIRE contains three variables: TREAT is a character variable containing values for treatment, OUTCOME is a character variable containing values for the outcome (f for favorable and u for unfavorable), and COUNT contains the number of observations that have the respective TREAT and OUTCOME values. Thus, COUNT effectively takes values corresponding to the cells of Table 1.1. The PROC FREQ statements request that a table be constructed using TREAT as the row variable and OUTCOME as the column variable. By default, PROC FREQ orders the values of the rows (columns) in alphanumeric order. The WEIGHT statement is necessary to tell the procedure that the data are count data, or frequency data; the variable listed in the WEIGHT statement contains the values of the count variable.

Output 1.1 contains the resulting frequency table.

Output 1.1   Frequency Table

```
              TABLE OF TREAT BY OUTCOME

          TREAT        OUTCOME

          Frequency|
          Percent  |
          Row Pct  |
          Col Pct  |f        |u        | Total
          ---------+--------+--------+
          placebo  |    16 |     48 |     64
                   | 12.90 | 38.71 | 51.61
                   | 25.00 | 75.00 |
                   | 28.57 | 70.59 |
          ---------+--------+--------+
          test     |    40 |     20 |     60
                   | 32.26 | 16.13 | 48.39
                   | 66.67 | 33.33 |
                   | 71.43 | 29.41 |
          ---------+--------+--------+
          Total         56       68      124
                      45.16    54.84   100.00
```

Suppose that a different sample produced the numbers displayed in Table 1.7.

Table 1.7   Respiratory Outcomes

Treatment	Favorable	Unfavorable	Total
Placebo	5	10	15
Test	8	20	28

These data may be stored in case record form, which means that each individual is represented by a single observation. You can also use this type of input with the FREQ procedure. The only difference is that the WEIGHT statement is not required.

The following statements create a SAS data set for these data and invoke PROC FREQ for case record data. The @@ symbol in the INPUT statement means that the data lines contain multiple observations.

```
data respire;
    input treat $ outcome $ @@ ;
    cards;
placebo f placebo f  placebo f
placebo f placebo f
placebo u placebo u  placebo u
placebo u placebo u  placebo u
placebo u placebo u  placebo u
placebo u
test    f test    f test    f
test    f test    f test    f
test    f test    f
test    u test    u test    u
test    u test    u test    u
test    u test    u test    u
test    u test    u test    u
```

```
test    u test    u  test    u
test    u test    u  test    u
test    u test    u
    ;
proc freq;
    tables treat*outcome;
run;
```

Output 1.2 displays the resulting frequency table.

Output 1.2   Frequency Table

```
            TABLE OF TREAT BY OUTCOME

        TREAT       OUTCOME

        Frequency|
        Percent  |
        Row Pct  |
        Col Pct  |f        |u       |  Total
        ---------+--------+--------+
        placebo  |     5 |     10 |     15
                 | 11.63 | 23.26 | 34.88
                 | 33.33 | 66.67 |
                 | 38.46 | 33.33 |
        ---------+--------+--------+
        test     |     8 |     20 |     28
                 | 18.60 | 46.51 | 65.12
                 | 28.57 | 71.43 |
                 | 61.54 | 66.67 |
        ---------+--------+--------+
        Total          13       30       43
                     30.23    69.77   100.00
```

In this book, the data are generally presented in count form.

When ordinal data are considered, it becomes quite important to ensure that the levels of the rows and columns are sorted correctly. By default, the data are going to be sorted alphanumerically. If this isn't suitable, then you need to alter the default behavior.

Consider the data displayed in Table 1.2. IMPROVE is the outcome variable, and the values marked, some, and none are listed in decreasing order. Suppose that the data set ARTHRIT is created with the following statements.

```
data arthrit;
   length treat $7. sex $6. ;
   input sex $ treat $ improve $ count @@ ;
   cards ;
female active  marked 16 female active  some 5 female active  none  6
female placebo marked  6 female placebo some 7 female placebo none 19
male   active  marked  5 male   active  some 2 male   active  none  7
male   placebo marked  1 male   placebo some 0 male   placebo none 10
;
run;
```

If you invoked PROC FREQ for this data set and used the default sort order, the levels of the columns would be ordered marked, none, and some, which would be incorrect. One

way to change this default sort order is to use the ORDER=DATA option in the PROC
FREQ statement. This specifies that the sort order is the same order in which the values
are encountered in the data set. Thus, since 'marked' comes first, it is first in the sort
order. Since 'some' is the second value for IMPROVE encountered in the data set, then it
is second in the sort order. And 'none' would be third in the sort order. This is the desired
sort order. The following PROC FREQ statements produce a table displaying the sort
order resulting from the ORDER=DATA option.

```
proc freq order=data;
    weight count;
    tables treat*improve;
run;
```

Output 1.3 displays the frequency table for the crossclassification of treatment and
improvement for these data; the values for IMPROVE are in the correct order.

Output 1.3   Frequency Table from ORDER=DATA option

```
                        TABLE OF TREAT BY IMPROVE

            TREAT       IMPROVE

            Frequency|
            Percent  |
            Row Pct  |
            Col Pct  |marked  |some    |none    | Total
            ---------+--------+--------+--------+
            active   |     21 |      7 |     13 |     41
                     |  25.00 |   8.33 |  15.48 |  48.81
                     |  51.22 |  17.07 |  31.71 |
                     |  75.00 |  50.00 |  30.95 |
            ---------+--------+--------+--------+
            placebo  |      7 |      7 |     29 |     43
                     |   8.33 |   8.33 |  34.52 |  51.19
                     |  16.28 |  16.28 |  67.44 |
                     |  25.00 |  50.00 |  69.05 |
            ---------+--------+--------+--------+
            Total          28       14       42       84
                        33.33    16.67    50.00   100.00
```

Other possible values for the ORDER= option include FORMATTED, which means sort
by the formatted values. The ORDER= option is also available with the CATMOD,
LOGISTIC, and GENMOD procedures. For information on the ORDER= option for the
FREQ procedure, refer to the *SAS/STAT User's Guide, Version 6, Fourth Edition*. This
option is used frequently in this book.

Often, you want to analyze sets of tables. For example, you may want to analyze the
crossclassification of treatment and improvement for both males and females. You do this
in PROC FREQ by using a three-way crossing of the variables SEX, TREAT, and
IMPROVE.

```
proc freq order=data;
    weight count;
    tables sex*treat*improve / nocol nopct;
run;
```

The two rightmost variables in the TABLES statement determine the rows and columns of the table, respectively. Separate tables are produced for the unique combination of values of the other variables in the crossing. Since SEX has two levels, one table is produced for males and one table is produced for females. If there were four variables in this crossing, with the two variables on the left having two levels each, then four tables would be produced, one for each unique combination of the two leftmost variables in the TABLES statement.

Note also that the options NOCOL and NOPCT are included. These options suppress the printing of column percentages and cell percentages, respectively. Since generally you are interested in row percentages, these options are often specified in the code displayed in this book.

Output 1.4 contains the two tables produced with the preceding statements.

Output 1.4   Producing Sets of Tables

```
              TABLE 1 OF TREAT BY IMPROVE
                 CONTROLLING FOR SEX=female

        TREAT      IMPROVE

        Frequency|
        Row Pct  |marked  |some    |none    |  Total
        ---------+--------+--------+--------+
        active   |    16  |     5  |     6  |    27
                 |  59.26 |  18.52 |  22.22 |
        ---------+--------+--------+--------+
        placebo  |     6  |     7  |    19  |    32
                 |  18.75 |  21.88 |  59.38 |
        ---------+--------+--------+--------+
        Total          22       12       25       59


              TABLE 2 OF TREAT BY IMPROVE
                 CONTROLLING FOR SEX=male

        TREAT      IMPROVE

        Frequency|
        Row Pct  |marked  |some    |none    |  Total
        ---------+--------+--------+--------+
        active   |     5  |     2  |     7  |    14
                 |  35.71 |  14.29 |  50.00 |
        ---------+--------+--------+--------+
        placebo  |     1  |     0  |    10  |    11
                 |   9.09 |   0.00 |  90.91 |
        ---------+--------+--------+--------+
        Total           6        2       17       25
```

This section reviewed some of the basic table management necessary for using the FREQ procedure. Other related options are discussed in the appropriate chapters.

1.6   Using This Book

This book is intended for a variety of audiences, including novice readers with some statistical background (solid understanding of regression analysis), those readers with substantial statistical background, and those readers with background in categorical data analysis. Therefore, not all of this material will have the same importance to all readers. Some chapters include a good deal of tutorial material, while others have a good deal of advanced material. This book is not intended to be a comprehensive treatment of categorical data analysis, so some topics are mentioned briefly for completeness and some other topics are emphasized because they are not generally well documented.

The data used in this book come from a variety of sources and represent a wide breadth of application. However, due to the biostatistical background of all three authors, there is a certain inevitable weighting of biostatistical examples. Most of the data come from practice, and the original sources are cited when this is true; however, due to confidentiality concerns and pedalogical requirements, some of the data are altered or created. However, they still represent realistic situations.

Chapters 2–4 are intended to be accessible to all readers, as is most of Chapter 5. Chapter 6 is an integration of Mantel-Haenszel methods at a more advanced level, but scanning it is probably a good idea for readers interested in the topic. In particular, the discussion about the analysis of repeated measurements data with extended Mantel-Haenszel methods is useful material for all readers comfortable with the Mantel-Haenszel technique.

Chapter 7 is a special interest chapter relating Mantel-Haenszel procedures to traditional nonparametric methods used for continuous data outcomes.

Chapters 8 and 9 on logistic regression are intended to be accessible to all readers, particularly Chapter 8. The last section of Chapter 8 describes the statistical methodology more completely for the advanced reader. Most of the material in Chapter 9 should be accessible to most readers. Chapter 10 is a specialized chapter that discusses conditional logistic regression and requires somewhat more statistical expertise. Chapter 11 discusses the use of logistic regression in analyzing bioassay data.

Chapter 12 discusses weighted least squares and is written at a somewhat higher statistical level than Chapters 8 and 9, but most readers should find this material useful, particularly the examples.

Chapters 13–15 discuss advanced topics and are necessarily written at a higher statistical level. Chapter 13 describes the analysis of repeated measurements data using weighted least squares and includes a section discussing the use of generalized estimating equations for repeated measurements data. The opening sections introduce repeated measurements analysis and discuss a basic example; this material is intended to be accessible to a wide range of readers. Chapter 14 discusses loglinear model analysis and Chapter 15 discusses the analysis of categorized time-to-event data.

This book describes statistical techniques and discusses their implementation with the SAS System. In some instances, statistics are computed by hand or other software is mentioned so that the methodological information presented is complete. All examples were executed with Release 6.10 of the SAS System; features new in that release are pointed out. A few features upcoming in Release 6.11 are also described.

Chapter 2
The 2 × 2 Table

Chapter Table of Contents

Chapter 2
The 2 × 2 Table

2.1 Introduction

The 2 × 2 contingency table is one of the most common ways to summarize categorical data. Categorizing patients by their favorable or unfavorable response to two different drugs, asking health survey participants whether they have regular physicians and regular dentists, and asking residents of two cities whether they desire more environmental regulations all result in data that can be summarized in a 2 × 2 table.

Generally, interest lies in whether there is an association between the row variable and the column variable that produce the table; sometimes there is further interest in describing the strength of that association. The data can arise from several different sampling frameworks, and the interpretation of the hypothesis of no association depends on the framework. Data in a 2 × 2 table can represent

- simple random samples from two groups that yield two independent binomial distributions for a binary response

  Asking residents from two cities whether they desire more environmental regulations is an example of this framework. This is a stratified random sampling setting, since the subjects from each city represent two independent random samples. Because interest lies in whether the proportion favoring regulation is the same for the two cities, the hypothesis of interest is the hypothesis of homogeneity. Is the distribution of the response the same in both groups ?

- a simple random sample from one group that yields a single multinomial distribution for the crossclassification of two binary responses

  Taking a random sample of subjects and asking whether they see both a regular physician and a regular dentist is an example of this framework. The hypothesis of interest is one of independence. Are having a regular dentist and having a regular physician independent of each other ?

- randomized assignment of patients to two equivalent treatments, resulting in the hypergeometric distribution

  This framework occurs when patients are randomly allocated to one of two drug treatments, and their response to that treatment is the binary outcome. Under the hypothesis that the effects of the two treatments are the same for each patient, a hypergeometric distribution applies to the response distributions for the two treatments. (A less frequent framework that produces data for the 2 × 2 table is the

Poisson distribution. Each count is considered to be the result of an independent Poisson process, and questions related to multiplicative effects in Poisson regression (discussed in Chapter 15) are addressed by testing the hypothesis of no association.)

Table 2.1 summarizes the information from a randomized clinical trial that compared two treatments (test, placebo) for a respiratory disorder.

Table 2.1   Respiratory Outcomes

Treatment	Favorable	Unfavorable	Total
Placebo	16	48	64
Test	40	20	60

The question of interest is whether the rates of favorable response for test (67 percent) and placebo (25 percent) are the same. You can address this question by investigating whether there is a statistical association between treatment and outcome. The null hypothesis is stated

H_0: There is no association between treatment and outcome.

There are several ways of testing this hypothesis; many of the tests are based on the chi-square statistic. Section 2.2 discusses these methods. However, sometimes the counts in the table cells are too small to meet the sample size requirements necessary for the chi-square distribution to apply, and exact methods based on the hypergeometric distribution are used to test the hypothesis of no association. Exact methods are discussed in Section 2.3.

In addition to testing the hypothesis concerning the presence of association, you may be interested in describing the association or gauging its strength. Section 2.4 discusses the estimation of the difference in proportions from 2 × 2 tables. Section 2.5 discusses measures of association, which assess strength of association, and Section 2.6 discusses measures called sensitivity and specificity, which are useful when the two responses correspond to two different methods for determining whether a particular disorder is present. Finally, 2 × 2 tables often display data for matched pairs, and Section 2.7 discusses McNemar's Test for assessing association for matched pairs data.

2.2   Chi-Square Statistics

Table 2.2 displays the generic 2 × 2 table, including row and column marginal totals.

Table 2.2   2 × 2 Contingency Table

Column	Row Levels		
Levels	1	2	Total
1	n_{11}	n_{12}	n_{1+}
2	n_{21}	n_{22}	n_{2+}
Total	n_{+1}	n_{+2}	n

Under the randomization framework that produced Table 2.1, the row marginal totals n_{1+} and n_{2+} are fixed since 60 patients were randomly allocated to one of the treatment groups and 64 to the other. The column marginal totals can be regarded as fixed under the null hypothesis of no treatment difference for each patient. Then, given that all of the marginal totals n_{1+}, n_{2+}, n_{+1}, and n_{+2} are fixed under the null hypothesis, the probability distribution from the randomized allocation of patients to treatment can be written

$$\Pr\{n_{ij}\} = \frac{n_{1+}!\,n_{2+}!\,n_{+1}!\,n_{+2}!}{n!\,n_{11}!\,n_{12}!\,n_{21}!\,n_{22}!}$$

which is the hypergeometric distribution. The expected value of n_{ij} is

$$E\{n_{ij}|H_0\} = \frac{n_{i+}n_{+j}}{n} = m_{ij}$$

and the variance is

$$V\{n_{ij}|H_0\} = \frac{n_{1+}n_{2+}n_{+1}n_{+2}}{n^2(n-1)} = v_{ij}$$

For a sufficiently large sample, n_{11} approximately has a normal distribution, which implies that

$$Q = \frac{(n_{11} - m_{11})^2}{v_{11}}$$

approximately has a chi-square distribution with one degree of freedom. It is the ratio of a squared difference from the expected value versus its variance, and such quantities follow the chi-square distribution when the variable is distributed normally. Q is often called the randomization chi-square. It doesn't matter how the rows and columns are arranged, Q takes the same value since

$$|n_{11} - m_{11}| = |n_{ij} - m_{ij}| = \frac{|n_{11}n_{22} - n_{12}n_{21}|}{n}$$

A related statistic is the Pearson chi-square statistic. This statistic is written

$$Q_P = \sum_{i=1}^{2}\sum_{j=1}^{2} \frac{(n_{ij} - m_{ij})^2}{m_{ij}} = \frac{n}{(n-1)}Q$$

If the cell counts are sufficiently large, Q_P is distributed as chi-square with one degree of freedom. As n grows large, Q_P and Q converge. A useful rule for determining adequate sample size for both Q and Q_P is that the expected value m_{ij} should exceed 5 for all of the cells (and preferably 10). While Q is discussed here in the framework of a randomized allocation of patients to two groups, Q and Q_P are also appropriate for investigating the hypothesis of no association for all of the sampling frameworks described previously.

The following PROC FREQ statements produce a frequency table and the chi-square statistics for the data in Table 2.1. The data are supplied in frequency, or count, form. An observation is supplied for each configuration of the values of the variables TREAT and OUTCOME. The variable COUNT holds the total number of observations that have that particular configuration. The WEIGHT statement tells the FREQ procedure that the data are in frequency form and names the variable that contains the frequencies.

The CHISQ option in the TABLES statement produces chi-square statistics.

```
data respire;
   input treat $ outcome $ count;
   cards;
   placebo f 16
   placebo u 48
   test    f 40
   test    u 20
   ;
proc freq;
   weight count;
   tables treat*outcome / chisq;
run;
```

Output 2.1 displays the data in a 2 × 2 table. With an overall sample size of 124, and all expected cell counts greater than 10, the sampling assumptions for the chi-square statistics are met. PROC FREQ prints out a warning message when more than twenty percent of the cells in a table have expected counts less than 5. (Note that you can specify the EXPECTED option in the TABLE statement to produce the expected cell counts along with the cell percentages.)

Output 2.1   Frequency Table

```
              TABLE OF TREAT BY OUTCOME

        TREAT       OUTCOME

        Frequency|
        Percent  |
        Row Pct  |
        Col Pct  |f        |u        |  Total
        ---------+--------+--------+
        placebo  |     16 |     48 |     64
                 |  12.90 |  38.71 |  51.61
                 |  25.00 |  75.00 |
                 |  28.57 |  70.59 |
        ---------+--------+--------+
        test     |     40 |     20 |     60
                 |  32.26 |  16.13 |  48.39
                 |  66.67 |  33.33 |
                 |  71.43 |  29.41 |
        ---------+--------+--------+
        Total          56       68      124
                    45.16    54.84   100.00
```

Output 2.2 contains the table with the chi-square statistics.

Output 2.2   Chi-Square Statistics

```
          STATISTICS FOR TABLE OF TREAT BY OUTCOME

     Statistic                     DF      Value        Prob
     -----------------------------------------------------------
     Chi-Square                     1      21.709       0.001
     Likelihood Ratio Chi-Square    1      22.377       0.001
     Continuity Adj. Chi-Square     1      20.059       0.001
     Mantel-Haenszel Chi-Square     1      21.534       0.001
     Fisher's Exact Test (Left)                       2.84E-06
                         (Right)                        1.000
                         (2-Tail)                     4.75E-06
     Phi Coefficient                       -0.418
     Contingency Coefficient                0.386
     Cramer's V                            -0.418

     Sample Size = 124
```

The randomization statistic Q is labeled "Mantel-Haenszel Chi-Square," and the Pearson chi-square Q_P is labeled "Chi-Square." Q has a value of 21.534 and $p = 0.001$; Q_P has a value of 21.709 and $p = 0.001$. Both of these statistics are clearly significant. There is a strong association between treatment and outcome such that the test treatment results in a more favorable response outcome than the placebo. The row percentages in Output 2.1 show that the test treatment resulted in 67 percent favorable response and the placebo treatment resulted in 25 percent favorable response.

Notice that the output also includes a statistic labeled "Likelihood Ratio Chi-Square." This statistic, often written Q_L, is asymptotically equivalent to Q and Q_P. The statistic Q_L is described later in chapters on modeling; it is not often used in the analysis of 2×2 tables. Some of the other statistics are discussed in the next section.

2.3   Exact Tests

Sometimes your data include small and zero cell counts. For example, consider the following data from a study on treatments for healing severe infections. A test treatment and a control are compared to determine whether the rates of favorable response are the same.

Table 2.3   Severe Infection Treatment Outcomes

Treatment	Favorable	Unfavorable	Total
Test	10	2	12
Control	2	4	6
Total	12	6	18

Obviously, the sample sizes requirements for the chi-square tests described in Section 2.2 are not met by these data. However, if you can consider the margins (12, 6, 12, 6) to be fixed, then you can assume that the data are distributed hypergeometrically and write

$$\Pr\{n_{ij}\} = \frac{n_{1+}!\,n_{2+}!\,n_{+1}!\,n_{+2}!}{n!\,n_{11}!\,n_{12}!\,n_{21}!\,n_{22}!}$$

The row margins may be fixed by the treatment allocation process; that is, subjects are randomly assigned to Test and Control. The column totals can be regarded as fixed by the null hypothesis; there are 12 patients with favorable response and 6 patients with unfavorable response, regardless of treatment. If the data are the result of a sample of convenience, you can still condition on marginal totals being fixed by addressing the null hypothesis that patients are interchangeable; that is, an individual patient is as likely to have a favorable response on Test as on Control.

Recall that a p-value is the probability of the observed data or more extreme data occurring under the null hypothesis. With Fisher's exact test, you determine the p-value for this table by summing the probabilities of the tables that are as likely or less likely, given the fixed margins. The following table includes all possible table configurations and their associated probabilities.

Table 2.4   Table Probabilities

Table Cell				
(1,1)	(1,2)	(2,1)	(2,2)	Probabilities
12	0	0	6	0.0001
11	1	1	5	0.0039
10	2	2	4	0.0533
9	3	3	3	0.2370
8	4	4	2	0.4000
7	5	5	1	0.2560
6	6	6	0	0.0498

To find the one-sided p-value, you sum the probabilities as small or smaller than those computed for the table observed, in the direction specified by the one-sided alternative. In this case, it would be those tables in which the Test treatment had the more favorable response, or

$$p = 0.0533 + 0.0039 + 0.0001 = 0.0573$$

To find the two-sided p-value, you sum all of the probabilities that are as small or smaller than that observed, or

$$p = 0.0533 + 0.0039 + 0.0001 + 0.0498 = 0.1071$$

Generally, you will be interested in the two-sided p-value. Note that when the row (or column) totals are nearly equal, the p-value for the two-sided Fisher's exact test is approximately twice the p-value for the one-sided Fisher's exact test. When the row (or column) totals are equal, the p-value for the two-sided Fisher's exact test is exactly twice the value of the p-value for the one-sided Fisher's exact test for the better treatment.

The following SAS code produces the 2 × 2 frequency table for Table 2.3. Specifying the CHISQ option also produces the Fisher's exact test for a 2 × 2 table. In addition, the ORDER=DATA option specifies that PROC FREQ orders the levels of the rows (columns) in the same order in which the values are encountered in the data set.

```
data severe;
   input treat $ outcome $ count;
```

```
      cards;
      Test     f 10
      Test     u 2
      Control  f 2
      Control  u 4
      ;
proc freq order=data;
      tables treat*outcome / chisq nocol;
      weight count;
run;
```

The NOCOL option suppresses the column percentages, as seen in Output 2.3.

Output 2.3   Frequency Table

```
              TABLE OF TREAT BY OUTCOME

        TREAT       OUTCOME

        Frequency|
        Percent  |
        Row Pct  |f        |u        | Total
        ---------+--------+--------+
        Test     |   10 |     2 |    12
                 | 55.56 | 11.11 | 66.67
                 | 83.33 | 16.67 |
        ---------+--------+--------+
        Control  |    2 |     4 |     6
                 | 11.11 | 22.22 | 33.33
                 | 33.33 | 66.67 |
        ---------+--------+--------+
        Total         12       6        18
                    66.67   33.33   100.00
```

Output 2.4 contains the chi-square statistics, including the exact test. Note that the sample size assumptions are not met for the chi-square tests: the warning beneath the table asserts that this is the case.

Output 2.4   Table Statistics

```
            STATISTICS FOR TABLE OF TREAT BY OUTCOME

     Statistic                      DF    Value      Prob
     --------------------------------------------------------
     Chi-Square                      1    4.500      0.034
     Likelihood Ratio Chi-Square     1    4.463      0.035
     Continuity Adj. Chi-Square      1    2.531      0.112
     Mantel-Haenszel Chi-Square      1    4.250      0.039
     Fisher's Exact Test (Left)                      0.996
                         (Right)                     0.057
                         (2-Tail)                    0.107
     Phi Coefficient                      0.500
     Contingency Coefficient              0.447
     Cramer's V                           0.500

     Sample Size = 18
     WARNING:  75% of the cells have expected counts less
               than 5. Chi-Square may not be a valid test.
```

Note that the SAS System produces both a left-tail and right-tail *p*-value for Fisher's exact test. The left-tail probability is the probability of all tables such that the (1,1) cell value is less than or equal to the one observed. The right-tail probability is the probability of all tables such that the (1,1) cell value is greater than or equal to the one observed. Thus, the one-sided *p*-value is the same as the right-tailed *p*-value in this case, since large values for the (1,1) cell correspond to better outcomes for Test treatment.

Both the two-sided *p*-value of 0.107 and the one-sided *p*-value of 0.057 are larger than the *p*-values associated with Q_P ($p = 0.034$) and Q ($p = 0.039$). Depending on your significance criterion, you may reach very different conclusions with these three test statistics. The sample size requirements for the chi-square distribution are not met with these data; hence the test statistics using this approximation are questionable. This example illustrates the usefulness of Fisher's exact test when the sample size requirements for the usual chi-square tests are not met.

The output also includes a statistic labeled the "Continuity Adj. Chi-Square"; this is the continuity-adjusted chi-square statistic suggested by Yates, which is intended to correct the Pearson chi-square statistic so that it more closely approximates Fisher's exact test. In this case, the correction produces a chi-square value of 2.531 with $p = 0.112$, which is certainly close to the two-sided Fisher's exact test value. However, many statisticians recommend that you should simply apply Fisher's exact test when the sample size requires it rather than try to approximate it. In particular, the continuity-corrected chi-square may be overly conservative for two-sided tests when the data are nonsymmetric, that is, the row (column) totals are very different, and the sample sizes are small.

Note that Fisher's exact test is always appropriate, even when the sample size is large.

2.4 Difference in Proportions

The previous sections have addressed the question of whether there is an association between the rows and columns of a 2 × 2 table. In addition, you may be interested in describing the association in the table. For example, once you have established that the proportions computed from a table are different, you may want to estimate their difference.

Consider the following table, which displays data from two independent groups:

Table 2.5   2 × 2 Contingency Table

	Yes	No	Total	Proportion Yes
Group 1	n_{11}	n_{12}	n_{1+}	$p_1 = n_{11}/n_{1+}$
Group 2	n_{21}	n_{22}	n_{2+}	$p_2 = n_{21}/n_{2+}$
Total	n_{+1}	n_{+2}	n	

If the two groups are simple random samples from populations with corresponding proportions "yes" as π_1 and π_2, you may be interested in estimating the difference between those proportions by $d = p_1 - p_2$. You can show that the expected value is

$$E\{p_1 - p_2\} = \pi_1 - \pi_2$$

and the variance is

$$V\{p_1 - p_2\} = \frac{\pi_1(1 - \pi_1)}{n_{1+}} + \frac{\pi_2(1 - \pi_2)}{n_{2+}}$$

for which an unbiased estimate is

$$v_d = \frac{p_1(1 - p_1)}{n_{1+} - 1} + \frac{p_2(1 - p_2)}{n_{2+} - 1}$$

A $100(1 - \alpha)$ percent confidence interval for $(\pi_1 - \pi_2)$ is written

$$d \pm \left\{ z_{\alpha/2}\sqrt{v_d} + \frac{1}{2}\left\{ \frac{1}{n_{1+}} + \frac{1}{n_{2+}} \right\} \right\}$$

where $z_{\alpha/2}$ is the $100(1 - \alpha/2)$ percentile of the standard normal distribution; this confidence interval is based on Fleiss (1981, p. 29).

For example, consider Table 2.6, which reproduces the data analyzed in Section 2.2. In addition to determining that there is a statistical association between treatment and response, you may be interested in estimating the difference between the rates of favorable response for the test and placebo treatments, including a 95 percent confidence interval.

Table 2.6   Respiratory Outcomes

Treatment	Favorable	Unfavorable	Total	Favorable Proportion
Placebo	16	48	64	0.250
Test	40	20	60	0.667
Total	56	68	124	0.452

The difference is $d = 0.667 - 0.25 = 0.417$, and the confidence interval is written

$$0.417 \pm \left\{ (1.96)\left[\frac{0.667(1 - 0.667)}{60 - 1} + \frac{0.25(1 - 0.25)}{64 - 1} \right]^{1/2} + \frac{1}{2}\left(\frac{1}{60} + \frac{1}{64} \right) \right\}$$
$$= 0.417 \pm 0.177$$

A related measure of association is the Pearson correlation coefficient. This statistic is proportional to the difference of proportions. Since the Pearson correlation coefficient is also proportional to $\sqrt{Q_P}$, this illustrates that Q_P is also proportional to the squared difference in proportions.

The Pearson correlation coefficient can be written

$$r = \left\{ (n_{11} - \frac{n_{1+}n_{+1}}{n})/\left[(n_{1+} - \frac{n_{1+}^2}{n})(n_{+1} - \frac{n_{+1}^2}{n}) \right]^{1/2} \right\}$$
$$= \left\{ (n_{11}n_{22} - n_{12}n_{21})/[(n_{1+}n_{2+}n_{+1}n_{+2})]^{1/2} \right\}$$
$$= [n_{1+}n_{2+}/n_{+1}n_{+2}]^{1/2}d$$
$$= (Q_P/n)^{1/2}$$

For the data in Table 2.6, r is computed as

$$r = [(60)(64)/(56)(68)]^{1/2}(0.417) = 0.419$$

2.5 Odds Ratio and Relative Risk

Measures of association are used to assess the strength of an association. There are numerous measures of association available for the contingency table, some of which are described in Chapter 5, "The $s \times r$ Table." For the 2×2 table, one measure of association is the *odds ratio*, and a related measure of association is the *relative risk*.

Consider Table 2.5. The *odds ratio* compares the odds of the yes proportion for Group 1 to the odds of the yes proportion for Group 2. It is computed as

$$OR = \frac{p_1/(1 - p_1)}{p_2/(1 - p_2)} = \frac{n_{11}n_{22}}{n_{12}n_{21}}$$

The odds ratio ranges from 0 to infinity. When OR is 1, there is no association between the row variable and the column variable. When OR is greater than 1, Group 1 is more likely than Group 2 to have the yes response; when OR is less than 1, Group 1 is less likely than Group 2 to have the yes response.

Define the *logit* for general p as

$$logit = log\left[\frac{p}{1 - p}\right]$$

If you take the log of the odds ratio,

$$
\begin{aligned}
f = log\{OR\} &= log\left\{\frac{p_1(1 - p_2)}{p_2(1 - p_1)}\right\} \\
&= log\{p_1/(1 - p_1)\} - log\{p_2/(1 - p_2)\}
\end{aligned}
$$

you see that the odds ratio can be written in terms of the difference between two logits. The logit is the function that is modeled in logistic regression. As you will see in Chapter 8, "Logistic Regression I: Dichotomous Response," the odds ratio and logistic regression are closely connected.

The estimate of the variance of f is

$$v_f = \left\{\frac{1}{n_{11}} + \frac{1}{n_{12}} + \frac{1}{n_{21}} + \frac{1}{n_{22}}\right\}$$

so a $100(1 - \alpha)$ confidence interval for OR can be written as

$$exp(f \pm z_{\alpha/2}\sqrt{v_f})$$

The odds ratio is a useful measure of association regardless of how the data are collected. However, it has special meaning for retrospective studies because it can be used to estimate a quantity called *relative risk*, which is commonly used in epidemiological work. The relative risk is the risk of developing a particular condition (often a disease) for one group compared to another group. For data collected prospectively, the relative risk is written

$$ RR = \frac{p_1}{p_2} $$

You can show that

$$ RR = OR \times \frac{\{1 + (n_{21}/n_{22})\}}{\{1 + (n_{11}/n_{12})\}} $$

or that OR approximates RR when n_{11} and n_{21} are small relative to n_{12} and n_{22}, respectively. This is called the *rare outcome assumption* . Usually, the outcome of interest needs to occur less than ten percent of the time for OR and RR to be similar. However, many times when the event under investigation is a relatively common occurrence, you are more interested in looking at the difference in proportions rather than the odds ratio or the relative risk.

For cross-sectional data, the quantity p_1/p_2 is called the *prevalence ratio*; it does not indicate risk since the disease and risk factor are assessed at the same time, but it does give you an idea of the prevalence of a condition in one group compared to another.

It is important to realize that the odds ratio can always be used as a measure of association, and that relative risk and the odds ratio as an estimator of relative risk have meaning for certain types of studies and require certain assumptions.

Table 2.7 contains data from a study on how general daily stress affects one's opinion on a proposed new health policy. Since information on stress level and opinion were collected at the same time, the data are cross-sectional.

Table 2.7   Opinions on New Health Policy

Stress	Favorable	Unfavorable	Total
Low	48	12	60
High	96	94	190

To produce the odds ratio and other measures of association from PROC FREQ, you specify the MEASURES option in the TABLES statement. The ORDER=DATA option is used in the PROC FREQ statement to produce a table that looks the same as that displayed in Table 2.7. Without this option, the row corresponding to high stress would come first and the row corresponding to low stress would come last.

```
data stress;
   input stress $ outcome $ count;
   cards;
   low  f 48
```

```
      low  u 12
      high f 96
      high u 94
      ;
  proc freq order=data;
      tables stress*outcome / chisq measures nocol nopct;
      weight count;
  run ;
```

Output 2.5 contains the resulting frequency table. Since the NOCOL and NOPCT options are specified, only the row percentages are printed. Eighty percent of the low stress group were favorable, while the high stress group was nearly evenly split between favorable and unfavorable.

Output 2.5   Frequency Table

```
                   TABLE OF STRESS BY OUTCOME

            STRESS         OUTCOME

            Frequency|
            Row Pct  |f        |u        | Total
            ---------+---------+---------+
            low      |    48 |      12 |     60
                     | 80.00 |   20.00 |
            ---------+---------+---------+
            high     |    96 |      94 |    190
                     | 50.53 |   49.47 |
            ---------+---------+---------+
            Total        144      106       250
```

Output 2.6 displays the chi-square statistics, measures of association, and a table labeled "Estimates of the Relative Risk (Row1/Row2)." The statistics Q and Q_P indicate a strong association, with values of 16.155 and 16.220, respectively. Note how close the values for these statistics are for a sample size of 250.

Measures of association such as Kendall's tau-b, the Pearson Correlation, Spearman Correlation, and uncertainty coefficients are listed in the second table printed. See Section 5.4 for more information about some of these measures.

The odds ratio value is listed beside "Case-Control" in the section labeled "Estimates of the Relative Risk (Row1/Row2)." The estimated OR is 3.917, which means that the odds of a favorable response are 3.917 times higher for those with low stress than those with high stress. The confidence intervals are labeled "Confidence Bounds" and are 95 percent confidence intervals by default. To change them, use the ALPHA= option in the TABLES statement.

The values listed for "Cohort (Col1 Risk)" and "Cohort (Col2 Risk)" are the estimates of relative risk for a cohort (prospective) study. Since these data are cross-sectional, you cannot estimate relative risk. However, the value 1.583 is the ratio of the prevalence of favorable opinions for the low stress group compared to the high stress group. (The value 0.404 is the prevalence ratio of the unfavorable opinions of the low stress group compared to the high stress group.)

Output 2.6   Table Statistics

```
           STATISTICS FOR TABLE OF STRESS BY OUTCOME

Statistic                    DF     Value       Prob
------------------------------------------------------------
Chi-Square                    1    16.220       0.001
Likelihood Ratio Chi-Square   1    17.352       0.001
Continuity Adj. Chi-Square    1    15.035       0.001
Mantel-Haenszel Chi-Square    1    16.155       0.001
Fisher's Exact Test (Left)                      1.000
                    (Right)                     3.25E-05
                    (2-Tail)                    4.55E-05
Phi Coefficient                     0.255
Contingency Coefficient             0.247
Cramer's V                          0.255


Statistic                          Value        ASE
------------------------------------------------------------
Gamma                               0.593       0.115
Kendall's Tau-b                     0.255       0.055
Stuart's Tau-c                      0.215       0.049

Somers' D C|R                       0.295       0.063
Somers' D R|C                       0.220       0.050

Pearson Correlation                 0.255       0.055
Spearman Correlation                0.255       0.055

Lambda Asymmetric C|R               0.000       0.000
Lambda Asymmetric R|C               0.000       0.000
Lambda Symmetric                    0.000       0.000

Uncertainty Coefficient C|R         0.051       0.023
Uncertainty Coefficient R|C         0.063       0.028
Uncertainty Coefficient Symmetric   0.056       0.025


           Estimates of the Relative Risk (Row1/Row2)

                                          95%
Type of Study          Value       Confidence Bounds
------------------------------------------------------------
Case-Control           3.917       1.958       7.837
Cohort (Col1 Risk)     1.583       1.310       1.913
Cohort (Col2 Risk)     0.404       0.239       0.684
```

Table 2.8 contains data that concern respiratory illness. Two groups having the same symptoms of respiratory illness were selected via simple random sampling: one group was treated with a test treatment, and one group was treated with a placebo. This is an example of a cohort study, since the comparison groups were chosen before the responses were measured. They are considered to come from independent binomial distributions.

Table 2.8   Respiratory Improvement

Treatment	Yes	No	Total
Test	29	16	45
Placebo	14	31	45

In order to produce chi-square statistics, odds ratios, and relative risk measures for these data, the following statements are submitted. The ALL option has the same action as specifying both the CHISQ and the MEASURES options (and the CMH option, discussed in Chapter 3).

```
data respire;
   input treat $ outcome $ count;
   cards;
   test     yes   29
   test     no    16
   placebo  yes   14
   placebo  no    31
   ;
proc freq order=data;
   tables treat*outcome / all nocol nopct;
   weight count;
run ;
```

For these data, $Q = 9.908$ and $Q_P = 10.020$. Clearly, there is a strong association between treatment and improvement.

Output 2.7   Table Statistics

```
       STATISTICS FOR TABLE OF TREAT BY OUTCOME

   Statistic                    DF    Value      Prob
   --------------------------------------------------
   Chi-Square                    1    10.020     0.002
   Likelihood Ratio Chi-Square   1    10.216     0.001
   Continuity Adj. Chi-Square    1     8.728     0.003
   Mantel-Haenszel Chi-Square    1     9.908     0.002
   Fisher's Exact Test (Left)                    1.000
                       (Right)               1.46E-03
                       (2-Tail)              2.92E-03
   Phi Coefficient                     0.334
   Contingency Coefficient             0.317
   Cramer's V                          0.334
```

Output 2.8 displays the estimates of relative risk and the odds ratio (other measures of association produced by the ALL option are not displayed here). Two versions of the relative risk are supplied: one is the relative risk of the attribute corresponding to the first column, or the risk of improvement. The column 2 risk is the risk of no improvement. The relative risk for improvement is 2.071, with a 95 percent confidence interval of (1.274, 3.367).

Note that if these data had been obtained retrospectively, the odds ratio couldn't be used as an estimate of the relative risk since the proportions with improvement are 0.36 and 0.69. The rare outcome assumption isn't satisfied.

Output 2.8   Odds Ratio and Relative Risk

```
            Estimates of the Relative Risk (Row1/Row2)

                                              95%
         Type of Study          Value    Confidence Bounds
         --------------------------------------------------
         Case-Control           4.013     1.668      9.656
         Cohort (Col1 Risk)     2.071     1.274      3.367
         Cohort (Col2 Risk)     0.516     0.333      0.801
```

2.6   Sensitivity and Specificity

Some other measures frequently calculated for 2×2 tables are *sensitivity* and *specificity*. These measures are of particular interest when you are determining the efficacy of screening tests for various disease outcomes. Sensitivity is the true proportion of positive results that a test elicits when performed on subjects known to have the disease; specificity is the true proportion of negative results that a test elicits when performed on subjects known to be disease free.

Often, a standard screening method is used to determine whether disease is present and compared to a new test method. Table 2.9 contains the results of a study investigating a new screening device for a skin disease. The distributions for positive and negative results for the test method are assumed to result from simple random samples from the corresponding populations of persons with disease present and those with disease absent.

Table 2.9   Skin Disease Screening Test Results

Status	Test +	Test −	Total
Disease Present	52	8	60
Disease Absent	20	100	120

Sensitivity and specificity for these data are estimated by

$$\text{sensitivity} = (n_{11}/n_{1+}) \doteq \Pr(\text{Test} + |\text{disease present})$$

and

$$\text{specificity} = (n_{22}/n_{2+}) \doteq \Pr(\text{Test} - |\text{disease absent})$$

For these data, sensitivity = 52/60 = 0.867 and specificity = 100/120 = 0.833.

You may know the underlying percentage of those with and without the disease in a population of interest. You may want to estimate the proportion of subjects with the disease among those who have a positive test. You can determine these proportions with the use of Bayes theorem.

Suppose that the underlying prevalence of disease for an appropriate target population for these data is 15 percent. That is, 15 percent of the population have the disease and 85 percent do not. You can compute joint probabilities by multiplying the conditional probabilities by the marginal probabilities.

$$Pr(T, D) = Pr(T|D) \times Pr(D)$$

Table 2.10   How Test Should Perform in General Population

Status	Test +	Test −	Total
Disease Present	$0.867(.15) = 0.130$	$0.133(.15) = 0.020$	0.15
Disease Absent	$0.167(.85) = 0.142$	$0.833(.85) = 0.708$	0.85
Total	$0.130 + 0.142 = 0.272$	$0.020 + 0.708 = 0.728$	

The values in the row titled "Total" are Pr(Test +) and Pr(Test −), respectively. You can now determine the probability of those with the disease among those with a positive test:

$$Pr(D|T) = \frac{Pr(T, D)}{Pr(T)}$$

Thus, Pr (disease|Test +) = 0.130/0.272 = 0.478 and Pr(no disease|Test −) = 0.708/0.728 = 0.972. Refer to Fleiss (1981, p. 4) for more detail, including the calculation of false negative and false positive rates.

2.7   McNemar's Test

The 2 × 2 table often contains information collected from *matched pairs*, experimental units for which two related responses are made. The sampling unit is no longer one individual but a pair of related individuals, which could be two locations on the same individual or two occasions for the same individual. For example, in case-control studies, cases are often matched to controls on the basis of demographic characteristics; interest lies in determining whether there is a difference between control exposure to a risk factor and case exposure to the same risk factor. Other examples of matched pairs are left eye and right eye measurements, and husband and wife voting preferences. Measurements at two different time points can also be considered a matched pair, such as before and after measurements.

Data from a study on matched pairs are represented in Table 2.11. The n_{11} in the (1,1) cell means that n_{11} pairs responded yes for both Response 1 and Response 2; the n_{21} in the (2,1) cell means that n_{21} pairs responded yes for Response 1 and no for Response 2.

Table 2.11   Matched Pairs Data

	Response 1		
Response 2	Yes	No	Total
Yes	n_{11}	n_{12}	n_{1+}
No	n_{21}	n_{22}	n_{2+}
Total	n_{+1}	n_{+2}	n

The question of interest for such data is whether the proportion of pairs responding yes for Response 1 is the same as the proportion of pairs responding yes for Response 2. This question cannot be addressed with the chi-square tests of association of previous sections, since the cell counts represent pairs instead of individuals.

The question is whether

$$p_1 = \frac{n_{+1}}{n}$$

and

$$p_2 = \frac{n_{1+}}{n}$$

are the same. McNemar (1947) developed a chi-square test based on the binomial distribution to address this situation. He shows that only the off-diagonal elements are important in determining whether there is a difference in these proportions. The test statistic is written

$$Q_M = \frac{(n_{12} - n_{21})^2}{(n_{12} + n_{21})}$$

and is approximately chi-square with one degree of freedom.

Table 2.12 displays data collected by political science researchers who polled husbands and wives on whether they approved of one of their U.S. senators. The cell counts represent the number of pairs of husbands and wives who fit the configurations indicated by the row and column levels.

Table 2.12   State Senator Approval Ratings

Husband	Wife Approval		
Approval	Yes	No	Total
Yes	20	5	25
No	10	10	20
Total	30	15	45

McNemar's test is easy to compute by hand.

$$Q_M = \frac{(5 - 10)^2}{(5 + 10)} = 1.67$$

Compared to a chi-square distribution with 1 df, this statistic is clearly nonsignificant.

Beginning with Release 6.10 of the SAS System, the FREQ procedure computes McNemar's Test with the AGREE option in the TABLE statement (see Section 5.5 for other analyses available with the AGREE option for tables of other dimensions). The following SAS statements request McNemar's test.

```
data approval;
   input hus_resp $ wif_resp $ count;
   cards;
   yes yes 20
   yes no   5
   no yes   10
```

```
     no no    10
     ;
proc freq order=data;
   weight count;
   tables hus_resp*wif_resp / agree;
run;
```

Output 2.9 displays the output that is produced. $Q_M = 1.67$, the same value as computed previously.

Output 2.9   McNemar's Test

```
               TABLE OF HUS_RESP BY WIF_RESP

          HUS_RESP      WIF_RESP

          Frequency|
          Percent  |
          Row Pct  |
          Col Pct  |yes     |no      |  Total
          ---------+--------+--------+
          yes      |    20  |     5  |    25
                   | 44.44  | 11.11  | 55.56
                   | 80.00  | 20.00  |
                   | 66.67  | 33.33  |
          ---------+--------+--------+
          no       |    10  |    10  |    20
                   | 22.22  | 22.22  | 44.44
                   | 50.00  | 50.00  |
                   | 33.33  | 66.67  |
          ---------+--------+--------+
          Total         30       15       45
                      66.67    33.33   100.00


          STATISTICS FOR TABLE OF HUS_RESP BY WIF_RESP

                        McNemar's Test
                        --------------
          Statistic = 1.667       DF = 1        Prob = 0.197


                    Simple Kappa Coefficient
                    ------------------------
                                       95% Confidence Bounds
          Kappa = 0.308   ASE = 0.140        0.033    0.583


          Sample Size = 45
```

Chapter 3
Sets of 2×2 Tables

Chapter Table of Contents

Chapter 3
Sets of 2 × 2 Tables

3.1 Introduction

The respiratory data displayed in Table 2.8 in the previous chapter are only a subset of the data collected in the clinical trial. The study included patients at two medical centers and produced the complete data shown in Table 3.1. These data comprise a set of two 2 × 2 tables.

Table 3.1   Respiratory Improvement

Center	Treatment	Yes	No	Total
1	Test	29	16	45
1	Placebo	14	31	45
Total		43	47	90
2	Test	37	8	45
2	Placebo	24	21	45
Total		61	29	90

Investigators were interested in whether there were overall differences in rates of improvement; however, they were concerned that the patient populations at the two centers were sufficiently different that center needed to be accounted for in the analysis. One strategy for examining the association between two variables while adjusting for the effects of others is *stratified analysis*.

In general, the strata may represent explanatory variables, or they may represent research sites or hospitals in a multicenter study. Each table corresponds to one stratum; the strata are determined by the levels of the explanatory variables (one for each unique combination of the levels of the explanatory variables). The idea is to evaluate the association between the row variable and the response variable, while *adjusting*, or *controlling*, for the effects of the stratification variables. In some cases, the stratification results from the study design, such as in the case of a multicenter clinical trial; in other cases, it may arise from a prespecified poststudy stratification performed to control for the effects of certain explanatory variables that are thought to be related to the response variable.

The analysis of sets of tables addresses the same questions as the analysis of a single table: is there an association between the row and column variables in the tables and what is the strength of that association ? These questions are investigated with similar strategies involving chi-square statistics and measures of association such as the odds ratios; the key difference is that you are investigating overall association instead of the association in just one table.

3.2   Mantel-Haenszel Test

For the data in Table 3.1, interest lies in determining whether there is a difference in the favorable rates between Test and Placebo. Patients in both centers were randomized into two treatment groups, which induces independent hypergeometric distributions for the within-center frequencies under the hypothesis that treatments have equal effects for all patients. Thus, the distribution for the two tables is the product of these two hypergeometric distributions. You can induce the hypergeometric distribution via conditional distribution arguments when you have postrandomization stratification or when you have independent binomial distributions from simple random sampling.

Consider the following table as representative of q 2 × 2 tables, $h = 1, 2, \ldots, q$.

Table 3.2 hth 2 × 2 Contingency Table

	Yes	No	Total
Group 1	n_{h11}	n_{h12}	n_{h1+}
Group 2	n_{h21}	n_{h22}	n_{h2+}
Total	n_{h+1}	n_{h+2}	n_h

Under the null hypothesis of no treatment difference, the expected value of n_{h11} is

$$E\{n_{h11}|H_0\} = \frac{n_{h1+} n_{h+1}}{n_h} = m_{h11}$$

and its variance is

$$V\{n_{h11}|H_0\} = \frac{n_{h1+} n_{h2+} n_{h+1} n_{h+2}}{n_h^2 (n_h - 1)} = v_{h11}$$

One method for assessing the overall association of group and response, adjusting for the stratification factor, is the Mantel-Haenszel (1959) statistic.

$$
\begin{aligned}
Q_{MH} &= \frac{\left\{ \sum_{h=1}^{q} n_{h11} - \sum_{h=1}^{q} m_{h11} \right\}^2}{\sum_{h=1}^{q} v_{h11}} \\
&= \frac{\left\{ \sum_{h=1}^{q} (n_{h1+} n_{h2+}/n_h)(p_{h11} - p_{h21}) \right\}^2}{\sum_{h=1}^{q} v_{h11}}
\end{aligned}
$$

where $p_{hi1} = n_{hi1}/n_{hi+}$ is the proportion of subjects from the hth stratum and the ith group who have a favorable response. Q_{MH} approximately has the chi-square distribution with one degree of freedom when the combined row sample sizes ($\sum_{h=1}^{q} n_{hi+} = n_{+i+}$) are large, for example, greater than 30. This means that individual cell counts and table sample sizes may be small, so long as the overall row sample sizes are large. For the case of two tables, such as for Table 3.1, $q = 2$.

The Mantel-Haenszel strategy potentially removes the confounding influence of the explanatory variables that comprise the stratification and so provides a gain of power for detecting association by comparing like subjects with like subjects. In some sense, the strategy is similar to adjustment for blocks in a two-way analysis of variance for randomized blocks; it is also like covariance adjustment for a categorical explanatory variable.

Q_{MH} is effective for detecting patterns of association across q strata when there is a strong tendency to expect the predominant majority of differences $\{p_{h11} - p_{h21}\}$ to have the same sign. For this reason, Q_{MH} is often called an *average partial association statistic*. Q_{MH} may fail to detect association when the differences are in opposite directions and are of similar magnitude. Q_{MH} as formulated here is directed at the n_{h11} cell; however, it is invariant to whatever cell is chosen.

Mantel and Fleiss (1980) proposed a criterion for determining whether the chi-square approximation is appropriate for the distribution of the Mantel-Haenszel statistic for q strata:

$$\min\left\{\left[\sum_{h=1}^{q} m_{h11} - \sum_{h=1}^{q}(n_{h11})_L\right], \left[\sum_{h=1}^{q}(n_{h11})_U - \sum_{h=1}^{q} m_{h11}\right]\right\} > 5$$

where $(n_{h11})_L = \max(0, n_{h1+} - n_{h+2})$ and $(n_{h11})_U = \min(n_{h+1}, n_{h1+})$. The criterion specifies that the across-strata sum of expected values for a particular cell have a difference of at least 5 from both the minimum possible sum and the maximum possible sum of the observed values.

3.2.1 Respiratory Data Example

For the data in Table 3.1, there is interest in the association between treatment and respiratory outcome, after adjusting for the effects of the centers. The following DATA step puts all the respiratory data into the SAS data set RESPIRE.

```
data respire;
   input center treatmnt $ response $ count @@;
   cards;
1 test    y 29 1 test    n 16
1 placebo y 14 1 placebo n 31
2 test    y 37 2 test    n  8
2 placebo y 24 2 placebo n 21
;
```

Producing a Mantel-Haenszel analysis from PROC FREQ requires the specification of multi-way tables. The triple crossing CENTER*TREATMNT*RESPONSE specifies that the data consists of sets of two-way tables. The two rightmost variables TREATMNT and RESPONSE determine the rows and columns of the tables, respectively, and the variables to the left (CENTER) determine the stratification scheme. There will be one table for each value of CENTER. If there are more variables to the left of the variables determining the rows and columns of the tables, there will be strata for each unique combination of values for those variables.

The CHISQ option specifies that chi-square statistics be printed for each table. The CMH option requests the Mantel-Haenszel statistics for the stratified analysis; these are also called summary statistics. The ORDER=DATA option specifies that PROC FREQ order the rows and columns according to the order in which the variable values are encountered in the input data.

```
proc freq order=data;
   weight count;
   tables center*treatmnt*response /
      nocol nopct chisq cmh;
run;
```

Output 3.1 and Output 3.2 display the frequency tables and chi-square statistics for each center. For Center 1, the favorable rate for test treatment is 64 percent, versus 31 percent for placebo. For Center 2, the favorable rate for test treatment is 82 percent, versus 53 percent for the placebo. Q (the randomization statistic discussed in Chapter 2) for Center 1 is 9.908; Q for Center 2 is 8.503. With 1 df, both of these statistics are strongly significant.

Output 3.1   Table 1 Results

```
              TABLE 1 OF TREATMNT BY RESPONSE
                  CONTROLLING FOR CENTER=1

        TREATMNT        RESPONSE

        Frequency|
        Row Pct  |y          |n         |  Total
        ---------+--------+--------+
        test     |     29 |     16 |     45
                 |  64.44 |  35.56 |
        ---------+--------+--------+
        placebo  |     14 |     31 |     45
                 |  31.11 |  68.89 |
        ---------+--------+--------+
        Total          43       47       90


          STATISTICS FOR TABLE 1 OF TREATMNT BY RESPONSE
                  CONTROLLING FOR CENTER=1


        Statistic                   DF      Value       Prob
        ----------------------------------------------------------
        Chi-Square                   1      10.020      0.002
        Likelihood Ratio Chi-Square  1      10.216      0.001
        Continuity Adj. Chi-Square   1       8.728      0.003
        Mantel-Haenszel Chi-Square   1       9.908      0.002
        Fisher's Exact Test (Left)                      1.000
                            (Right)                     1.46E-03
                            (2-Tail)                    2.92E-03
        Phi Coefficient                      0.334
        Contingency Coefficient              0.317
        Cramer's V                           0.334

        Sample Size = 90
```

Output 3.2   Table 2 Results

```
                TABLE 2 OF TREATMNT BY RESPONSE
                   CONTROLLING FOR CENTER=2

     TREATMNT      RESPONSE

     Frequency|
     Row Pct  |y        |n        | Total
     ---------+--------+--------+
     test     |    37 |      8 |     45
              | 82.22 |  17.78 |
     ---------+--------+--------+
     placebo  |    24 |     21 |     45
              | 53.33 |  46.67 |
     ---------+--------+--------+
     Total         61       29      90


           STATISTICS FOR TABLE 2 OF TREATMNT BY RESPONSE
                   CONTROLLING FOR CENTER=2

     Statistic                   DF    Value     Prob
     --------------------------------------------------
     Chi-Square                   1    8.598     0.003
     Likelihood Ratio Chi-Square  1    8.832     0.003
     Continuity Adj. Chi-Square   1    7.326     0.007
     Mantel-Haenszel Chi-Square   1    8.503     0.004
     Fisher's Exact Test (Left)                  0.999
                        (Right)              3.14E-03
                        (2-Tail)             6.28E-03
     Phi Coefficient                   0.309
     Contingency Coefficient           0.295
     Cramer's V                        0.309

     Sample Size = 90
```

Following the information for the individual tables, PROC FREQ prints out a section titled "SUMMARY STATISTICS FOR TREATMNT BY RESPONSE, CONTROLLING FOR CENTER." This includes tables containing Mantel-Haenszel (MH) statistics, estimates of the common relative risk, and the Breslow-Day test for homogeneity of the odds ratio.

Output 3.3   Summary Statistics

```
      SUMMARY STATISTICS FOR TREATMENT BY RESPONSE
                 CONTROLLING FOR CENTER


      Cochran-Mantel-Haenszel Statistics (Based on Table Scores)

   Statistic   Alternative Hypothesis    DF      Value      Prob
   --------------------------------------------------------------
       1         Nonzero Correlation      1      18.411     0.000
       2         Row Mean Scores Differ   1      18.411     0.000
       3         General Association      1      18.411     0.000



       Estimates of the Common Relative Risk (Row1/Row2)
                                                    95%
   Type of Study   Method          Value    Confidence Bounds
   --------------------------------------------------------------
   Case-Control    Mantel-Haenszel  4.029    2.132      7.614
     (Odds Ratio)  Logit            4.029    2.106      7.707

   Cohort          Mantel-Haenszel  1.737    1.350      2.235
     (Col1 Risk)   Logit            1.676    1.294      2.170

   Cohort          Mantel-Haenszel  0.462    0.324      0.657
     (Col2 Risk)   Logit            0.474    0.326      0.688

   The confidence bounds for the M-H estimates are test-based.


       Breslow-Day Test for Homogeneity of the Odds Ratios


   Chi-Square =   0.000        DF =   1         Prob = 0.990

   Total Sample Size = 180
```

To find the value of Q_{MH}, read the value for any of the statistics in the table labeled "Cochran-Mantel-Haenszel Statistics": "Nonzero Correlation," "Row Mean Scores Differ," or "General Association." These statistics pertain to the situation where you have sets of tables with two or more rows or columns: they are discussed in Chapter 6, "Sets of $s \times r$ Tables." However, they all reduce to the MH statistic when you have 2×2 tables and use the CMH option in its default mode (that is, no SCORE= option specified).

Q_{MH} for these data is $Q_{MH} = 18.411$, with 1 df. This is clearly significant. The associations in the individual tables reinforce each other so that the overall association is stronger than that seen in the individual tables. There is a strong association between treatment and response, adjusting for center. The test treatment had a significantly higher favorable response rate than placebo.

The information in the rest of the summary statistics output is discussed later in this chapter. Note that for these data, the Mantel-Fleiss criterion is satisfied:

$$\sum_{h=1}^{2} m_{h11} = 21.5 + 30.5 = 52$$

$$\sum_{h=1}^{2}(n_{h11})_L = 0 + 16 = 16$$

$$\sum_{h=1}^{2}(n_{h11})_U = 43 + 45 = 88$$

so that $(52 - 16) \geq 5$ and $(88 - 52) \geq 5$.

3.2.2   Health Policy Data

Another data set discussed in Chapter 2 was also a subset of the complete data. The health policy data displayed in Table 2.7 comes from a study that included interviews with subjects from both rural and urban geographic regions. Table 2.7 displays the information from the rural region, and Table 3.3 includes the complete data.

Table 3.3   Health Policy Opinion Data

Residence	Stress	Favorable	Unfavorable	Total
Urban	Low	48	12	60
Urban	High	96	94	190
	Total	144	106	250
Rural	Low	55	135	190
Rural	High	7	53	60
	Total	62	188	250

If you ignored region and pooled these two tables, you would obtain Table 3.4.

Table 3.4   Pooled Health Policy Opinion Data

Stress	Favorable	Unfavorable	Total
Low	103	147	250
High	103	147	250
Total	206	294	500

There is clearly no association in this table; the proportions for favorable opinion are the same for low stress and high stress. For this table, Q_P and Q take the value 0, and the odds ratio is exactly 1. These data illustrate the need to consider the sampling framework in any data analysis. If you note the row totals in Table 3.3, you see that high stress subjects were oversampled for the urban region, and the low stress subjects were oversampled for the rural region. This oversampling causes the pooled table to take its form, even though favorable response is more likely for low stress persons in both regions.

The fact that a marginal table (pooled over residence) may exhibit an association completely different from the partial tables (individual tables for urban and rural) is known as *Simpson's Paradox* (Simpson 1951, Yule 1903).

The following statements request a Mantel-Haenszel analysis for the health policy data.

```
data stress;
   input region $ stress $ outcome $ count @@;
   cards;
urban low  f 48 urban  low  u  12
urban high f 96 urban  high u  94
rural low  f 55 rural  low  u 135
rural high f  7 rural  high u  53
;
proc freq order=data;
   weight count;
   tables region*stress*outcome / chisq cmh nocol nopct;
run;
```

Output 3.4 and Output 3.5 display the results for the individual tables. The urban region has a Q of 16.155 for the association of stress level and health policy opinion; the Q for the rural region is 7.272. The rate of favorable response is higher for the low stress group than for the high stress group in each region.

Output 3.4   Table 1 Results

```
                 TABLE 1 OF STRESS BY OUTCOME
                 CONTROLLING FOR REGION=urban

         STRESS       OUTCOME

         Frequency|
         Row Pct  |f        |u        |  Total
         ---------+---------+---------+
         low      |     48 |     12 |    60
                  |  80.00 |  20.00 |
         ---------+---------+---------+
         high     |     96 |     94 |   190
                  |  50.53 |  49.47 |
         ---------+---------+---------+
         Total         144      106      250


             STATISTICS FOR TABLE 1 OF STRESS BY OUTCOME
                    CONTROLLING FOR REGION=rural

         Statistic                  DF      Value        Prob
         -------------------------------------------------------
         Chi-Square                  1      16.220       0.000
         Likelihood Ratio Chi-Square 1      17.352       0.000
         Continuity Adj. Chi-Square  1      15.035       0.000
         Mantel-Haenszel Chi-Square  1      16.155       0.000
         Fisher's Exact Test (Left)                      1.000
                             (Right)                     3.25E-05
                             (2-Tail)                    4.55E-05
         Phi Coefficient                     0.255
         Contingency Coefficient             0.247
         Cramer's V                          0.255

         Sample Size = 250
```

Output 3.5   Table 2 Results

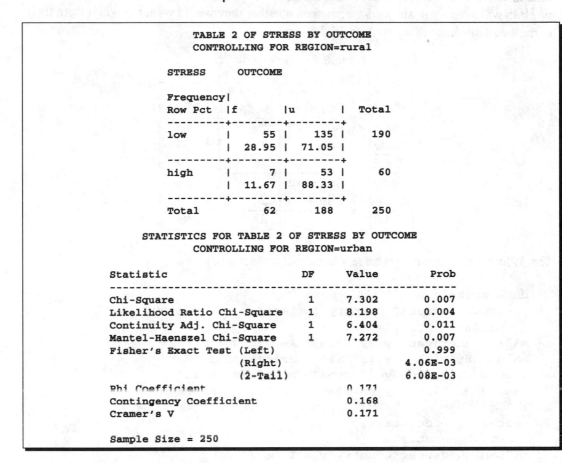

```
               TABLE 2 OF STRESS BY OUTCOME
               CONTROLLING FOR REGION=rural

       STRESS      OUTCOME

       Frequency|
       Row Pct  |f        |u       |  Total
       ---------+--------+--------+
       low      |     55 |    135 |    190
                |  28.95 |  71.05 |
       ---------+--------+--------+
       high     |      7 |     53 |     60
                |  11.67 |  88.33 |
       ---------+--------+--------+
       Total         62      188      250

         STATISTICS FOR TABLE 2 OF STRESS BY OUTCOME
                 CONTROLLING FOR REGION=urban

    Statistic                    DF    Value      Prob
    -----------------------------------------------------
    Chi-Square                    1    7.302      0.007
    Likelihood Ratio Chi-Square   1    8.198      0.004
    Continuity Adj. Chi-Square    1    6.404      0.011
    Mantel-Haenszel Chi-Square    1    7.272      0.007
    Fisher's Exact Test (Left)                    0.999
                        (Right)                4.06E-03
                        (2-Tail)               6.08E-03
    Phi Coefficient                    0.171
    Contingency Coefficient            0.168
    Cramer's V                         0.171

    Sample Size = 250
```

From Output 3.6 you can see that Q_{MH} has the value 23.050, which is strongly significant. Stress is highly associated with health policy opinion, adjusting for regional effects.

Output 3.6   Summary Statistics

```
          SUMMARY STATISTICS FOR STRESS BY OUTCOME
                  CONTROLLING FOR REGION


     Cochran-Mantel-Haenszel Statistics (Based on Table Scores)

     Statistic  Alternative Hypothesis   DF    Value    Prob
     -------------------------------------------------------
         1      Nonzero Correlation       1    23.050   0.000
         2      Row Mean Scores Differ    1    23.050   0.000
         3      General Association       1    23.050   0.000
```

3.2.3   Soft Drink Example

The following data come from a study on soft drink tastes by a company interested in reactions to a new soft drink that was being targeted for both the United States and Great Britain. Investigators poststratified on gender because they thought it was potentially related to the response. After receiving a supply of the new soft drink and being given a week in which to try it, subjects were asked whether they would want to switch from their current soft drinks to this new soft drink.

Table 3.5   Soft Drink Data

Gender	Country	Switch ? Yes	No	Total
Male	American	29	6	35
Male	British	19	15	34
Total		48	21	69
Female	American	7	23	30
Female	British	24	29	53
Total		31	52	83

The following statements produce a Mantel-Haenszel analysis.

```
data soft;
   input gender $ country $ question $ count @@;
   cards;
male    American  y 29 male    American  n  6
male    British   y 19 male    British   n 15
female American   y  7 female American   n 23
female British    y 24 female British    n 29
;
proc freq order=data;
   weight count;
   tables gender*country*question /
       chisq cmh nocol nopct;
run;
```

Output 3.7 and Output 3.8 display the table results for males and females.

Output 3.7   Summary Statistics for Males

```
              TABLE 1 OF COUNTRY BY QUESTION
                 CONTROLLING FOR GENDER=male

     COUNTRY      QUESTION

     Frequency|
     Row Pct  |y        |n        | Total
     ---------+--------+--------+
     American |    29 |     6 |    35
              | 82.86 | 17.14 |
     ---------+--------+--------+
     British  |    19 |    15 |    34
              | 55.88 | 44.12 |
     ---------+--------+--------+
     Total         48       21       69


        STATISTICS FOR TABLE 1 OF COUNTRY BY QUESTION
                 CONTROLLING FOR GENDER=male

     Statistic                   DF     Value     Prob
     ------------------------------------------------------
     Chi-Square                   1     5.927     0.015
     Likelihood Ratio Chi-Square  1     6.069     0.014
     Continuity Adj. Chi-Square   1     4.722     0.030
     Mantel-Haenszel Chi-Square   1     5.841     0.016
     Fisher's Exact Test (Left)                   0.997
                         (Right)                  0.014
                         (2-Tail)                 0.019
     Phi Coefficient                    0.293
     Contingency Coefficient            0.281
     Cramer's V                         0.293

     Sample Size = 69
```

Output 3.8   Summary Statistics for Females

```
                TABLE 2 OF COUNTRY BY QUESTION
                CONTROLLING FOR GENDER=female

        COUNTRY      QUESTION

        Frequency|
        Row Pct  |y        |n        |  Total
        ---------+--------+--------+
        American |      7  |     23  |    30
                 |  23.33  |  76.67  |
        ---------+--------+--------+
        British  |     24  |     29  |    53
                 |  45.28  |  54.72  |
        ---------+--------+--------+
        Total          31        52       83


           STATISTICS FOR TABLE 2 OF COUNTRY BY QUESTION
                   CONTROLLING FOR GENDER=female

      Statistic                    DF      Value      Prob
      ------------------------------------------------------
      Chi-Square                    1       3.944      0.047
      Likelihood Ratio Chi-Square   1       4.093      0.043
      Continuity Adj. Chi-Square    1       3.062      0.080
      Mantel-Haenszel Chi-Square    1       3.897      0.048
      Fisher's Exact Test (Left)                       0.039
                          (Right)                      0.988
                          (2-Tail)                     0.060
      Phi Coefficient                      -0.218
      Contingency Coefficient               0.213
      Cramer's V                           -0.218

      Sample Size = 83
```

As indicated by Q for males (5.841) and Q for females (3.897), there is significant association in both tables between country and willingness to switch. However, look at Q_{MH} in the following output.

Output 3.9   Summary Statistics

```
            SUMMARY STATISTICS FOR COUNTRY BY QUESTION
                    CONTROLLING FOR GENDER


      Cochran-Mantel-Haenszel Statistics (Based on Table Scores)

      Statistic  Alternative Hypothesis    DF     Value     Prob
      -------------------------------------------------------------
          1      Nonzero Correlation        1     0.024     0.876
          2      Row Mean Scores Differ      1     0.024     0.876
          3      General Association         1     0.024     0.876
```

Q_{MH} takes the value 0.024, indicating that there is no association between country and willingness to switch, after adjusting for gender. However, if you examine the individual tables more closely, you see that the association is manifested in opposite directions. For males, Americans are overwhelming favorable, and the British are a little more favorable than unfavorable. For females, Americans are very opposed, while the British are mildly opposed.

Thus, for these data, Q_{MH} fails to detect an association because the association is of opposite directions with roughly the same magnitude. As discussed previously, Q_{MH} has power against the alternative hypothesis of consistent patterns of association; it has low power for detecting association in opposite directions. (However, regardless of these matters of power, the method always performs at the specified significance level (or less) under the null hypothesis, so it is always valid.)

Generally, this isn't a problem because if there is association, it is usually in the same direction across a set of tables, although often to varying degrees. However, you should always examine the individual tables, especially if your results are questionable, to determine if you have a situation in which the association is inconsistent and the Q_{MH} statistic is not very powerful.

3.3   Measures of Association

Section 2.5 discusses the odds ratio as a measure of association for the 2×2 table. You can compute average odds ratios for sets of 2×2 tables. For the hth stratum,

$$\mathrm{OR}_h = \frac{p_{h1}/(1 - p_{h1})}{p_{h2}/(1 - p_{h2})} = \frac{n_{h11} n_{h22}}{n_{h12} n_{h21}}$$

so OR_h estimates ψ_h, the population odds ratio for the hth stratum. If the ψ_h are homogeneous, then you can compute the Mantel-Haenszel estimator for the common odds ratio ψ.

$$\hat{\psi}_{MH} = \sum_{h=1}^{q} \frac{n_{h11} n_{h22}}{n_h} \bigg/ \sum_{h=1}^{q} \frac{n_{h12} n_{h21}}{n_h}$$

The quantity $\hat{\psi}_{MH}$ does not have a very straightforward standard error estimate. The Mantel-Haenszel estimator is provided by the SAS System; however, its standard error is test based, which means that it only applies if the null hypothesis is true (that the odds ratio is no different from 1). It should be used with great caution. However, the estimator is useful for description, even when cell sizes are small. A more widely applicable estimator for the standard error is that of Robins, Breslow, and Greenland (1986), but it is not currently provided in the FREQ procedure.

Another estimator of ψ is the logit estimator. This is a weighted regression estimate with the form

$$\hat{\psi}_L = \exp\left\{ \sum_{h=1}^{q} w_h f_h \bigg/ \sum_{h=1}^{q} w_h \right\} = \exp\{\bar{f}\}$$

where $f_h = \log \mathrm{OR}_h$ and

$$w_h = \left\{ \frac{1}{n_{h11}} + \frac{1}{n_{h12}} + \frac{1}{n_{h21}} + \frac{1}{n_{h22}} \right\}^{-1}$$

You can write a $100\%(1 - \alpha)$ confidence interval for $\hat{\psi}_L$ as

$$\exp\left\{\bar{f} \pm z_{\alpha/2}\left[\sum_{h=1}^{q} w_h\right]^{-1/2}\right\}$$

The logit estimator is also reasonable but requires adequate sample sizes (all $n_{hij} \geq 5$); it has problems with zero cells for the n_{hij}, in which case you should proceed cautiously.

Note that logistic regression provides a better strategy to estimate the common odds ratio and produces a confidence interval based on maximum likelihood methods. This is discussed in Chapter 8, "Logistic Regression I: Dichotomous Response."

3.3.1   Homogeneity of Odds Ratios

You are generally interested in whether the odds ratios in a set of tables are homogeneous. There are several test statistics that address the hypothesis of homogeneity, one of which is the Breslow-Day statistic.

Consider Table 3.6. The top table shows the expected counts m_{ij} for a 2×2 table, and the bottom table shows how you can write the expected counts for the rest of the cells if you know the $(1,1)$ expected count m_{11}.

Table 3.6   Odds Ratios

	Yes	No	Total
Group 1	m_{11}	m_{12}	n_{1+}
Group 2	m_{21}	m_{22}	n_{2+}
Total	n_{+1}	n_{+2}	n
Group 1	m_{11}	$n_{1+} - m_{11}$	n_{1+}
Group 2	$n_{+1} - m_{11}$	$n - n_{1+} - n_{+1} + m_{11}$	$n - n_{1+}$
Total	n_{+1}	$n - n_{+1}$	n

If you assume that the odds ratio takes a certain value, $\psi = \psi_0$, then

$$\frac{m_{11}(n - n_{1+} - n_{+1} + m_{11})}{(n_{+1} - m_{11})(n_{1+} - m_{11})} = \psi_0$$

You can put this expression into the form of a quadratic equation and then solve for m_{11}; once you have m_{11}, you can solve for the other expected counts.

To compute the Breslow-Day statistic, you use ψ_{MH} as ψ_0 for each stratum and perform the preceding computations for the expected counts for each table; that is, you compute the m_{hij}. Then,

$$Q_{BD} = \sum_{h=1}^{q}\sum_{i=1}^{2}\sum_{j=1}^{2}\frac{(n_{hij} - m_{hij})^2}{m_{hij}}$$

Under the null hypothesis of homogeneity, Q_{BD} approximately has a chi-square distribution with $(q - 1)$ degrees of freedom. In addition, the cells in all of the tables must have expected cell counts greater than 5 (or at least 80 percent of them should). Note that a chi-square approximation for Q_{MH} requires only the total sample size to be large, but the chi-square approximation for Q_{BD} requires each table to have a large sample size. If the odds ratios are not homogeneous, then the overall odds ratio should not be presented; only the within-strata odds ratios should be displayed.

Note that the Mantel-Haenszel statistics do not require homogeneous odds ratios, so the Breslow-Day test should not be interpreted as an indicator of their validity. Refer to Breslow and Day (1980, p. 182) for more information.

3.3.2 Coronary Artery Disease Data Example

The following data are based on a study on coronary artery disease (Koch, Imrey, et al. 1985). The sample is one of convenience since the patients studied were people who came to a clinic and requested an evaluation.

Table 3.7 Coronary Artery Disease Data

Sex	ECG	Disease	No Disease	Total
Female	< 0.1 ST segment depression	4	11	15
Female	≥ 0.1 ST segment depression	8	10	18
Male	< 0.1 ST segment depression	9	9	18
Male	≥ 0.1 ST segment depression	21	6	27

Investigators were interested in whether electrocardiogram (ECG) measurement was associated with disease status. Gender was thought to be associated with disease status, so investigators poststratified the data into male and female groups. In addition, there was interest in examining the odds ratios.

The following statements produce the SAS data set CA and request a stratified analysis. The first TABLES statement requests chi-square tests for the association of gender and disease status. The second TABLES statement requests the stratified analysis, including the generation of odds ratios with the MEASURES option.

```
data ca;
    input gender $ ECG $ disease $ count;
    cards;
female <0.1   yes    4
female <0.1   no    11
female >=0.1  yes    8
female >=0.1  no    10
male   <0.1   yes    9
male   <0.1   no     9
male   >=0.1  yes   21
male   >=0.1  no     6
;
proc freq;
    weight count;
```

```
      tables gender*disease / nocol nopct chisq;
      tables gender*ECG*disease / nocol nopct cmh chisq measures;
   run;
```

Output 3.10 contains the table of GENDER by DISEASE. Q takes the value 6.944 and Q_P takes the value 7.035. Obviously there is a strong association between gender and disease status. Males are much more likely to have symptoms of coronary artery disease than females. The idea to control for gender in a stratified analysis is a good one.

Note that you are controlling for confounding in this example, which is different from the adjustment performed in previous examples. Confounding variables are those related to both the response and the factor under investigation. In previous examples, the stratification variable was part of the study design (center) or thought to be related to the response (gender in soft drink analysis). Adjusting for confounding is often required in epidemiological studies.

Output 3.10   GENDER × DISEASE

```
                TABLE OF GENDER BY DISEASE

        GENDER       DISEASE

        Frequency|
        Row Pct  |no       |yes      |  Total
        ---------+--------+--------+
        female   |     21 |     12 |     33
                 |  63.64 |  36.36 |
        ---------+--------+--------+
        male     |     15 |     30 |     45
                 |  33.33 |  66.67 |
        ---------+--------+--------+
        Total          36       42       78

           STATISTICS FOR TABLE OF GENDER BY DISEASE

        Statistic                    DF    Value      Prob
        --------------------------------------------------------
        Chi-Square                    1    7.035      0.008
        Likelihood Ratio Chi-Square   1    7.121      0.008
        Continuity Adj. Chi-Square    1    5.868      0.015
        Mantel-Haenszel Chi-Square    1    6.944      0.008
        Fisher's Exact Test (Left)                    0.998
                            (Right)              7.51E-03
                            (2-Tail)                  0.011
        Phi Coefficient                    0.300
        Contingency Coefficient            0.288
        Cramer's V                         0.300
```

Output 3.11 and Output 3.12 display the individual tables results for ECG × disease status; included are the table of chi-square statistics generated by the CHISQ option and only the "Estimates of the Relative Risk" table part of the output generated by the MEASURES option.

Output 3.11   Results for Females

```
        STATISTICS FOR TABLE 1 OF ECG BY DISEASE
               CONTROLLING FOR GENDER=female

     Statistic                      DF     Value       Prob
     -------------------------------------------------------
     Chi-Square                     1      1.117       0.290
     Likelihood Ratio Chi-Square    1      1.134       0.287
     Continuity Adj. Chi-Square     1      0.481       0.488
     Mantel-Haenszel Chi-Square     1      1.084       0.298
     Fisher's Exact Test (Left)                        0.923
                         (Right)                       0.245
                         (2-Tail)                      0.469
     Phi Coefficient                       0.184
     Contingency Coefficient               0.181
     Cramer's V                            0.184


        Estimates of the Relative Risk (Row1/Row2)


                                             95%
     Type of Study          Value      Confidence Bounds
     -------------------------------------------------------
     Case-Control           2.200      0.504      9.611
     Cohort (Col1 Risk)     1.320      0.790      2.206
     Cohort (Col2 Risk)     0.600      0.224      1.607
```

Q_{MH} is 1.084 for females, with a p-value of 0.298. The odds ratio for the females is OR = 2.2, with a 95 percent confidence interval that includes 1. Those females with higher ST segment depression levels had 2.2 times the odds of CA disease than those with lower levels.

Output 3.12   Results for Males

```
        STATISTICS FOR TABLE 2 OF ECG BY DISEASE
               CONTROLLING FOR GENDER=male

     Statistic                      DF     Value       Prob
     -------------------------------------------------------
     Chi-Square                     1      3.750       0.053
     Likelihood Ratio Chi-Square    1      3.729       0.053
     Continuity Adj. Chi-Square     1      2.604       0.107
     Mantel-Haenszel Chi-Square     1      3.667       0.056
     Fisher's Exact Test (Left)                        0.988
                         (Right)                       0.054
                         (2-Tail)                      0.105
     Phi Coefficient                       0.289
     Contingency Coefficient               0.277
     Cramer's V                            0.289

        Estimates of the Relative Risk (Row1/Row2)

                                             95%
     Type of Study          Value      Confidence Bounds
     -------------------------------------------------------
     Case-Control           3.500      0.959      12.778
     Cohort (Col1 Risk)     2.250      0.968      5.230
     Cohort (Col2 Risk)     0.643      0.388      1.064
```

Q_{MH} is 3.667 for males, with a p-value of 0.056. The odds ratio for the males is OR = 3.5, with a 95 percent confidence interval that barely contains the value 1. Those men with higher ST segment depression levels had 3.5 times the odds of CA disease than those with lower levels.

Output 3.13 contains the Q_{MH} statistic, which takes the value 4.503 with a p-value of 0.034. By combining the genders, the power has been increased so that the association detected by Q_{MH} is significant at the $\alpha = 0.05$ level of significance.

Output 3.13   Stratified Analysis

```
                SUMMARY STATISTICS FOR ECG BY DISEASE
                      CONTROLLING FOR GENDER

      Cochran-Mantel-Haenszel Statistics (Based on Table Scores)

    Statistic   Alternative Hypothesis     DF     Value     Prob
    ------------------------------------------------------------
        1        Nonzero Correlation        1      4.503     0.034
        2        Row Mean Scores Differ     1      4.503     0.034
        3        General Association        1      4.503     0.034
```

Output 3.14 contains the estimates of the common odds ratios. $\hat{\psi}_{MH} = 2.847$ and $\hat{\psi}_L = 2.859$. The confidence interval for the logit estimator does not contain the value 1; note that since Q_{MH} is significant, the confidence interval listed for $\hat{\psi}_{MH}$ should be viewed cautiously. Note the message that the MH confidence bounds are test based.

Output 3.14   Odds Ratios

```
          Estimates of the Common Relative Risk (Row1/Row2)
                                              95%
       Type of Study   Method        Value  Confidence Bounds
       ------------------------------------------------------
       Case-Control    Mantel-Haenszel  2.847   1.083   7.482
         (Odds Ratio)  Logit            2.859   1.081   7.565

       Cohort          Mantel-Haenszel  1.641   1.039   2.594
         (Col1 Risk)   Logit            1.525   0.983   2.365

       Cohort          Mantel-Haenszel  0.630   0.411   0.965
         (Col2 Risk)   Logit            0.634   0.405   0.993

       The confidence bounds for the M-H estimates are test-based.


          Breslow-Day Test for Homogeneity of the Odds Ratios


       Chi-Square =   0.215        DF =   1         Prob = 0.643
```

Common measures of relative risk are also printed by the FREQ procedure. However, since these data do not come from a prospective study, these statistics are not relevant and should be ignored.

Finally, the Breslow-Day test is printed at the bottom and does not contradict the assumption of homogeneous odds ratios for these data. $Q_{BD} = 0.215$ with $p = 0.643$.

Chapter 4
Sets of $2 \times r$ and $s \times 2$ Tables

Chapter Table of Contents

Chapter 4
Sets of $2 \times r$ and $s \times 2$ Tables

4.1   Introduction

While sets of 2×2 tables are very common, many sets of tables have other dimensions. This chapter focuses on sets of tables that also occur frequently: sets of $2 \times r$ tables in which the column variable is ordinally scaled and sets of $s \times 2$ tables in which the row variable is ordinally scaled. For $2 \times r$ tables, there is interest in investigating a response variable with multiple ordered outcomes for a combined set of strata. For example, you may be comparing a new treatment and a placebo on the extent of patient improvement that is rated as minimal, moderate, or substantial. For $s \times 2$ tables, there is interest in the trend of proportions across ordered groups for a combined set of strata. For example, you may be comparing the proportion of successful outcomes for different dosage levels of a new drug.

Extensions of the Mantel-Haenszel strategy address association in sets of tables with these characteristics. Section 4.2 addresses $2 \times r$ tables and Section 4.3 addresses $s \times 2$ tables. Each of these sections begins by discussing the assessment of association in a single table where the column (row) variable is ordinally scaled and the row (column) variable is dichotomous.

4.2   Sets of $2 \times r$ Tables

Consider the data from Koch and Edwards (1988) displayed in Table 4.1. The information comes from a randomized, double-blind clinical trial investigating a new treatment for rheumatoid arthritis. Investigators compared the new treatment with a placebo; the response measured was whether there was no, some, or marked improvement in the symptoms of rheumatoid arthritis.

Table 4.1   Rheumatoid Arthritis Data

Gender	Treatment	Improvement None	Some	Marked	Total
Female	Test Drug	6	5	16	27
Female	Placebo	19	7	6	32
Total		25	12	22	59
Male	Test Drug	7	2	5	14
Male	Placebo	10	0	1	11
Total		17	2	6	25

These data comprise a set of two 2×3 tables. There is interest in the association between treatment and degree of improvement, adjusting for gender effects. Degree of improvement is an ordinal response, since none, some, and marked are gradations of improvement.

Mantel (1963) proposed an extension of the Mantel-Haenszel strategy for the analysis of $2 \times r$ tables when the response variable is ordinal. The extension involves computing mean scores for the responses and using the mean score differences across tables in the computation of a suitable test statistic, much like the difference in proportions across tables was the basis of the Mantel-Haenszel statistic.

4.2.1   The $2 \times r$ Table

Before discussing the strategies for assessing association in sets of $2 \times r$ tables, it is necessary to discuss the assessment of association in a single $2 \times r$ table that has an ordinal outcome. Consider the table corresponding to patients pooled over gender for the rheumatoid arthritis data.

Table 4.2   Combined Rheumatoid Arthritis Data

Treatment	Improvement None	Some	Marked	Total
Test Drug	13	7	21	41
Placebo	29	7	7	43
Total	42	14	28	84

As discussed in Chapter 1, "Introduction," you want to take advantage of the ordinality of the column variable in forming a test statistic. This involves assigning scores to the response levels, forming means, and then examining location shifts of the means across the levels of the row variable.

Define the mean for the Test Drug group as

$$\bar{f}_1 = \sum_{j=1}^{3} \frac{a_j n_{1j}}{n_{1+}}$$

where $\mathbf{a} = \{a_j\} = (a_1, a_2, a_3)$ are a set of scores reflecting the response levels. Then

$$E\{\bar{f}_1|H_0\} = \sum_{j=1}^{3} \left(a_j \frac{n_{1+}n_{+j}}{n_{1+}n} \right) = \sum_{j=1}^{3} a_j \frac{n_{+j}}{n} = \mu_{\mathbf{a}}$$

It can be shown that

$$
\begin{aligned}
V\{\bar{f}_1|H_0\} &= \frac{n - n_{1+}}{n_{1+}(n-1)} \sum_{j=1}^{3} (a_j - \mu_{\mathbf{a}})^2 \left(\frac{n_{+j}}{n} \right) \\
&= \frac{(n - n_{1+})v_{\mathbf{a}}}{n_{1+}(n-1)}
\end{aligned}
$$

where $\mu_{\mathbf{a}}$ and $v_{\mathbf{a}}$ are the finite population mean and variance of scores $\mathbf{a}$ for the patients in the study. The quantity $\bar{f}_1$ approximately has a normal distribution by randomization central limit theory, so the quantity

$$Q_S = \frac{(\bar{f}_1 - \mu_{\mathbf{a}})^2}{\{(n - n_{1+})/[n_{1+}(n-1)]\}v_{\mathbf{a}}}$$

approximately has the chi-square distribution with one degree of freedom. Q_S is called the mean score statistic. By taking advantage of the ordinality of the response variable, Q_S can target the alternative hypothesis of location shifts to the hypothesis of no association with fewer degrees of freedom. While Q and Q_P are useful for detecting general types of association, they are not as effective as Q_S in detecting location shifts. Q_S is also a trend statistic for the tendency for the patients in one treatment group to have better scores than the patients in the other treatment group.

A very conservative sample size guideline is the guideline used for the Pearson chi-square statistic (that is, all expected values $n_{i+}n_{+j}/n = m_{ij}$ being greater than or equal to 5). However, one of the advantages of the mean score statistic is that it has less stringent sample size requirements. A more realistic but still conservative sample size guideline is to choose one or more cutpoints $j = (2, \ldots, (r-1))$, add the 1st through jth columns together and add the $(j+1)$th through rth columns together. If most of these sums are 5 or greater for both rows, then the sample size is adequate.

For example, for Table 4.2, choose $j = 2$. Adding the first and second columns together yields the sums 20 for the first row and 36 for the second; the remaining sums are just the third column cells (21 and 7, respectively). Thus, according to this criterion, the sample size is adequate.

The following PROC FREQ statements generate Q_S. Note the use of the ORDER=DATA option to ensure that the values for the variable RESPONSE are put in the correct order. If they are not, the resulting statistics are incorrect. Ensuring the correct sort order is critical when you are using statistics that assume ordered values.

```
data arth;
   input gender $ treat $ response $ count @@;
   cards;
female test      none 6  female test      some 5  female test      marked 16
female placebo none 19 female placebo some 7  female placebo marked 6
male    test      none 7  male    test      some 2  male    test      marked 5
male    placebo none 10 male    placebo some 0  male    placebo marked 1
;
proc freq data=arth order=data;
   weight count;
   tables treat*response / chisq nocol nopct;
run;
```

The results are contained in Output 4.1.

Output 4.1   Mean Score Statistic

```
              TABLE OF TREAT BY RESPONSE

      TREAT      RESPONSE

      Frequency|
      Row Pct  |none    |some    |marked  |  Total
      ---------+--------+--------+--------+
      test     |    13 |     7 |    21 |     41
               | 31.71 | 17.07 | 51.22 |
      ---------+--------+--------+--------+
      placebo  |    29 |     7 |     7 |     43
               | 67.44 | 16.28 | 16.28 |
      ---------+--------+--------+--------+
      Total          42       14       28       84


      STATISTICS FOR TABLE OF TREAT BY RESPONSE

      Statistic                    DF     Value      Prob
      --------------------------------------------------------
      Chi-Square                    2     13.055     0.001
      Likelihood Ratio Chi-Square   2     13.530     0.001
      Mantel-Haenszel Chi-Square    1     12.859     0.001
      Phi Coefficient                      0.394
      Contingency Coefficient              0.367
      Cramer's V                           0.394

      Sample Size = 84
```

For a $2 \times r$ table, the statistic labeled "Mantel-Haenszel Chi-Square" is Q_S. The scores
(1, 2, 3) are used for the response levels none, some, and marked in Table 4.2. Q_S takes
the value 12.859, which is strongly significant. The test treatment performs better than the
placebo treatment.

You can also produce Q_S by specifying the CMH option and generating the summary
statistics, which will be for just one stratum. Q_S is the statistic labeled "Row Mean Scores
Differ" in the resulting summary statistics table.

4.2.2 Extension to Q_{MH}

Assessing association for sets of $2 \times r$ tables where the response is ordinal also involves a strategy of computing means based on a scoring system and looking at shifts in location.

Consider the following table as representative of q $2 \times r$ tables, $h = 1, 2, \ldots, q$.

Table 4.3 hth $2 \times r$ Contingency Table

	Level of Column Variable				
	1	2	...	r	Total
Group 1	n_{h11}	n_{h12}	...	n_{h1r}	n_{h1+}
Group 2	n_{h21}	n_{h22}	...	n_{h2r}	n_{h2+}
Total	n_{h+1}	n_{h+2}	...	n_{h+r}	n_h

For the rheumatoid arthritis data in Table 4.1, $r = 3$ and $q = 2$. Under the null hypothesis of no difference in treatment effects for each patient, the appropriate probability model is

$$Pr\{n_{hij}\} = \prod_{h=1}^{2} \frac{\prod_{i=1}^{2} n_{hi+}! \prod_{j=1}^{3} n_{h+j}!}{n_h! \prod_{i=1}^{2} \prod_{j=1}^{3} n_{hij}!}$$

Here, n_{hij} represents the number of patients in the hth stratum who received the ith treatment and had the jth response.

Suppose $\{a_{hj}\}$ is a set of scores for the response levels in the hth stratum. Then you can compute the sum of strata scores for the 1st treatment, test, as

$$f_{+1+} = \sum_{h=1}^{2} \sum_{j=1}^{3} a_{hj} n_{h1j} = \sum_{h=1}^{2} n_{h1+} \bar{f}_{h1}$$

where

$$\bar{f}_{h1} = \sum_{j=1}^{3} (a_{hj} n_{h1j} / n_{h1+})$$

is the mean score for Group 1 in the hth stratum. Under the null hypothesis of no association, f_{+1+} has the expected value

$$E\{f_{+1+}|H_0\} = \sum_{h=1}^{2} n_{h1+} \mu_h = \mu_*$$

and variance

$$V\{f_{+1+}|H_0\} = \sum_{h=1}^{2} \frac{n_{h1+}(n_h - n_{h1+})}{(n_h - 1)} v_h = v_*$$

where $\mu_h = \sum_{j=1}^{3}(a_{hj}n_{h+j}/n_h)$ is the finite subpopulation mean and

$$v_h = \sum_{j=1}^{3}(a_{hj} - \mu_h)^2(n_{h+j}/n_h)$$

is the variance of scores for the hth stratum.

If the across-strata sample sizes $n_{+i+} = \sum_{h=1}^{q}\sum_{j=1}^{r} n_{hij}$ are sufficiently large, then f_{+1+} approximately has a normal distribution, and so the quantity

$$Q_{SMH} = \frac{(f_{+1+} - \mu_*)^2}{v_*}$$

approximately has a chi-square distribution with one degree of freedom. Q_{SMH} is known as the extended Mantel-Haenszel mean score statistic; it is sometimes called the ANOVA statistic. You can show that Q_{SMH} is a linear function of the differences in the mean scores of the two treatments for the q strata.

$$
\begin{aligned}
Q_{SMH} &= \frac{\{\sum_{h=1}^{q} n_{h1+}(\bar{f}_{h1} - \mu_h)\}^2}{\sum_{h=1}^{q} n_{h1+}n_{h2+} v_h/(n_h - 1)} \\
&= \frac{\{\sum_{h=1}^{q}(n_{h1+}n_{h2+}/n_h)(\bar{f}_{h1} - \bar{f}_{h2})\}^2}{\sum_{h=1}^{q}(n_{h1+}n_{h2+}/n_h)^2 \bar{v}_h}
\end{aligned}
$$

where the

$$\bar{v}_h = \left\{\frac{1}{n_{h1+}} + \frac{1}{n_{h2+}}\right\}\frac{n_h v_h}{n_h - 1}$$

are the variances of the mean score differences $\{\bar{f}_{h1} - \bar{f}_{h2}\}$ for the respective strata.

Q_{SMH} is effective for detecting consistent patterns of differences across the strata when the $(\bar{f}_{h1} - \bar{f}_{h2})$ predominantly have the same sign.

Besides the guideline that the across strata row totals (n_{+i+}) be sufficiently large, another guideline for sample size requirements for Q_{SMH} is to choose cutpoints and add columns together so that each stratum table is collapsed to a 2×2 table, similar to what is described in Section 4.2.1; the cutpoints don't have to be the same for each table. Then, you apply the Mantel-Fleiss criterion to these 2×2 tables (see Section 3.2).

4.2.3   Choosing Scores

Ordinal data analysis strategies do involve some choice on the part of the analyst, and that is the choice of scores to apply to the response levels. There are a variety of scoring systems to consider; the following are often used.

- *integer scores*

  Integer scores are defined as $a_j = j$ for $j = 1, 2, \ldots, r$. They are useful when the response levels are ordered categories that can be viewed as equally spaced and when the response levels correspond to discrete counts. They are also useful if you have equal interest in detecting group differences for any binary partition $\leq j$ versus $> j$ of outcomes for $j = 1, 2, \ldots, r$. Note that if you add the same number to a set of scores, or multiply a set of scores by the same number, both sets of scores produce the same test statistic because multiplication is cancelled by division by the same factor in the variance and addition is cancelled by subtraction of the same factor in the expected value. Thus, the integer scores $(1, 2, 3, \ldots)$ and $(0, 1, 2, \ldots)$ produce the same results.

- *standardized midranks*

  These scores are defined as

  $$a_j = \frac{2[\sum_{k=1}^{j} n_{+k}] - n_{+j} + 1}{2(n+1)}$$

  The $\{a_j\}$ are constrained to lie between 0 and 1. Their advantage over integer scores is that they require no scaling of the response levels other than that implied by their relative ordering. For sets of $2 \times r$ tables, they provide somewhat more power than actual midranks since they produce the van Elteren (1960) extension of the Wilcoxon rank sum test (refer to Lehmann, 1975 for a discussion). Standardized midranks are also known as *modified ridit scores*.

- *logrank scores*

  $$a_j = 1 - \sum_{k=1}^{j} \left(\frac{n_{+k}}{\sum_{m=k}^{r} n_{+m}} \right)$$

  Logrank scores are useful when the distribution is thought to be L-shaped, and there is greater interest in treatment differences for response levels with higher values than with lower values.

  Other scores that are sometimes used are ridit and rank scores. For a single stratum, rank, ridit, and modified ridit scores produce the same result, which is the categorical counterpart of the Wilcoxon rank sum test. For stratified analyses, modified ridit scores produce van Elteren's extension of the Wilcoxon rank sum test, a property that makes them the preferred of these three types of scores. A possible shortcoming of rank scores, relative to ridit or modified ridit scores, is that their use tends to make the large strata overly influence the test statistic. See page 132 for additional discussion on choosing scores.

  You specify the choice of scores in the FREQ procedure by using the SCORES= option in the TABLES statement. If you don't specify SCORES=, then you get the default table scores. The column (row) numbers are the table scores for character data and the actual variable values are used as scores for numeric variables. Other SCORES= values are RANK, MODRIDIT, and RIDIT. If you are interested in using logrank scores, then you need to compute them in a DATA step and make them the values of the row and column variables you list in the TABLES statement.

4.2.4   Analyzing the Respiratory Data

Applying the extension of the Mantel-Haenzsel strategy involves no new steps in the SAS System. You specify the CMH option in the TABLES statement of the FREQ procedure. Notice that the ORDER=DATA option is specified in the PROC statement to ensure that the levels of RESPONSE are sorted correctly. The columns will be ordered none, some, and marked; and the rows will be ordered test and placebo.

```
data arth;
   input gender $ treat $ response $ count @@;
   cards;
female test    none 6  female test    some 5  female test    marked 16
female placebo none 19 female placebo some 7  female placebo marked 6
male    test   none 7  male    test   some 2  male    test    marked 5
male    placebo none 10 male   placebo some 0  male   placebo marked 1
;
proc freq data=arth order=data;
   weight count;
   tables gender*treat*response / cmh nocol nopct;
run;
```

Output 4.2   Tables by Gender

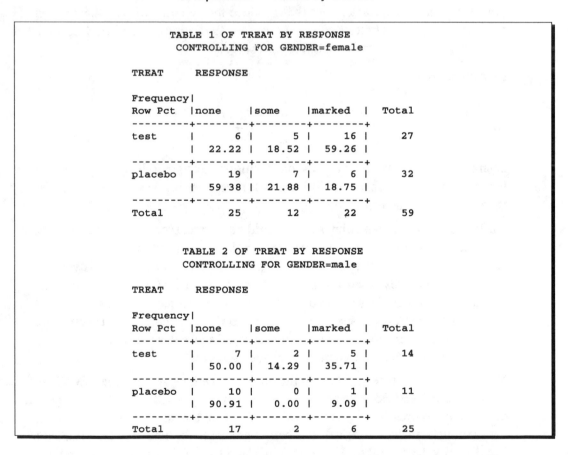

```
               TABLE 1 OF TREAT BY RESPONSE
               CONTROLLING FOR GENDER=female

      TREAT       RESPONSE

      Frequency|
      Row Pct  |none    |some    |marked  |  Total
      ---------+--------+--------+--------+
      test     |     6 |     5 |    16 |    27
               | 22.22 | 18.52 | 59.26 |
      ---------+--------+--------+--------+
      placebo  |    19 |     7 |     6 |    32
               | 59.38 | 21.88 | 18.75 |
      ---------+--------+--------+--------+
      Total         25      12      22       59


               TABLE 2 OF TREAT BY RESPONSE
               CONTROLLING FOR GENDER=male

      TREAT       RESPONSE

      Frequency|
      Row Pct  |none    |some    |marked  |  Total
      ---------+--------+--------+--------+
      test     |     7 |     2 |     5 |    14
               | 50.00 | 14.29 | 35.71 |
      ---------+--------+--------+--------+
      placebo  |    10 |     0 |     1 |    11
               | 90.91 |  0.00 |  9.09 |
      ---------+--------+--------+--------+
      Total         17       2       6       25
```

Output 4.2 displays the frequency tables for females and males. Output 4.3 displays the table of Mantel-Haenszel statistics. Note that the table heading includes "Table Scores" in parentheses. Q_{SMH} is the "Row Mean Scores Differ" statistic. It has the value 14.632, with 1 df, and is clearly significant.

Note the small cell counts for several cells in the table for males. This is not a problem for Q_{SMH} since the adequacy of the sample sizes is determined by the across strata sample sizes n_{+i+}, which are $n_{+1+} = 41$ and $n_{+2+} = 43$ for these data.

Output 4.3   Mantel-Haenszel Results

```
           SUMMARY STATISTICS FOR TREAT BY RESPONSE
                     CONTROLLING FOR GENDER


     Cochran-Mantel-Haenszel Statistics (Based on Table Scores)

     Statistic   Alternative Hypothesis    DF      Value      Prob
     ---------------------------------------------------------------
         1        Nonzero Correlation       1      14.632     0.000
         2        Row Mean Scores Differ    1      14.632     0.000
         3        General Association       2      14.632     0.001
```

If you can't make the case that the response levels for degree of improvement are equally spaced, then modified ridit scores are an alternative strategy. The following PROC FREQ invocation requests that modified ridit scores be used in the computation of Q_{SMH} through the use of the SCORES=MODRIDIT option in the TABLES statement.

```
proc freq data=arth order=data;
   weight count;
   tables gender*treat*response/cmh scores=modridit nocol nopct;
run;
```

Output 4.4 contains the table of CMH statistics using modified ridit scores. Q_{SMH} takes the value 15.004 with 1 df, which is clearly significant. Note that the different scoring systems produced similar results. This is often the case.

Output 4.4   Mantel-Haenszel Results for Modified Ridit Scores

```
           SUMMARY STATISTICS FOR TREAT BY RESPONSE
                     CONTROLLING FOR GENDER


     Cochran-Mantel-Haenszel Statistics (Modified Ridit Scores)

     Statistic   Alternative Hypothesis    DF      Value      Prob
     ---------------------------------------------------------------
         1        Nonzero Correlation       1      14.992     0.000
         2        Row Mean Scores Differ    1      15.004     0.000
         3        General Association       2      14.632     0.001
```

4.2.5   Colds Example

The following data come from a study on the presence of colds in children in two regions (Stokes 1986). Researchers visited children several times and noted whether they had any symptoms of colds. The outcome measure is the number of periods in which a child exhibited cold symptoms.

Table 4.4 Number of Periods with Colds by Gender and Residence

Gender	Residence	Periods With Colds			Total
		0	1	2	
Female	Urban	45	64	71	180
Female	Rural	80	104	116	300
Total		125	168	187	480
Male	Urban	84	124	82	290
Male	Rural	106	117	87	310
Total		190	141	169	600

These data consist of two 2×3 tables; there is interest in determining whether there is association between residence (urban or rural) and number of periods with colds (0, 1 or 2) while controlling for gender. The response levels for these data consist of small discrete counts, so number of colds can be considered an ordinal variable in which the levels are equally spaced. The usual ANOVA strategy for interval-scaled response variables is not appropriate since there is no reason to think that the number of periods with colds is normally distributed with homogeneous variance.

The following statements produce an extended Mantel-Haenszel analysis. The default table scores are used, which will be the actual scores of the variable PER_COLD (0, 1, 2).

```
data colds;
   input gender $ residnce $ per_cold count @@;
   cards;
female urban 0    45   female urban  1  64   female urban 2  71
female rural 0    80   female rural  1 104   female rural 2 116
male    urban 0   84   male    urban 1 124   male    urban 2  82
male    rural 0  106   male    rural 1 117   male    rural 2  87
;
proc freq data=colds order=data;
   weight count;
   tables gender*residnce*per_cold / all nocol nopct;
run;
```

Output 4.5 and Output 4.6 contain the frequency tables for females and males and their associated chi-square statistics. There is no significant association between residence and number of periods with colds for females or males; $Q = 0.106$ ($p = 0.745$) for females and $Q = 0.741$ ($p = 0.389$) for males.

Output 4.5   Results for Females

```
              TABLE 1 OF RESIDNCE BY PER_COLD
                 CONTROLLING FOR GENDER=female

         RESIDNCE     PER_COLD

         Frequency|
         Row Pct  |       0|       1|       2|  Total
         ---------+--------+--------+--------+
         urban    |    45  |    64  |    71  |   180
                  |  25.00 |  35.56 |  39.44 |
         ---------+--------+--------+--------+
         rural    |    80  |   104  |   116  |   300
                  |  26.67 |  34.67 |  38.67 |
         ---------+--------+--------+--------+
         Total        125      168      187      480

         STATISTICS FOR TABLE 1 OF RESIDNCE BY PER_COLD
                 CONTROLLING FOR GENDER=female

    Statistic                       DF     Value      Prob
    ------------------------------------------------------------
    Chi-Square                       2     0.163      0.922
    Likelihood Ratio Chi-Square      2     0.163      0.922
    Mantel-Haenszel Chi-Square       1     0.106      0.745
    Phi Coefficient                        0.018
    Contingency Coefficient                0.018
    Cramer's V                             0.018
```

Output 4.6   Results for Males

```
              TABLE 2 OF RESIDNCE BY PER_COLD
                 CONTROLLING FOR GENDER=male

         RESIDNCE     PER_COLD

         Frequency|
         Row Pct  |       0|       1|       2|  Total
         ---------+--------+--------+--------+
         urban    |    84  |   124  |    82  |   290
                  |  28.97 |  42.76 |  28.28 |
         ---------+--------+--------+--------+
         rural    |   106  |   117  |    87  |   310
                  |  34.19 |  37.74 |  28.06 |
         ---------+--------+--------+--------+
         Total        190      241      169      600

         STATISTICS FOR TABLE 2 OF RESIDNCE BY PER_COLD
                 CONTROLLING FOR GENDER=male

    Statistic                       DF     Value      Prob
    ------------------------------------------------------------
    Chi-Square                       2     2.234      0.327
    Likelihood Ratio Chi-Square      2     2.238      0.327
    Mantel-Haenszel Chi-Square       1     0.741      0.389
    Phi Coefficient                        0.061
    Contingency Coefficient                0.061
    Cramer's V                             0.061
```

Output 4.7 contains the Mantel-Haenszel statistics. Q_{SMH} has the value 0.738, with $p = 0.390$. Even controlling for gender, there appears to be no association between residence and number of periods with colds for these data.

Output 4.7 Q_{SMH} Statistic

```
          SUMMARY STATISTICS FOR RESIDNCE BY PER_COLD
                    CONTROLLING FOR GENDER


        Cochran-Mantel-Haenszel Statistics (Based on Table Scores)

        Statistic   Alternative Hypothesis   DF     Value    Prob
        ----------------------------------------------------------
            1        Nonzero Correlation       1     0.738    0.390
            2        Row Mean Scores Differ    1     0.738    0.390
            3        General Association       2     1.971    0.373
```

4.3   Sets of $s \times 2$ Tables

The following data come from a study on adolescent usage of smokeless tobacco
(Bauman, Koch, and Lentz, 1989). Interest focused on factors that affected usage, such as
perception of risk, father's usage of smokeless tobacco, and educational background.
Table 4.5 contains two $s \times 2$ tables of risk perception (minimal, moderate, and substantial)
and adolescent usage by father's usage. This time, the row variable is ordinally scaled. The
question of interest is whether there is a discernable trend in the proportions of adolescent
usage over the levels of risk perception. Does usage decline with higher risk perception ?

Table 4.5   Adolescent Smokeless Tobacco Usage

| Father's | Risk | Adolescent Usage | | |
Usage	Perception	No	Yes	Total
No	Minimal	59	25	84
No	Moderate	169	29	198
No	Substantial	196	9	205
Yes	Minimal	11	8	19
Yes	Moderate	33	11	44
Yes	Substantial	22	2	24

Since the response variable is dichotomous, both risk perception and adolescent usage can
be considered ordinal variables. The strategy for assessing association when both row and
column variables are ordinal involves assigning scores to the levels of both variables and
evaluating their correlation.

4.3.1   The $s \times 2$ Table

Table 4.6 contains the data for those adolescents interviewed whose fathers did not use
smokeless tobacco.

Table 4.6   Adolescent Smokeless Tobacco Usage When Fathers Did Not Use

| Risk | Adolescent Usage | | |
Perception	No	Yes	Total
Minimal	59	25	84
Moderate	169	29	198
Substantial	196	9	205

Form the linear function

$$\bar{f} = \sum_{i=1}^{3} c_i \bar{f}_i \left(\frac{n_{i+}}{n} \right) = \sum_{i=1}^{3} \sum_{j=1}^{2} \frac{c_i a_j n_{ij}}{n}$$

where $\mathbf{c} = (c_1, c_2, c_3)$ represents scores for the groups and $\mathbf{a} = (a_1, a_2)$ represents scores for the columns (effectively 0, 1). Under H_0,

$$E\{\bar{f}|H_0\} = \sum_{i=1}^{3} c_i \left(\frac{n_{i+}}{n} \right) \sum_{j=1}^{2} a_j \left(\frac{n_{+j}}{n} \right) = \mu_{\mathbf{c}} \mu_{\mathbf{a}}$$

and

$$V\{\bar{f}|H_0\} = \left\{ \sum_{i=1}^{3} (c_i - \mu_{\mathbf{c}})^2 \left(\frac{n_{i+}}{n} \right) \sum_{j=1}^{2} \frac{(a_j - \mu_{\mathbf{a}})^2 (n_{+j}/n)}{(n-1)} \right\}$$

$$= \frac{v_{\mathbf{c}} v_{\mathbf{a}}}{(n-1)}$$

The quantity $\bar{f}$ has an approximate normal distribution for large samples, so for these situations

$$\begin{aligned} Q_{CS} &= \frac{(\bar{f} - E\{\bar{f}|H_0\})^2}{\text{Var}\{\bar{f}|H_0\}} \\ &= \frac{(n-1)[\sum_{i=1}^{3} \sum_{j=1}^{2} (c_i - \mu_{\mathbf{c}})(a_j - \mu_{\mathbf{a}}) n_{ij}]^2}{[\sum_{i=1}^{2} (c_i - \mu_{\mathbf{c}})^2 n_{i+}][\sum_{j=1}^{2} (a_i - \mu_{\mathbf{a}})^2 n_{+j}]} \\ &= (n-1) r_{\mathbf{ac}}^2 \end{aligned}$$

where $r_{\mathbf{ac}}$ is the Pearson correlation coefficient. Thus, Q_{CS} is known as the correlation statistic. It is approximately chi-square with one degree of freedom. This test is comparable to the Cochran-Armitage trend test (Cochran 1954, Armitage 1955). In fact, multiplying Q_{CS} by $n/(n-1)$ yields the same value as the z^2 of the Cochran-Armitage test.

For Table 4.6, $Q_{CS} = 41.058$. This is obtained by inputting the table into PROC FREQ, specifying the CHISQ option, and reading the value for the Mantel-Haenszel statistic.

4.3.2   Correlation Statistic

Mantel (1963) also proposed a statistic for the association of two variables that were ordinal for a combined set of strata, based on assigning scores $\{\mathbf{a}\}$ and $\{\mathbf{c}\}$ to the columns and rows of the tables.

$$
\begin{aligned}
Q_{CSMH} &= \frac{\{\sum_{h=1}^{q} n_h(\bar{f}_h - E\{\bar{f}_h|H_0\})\}^2}{\sum_{h=1}^{q} n_h^2 \mathrm{var}\{f_h|H_0\}} \\
&= \frac{\{\sum_{h=1}^{q} n_h(v_{hc}v_{ha})^{1/2}r_{\mathbf{ca},h}\}^2}{\sum_{h=1}^{q}[n_h^2 v_{hc}v_{ha}/(n_h - 1)]}
\end{aligned}
$$

Q_{CSMH} is called the extended Mantel-Haenszel correlation statistic. It approximately follows the chi-square distribution with one degree of freedom when the combined strata sample sizes are sufficiently large, that is,

$$
\sum_{h=1}^{q} n_h \geq 40
$$

4.3.3   Analysis of Smokeless Tobacco Data

The following SAS statements request that Mantel-Haenszel correlation statistics be computed for the smokeless tobacco data. Two TABLE statements are included to specify analyses using both integer scores and modified ridit scores. You can include as many TABLE statements in a PROC FREQ invocation as you like.

```
data tobacco;
   length risk $11. ;
   input f_usage $ risk $ usage $ count @@;
   cards;
no minimal        no    59 no   minimal     yes 25
no moderate       no   169 no   moderate    yes 29
no substantial    no   196 no   substantial yes  9
yes minimal       no    11 yes minimal      yes  8
yes moderate      no    33 yes moderate     yes 11
yes substantial no    22 yes substantial yes  2
;
proc freq;
   weight count;
   tables f_usage*risk*usage /cmh chisq measures;
   tables f_usage*risk*usage /cmh scores=modridit;
run;
```

Output 4.8 contains the statistics for the table of risk perception by adolescent usage when there is no father's usage. Note that $Q_{CS} = 34.284$, with 1 df, signifying a strong correlation between risk perception and smokeless tobacco usage.

Output 4.8   Results for No Father's Usage

```
            STATISTICS FOR TABLE 1 OF RISK BY USAGE
                  CONTROLLING FOR F_USAGE=no

   Statistic                       DF      Value       Prob
   -----------------------------------------------------------
   Chi-Square                       2      34.922      0.000
   Likelihood Ratio Chi-Square      2      34.068      0.000
   Mantel-Haenszel Chi-Square       1      34.284      0.000
   Phi Coefficient                          0.268
   Contingency Coefficient                  0.259
   Cramer's V                               0.268
```

Output 4.9 contains the same results for those whose fathers used smokeless tobacco.

Output 4.9   Results for Father's Usage

```
            STATISTICS FOR TABLE 2 OF RISK BY USAGE
                 CONTROLLING FOR F_USAGE=yes

   Statistic                       DF      Value       Prob
   -----------------------------------------------------------
   Chi-Square                       2      6.641       0.036
   Likelihood Ratio Chi-Square      2      7.046       0.030
   Mantel-Haenszel Chi-Square       1      6.564       0.010
   Phi Coefficient                          0.276
   Contingency Coefficient                  0.266
   Cramer's V                               0.276
```

There is still a correlation between risk perception and adolescent usage, although it is not as strong.

Output 4.10 contains the results for the combined tables. Q_{CSMH} is Statistic 1 in the table, labeled the "Nonzero Correlation" statistic. It takes the value 40.664 for integer scores, and it takes the value 39.305 for modified ridit scores. Both results are similar, with strongly significant statistics; often, different sets of scores produce essentially the same results.

Output 4.10   Results for Combined Tables

```
              SUMMARY STATISTICS FOR RISK BY USAGE
                    CONTROLLING FOR F_USAGE


         Cochran-Mantel-Haenszel Statistics (Based on Table Scores)

         Statistic   Alternative Hypothesis   DF      Value      Prob
         ---------------------------------------------------------------
            1         Nonzero Correlation       1     40.664     0.000
            2         Row Mean Scores Differ     2     41.058     0.000
            3         General Association        2     41.058     0.000



         Total Sample Size = 574



              SUMMARY STATISTICS FOR RISK BY USAGE
                    CONTROLLING FOR F_USAGE


         Cochran-Mantel-Haenszel Statistics (Modified Ridit Scores)

         Statistic   Alternative Hypothesis   DF      Value      Prob
         ---------------------------------------------------------------
            1         Nonzero Correlation       1     39.305     0.000
            2         Row Mean Scores Differ     2     41.083     0.000
            3         General Association        2     41.058     0.000



         Total Sample Size = 574
```

4.3.4   Pain Data Analysis

Clinical trials not only investigate measures of efficacy, or how well a drug works for its
designed purpose, but also address the matter of adverse effects, or whether the drug has
harmful side effects. Table 4.7 contains data from a study concerned with measuring the
adverse effects of a pain relief treatment that was given at five different dosages, including
placebo, to patients with one of two diagnoses. Investigators were interested in whether
there was a trend in the proportions with adverse effects.

Table 4.7   Adverse Effects for Pain Treatment

	Diagnosis			
	I		II	
	Adverse Effects		Adverse Effects	
Treatment	No	Yes	No	Yes
Placebo	26	6	26	6
Dosage1	26	7	12	20
Dosage2	23	9	13	20
Dosage3	18	14	1	31
Dosage4	9	23	1	31

The following SAS statements request a Q_{CSMH} statistic from PROC FREQ, using both integer scores and modified ridit scores. First, a TABLES statement requesting the table of treatment by response pooled over the two diagnoses is requested. Note the use of the ORDER=DATA option in the PROC statement. If this option was omitted, the levels of TREATMNT would be ordered incorrectly, with placebo being placed last instead of first.

```
data pain;
   input dgnosis $ treatmnt $ response $ count @@;
   cards;
   I placebo  no 26 I  placebo yes  6
   I dosage1  no 26 I  dosage1 yes  7
   I dosage2  no 23 I  dosage2 yes  9
   I dosage3  no 18 I  dosage3 yes 14
   I dosage4  no  9 I  dosage4 yes 23
   II placebo no 26 II placebo yes  6
   II dosage1 no 12 II dosage1 yes 20
   II dosage2 no 13 II dosage2 yes 20
   II dosage3 no  1 II dosage3 yes 31
   II dosage4 no  1 II dosage4 yes 31
;
proc freq order=data;
   weight count;
   tables treatmnt*response / chisq;
   tables dgnosis*treatmnt*response /
             chisq cmh;
   tables dgnosis*treatmnt*response /
             scores=modridit cmh;
run;
```

Q_{CS} for the combined table is strongly significant, with a value of 65.473 and 1 df.

Output 4.11   Results for Combined Diagnoses

```
                   TABLE OF TREATMNT BY RESPONSE

               TREATMNT      RESPONSE

               Frequency|
               Percent  |
               Row Pct  |
               Col Pct  |no      |yes     |  Total
               ---------+--------+--------+
               placebo  |    52  |    12  |     64
                        | 16.15  |  3.73  |  19.88
                        | 81.25  | 18.75  |
                        | 33.55  |  7.19  |
               ---------+--------+--------+
               dosage1  |    38  |    27  |     65
                        | 11.80  |  8.39  |  20.19
                        | 58.46  | 41.54  |
                        | 24.52  | 16.17  |
               ---------+--------+--------+
               dosage2  |    36  |    29  |     65
                        | 11.18  |  9.01  |  20.19
                        | 55.38  | 44.62  |
                        | 23.23  | 17.37  |
               ---------+--------+--------+
               dosage3  |    19  |    45  |     64
                        |  5.90  | 13.98  |  19.88
                        | 29.69  | 70.31  |
                        | 12.26  | 26.95  |
               ---------+--------+--------+
               dosage4  |    10  |    54  |     64
                        |  3.11  | 16.77  |  19.88
                        | 15.63  | 84.38  |
                        |  6.45  | 32.34  |
               ---------+--------+--------+
               Total        155      167      322
                          48.14    51.86   100.00


            STATISTICS FOR TABLE OF TREATMNT BY RESPONSE

       Statistic                      DF      Value      Prob
       --------------------------------------------------------
       Chi-Square                      4      68.075     0.000
       Likelihood Ratio Chi-Square     4      73.253     0.000
       Mantel-Haenszel Chi-Square      1      65.473     0.000
       Phi Coefficient                        0.460
       Contingency Coefficient                0.418
       Cramer's V                             0.460

       Sample Size = 322
```

Output 4.12 contains the statistics for the individual tables. Q_{CS} takes the value 22.819 for Diagnosis I and the value 52.331 for Diagnosis II.

Output 4.12   Results for Separate Diagnoses

```
        STATISTICS FOR TABLE 1 OF TREATMNT BY RESPONSE
                  CONTROLLING FOR DGNOSIS=I

Statistic                        DF      Value       Prob
---------------------------------------------------------
Chi-Square                        4      26.603      0.000
Likelihood Ratio Chi-Square       4      26.669      0.000
Mantel-Haenszel Chi-Square        1      22.819      0.000
Phi Coefficient                          0.406
Contingency Coefficient                  0.377
Cramer's V                               0.406


        STATISTICS FOR TABLE 2 OF TREATMNT BY RESPONSE
                 CONTROLLING FOR DGNOSIS=II

Statistic                        DF      Value       Prob
---------------------------------------------------------
Chi-Square                        4      60.507      0.000
Likelihood Ratio Chi-Square       4      68.745      0.000
Mantel-Haenszel Chi-Square        1      52.331      0.000
Phi Coefficient                          0.613
Contingency Coefficient                  0.523
Cramer's V                               0.613
```

Output 4.13 contains the stratified analysis results. Integer scores produce a Q_{CSMH} of 71.726, and modified ridit scores produce a Q_{CSMH} of 71.647. These statistics are clearly significant. The proportion of patients with adverse effects is correlated with level of dosage; higher dosages produce more reports of adverse effects.

Output 4.13   Combined Results

```
            SUMMARY STATISTICS FOR TREATMNT BY RESPONSE
                    CONTROLLING FOR DGNOSIS


  Cochran-Mantel-Haenszel Statistics (Based on Table Scores)

  Statistic   Alternative Hypothesis   DF      Value       Prob
  ------------------------------------------------------------
      1       Nonzero Correlation       1      71.726      0.000
      2       Row Mean Scores Differ    4      74.531      0.000
      3       General Association       4      74.531      0.000

            SUMMARY STATISTICS FOR TREATMNT BY RESPONSE
                    CONTROLLING FOR DGNOSIS


  Cochran-Mantel-Haenszel Statistics (Modified Ridit Scores)

  Statistic   Alternative Hypothesis   DF      Value       Prob
  ------------------------------------------------------------
      1       Nonzero Correlation       1      71.647      0.000
      2       Row Mean Scores Differ    4      74.531      0.000
      3       General Association       4      74.531      0.000
```

4.4   Relationships Between Sets of Tables

Suppose you transposed the rows and columns of Table 4.7. You would obtain the following:

Table 4.8   Adverse Effects for Pain Treatment

Diagnosis	Adverse Effects	Placebo	Dosage1	Dosage2	Dosage3	Dosage4
I	No	26	26	23	18	9
I	Yes	6	7	9	14	23
II	No	26	12	13	1	1
II	Yes	6	20	20	31	31

Furthermore, suppose you analyzed these tables as two $2 \times r$ tables, making the response variable the row variable and the grouping variable the column variable.

```
proc freq order=data;
   weight count;
   tables dgnosis*response*treatmnt /
          cmh;
run;
```

Look at the resulting table of Mantel-Haenszel statistics for DGNOSIS by RESPONSE by TREATMNT and compare it to the reprinted table of DGNOSIS by TREATMENT by RESPONSE.

Output 4.14   Combined Results

```
            SUMMARY STATISTICS FOR RESPONSE BY TREATMNT
                    CONTROLLING FOR DGNOSIS


     Cochran-Mantel-Haenszel Statistics (Based on Table Scores)

     Statistic   Alternative Hypothesis    DF      Value      Prob
     ------------------------------------------------------------------
         1         Nonzero Correlation       1      71.726     0.000
         2         Row Mean Scores Differ     1      71.726     0.000
         3         General Association        4      74.531     0.000


            SUMMARY STATISTICS FOR TREATMNT BY RESPONSE
                    CONTROLLING FOR DGNOSIS


     Cochran-Mantel-Haenszel Statistics (Based on Table Scores)

     Statistic   Alternative Hypothesis    DF      Value      Prob
     ------------------------------------------------------------------
         1         Nonzero Correlation       1      71.726     0.000
         2         Row Mean Scores Differ     4      74.531     0.000
         3         General Association        4      74.531     0.000
```

Q_{SMH} and Q_{CSMH} are identical here. One degree of freedom is needed to compare the mean differences across two groups, in the case of Q_{SMH}, and one degree of freedom is needed to assess correlation, in the case of Q_{CSMH}.

In Chapter 6, "Sets of $s \times r$ Tables," the Mantel-Haenszel statistic is extended to sets of $s \times r$ tables. The mean score statistic for the case of more than two groups has $(s - 1)$ degrees of freedom, since you are comparing mean differences across s groups. Thus, Q_S for the $2 \times r$ table is a special case of the more general mean score statistic and has $(s - 1) = (2 - 1) = 1$ degree of freedom. When $s = 2$, Q_{SMH} and Q_{CSMH} take the same value with table scores and can be used interchangeably. Thus, transposing the Table 4.7 data and computing these statistics produced identical mean score and correlation statistics, since the transposed data produced a mean score statistic with one degree of freedom.

Similarly, when $s = 2$, Q_S and Q_{CS} take the same value. This is why, in Section 4.2.1, you are able to use the Mantel-Haenszel statistic produced by the CHISQ option of PROC FREQ. That statistic is actually Q_{CS}, but for $2 \times r$ tables it is also the mean score statistic.

Table 4.9 summarizes the Mantel-Haenszel statistics for the tables discussed in this chapter; it also lists the labels associated with these statistics in PROC FREQ output.

Table 4.9   Summary of Extended Mantel-Haenszel Statistics

Table Dimensions	Statistic	DF	Corresponding PROC FREQ MH Label
2×2	Q_{MH}	1	Nonzero Correlation Row Mean Scores Differ General Association
$2 \times r$	Q_{SMH}	1	Nonzero Correlation Row Mean Scores Differ
$s \times 2$	Q_{CSMH}	1	Nonzero Correlation

Chapter 5
The s × r Table

Chapter Table of Contents

Chapter 5
The s × r Table

5.1 Introduction

Previous chapters address the concepts of association and measures of association in 2×2 tables and association in $2 \times r$ and $s \times 2$ tables. This chapter extends these concepts to the general $s \times r$ table. The main difference from these earlier chapters is that scale of measurement is always a consideration; the statistics you choose depend on whether the rows and columns of the table are nominally or ordinally scaled. This is true for investigating whether association exists and for summarizing the degree of association.

In addition, this chapter discusses measures of agreement. Often, subjects or experimental units are observed by two or more researchers, and the question of interest is how closely their evaluation agrees. Such studies are called *observer agreement* studies. The columns of the resulting table are the classifications of one observer, and the rows are the classifications of the other observer. Subjects are crossclassified into table cells according to their observed profiles.

Section 5.2 addresses tests for association, and Section 5.4 addresses measures of association. The exact test for $s \times r$ tables is discussed in Section 5.3, and observer agreement is discussed in Section 5.5.

5.2 Association

5.2.1 Tests for General Association

Table 5.1 contains data from a study concerning the distribution of party affiliation in a city suburb. There was interest in whether there was an association between registered political party and neighborhood.

Table 5.1 Distribution of Parties in Neighborhoods

Party	Neighborhood			
	Bayside	Highland	Longview	Sheffeld
Democrat	221	160	360	140
Independent	200	291	160	311
Republican	208	106	316	97

For these data, both row and column variables are nominally scaled; there is no inherent ordering of the response values for either neighborhood or political party. Thus, the alternative to the null hypothesis of no association is general association, defined as heterogeneous patterns of distribution of the response (column) levels across the row levels. The following table represents the general $s \times r$ table.

Table 5.2   s × r Contingency Table

Group	Response Variable Categories				Total
	1	2	...	r	
1	n_{11}	n_{12}	...	n_{1r}	n_{1+}
2	n_{21}	n_{22}	...	n_{2r}	n_{2+}
⋮	⋮	⋮		⋮	⋮
s	n_{s1}	n_{s2}	...	n_{sr}	n_{s+}
Total	n_{+1}	n_{+2}	...	n_{+r}	n

One test statistic for the hypothesis of no general association is the Pearson chi-square. This statistic is defined the same as for the 2×2 table, except that the summation for i is from 1 to s, and the summation for j is from 1 to r.

$$Q_P = \sum_{i=1}^{s} \sum_{j=1}^{r} \frac{(n_{ij} - m_{ij})^2}{m_{ij}}$$

where

$$m_{ij} = E\{n_{ij}|H_0\} = \frac{n_{i+}n_{+j}}{n}$$

is the expected value of the frequencies in the ith row and jth column.

If the sample size is sufficiently large, that is, all expected cell counts $m_{ij} \geq 5$, then Q_P approximately has the chi-square distribution with $(s-1)(r-1)$ degrees of freedom. In the case of the 2×2 table, $r = 2$ and $s = 2$ so that Q_P has 1 df.

Just as for 2×2 tables, the randomization statistic Q can be written

$$Q = \frac{n-1}{n}Q_P$$

and it also has an approximate chi-square distribution with $(s-1)(r-1)$ degrees of freedom under the null hypothesis.

For more detail, recall from Chapter 2, "The 2×2 Table," that the derivation of Q depends on the assumption of fixed marginal totals such that the table frequencies have a hypergeometric distribution. For the $s \times r$ table, the distribution is multivariate hypergeometric under the null hypothesis of no association.

You can write the probability distribution as

$$Pr\{n_{ij}\} = \frac{\prod_{i=1}^{s} n_{i+}! \prod_{j=1}^{r} n_{+j}!}{n! \prod_{i=1}^{s} \prod_{j=1}^{r} n_{ij}!}$$

The covariance structure under H_0 is

$$\text{Cov}\{n_{ij}, n_{i'j'}|H_0\} = \frac{m_{ij}(n\delta_{ii'} - n_{i'+})(n\delta_{jj'} - n_{+j'})}{n(n-1)}$$

where $\delta_{kk'} = 1$ if $k = k'$ and $\delta_{kk'} = 0$ if $k \neq k'$.

Q is computed from the quadratic form

$$Q = (\mathbf{n} - \mathbf{m})'\mathbf{A}'(\mathbf{AVA}')^{-1}\mathbf{A}(\mathbf{n} - \mathbf{m})$$

where $\mathbf{n} = (n_{11}, n_{12}, \ldots, n_{1r}, \ldots, n_{s1}, \ldots, n_{sr})'$ is the compound vector of observed frequencies, $\mathbf{m}$ is the corresponding vector of expected frequencies, $\mathbf{V}$ is the covariance matrix, and $\mathbf{A}$ is a matrix of coefficients defined such that $\mathbf{AVA}'$ is nonsingular. The symbol $\otimes$ denotes the left-hand Kronecker product (the matrix on the left of the $\otimes$ multiplies each element in the matrix on the right).

The usual choice for $\mathbf{A}$ for testing general association is

$$\mathbf{A} = \left[\mathbf{I}_{(r-1)}, \mathbf{0}_{(r-1)}\right] \otimes \left[\mathbf{I}_{(s-1)}, \mathbf{0}_{(s-1)}\right]$$

where $\mathbf{I}_{(j-1)}$ is the $(j-1) \times (j-1)$ identity matrix and $\mathbf{0}_{(j-1)}$ is a $(j-1)$ vector of 0s.

For example, for a 2×3 table,

$$\mathbf{A} = \begin{bmatrix} 1 & 0 & 0 & 0 & 0 & 0 \\ 0 & 1 & 0 & 0 & 0 & 0 \end{bmatrix}$$

Generating Q_P and Q from the SAS System requires no new PROC FREQ features. The CHISQ option in the TABLES statement produces Q_P, and the CMH option produces Q. The following statements produce these statistics for the neighborhood data.

```
data neighbor;
   length party $ 11 nei_hood $ 10;
   input party $ nei_hood $ count @@;
   cards;
democrat     longview  360 democrat     bayside  221
democrat     sheffeld  140 democrat     highland 160
republican   longview  316 republican   bayside  208
republican   sheffeld   97 republican   highland 106
independent  longview  160 independent  bayside  200
independent  sheffeld  311 independent  highland 291
;
proc freq ;
   weight count;
   tables party*nei_hood / chisq cmh;
run;
```

Output 5.1 contains the frequency table.

Output 5.1   Frequency Table

```
                    TABLE OF PARTY BY NEI_HOOD

         PARTY        NEI_HOOD

         Frequency  |
         Percent    |
         Row Pct    |
         Col Pct    |bayside |highland|longview|sheffeld|  Total
         -----------+--------+--------+--------+--------+
         democrat   |    221 |    160 |    360 |    140 |    881
                    |   8.60 |   6.23 |  14.01 |   5.45 |  34.28
                    |  25.09 |  18.16 |  40.86 |  15.89 |
                    |  35.14 |  28.73 |  43.06 |  25.55 |
         -----------+--------+--------+--------+--------+
         independent|    200 |    291 |    160 |    311 |    962
                    |   7.78 |  11.32 |   6.23 |  12.10 |  37.43
                    |  20.79 |  30.25 |  16.63 |  32.33 |
                    |  31.80 |  52.24 |  19.14 |  56.75 |
         -----------+--------+--------+--------+--------+
         republican |    208 |    106 |    316 |     97 |    727
                    |   8.09 |   4.12 |  12.30 |   3.77 |  28.29
                    |  28.61 |  14.58 |  43.47 |  13.34 |
                    |  33.07 |  19.03 |  37.80 |  17.70 |
         -----------+--------+--------+--------+--------+
         Total          629      557      836      548     2570
                       24.47    21.67    32.53    21.32   100.00
```

Output 5.2 displays the table statistics. $Q_P = 273.919$ with 6 df, $p < 0.001$.

Output 5.2   Pearson Chi-Square

```
         STATISTICS FOR TABLE OF PARTY BY NEI_HOOD

         Statistic                   DF    Value      Prob
         ------------------------------------------------------
         Chi-Square                   6   273.919    0.001
         Likelihood Ratio Chi-Square  6   282.327    0.001
         Mantel-Haenszel Chi-Square   1     0.812    0.367
         Phi Coefficient                    0.326
         Contingency Coefficient            0.310
         Cramer's V                         0.231
```

Output 5.3 contains the MH statistics. PROC FREQ computes Q as the extended Mantel-Haenszel statistic for one stratum. Q is the ''General Association'' statistic, with a value of 273.812 and 6 df. Notice how close the values of Q and Q_P are for these data; this is expected since the sample size is large (2570).

Output 5.3   Randomization Q

```
┌─────────────────────────────────────────────────────────────────┐
│              SUMMARY STATISTICS FOR PARTY BY NEI_HOOD             │
│                                                                   │
│                                                                   │
│         Cochran-Mantel-Haenszel Statistics (Based on Table Scores)│
│                                                                   │
│      Statistic   Alternative Hypothesis    DF      Value    Prob  │
│      ------------------------------------------------------------ │
│          1        Nonzero Correlation       1      0.812    0.367 │
│          2        Row Mean Scores Differ     2     13.894    0.001 │
│          3        General Association        6    273.812    0.001 │
└─────────────────────────────────────────────────────────────────┘
```

Political party and neighborhood are statistically associated. If you study the column percentages, you can see that the neighborhoods that have relatively high numbers of Democrats (Bayside, Longview) also have high numbers of Republicans. The neighborhoods that have relatively high numbers of Independents, Highland and Sheffeld, also have low numbers of both Democrats and Republicans.

5.2.2   Mean Score Test

The following data come from a study on headache pain relief. A new treatment was compared with the standard treatment and a placebo. Researchers measured the number of hours of substantial relief from headache pain.

Table 5.3   Pain Study Data

Treatment	Hours of Relief				
	0	1	2	3	4
Placebo	6	9	6	3	1
Standard	1	4	6	6	8
Test	2	5	6	8	6

Clearly, number of hours of relief is an ordinally scaled response measure. While Q and Q_P are good strategies for detecting general association, they aren't as good as other strategies when the response variable is ordinally scaled and the alternative to no association is location shifts. Section 4.2.1 discusses the mean score test for a $2 \times r$ table. Scores are assigned to the levels of the response variable, and row mean scores are computed. The statistic Q_S is then derived. Q_S also applies to $s \times r$ tables, in which case it has $(s - 1)$ degrees of freedom since you are comparing mean scores across s groups.

For more detail, the statistic Q_S is derived from the same general quadratic form as Q discussed in Section 5.2. You choose A so that it assigns scores to the response levels and then compares the resulting linear functions of scores for $(s - 1)$ groups to their expected values. A is the $(s - 1) \times sr$ matrix

$$
A = \begin{bmatrix}
a' & 0' & \cdots & 0' & 0' \\
0' & a' & \cdots & 0' & 0' \\
\vdots & \vdots & & & \vdots \\
0' & 0' & \cdots & a' & 0'
\end{bmatrix}
$$

For example, if the actual values were used as scores for the columns in Table 5.3, then $a' = (0\ 1\ 2\ 3\ 4)$.

It is interesting to note that Q_S can be written in a one-way analysis of variance form

$$
Q_S = \frac{(n-1)\sum_{i=1}^{s} n_{i+}(\bar{f}_i - \mu_{\mathbf{a}})^2}{n v_{\mathbf{a}}}
$$

where, as discussed in Section 4.2.1,

$$
\bar{f}_i = \sum_{j=1} \frac{a_j n_{ij}}{n_{i+}}
$$

and $\mu_{\mathbf{a}}$ is its expected value

$$
\mu_{\mathbf{a}} = E\{\bar{f}_i | H_0\} = \sum_{j=1}^{r} \frac{a_j n_{+j}}{n}
$$

$$
v_{\mathbf{a}} = \sum_{j=1}^{r} (a_j - \mu_{\mathbf{a}})^2 \left(\frac{n_{+j}}{n} \right)
$$

See Section 4.2.3 for choices of scoring systems. For the pain data, integer scores make sense. The following statements request the mean score test Q_S for the pain data.

```
data pain;
   input treatmnt $ hours count @@;
   cards;
   placebo  0 6 placebo  1  9 placebo  2 6 placebo  3 3 placebo  4 1
   standard 0 1 standard 1  4 standard 2 6 standard 3 6 standard 4 8
   test     0 2 test     1  5 test     2 6 test     3 8 test     4 6
   ;
proc freq;
   weight count;
   tables treatmnt*hours/ cmh nocol nopct;
run;
```

Output 5.4 contains the frequency table produced by PROC FREQ.

Output 5.4   Frequency Table

```
                    TABLE OF TREATMNT BY HOURS

        TREATMNT      HOURS

        Frequency|
        Row Pct  |      0|      1|      2|      3|      4|  Total
        ---------+--------+--------+--------+--------+--------+
        placebo  |    6  |    9  |    6  |    3  |    1  |    25
                 |  24.00 |  36.00 |  24.00 |  12.00 |   4.00 |
        ---------+--------+--------+--------+--------+--------+
        standard |    1  |    4  |    6  |    6  |    8  |    25
                 |   4.00 |  16.00 |  24.00 |  24.00 |  32.00 |
        ---------+--------+--------+--------+--------+--------+
        test     |    2  |    5  |    6  |    8  |    6  |    27
                 |   7.41 |  18.52 |  22.22 |  29.63 |  22.22 |
        ---------+--------+--------+--------+--------+--------+
        Total         9      18      18      17      15      77
```

Output 5.5 displays the summary statistics.

Output 5.5   Mean Score Statistic

```
              SUMMARY STATISTICS FOR TREATMNT BY HOURS

       Cochran-Mantel-Haenszel Statistics (Based on Table Scores)

       Statistic   Alternative Hypothesis    DF     Value     Prob
       ------------------------------------------------------------
           1       Nonzero Correlation        1     8.067    0.005
           2       Row Mean Scores Differ     2    13.735    0.001
           3       General Association        8    14.403    0.072
```

Q_S is the "Row Mean Scores Differ" statistic. $Q_S = 13.735$, with 2 df, and is clearly significant. Note that Q for these data takes the value 14.403, which has a p-value of 0.072 with 8 df. In fact, there are a number of cells whose expected values are less than or equal to 5, so the chi-square approximation for the test for general association may not even be valid. However, since the row totals of the table are all greater than 20, and each row has counts ≥ 5 for both outcomes ≤ 1 and ≥ 2, there is sufficient sample size for Q_S. This is an example of where taking advantage of the ordinality of the data not only is the more appropriate approach, it may be the only possible Mantel-Haenszel strategy due to sample size constraints.

5.2.3   Correlation Test

Sometimes, both the row variable and the column variable are ordinally scaled. This is common when you are studying responses that are evaluated on an ordinal scale and what is being compared are different dosage levels, which are also ordinally scaled. Consider the data in Table 5.4. A water treatment company is studying water additives and investigating how they affect clothes washing. The treatments studied were no treatment (plain water), the standard treatment, and a double dose of the standard treatment, called super. Washability was measured as low, medium, and high.

Table 5.4   Washability Data

| | Washability | | | |
Treatment	Low	Medium	High	Total
Water	27	14	5	46
Standard	10	17	26	53
Super	5	12	50	67

As discussed in Section 4.2.1, the appropriate statistic to investigate association for this situation is one that takes advantage of the ordinality of both the row variable and the column variable and tests the null hypothesis of no association against the alternative of linear association. In Chapter 4, "Sets of $2 \times r$ and $s \times 2$ Tables," the test statistic Q_{CS} was developed for the $s \times 2$ table and was shown to have one degree of freedom. A similar strategy applies to the $s \times r$ table. You assign scores both to the levels of the response variable and to the levels of the grouping variable to obtain Q_{CS}, which is approximately chi-square with one degree of freedom. Thus, whether the table is 2×2, $s \times 2$, or $s \times r$, Q_{CS} always has one degree of freedom. (See Section 4.4 for a related discussion.)

For more detail, this statistic is also derived from the general quadratic form

$$Q = (n - m)'A'(AVA')^{-1}A(n - m)$$

You obtain Q_{CS} by choosing A to be

$$A = [a' \otimes c'] = [a_1 c_1, \ldots, a_r c_1, \ldots, a_r c_s]$$

where $a' = (a_1, a_2, \ldots, a_r)$ are scores for the response levels and $c' = (c_1, c_2, \ldots, c_s)$ are scores for the levels of the grouping variable. A has dimension $1 \times sr$.

The following PROC FREQ invocation produces the correlation statistic for the washability data. It is of interest to use both integer scores and modified ridit scores and compare the results. The following statements request both integer scores (the default) and modified ridit scores. The ORDER= option maintains the desired order of the levels of the rows and columns; it is the same as the order in which the variable values are encountered in the DATA step. The NOPRINT option suppresses the printing of the individual tables.

```
data wash;
   input treatmnt $ washblty $ count @@;
   cards;
   water low 27 water medium 14 water high 5
   standard low 10 standard medium 17 standard high 26
   super low 5 super medium 12 super high 50
   ;
proc freq order=data;
   weight count;
   tables treatmnt*washblty / chisq cmh;
   tables treatmnt*washblty / scores=modridit cmh noprint;
run;
```

Output 5.6 displays the frequency table.

Output 5.6   Frequency Table

```
            TABLE OF TREATMNT BY WASHBLTY

      TREATMNT      WASHBLTY

      Frequency|
      Percent  |
      Row Pct  |
      Col Pct  |low     |medium  |high    |  Total
      ---------+--------+--------+--------+
      water    |    27  |    14  |     5  |    46
               | 16.27  |  8.43  |  3.01  | 27.71
               | 58.70  | 30.43  | 10.87  |
               | 64.29  | 32.56  |  6.17  |
      ---------+--------+--------+--------+
      standard |    10  |    17  |    26  |    53
               |  6.02  | 10.24  | 15.66  | 31.93
               | 18.87  | 32.08  | 49.06  |
               | 23.81  | 39.53  | 32.10  |
      ---------+--------+--------+--------+
      super    |     5  |    12  |    50  |    67
               |  3.01  |  7.23  | 30.12  | 40.36
               |  7.46  | 17.91  | 74.63  |
               | 11.90  | 27.91  | 61.73  |
      ---------+--------+--------+--------+
      Total         42       43       81      166
                  25.30    25.90    48.80   100.00
```

The CHISQ option always produces the correlation statistic Q_{CS}. Compare its value, $Q_{CS} = 50.602$ (displayed in Output 5.7), with the statistic displayed under "Nonzero Correlation" in Output 5.8. These statistics are the same. Thus, you don't need to specify CMH to obtain Q_{CS} for a single table. For a 2×2 table, Q_{CS} is equivalent to Q and Q_S; for a $2 \times r$ table, Q_{CS} is equivalent to Q_S.

Output 5.7   Statistics for Table

```
      STATISTICS FOR TABLE OF TREATMNT BY WASHBLTY

      Statistic                   DF    Value    Prob
      ---------------------------------------------------
      Chi-Square                   4    55.088   0.001
      Likelihood Ratio Chi-Square  4    58.037   0.001
      Mantel-Haenszel Chi-Square   1    50.602   0.001
      Phi Coefficient                   0.576
      Contingency Coefficient           0.499
      Cramer's V                        0.407
```

Output 5.8 Q_{CS} for Integer Scores

```
SUMMARY STATISTICS FOR TREATMNT BY WASHBLTY


Cochran-Mantel-Haenszel Statistics (Based on Table Scores)

Statistic    Alternative Hypothesis    DF      Value      Prob
-------------------------------------------------------------------
    1        Nonzero Correlation        1      50.602     0.001
    2        Row Mean Scores Differ     2      52.779     0.001
    3        General Association        4      54.756     0.001
```

Q_{CS} is clearly significant. Washability increases with the degree of additive to the water. Output 5.9 displays Q_{CS} for the modified ridit scores. It has the value 49.541, which is clearly significant.

Output 5.9 Q_{CS} for Modified Ridit Scores

```
SUMMARY STATISTICS FOR TREATMNT BY WASHBLTY

Cochran-Mantel-Haenszel Statistics (Modified Ridit Scores)

Statistic    Alternative Hypothesis    DF      Value      Prob
-------------------------------------------------------------------
    1        Nonzero Correlation        1      49.541     0.001
    2        Row Mean Scores Differ     2      52.515     0.001
    3        General Association        4      54.756     0.001
```

5.3   Exact Tests

In some cases, there is not sufficient sample size for the chi-square statistics discussed earlier in this chapter to be valid (several $m_{ij} \leq 5$). An alternative strategy for these situations is the exact test for $s \times r$ tables. This method follows the same principles as Fisher's exact test, except that the probabilities that are summed are taken from the multivariate hypergeometric distribution. Mehta and Patel (1983) describe an algorithm for obtaining exact p-values; Baglivo et al. (1988), Cox and Plackett (1980), and Pagano and Halvorsen (1981) have also done work in this area.

Consider Table 5.5. A marketing research firm organized a focus group to consider issues of new car marketing. Members of the group included those persons who had purchased a car from a local dealer in the last month. Researchers were interested in whether there was an association between the type of car bought and the manner in which group members found out about the car in the media. Cars were classified as sedans, sporty, and utility. The types of media included television, magazines, newspapers, and radio.

Table 5.5   Car Marketing Data

| Type of Car | Advertising Source | | | | Total |
	TV	Magazine	Newspaper	Radio	
Sedan	4	0	0	2	6
Sporty	0	3	3	4	10
Utility	5	5	2	2	14

It is clear that the data do not meet the requirements for the usual tests of association via the Pearson chi-square or the randomization chi-square. There are a number of zero cells and a number of other cells whose expected values are less than 5. Under these circumstances, the exact test for no association is an appropriate strategy.

The following SAS statements produce the exact test for the car marketing data. Recall that Fisher's exact test is produced automatically for 2×2 tables with the CHISQ option; to generate the exact test for $s \times r$ tables, you need to specify the EXACT option in the TABLES statement. This generates the usual statistics produced with the CHISQ option and the exact test. Since the ORDER= option isn't specified, the columns of the resulting table will be ordered alphabetically. No ordering is assumed for this test, so this does not matter.

```
data market;
   length ad_sourc $ 9. ;
   input car $ ad_sourc $ count @@;
   cards;
   sporty  paper 3 sporty  radio 4 sporty  tv 0 sporty  magazine 3
   sedan   paper 0 sedan   radio 2 sedan   tv 4 sedan   magazine 0
   utility paper 2 utility radio 2 utility tv 5 utility magazine 5
   ;
proc freq;
   weight count;
   table car*ad_sourc / exact norow nocol nopct;
run;
```

Output 5.10 contains the frequency table.

Output 5.10   Car Marketing Frequency Table

```
                       TABLE OF CAR BY AD_SOURC

          CAR        AD_SOURC

          Frequency|magazine|paper   |radio   |tv     |  Total
          ---------+--------+--------+--------+--------+
          sedan    |    0 |     0 |     2 |     4 |     6
          ---------+--------+--------+--------+--------+
          sporty   |    3 |     3 |     4 |     0 |    10
          ---------+--------+--------+--------+--------+
          utility  |    5 |     2 |     2 |     5 |    14
          ---------+--------+--------+--------+--------+
          Total         8       5       8       9       30
```

Output 5.11 displays the statistics for the table. The p-value for the exact test is listed for "Fisher's Exact Test (2-Tail)." For these data, $p = 0.047$. Note that the value for Q_P is 11.598 with 6 df, $p = 0.072$, and the likelihood ratio chi-square has the value 16.309 with $p = 0.012$. Q_P tends to be more conservative and Q_L tends to be more liberal than the exact test. Note that since the alternative hypothesis is general association, there is no analogy to the left-tail or right-tail like there is for Fisher's exact test for 2×2 tables, when the alternative can be directional association.

Output 5.11   Exact Test Results

```
              STATISTICS FOR TABLE OF CAR BY AD_SOURC

          Statistic                  DF      Value      Prob
          ------------------------------------------------------
          Chi-Square                  6      11.598     0.072
          Likelihood Ratio Chi-Square 6      16.309     0.012
          Mantel-Haenszel Chi-Square  1       0.191     0.662
          Fisher's Exact Test (2-Tail)                  0.047
          Phi Coefficient                     0.622
          Contingency Coefficient             0.528
          Cramer's V                          0.440

          Sample Size = 30
          WARNING: 100% of the cells have expected counts less
                   than 5. Chi-Square may not be a valid test.
```

This method is computationally intensive. The memory requirements and CPU time requirements can be quite high. As the sample size becomes larger, the test is likely to become computationally infeasible. This test is mainly useful when significance is suggested by the approximate results of Q_P and Q_L. Also, in these situations the computations are not overly lengthy. Computations are lengthy when the p-value is somewhere around 0.5, and in this situation, the exact p-value is usually not needed.

5.4   Measures of Association

Analysts are sometimes interested in assessing the strength of association in $s \times r$ tables. Although there is no counterpart to the odds ratios in 2×2 tables, there are several measures of association available, and, as you might expect, their choice depends on the scale of measurement.

5.4.1 Ordinal Measures of Association

If the data in the table have an interval scale or have scores that are equally spaced, then the Pearson correlation coefficient is an appropriate measure of association, and one that is familiar to most readers.

If the data do not lie on an obvious scale, but are ordinal in nature, then there are other measures of association that apply. Most of these are based on the classification of all possible pairs of subjects in the table as *concordant* or *discordant* pairs. If a pair is concordant, then the subject ranking higher on the row variable also ranks higher on the column variable. If a pair is discordant, then the subject ranking higher on the row variable ranks lower on the column variable. The pair can also be tied on the row and column variables.

The gamma, Kendall's tau-b, tau-c, and Somer's D statistics are all based on concordant and discordant pairs; that is, they use the relative ordering on the levels of the variables to determine whether association is negative, positive, or present at all. For example, gamma is estimated by

$$\hat{\gamma} = \frac{(C - D)}{(C + D)}$$

where C is the total number of concordant pairs, and D is the total number of discordant pairs.

These measures, like the Pearson correlation coefficient, take values between -1 and 1. They differ mainly on their strategies for adjusting for ties and sample size. Somer's D depends on which variable is considered to be independent (the grouping variable—adjustments for ties are made only on it). Somer's D, Stuart's tau-c, and Kendall's tau-b are generally more conservative than gamma. See the *SAS/STAT User's Guide, Version 6, Fourth Edition, Volume I* for more information on these statistics.

5.4.2 Nominal Measures of Association

Measures of association when one or both variables are nominally scaled are more difficult to define, since you can't think of association in these circumstances as negative or positive in any sense. However, indices of association in the nominal case have been constructed, and most are based on mimicking R-squared in some fashion. One such measure is the uncertainty coefficient, and another is the lambda coefficient. More information about these statistics can be obtained in the *SAS/STAT User's Guide, Volume I*, including the appropriate references. Agresti (1990) also discusses some of these measures.

5.4.3 Examples

Measures of association are produced in the PROC FREQ output by specifying
MEASURES as an option in the TABLES statement. The following statements produce
measures of association for the washability data. Using SCORES=RANK on the second
TABLES statement specifies that rank scores are to be used in calculating Pearson's
correlation coefficient to produce a Spearman's rank correlation coefficient.

```
data wash;
   input treatmnt $ washblty $ count @@;
   cards;
   water     low 27 water     medium 14 water     high  5
   standard low 10 standard medium 17 standard high 26
   super     low  5 super     medium 12 super     high 50
   ;
proc freq order=data;
   weight count;
   tables treatmnt*washblty / measures noprint;
   tables treatmnt*washblty / measures scores=rank noprint;
run;
```

Output 5.12 contains the table produced by the first PROC FREQ invocation. All of the
measures of ordinal association indicate a positive association. Note also that the Somer's
D statistics, Kendall's tau-b, and Stuart's tau-c all have smaller values than gamma.
Somer's D statistic has two forms: Somer's D C|R means that the column variable is
considered the dependent, or response, variable and Somer's D R|C means that the row
variable is considered the response variable.

Output 5.12   Measures of Association

```
            STATISTICS FOR TABLE OF TREATMNT BY WASHBLTY

        Statistic                          Value       ASE
        ---------------------------------------------------
        Gamma                              0.697      0.064
        Kendall's Tau-b                    0.497      0.055
        Stuart's Tau-c                     0.480      0.055

        Somers' D C|R                      0.486      0.054
        Somers' D R|C                      0.508      0.057

        Pearson Correlation                0.554      0.059
        Spearman Correlation               0.548      0.060

        Lambda Asymmetric C|R              0.259      0.057
        Lambda Asymmetric R|C              0.273      0.067
        Lambda Symmetric                   0.266      0.056

        Uncertainty Coefficient C|R        0.167      0.039
        Uncertainty Coefficient R|C        0.161      0.037
        Uncertainty Coefficient Symmetric  0.164      0.038
```

Printed next to each statistic is the asymptotic standard error (ASE). Although the measure
of association is always valid, these standard errors are only valid if the sample size is
large. Very conservative guidelines are the usual requirements for the Pearson chi-square

that the expected cell counts is 5 or greater. A more realistic guideline is to collapse the $s \times r$ table to a 2×2 table by choosing cutpoints and then adding the appropriate rows and columns. You can think of this as drawing a line under one row and beside one column. The 2×2 table is the result of summing the cells in the resulting quadrants. The sample size is adequate if each of the cells of this 2×2 table is 5 or greater.

If the sample size is adequate, then the measure of association is approximately normally distributed and you can form the confidence intervals of interest. For example,

$$\text{measure} \pm 1.96 \times \text{ASE}$$

forms the bounds of a 95 percent confidence interval.

Output 5.13 contains the output produced by the second PROC FREQ invocation. The only difference is that rank scores were used in the calculation of Pearson's correlation coefficient. When rank scores are used, Pearson's correlation coefficient is equivalent to Spearman's correlation, as illustrated in the output. (However, the asymptotic standard errors are not equivalent.)

Output 5.13   Rank Scores for Pearson's Correlation

```
             STATISTICS FOR TABLE OF TREATMNT BY WASHBLTY

             Statistic                        Value      ASE
             ----------------------------------------------------
             Gamma                            0.697      0.064
             Kendall's Tau-b                  0.497      0.055
             Stuart's Tau-c                   0.480      0.055

             Somers' D C|R                    0.486      0.054
             Somers' D R|C                    0.508      0.057

             Pearson Correlation (Rank Scores) 0.548     0.059
             Spearman Correlation             0.548      0.060

             Lambda Asymmetric C|R            0.259      0.057
             Lambda Asymmetric R|C            0.273      0.067
             Lambda Symmetric                 0.266      0.056

             Uncertainty Coefficient C|R      0.167      0.039
             Uncertainty Coefficient R|C      0.161      0.037
             Uncertainty Coefficient Symmetric 0.164     0.038
```

The next PROC FREQ invocation produces nominal measures of association for the neighborhood data.

```
data neighbor;
   length party $ 11 nei_hood $ 10;
   input party $ nei_hood $ count @@;
   cards;
democrat      longview    360 democrat      bayside  221
democrat      sheffeld    140 democrat      highland 160
republican    longview    316 republican    bayside  208
republican    sheffeld     97 republican    highland 106
independent   longview    160 independent   bayside  200
```

```
independent sheffeld    311 independent highland 291
;
proc freq ;
   weight count;
   tables party*nei_hood / chisq measures;
run;
```

Output 5.14 displays the resulting table.

Output 5.14   Nominal Measures of Association

```
          STATISTICS FOR TABLE OF PARTY BY NEI_HOOD

     Statistic                           Value       ASE
     -------------------------------------------------------
     Gamma                              -0.018      0.023
     Kendall's Tau-b                    -0.013      0.016
     Stuart's Tau-c                     -0.014      0.017

     Somers' D C|R                      -0.014      0.017
     Somers' D R|C                      -0.012      0.015

     Pearson Correlation                -0.018      0.019
     Spearman Correlation               -0.015      0.019

     Lambda Asymmetric C|R               0.087      0.012
     Lambda Asymmetric R|C               0.137      0.018
     Lambda Symmetric                    0.111      0.012

     Uncertainty Coefficient C|R         0.040      0.005
     Uncertainty Coefficient R|C         0.050      0.006
     Uncertainty Coefficient Symmetric   0.045      0.005
```

You should ignore the ordinal measures of association here since the data are not ordinally scaled. There are three versions of both the lambda coefficient and the uncertainty coefficient: column variable as the response variable, row variable as the response variable, and a symmetric version. Obviously, this makes a difference in the resulting statistic.

5.5   Observer Agreement

For many years, researchers in medicine, epidemiology, psychiatry, and psychological measurement and testing have been aware of the importance of observer error as a major source of measurement error. In many cases, different observers, or even the same observer at a different time, may examine an x-ray or perform a physical examination and reach different conclusions. It is important to evaluate observer agreement, both to understand the possible contributions to measurement error and as part of the evaluation of testing new instruments and procedures.

Often, the data collected as part of an observer agreement study form a contingency table, where the column levels represent the ratings of one observer and the row levels represent the ratings of another observer. Each cell represents one possible profile of the observers' ratings. The cells on the diagonal represent the cases where the observers agree.

Consider Table 5.6. These data come from a study concerning the diagnostic classification of multiple sclerosis patients. Patients from Winnipeg and News Orleans were classified into one of four diagnostic classes by both a Winnipeg neurologist and a New Orleans neurologist. Table 5.6 contains the data for the Winnipeg patients (Landis and Koch 1977).

Table 5.6   Ratings of Neurologists

New Orleans Neurologist	Winnipeg Neurologist			
	1	2	3	4
1	38	5	0	1
2	33	11	3	0
3	10	14	5	6
4	3	7	3	10

Certainly one way to assess the association between these two raters is to compute the usual measures of association. However, while measures of association can reflect the strength of the predictable relationship between two raters or observers, they don't target how well they agree. Agreement can be considered a special case of association—to what degree do different observers classify a particular subject into the identical category. All measures of agreement target the diagonal cells of a contingency table in their computations, and some measures take into consideration how far away from the diagonal elements other cells fall.

Suppose π_{ij} is the probability of a subject being classified in the ith category by the first observer and the jth category by the second observer. Then

$$\Pi_o = \sum \pi_{ii}$$

is the probability that the observers agree. If the ratings are independent, then the probability of agreement is

$$\Pi_e = \sum \pi_{i+}\pi_{+i}$$

So, $\Pi_o - \Pi_e$ is the amount of agreement beyond that expected by chance. The *kappa coefficient* (Cohen 1960) is defined as

$$\kappa = \frac{\Pi_o - \Pi_e}{1 - \Pi_e}$$

Since $\Pi_o = 1$ when there is perfect agreement (all non-diagonal elements are zero), κ equals 1 when there is perfect agreement, and κ equals 0 when the agreement equals that expected by chance. The closer the value is to 1, the more agreement there is in the table. It is possible to obtain negative values, but that rarely occurs. Note that κ is analogous to the intraclass correlation coefficient obtained from ANOVA models for quantitative measurements; it can be used as a measure of reliability of multiple determinations on the same subject (Fleiss and Cohen 1973, Fleiss 1975).

You may be interested in distinguishing degrees of agreement in a table, particularly if the categories are ordered in some way. For example, you may want to take into account those disagreements that are just one category away. A weighted form of the kappa statistic allows you to assign weights, or scores, to the various categories so that you can incorporate such considerations into the construction of the test statistic.

Weighted κ is written

$$\kappa_w = \frac{\sum\sum w_{ij}\pi_{ij} - \sum\sum w_{ij}\pi_{i+}\pi_{+j}}{1 - \sum\sum_{ij} w_{ij}\pi_{i+}\pi_{+j}}$$

where w_{ij} represents weights with values between 0 and 1. One possible set of weights is

$$w_{ij} = 1 - \frac{|\text{score}(i) - \text{score}(j)|}{\text{score}(dim) - \text{score}(1)}$$

where score(i) is the score for the ith row, score(j) is the score for the jth column, and dim is the dimension of an $s \times s$ table. This scoring system puts more weight on those cells closest to the diagonal.

The following SAS statements generate kappa statistics for the Winnipeg data. To produce measures of agreement, you specify AGREE in the TABLES statement. (Note: This feature is available with Release 6.10 of the SAS System.)

```
data classify;
   input no_rater w_rater count @@;
   cards;
   1 1 38 1 2  5 1 3 0 1 4  1
   2 1 33 2 2 11 2 3 3 2 4  0
   3 1 10 3 2 14 3 3 5 3 4  6
   4 1  3 4 2  7 4 3 3 4 4 10
   ;
proc freq;
   weight count;
   tables no_rater*w_rater / agree ;
run;
```

Output 5.15 contains the table.

Output 5.15   Winnipeg Data

```
                    TABLE OF NO_RATER BY W_RATER

    NO_RATER       W_RATER

    Frequency|
    Percent  |
    Row Pct  |
    Col Pct  |       1|       2|       3|       4| Total
    ---------+--------+--------+--------+--------+
          1 |     38 |      5 |      0 |      1 |    44
            |  25.50 |   3.36 |   0.00 |   0.67 | 29.53
            |  86.36 |  11.36 |   0.00 |   2.27 |
            |  45.24 |  13.51 |   0.00 |   5.88 |
    ---------+--------+--------+--------+--------+
          2 |     33 |     11 |      3 |      0 |    47
            |  22.15 |   7.38 |   2.01 |   0.00 | 31.54
            |  70.21 |  23.40 |   6.38 |   0.00 |
            |  39.29 |  29.73 |  27.27 |   0.00 |
    ---------+--------+--------+--------+--------+
          3 |     10 |     14 |      5 |      6 |    35
            |   6.71 |   9.40 |   3.36 |   4.03 | 23.49
            |  28.57 |  40.00 |  14.29 |  17.14 |
            |  11.90 |  37.84 |  45.45 |  35.29 |
    ---------+--------+--------+--------+--------+
          4 |      3 |      7 |      3 |     10 |    23
            |   2.01 |   4.70 |   2.01 |   6.71 | 15.44
            |  13.04 |  30.43 |  13.04 |  43.48 |
            |   3.57 |  18.92 |  27.27 |  58.82 |
    =========+========+========+========+========+
    Total          84       37       11       17    149
                56.38    24.83     7.38    11.41 100.00
```

Output 5.16 displays the measures of association.

Output 5.16   Kappa Statistics

```
         STATISTICS FOR TABLE OF NO_RATER BY W_RATER

                      Test of Symmetry
                      ----------------
    Statistic = 46.749       DF = 6        Prob = 0.001


                      Kappa Coefficients

    Statistic        Value     ASE    95% Confidence Bounds
    ----------------------------------------------------------
    Simple Kappa     0.208    0.050      0.109     0.307
    Weighted Kappa   0.380    0.052      0.278     0.481
```

$\hat{\kappa}$ has the value 0.208. This is indicative of slight agreement. Values of 0.4 or above are considered to indicate moderate agreement, and values of 0.8 or higher indicate excellent agreement. The asymptotic standard error is also printed, as well as confidence bounds. Since the confidence bounds do not contain the value 0, you can reject the hypothesis that κ is 0 for these data (no agreement) at the $\alpha = 0.05$ level of significance.

Using the default scores, $\hat{\kappa}_w$ takes the value 0.380. This means that if you consider disagreement close to the diagonals less heavily than disagreement further away from the diagonals, you get higher agreement. $\hat{\kappa}$ treats all off-diagonal cells the same. When $\hat{\kappa}_w$ is high, for example, ≥ 0.6 for moderate sample size, it may be preferable to produce confidence bounds on a transformed scale like logarithms and then exponentiate to compute the limits.

The test of symmetry that is printed is Bowker's test of symmetry (Bowker 1948).

Chapter 6
Sets of s × r Tables

Chapter Table of Contents

Chapter 6
Sets of s × r Tables

6.1 Introduction

Previous chapters address stratified analysis as the assessment of association in sets of 2×2 tables, $2 \times r$ tables where the response variable, represented in the table columns, is ordinally scaled, and $s \times 2$ tables where the groups for the row variable are ordinally scaled. Such analyses are special cases of the analysis of sets of $s \times r$ tables, which includes the cases where the row and column variables are both nominally scaled, the row variable is nominally scaled and the column variable is ordinally scaled, and the row variable and the column variable are both ordinally scaled. The Mantel-Haenszel procedure can be extended to handle these situations. It provides statistics that detect general association, mean score differences, and linear correlation as alternatives to the null hypothesis of no association; the choice of statistic depends on the scale of the row and column variables.

The general idea of stratified analyses is that you control for the effects of factors that are part of the research design, such as medical centers or hospitals in a randomized clinical trial, or factors that represent a prespecified poststudy stratification to adjust for explanatory variables that are thought to be related to the response variable. This is a common strategy for retrospective and observational studies. As mentioned in previous chapters, the Mantel-Haenszel procedure potentially removes the confounding influence of the explanatory variables that comprise the stratification and provides a gain of power for detecting association by comparing like subjects. In some sense, the strategy is similar to adjustment for blocks in a two-way analysis of variance for randomized blocks; it is also similar to covariance adjustment for a categorical explanatory variable.

Historically, the principle of combining information across strata was identified by Cochran (1954): this was in the context of combining differences of proportions from binomial distributions. Mantel and Haenszel (1959) refined the procedure to apply to hypergeometric distributions and produced a statistic to which central limit theory was more applicable for the combined strata. Thus, only the overall sample size needed to be reasonably large. The Mantel-Haenszel statistic proved more useful than Cochran's method. (Cochran's influence is why the PROC FREQ output is labeled ''Cochran-Mantel-Haenszel Statistics''; current literature tends to use the terms 'extended Mantel-Haenszel statistics' and 'Mantel-Haenszel statistics.')

Mantel (1963) discussed extensions to the MH strategy, including strategies for sets of $2 \times r$ tables, sets of $s \times 2$ tables, and the correlation statistic for $s \times r$ tables. The method was further elaborated by Landis, Heyman, and Koch (1978) to encompass the family of

Mantel-Haenzsel statistics, which included the statistics for general association, nonparametric ANOVA (mean score), the correlation statistic, and other special cases. Kuritz, Landis, and Koch (1988) present a useful overview of the Mantel-Haenszel strategy.

The Mantel-Haenszel procedure requires minimal assumptions. The methods it encompasses are based on randomization considerations; the only assumptions required are the randomization of the subjects to levels of the row variable. This can be done explicitly, such as for randomized clinical trials, implicitly, via hypothesis, or conditionally, such as for retrospective studies or observational data. The minimal assumptions often allow you to perform hypothesis tests on data that do not meet the more rigorous assumptions concerning random sampling or underlying distributions that are required for statistical modeling. However, the conclusions of the analysis may be restricted to the study population at hand, versus inference to a larger population. Most often, a complete analysis includes the applications of these minimal assumption methods to perform hypothesis tests and then statistical modeling to describe more completely the variation in the data.

Another advantage of the Mantel-Haenszel procedure is the fact that sample size requirements are based on total frequencies, or quantities summed across tables, rather than on individual cell sizes. This is partly because the Mantel-Haenszel methods are targeted at detecting average effects across strata; they are often called methods of assessing average partial association.

Section 6.2 discusses the formulation of the Mantel-Haenszel statistics in matrix terminology. Section 6.3 illustrates the use of the Mantel-Haenszel strategy for several applications. Finally, Section 6.4 includes the advanced topic of the use of the Mantel-Haenszel procedure in repeated measurements analysis.

6.2   General Mantel-Haenszel Methodology

The following table represents the generic $s \times r$ table in a set of q $s \times r$ tables.

Table 6.1 hth s × r Contingency Table

Group	Response Variable Categories 1	2	...	r	Total
1	n_{h11}	n_{h12}	...	n_{h1r}	n_{h1+}
2	n_{h21}	n_{h22}	...	n_{h2r}	n_{h2+}
⋮	⋮	⋮		⋮	⋮
s	n_{hs1}	n_{hs2}	...	n_{hsr}	n_{hs+}
Total	n_{h+1}	n_{h+2}	...	n_{h+r}	n_h

Under the assumption that the marginal totals n_{hi+} and n_{n+j} are fixed, the overall null hypothesis of no partial association can be stated as follows:

For each of the levels of the stratification variable $h = 1, 2, \ldots, q$, the response variable is distributed at random with respect to the groups (row variable levels).

Suppose $\mathbf{n}'_h = (n_{h11}, n_{h12}, \ldots, n_{h1r}, \ldots, n_{hs1}, \ldots, n_{hsr})$, where n_{hij} is the number of subjects in the hth stratum in the ith group in the jth response category. The probability distribution for the vector $\mathbf{n}_h$ under H_0 can be written

$$Pr\{\mathbf{n}_h|H_0\} = \frac{\prod_{i=1}^{s} n_{hi+}! \prod_{j=1}^{r} n_{h+j}!}{n_h! \prod_{i=1}^{s} \prod_{j=1}^{r} n_{hij}!}$$

For the hth stratum, suppose that $p_{hi+} = n_{hi+}/n_h$ denotes the marginal proportion of subjects belonging to the ith group and suppose that $p_{h+j} = n_{h+j}/n_h$ denotes the marginal proportion of subjects classified as belonging to the jth response category. These proportions can be denoted in vector notation as

$$\mathbf{p}'_{h*+} = (p_{h1+}, \ldots, p_{hs+})$$

$$\mathbf{p}'_{h+*} = (p_{h+1}, \ldots, p_{h+r})$$

Then,

$$E\{n_{hij}|H_0\} = m_{hij} = n_h p_{hi+} p_{h+j}$$

and the expected value of $\mathbf{n}_h$ can be written

$$E\{\mathbf{n}_h|H_0\} = \mathbf{m}_h = n_h \left[\mathbf{p}_{h+*} \otimes \mathbf{p}_{h*+}\right]$$

where $\otimes$ denotes the left-hand Kronecker product (the matrix on the left of the $\otimes$ multiplies each element of the matrix on the right).

The variance of $\mathbf{n}_h$ under H_0 is

$$V_h = \mathrm{Var}\{\mathbf{n}_h|H_0\} = \frac{n_h^2}{(n_h - 1)} \left\{[\mathbf{D}_{\mathbf{p}_{h+*}} - \mathbf{p}_{h+*}\mathbf{p}'_{h+*}] \otimes [\mathbf{D}_{\mathbf{p}_{h*+}} - \mathbf{p}_{h*+}\mathbf{p}'_{h*+}]\right\}$$

where $\mathbf{D}_{\mathbf{p}_{h+*}}$ and $\mathbf{D}_{\mathbf{p}_{h*+}}$ are diagonal matrices with elements of the vectors $\mathbf{p}_{h+*}$ and $\mathbf{p}_{h*+}$ as the main diagonals.

The general form of the extended Mantel-Haenszel statistic for $s \times r$ tables is

$$Q_{EMH} = \left\{\sum_{h=1}^{q} (\mathbf{n}_h - \mathbf{m}_h)' \mathbf{A}'_h\right\} \left\{\sum_{h=1}^{q} \mathbf{A}_h \mathbf{V}_h \mathbf{A}'_h\right\}^{-1} \left\{\sum_{h=1}^{q} \mathbf{A}_h (\mathbf{n}_h - \mathbf{m}_h)\right\}$$

where $\mathbf{A}_h$ is a matrix that specifies the linear functions of the $\{\mathbf{n}_h - \mathbf{m}_h\}$ at which the test statistic is directed. Choices of the $\{\mathbf{A}_h\}$ provide stratification-adjusted counterparts to the randomization chi-square statistic Q, the mean score statistic Q_S, and the correlation statistic Q_{CS} that are discussed in Chapter 5, "The $s \times r$ Table."

6.2.1   General Association Statistic

When both the row and column variables are nominally scaled, the alternative hypothesis of interest is that of general association, where the pattern of distribution of the response levels across the row levels is heterogeneous. This is the most general alternative hypothesis and is always valid, no matter how the row and column variables are scaled.

In this case,

$$\mathbf{A}_h = \left\{ [\mathbf{I}_{(r-1)}, \mathbf{0}_{(r-1)}] \otimes [\mathbf{I}_{(s-1)}, \mathbf{0}_{(s-1)}] \right\}$$

which, applied to $(\mathbf{n}_h - \mathbf{m}_h)$, produces the differences between the observed and expected frequencies under H_0 for the $(s-1)(r-1)$ cells of the table after eliminating the last row and column. This results in Q_{GMH}, which is approximately chi-square with $(s-1)(r-1)$ degrees of freedom. Q_{GMH} is often called the test of general association.

6.2.2   Mean Score Statistic

When the response levels are ordinally scaled, you can assign scores to them to compute row mean scores. In this case, the alternative hypothesis to the null hypothesis of no association is that there are location shifts for these mean scores across the levels of the row variables.

Here,

$$\mathbf{A}_h = \mathbf{a}'_h \otimes [\mathbf{I}_{(s-1)}, \mathbf{0}_{(s-1)}]$$

where $\{\mathbf{a}_h\} = (a_{h1}, a_{h2}, \ldots, a_{hr})$ specifies scores for the jth response level in the hth stratum, from which the means

$$\bar{y}_{hi} = \sum_{j=1}^{r} (a_{hj} n_{hij} / n_{hi+})$$

are created for comparisons of the s populations across the strata.

This produces the extended Mantel-Haenszel Q_{SMH}, which is approximately chi-square with $(s-1)$ degrees of freedom under H_0. Q_{SMH} is called the mean score statistic and is the general form of the Q_{SMH} statistic for $2 \times r$ tables discussed in Chapter 4, "Sets of $2 \times \mathbf{r}$ and $\mathbf{s} \times 2$ Tables," where $(s-1) = 1$. If marginal rank or ridit scores are used, with midranks assigned for ties, Q_{SMH} is equivalent to an extension of the Kruskal-Wallis ANOVA test on ranks to account for strata and the Friedman ANOVA test on ranks to account for more than one subject per group within strata. See Chapter 7, "Nonparametric Methods," for further discussion on nonparametric tests that are special cases of Mantel-Haenszel strategies.

6.2.3 Correlation Statistic

When both the response variable (columns) and the row variable (or groups) are ordinally scaled, you can assign scores to both the response levels and the row levels in the hth stratum. The alternative hypothesis to no association in this situation is a linear trend on the mean scores across the levels of the row variable. In this case,

$$\mathbf{A}_h = [\mathbf{a}_h' \otimes \mathbf{c}_h']$$

where the $\{\mathbf{a}_h\}$ are defined as before and the $\{\mathbf{c}_h\} = (c_{h1}, c_{h2}, \ldots, c_{hs})$ specify a set of scores for the ith level of the row variable in the hth stratum. This produces the differences between the observed and expected sum of products of the row and column scores with the frequencies n_{hij}, so that the resulting test statistic is directed at detecting correlation.

This test statistic is Q_{CSMH}, which is approximately chi-square with one degree of freedom under H_0. It is the general form of Q_{CSMH} discussed in Chapter 4 for stratified $s \times 2$ tables where the row variable is ordinally scaled. It has increased power relative to Q_{GMH} or Q_{SMH} for linear association alternatives to the null hypothesis of no association.

6.2.4 Summary

The following table summarizes the various types of extended Mantel Haenszel statistics.

Table 6.2 Extended Mantel Haenszel Statistics

MH Statistic	Alternative Hypothesis	SAS Output Label	Degrees of Freedom	Scale Requirements	Nonparametric Equivalents
Q_{GMH}	general association	General Association	$(s-1) \times (r-1)$	none	
Q_{SMH}	mean score location shifts	Row Means Scores Differ	$(s-1)$	column variable ordinal	Kruskal-Wallis
Q_{CSMH}	linear association	Nonzero Correlation	1	row and column variable ordinal	Spearman correlation

6.3 Mantel-Haenszel Applications

The Mantel-Haenszel strategy has applications in many different settings, including a number of different sampling frameworks. Chapter 3, "Sets of 2×2 Tables," demonstrates the use of this strategy for analyzing sets of 2×2 tables, and Chapter 4 demonstrates the use of the strategy for sets of $2 \times r$ and $s \times 2$ tables. If you haven't read these chapters, you should review them since they contain many general remarks on the application of Mantel-Haenszel methods. Section 6.3 illustrates the use of these methods for sets of $s \times r$ tables, including examples from clinical trials, observational studies, and prospective studies.

6.3.1 Dumping Syndrome Data

Table 6.3 displays the dumping syndrome data, which have appeared frequently in the categorical data analysis literature, beginning with Grizzle, Starmer, and Koch (1969). Investigators conducted a randomized clinical trial in four hospitals, where patients were assigned to one of four surgical procedures for the treatment of severe duodenal ulcers. The treatments include:

v + d: vagotomy and drainage

v + a: vagotomy and antrectomy (removal of 25% of gastric tissue)

v + h: vagatomy and hemigastrectomy (removal of 50% of gastric tissue)

gre: gastric resection (removal of 75% of gastric tissue)

The response measured was the severity (none, slight, moderate) of the dumping syndrome, which is expected to increase directly with the proportion of gastric tissue removed. This response, an adverse effect of surgery, can be considered ordinally scaled, as can operation. Investigators wanted to determine if type of operation was associated with severity of dumping syndrome, after adjusting for hospital.

Table 6.3   Dumping Syndrome Data

Hospital	Operation	Severity of Symptoms			Total
		None	Slight	Moderate	
1	v + d	23	7	2	32
1	v + a	23	10	5	38
1	v + h	20	13	5	38
1	gre	24	10	6	40
2	v + d	18	6	1	25
2	v + a	18	6	2	26
2	v + h	13	13	2	28
2	gre	9	15	2	26
3	v + d	8	6	3	17
3	v + a	12	4	4	20
3	v + h	11	6	2	19
3	gre	7	7	4	18
4	v + d	12	9	1	22
4	v + a	15	3	2	20
4	v + h	14	8	3	25
4	gre	13	6	4	23

Since both the row and column variables are ordinally scaled, you can use the correlation statistic Q_{CSMH} to assess the null hypothesis of no association against the alternative that type of operation and severity of response are linearly associated.

The following SAS statements input the data into the SAS data set OPERATE and request the MH analysis. Note the use of the option ORDER=DATA, as well as the request for both integer scores (the default table scores) and standardized midrank scores (SCORES=MODRIDIT).

```
data operate;
   input hospital trt $ severity $ wt @@;
   cards;
1 v+d none 23    1 v+d slight  7    1 v+d moderate 2
1 v+a none 23    1 v+a slight 10    1 v+a moderate 5
1 v+h none 20    1 v+h slight 13    1 v+h moderate 5
1 gre none 24    1 gre slight 10    1 gre moderate 6
2 v+d none 18    2 v+d slight  6    2 v+d moderate 1
2 v+a none 18    2 v+a slight  6    2 v+a moderate 2
2 v+h none 13    2 v+h slight 13    2 v+h moderate 2
2 gre none  9    2 gre slight 15    2 gre moderate 2
3 v+d none  8    3 v+d slight  6    3 v+d moderate 3
3 v+a none 12    3 v+a slight  4    3 v+a moderate 4
3 v+h none 11    3 v+h slight  6    3 v+h moderate 2
3 gre none  7    3 gre slight  7    3 gre moderate 4
4 v+d none 12    4 v+d slight  9    4 v+d moderate 1
4 v+a none 15    4 v+a slight  3    4 v+a moderate 2
4 v+h none 14    4 v+h slight  8    4 v+h moderate 3
4 gre none 13    4 gre slight  6    4 gre moderate 4
;
```

```
proc freq order=data;
   weight wt;
   tables hospital*trt*severity / cmh;
   tables hospital*trt*severity / cmh scores=modridit;
run;
```

Output 6.1 contains the results for the extended Mantel-Haenszel analysis using integer scores. Q_{CSMH} takes the value 6.340, which is significant at the $\alpha = 0.05$ level; note that the statistics for general association, Q_{GMH}, and mean score differences, Q_{SMH}, are not significant at the $\alpha = 0.05$ level of significance. This is an example of the utility of taking advantage of the correlation statistic when it is appropriate; its greater power against the alternative hypothesis of linear association has detected significant evidence against the null hypothesis.

Output 6.1   Table Scores

```
              SUMMARY STATISTICS FOR TRT BY SEVERITY
                   CONTROLLING FOR HOSPITAL


       Cochran-Mantel-Haenszel Statistics (Based on Table Scores)

     Statistic   Alternative Hypothesis    DF      Value     Prob
     --------------------------------------------------------------
         1       Nonzero Correlation        1      6.340     0.012
         2       Row Mean Scores Differ     3      6.590     0.086
         3       General Association        6     10.598     0.102
```

Output 6.2 contains the results for the standardized midrank scores. $Q_{CSMH} = 6.927$, with $p = 0.008$. As with the integer scores, the other statistics do not detect as much evidence against the null hypothesis of no association. Since the response variable levels are subjective and undoubtedly not equally spaced, the analysis of standardized midrank scores may provide the most appropriate test.

Output 6.2   Standardized Midrank Scores

```
              SUMMARY STATISTICS FOR TRT BY SEVERITY
                   CONTROLLING FOR HOSPITAL


       Cochran-Mantel-Haenszel Statistics (Modified Ridit Scores)

     Statistic   Alternative Hypothesis    DF      Value     Prob
     --------------------------------------------------------------
         1       Nonzero Correlation        1      6.927     0.008
         2       Row Mean Scores Differ     3      7.637     0.054
         3       General Association        6     10.598     0.102
```

This analysis shows that, adjusting for hospital, there is a clear monotonic association between degree of gastric tissue removal and severity of dumping syndrome. The greater the degree of gastric tissue removal, the worse the dumping syndrome.

6.3.2   Shoulder Harness Data

The following data were collected in a study of shoulder harness usage in observations for a sample of North Carolina cars (Hochberg, Stutts, and Reinfurt, 1977).

Table 6.4   Shoulder Harness Data

Area	Location	Larger Cars No	Larger Cars Yes	Medium No	Medium Yes	Smaller Cars No	Smaller Cars Yes	Total
Coast	Urban	174	69	134	56	150	54	637
Coast	Rural	52	14	31	14	25	17	153
Piedmont	Urban	127	62	94	63	112	93	551
Piedmont	Rural	35	29	32	30	46	34	206
Mountains	Urban	111	26	120	47	145	68	517
Mountains	Rural	62	31	44	32	85	43	297

For these data, researchers were interested in whether there was an association between the size of car and shoulder harness usage, after controlling for geographic area and location. First, there is interest in looking at the pooled table of car size × usage. Then, a Mantel-Haenszel analysis is requested for a stratification consisting of the combinations of levels of area and location, resulting in six strata. Finally, Mantel-Haenszel analyses are requested for the association of size with usage stratified on area and location, singly. Standardized midrank scores are specified.

The following SAS statements request these analyses. Note that the NOPRINT option is specified in the last two TABLES statements to suppress the printing of tables.

```
data shoulder;
   input area $ location $ size $ usage $ count @@;
   cards;
   coast    urban large  no 174 coast    urban large  yes 69
   coast    urban medium no 134 coast    urban medium yes 56
   coast    urban small  no 150 coast    urban small  yes 54
   coast    rural large  no  52 coast    rural large  yes 14
   coast    rural medium no  31 coast    rural medium yes 14
   coast    rural small  no  25 coast    rural small  yes 17
   piedmont urban large  no 127 piedmont urban large  yes 62
   piedmont urban medium no  94 piedmont urban medium yes 63
   piedmont urban small  no 112 piedmont urban small  yes 93
   piedmont rural large  no  35 piedmont rural large  yes 29
   piedmont rural medium no  32 piedmont rural medium yes 30
   piedmont rural small  no  46 piedmont rural small  yes 34
   mountain urban large  no 111 mountain urban large  yes 26
   mountain urban medium no 120 mountain urban medium yes 47
   mountain urban small  no 145 mountain urban small  yes 68
   mountain rural large  no  62 mountain rural large  yes 31
   mountain rural medium no  44 mountain rural medium yes 32
   mountain rural small  no  85 mountain rural small  yes 43
   ;
proc freq;
   weight count;
   tables size*usage / chisq;
```

```
      tables area*location*size*usage / cmh scores=modridit;
      tables area*size*usage / noprint cmh scores=modridit;
      tables location*size*usage / noprint cmh scores=modridit;
   run;
```

Output 6.3 displays the pooled frequency table. The "Mantel-Haenszel Chi-Square," Q_{CS}, is valid for these data since SIZE is ordinally scaled, and the response is dichotomous; it indicates that there is a strong association between size of car and shoulder harness usage ($Q_{CS} = 7.205$). By looking at the row percentages in the table cells, you can see that drivers of small and medium sized cars exhibit a greater tendency to use shoulder harnesses than the drivers of large cars.

Output 6.3   Pooled Table

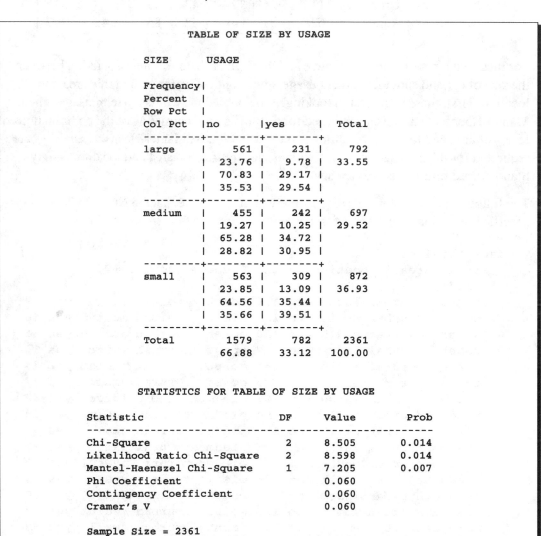

```
                   TABLE OF SIZE BY USAGE

         SIZE       USAGE

         Frequency|
         Percent  |
         Row Pct  |
         Col Pct  |no       |yes      |   Total
         ---------+---------+---------+
         large    |    561  |    231  |    792
                  |  23.76  |   9.78  |  33.55
                  |  70.83  |  29.17  |
                  |  35.53  |  29.54  |
         ---------+---------+---------+
         medium   |    455  |    242  |    697
                  |  19.27  |  10.25  |  29.52
                  |  65.28  |  34.72  |
                  |  28.82  |  30.95  |
         ---------+---------+---------+
         small    |    563  |    309  |    872
                  |  23.85  |  13.09  |  36.93
                  |  64.56  |  35.44  |
                  |  35.66  |  39.51  |
         ---------+---------+---------+
         Total        1579      782      2361
                      66.88    33.12    100.00


             STATISTICS FOR TABLE OF SIZE BY USAGE

         Statistic                 DF    Value     Prob
         -------------------------------------------------
         Chi-Square                 2    8.505     0.014
         Likelihood Ratio Chi-Square 2   8.598     0.014
         Mantel-Haenszel Chi-Square  1   7.205     0.007
         Phi Coefficient                 0.060
         Contingency Coefficient         0.060
         Cramer's V                      0.060

         Sample Size = 2361
```

This association holds when you control for area and location. Output 6.4 contains the frequency table for rural locations in the coast region (the other tables are not reproduced here).

Output 6.4   Table for AREA=coast and LOCATION=rural

```
                 TABLE 1 OF SIZE BY USAGE
             CONTROLLING FOR AREA=coast LOCATION=rural

          SIZE       USAGE

          Frequency|
          Percent  |
          Row Pct  |
          Col Pct  |no       |yes      |  Total
          ---------+--------+--------+
          large    |     52 |     14 |     66
                   |  33.99 |   9.15 |  43.14
                   |  78.79 |  21.21 |
                   |  48.15 |  31.11 |
          ---------+--------+--------+
          medium   |     31 |     14 |     45
                   |  20.26 |   9.15 |  29.41
                   |  68.89 |  31.11 |
                   |  28.70 |  31.11 |
          ---------+--------+--------+
          small    |     25 |     17 |     42
                   |  16.34 |  11.11 |  27.45
                   |  59.52 |  40.48 |
                   |  23.15 |  37.78 |
          ---------+--------+--------+
          Total         108       45      153
                      70.59    29.41   100.00
```

Output 6.5 displays the Mantel-Haenszel results for the stratified analysis where the strata are all combinations of area and location. $Q_{CSMH} = 6.640$, which is strongly significant. Controlling for area and location, shoulder harness usage is clearly associated with size of car.

Output 6.5   Stratified by Area and Location

```
              SUMMARY STATISTICS FOR SIZE BY USAGE
                CONTROLLING FOR AREA AND LOCATION


   Cochran-Mantel-Haenszel Statistics (Modified Ridit Scores)

   Statistic   Alternative Hypothesis    DF     Value    Prob
   ----------------------------------------------------------------
       1        Nonzero Correlation        1     6.640    0.010
       2        Row Mean Scores Differ      2     8.423    0.015
       3        General Association         2     8.426    0.015
```

Output 6.6 and Output 6.7 contain the Mantel-Haenszel results for the association of size and shoulder harness usage controlling for area and location singly. $Q_{CSMH} = 6.510$ and 7.070, respectively. Controlling only for area or location, the significant association between shoulder harness and size of car remains evident. Q_{GMH} and Q_{SMH} are significant too, for the preceding analyses, but most of the information is contained in the correlation statistic Q_{CSMH}.

However, you should use caution in interpreting the mean score statistic for modified ridit scores when the outcome is a dichotomous response. Ordinarily, you would want the values 0 and 1 to be maintained in such an analysis; by using modified ridit scores you are effectively assigning different values from 0 and 1 to the columns, and these scores will be different in the different strata.

Also, the fact that Q_{GMH} and Q_{SMH} have very close values in Output 6.5 and the same values in Output 6.6 and Output 6.7 is an artifact. However, these statistics are identical for sets of $s \times 2$ tables when integer scores are used.

Output 6.6   Stratified By Area

```
            SUMMARY STATISTICS FOR SIZE BY USAGE
                   CONTROLLING FOR AREA


     Cochran-Mantel-Haenszel Statistics (Modified Ridit Scores)

     Statistic   Alternative Hypothesis    DF     Value     Prob
     -------------------------------------------------------------
        1        Nonzero Correlation        1     6.510     0.011
        2        Row Mean Scores Differ     2     8.120     0.017
        3        General Association        2     8.120     0.017
```

Output 6.7   Stratified By Location

```
            SUMMARY STATISTICS FOR SIZE BY USAGE
                 CONTROLLING FOR LOCATION


     Cochran-Mantel-Haenszel Statistics (Modified Ridit Scores)

     Statistic   Alternative Hypothesis    DF     Value     Prob
     -------------------------------------------------------------
        1        Nonzero Correlation        1     7.070     0.008
        2        Row Mean Scores Differ     2     8.579     0.014
        3        General Association        2     8.579     0.014
```

6.3.3   Learning Preference Data

In this study, educational researchers compared three different approaches to mathematics instruction for third graders. During the year, students were rotated through three different styles: a self-instructional mode that was largely based on computer use, a team approach in which students solved problems in groups of four students, and a traditional class approach. Researchers were interested in how other school programs influenced the effectiveness of the styles, as well as how they influenced the students' perceptions of the different styles. Table 6.5 displays data that reflect the students' preferences of styles, cross-classified by the school program they are in: Regular, which is a regular school schedule, and After, which supplements the regular school day with an afternoon school program involving the same classmates. The study included three different schools.

Table 6.5   School Program Data

School	Program	Learning Style Preference		
		Self	Team	Class
1	Regular	10	17	26
1	After	5	12	50
2	Regular	21	17	26
2	After	16	12	36
3	Regular	15	15	16
3	After	12	12	20

The question of interest is whether students' learning style preference is associated with their school day program, after adjusting for any effects of individual school. There may be some ordinality to the response measure, in the sense of increasing group participation, but that doesn't stand up when you try to distinguish the team approach from the classroom approach. Thus, the appropriate extended Mantel-Haenszel statistic for the stratified analysis of these data is the test for general association. Since $(s - 1)(r - 1)$ for these data is equal to 2, Q_{GMH} has two degrees of freedom.

The following SAS statements request the appropriate analysis.

```
data school;
   input school program $ style $ count @@;
   cards;
   1 regular   self 10  1 regular   team 17 1 regular class   26
   1 after     self  5  1 after     team 12 1 after   class   50
   2 regular   self 21  2 regular   team 17 2 regular class   26
   2 after     self 16  2 after     team 12 2 after   class   36
   3 regular   self 15  3 regular   team 15 3 regular class   16
   3 after     self 12  3 after     team 12 3 after   class   20
   ;
proc freq;
   weight count;
   tables school*program*style / cmh chisq measures;
run;
```

Output 6.8 contains the results for the stratified analysis. Q_{GMH} has a value of 10.958, with 2 df, $p = 0.004$. School program and learning style preference are strongly associated. Note that for these data, the general association statistic is most appropriate. The other statistics printed in this table are not applicable since the scale of the row and column variables of these tables do not justify their use. Note that since the ORDER=DATA option is not specified, the columns and rows of the tables are arranged alphabetically. This has no bearing on the general association statistic. However, if you wanted to order the rows and columns of the table as displayed in Table 6.5, then you would use ORDER=DATA.

Output 6.8   Stratified Analysis

```
            SUMMARY STATISTICS FOR PROGRAM BY STYLE
                    CONTROLLING FOR SCHOOL

    Cochran-Mantel-Haenszel Statistics (Based on Table Scores)

    Statistic   Alternative Hypothesis    DF     Value     Prob
    -------------------------------------------------------------
        1       Nonzero Correlation        1     9.007     0.003
        2       Row Mean Scores Differ     1     9.007     0.003
        3       General Association        2    10.958     0.004
```

Output 6.9, Output 6.10, and Output 6.11 contain the results for the individual tables. Note that most of the association seems to be occurring in school 1, judging by Q_P.

Output 6.9   Results for School 1

```
                    TABLE 1 OF PROGRAM BY STYLE
                    CONTROLLING FOR SCHOOL=1

       PROGRAM     STYLE

       Frequency|
       Percent  |
       Row Pct  |
       Col Pct  |class   |self    |team    |  Total
       ---------+--------+--------+--------+
       after    |    50  |     5  |    12  |     67
                | 41.67  |  4.17  | 10.00  |  55.83
                | 74.63  |  7.46  | 17.91  |
                | 65.79  | 33.33  | 41.38  |

       ---------+--------+--------+--------+
       regular  |    26  |    10  |    17  |     53
                | 21.67  |  8.33  | 14.17  |  44.17
                | 49.06  | 18.87  | 32.08  |
                | 34.21  | 66.67  | 58.62  |

       ---------+--------+--------+--------+
       Total         76       15       29      120
                   63.33    12.50    24.17   100.00


         STATISTICS FOR TABLE 1 OF PROGRAM BY STYLE
                 CONTROLLING FOR SCHOOL=1


       Statistic                    DF     Value     Prob
       ----------------------------------------------------
       Chi-Square                    2     8.591     0.014
       Likelihood Ratio Chi-Square   2     8.639     0.013
       Mantel-Haenszel Chi-Square    1     6.421     0.011
       Phi Coefficient                     0.268
       Contingency Coefficient             0.258
       Cramer's V                          0.268
```

Output 6.10   Results for School 2

```
               TABLE 2 OF PROGRAM BY STYLE
                 CONTROLLING FOR SCHOOL=2

         PROGRAM      STYLE

         Frequency|
         Percent  |
         Row Pct  |
         Col Pct  |class   |self    |team    |   Total
         ---------+--------+--------+--------+
         after    |     36 |     16 |     12 |      64
                  |  28.13 |  12.50 |   9.38 |   50.00
                  |  56.25 |  25.00 |  18.75 |
                  |  58.06 |  43.24 |  41.38 |
         ---------+--------+--------+--------+
         regular  |     26 |     21 |     17 |      64
                  |  20.31 |  16.41 |  13.28 |   50.00
                  |  40.63 |  32.81 |  26.56 |
                  |  41.94 |  56.76 |  58.62 |
         ---------+--------+--------+--------+
         Total          62       37       29      128
                     48.44    28.91    22.66   100.00


          STATISTICS FOR TABLE 2 OF PROGRAM BY STYLE
                 CONTROLLING FOR SCHOOL=2

    Statistic                    DF     Value      Prob
    -----------------------------------------------------

    Chi-Square                    2     3.151      0.207
    Likelihood Ratio Chi-Square   2     3.164      0.206
    Mantel-Haenszel Chi-Square    1     2.706      0.100
    Phi Coefficient                     0.157
    Contingency Coefficient             0.155
    Cramer's V                          0.157
```

Output 6.11   Results for School 3

```
              TABLE 3 OF PROGRAM BY STYLE
              CONTROLLING FOR SCHOOL=3

    PROGRAM      STYLE

    Frequency|
    Percent  |
    Row Pct  |
    Col Pct  |class   |self    |team    |  Total
    ---------+--------+--------+--------+
    after    |    20  |    12  |    12  |    44
             |  22.22 |  13.33 |  13.33 |  48.89
             |  45.45 |  27.27 |  27.27 |
             |  55.56 |  44.44 |  44.44 |
    ---------+--------+--------+--------+
    regular  |    16  |    15  |    15  |    46
             |  17.78 |  16.67 |  16.67 |  51.11
             |  34.78 |  32.61 |  32.61 |
             |  44.44 |  55.56 |  55.56 |
    ---------+--------+--------+--------+
    Total         36       27       27       90
                40.00    30.00    30.00   100.00

       STATISTICS FOR TABLE 3 OF PROGRAM BY STYLE
              CONTROLLING FOR SCHOOL=3

    Statistic                   DF    Value      Prob
    -----------------------------------------------------
    Chi-Square                   2    1.067     0.586
    Likelihood Ratio Chi-Square  2    1.069     0.586
    Mantel-Haenszel Chi-Square   1    0.826     0.363
    Phi Coefficient                   0.109
    Contingency Coefficient           0.108
    Cramer's V                        0.109
```

6.4   Advanced Topic: Application to Repeated Measures

6.4.1   Introduction

The Mantel-Haenszel strategy has a useful application to the analysis of repeated measurements data. Such data occur when measurements are obtained over time, when responses from experimental units are measured under multiple conditions, such as multiple teeth in the same subject, and when multiple measurements are obtained from the same experimental unit, such as from two or more observers. Using repeated measurements enables comparisons among different times or conditions to avoid being obscured by subject-to-subject variability.

By specifying the appropriate tables for the data, you construct a setting in which Mantel-Haenszel methods can address the hypothesis of no association between a repeated measurement factor, such as time or condition, and a response variable, adjusting for the effect of subject. This type of analysis may be sufficient, or there may also be interest in statistical modeling of the repeated measurements data, which is discussed in Chapter 13, "Modeling Repeated Measurements Data."

Consider the general situation in which t measurements of a univariate response variable Y are obtained from each of n experimental units. One common application is to longitudinal studies, in which repeated measurements are obtained at t time points for each subject. In other applications, the responses from each experimental unit are measured under multiple conditions rather than at multiple time points. In some settings in which repeated measures data are obtained, the independent experimental units are not individual subjects. For example, in a matched case-control study, the experimental units are matched sets and responses are obtained from the individual members of each set. In a toxicological study, the experimental units may be litters; responses are then obtained from the multiple newborns in each litter. In a genetic study, experimental units may be defined by families; responses are then obtained from the members of each family.

Although interest will focus primarily on the situation in which Y is categorical, the response may be either continuous or categorical. Let y_{ij} denote the response for subject i at time (or condition) j. The resulting data are commonly displayed in an $n \times t$ data matrix, as shown in Table 6.6.

Table 6.6   One-Sample Repeated Measures Data

Subject	Time point				
	1	$\dots$	j	$\dots$	t
1	y_{11}	$\dots$	y_{1j}	$\dots$	y_{1t}
$\vdots$	$\vdots$	$\ddots$	$\vdots$	$\ddots$	$\vdots$
i	y_{i1}	$\dots$	y_{ij}	$\dots$	y_{it}
$\vdots$	$\vdots$	$\ddots$	$\vdots$	$\ddots$	$\vdots$
n	y_{n1}	$\dots$	y_{nj}	$\dots$	y_{nt}

Alternatively, suppose c denotes the number of distinct values of Y and suppose indicator variables

$$n_{ijk} = \begin{cases} 1 & \text{if subject } i \text{ is classified in response category } k \text{ at time } j \\ 0 & \text{otherwise} \end{cases}$$

for $i = 1, \dots, n$; $j = 1, \dots, t$; and $k = 1, \dots, c$. In this case, the data from subject i can be displayed in a $t \times c$ contingency table, as shown in Table 6.7. Thus, the data from a one-sample repeated measures study can be viewed as a set of n independent two-way contingency tables, where each table has t rows and c columns.

Table 6.7   Contingency Table Layout for Subject i

Time	Response category			
Point	1	$\dots$	c	Total
1	n_{i11}	$\dots$	n_{i1c}	n_{i1+}
$\vdots$	$\vdots$	$\ddots$	$\vdots$	$\vdots$
t	n_{it1}	$\dots$	n_{itc}	n_{it+}
Total	n_{i+1}	$\dots$	n_{i+c}	n_i

If the response variable Y is categorical with a limited number of possible values, the number of columns in each table, c, will be relatively small. On the other hand, if Y is a continuous variable, the number of distinct values of Y may be very large. The most extreme case results when each of the n subjects has a unique response at each time. In this situation, c is equal to nt and every column marginal total n_{i+k} is equal to zero or one.

When the data are complete, the total sample size for each of the n tables is $n_i = t$ and every row marginal total n_{ij+} is equal to 1. In this case, each row of Table 6.7 has exactly one n_{ijk} value equal to 1 and the remaining values are equal to 0. This situation occurs when the outcome variable is measured once at every time point for each subject.

However, if a particular subject has a missing response at one or more time points, the corresponding row of the subject's table will have each n_{ijk} value equal to 0 and the marginal total n_{ij+} will consequently equal 0. In this case, the total sample size n_i equals t minus the number of missing observations.

Based on the framework displayed in Table 6.7, Mantel-Haenszel statistics can be used to test the null hypothesis of no association between the row dimension (time) and the column dimension (response), adjusted for subject. Under the assumption that the marginal totals $\{n_{ij+}\}$ and $\{n_{i+k}\}$ of each table are fixed, the null hypothesis is that, for each subject, the response variable Y is distributed at random with respect to the t time points. As discussed in Landis et al. (1988), this null hypothesis is precisely the interchangeability hypothesis of Madansky (1963). Interchangeability states that all permutations of responses across conditions within a subject are equally likely. In turn, the hypothesis of interchangeability implies *marginal homogeneity* in the distribution of Y across the t time points; that is, the marginal distribution of Y is the same at each of the t time points.

Although the interchangeability hypothesis is a somewhat stronger condition than marginal homogeneity, the general association statistic Q_{GMH}, mean score statistic Q_{SMH}, and correlation statistic Q_{CSMH} are directed at alternatives that correspond to various types of departures from marginal homogeneity. The following examples demonstrate the use of MH statistics in testing marginal homogeneity for repeated measures.

6.4.2 Dichotomous Response, Two Time Points (McNemar's Test)

A running shoe company produces a new model of running shoe that includes a harder material for the insert that corrects for overpronation. However, the company is concerned that the material will induce heel tenderness as a result of some loss of cushioning on the strike of each step. It conducted a study on 87 runners who used the new shoe for a month. Researchers asked the participants whether they experienced occasional heel tenderness before and after they used the new shoe.

The data was collected as one observation per time period, that is, two measurements were collected for each subject, and they included the time period (before or after) and whether heel tenderness was experienced (yes or no). Table 6.8 contains the contingency table summarizing these data.

Table 6.8 Heel Tenderness for Runners

Before	After No	After Yes	Total
No	48	15	63
Yes	5	19	24

However, you can think of the measurements for each subject as being one of four 2×2 tables, corresponding to the four cells of Table 6.8. These tables are displayed in Table 6.9 through Table 6.12. Each subject's set of responses can be represented by one of these tables.

Table 6.9   (No,No) Configuration Table (48)

Time	Heel Tenderness No	Heel Tenderness Yes	Total
Before	1	0	1
After	1	0	1

Table 6.10   (No, Yes) Configuration Table (15)

Time	Heel Tenderness No	Heel Tenderness Yes	Total
Before	1	0	1
After	0	1	1

Table 6.11   (Yes, No) Configuration Table (5)

Time	Heel Tenderness No	Heel Tenderness Yes	Total
Before	0	1	1
After	1	0	1

Table 6.12   (Yes, Yes) Configuration Table (19)

Time	Heel Tenderness No	Heel Tenderness Yes	Total
Before	0	1	1
After	0	1	1

You can determine whether there is an association between the response and time for before and after responses by performing a stratified analysis where each subject constitutes a stratum. There are 87 tables altogether: 48 with the (no, no) configuration, 15 with the (no, yes) configuration, 5 with the (yes, no) configuration, and 19 with the (yes, yes) configuration.

If you study Table 6.8, you can see that these data effectively have the matched pairs framework that was discussed in Section 2.7. In fact, the Mantel-Haenszel statistic for the described analysis is equivalent to McNemar's test. The following analysis demonstrates the Mantel-Haenszel approach to analyzing these repeated measurements data. The same strategy is followed when the tables involved have dimensions greater than 2 × 2 and there is no alternative strategy such as McNemar's Test.

The following SAS statements input the running shoes data. The data are in case record form: one observation per time point per subject. Thus, there are 174 observations altogether.

```
data pump;
   input subject time $ response $ @@;
   cards;
 1 before no    1 after no    2 before no    2 after no
 3 before no    3 after no    4 before no    4 after no
 5 before no    5 after no    6 before no    6 after no
 7 before no    7 after no    8 before no    8 after no
 9 before no    9 after no   10 before no   10 after no
11 before no   11 after no   12 before no   12 after no
13 before no   13 after no   14 before no   14 after no
15 before no   15 after no   16 before no   16 after no
17 before no   17 after no   18 before no   18 after no
19 before no   19 after no   20 before no   20 after no
21 before no   21 after no   22 before no   22 after no
23 before no   23 after no   24 before no   24 after no
25 before no   25 after no   26 before no   26 after no
27 before no   27 after no   28 before no   28 after no
29 before no   29 after no   30 before no   30 after no
31 before no   31 after no   32 before no   32 after no
33 before no   33 after no   34 before no   34 after no
35 before no   35 after no   36 before no   36 after no
37 before no   37 after no   38 before no   38 after no
39 before no   39 after no   40 before no   40 after no
41 before no   41 after no   42 before no   42 after no
43 before no   43 after no   44 before no   44 after no
45 before no   45 after no   46 before no   46 after no
47 before no   47 after no   48 before no   48 after no
49 before no   49 after yes  50 before no   50 after yes
51 before no   51 after yes  52 before no   52 after yes
53 before no   53 after yes  54 before no   54 after yes
55 before no   55 after yes  56 before no   56 after yes
57 before no   57 after yes  58 before no   58 after yes
59 before no   59 after yes  60 before no   60 after yes
61 before no   61 after yes  62 before no   62 after yes
63 before no   63 after yes  64 before yes  64 after no
65 before yes  65 after no   66 before yes  66 after no
67 before yes  67 after no   68 before yes  68 after no
69 before yes  69 after yes  70 before yes  70 after yes
71 before yes  71 after yes  72 before yes  72 after yes
73 before yes  73 after yes  74 before yes  74 after yes
75 before yes  75 after yes  76 before yes  76 after yes
77 before yes  77 after yes  78 before yes  78 after yes
79 before yes  79 after yes  80 before yes  80 after yes
81 before yes  81 after yes  82 before yes  82 after yes
83 before yes  83 after yes  84 before yes  84 after yes
```

```
   85 before yes 85 after yes 86 before yes 86 after yes
   87 before yes 87 after yes
;
```

The next statements request the Mantel-Haenszel analysis. Since the data are in case record form, no WEIGHT statement is required. Since 87 tables are to be computed, the NOPRINT option is specified so that the tables are not printed.

```
proc freq;
   tables subject*time*response/ noprint cmh out=freqtab;
run;
```

Output 6.12 contains the Mantel-Haenszel results. Q_{MH} has the value 5.00 with $p=0.025$. This is clearly significant. Runners reported more heel tenderness with the new running shoes than with their old running shoes.

Output 6.12   Mantel-Haenszel Results

```
              SUMMARY STATISTICS FOR TIME BY RESPONSE
                      CONTROLLING FOR SUBJECT


       Cochran-Mantel-Haenszel Statistics (Based on Table Scores)

     Statistic   Alternative Hypothesis   DF     Value      Prob
     ==================================================================
         1       Nonzero Correlation       1     5.000      0.025
         2       Row Mean Scores Differ    1     5.000      0.025
         3       General Association       1     5.000      0.025
```

Note that the CMH option always produces the "Estimates of Relative Risk" table and the "Breslow-Day Test for Homogeneity" for sets of 2×2 tables. However, Q_{BD} is not valid here.

Another way of obtaining these results for sets of 2×2 tables is to input the original 2×2 table and specify the AGREE option to obtain McNemar's Test (available in Release 6.10 of the SAS System).

```
data shoes;
   input before $ after $ count ;
   cards;
   yes yes 19
   yes no  5
   no yes  15
   no no   48
   ;
proc freq;
   weight count;
   tables before*after / agree;
run;
```

Output 6.13 contains the resulting frequency table and McNemar's Test. $Q_M = 5.00$, the same value as was obtained for Q_{MH}.

Output 6.13   Frequency Table and McNemar's Test

```
                    TABLE OF BEFORE BY AFTER

          BEFORE      AFTER

          Frequency|
          Percent  |
          Row Pct  |
          Col Pct  |no      |yes     |  Total
          ---------+--------+--------+
          no       |     48 |     15 |     63
                   |  55.17 |  17.24 |  72.41
                   |  76.19 |  23.81 |
                   |  90.57 |  44.12 |
          ---------+--------+--------+
          yes      |      5 |     19 |     24
                   |   5.75 |  21.84 |  27.59
                   |  20.83 |  79.17 |
                   |   9.43 |  55.88 |
          ---------+--------+--------+
          Total           53       34       87
                       60.92    39.08   100.00


          STATISTICS FOR TABLE OF BEFORE BY AFTER

                      McNemar's Test
                      --------------
     Statistic = 5.000        DF = 1         Prob = 0.025
```

Recall that McNemar's Test did not make use of the diagonal cells, that is, the (no, no) and (yes, yes) cells. Thus, if you repeated the Mantel-Haenszel analysis and eliminated the tables corresponding to the (no, no) and (yes, yes) configurations, you would obtain identical results.

6.4.3   Dichotomous Response: Three Repeated Measurements

Grizzle, Starmer, and Koch (1969) analyze data in which 46 patients were each treated with three drugs (A, B, and C). The response to each drug was recorded as favorable (F) or unfavorable (U). Table 6.13 summarizes the eight possible combinations of favorable or unfavorable response for the three drugs and the number of patients with each response pattern.

Table 6.13   Drug Response Data

Drug			
A	B	C	Frequency
F	F	F	6
F	F	U	16
F	U	F	2
F	U	U	4
U	F	F	2
U	F	U	4
U	U	F	6
U	U	U	6

The objective of the analysis is to determine whether the three drugs have similar probabilities for favorable response. Thus, the null hypothesis is interchangeability (that is, no association between drug and response for each patient), which implies equality of the marginal probabilities of a favorable response for the three drugs across patients. This hypothesis can be tested using the general association statistic Q_{GMH}. The data in Table 6.13 must first be restructured so that there are forty-six 3×2 contingency tables, one for each of the 46 patients. For example, Table 6.14 shows the underlying table for a patient who responded favorably to drugs A and C and unfavorably to drug B.

Table 6.14   Sample Contingency Table for a Single Patient

	Response		
Drug	F	U	Total
A	1	0	1
B	0	1	1
C	1	0	1
Total	2	1	3

To apply the Mantel-Haenszel strategy to this data, you have to create a SAS data set that contains $46 \times 3 = 138$ observations (one observation per measurement) and three variables representing patient, drug, and measurement, respectively. If the data are supplied in frequency count form, they must be rearranged. The following SAS statements read the data in frequency form, as displayed in Table 6.13, and rearrange them into the form displayed in Table 6.14. Thus, three observations are created for each patient, one for each drug. Each of the observations in data set DRUG2 contains an arbitrary patient identifier (numbered from 1 to 46), the drug code (A, B, or C), and the response (F or U).

Finally, the FREQ procedure computes the MH statistics that assess the association of drug and response, adjusting for patient. The NOPRINT option of the TABLES statement suppresses the printing of the 46 individual contingency tables. You almost always use this option when analyzing repeated measures data using MH methods.

```
data drug;
   input druga $ drugb $ drugc $ count;
```

```
      cards;
F  F  F   6
F  F  U  16
F  U  F   2
F  U  U   4
U  F  F   2
U  F  U   4
U  U  F   6
U  U  U   6
;
data drug2; set drug;
   keep patient drug response;
   retain patient 0;
   do i=1 to count;
   patient=patient+1;
   drug='A';   response=druga;   output;
   drug='B';   response=drugb;   output;
   drug='C';   response=drugc;   output;
   end;
proc freq;
   tables patient*drug*response / noprint cmh;
run;
```

Output 6.14 displays the results from PROC FREQ. Since the response is dichotomous, the general association and mean score statistics both have 2 df. With table scores, their values are identical. Since the repeated measures factor (drug) is not ordered, the correlation statistic does not apply.

Output 6.14   Test of Marginal Homogeneity

```
              SUMMARY STATISTICS FOR DRUG BY RESPONSE
                     CONTROLLING FOR PATIENT


      Cochran-Mantel-Haenszel Statistics (Based on Table Scores)

    Statistic   Alternative Hypothesis    DF     Value     Prob
    -----------------------------------------------------------------
        1        Nonzero Correlation       1      6.353    0.012
        2        Row Mean Scores Differ    2      8.471    0.014
        3        General Association       2      8.471    0.014



    Total Sample Size = 138
```

The value of Q_{GMH} is 8.471. With reference to the approximate chi-square distribution with 2 df, there is a clearly significant association between drug and response. This test is the same as Cochran's Q statistic (Cochran 1950). In order to summarize the nature of the association, it is helpful to report the estimated marginal probabilities of a favorable response for drugs A, B, and C. These can be computed from Table 6.13 and are equal to 28/46 = 0.61, 28/46 = 0.61, and 16/46 = 0.35, respectively. It is evident that the marginal proportion for drug C differs considerably from that of drugs A and B. Drugs A and B have a much greater probability of favorable response than Drug C.

6.4.4 Ordinal Response

The same Mantel-Haenszel strategy is appropriate when the repeated measurements response variable is ordinally scaled. In this case, the statistic of interest is Q_{SMH}, the mean score statistic.

Macknin, Mathew, and Medendorp (1990) studied the efficacy of steam inhalation in the treatment of common cold symptoms. Thirty patients with colds of recent onset (symptoms of nasal drainage, nasal congestion, and sneezing for three days or less) received two 20-minute steam inhalation treatments. On four successive days, these patients self-assessed the severity of nasal drainage on a four-point ordinal scale (0=no symptoms, 1=mild symptoms, 2=moderate symptoms, 3=severe symptoms). Table 6.15 displays the resulting data.

Table 6.15   Nasal Drainage Data

Patient ID	Study day 1	2	3	4	Patient ID	Study day 1	2	3	4
1	1	1	2	2	16	2	1	1	1
2	0	0	0	0	17	1	1	1	1
3	1	1	1	1	18	2	2	2	2
4	1	1	1	1	19	3	1	1	1
5	0	2	2	0	20	1	1	2	1
6	2	0	0	0	21	2	1	1	2
7	2	2	1	2	22	2	2	2	2
8	1	1	1	0	23	1	1	1	1
9	3	2	1	1	24	2	2	3	1
10	2	2	2	3	25	2	0	0	0
11	1	0	1	1	26	1	1	1	1
12	2	3	2	2	27	0	1	1	0
13	1	3	2	1	28	1	1	1	1
14	2	1	1	1	29	1	1	1	0
15	2	3	3	3	30	3	3	3	3

The objective of the study was to determine if nasal drainage becomes less severe following steam inhalation treatment. Thus, the relevant null hypothesis is that the distribution of the symptom severity scores is the same on each of the four study days for each patient. Since there are only four possible values of the response variable, the assumptions for the usual parametric methods are not directly applicable. In addition, the sample size is too small to justify analysis of the full 4^4 contingency table obtained by the joint crossclassification of the four-level response variable on four days. Thus, randomization model MH methods seem appropriate.

Although the general association statistic Q_{GMH} may be considered for this example, its use of 9 df would have low power to detect departures from marginal homogeneity in a sample of only 30 patients. Since the response is ordinal, the mean score statistic Q_{SMH}, with 3 df, can be used to compare the average symptom scores across the four days. The adequacy of the sample size to support the use of this statistic may also be questionable. Alternatively, since the repeated measures factor (study day) is also ordinal, you could test for a linear trend over study day for symptom severity using the correlation statistic Q_{CSMH}.

Both Q_{SMH} and Q_{CSMH} require that scores be assigned to the values of the repeated measures and response variables. Since study day is quantitative, it is natural to use the scores 1–4 for this variable. If it is reasonable to assume that the symptom severity ratings are equally spaced, the actual scores 0–3 can be used. You could also assign scores that incorporate unequal spacing between the four levels of symptom severity.

Another possibility is to use rank scores for the symptom severity ratings. In PROC FREQ, the SCORES=RANK option of the TABLES statement uses rank scores for both the row and column variables. However, since each patient contributes exactly one observation on each of the four days, the rank scores for study day are also 1, 2, 3, and 4. Thus, this option only affects the scoring of the symptom severity levels. The SCORES=RIDIT and SCORES=MODRIDIT options compute rank scores that are standardized by a function of the stratum-specific sample size. Since the sample sizes in the 30 underlying 4×4 contingency tables are all equal to 4, the results from the SCORES=RANK, SCORES=RIDIT, and SCORES=MODRIDIT options would be identical.

The following SAS statements read in the data in case record form with responses for all days on the same record and rearrange it so that there are four observations per patient. PROC FREQ computes the MH statistics, first using equally-spaced table scores and then using rank scores.

```
data cold;
   keep id day drainage;
   input id day1-day4;
   day=1; drainage=day1; output;
   day=2; drainage=day2; output;
   day=3; drainage=day3; output;
   day=4; drainage=day4; output;
   cards;
 1 1 1 2 2
 2 0 0 0 0
 3 1 1 1 1
 4 1 1 1 1
 5 0 2 2 0
 6 2 0 0 0
 7 2 2 1 2
 8 1 1 1 0
 9 3 2 1 1
10 2 2 2 3
11 1 0 1 1
12 2 3 2 2
13 1 3 2 1
14 2 1 1 1
15 2 3 3 3
16 2 1 1 1
17 1 1 1 1
18 2 2 2 2
19 3 1 1 1
20 1 1 2 1
21 2 1 1 2
```

```
22 2 2 2 2
23 1 1 1 1
24 2 2 3 1
25 2 0 0 0
26 1 1 1 1
27 0 1 1 0
28 1 1 1 1
29 1 1 1 0
30 3 3 3 3
;
proc freq;
    tables id*day*drainage / cmh noprint;
    tables id*day*drainage / cmh noprint scores=rank;
run;
```

Output 6.15 displays the MH statistics based on table scores, and Output 6.16 displays the corresponding results using rank scores. Using the default table scores, the test statistic that the mean symptom severity scores are the same at all four days is not statistically significant ($Q_{SMH} = 4.935$, $p = 0.177$). However, there is a statistically significant trend between study day and nasal drainage severity ($Q_{CSMH} = 4.355$, $p = 0.037$). The observed mean scores at days 1–4 are 1.50, 1.37, 1.37, and 1.17; thus, symptom severity is decreasing over time.

Output 6.15   MH Tests Using Table Scores

```
                 SUMMARY STATISTICS FOR DAY BY DRAINAGE
                          CONTROLLING FOR ID


     Cochran-Mantel-Haenszel Statistics (Based on Table Scores)

     Statistic   Alternative Hypothesis   DF     Value    Prob
     ---------------------------------------------------------------
         1       Nonzero Correlation       1     4.355    0.037
         2       Row Mean Scores Differ    3     4.935    0.177
         3       General Association       9    10.127    0.340


     Total Sample Size = 120
```

Output 6.16   MH Tests Using Rank Scores

```
                 SUMMARY STATISTICS FOR DAY BY DRAINAGE
                          CONTROLLING FOR ID


          Cochran-Mantel-Haenszel Statistics (Based on Rank Scores)

          Statistic    Alternative Hypothesis    DF    Value    Prob
          ------------------------------------------------------------
              1        Nonzero Correlation        1    2.682    0.101
              2        Row Mean Scores Differ      3    3.350    0.341
              3        General Association         9   10.127    0.340



          Total Sample Size = 120
```

In this example, the use of rank scores leads to a less clear conclusion regarding the statistical significance of the correlation statistic ($Q_{CSMH} = 2.682, p = 0.101$). Some authors recommend the routine use of rank scores in preference to the arbitrary assignment of scores (for example, Fleiss 1986, pp. 83–84). However, as demonstrated by Graubard and Korn (1987), rank scores can be a poor choice when the column margin is far from uniformly distributed. This occurs because rank scores also assign a spacing between the levels of the categories. This spacing is generally not known by the analyst and may not be as powerful as other spacings for certain patterns of differences among distributions. Graubard and Korn (1987) recommend that you specify the scores whenever possible. If the choice of scores is not apparent, they recommend integer (or equally spaced) scores.

When there is no natural set of scores, Agresti (1990, p. 294) recommends that the data be analyzed using several reasonably assigned sets of scores to determine whether substantive conclusions depend on the choice of scores. This type of sensitivity analysis seems especially appropriate in this example, since the results assuming equally spaced scores differ from those obtained using rank scores. For example, the scores 0, 1, 3, 5 assume that the moderate category is equally spaced between the mild and severe categories, while none and mild are less far apart. Another possibility would be 0, 1, 2, 4; this choice places severe symptoms further from the other three categories. These alternative scoring specifications are easily implemented by redefining the values of the DRAINAGE variable in the DATA step and then using the default table scores, which are just the input numeric values for drainage.

Note that since the general association statistic does not use scores, the value of Q_{GMH} is the same in both analyses.

6.4.5   Ordinal Response with Missing Data

Researchers at the C. S. Mott Children's Hospital, Ann Arbor, Michigan, investigated the effect of pulse duration on the development of acute electrical injury during transesophageal atrial pacing in animals. In brief, this procedure involves placing a pacemaker in the esophagus. Each of the 14 animals available for experimentation then received atrial pacing at pulse durations of 2, 4, 6, 8, and 10 milliseconds (ms), with each pulse delivered at a separate site in the esophagus for 30 minutes. The response variable, lesion severity, was classified according to depth of injury by histologic examination using an ordinal staging scale from 0 to 5 (0=no lesion, 5=acute inflammation of extraesophageal fascia). Table 6.16 displays the resulting data (missing observations are denoted by –). Landis et al. (1988) previously analyzed the data from the first 11 animals.

Table 6.16 Lesion Severity Data

	Pulse duration (ms)				
ID	2	4	6	8	10
6	0	0	5	0	3
7	0	3	3	4	5
8	0	3	4	3	2
9	2	2	3	0	4
10	0	0	4	4	3
12	0	0	0	4	4
13	0	4	4	4	0
15	0	4	0	0	0
16	0	3	0	1	1
17	–	–	0	1	0
19	0	0	1	1	0
20	–	0	0	2	2
21	0	0	2	3	3
22	–	0	0	3	0

The investigators were primarily interested in determining the extent to which increasing the pulse duration from 2 to 10 ms tends to increase the severity of the lesion. In an experiment in which five repeated measurements of a six-category ordinal response are obtained from only 14 experimental units, the choice of statistical methodology is limited. The study is further complicated by the fact that three of the 14 animals have incomplete data.

The general association statistic Q_{GMH} has 20 df in this case ($s = 5$, $r = 6$). In addition to the fact that Q_{GMH} will not have a chi-square distribution when the sample size is so small relative to the degrees of freedom, there will be very low power to detect general departures from the null hypothesis of interchangeability. Although the alternative of location shift for mean responses across the five pulse durations can be addressed using the mean score statistic Q_{SMH}, this statistic does not take into account the ordering of the pulse durations. The 1 df correlation statistic Q_{CSMH} specifically focuses on the narrow alternative of a monotone relationship between lesion severity and pulse duration. This test addresses the objective of the investigators and is also best justified given the small sample size.

The following SAS statements read in the data in the format shown in Table 6.16, rearrange them so that each subject has five observations, one for each pulse duration, and request the MH statistics using table scores and all three types of rank scores. Since Q_{GMH} is unaffected by the choice of scores, the CMH2 option is used in all but the first TABLES statement. This option specifies that only the Mantel-Haenszel statistics Q_{SMH} and Q_{CSMH} be computed. (The CMH1 option specifies that only the correlation statistic

Q_{CSMH} be computed.)

```
data animals;
   keep id pulse severity;
   input id sev2 sev4 sev6 sev8 sev10;
   pulse=2;  severity=sev2;  output;
   pulse=4;  severity=sev4;  output;
   pulse=6;  severity=sev6;  output;
   pulse=8;  severity=sev8;  output;
   pulse=10; severity=sev10; output;
   cards;
  6 0 0 5 0 3
  7 0 3 3 4 5
  8 0 3 4 3 2
  9 2 2 3 0 4
 10 0 0 4 4 3
 12 0 0 0 4 4
 13 0 4 4 4 0
 15 0 4 0 0 0
 16 0 3 0 1 1
 17 . . 0 1 0
 19 0 0 1 1 0
 20 . 0 0 2 2
 21 0 0 2 3 3
 22 . 0 0 3 0
 ;
proc freq;
   tables id*pulse*severity / noprint cmh;
   tables id*pulse*severity / noprint cmh2 scores=rank;
   tables id*pulse*severity / noprint cmh2 scores=ridit;
   tables id*pulse*severity / noprint cmh2 scores=modridit;
run;
```

Output 6.17 displays the results using the default table scores. In this case, lesion severity is scored using the integers $0, \ldots, 5$ in computing both the mean score statistic Q_{SMH} and the correlation statistic Q_{CSMH}. In addition, pulse duration is scored as 2, 4, 6, 8, or 10 in computing Q_{CSMH}. The correlation statistic Q_{CSMH} shows a highly significant monotone association (trend) between pulse duration and lesion severity; the results from the mean score statistic are also statistically significant.

Output 6.17   MH Tests Using Table Scores

```
                SUMMARY STATISTICS FOR PULSE BY SEVERITY
                         CONTROLLING FOR ID


       Cochran-Mantel-Haenszel Statistics (Based on Table Scores)

       Statistic   Alternative Hypothesis    DF      Value      Prob
       ------------------------------------------------------------
          1        Nonzero Correlation         1      8.804     0.003
          2        Row Mean Scores Differ       4     12.347     0.015
          3        General Association         20     22.846     0.296



       Frequency Missing = 4           Effective Sample Size = 66
```

Output 6.18, Output 6.19, and Output 6.20 display the corresponding results using rank, ridit, and modified ridit scores, respectively. In this example, the values of the mean score and correlation statistics differ slightly among the three types of rank statistics. This is due to the fact that the sample sizes are no longer the same across the 14 tables (due to the occurrence of missing data).

Output 6.18   MH Tests Using Rank Scores

```
                SUMMARY STATISTICS FOR PULSE BY SEVERITY
                         CONTROLLING FOR ID


       Cochran-Mantel-Haenszel Statistics (Based on Rank Scores)

       Statistic   Alternative Hypothesis    DF      Value      Prob
       ------------------------------------------------------------
          1        Nonzero Correlation         1      9.976     0.002
          2        Row Mean Scores Differ       4     13.680     0.008



       Frequency Missing = 4           Effective Sample Size = 66
```

Output 6.19   MH Tests Using Ridit Scores

```
                SUMMARY STATISTICS FOR PULSE BY SEVERITY
                         CONTROLLING FOR ID


       Cochran-Mantel-Haenszel Statistics (Based on Ridit Scores)

       Statistic   Alternative Hypothesis    DF      Value      Prob
       ------------------------------------------------------------
          1        Nonzero Correlation         1     10.034     0.002
          2        Row Mean Scores Differ       4     14.263     0.007



       Frequency Missing = 4           Effective Sample Size = 66
```

Output 6.20   MH Tests Using Modified Ridit Scores

```
        SUMMARY STATISTICS FOR PULSE BY SEVERITY
                   CONTROLLING FOR ID


    Cochran-Mantel-Haenszel Statistics (Modified Ridit Scores)

Statistic   Alternative Hypothesis     DF      Value     Prob
-----------------------------------------------------------------
    1       Nonzero Correlation         1      10.110    0.001
    2       Row Mean Scores Differ      4      14.133    0.007



Frequency Missing = 4                 Effective Sample Size = 66
```

As shown in Table 6.16, three of the 14 animals had incomplete data. Table 6.17 through Table 6.19 display the underlying contingency tables for these strata (ID numbers 17, 20, and 22). Although each of these three tables has one or more rows with a marginal total of zero, the remaining rows provide useful information concerning the association between pulse duration and lesion severity.

Table 6.17   Contingency Table for ID 17

Pulse Duration	Lesion Severity						Total
	0	1	2	3	4	5	
2	0	0	0	0	0	0	0
4	0	0	0	0	0	0	0
6	1	0	0	0	0	0	1
8	0	1	0	0	0	0	1
10	1	0	0	0	0	0	1
Total	2	1	0	0	0	0	3

Table 6.18   Contingency Table for ID 20

Pulse Duration	Lesion Severity						Total
	0	1	2	3	4	5	
2	0	0	0	0	0	0	0
4	1	0	0	0	0	0	1
6	1	0	0	0	0	0	1
8	0	0	1	0	0	0	1
10	0	0	1	0	0	0	1
Total	2	0	2	0	0	0	4

Table 6.19   Contingency Table for ID 22

Pulse	Lesion Severity						
Duration	0	1	2	3	4	5	Total
2	0	0	0	0	0	0	0
4	1	0	0	0	0	0	1
6	1	0	0	0	0	0	1
8	0	0	0	1	0	0	1
10	1	0	0	0	0	0	1
Total	3	0	0	1	0	0	4

The following statements exclude these three animals from the analysis and compute the test statistics for the subset of complete cases. In this case, all three types of rank scores produce the same results; thus, only the SCORES=RANK option is used. The WHERE clause is used to delete those observations with ID equal to 17, 20, or 22.

```
proc freq data=animals;
    where id notin(17,20,22);
    tables id*pulse*severity / noprint cmh;
    tables id*pulse*severity / noprint cmh scores=rank;
run;
```

Output 6.21 and Output 6.22 display the results from the analysis of complete cases. The value of each of the test statistics is somewhat smaller than the corresponding value computed using all available data. Thus, the partial data from the incomplete cases strengthen the evidence in favor of the existence of a significant trend between pulse duration and lesion severity.

Output 6.21   MH Tests Using Table Scores: Complete Cases Only

```
                 SUMMARY STATISTICS FOR PULSE BY SEVERITY
                         CONTROLLING FOR ID


    Cochran-Mantel-Haenszel Statistics (Based on Table Scores)

    Statistic   Alternative Hypothesis     DF      Value      Prob
    -----------------------------------------------------------------
        1        Nonzero Correlation         1      7.561     0.006
        2        Row Mean Scores Differ      4     11.593     0.021
        3        General Association        20     21.249     0.383


    Total Sample Size = 55
```

Output 6.22   MH Tests Using Rank Scores: Complete Cases Only

```
                SUMMARY STATISTICS FOR PULSE BY SEVERITY
                          CONTROLLING FOR ID


        Cochran-Mantel-Haenszel Statistics (Based on Rank Scores)

        Statistic   Alternative Hypothesis    DF      Value     Prob
        --------------------------------------------------------------
            1        Nonzero Correlation        1      8.510     0.004
            2        Row Mean Scores Differ     4     12.264     0.015



        Total Sample Size = 55
```

6.4.6   Continuous Response

Table 6.20 displays artificial data collected for the purpose of determining if pH level
alters action potential characteristics following administration of a drug (Harrell 1989).
The response variable of interest (Vmax) was measured at up to four pH levels for each of
25 patients. While at least two measurements were obtained from each patient, only three
patients provided data at all four pH levels.

Table 6.20   Action Potential Data

Patient	pH Level 6.5	6.9	7.4	7.9	Patient	pH Level 6.5	6.9	7.4	7.9
1		284	310	326	14	204	234	268	
2			261	292	15			258	267
3		213	224	240	16		193	224	235
4		222	235	247	17	185	222	252	263
5			270	286	18		238	301	300
6			210	218	19		198	240	
7		216	234	237	20		235	255	
8		236	273	283	21		216	238	
9	220	249	270	281	22		197	212	219
10	166	218	244		23		234	238	
11	227	258	282	286	24			295	281
12	216		284		25			261	272
13			257	284					

Although the response is a continuous measurement, MH statistics can still be used to
determine if the average Vmax differs among the four pH values (Q_{SMH}) and if there is a
trend between Vmax and pH (Q_{CSMH}). This approach offers the advantage of not
requiring any assumptions concerning the distribution of Vmax. In addition, the MH
methodology accommodates the varying numbers of observations per patient (under the
assumption that missing values are missing completely at random and the test statistic is

specified with either table scores or ranks).

The following SAS statements read in the data in the format shown in Table 6.20, restructure the data set for PROC FREQ, and compute the MH mean score and correlation statistics. The CMH2 option is used since it is not possible (or sensible) to compute the general association statistic Q_{GMH}. Since both pH and Vmax are quantitative variables, the default table scores are used. In addition, the trend is also assessed using modified ridit scores.

```
data ph_vmax;
    keep subject ph vmax;
    input subject vmax1-vmax4;
    ph=6.5;   vmax=vmax1;   output;
    ph=6.9;   vmax=vmax2;   output;
    ph=7.4;   vmax=vmax3;   output;
    ph=7.9;   vmax=vmax4;   output;
    cards;
 1   .   284 310 326
 2   .    .  261 292
 3   .   213 224 240
 4   .   222 235 247
 5   .    .  270 286
 6   .    .  210 218
 7   .   216 234 237
 8   .   236 273 283
 9 220 249 270 281
10 166 218 244  .
11 227 258 282 286
12 216  .  284  .
13   .   .  257 284
14 204 234 268  .
15   .   .  258 267
16   .  193 224 235
17 185 222 252 263
18   .  238 301 300
19   .  198 240  .
20   .  235 255  .
21   .  216 238  .
22   .  197 212 219
23   .  234 238  .
24   .   .  295 281
25   .   .  261 272
 ;
proc freq;
    tables subject*ph*vmax / noprint cmh2;
    tables subject*ph*vmax / noprint cmh2 scores=modridit;
run;
```

Output 6.23 shows that the mean Vmax differs significantly among the four pH levels ($Q_{SMH} = 27.7$, 3 df, $p < 0.001$). In addition, there is a highly significant linear trend between pH and Vmax ($Q_{CSMH} = 27.4$, 1 df, $p < 0.001$).

Output 6.23   MH Mean Score and Correlation Tests: Table Scores

```
                    SUMMARY STATISTICS FOR PH BY VMAX
                        CONTROLLING FOR SUBJECT


           Cochran-Mantel-Haenszel Statistics (Based on Table Scores)

        Statistic   Alternative Hypothesis     DF      Value      Prob
        -------------------------------------------------------------------
            1       Nonzero Correlation         1      27.389     0.000
            2       Row Mean Scores Differ      3      27.743     0.000



        Frequency Missing = 34            Effective Sample Size = 66

        ********** WARNING:   34% of the data are missing ************
```

The mean score and correlation statistics are even more significant when modified ridit scores are used (Output 6.24). Note that Vmax tends to progressively increase with PH for almost all patients (patients 18 and 24 are the exception).

Output 6.24   MH Mean Score and Correlation Tests: Modified Ridit Scores

```
                    SUMMARY STATISTICS FOR PH BY VMAX
                        CONTROLLING FOR SUBJECT


           Cochran-Mantel-Haenszel Statistics (Modified Ridit Scores)

        Statistic   Alternative Hypothesis     DF      Value      Prob
        -------------------------------------------------------------------
            1       Nonzero Correlation         1      35.382     0.000
            2       Row Mean Scores Differ      3      34.794     0.000



        Frequency Missing = 34            Effective Sample Size = 66

        ********** WARNING:   34% of the data are missing ************
```

In this example, the column variable of each table was continuous and the row variable, although quantitative, had only four possible values. Thus, both Q_{SMH} and Q_{CSMH} could be used. The MH approach to the analysis of one-sample repeated measures can also be very useful when the row and column variables are both continuous. In this case, only Q_{CSMH} can be used. This can be specified by using the CMH1 option in the TABLES statement.

The methodology is also applicable when there are multiple groups (samples). However, the observations are viewed as a single group when comparing conditions within subjects.

Chapter 7
Nonparametric Methods

Chapter Table of Contents

Chapter 7
Nonparametric Methods

7.1 Introduction

Parametric methods of statistical inference require you to assume that your data come from some underlying distribution whose general form is known, such as the normal, binomial, Poisson, or Weibull distribution. Statistical methods for estimation and hypothesis testing are then based on these assumptions. The focus is on estimating parameters and testing hypotheses about them.

In contrast, nonparametric statistical methods make few assumptions about the underlying distribution from which the data are sampled. One of their main advantages is that inference is not focused on specific population parameters, and it is thus possible to test hypotheses that are more general than statements about parameters. For example, they allow you to test whether two distributions are the same without having to test hypotheses concerning population parameters. Nonparametric procedures can also be used when the underlying distribution is unknown or when parametric assumptions are not valid.

The main disadvantage is that a nonparametric test is generally less powerful than the corresponding parametric test when the assumptions are satisfied. However, for many of the commonly used nonparametric methods, the decrease in power is not large.

Most of this book concentrates on the analysis of categorical response variables measured on nominal or ordinal scales. This chapter focuses on the analysis of continuous response variables with the use of nonparametric statistical methods. The reason for considering these methods is that many of the commonly used nonparametric tests, such as the Wilcoxon-Mann-Whitney, Kruskal-Wallis, Spearman correlation, Friedman, and Durbin tests, can be computed using Mantel-Haenszel procedures. While previous chapters have shown how to use Mantel-Haenszel procedures to analyze two-way tables and sets of two-way tables, this chapter shows how to use the same procedures to perform nonparametric analyses of continuous response variables.

7.2 Wilcoxon-Mann-Whitney Test

The Wilcoxon-Mann-Whitney test is a nonparametric test of the null hypothesis that the distribution of an ordinally scaled response variable is the same in two independently sampled populations. It is sensitive to the alternative hypothesis that there is a location difference between the two populations. This test was first proposed for the case of two samples of equal size by Wilcoxon (1945). Mann and Whitney (1947) introduced an equivalent statistic, and they were the first to consider unequal sample sizes and to furnish tables suitable for use with small samples. (Such tables are found in the appendices of standard statistics textbooks.)

The Wilcoxon-Mann-Whitney test can be used whenever the two-sample t-test is appropriate. One approach to comparing the nonparametric Wilcoxon-Mann-Whitney test to the parametric two-sample t-test is based on the concept of asymptotic relative efficiency, as developed by Pitman (1948) in a series of unpublished lecture notes. In brief, the efficiency of a test T_2 relative to a test T_1 is the ratio n_1/n_2 of the sample sizes needed to obtain the same power for the two tests. For normal distributions with a shift in the mean, the asymptotic efficiency of the Wilcoxon-Mann-Whitney test relative to the two-sample t-test is 0.955. Thus, a small price is paid for using the nonparametric test, in return for greater applicability. If the underlying populations are not normally distributed (for example, they have asymmetric distributions), the power of the Wilcoxon-Mann-Whitney test can be much higher than that of the two-sample t-test. In fact, the asymptotic relative efficiency can be as high as infinity.

When the sample sizes in the two groups are small, tables of the exact distribution of the test statistic should be used. Alternatively, you can carry out exact tests of significance for small sample sizes by using the new EXACT statement in the NPAR1WAY procedure, which is available with Release 6.11 of the SAS System, or by using specialized software packages such as StatXact© (Mehta and Patel 1991). If there are at least 10 observations per group, the p-value can be approximated using the asymptotic normal distribution of the test criteria. The asymptotic test is simply the Mantel-Haenszel mean score statistic for the special case of one stratum when rank scores are used.

Table 7.1 displays data from a study of the relationship between sodium chloride preference and hypertension (Schechter, Horwitz, and Henkin 1973). Two groups of subjects, 12 normal and 10 hypertensive, were isolated for a week and compared with respect to their average daily Na^+ intakes.

Table 7.1   Sodium Chloride Preference Data

Normal Group		Hypertensive Group	
Subject	NA^+	Subject	NA^+
1	10.2	1	92.8
2	2.2	2	54.8
3	0.0	3	51.6
4	2.6	4	61.7
5	0.0	5	250.8
6	43.1	6	84.5
7	45.8	7	34.7
8	63.6	8	62.2
9	1.8	9	11.0
10	0.0	10	39.1
11	3.7		
12	0.0		

The following statements create a SAS data set containing the data of Table 7.1 and compare the two groups using the Wilcoxon-Mann-Whitney test. The statistic is computed using the Mantel-Haenszel mean score test based on rank scores.

```
data sodium;
   input group $ subject intake;
   cards;
Normal     1  10.2
Normal     2   2.2
Normal     3   0.0
Normal     4   2.6
Normal     5   0.0
Normal     6  43.1
Normal     7  45.8
Normal     8  63.6
Normal     9   1.8
Normal    10   0.0
Normal    11   3.7
Normal    12   0.0
Hyperten   1  92.8
Hyperten   2  54.8
Hyperten   3  51.6
Hyperten   4  61.7
Hyperten   5 250.8
Hyperten   6  84.5
Hyperten   7  34.7
Hyperten   8  62.2
Hyperten   9  11.0
Hyperten  10  39.1
;
proc freq;
   tables group*intake / noprint cmh2 scores=rank;
run;
```

The CMH2 option in the TABLES statement specifies that only the Mantel-Haenszel correlation and mean score statistics are to be computed, since the general association statistic is not useful in this example (for example, its use is for strictly categorical data). As shown in Output 7.1, the mean score statistic indicates that there is a significant difference between normal and hypertensive subjects (chi-square=9.659, 1 df, $p = 0.002$). Since there are only two groups, the correlation and mean score statistics are identical.

Output 7.1   Wilcoxon-Mann-Whitney Test Using the MH Mean Score Statistic

```
           SUMMARY STATISTICS FOR GROUP BY INTAKE


    Cochran-Mantel-Haenszel Statistics (Based on Rank Scores)

   Statistic   Alternative Hypothesis     DF     Value     Prob
   --------------------------------------------------------------
       1        Nonzero Correlation        1      9.659    0.002
       2        Row Mean Scores Differ     1      9.659    0.002


   Total Sample Size = 22
```

The Wilcoxon-Mann-Whitney test is also equivalent to the extended Mantel-Haenszel correlation statistic in the tests of no association for a two-way contingency table (with $s \times 2$ or $2 \times r$ structure), provided that rank scores are specified. The following SAS statements produce the results shown in Output 7.2.

```
proc freq;
    tables group*intake / noprint chisq scores=rank;
run;
```

The chi-square test statistic labeled "MH Chi-Square (Rank Scores)" is also equal to 9.659. Note that chi-square and other contingency table results for this specification should be ignored because of insufficient cell sizes.

Output 7.2   Wilcoxon-Mann-Whitney Test Using the MH Chi-Square Statistic

```
              STATISTICS FOR TABLE OF GROUP BY INTAKE

       Statistic                    DF     Value       Prob
       --------------------------------------------------------
       Chi-Square                   18     22.000      0.232
       Likelihood Ratio Chi-Square  18     30.316      0.034
       MH Chi-Square (Rank Scores)   1      9.659      0.002
       Phi Coefficient                     1.000
       Contingency Coefficient             0.707
       Cramer's V                          1.000


       Sample Size = 22
       WARNING: 100% of the cells have expected counts less
                than 5. Chi-Square may not be a valid test.
```

You can also use the NPAR1WAY procedure to compute the Wilcoxon-Mann-Whitney statistic. You specify the WILCOXON option in the PROC statement, list GROUP in the CLASS statement, and list INTAKE in the VAR statement. Output 7.3 displays the results of the following statements.

```
proc npar1way wilcoxon;
    class group;
    var intake;
run;
```

Output 7.3   Wilcoxon-Mann-Whitney Test Using PROC NPAR1WAY

```
                    N P A R 1 W A Y   P R O C E D U R E

              Wilcoxon Scores (Rank Sums) for Variable INTAKE
                       Classified by Variable GROUP


                         Sum of      Expected      Std Dev        Mean
     GROUP        N      Scores      Under H0      Under H0       Score

     Normal      12        91.0        138.0     15.1228734    7.5833333
     Hyperten    10       162.0        115.0     15.1228734   16.2000000
                     Average Scores were used for Ties
              Wilcoxon 2-Sample Test (Normal Approximation)
              (with Continuity Correction of .5)

              S=   162.000      Z=  3.07481       Prob > |Z| =    0.0021


              T-Test approx. Significance =       0.0057


              Kruskal-Wallis Test (Chi-Square Approximation)
              CHISQ=  9.6589       DF=  1       Prob > CHISQ=    0.0019
```

The NPAR1WAY procedure computes a continuity-corrected Wilcoxon-Mann-Whitney test that yields slightly different results from PROC FREQ. The normal approximation statistic is $Z = 3.07481$ with a two-sided p-value of 0.0021. Output 7.3 also displays a chi-square statistic labeled "Kruskal-Wallis Test (Chi-Square Approximation)." The value of this statistic is identical to that resulting from the tests computed by the FREQ procedure.

7.3   Kruskal-Wallis Test

The Kruskal-Wallis (1952) test is a generalization of the two-sample Wilcoxon-Mann-Whitney test to three or more groups. It is a nonparametric test of the null hypothesis that the distribution of a response variable is the same in multiple independently sampled populations. The test requires an ordinally scaled response variable and is sensitive to the alternative hypothesis that there is a location difference among the populations. The Kruskal-Wallis test can be used whenever a one-way analysis of variance (ANOVA) model is appropriate.

When the sample sizes in the groups are small, tables of the exact distribution of the test statistic should be used. Alternatively, you can carry out exact tests of significance for small sample sizes (see page 144). If there are at least five observations per group, the p-value can be approximated using the asymptotic chi-square distribution with $s - 1$ degrees of freedom, where s is the number of groups. The approximate test is simply the Mantel-Haenszel mean score statistic for the special case of one stratum when rank scores are used.

Table 7.2 displays data from a study of antecubital vein cortisol levels at time of delivery in pregnant women (Cawson et al. 1974). The investigators wanted to determine if median cortisol levels differed among three groups of women, all of whom had delivery between 38 and 42 weeks gestation. The data were obtained before the onset of labor at elective

Caesarean section (Group I), at emergency Caesarean section during induced labor (Group II), or at the time of vaginal or Caesarean delivery in women in whom spontaneous labor occurred (Group III).

Table 7.2   Antecubital Vein Cortisol Levels at Time of Delivery

Group I		Group II		Group III	
Patient	Level	Patient	Level	Patient	Level
1	262	1	465	1	343
2	307	2	501	2	772
3	211	3	455	3	207
4	323	4	355	4	1048
5	454	5	468	5	838
6	339	6	362	6	687
7	304				
8	154				
9	287				
10	356				

The following statements create a SAS data set containing the data of Table 7.2 and request the Mantel-Haenszel mean score statistic comparing the mean rank scores in the three groups of subjects.

```
data cortisol;
   input group $ subject cortisol;
   cards;
I     1   262
I     2   307
I     3   211
I     4   323
I     5   454
I     6   339
I     7   304
I     8   154
I     9   287
I    10   356
II    1   465
II    2   501
II    3   455
II    4   355
II    5   468
II    6   362
III   1   343
III   2   772
III   3   207
III   4  1048
III   5   838
III   6   687
;
```

```
proc freq;
    tables group*cortisol / noprint cmh2 scores=rank;
run;
```

The Kruskal-Wallis statistic, labeled "Row Mean Scores Differ" in Output 7.4, is equal to 9.232 with 2 df, corresponding to a p-value of 0.010. Thus, the cortisol level distributions differ among the three groups of patients. Since there are more than two groups, the Mantel-Haenszel correlation statistic, labeled "Nonzero Correlation," does not produce the same results as the Kruskal-Wallis test. The correlation statistic uses rank scores to test the null hypothesis that there is no association between group and cortisol level, versus the alternative hypothesis of a monotone association between the two variables. Thus, this statistic is only valid if the three groups are ordered (which might be realistic for this example in terms of the timing for cortisol level determination).

Output 7.4   Kruskal-Wallis Test Using PROC FREQ

```
                   SUMMARY STATISTICS FOR GROUP BY CORTISOL


        Cochran-Mantel-Haenszel Statistics (Based on Rank Scores)

        Statistic   Alternative Hypothesis    DF     Value    Prob
        -----------------------------------------------------------------
            1        Nonzero Correlation        1     8.286    0.004
            2        Row Mean Scores Differ     2     9.232    0.010


        Total Sample Size = 22
```

The Kruskal-Wallis test can also be computed using the WILCOXON option of the NPAR1WAY procedure.

```
proc nparlway wilcoxon;
    class group;
    var cortisol;
run;
```

The Kruskal-Wallis test displayed in Output 7.5 is identical to the value shown in Output 7.4. The NPAR1WAY procedure gives additional results showing that the mean rank scores in groups II and III are nearly equivalent and are substantially greater than the mean rank score in group I.

Output 7.5   Kruskal-Wallis Test Using PROC NPAR1WAY

```
                    N P A R 1 W A Y   P R O C E D U R E

            Wilcoxon Scores (Rank Sums) for Variable CORTISOL
                       Classified by Variable GROUP


                     Sum of      Expected     Std Dev        Mean
        GROUP    N    Scores     Under H0      Under H0      Score

        I       10     69.0       115.0      15.1657509    6.9000000
        II       6     90.0        69.0      13.5646600   15.0000000
        III      6     94.0        69.0      13.5646600   15.6666667



          Kruskal-Wallis Test (Chi-Square Approximation)
            CHISQ=  9.2316     DF=  2     Prob > CHISQ=      0.0099
```

7.4   Friedman's Chi-Square Test

Friedman's test (1937) is a nonparametric method for analyzing a randomized complete block design. This type of study design is applicable when interest is focused on one particular factor, but there are other factors whose effects you want to control. The experimental units are first divided into blocks (groups) in such a way that units within a block are relatively homogeneous. The size of each block is equal to the number of treatments or conditions under study. The treatments are then assigned at random to the experimental units within each block so that each treatment is given once and only once per block. The basic design principle is to partition the experimental units in such a way that background variability between blocks is maximized so that the variability within blocks is minimized.

The standard parametric ANOVA methods for analyzing randomized complete block designs require the assumption that the experimental errors are normally distributed. The Friedman test, which does not require this assumption, depends only on the ranks of the observations within each block and is sometimes called the two-way analysis of variance by ranks.

For small randomized complete block designs, the exact distribution of the Friedman test statistic should be used; for example, Odeh et al. (1977) tabulate the critical values of the Friedman test for up to six blocks and up to six treatments. Alternatively, you can carry out exact tests of significance for small sample sizes (see page 144). As the number of blocks increases, the distribution of the Friedman statistic approaches that of a chi-square random variable with $s - 1$ degrees of freedom, where s is the number of treatments. The approximate test is simply the Mantel-Haenszel mean score statistic for the special case of rank scores and one subject per treatment group in each block.

Table 7.3 displays data from an experiment designed to determine if five electrode types performed similarly (Berry 1987). In this study, all five types were applied to the arms of 16 subjects and the resistance was measured. Each subject is a block in this example, and all five treatments are applied once and only once per block.

Table 7.3 Electrical Resistance Data

	Electrode Type				
Subject	1	2	3	4	5
1	500	400	98	200	250
2	660	600	600	75	310
3	250	370	220	250	220
4	72	140	240	33	54
5	135	300	450	430	70
6	27	84	135	190	180
7	100	50	82	73	78
8	105	180	32	58	32
9	90	180	220	34	64
10	200	290	320	280	135
11	15	45	75	88	80
12	160	200	300	300	220
13	250	400	50	50	92
14	170	310	230	20	150
15	66	1000	1050	280	220
16	107	48	26	45	51

The following statements read in one record per subject and create a SAS data set containing one observation per electrode per subject. The Mantel-Haenszel mean score statistic is then computed using rank scores, where the 16 subjects define 16 strata.

```
data electrod;
   input subject resist1-resist5;
   type=1;  resist=resist1;  output;
   type=2;  resist=resist2;  output;
   type=3;  resist=resist3;  output;
   type=4;  resist=resist4;  output;
   type=5;  resist=resist5;  output;
   cards;
 1   500   400    98   200   250
 2   660   600   600    75   310
 3   250   370   220   250   220
 4    72   140   240    33    54
 5   135   300   450   430    70
 6    27    84   135   190   180
 7   100    50    82    73    78
 8   105   180    32    58    32
 9    90   180   220    34    64
10   200   290   320   280   135
11    15    45    75    88    80
12   160   200   300   300   220
13   250   400    50    50    92
14   170   310   230    20   150
15    66  1000  1050   280   220
16   107    48    26    45    51
;
proc freq;
```

```
        tables subject*type*resist / noprint cmh2 scores=rank;
   run;
```

Output 7.6 displays the results. The value of the test statistic is 5.452 with 4 df. The *p*-value of 0.244 indicates that there is little evidence of a statistically significant difference among the five types of electrodes.

Output 7.6   Friedman Test

```
                        The SAS System

              SUMMARY STATISTICS FOR TYPE BY RESIST
                    CONTROLLING FOR SUBJECT


      Cochran-Mantel-Haenszel Statistics (Based on Rank Scores)

     Statistic   Alternative Hypothesis   DF     Value    Prob
     ------------------------------------------------------------
         1         Nonzero Correlation      1     2.775    0.096
         2         Row Mean Scores Differ    4     5.452    0.244


     Total Sample Size = 80
```

In experimental situations with more than one subject per group in each block, PROC FREQ can be used to compute generalizations of the Friedman test. The general principle is that the strata are defined by the blocks and the treatments or groups define the rows of each table.

7.5   Aligned Ranks Test for Randomized Complete Blocks

When the number of blocks or treatments is small, the Friedman test has relatively low power. This results from the fact that the test statistic is based on ranking the observations within each block, which provides comparisons only of the within-block responses. Thus, direct comparison of responses in different blocks is not meaningful, due to variation between blocks. If the blocks are small, there are too few comparisons to permit an effective overall comparison of the treatments. As an example, the Friedman test reduces to the sign test if there are only two treatments. This disadvantage becomes less serious as the number of treatments increases or as the number of subjects per block increases for a fixed number *s* of treatments.

An alternative to the Friedman test is to use *aligned ranks*. The basic idea is to make the blocks more comparable by subtracting from each observation within a block some estimate of the location of the block, such as the average or median of the observations. The resulting differences are called *aligned observations*. Instead of separately ranking the observations within each block, you rank the complete set of aligned observations relative to each other. Thus, the ranking scheme is the same as that used in computing the Kruskal-Wallis statistic. The resulting ranks are called aligned ranks.

The aligned rank test was introduced by Hodges and Lehmann (1962). Koch and Sen (1968) considered four cases of interest in the analysis of randomized complete block experiments and independently proposed the aligned rank procedure for their Case IV. Apart from the fact that one set of aligned ranks is used instead of separate within-block ranks, the computation of the aligned rank statistic is the same as for the Friedman test.

The exact distribution of the test statistic is cumbersome to compute. In addition, tables are not feasible since the distribution depends on the way the aligned ranks are distributed over the blocks. However, the null distribution of the test statistic is approximately chi-square with $s - 1$ degrees of freedom, where s is the number of treatments (or block size when there is one observation per treatment in each block). Tardif (1980, 1981, 1985) studied the asymptotic efficiency and other aspects of aligned rank tests in randomized block designs.

In Section 7.4, Friedman's test was used to analyze data from an experiment designed to determine if five electrode types performed similarly (Table 7.3). Using the SAS data set created in Section 7.4, the following statements compute the aligned rank statistic.

```
proc standard mean=0;
   by subject;
   var resist;
proc rank;
   var resist;
proc freq;
   tables subject*type*resist / noprint cmh2;
run;
```

The STANDARD procedure standardizes the observations within each block (subject) to have mean zero. Thus, the subject-specific sample mean is subtracted from each response. The RANK procedure computes a single set of rankings for the combined aligned observations. Using the resulting aligned ranks as scores, the FREQ procedure computes the aligned rank statistic.

Output 7.7 displays the results. The test statistic is equal to 13.6 with 4 df. With reference to the chi-square distribution with four degrees of freedom, there is a clearly significant difference among the five electrode types. Recall that the Friedman test (Output 7.6) was not statistically significant. Thus, this example illustrates the potentially greater power of the aligned ranks test.

Output 7.7   Aligned Ranks Test

```
                SUMMARY STATISTICS FOR TYPE BY RESIST
                      CONTROLLING FOR SUBJECT


    Cochran-Mantel-Haenszel Statistics (Based on Table Scores)

    Statistic   Alternative Hypothesis    DF     Value     Prob
    ----------------------------------------------------------------
        1        Nonzero Correlation        1     4.978    0.026
        2        Row Mean Scores Differ     4    13.600    0.009


    Total Sample Size = 80
```

7.6 Durbin's Test for Balanced Incomplete Blocks

In the randomized complete block design, every treatment is applied in every block. However, it is sometimes impractical or impossible for all of the treatments to be applied to each block, especially when the number of treatments is large and the block size is limited. Experimental designs in which not all treatments are applied to each block are called incomplete block designs. If the design is balanced so that every block contains c experimental units, every treatment appears in u blocks, and every treatment appears with every other treatment an equal number of times, the design is then called a balanced incomplete block design.

Durbin (1951) presented a rank test that can be used to test the null hypothesis of no differences among treatments in a balanced incomplete block design. This test can be computed using the stratified Mantel-Haenszel mean score statistic based on rank scores. The Durbin test reduces to the Friedman test if the number of treatments equals the number of experimental units per block.

As an example, Table 7.4 displays data taken from a mirror drawing experiment conducted in 20 psychiatric patients (Ogilvie 1965). The subject's task was to trace along a straight line, seen in a mirror, with his or her hand hidden. The straight lines were oriented at five different angles to the median plane of the subject ($0°$, $22.5°$, $45°$, $67.5°$, and $90°$), and the outcome variable was the time (in seconds) taken to complete the task. Ideally, every subject should draw lines at each angle. However, the effect of practice on performance could be considerable. In addition, it was difficult to maintain the subject's interest and cooperation in the experiment for more than a brief period. Consequently, a balanced incomplete block design was used. Each of the 20 subjects completed the experiment at two of the five angles; thus, each angle was studied eight times.

Table 7.4   Drawing Times (Seconds) from a Mirror Tracing Experiment

Subject	Angle (degrees)					Subject	Angle (degrees)				
	0	22.5	45	67.5	90		0	22.5	45	67.5	90
1	7	15				11				17	9
2	20		72			12			100		15
3	8			26		13	16			32	
4	33				36	14		19		32	
5	7	16				15			36	39	
6		68	67			16				44	54
7		33		64		17	16				38
8		34			12	18		17			12
9	10		96			19			37		11
10		29	59			20				56	6

The following statements read in one record per subject. The four input variables for each subject contain the two angles used and the drawing times at these angles. The resulting SAS data set contains two observations per subject and three variables per observation: subject identifier, angle, and drawing time. The PROC FREQ statements compute the extended Mantel-Haenszel mean score statistic, with one stratum for each subject. The rows of each table are defined by the five angles studied, and rank scores are used for the response variable (drawing time).

```
data tracing;
   keep subject angle time;
   input subject angle1 angle2 time1 time2;
   angle=angle1;  time=time1;  output;
   angle=angle2;  time=time2;  output;
   cards;
 1  0.0 22.5    7   15
 2  0.0 45.0   20   72
 3  0.0 67.5    8   26
 4  0.0 90.0   33   36
 5 22.5  0.0   16    7
 6 22.5 45.0   68   67
 7 22.5 67.5   33   64
 8 22.5 90.0   34   12
 9 45.0  0.0   96   10
10 45.0 22.5   59   29
11 45.0 67.5   17    9
12 45.0 90.0  100   15
13 67.5  0.0   32   16
14 67.5 22.5   32   19
15 67.5 45.0   39   36
16 67.5 90.0   44   54
17 90.0  0.0   38   16
18 90.0 22.5   12   17
19 90.0 45.0   11   37
20 90.0 67.5    6   56
;
proc freq;
   tables subject*angle*time / noprint cmh2 scores=rank;
run;
```

Output 7.8 displays the results of Durbin's test. The chi-square statistic is 10.4 with 4 df (since there are five groups). The p-value of 0.034 indicates that there is a significant difference among the drawing time distributions at the five angles.

Output 7.8   Results of Durbin's Test

```
              SUMMARY STATISTICS FOR ANGLE BY TIME
                    CONTROLLING FOR SUBJECT


    Cochran-Mantel-Haenszel Statistics (Based on Rank Scores)

    Statistic   Alternative Hypothesis    DF     Value     Prob
    ------------------------------------------------------------
        1       Nonzero Correlation        1     1.800     0.180
        2       Row Mean Scores Differ     4    10.400     0.034



    Total Sample Size = 40
```

While Durbin's test uses within-block ranks, you could perform a similar test using aligned ranks, as described in Section 7.5. In addition, Benard and van Elteren (1953) generalized the Durbin test to the case where some experimental units may contain several observations per treatment. This generalization can also be computed using the CMH option of PROC FREQ.

7.7 Rank Analysis of Covariance

The analysis of covariance (ANCOVA) is a standard statistical methodology that combines the features of analysis of variance (ANOVA) and linear regression to determine if there is a difference in some response variable between two or more groups. The basic idea is to augment the ANOVA model containing the group effects with one or more additional categorical or quantitative variables that are related to the response variable. These additional variables *covary* with the response and so are called covariables or covariates.

One of the main uses of ANCOVA is to increase precision in randomized experiments by using the relationship between the response variable and the covariates to reduce the error variability in comparing treatment groups. In this setting, ANCOVA often results in more powerful tests, shorter confidence intervals, and a reduction in the sample size required to establish differences among treatment groups. ANCOVA is also useful in adjusting for sources of bias in observational studies.

The validity of classical parametric ANCOVA depends on several assumptions, including normality of error terms, equality of error variances for different treatments, equality of slopes for the different treatment regression lines, and linearity of regression. For situations in which these assumptions may not be satisfied, Quade (1967) proposed the use of rank analysis of covariance. This technique can be combined with the randomization model framework of extended Mantel-Haenszel statistics to carry out nonparametric comparisons between treatment groups, after adjusting for the effects of one or more covariates. The methodology, which has been described by Koch et al. (1982, 1990), can be easily implemented using the SAS System.

Table 7.5 displays exercise data from treadmill testing of healthy males and females (Bruce, Kusumi, and Hosmer 1973; Fisher and van Belle 1993). The purpose of the analysis is to determine if men and women use the same amount of oxygen. The outcome, VO_2MAX, is computed by determining the volume of oxygen used per minute per kilogram of body weight. Since the effort expended to go further on the treadmill increases with the duration of time on the treadmill, there should be some relationship between VO_2MAX and duration on the treadmill; thus, this variable is used as a covariate.

Table 7.5   Exercise Data for Healthy Males and Females

	Males						Females				
ID	Durat.	VO_2	ID	Durat.	VO_2	ID	Durat.	VO_2	ID	Durat.	VO_2
1	706	41.5	23	582	35.8	1	660	38.1	23	461	30.5
2	732	45.9	24	503	29.1	2	628	38.4	24	540	25.9
3	930	54.5	25	747	47.2	3	637	41.7	25	588	32.7
4	900	60.3	26	600	30.0	4	575	33.5	26	498	26.9
5	903	60.5	27	491	34.1	5	590	28.6	27	483	24.6
6	976	64.6	28	694	38.1	6	600	23.9	28	554	28.8
7	819	47.4	29	586	28.7	7	562	29.6	29	521	25.9
8	922	57.0	30	612	37.1	8	495	27.3	30	436	24.4
9	600	40.2	31	610	34.5	9	540	33.2	31	398	26.3
10	540	35.2	32	539	34.4	10	470	26.6	32	366	23.2
11	560	33.8	33	559	35.1	11	408	23.6	33	439	24.6
12	637	38.8	34	653	40.9	12	387	23.1	34	549	28.8
13	593	38.9	35	733	45.4	13	564	36.6	35	360	19.6
14	719	49.5	36	596	36.9	14	603	35.8	36	566	31.4
15	615	37.1	37	580	41.6	15	420	28.0	37	407	26.6
16	589	32.2	38	550	22.7	16	573	33.8	38	602	30.6
17	478	31.3	39	497	31.9	17	602	33.6	39	488	27.5
18	620	33.8	40	605	42.5	18	430	21.0	40	526	30.9
19	710	43.7	41	552	37.4	19	508	31.2	41	524	33.9
20	600	41.7	42	640	48.2	20	565	31.2	42	562	32.3
21	660	41.0	43	500	33.6	21	464	23.7	43	496	26.9
22	644	45.9	44	603	45.0	22	495	24.5			

The following statements create a SAS data set containing the sex, subject ID, duration of exercise (seconds), and VO_2MAX values for each subject.

```
data exercise;
   input sex $ case duration vo2max @@;
   cards;
M  1 706 41.5    M  2 732 45.9    M  3 930 54.5    M  4 900 60.3
M  5 903 60.5    M  6 976 64.6    M  7 819 47.4    M  8 922 57.0
M  9 600 40.2    M 10 540 35.2    M 11 560 33.8    M 12 637 38.8
M 13 593 38.9    M 14 719 49.5    M 15 615 37.1    M 16 589 32.2
M 17 478 31.3    M 18 620 33.8    M 19 710 43.7    M 20 600 41.7
M 21 660 41.0    M 22 644 45.9    M 23 582 35.8    M 24 503 29.1
M 25 747 47.2    M 26 600 30.0    M 27 491 34.1    M 28 694 38.1
M 29 586 28.7    M 30 612 37.1    M 31 610 34.5    M 32 539 34.4
M 33 559 35.1    M 34 653 40.9    M 35 733 45.4    M 36 596 36.9
M 37 580 41.6    M 38 550 22.7    M 39 497 31.9    M 40 605 42.5
M 41 552 37.4    M 42 640 48.2    M 43 500 33.6    M 44 603 45.0
F  1 660 38.1    F  2 628 38.4    F  3 637 41.7    F  4 575 33.5
F  5 590 28.6    F  6 600 23.9    F  7 562 29.6    F  8 495 27.3
F  9 540 33.2    F 10 470 26.6    F 11 408 23.6    F 12 387 23.1
F 13 564 36.6    F 14 603 35.8    F 15 420 28.0    F 16 573 33.8
F 17 602 33.6    F 18 430 21.0    F 19 508 31.2    F 20 565 31.2
F 21 464 23.7    F 22 495 24.5    F 23 461 30.5    F 24 540 25.9
```

```
F 25 588 32.7      F 26 498 26.9      F 27 483 24.6      F 28 554 28.8
F 29 521 25.9      F 30 436 24.4      F 31 398 26.3      F 32 366 23.2
F 33 439 24.6      F 34 549 28.8      F 35 360 19.6      F 36 566 31.4
F 37 407 26.6      F 38 602 30.6      F 39 488 27.5      F 40 526 30.9
F 41 524 33.9      F 42 562 32.3      F 43 496 26.9
;
run;
```

The first step of the analysis is to compute the ranks of the response variable and covariate in the combined group of males and females. You do this using PROC RANK, as follows:

```
proc rank out=ranks;
   var duration vo2max;
run;
```

The next step is to calculate the residuals from the linear regression of the VO_2MAX ranks on the duration ranks using PROC REG. The residuals are saved in an output data set.

```
proc reg noprint;
   model vo2max=duration;
   output out=residual r=resid;
run;
```

Finally, the Mantel-Haenszel mean score statistic is used to compare the mean values of the residuals in males and females using TABLE scores.

```
proc freq;
   tables sex*resid / noprint cmh2;
run;
```

Output 7.9 displays the results, which indicate a clearly significant difference between males and females (chi-square=11.763, 1 df, $p = 0.001$).

Output 7.9   Rank Analysis of Covariance Results

```
                SUMMARY STATISTICS FOR SEX BY RESID


     Cochran-Mantel-Haenszel Statistics (Based on Table Scores)

     Statistic   Alternative Hypothesis     DF     Value     Prob
     ----------------------------------------------------------------
         1        Nonzero Correlation        1     11.763    0.001
         2        Row Mean Scores Differ     1     11.763    0.001


     Total Sample Size = 87
```

The methodology can also be modified for the situation in which there are multiple strata. Table 7.6 displays data from an experiment to evaluate the effectiveness of topically applied stannous fluoride and acid phosphate fluoride in reducing the incidence of dental caries, as compared with a placebo treatment of distilled water (Cartwright, Lindahl, and

Bawden 1968, Quade 1982). These data are from 69 female children from three centers who completed the two year study. The stannous fluoride, acid phosphate fluoride, and distilled water treatment groups are denoted by SF, APF, and W. The columns labeled B and A represent the number of decayed, missing, or filled teeth (DMFT) before and after the study, respectively. In this example, the response to be compared among the three groups is the number of DMFT after treatment; the number of DMFT before treatment is used as a covariate. In addition, the analysis is stratified by center.

Table 7.6 Dental Caries Data

	Center 1				Center 2				Center 3						
ID	Grp	B	A	ID	Grp	B	A	ID	Grp	B	A	ID	Grp	B	A
1	W	7	11	1	W	10	14	1	W	2	4	18	APF	10	12
2	W	20	24	2	W	13	17	2	W	13	18	19	APF	7	11
3	W	21	25	3	W	3	4	3	W	9	12	20	APF	13	12
4	W	1	2	4	W	4	7	4	W	15	18	21	APF	5	8
5	W	3	7	5	W	4	9	5	W	13	17	22	APF	1	3
6	W	20	23	6	SF	15	18	6	W	2	5	23	APF	8	9
7	W	9	13	7	SF	6	8	7	W	9	12	24	APF	4	5
8	W	2	4	8	SF	4	6	8	SF	4	6	25	APF	4	7
9	SF	11	13	9	SF	18	19	9	SF	10	14	26	APF	14	14
10	SF	15	18	10	SF	11	12	10	SF	7	11	27	APF	8	10
11	APF	7	10	11	SF	9	9	11	SF	14	15	28	APF	3	5
12	APF	17	17	12	SF	4	7	12	SF	7	10	29	APF	11	12
13	APF	9	11	13	SF	5	7	13	SF	3	6	30	APF	16	18
14	APF	1	5	14	SF	11	14	14	SF	9	12	31	APF	8	8
15	APF	3	7	15	SF	4	6	15	SF	8	10	32	APF	0	1
				16	APF	4	4	16	SF	19	19	33	APF	3	4
				17	APF	7	7	17	SF	10	13				
				18	APF	0	4								
				19	APF	3	3								
				20	APF	0	1								
				21	APF	8	8								

The following SAS statements read in the variables CENTER, ID, GROUP, BEFORE, and AFTER, whose values are displayed in Table 7.6.

```
data caries;
   input center id group $ before after @@;
   cards;
   1  1 W     7 11     1  2 W    20 24     1  3 W    21 25     1  4 W     1  2
   1  5 W     3  7     1  6 W    20 23     1  7 W     9 13     1  8 W     2  4
   1  9 SF   11 13     1 10 SF   15 18     1 11 APF   7 10     1 12 APF  17 17
   1 13 APF   9 11     1 14 APF   1  5     1 15 APF   3  7     2  1 W    10 14
   2  2 W    13 17     2  3 W     3  4     2  4 W     4  7     2  5 W     4  9
   2  6 SF   15 18     2  7 SF    6  8     2  8 SF    4  6     2  9 SF   18 19
   2 10 SF   11 12     2 11 SF    9  9     2 12 SF    4  7     2 13 SF    5  7
```

```
      2 14 SF   11 14      2 15 SF    4  6      2 16 APF   4  4      2 17 APF   7  7
      2 18 APF   0  4      2 19 APF   3  3      2 20 APF   0  1      2 21 APF   8  8
      3  1 W     2  4      3  2 W    13 18      3  3 W     9 12      3  4 W    15 18
      3  5 W    13 17      3  6 W     2  5      3  7 W     9 12      3  8 SF    4  6
      3  9 SF   10 14      3 10 SF    7 11      3 11 SF   14 15      3 12 SF    7 10
      3 13 SF    3  6      3 14 SF    9 12      3 15 SF    8 10      3 16 SF   19 19
      3 17 SF   10 13      3 18 APF  10 12      3 19 APF   7 11      3 20 APF  13 12
      3 21 APF   5  8      3 22 APF   1  3      3 23 APF   8  9      3 24 APF   4  5
      3 25 APF   4  7      3 26 APF  14 14      3 27 APF   8 10      3 28 APF   3  5
      3 29 APF  11 12      3 30 APF  16 18      3 31 APF   8  8      3 32 APF   0  1
      3 33 APF   3  4
   ;
   run;
```

The next statements produce standardized ranks for the covariate BEFORE and the response variable AFTER in each of the three centers. Standardized ranks are used to adjust for the fact that the number of patients differs among centers.

```
   proc rank nplus1 ties=mean out=ranks;
      by center;
      var before after;
   run;
```

The NPLUS1 option of the RANK procedure requests fractional ranks using the denominator $n + 1$, where n is the center-specific sample size. The TIES=MEAN option requests that tied values receive the mean of the corresponding ranks (midranks). Since TIES=MEAN is the default for PROC RANK, this option was not specified in the previous example. However, when fractional ranks are requested using either the FRACTION (denominator is n) or NPLUS1 (denominator is $n + 1$) options, the TIES=HIGH option is the default. Thus, you must specify both the NPLUS1 and TIES=MEAN options.

PROC REG is then used to fit separate linear regression models for the three centers. In each model, the standardized ranks of the AFTER and BEFORE variables are used as the dependent and independent variables, respectively. The following statements request these models and output the corresponding residuals into an output data set named RESIDUAL.

```
   proc reg noprint;
      by center;
      model after=before;
      output out=residual r=resid;
   run;
```

Finally, the stratified mean score test, using the values of the residuals as scores, compares the three groups.

```
   proc freq;
      tables center*group*resid / noprint cmh2;
   run;
```

Output 7.10 displays the results. The difference among the three treatment groups, after adjusting for the baseline number of DMFT and center, is clearly significant (row mean score chi-square=17.593, 2 df, $p < 0.001$).

Output 7.10   Results of Stratified Rank Analysis of Covariance

```
                  SUMMARY STATISTICS FOR GROUP BY RESID
                       CONTROLLING FOR CENTER


        Cochran-Mantel-Haenszel Statistics (Based on Table Scores)

        Statistic   Alternative Hypothesis   DF    Value    Prob
        ----------------------------------------------------------
            1        Nonzero Correlation       1    17.172   0.001
            2        Row Mean Scores Differ     2    17.593   0.001


        Total Sample Size = 69
```

The analyses described in this section are generally limited to randomized clinical trials, since the covariables should have similar distributions in the groups being compared. In the dental caries example, patients were randomly assigned to one of the three treatment groups, and Cartwright, Lindahl, and Bawden (1968) reported that the groups were comparable with respect to the number of DMFT at baseline, as well as with respect to other baseline variables. Although the patients in the APF group appear to have fewer DMFT at baseline than the patients in the SF and W groups (the corresponding medians were 7, 9, and 9, respectively), there is insufficient evidence to conclude that the distributions are significantly different (Kruskal-Wallis chi-square=4.4 with 2 df, $p = 0.11$); thus, rank analysis of covariance methods are appropriate.

In contrast, the exercise data (Table 7.5) were obtained from a nonrandomized experiment comparing men and women, and the distributions of the covariate, duration of time on the treadmill, differ significantly in the two samples. In particular, the average durations in males and females are 647.4 and 514.9 seconds, respectively ($p < 0.001$ from the two-sample t-test). Therefore, although the analysis presented in this section is a useful illustration of the rank analysis of covariance methodology, its results should be interpreted cautiously.

Chapter 8
Logistic Regression I: Dichotomous Response

Chapter Table of Contents

Chapter 8
Logistic Regression I: Dichotomous Response

8.1 Introduction

The previous chapters discussed the investigation of statistical association, primarily by testing the hypothesis of no association. Recall that Mantel-Haenszel strategies produced tests for specific alternatives to no association: general association, mean location shifts, and linear trends. This chapter shifts the focus to statistical models, methods aimed at describing the nature of the association in terms of a parsimonious number of parameters. Besides describing the variation in the data, statistical modeling allows you to address questions about association in terms of hypotheses concerning model parameters.

If certain sampling assumptions are plausible, a statistical model can be used to make inferences from a study population to a larger target population. If you are analyzing a clinical trial that assigned its subjects to a randomized protocol, then you can generalize your results to the population from which the subjects were selected and possibly to a more general target population. If you are analyzing observational data, and you can argue that your study subjects are conceptually representative of some larger target population, then you may make inferences to that target population.

Logistic regression is a form of statistical modeling that is often appropriate for categorical outcome variables. It describes the relationship between a categorical response variable and a set of explanatory variables. The response variable is usually dichotomous, but it may be polytomous, that is, have more than two response levels. These multiple-level response variables can be nominally or ordinally scaled. This chapter addresses logistic regression when the response is dichotomous; typically the two outcomes are yes and no. Logistic regression with more than two response variable levels is covered in Chapter 9, "Logistic Regression II: Polytomous Response."

The explanatory variables in logistic regression can be categorical or continuous. Sometimes the term 'logistic regression' is restricted to analyses that include continuous explanatory variables, and the term 'logistic analysis' is used for those situations where all the explanatory variables are categorical. In this book, logistic regression refers to both cases. Logistic regression has applications in fields such as epidemiology, medical research, banking, market research, and social research. As you will see, one of its advantages is that model interpretation is possible through odds ratios, which are functions of model parameters.

Several procedures in the SAS System can be used to perform logistic regression, including the LOGISTIC procedure, the CATMOD procedure, and the GENMOD procedure. The LOGISTIC procedure is designed primarily for logistic regression analysis, and it provides useful information such as odds ratio estimates and model diagnostics. The CATMOD procedure is a general procedure designed to fit models to functions of categorical response variables, and it may be convenient when the explanatory variables are all categorical. PROC GENMOD is a procedure for analyzing generalized linear models, of which logistic regression is a simple case. In this chapter, attention is focused on the use of the LOGISTIC procedure to perform logistic regression; however, included are sections that discuss the use of the CATMOD and GENMOD procedures for the same purpose.

8.2 Dichotomous Explanatory Variables

8.2.1 Logistic Model

Table 8.1 displays the coronary artery disease data that were analyzed in Chapter 3, "Sets of 2×2 Tables." Recall that the study population consists of people who visited a clinic on a walk-in basis and required a catheterization. The response, presence of coronary artery disease (CA), is dichotomous, as are the explanatory variables, sex and ECG. These data were analyzed in Section 3.3.2 with Mantel-Haenszel methods; also, odds ratios and the common odds ratio were computed. Recall that ECG was clearly associated with disease status, adjusted for gender.

Table 8.1 Coronary Artery Disease Data

Sex	ECG	Disease	No Disease	Total
Female	< 0.1 ST segment depression	4	11	15
Female	≥ 0.1 ST segment depression	8	10	18
Male	< 0.1 ST segment depression	9	9	18
Male	≥ 0.1 ST segment depression	21	6	27

Assume that these data arise from a stratified simple random sample so that presence of coronary artery disease is distributed binomially for each sex $\times$ ECG combination, that is, for each row of Table 8.1. These rows are called groups or subpopulations. You can then write a model for the probability, or the likelihood, of these data. The sex by ECG by disease status classification has the product binomial distribution

$$\Pr\{n_{hij}\} = \prod_{h=1}^{2} \prod_{i=1}^{2} \frac{n_{hi+}!}{n_{hi1}!n_{hi2}!} \theta_{hi}^{n_{hi1}} (1 - \theta_{hi})^{n_{hi2}}$$

The quantity θ_{hi} is the probability that a person of the hth sex with an ith ECG status has coronary artery disease, and n_{hi1} and n_{hi2} are the numbers of persons of the hth sex and ith ECG with and without coronary artery disease, respectively ($h = 1$ for females, $h = 2$ for males; $i = 1$ for ECG < 0.1, $i = 2$ for ECG ≥ 0.1; $j = 1$ for disease, $j = 2$ for no disease, and $n_{hi+} = (n_{hi1} + n_{hi2})$). You can apply the logistic model to describe the variation among the $\{\theta_{hi}\}$.

$$\theta_{hi} = \frac{1}{1 + \exp\{-(\alpha + \sum_{k=1}^{t} \beta_k x_{hik})\}}$$

Another form of this equation that is often used is

$$\theta_{hi} = \frac{\exp\{\alpha + \sum_{k=1}^{t} \beta_k x_{hik}\}}{1 + \exp\{\alpha + \sum_{k=1}^{t} \beta_k x_{hik}\}}$$

The quantity α is the intercept parameter; the $\{x_{hik}\}$ are the t explanatory variables for the hth sex and ith ECG; $k = 1, \ldots, t$; and the $\{\beta_k\}$ are the t regression parameters.

The matrix form of this equation is

$$\theta_{hi} = \frac{\exp(\mathbf{x}'_{hi}\boldsymbol{\beta})}{1 + \exp(\mathbf{x}'_{hi}\boldsymbol{\beta})}$$

where the quantity $\boldsymbol{\beta}$ is a vector of $t + 1$ regression parameters (including α), and $\mathbf{x}_{hi}$ is a vector of explanatory variables corresponding to the hith group.

You can show that the odds of CA disease for the hith group is

$$\frac{\theta_{hi}}{1 - \theta_{hi}} = \exp\{\alpha + \sum_{k=1}^{t} \beta_k x_{hik}\}$$

By taking logs on both sides, you obtain a linear model for the *logit*:

$$\log\left\{\frac{\theta_{hi}}{1 - \theta_{hi}}\right\} = \alpha + \sum_{k=1}^{t} \beta_k x_{hik}$$

Since the logit is the log of an odds, this model is for the log odds of coronary artery disease versus no coronary artery disease for the hith group. The log odds for the hith group can be written as an intercept and a combination of explanatory variable values multiplied by the appropriate parameter value. This result allows you to obtain the model-predicted odds ratios by exponentiating model parameter estimates, as explained below.

Besides taking the familiar linear form, the logistic model has the useful property that all possible values of $(\mathbf{x}'_{hi}\boldsymbol{\beta})$ in $(-\infty, \infty)$ map into $(0, 1)$ for θ_{hi}. Thus, predicted probabilities produced by this model are constrained to lie between 0 and 1. This model produces no negative predicted probabilities and no predicted probabilities greater than 1. Maximum likelihood methods are generally used to estimate α and $\boldsymbol{\beta}$. PROC LOGISTIC uses the Fisher scoring method, which is equivalent to model fitting with iteratively weighted least squares. PROC CATMOD and PROC GENMOD use Newton-Raphson algorithms. See Section 8.10 for more methodological detail.

8.2.2   Model Fitting

A useful first model for the coronary disease data is one that includes main effects for sex and ECG. Since these effects are dichotomous, there are three parameters in this model, including the intercept.

You can write this main effects model as

$$
\begin{bmatrix} \text{logit}(\theta_{11}) \\ \text{logit}(\theta_{12}) \\ \text{logit}(\theta_{21}) \\ \text{logit}(\theta_{22}) \end{bmatrix} = \begin{bmatrix} \alpha & & & \\ \alpha & & + & \beta_2 \\ \alpha & + & \beta_1 & \\ \alpha & + & \beta_1 & + & \beta_2 \end{bmatrix} = \begin{bmatrix} 1 & 0 & 0 \\ 1 & 0 & 1 \\ 1 & 1 & 0 \\ 1 & 1 & 1 \end{bmatrix} \begin{bmatrix} \alpha \\ \beta_1 \\ \beta_2 \end{bmatrix}
$$

This type of parameterization is often called *incremental effects* parameterization. It has a model matrix (also called a design matrix) composed of 0s and 1s. The quantity α is the log odds of coronary artery disease for females with an ECG of less than 0.1. Since females with ST segment depression less than 0.1 are described by the intercept, this group is known as the reference cell in this parameterization. The parameter β_1 is the increment in log odds for males, and β_2 is the increment in log odds for having an ECG of at least 0.1. Table 8.2 displays the probabilities and odds predicted by this model.

Table 8.2   Model-Predicted Probabilities and Odds

Sex	ECG	Pr{CA Disease}=θ_{hi}	Odds of CA Disease
Females	< 0.1	$e^{\alpha}/(1+e^{\alpha})$	e^{α}
Females	≥ 0.1	$e^{\alpha+\beta_2}/(1+e^{\alpha+\beta_2})$	$e^{\alpha+\beta_2}$
Males	< 0.1	$e^{\alpha+\beta_1}/(1+e^{\alpha+\beta_1})$	$e^{\alpha+\beta_1}$
Males	≥ 0.1	$e^{\alpha+\beta_1+\beta_2}/(1+e^{\alpha+\beta_1+\beta_2})$	$e^{\alpha+\beta_1+\beta_2}$

You can calculate the odds ratio for males versus females by forming the ratio of male odds of CA disease to female odds of CA disease for either low or high ECG (see Chapter 2 for a discussion of odds ratios):

$$
\frac{e^{\alpha+\beta_1}}{e^{\alpha}} = e^{\beta_1} \quad \text{or} \quad \frac{e^{\alpha+\beta_1+\beta_2}}{e^{\alpha+\beta_2}} = e^{\beta_1}
$$

Similarly, the odds ratio for high ECG versus low ECG is determined by forming the ratio of the odds of CA disease for either sex:

$$
\frac{e^{\alpha+\beta_1+\beta_2}}{e^{\alpha+\beta_1}} = e^{\beta_2} \quad \text{or} \quad \frac{e^{\alpha+\beta_2}}{e^{\alpha}} = e^{\beta_2}
$$

Thus, you can obtain odds ratios as functions of the model parameters in logistic regression. With incremental effects parameterization, you simply exponentiate the parameter estimates. However, unlike the odds ratios you calculate from individual 2×2 tables, these odds ratios have been adjusted for all other explanatory variables in the model.

8.2.3   Goodness of Fit

Once you have applied the model, you need to assess how well it fits the data, or how close the model-predicted values are to the corresponding observed values. Test statistics that assess fit in this manner are known as *goodness-of-fit statistics*. They address the differences between observed and predicted values, or their ratio, in some appropriate manner. Departures of the predicted proportions from the observed proportions should be essentially random. The test statistics have approximate chi-square distributions. If they are larger than a tolerable value, then you have an oversimplified model and you need to identify some other factors to better explain the variation in the data.

Two traditional goodness-of-fit tests are the Pearson chi-square, Q_P, and the likelihood ratio chi-square, Q_L, also known as the *deviance*.

$$Q_P = \sum_{h=1}^{2} \sum_{i=1}^{2} \sum_{j=1}^{2} (n_{hij} - m_{hij})^2 / m_{hij}$$

$$Q_L = \sum_{h=1}^{2} \sum_{i=1}^{2} \sum_{j=1}^{2} 2 n_{hij} \log \left(\frac{n_{hij}}{m_{hij}} \right)$$

where m_{ij} are the model-predicted counts defined as

$$m_{hij} = \begin{cases} n_{hi+} \hat{\theta}_{hi} & \text{for j=1} \\ n_{hi+} (1 - \hat{\theta}_{hi}) & \text{for j=2} \end{cases}$$

The quantity $\hat{\theta}_{hi}$ is the estimate of θ_{hi}. If the model fits, both Q_P and Q_L are distributed as chi-square with degrees of freedom equal to the number of rows in the table minus the number of parameters. For the main effects model being discussed, there are four rows in the table (four groups) and three parameters, including the intercept, and so Q_P and Q_L have $4 - 3 = 1$ degree of freedom. Sample size guidelines for these statistics to be approximately chi-square include

- at least 10 subjects in each of the groups ($n_{hi+} \geq 10$)
- 80 percent of the predicted counts (m_{hij}) are at least 5
- all other expected counts are greater than 2, with essentially no 0 counts

8.2.4   Using PROC LOGISTIC

The LOGISTIC procedure was designed specifically to fit logistic regression models. You specify the response variable and the explanatory variables in a MODEL statement, and it fits the model via maximum likelihood estimation. PROC LOGISTIC produces the parameter estimates, their standard errors, and statistics to assess model fit. In addition, it also provides several model selection methods, puts predicted values and other statistics into output data sets, and includes a number of options for controlling the model-fitting process.

The following SAS code creates the data set CORONARY.

```
data coronary;
   input sex ecg ca count @@;
   sexecg=sex*ecg;
   cards;
   0 0 0   11 0 0 1   4
   0 1 0   10 0 1 1   8
   1 0 0    9 1 0 1   9
   1 1 0    6 1 1 1  21
   ;
run;
```

The variable CA is the response variable, and SEX and ECG are the explanatory variables. The variable SEX takes the value 0 for females and 1 for males, and ECG takes the value 0 for lower ST segment depression and 1 for higher ST segment depression. Thus, these variables provide the values for the model matrix. Such coding is known as *dummy-coding* or *indicator-coding*.

CA is 1 if CA disease is present and is 0 otherwise. By default, PROC LOGISTIC orders the response variable values alphanumerically so that, for these data, it bases its model on the probability of the smallest value, Pr{CA=0}, which is Pr{no coronary artery disease}; this means that it models the log odds of {no coronary artery disease}. If you want to change the basis of the model to be Pr{CA=1}, which is Pr{coronary artery disease}, you have to alter this default behavior. Data analysts usually want their models to be based on the probability of the event (disease, success), often coded as 1.

The DESCENDING option in the PROC LOGISTIC statement requests that the response value ordering be reversed. For these data, this means that PROC LOGISTIC will model Pr{coronary artery disease}. For a dichotomous response variable, the effect of reversing the order of the response values is to change the sign of the parameter estimates. Thus, if your parameters have opposite signs from another logistic regression run, you have modeled opposite forms for the dichotomous response variable.

The next group of SAS statements invokes PROC LOGISTIC. (Note the use of the DESCENDING option.) Since the data are in frequency, or count form, you need to indicate that to PROC LOGISTIC. This is done with the FREQ statement, which is similar in use to the WEIGHT statement in PROC FREQ. (Note that a WEIGHT statement is available with the LOGISTIC procedure; however, it is used somewhat differently.) The main effects model is specified in the MODEL statement, which also includes the options SCALE=NONE and AGGREGATE. The SCALE option produces goodness-of-fit statistics; the AGGREGATE option requests that PROC LOGISTIC treat each unique combination of the explanatory variable values as a distinct group in computing the goodness-of-fit statistics. (These options became available with Release 6.10 of the SAS System.)

```
proc logistic descending;
   freq count;
   model ca=sex ecg / scale=none aggregate;
run;
```

Output 8.1 displays the resulting "Response Profile" table. The response variable values are listed according to their PROC LOGISTIC *ordered values*. The DESCENDING option has made CA=1 the first ordered value (1) and CA=0 the second ordered value (2). Thus, the model is based on Pr{coronary artery disease}. It is always important to check the "Response Profile" table to ensure that PROC LOGISTIC is ordering response variable values the way you want. You can also use the ORDER= option in the PROC LOGISTIC statement to establish a different set of ordered values, for example, by creating formats for the levels of the response variable and using ORDER=FORMATTED.

Output 8.1   Response Profile

	Response Profile		
Ordered Value		CA	Count
1		1	42
2		0	36

Output 8.2 contains the goodness of fit statistics. Q_P has the value 0.2155, and Q_L has the value 0.2141. Compared to a chi-square distribution with 1 df, these values suggest that the model fits the data adequately. The note that the number of unique profiles is 4 means that these statistics are computed based on the 4 groups that are the rows of Table 8.1, the result of the AGGREGATE option.

Output 8.2   Goodness-of-Fit Statistics

Deviance and Pearson Goodness-of-Fit Statistics				
Criterion	DF	Value	Value/DF	Pr > Chi-Square
Deviance	1	0.2141	0.2141	0.6436
Pearson	1	0.2155	0.2155	0.6425
Number of unique profiles: 4				

Output 8.3 lists various criteria for assessing model fit through the quality of the explanatory capacity of the model; for $-2 \log L$ and the score statistic, this is done by testing whether the explanatory variables are jointly significant relative to the chi-square distribution. AIC and SC serve a similar purpose while adjusting for the number of explanatory variables in the model. All of these statistics are analogous to the overall F test for the model parameters in a linear regression setting. Refer to the *SAS/STAT User's Guide, Version 6, Fourth Edition, Volume II* for more information on these statistics.

Output 8.3   Testing Joint Significance of the Explanatory Variables

```
                 Testing Global Null Hypothesis: BETA=0

                              Intercept
                 Intercept       and
Criterion          Only       Covariates    Chi-Square for Covariates

AIC              109.669       101.900            .
SC               112.026       108.970            .
-2 LOG L         107.669        95.900        11.769 with 2 DF (p=0.0028)
Score                .             .          11.241 with 2 DF (p=0.0036)
```

8.2.5   Interpretation of Main Effects Model

With the satisfactory goodness of fit, it is appropriate to examine the parameter estimates from the model. Note that these results apply only to the population consisting of those persons who visited this medical clinic and required catheterization. The "Analysis of Maximum Likelihood Estimates" table lists the estimated model parameters, their standard errors, Wald tests, and odds ratios. A Wald test is a statistic that takes the form of a squared ratio of an estimate to its standard error; it follows an approximate chi-square distribution when the sample size is sufficiently large. Wald statistics are easy to compute and are based on normal theory; however, their statistical properties are somewhat less optimal than those of the likelihood ratio statistics for small samples.

Output 8.4   Main Effects Model: ANOVA Table

```
          Analysis of Maximum Likelihood Estimates

          Parameter Standard    Wald        Pr >     Standardized
Variable DF Estimate  Error  Chi-Square Chi-Square   Estimate

INTERCPT 1   -1.1747  0.4854    5.8572     0.0155         .
SEX      1    1.2770  0.4980    6.5750     0.0103      0.350072
ECG      1    1.0545  0.4980    4.4844     0.0342      0.289086

                   The LOGISTIC Procedure

     Analysis of
       Maximum
     Likelihood
      Estimates


                 Odds
    Variable     Ratio

    INTERCPT       .
    SEX          3.586
    ECG          2.871
```

The variable SEX is significant compared to a significance level of 0.05, with a Wald statistic (usually denoted Q_W) of 6.575. The variable ECG is also significant, with $Q_W = 4.484$.

The model equation can be written as follows:

$$\text{logit}(\theta_{hi}) = -1.1747 + 1.2770\,\text{SEX} + 1.0545\,\text{ECG}$$

The output also includes the odds ratios. Table 8.3 lists the parameter interpretations, and Table 8.4 displays the predicted logits and odds of coronary disease.

Table 8.3   Interpretation of Parameters

Parameter	Estimate	Standard Error	Interpretation
α	−1.1747	0.485	log odds of coronary disease for females with low ECG
β_1	1.2770	0.498	increment to log odds for males
β_2	1.0545	0.498	increment to log odds for high ECG

Table 8.4   Model-Predicted Logits and Odds of CA Disease

Sex	ECG	Logit	Odds of Coronary Artery Disease
Female	< 0.1	$\hat{\alpha} = -1.1747$	$e^{\hat{\alpha}} = e^{-1.1747} = 0.3089$
Female	≥ 0.1	$\hat{\alpha} + \hat{\beta}_2 = -0.1202$	$e^{\hat{\alpha}+\hat{\beta}_2} = e^{-.1202} = 0.8867$
Male	< 0.1	$\hat{\alpha} + \hat{\beta}_1 = 0.1023$	$e^{\hat{\alpha}+\hat{\beta}_1} = e^{0.1023} = 1.1077$
Male	≥ 0.1	$\hat{\alpha} + \hat{\beta}_1 + \hat{\beta}_2 = 1.1568$	$e^{\hat{\alpha}+\hat{\beta}_1+\hat{\beta}_2} = e^{1.1568} = 3.1797$

The odds ratio for males compared to females is the ratio of the predicted odds of CA disease for males versus females, which has been shown to be

$$e^{\hat{\beta}_1} = e^{1.2770} = 3.586$$

Men in the study have three times higher odds for coronary artery disease than women in the study.

The odds ratio for high ECG versus low ECG is the ratio of the predicted odds of CA disease for high ECG versus low ECG, which has been shown to be

$$e^{\hat{\beta}_2} = e^{1.0545} = 2.871$$

Those persons with high ECG are nearly three times as likely to have coronary artery disease as those with a low ECG. This quantity is very similar to the common odds ratio estimates computed by PROC FREQ and displayed in Section 3.3.2 ($\hat{\psi}_{MH} = 2.847$ and $\hat{\psi}_L = 2.859$).

Output 8.4 also contains the adjusted odds ratios. Note that a missing value is printed for INTERCPT, since exponentiating $\hat{\alpha}$ does not produce an odds ratio but the odds of coronary artery disease for the reference group, females with a low ECG, as listed in Table 8.4.

Both predicted values and confidence limits for odds ratios estimates are available as optional PROC LOGISTIC output. The RISKLIMITS option produces the confidence limits for the odds ratio. The OUTPUT statement specifies that predicted values for the first ordered value (CA=1) be put into the variable PROB and output into the SAS data set PREDICT along with the variables from the input data set.

```
proc logistic descending;
   freq count;
   model ca=sex ecg / risklimits;
   output out= predict pred=prob;
run;
proc print data=predict;
run;
```

Output 8.5   Confidence Limits for Odds Ratios

			Wald Confidence Limits	
Variable	Unit	Odds Ratio	Lower	Upper
SEX	1.0000	3.586	1.351	9.516
ECG	1.0000	2.871	1.082	7.618

Conditional Odds Ratios and 95% Confidence Intervals

The data set PREDICT contains model-predicted values for each observation in the input data set. The created variable named PROB contains these predicted values; the created variable _LEVEL_ tells you that they are the predicted values for the first ordered value, or Pr{coronary artery disease}. Observations 7 and 8 display the predicted value 0.76075 for males with high ECG.

Output 8.6   Predicted Values Output Data Set

OBS	SEX	ECG	CA	COUNT	SEXECG	_LEVEL_	PROB
1	0	0	0	11	0	1	0.23601
2	0	0	1	4	0	1	0.23601
3	0	1	0	10	0	1	0.46999
4	0	1	1	8	0	1	0.46999
5	1	0	0	9	0	1	0.52555
6	1	0	1	9	0	1	0.52555
7	1	1	0	6	1	1	0.76075
8	1	1	1	21	1	1	0.76075

In conclusion, the main effects model is satisfactory. Being male and having a high ECG are risk indicators for the presence of coronary artery disease for these data. If you can make the argument that this convenience sample is representative of a target group of coronary artery disease patients, possibly those persons who visit clinics on a walk-in basis, then these results may also apply to that population.

8.2.6 Alternative Methods of Assessing Goodness of Fit

There are other strategies available for assessing goodness of fit; these are based on fitting an appropriate expanded model and then testing whether the contribution of the additional terms is nonsignificant. If so, you then conclude that the original model has an adequate fit. You can compute likelihood ratio tests for the significance of the additional terms by taking the difference in the log likelihood for both models (-2 LOG L in the "Testing Global Null Hypothesis: BETA=0" table); this difference has an approximate chi-square distribution with degrees of freedom equal to the difference in the number of parameters in the models. You can also examine the Wald statistic for the additional parameters in order to assess goodness of fit.

For these data, the expanded model would be the one that contains the main effects for sex and ECG and their interaction. The desired likelihood ratio statistic tests the significance of the interaction term and thus serves as a goodness-of-fit test for the main effects model.

You can write this model as

$$
\begin{bmatrix} \text{logit}(\theta_{11}) \\ \text{logit}(\theta_{12}) \\ \text{logit}(\theta_{21}) \\ \text{logit}(\theta_{22}) \end{bmatrix} = \begin{bmatrix} \alpha & & & \\ \alpha & + & & \beta_2 \\ \alpha & + & \beta_1 & \\ \alpha & + & \beta_1 & + & \beta_2 & + & \beta_3 \end{bmatrix} = \begin{bmatrix} 1 & 0 & 0 & 0 \\ 1 & 0 & 1 & 0 \\ 1 & 1 & 0 & 0 \\ 1 & 1 & 1 & 1 \end{bmatrix} \begin{bmatrix} \alpha \\ \beta_1 \\ \beta_2 \\ \beta_3 \end{bmatrix}
$$

The model matrix column corresponding to β_3, the interaction term, is constructed by multiplying the columns for β_1 and β_2 together. Note that this model is a *saturated* model, since there are as many parameters as there are logit functions being modeled.

The following SAS code fits this model. Since PROC LOGISTIC builds its model matrix from the explanatory variables, you need to create a variable that has the correct values. The DATA step displayed in Section 8.2.4 computes the variable SEXECG for data set CORONARY by multiplying SEX and ECG together. It has the value 1 if both SEX and ECG are 1; otherwise, it is 0.

```
proc logistic descending;
   freq count;
   model ca=sex ecg sexecg;
run;
```

The resulting tables titled "Testing Global Null Hypothesis: BETA=0" and "Analysis of Maximum Likelihood Estimates" follow.

Output 8.7   Results for Saturated Model

```
                Testing Global Null Hypothesis: BETA=0

                            Intercept
                Intercept      and
  Criterion       Only     Covariates    Chi-Square for Covariates

  AIC            109.669     103.686            .
  SC             112.026     113.112            .
  -2 LOG L       107.669      95.686        11.983 with 3 DF (p=0.0074)
  Score             .           .           11.428 with 3 DF (p=0.0096)



                Analysis of Maximum Likelihood Estimates

              Parameter Standard    Wald        Pr >      Standardized
  Variable DF Estimate   Error   Chi-Square  Chi-Square     Estimate

  INTERCPT 1  -1.0116    0.5839    3.0018      0.0832           .
  SEX      1   1.0116    0.7504    1.8172      0.1776       0.277326
  ECG      1   0.7885    0.7523    1.0985      0.2946       0.216152
  SEXECG   1   0.4643    1.0012    0.2151      0.6428       0.122571
```

The value for -2(log likelihood) is 95.686 for the saturated model; this is the value for -2 LOG L listed under ''Intercept and Covariates.'' The value for the main effects model is 95.900 (see Output 8.3), yielding a difference of 0.214. This difference is the likelihood ratio test value, with 1 df (4 parameters for the expanded model $-$ 3 parameters for the main effects model). Compared with a chi-square distribution with 1 df, this statistic supports the adequacy of the main effects model. Note that you can always compute a likelihood ratio test in this manner for the contribution of a particular model term or a set of model terms.

This likelihood ratio test value is the same as the deviance reported for the main effects model in Output 8.2. This is because the deviance statistic is effectively comparing the model for which it is computed with a saturated model.

Note that the value of the Wald statistic is 0.2151 for the interaction listed in the ''Analysis of Maximum Likelihood Estimates'' table. Both the likelihood ratio statistic and the Wald statistic are evaluating the same thing: whether or not the interaction explains any of the variation among the different log odds beyond that explained by the main effects. They support goodness of fit of the main effects model by indicating nonsignificance of the interaction between sex and ECG. The Wald statistic and the likelihood ratio statistic are essentially equivalent for large samples.

8.2.7   Overdispersion

Sometimes a logistic model is considered reasonable, but the goodness-of-fit statistics indicate too much variation remains (usually the deviance or deviance/df is examined). This condition is known as *overdispersion*, and it occurs when the data do not follow a binomial distribution well; the condition is also known as heterogeneity.

You can model the overdispersion by adjusting, or scaling, the covariance matrix to account for it. This involves the additional estimation of a dispersion parameter, often called a scaling parameter. In Release 6.10, PROC LOGISTIC allows you to specify a scaling parameter through the use of the SCALE= option; this explains why the SCALE=NONE option is used to generate the goodness-of-fit statistics, including the deviance, when no scale adjustment is desired. McCullagh and Nelder (1989) and Collett (1991) discuss overdispersion comprehensively. The SAS Institute publication *SAS/STAT Software: Changes and Enhancements, Release 6.10* describes these options in detail.

8.3 Setting Up Dummy Variables

In the previous example, PROC LOGISTIC used the values of the explanatory variables to construct the model matrix. These values were already coded as 0s and 1s and thus were appropriate for this use. However, sometimes your SAS data set contains a response variable or explanatory variables that are character valued. The LOGISTIC procedure handles character-valued response variables by creating ordered values based on the alphabetical order of the response variable values. However, you must recode character-valued explanatory variables. This section illustrates how to create dummy variables to produce the correct model parameterization and shows how PROC LOGISTIC treats character-valued response variables. In addition, this section discusses what to do when an effect in a model is not clearly statistically significant but has a modest influence.

8.3.1 Analysis of Sentencing Data

Table 8.5 displays data based on a study on prison sentencing for persons convicted of a burglary or larceny. Investigators collected information on whether there was a prior arrest record and whether the crime was a nonresidential burglary, residential burglary, or something else—usually some sort of larceny. Here, type of crime is divided into nonresidential burglary versus all others. Sentence was recorded as whether the offender was sent to prison.

Table 8.5 Sentencing Data

Type	Prior Arrest	Prison	No Prison	Total
Nonresidential	Some	42	109	151
Nonresidential	None	17	75	92
Other	Some	33	175	208
Other	None	53	359	412

Assume that these data arise from a stratified simple random sample so that sentence is distributed binomially for each offense type $\times$ prior arrest record combination, that is, for each row of Table 8.5. The type of offense by prior arrest status by sentence classification has the product binomial distribution.

$$\Pr\{n_{hij}\} = \prod_{h=1}^{2} \prod_{i=1}^{2} \frac{n_{hi+}!}{n_{hi1}!n_{hi2}!} \theta_{hi}^{n_{hi1}} (1 - \theta_{hi})^{n_{hi2}}$$

The quantity θ_{hi} is the probability that a person arrested for a crime of type h with an ith prior arrest record receives a prison sentence, and n_{hi1} and n_{hi2} are the number of persons of the hth type and ith prior record who did and did not receive prison sentences, respectively (h=1 for nonresidential, h=2 for other; i=1 for prior arrest, i=2 for no arrest).

Similar to the previous analysis, a useful preliminary model for the sentencing data is one that includes main effects for type of offense and prior arrest record. There are three parameters in this model. The parameter α is the intercept, β_1 is the increment in log odds for committing a nonresidential burglary, and β_2 is the increment in log odds for having a prior arrest record. The probabilities and odds predicted by this model are identical to those presented in Table 8.2, replacing the first column with the values Nonresidential and Other and replacing the second column with the values Some and None.

The following DATA step prepares this data for use with PROC LOGISTIC.

```
data sentence;
   input type $ prior $ sentence $ count @@;
   iprior=(prior='some');
   itype=(type= 'nrb');
   itypepri=itype*iprior;
   cards;
   nrb     some   y  42 nrb     some   n 109
   nrb     none   y  17 nrb     none   n  75
   other   some   y  33 other   some   n 175
   other   none   y  53 other   none   n 359
   ;
run;
```

The variable SENTENCE is the response variable, and TYPE and PRIOR are the explanatory variables. Note that SENTENCE is character valued, with values 'y' for prison sentence and 'n' for no prison sentence. PROC LOGISTIC orders these values alphabetically by default so that it bases its model on the probability of the value 'n', or Pr{no prison sentence}. If you want to change the basis of the model to be Pr{prison sentence}, you have to alter this default behavior.

The values for the model matrix are determined from the values of the variables listed as explanatory variables in the MODEL statement. Since the explanatory variables in the previous example were coded as 0s and 1s, they were simply listed in the MODEL statement. However, for these data, the explanatory variables are character valued, so they cannot be listed on the MODEL statement. Those SAS procedures that support a CLASS statement, like PROC GLM, can create appropriate model matrices when the values of the explanatory variables are character. However, with PROC LOGISTIC, you need to put the values into the model matrix yourself by recoding explanatory variables or creating new indicator variables. When the CLASS statement is implemented in a future release of PROC LOGISTIC, this step can be eliminated.

For these data, indicator variables IPRIOR and ITYPE are created in the preceding DATA step. Variable IPRIOR takes the value 1 if PRIOR='some' and 0 otherwise. Similarly, ITYPE takes the value 1 if TYPE='nrb' and 0 otherwise. Your choice of coding determines which group becomes the reference group. This coding makes other crime and no prior record the reference group (when ITYPE and IPRIOR are both 0). Incremental effects will be estimated for nonresidential burglary and prior record, respectively.

The following group of SAS statements invoke PROC LOGISTIC. Note that since the desired model is based on Pr{prison sentence}, the DESCENDING option is specified to request that 'y' be the first ordered value.

```
proc logistic descending;
   freq count;
   model sentence = itype iprior / scale=none aggregate;
run;
```

The "Response Profile" table indicates that SENTENCE='y' corresponds to the first ordered value. Thus, the model is based on Pr{prison sentence}. The goodness-of-fit statistics $Q_L = 0.5076$ and $Q_P = 0.5025$ indicate an adequate model fit. Note that if these statistics have values that are not similar, it is an indication that sample sizes in the groups are not large enough to support their use as goodness-of-fit statistics.

Output 8.8   Response Profiles and Goodness of Fit

```
                        Response Profile

                Ordered
                Value   SENTENCE      Count

                  1   y                145
                  2   n                718


             Goodness of Fit Statistics

                                                    Pr >
        Criterion       DF      Value   Value/DF  Chi-Square

        Deviance        1      0.5076    0.5076     0.4762
        Pearson         1      0.5025    0.5025     0.4784

         Number of unique covariates profiles:  4
```

The "Analysis of Maximum Likelihood Estimates" table for this model is displayed in Output 8.9. The variable ITYPE is clearly significant, with $Q_W = 9.0509$. The variable IPRIOR nearly approaches significance, with $Q_W = 3.3127$ and $p = 0.0687$. While some analysts might delete any effects that do not meet their designated 0.05 significance level, it is sometimes reasonable to keep modestly suggestive effects in the model to avoid potential bias for estimates of the other effects. In fact, for main effects models where presumably each explanatory variable chosen has some potential basis for its inclusion, many analysts keep all effects in the model, regardless of their significance. The model still appropriately describes the data, and it is easier to compare with other researchers' models where those nonsignificant effects may prove to be more important.

Output 8.9   Main Effects Model

```
          Analysis of Maximum Likelihood Estimates

              Parameter Standard    Wald      Pr >    Standardized
Variable DF   Estimate   Error   Chi-Square Chi-Square  Estimate

INTERCPT 1     -1.9523   0.1384   199.0994    0.0001        .
ITYPE    1      0.5920   0.1968     9.0509    0.0026    0.146873
IPRIOR   1      0.3469   0.1906     3.3127    0.0687    0.094332

                    The SAS System                            2

                  The LOGISTIC Procedure

    Analysis of
      Maximum
    Likelihood
     Estimates

                  Odds
Variable         Ratio

INTERCPT           .
ITYPE            1.808
IPRIOR           1.415
```

However, you may want to consider removing modest or clearly nonsignificant effects if some of them are redundant; that is, they are reflecting essentially the same factor. This can induce collinearity, and sometimes the association of explanatory variables with each other may mask the true effect. The additional model terms can result in a poorer quality of the individual parameter estimates since they will be less precise (higher standard errors). In this case, IPRIOR is kept in the model.

The model equation can be written as follows:

$$\text{logit}(\theta_{hi}) = -1.9523 + 0.5920 \,\text{ITYPE} + 0.3469 \,\text{IPRIOR}$$

The odds ratios are 1.808 ($e^{0.5920}$) for type of offense and 1.415 ($e^{0.3469}$) for prior arrest record. Thus, those persons committing a nonresidential burglary are nearly twice as likely to receive prison sentences as those committing another offense. Those with a prior arrest record are somewhat more likely to receive a prison sentence than those with no prior record.

8.3.2   Requesting Goodness-of-Fit Statistics for Single Main Effect Model

Suppose that you did decide to fit the model with a single main effect, ITYPE, and you wanted to generate the appropriate goodness-of-fit statistics for that model. Using the SCALE=NONE and AGGREGATE options would not work for this model, since the AGGREGATE option creates groups on which to base the goodness-of-fit statistic according to the values of the explanatory variables. Since there is just one dichotomous explanatory variable remaining in the model, only two groups would be created. To produce the groups consistent with the sampling framework, you need to specify

AGGREGATE=(ITYPE IPRIOR), where the list of variables inside the parentheses are those whose unique values determine the rows of Table 8.5.

The following statements request the main effects model.

```
proc logistic  descending;
   freq count;
   model sentence = itype / scale=none aggregate=(itype iprior);
run;
```

Output 8.10 includes the goodness-of-fit statistics. Note the SAS message that there are 4 unique covariate profiles; this tells you that the correct groups were formed and that the statistics are based on the intended subpopulations.

Output 8.10   Single Effect Model

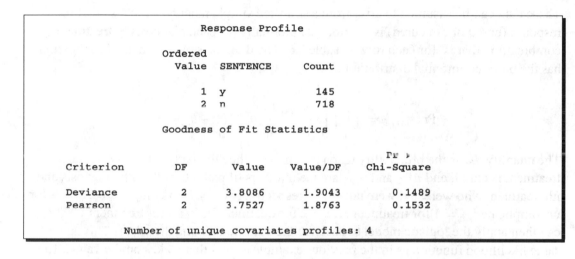

```
                        Response Profile

                  Ordered
                  Value    SENTENCE        Count

                      1  y                 145
                      2  n                 718

                  Goodness of Fit Statistics

                                                     Pr >
        Criterion       DF      Value    Value/DF  Chi-Square

        Deviance         2      3.8086    1.9043     0.1489
        Pearson          2      3.7527    1.8763     0.1532

           Number of unique covariates profiles: 4
```

Since $Q_L = 3.8086$ and $Q_P = 3.7527$, both with 2 df, this single main effect model has a satisfactory fit.

8.4   Qualitative Explanatory Variables

The previous examples have been concerned with analyses of dichotomous outcomes when the explanatory variables were also dichotomous. However, explanatory variables can be nominal (qualitative) with three or more levels, ordinal, or continuous. Logistic regression allows for any combination of these types of explanatory variables. This section is concerned with handling explanatory variables that are qualitative and contain three or more levels.

The following data come from a study on urinary tract infections (Koch, Imrey, et al. 1985). Investigators applied three treatments to patients who had either a complicated or uncomplicated diagnosis of urinary tract infection. Since complicated cases of urinary tract infections are difficult to cure, investigators were interested in whether the pattern of treatment differences are the same across diagnoses: did the diagnosis status of the patients affect the relative effectiveness of the three treatments ? This is the same as determining whether there is a treatment $\times$ diagnosis interaction. Diagnosis is a dichotomous explanatory variable and treatment is a nominal explanatory variable consisting of levels for treatments A, B, and C. Table 8.6 displays the data.

Table 8.6   Urinary Tract Infection Data

Diagnosis	Treatment	Cured	Not Cured	Proportion Cured
Complicated	A	78	28	0.736
Complicated	B	101	11	0.902
Complicated	C	68	46	0.596
Uncomplicated	A	40	5	0.889
Uncomplicated	B	54	5	0.915
Uncomplicated	C	34	6	0.850

These data can be assumed to arise from a stratified simple random sample so that the response (cured or not cured) is distributed binomially for each diagnosis $\times$ treatment combination, that is, for each row of Table 8.6. The diagnosis by treatment classification has the product binomial distribution.

$$\Pr\{n_{hij}\} = \prod_{h=1}^{2} \prod_{i=1}^{3} \frac{n_{hi+}!}{n_{hi1}!n_{hi2}!} \theta_{hi}^{n_{hi1}} (1 - \theta_{hi})^{n_{hi2}}$$

The quantity θ_{hi} is the probability that a person with the hth diagnosis receiving the ith treatment is cured, and n_{hi1} and n_{hi2} are the numbers of patients of the hth diagnosis and ith treatment who were and were not cured, respectively ($h = 1$ for complicated, $h = 2$ for uncomplicated; $i = 1$ for treatment A, $i = 2$ for treatment B, $i = 3$ for treatment C). You can then apply the logistic model to describe the variation among the $\{\theta_{hi}\}$. This is the same likelihood function as in the previous example except that i takes on the values 1, 2, and 3 instead of 1, 2.

8.4.1   Model Fitting

Since there is interest in the interaction term, the preliminary model includes main effects and their interaction (saturated model). There is one parameter for the intercept (α), which is the reference parameter corresponding to the log odds of being cured if you have an uncomplicated diagnosis and are getting treatment C. The parameter β_1 is the increment for complicated diagnosis. The effect for treatment consists of two parameters: β_2 is the incremental effect for treatment A, and β_3 is the incremental effect for treatment B.

There is no particular reason to choose a parameterization that includes incremental effects for treatments A and B; you could choose to parameterize the model by including incremental effects for treatments A and C. Often, data analysts choose the reference parameter to be the control group, with incremental effects representing various exposure effects. However, it's important to note that an effect with L levels must be represented by $(L - 1)$ parameters.

The interaction effect is comprised of two additional parameters, β_4 and β_5, which represent the interaction terms for complicated diagnosis and treatment A, and complicated diagnosis and treatment B, respectively. When you are creating interaction terms from two effects, you create a number of terms equal to the product of the number of terms for both effects.

You can write this saturated model in matrix formulation as

$$\begin{bmatrix} \text{logit}(\theta_{11}) \\ \text{logit}(\theta_{12}) \\ \text{logit}(\theta_{13}) \\ \text{logit}(\theta_{21}) \\ \text{logit}(\theta_{22}) \\ \text{logit}(\theta_{23}) \end{bmatrix} = \begin{bmatrix} \alpha + \beta_1 + \beta_2 \quad\quad + \beta_4 \\ \alpha + \beta_1 \quad\quad + \beta_3 \quad\quad + \beta_5 \\ \alpha + \beta_1 \\ \alpha \quad\quad + \beta_2 \\ \alpha \quad\quad\quad\quad + \beta_3 \\ \alpha \end{bmatrix} = \begin{bmatrix} 1 & 1 & 1 & 0 & 1 & 0 \\ 1 & 1 & 0 & 1 & 0 & 1 \\ 1 & 1 & 0 & 0 & 0 & 0 \\ 1 & 0 & 1 & 0 & 0 & 0 \\ 1 & 0 & 0 & 1 & 0 & 0 \\ 1 & 0 & 0 & 0 & 0 & 0 \end{bmatrix} \begin{bmatrix} \alpha \\ \beta_1 \\ \beta_2 \\ \beta_3 \\ \beta_4 \\ \beta_5 \end{bmatrix}$$

Note that if you had parameterized the model so that there were three columns for treatment effects, each consisting of 1s corresponding to those logits representing the respective treatments, the columns would add up to a column of 1s. This would be redundant with the column of 1s for the intercept, and so PROC LOGISTIC would set the parameter corresponding to the third column of the effect equal to zero, since it is a linear combination of other columns.

8.4.2   PROC LOGISTIC for Nominal Effects

Fitting this model with PROC LOGISTIC requires you to create dummy variables both for the effects and for their interactions. The following DATA step creates SAS data set UTI and creates the dummy variables IDIAG, IATREAT, IBTREAT, IACOMP, and IBCOMP. The variable IACOMP is the interaction of treatment A with complicated diagnosis, and IBCOMP is the interaction of treatment B with complicated diagnosis.

```
data uti;
    input diagnoss : $13. treat $ response $ count @@;
    idiag=(diagnoss='complicated');
    iatreat=(treat='A');
    ibtreat=(treat='B');
    iacomp=idiag*iatreat;
    ibcomp=idiag*ibtreat;
    cards;
complicated     A   cured 78   complicated     A not 28
complicated     B   cured 101  complicated     B not 11
complicated     C   cured 68   complicated     C not 46
uncomplicated   A   cured 40   uncomplicated A not 5
uncomplicated   B   cured 54   uncomplicated B not 5
uncomplicated   C   cured 34   uncomplicated C not 6
;
run;
```

Since this model is saturated, the goodness-of-fit statistics don't apply; there are no available degrees of freedom because the number of groups and the number of parameters are the same (6). PROC LOGISTIC prints out near-zero values and zero df for saturated models. However, fitting this model does allow you to determine whether there is an interaction effect. Fitting the reduced model without the interaction terms and taking the difference in the likelihoods allows you to determine whether the interaction is meaningful. The following PROC LOGISTIC statements fit the full and reduced models.

```
proc logistic;
   freq count;
   model response = idiag iatreat ibtreat iacomp ibcomp;
run;
proc logistic;
   freq count;
   model response = idiag iatreat ibtreat / scale=none
   aggregate risklimits;
run;
```

Output 8.11 contains -2 LOG L for the full model, and Output 8.12 contains the -2 LOG L for the reduced model.

Output 8.11   Log Likelihood for the Full Model

```
                    Testing Global Null Hypothesis: BETA=0

                                  Intercept
                      Intercept      and
Criterion               Only      Covariates    Chi-Square for Covariates

AIC                   494.029       459.556            .
SC                    498.194       484.549            .
-2 LOG L              492.029       447.556      44.473 with 5 DF (p=0.0001)
Score                    .             .        44.786 with 5 DF (p=0.0001)
```

Output 8.12   Log Likelihood for the Reduced Model

```
                    Testing Global Null Hypothesis: BETA=0

                                  Intercept
                      Intercept      and
Criterion               Only      Covariates    Chi-Square for Covariates

AIC                   494.029       458.071            .
SC                    498.194       474.733            .
-2 LOG L              492.029       450.071      41.958 with 3 DF (p=0.0001)
Score                    .             .        38.846 with 3 DF (p=0.0001)
```

The difference between 447.556 (full) and 450.071 (reduced) is 2.515; since the difference in the number of parameters in these models is 2, this value should be compared to a chi-square distribution with 2 df (you can use the PROBCHI function to compute the probability with the DATA step). Thus, the likelihood ratio test for the hypothesis that the additional terms in the expanded model are essentially zero cannot be rejected. The interaction between treatment and diagnosis is not significant. This test also serves as the goodness-of-fit test for the reduced model, which is the main effects model; it supports the model's adequacy.

Output 8.13 contains the goodness-of-fit statistics Q_P and Q_L. Note that Q_L has the same value as the likelihood ratio statistic; thus, you could have simply fit the main effects model and used Q_L as the test for interaction, knowing that the two omitted terms were the two interaction terms.

Output 8.13   Goodness-of-Fit Statistics

```
            Goodness of Fit Statistics

                                            Pr >
    Criterion      DF      Value   Value/DF  Chi-Square

    Deviance        2     2.5147    1.2573    0.2844
    Pearson         2     2.7574    1.3787    0.2519
```

The following ''Analysis of Maximum Likelihood Estimates'' table is from the main effects model.

Output 8.14   Main Effects Model

```
         Analysis of Maximum Likelihood Estimates

           Parameter Standard   Wald       Pr >    Standardized
    Variable DF Estimate  Error  Chi-Square Chi-Square  Estimate

    INTERCPT 1    1.4184   0.2987   22.5505   0.0001        .
    IDIAG    1   -0.9616   0.2998   10.2885   0.0013    -0.243789
    IATREAT  1    0.5847   0.2641    4.9020   0.0268     0.150196
    IBTREAT  1    1.5608   0.3160   24.4010   0.0001     0.413281


                 The LOGISTIC Procedure

    Analysis of
      Maximum
     Likelihood
      Estimates


                  Odds
    Variable     Ratio

    INTERCPT       .
    IDIAG        0.382
    IATREAT      1.795
    IBTREAT      4.762
```

Note that in the previous examples, the Wald test for the interaction term could also be used as a goodness-of-fit test for the main effects model. However, since in this case the interaction consists of two terms, you can't get a test for the total interaction effect from this table. However, if both interaction terms are significant, you can often assume that the overall interaction is also significant (Section 8.4.3 shows how to construct a test for the total interaction using the TEST statement).

The odds ratios printed out for IATREAT and IBTREAT indicate higher odds of being cured for treatment A compared to treatment C, and higher odds of being cured for treatment B compared to treatment C, since treatment C is the reference treatment. To clarify this, look at the model-predicted probabilities and odds listed in Table 8.7. Taking the ratio of odds for complicated diagnosis and treatment A versus complicated diagnosis and treatment C yields e^{β_2}. A similar exercise for treatment B yields e^{β_3}. To determine the odds ratio for complicated diagnosis to uncomplicated diagnosis, take the ratio of the odds for complicated to uncomplicated diagnosis at any level of treatment. You should get e^{β_1}.

Table 8.7   Model-Predicted Probabilities and Odds

Diagnosis	Treatment	Pr{Cured}	Odds of Cured
Complicated	A	$e^{\alpha+\beta_1+\beta_2}/(1+e^{\alpha+\beta_1+\beta_2})$	$e^{\alpha+\beta_1+\beta_2}$
Complicated	B	$e^{\alpha+\beta_1+\beta_3}/(1+e^{\alpha+\beta_1+\beta_3})$	$e^{\alpha+\beta_1+\beta_3}$
Complicated	C	$e^{\alpha+\beta_1}/(1+e^{\alpha+\beta_1})$	$e^{\alpha+\beta_1}$
Uncomplicated	A	$e^{\alpha+\beta_2}/(1+e^{\alpha+\beta_2})$	$e^{\alpha+\beta_2}$
Uncomplicated	B	$e^{\alpha+\beta_3}/(1+e^{\alpha+\beta_3})$	$e^{\alpha+\beta_3}$
Uncomplicated	C	$e^{\alpha}/(1+e^{\alpha})$	e^{α}

The values listed in the output suggest that you have 4.8 times higher odds of being cured if you get treatment B compared with treatment C, and 1.8 times higher odds of being cured if you get treatment A compared to treatment C. You have 0.38 times lower odds of being cured if you have a complicated diagnosis as compared to an uncomplicated diagnosis; you have $(1/0.382) = 2.6$ times higher odds of being cured if you have uncomplicated diagnosis compared with complicated diagnosis. Note that all these odds ratios have been adjusted for the other explanatory variable.

Output 8.15 contains the output produced by the RISKLIMITS option, which is the 95 percent Wald confidence limits for the odds ratios. None of these limits contain the value 1, indicating that there is a significant treatment effect.

Output 8.15   Confidence Limits for Odds Ratios

```
    Conditional Odds Ratios and 95% Confidence Intervals

                                           Wald
                                    Confidence Limits
                            Odds
    Variable     Unit       Ratio     Lower      Upper

    IDIAG        1.0000     0.382     0.212      0.688
    IATREAT      1.0000     1.795     1.069      3.011
    IBTREAT      1.0000     4.762     2.564      8.847
```

PROC LOGISTIC can also produce confidence limits for the odds ratios that are likelihood-ratio based (beginning with Release 6.10). These are also known as profile likelihood confidence intervals. They are particularly desirable when the sample sizes are moderately large. The following PROC LOGISTIC invocation requests profile likelihood confidence intervals for the odds ratios with the PLRL option. It also requests profile likelihood confidence intervals for the regression parameters with the PLCL option (the

WALDCL option specifies confidence intervals for the parameters based on asymptotic normality of the parameter estimates).

```
proc logistic;
   freq count;
   model response = idiag iatreat ibtreat /
      scale=none aggregate risklimits plcl plrl;
run;
```

Output 8.16 displays the output produced by the PLCL and PLRL options.

Output 8.16   Confidence Limits for Odds Ratios

```
    Parameter Estimates and 95% Confidence Intervals

                                    Profile Likelihood
                                     Confidence Limits
                      Parameter
          Variable     Estimate      Lower      Upper

          INTERCPT       1.4184      0.8581     2.0358
          IDIAG         -0.9616     -1.5794    -0.3973
          IATREAT        0.5847      0.0712     1.1089
          IBTREAT        1.5608      0.9614     2.2067

    Conditional Odds Ratios and 95% Confidence Intervals

                                    Profile Likelihood
                                     Confidence Limits
                           Odds
      Variable     Unit    Ratio     Lower      Upper

      IDIAG       1.0000   0.382     0.206      0.672
      IATREAT     1.0000   1.795     1.074      3.031
      IBTREAT     1.0000   4.762     2.615      9.085
```

If you compare the confidence intervals in Output 8.16 and Output 8.15, you will find that they are similar.

8.4.3   Testing Hypotheses about the Parameters

In the previous analysis, both effects for treatment, the incremental effects for treatment A and treatment B, were significant. Therefore, the overall effect for treatment should be significant as well. If you recall the likelihood ratio test strategies, it should be clear that you can generate this test by computing the likelihood ratio test for the main effects model compared to the model containing the diagnosis effect only. In fact, if you do this, you will obtain a likelihood ratio test of $478.185 - 450.071 = 28.114$, clearly significant with 2 df.

However, you may also be interested in determining whether the effects of treatment A and treatment B are the same, or whether the effects of treatment B and treatment C are the same. With Release 6.10 of the LOGISTIC procedure, you can address such questions through the use of the TEST statement. (See Section 9.2.4 for an alternative strategy for performing these tests using SAS/IML with output data sets from PROC LOGISTIC.)

In order to assess whether any of the treatments are similar, linear combinations of the parameters are tested to see if they are significantly different from zero.

$$H_0: \mathbf{L}\boldsymbol{\beta} = \mathbf{0}$$

By choosing the appropriate elements of $\mathbf{L}$, you can construct linear combinations of the parameters that will produce the test of interest. The Wald statistic for a given linear combination $\mathbf{L}$ is computed as

$$Q_W = (\mathbf{L}\hat{\boldsymbol{\beta}})'(\mathbf{L}\mathbf{V}(\hat{\boldsymbol{\beta}})\mathbf{L}')^{-1}(\mathbf{L}\hat{\boldsymbol{\beta}})$$

where $\hat{\boldsymbol{\beta}}$ is the vector of parameter estimates. Q_W follows the chi-square distribution with degrees of freedom equal to the number of linearly independent rows of $\mathbf{L}$.

The test for whether treatment A is equivalent to treatment B is expressed as

$$H_0: \beta_2 - \beta_3 = 0$$

and the test for whether treatment A is equivalent to treatment C is expressed as

$$H_0: \beta_2 = 0$$

since, according to the model parameterization, β_2 is an incremental effect for treatment A in reference to Treatment C. If β_2 equals zero, then treatment A is the same as treatment C, and the intercept represents the logit for uncomplicated diagnosis for either treatment A or treatment C.

To compute the Wald test for the joint effect of treatment A and treatment B relative to Treatment C (or the equality of Treatments A, B, and C to one another), you test the hypothesis

$$H_0: \beta_2 = \beta_3 = 0$$

You compose the hypotheses in the TEST statement by using the variable names for the corresponding effects. Since all the tests are displayed in a single table, it is good practice to label them by including a descriptor up to 8 characters, followed by a colon, at the beginning of each TEST statement. The following statements produce these tests.

```
proc logistic;
   freq count;
   model response = idiag iatreat ibtreat;
   test1: test iatreat = ibtreat;
   test2: test iatreat = 0;
   test3: test iatreat = ibtreat = 0;
run;
```

Output 8.17 contains the expected results.

Output 8.17   Main Effects Model Contrasts

```
                     Linear Hypotheses Testing

                          Wald                        Pr >
         Label          Chi-Square          DF      Chi-Square

         TEST1            8.6919             1        0.0032
         TEST2            4.9020             1        0.0268
         TEST3           24.6219             2        0.0001
```

Since both effects for treatment A and treatment B are singly significant, as seen in Output 8.14, you would expect that the joint test is also significant. Q_W for this joint test (TEST3) is 24.6219, with 2 df. This is clearly significant. Similarly, these tests confirm that all of the treatments are different from each other: $Q_W = 8.6919$ for no difference in treatments A and B, and $Q_W = 4.9020$ for no difference between treatments A and C. Note that this latter test is exactly the same test as reported in the "Analysis of Maximum Likelihood Estimates" for IATREAT, since both of these tests are assessing whether the parameter for treatment A is zero.

8.5 Continuous and Ordinal Explanatory Variables

8.5.1 Goodness of Fit

Frequently, some or all of the explanatory variables in a logistic regression analysis are continuous. Analysis strategies are the same as those described in previous sections, except in the evaluation of goodness of fit.

The following data are from a study on coronary artery disease that is similar to that previously analyzed; in addition, the continuous variable AGE is an explanatory variable. The variable ECG is now treated as an ordinal variable, with values 0, 1, and 2. ECG is coded 0 if the ST segment depression is less than 0.1, 1 if it equals 0.1 or higher but less than 0.2, and 2 if the ST segment depression is greater than or equal to 0.2. The variable AGE is age in years.

```
data coronary;
   input sex ecg age ca @@  ;
   ecg2=ecg*ecg ; age2=age*age ;
   sexecg=sex*ecg; sexage=sex*age; ecgage=ecg*age ;
   cards;
0 0 28 0   1 0 42 1    0 1 46 0   1 1 45 0
0 0 34 0   1 0 44 1    0 1 48 1   1 1 45 1
0 0 38 0   1 0 45 0    0 1 49 0   1 1 45 1
0 0 41 1   1 0 46 0    0 1 49 0   1 1 46 1
0 0 44 0   1 0 48 0    0 1 52 0   1 1 48 1
0 0 45 1   1 0 50 0    0 1 53 1   1 1 57 1
0 0 46 0   1 0 52 1    0 1 54 1   1 1 57 1
0 0 47 0   1 0 52 1    0 1 55 0   1 1 59 1
0 0 50 0   1 0 54 0    0 1 57 1   1 1 60 1
0 0 51 0   1 0 55 0    0 2 46 1   1 1 63 1
```

```
0  0  51  0     1  0  59  1     0  2  48  0     1  2  35  0
0  0  53  0     1  0  59  1     0  2  57  1     1  2  37  1
0  0  55  1     1  1  32  0     0  2  60  1     1  2  43  1
0  0  59  0     1  1  37  0     1  0  30  0     1  2  47  1
0  0  60  1     1  1  38  1     1  0  34  0     1  2  48  1
0  1  32  1     1  1  38  1     1  0  36  1     1  2  49  0
0  1  33  0     1  1  42  1     1  0  38  1     1  2  58  1
0  1  35  0     1  1  43  0     1  0  39  0     1  2  59  1
0  1  39  0     1  1  43  1     1  0  42  0     1  2  60  1
0  1  40  0     1  1  44  1
;
```

Look at the values listed for AGE. While some observations share the same AGE value, most of these values are unique. Thus, there will be only one observation in most of the cells created by the cross-classification of the explanatory variable values. In fact, the SEX by ECG by AGE cross-classification produces 68 groups from these 78 observations. This means that the sample size requirement for the use of the Pearson chi-square goodness of fit test and the likelihood ratio goodness-of-fit test—that each predicted cell count tends to be at least 5—is not met. This is almost always the case when you have continuous explanatory variables.

There are several alternative strategies. First, you can fit the desired model, fit an appropriate expanded model with additional explanatory variables, and look at the differences in the log likelihood ratio statistics. This difference is distributed as chi-square with degrees of freedom equal to the difference of degrees in freedom in the two models (given sufficiently large samples to support approximate normal estimates from the expanded model).

The second strategy is to examine the residual score statistic, Q_{RS} (Breslow and Day 1980). This criterion is directed at the extent to which the residuals from the model are linearly associated with other potential explanatory variables. If there is an association, this is an indication that these variables should also be included in the model. Thus, to compute the residual score statistic, you need to have access to the variables that comprise the potential expansion. Q_{RS} is distributed as chi-square, with degrees of freedom equal to the difference in the number of parameters for the two models.

However, unlike computing the log likelihood ratio statistic where you have to execute PROC LOGISTIC twice and form the difference of the log likelihood ratio statistics, you can generate this score goodness-of-fit statistic with one invocation of PROC LOGISTIC. You do this by taking advantage of the LOGISTIC procedure's model-building capabilities. The SELECTION=FORWARD method adds variables to your model in the manner in which you specify, computing model assessment statistics for each of the models it fits. In addition, it prints a score statistic that assesses the joint contribution of the remaining model effects that have not yet been incorporated into the model. With the right choice of model effects in the MODEL statement, this is the score goodness-of-fit statistic. You can also generate the constituent one degree of freedom score tests by including the DETAILS option in the MODEL statement.

A third strategy is to compute an alternative goodness-of-fit statistic proposed by Hosmer and Lemeshow (1989). This test places subjects into deciles based on the model-predicted probabilities, then computes a Pearson chi-square test based on the observed and expected number of subjects in the deciles. The statistic is compared to a chi-square distribution with t degrees of freedom, where t is the number of decile groups minus 2. Depending on the number of observations, there may be less than ten groups. PROC LOGISTIC prints this statistic when you specify the LACKFIT option in the MODEL statement. You should note that this method may have low power for detecting departures from goodness of fit, and so some caution may be needed in its interpretation.

8.5.2   Fitting a Main Effects Model

A model of interest for these data is a main effects model with terms for sex, ECG, and age. To generate a score statistic, you need to choose the effects that constitute the expanded model. Your choice depends partially on the sample size. There should be at least 5 observations for the rarer outcome per parameter being considered in the expanded model. Some analysts would prefer at least 10. In this data set, there are 37 observations with no coronary artery disease and 41 observations with coronary artery disease. Thus, no coronary artery disease is the rarer event, and the quotient 37/5 suggests that 7–8 parameters can be supported.

For these data, an appropriate expanded model consists of all second-order terms, which are the squared terms for age and ECG plus all pairwise interactions. See the DATA step statements in Section 8.5.1 for the construction of these terms. This creates eight parameters beyond the intercept. One might also include the third-order terms, but their inclusion would result in too few observations per parameter for the necessary sample size requirements for these statistics. If there did happen to be substantial third-order variation, this approach would not be appropriate.

The following PROC LOGISTIC statements fit the main effects model and compute the score test. The first- and second-order terms are listed on the right-hand side of the MODEL statement, with CA as the response variable. SELECTION=FORWARD is specified as a MODEL statement option after a '/'. The option INCLUDE=3 requests that the first three terms listed in the MODEL statement are to be included in each fitted model. PROC LOGISTIC first fits this model, which is the main effects model, and then produce the score goodness-of-fit statistic.

```
proc logistic descending;
   model ca=sex ecg age
          ecg2 age2
          sexecg sexage ecgage /
          selection=forward include=3 details lackfit;
run ;
```

Note that 1 is the first ordered value, since the DESCENDING option was specified on the PROC statement, so the model is based on Pr{coronary artery disease}.

Output 8.18   Response Profile

```
                    Forward Selection Procedure

The following variables will be included in each model:

        INTERCPT SEX       ECG        AGE


Step  0. The INCLUDE variables were entered.


              Testing Global Null Hypothesis: BETA=0

                              Intercept
                 Intercept      and
Criterion          Only      Covariates   Chi-Square for Covariates

AIC              109.926      94.811           .
SC               112.282     104.238           .
-2 LOG L         107.926      86.811      21.114 with 3 DF (p=0.0001)
Score               .            .        18.562 with 3 DF (p=0.0003)
```

After the "Response Profile" table, PROC LOGISTIC prints a list of the variables
included in each model. Note that the score statistic printed in the table "Testing Global
Null Hypothesis: BETA=0" is not the score goodness-of-fit statistic. This score statistic is
strictly testing the hypothesis that the specified model effects are jointly equal to zero.

Output 8.19   Assessing Fit

```
   Association of Predicted Probabilities and Observed Responses

              Concordant = 78.2%        Somers' D = 0.568
              Discordant = 21.5%        Gamma     = 0.569
              Tied       =  0.3%        Tau-a     = 0.287
              (1517 pairs)              c         = 0.784


     Residual Chi-Square = 2.3277 with 5 DF (p=0.8022)

          Analysis of Variables Not in the Model

                          Score          Pr >
            Variable    Chi-Square     Chi-Square

            ECG2          0.3766         0.5394
            AGE2          0.7712         0.3798
            SEXECG        0.0352         0.8513
            SEXAGE        0.0290         0.8647
            ECGAGE        0.8825         0.3475


NOTE: No (additional) variables met the 0.05 significance level for
      entry into the model.
```

The "Residual Chi-Square" is printed after the "Association of Predicted Probabilities
and Observed Responses" table. This is the score goodness-of-fit statistic. Since the
difference between the number of parameters for the expanded model and the main effects
model is $9 - 4 = 5$, it has 5 degrees of freedom. Since $Q_{RS} = 2.3277$ and $p = 0.8022$, the
main effects model fits adequately. The DETAILS option causes the "Analysis of

Variables Not in the Model'' table to be printed. These tests are the score tests for the addition of the single effects to the model. Each of these tests has one degree of freedom. As one might expect, all these tests indicate that the single effects add little to the main effects model. Since the sample size requirements for the global test are very roughly met, the confirmation of goodness of fit with the single tests is reasonable, since sample size requirements for these individual expanded models are easily met.

Note that this testing process is conservative with respect to confirming model fit. Inadequate sample size may produce spuriously large chi-squares and correspondingly small p-values. However, this would mean that you decide that the fit is not adequate, and you search for another model. Small sample sizes will not misleadingly cause these methods to suggest that poor fit is adequate, although they would have the limitation of low power to detect real departures from a model.

You may have a concern with the evelution of multiple tests to assess model goodness of fit. However, by requiring the global test and most single tests to be nonsignificant, the assessment of goodness of fit is more stringent. Also, the multiplicity can be evaluated relative to what might be expected by chance in an assessment of goodness of fit.

Output 8.20 displays the results produced by the LACKFIT option.

Output 8.20   Results from the LACKFIT Option

```
              Hosmer and Lemeshow Goodness-of-Fit Test

                            CA = 1                    CA = 0
                      ---------------------     ---------------------
     Group    Total   Observed    Expected      Observed    Expected

       1        8        2         1.02            6           6.98
       2        8        1         1.80            7           6.20
       3        8        3         2.59            5           5.41
       4        8        3         3.42            5           4.58
       5        8        4         4.07            4           3.93
       6        9        6         5.38            3           3.62
       7        9        4         5.97            5           3.03
       8        8        7         5.99            1           2.01
       9        8        7         6.98            1           1.02
      10        4        4         3.77            0           0.23

      Goodness-of-fit Statistic = 4.7766 with 8 DF (p=0.7812)
```

The Hosmer and Lemeshow statistic has a value of 4.7766 with 8 df; $p = 0.7812$. Thus, this measure also supports the model's adequacy for these data. The output also includes the observed and expected counts for each predicted probability decile for each value of the response variable. This criterion can also be used as a measure of goodness of fit for the strictly qualitative explanatory variable situation.

Output 8.21   Main Effects Parameter Estimates

```
                      The LOGISTIC Procedure

                Analysis of Maximum Likelihood Estimates

               Parameter Standard    Wald      Pr >    Standardized
    Variable DF Estimate   Error  Chi-Square Chi-Square  Estimate

    INTERCPT 1   -5.6418   1.8061    9.7572     0.0018        .
    SEX      1    1.3564   0.5464    6.1616     0.0131     0.371858
    ECG      1    0.8732   0.3843    5.1619     0.0231     0.350744
    AGE      1    0.0929   0.0351    7.0003     0.0081     0.437780

        Analysis of

         Maximum
        Likelihood
         Estimates

                   Odds
    Variable      Ratio

    INTERCPT      0.004
    SEX          3.882
    ECG          2.395
    AGE          1.097
```

The satisfactory goodness of fit statistics make it reasonable to examine the main effects parameter estimates. The parameter estimates are all significant at the 0.05 level, as judged by the accompanying Wald statistics. Thus, the estimated equation for the log odds is

$$\text{logit}(\theta_{hi}) = -5.6418 + 1.3564 \text{ SEX} + 0.8732 \text{ ECG} + 0.0929 \text{ AGE}$$

Coronary artery disease is positively associated with age and ST segment depression, and it is more likely for males in this population. The odds ratio listed for SEX, 3.882, is the odds of coronary disease presence for males relative to females adjusted for age and ST segment depression. The value listed for ECG, 2.395, is the extent to which the odds of coronary artery disease increase per level increase in ST segment depression. The value 1.097 for AGE is the extent to which the odds increase each year. A more desirable statistic may be the extent to which the odds of coronary artery disease increase per ten years of age; instead of exponentiating the parameter estimate 0.0929, you compute $e^{10 \times 0.0929}$ to obtain 2.53. Thus, the odds of coronary artery disease increase by a factor of 2.53 every ten years. However, note that this model is useful for prediction only for persons in the walk-in population who fall into the age range of those in this study—ages 28 to 60.

Release 6.10 of PROC LOGISTIC includes a UNITS statement that enables you to specify the units of change for which you want the odds ratios computed. To obtain the odds ratio for AGE for 10 year units of change, you specify

```
proc logistic descending;
   model ca=sex ecg age;
   units age=10;
run;
```

The following results agree with those calculated by hand.

Output 8.22   Odds Ratios for Units of 10

```
                     Conditional Odds Ratio

                                        Odds
          Variable          Unit        Ratio

           AGE            10.0000        2.531
```

8.6   A Note on Diagnostics

While goodness-of-fit statistics can tell you how well a particular model fits the data, they tell you little about the lack of fit, or where a particular model fails to fit the data. Measures called regression diagnostics have long been useful tools to assess lack of fit for linear regression models, and in the 1980s researchers proposed similar measures for the analysis of binary data. In particular, work by Pregibon (1981) provided the theoretical basis of extending diagnostics used in linear regression to logistic regression. Both Hosmer and Lemeshow (1989) and Collett (1991) include lengthy discussions on model-checking for logistic regression models; Collett includes many references for recent work in this area. Standard texts on regression analysis like Draper and Smith (1981) discuss model-checking strategies for linear regression; Cook and Weisberg (1982) discuss residual analysis and diagnostics extensively.

This section presents a basic description of a few diagnostic tools and an example of their application with the urinary tract data set. The Pearson and deviance chi-square tests are two measures that assess overall model fit. It makes some sense that by looking at the individual components of these statistics, which are functions of the observed group counts and their model-predicted values, you will gain insight into a model's lack of fit.

Suppose that you have s groups, $i = 1, \ldots, s$, and n_i total subjects for the ith group. If y_i is the number of events (success, yes) for the ith group, and $\hat{\theta}_i$ denotes the predicted probability of success for the ith group, then define the ith residual as

$$e_i = \frac{y_i - n_i\hat{\theta}_i}{\sqrt{n_i\hat{\theta}_i(1 - \hat{\theta}_i)}}$$

These residuals are known as Pearson residuals, since the sum of their squares is Q_P. They compare the differences between observed counts and their predicted values, scaled by the observed count's standard deviation. By examining the e_i, you can determine how well the model fits the individual groups. Often, the residual values are considered to be indicative of lack of fit if they exceed 2 in size.

Similarly, the deviance residual is a component of the deviance statistic. The deviance residual is written

$$d_i = \text{sgn}(y_i - \hat{y}_i)\left[2y_i \log\left(\frac{y_i}{\hat{y}_i}\right) + 2(n_i - y_i) \log\left(\frac{n_i - y_i}{n_i - \hat{y}_i}\right)\right]^{\frac{1}{2}}$$

where $\hat{y}_i = n\hat{\theta}_i$. The sum of squares of the d_i values is the deviance statistic.

These residuals are often presented in tabular form; however graphical display usually aids their inspection. One simple plot is called an *index plot*, in which the residuals are plotted against the corresponding observation number, the index. By examining these plots, you can determine if there are unusually large residuals, possibly indicative of outliers, or systematic patterns of variation, possibly indicative of a poor model choice.

These residuals are examined for the urinary tract data. As you will recall, the main effects model was considered to have an adequate fit. The INFLUENCE option requests that PROC LOGISTIC provide regression diagnostics.

Notice that the data are input differently than they were in Section 8.4. The variable RESPONSE is now the number of cures in a group, and the variable TRIALS is the total number of patients in that group, the sum of those who were cured and those who were not. The *events/trials* MODEL statement syntax allows you to specify the response as a ratio of two variables, the *events* variable and the *trials* variable. When the response is specified this way, developed to support the binomial trials framework, the residuals are calculated using an n_i that is based on the group size, which is desired. (If you specify a single response, called *actual model* syntax, when you compute residuals, the residuals are calculated using a group size of 1.)

```
data uti;
   input diagnoss : $13. treat $ response trials;
   idiag=(diagnoss='complicated');
   iatreat=(treat='A');
   ibtreat=(treat='B');
   iacomp=idiag*iatreat;
   ibcomp=idiag*ibtreat;
   cards;
complicated    A   78   106
complicated    B   101  112
complicated    C   68   114
uncomplicated  A   40   45
uncomplicated  B   54   59
uncomplicated  C   34   40
;
proc logistic;
   model response/trials = idiag iatreat ibtreat /
   influence;
run;
```

Output 8.23 displays the table of covariate profiles that is first printed in the diagnostics output. There should be one case for each group in your data.

Output 8.23   Covariates

```
                         Covariates
           Case
          Number     IDIAG      IATREAT      IBTREAT

             1       1.0000     1.0000            0
             2       1.0000          0       1.0000
             3       1.0000          0            0
             4            0     1.0000            0
             5            0          0       1.0000
             6            0          0            0
```

Output 8.24 contains the Pearson and Deviance residuals for this model. The
INFLUENCE option produces other diagnostics as well; these are not reproduced here.

Output 8.24   Residuals

```
                    Regression Diagnostics

                     Pearson Residual

          Case                   (1 unit = 0.16)
         Number     Value     -8  -4  0 2 4 6 8

            1      -0.0773    |         *     |
            2       0.6300    |        |  *   |
            3      -0.3453    |       * |     |
            4       0.1609    |        |*     |
            5      -1.3020    |*       |      |
            6       0.7171    |        |   *  |

                    Regression Diagnostics

                     Deviance Residual

          Case                   (1 unit = 0.15)
         Number     Value     -8  -4  0 2 4 6 8

            1      -0.0772    |        *|     |
            2       0.6460    |        |  *   |
            3      -0.3445    |       * |     |
            4       0.1624    |        |*     |
            5      -1.1823    |*       |      |
            6       0.7406    |        |   *  |
```

Note that the largest Pearson residual for the main effects model is −1.3020 for the fifth
group (uncomplicated diagnosis, Treatment B) and the largest deviance residual is
−1.1823, also for the fifth group. The other residuals are all less than 1 (in absolute
value). All these residuals are acceptable.

To see what happens in a model that doesn't fit, the model with the single main effect
IDIAG is requested. The IPLOTS option is specified to produce index plots.

```
proc logistic;
   model response/trials = idiag /
     scale=none aggregate=(iatreat ibtreat idiag) influence iplots;
run;
```

The goodness-of-fit tests are displayed in Output 8.25.

Output 8.25   Goodness-of-Fit Statistics

```
             Deviance and Pearson Goodness-of-Fit Statistics

                                                    Pr >
        Criterion       DF      Value    Value/DF   Chi-Square

        Deviance        4     30.6284    7.6571      0.0001
        Pearson         4     28.7265    7.1816      0.0001

                Number of unique profiles: 6
```

With values of 30.6284 and 28.7265, respectively, Q_L and Q_P clearly do not support the model.

The residuals for this model are displayed in Output 8.26.

Output 8.26   Residuals

```
                                Regression Diagnostics

                                 Pearson Residual
              Covariates
     Case                                (1 unit = 0.48)
     Number      IDIAG       Value    -8   -4   0 2 4 6 8

         1      1.0000     -0.1917    |            *          |
         2      1.0000      3.8267    |            |         *|
         3      1.0000     -3.6081    |*           |          |
         4           0    1.058E-9    |            *          |
         5           0      0.6444    |            |*         |
         6           0     -0.7826    |         *  |          |

                                Regression Diagnostics

                                Deviance Residual

     Case                           (1 unit = 0.53)
     Number     Value           -8   -4   0 2 4 6 8

         1     -0.1911        |            *          |
         2      4.2166        |            |        *|
         3     -3.4358        |  *         |          |
         4          0        |            *          |
         5      0.6694        |            |*         |
         6     -0.7478        |          *|          |
```

This model appears to fit very poorly for groups 2 and 3; the Pearson residuals take the values 3.8267 and −3.6081, respectively, and the deviance residuals take the values 4.2166 and −3.4358 for the same groups. Output 8.27 displays the index plot for the Pearson residuals.

This display obviously makes it easy to spot those residuals that are outside a desirable range and then identify the corresponding group. The points for the second and third observations stand out clearly.

The Pearson and deviance residuals need to be used cautiously when the data contain continuous explanatory variables so that most of the group sizes are 1. This is for the same reason that Q_P and the deviance are inappropriate—the sample size requirements for approximate chi-square distributions are not met. However, these residuals are often considered useful as a rough indicator of model fit in this situation, and they are often examined.

Other types of diagnostics include changes in the Q_P and deviance when the ith observation is excluded; the ith leverage; and distances between estimated parameters and the estimated parameters when the ith observation is excluded. In addition, there are a variety of plots that have been devised to assist in evaluating model adequacy. Refer to the *SAS/STAT User's Guide, Volume II* for information on what diagnostics are provided by the LOGISTIC procedure. Diagnostics development is an active research area, particularly for assessing model fit for generalized linear models, and additional tools will be available in the future.

Output 8.27   Index Plot for Pearson Residuals

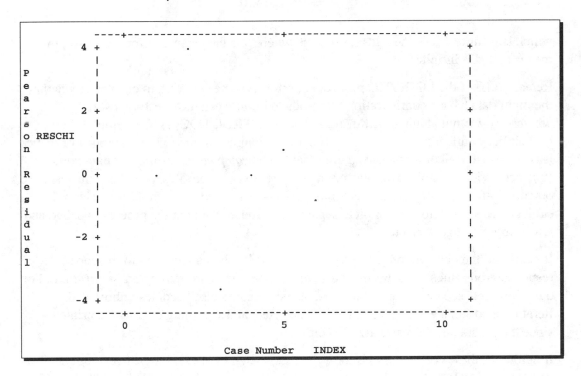

8.7   Maximum Likelihood Estimation Problems and Alternatives

If you perform enough logistic regressions, you will encounter data for which maximum likelihood estimation does not produce a unique solution for the parameters; you do not obtain convergence. In addition, for data with small cell counts, large sample theory may not be applicable and thus tests based on the asymptotic normality of the maximum likelihood estimates may be unreliable. This section discusses some of the situations in which maximum likelihood methods may not produce solutions and also summarizes the alternative strategies based on exact methods that are available today.

8.7.1 Examples of Non-Convergence

To gain insight into the possible data configurations that result in non-convergence, consider the following table:

Table 8.8   Infinite Odds Ratio Example

Factor	Response=Yes	Response=No
Factor 1	15	0
Factor 2	0	34

Computing the odds ratio for these data results in the quantity

$$\frac{a \times d}{b \times c} = \frac{15 \times 34}{0 \times 0}$$

which is infinite. Since the odds ratio is e^β, where β is the parameter for the factor, this means that β is infinite.

Release 6.10 of the LOGISTIC procedure performs some checking to determine whether the input data have a configuration that leads to infinite parameter estimates. If convergence is not attained within eight iterations, PROC LOGISTIC computes the probability of allocating each observation to the correct response group. If this probability is equal to 1 for all observations, there is said to be *complete separation* of data points (this occurs if all the observations having unique covariate profiles have the same response outcome—for example, all the Factor=1 subjects responded yes, and all the Factor=2 subjects responded no). If complete separation is found, the iterative process is halted and a warning message is printed.

If nearly all the observations have a probability of 1 of being allocated to the correct response group, then the data configuration may be one of *quasicomplete separation*. (For quasicomplete separation to occur, the dispersion matrix also becomes unbounded.) Iteration also stops when this condition is detected, and a warning message is printed, since the parameter estimates are also infinite.

If neither of these conditions exists for the data, then they are said to be *overlapping*. The data points overlap so that observations with the same covariate profile have all possible responses. Maximum likelihood estimates exist and are unique for overlapping configurations. The problems of complete separation and quasi-complete separation generally occur for small data sets. Usually quasi-complete separation does not occur if you have a continuous explanatory variable; complete separation can always occur. Refer to Albert and Anderson (1984) for more information about infinite parameters and the data configurations that produce them; refer to Silvapulle (1981) for a discussion of the necessary and sufficient conditions for the existence of maximum likelihood estimators in binomial response models.

Earlier releases of PROC LOGISTIC did not check for these conditions, and if the data configuration produced no unique solutions, then the procedure printed a message saying that convergence was not attained. You then had the option of finetuning the estimation process by increasing the number of iterations or changing the convergence criterion, or assuming that the parameter estimates were infinite. Occasionally, unique parameter estimates exist that require more iterations or a different convergence criterion for their estimation than the default.

The following statements input a data set with several zero values for the response outcome counts.

```
data quasi;
   input treatA treatB response count @@;
   cards;
   0 0 0 0  0 0 1  0
   0 1 0 2  0 1 1  0
   1 0 0 0  1 0 1  8
   1 1 0 6  1 1 1 21
   ;
proc logistic;
   freq count;
   model response= TreatA TreatB;
run;
```

Output 8.28 contains the results from PROC LOGISTIC. Since there is quasi-complete separation, the maximum likelihood solution may not exist.

Output 8.28   Quasi-Complete Separation Note

```
                        Response Profile

                 Ordered
                 Value   RESPONSE      Count

                   1         0           8
                   2         1          29

NOTE: 4 observation(s) having zero frequencies or weights were
      excluded since they do not contribute to the analysis.


WARNING: There is possibly a quasicomplete separation in the sample
         points.  The maximum likelihood estimate may not exist.
```

The next statements input a data set that also includes two dichotomous explanatory variables and the same number of zero counts; however, the placement of the zero counts results in complete separation of the data points.

```
data complete;
   input gender region count response @@;
   cards;
   0 0 0  1  0 0 5    0
   0 1 1  1  0 1 0    0
   1 0 0  1  1 0 175  0
   1 1 53 1  1 1 0    0
   ;
proc logistic;
```

```
        freq count;
        model response = gender region;
   run;
```

Output 8.29 contains the results. Since there is complete separation, the maximum likelihood solution does not exist.

Output 8.29   Complete Separation Note

```
                        Response Profile

                   Ordered
                     Value  RESPONSE       Count

                       1        0          180
                       2        1           54

NOTE: 4 observation(s) having zero frequencies or weights were
      excluded since they do not contribute to the analysis.


WARNING: There is a complete separation in the sample points. The
         maximum likelihood estimate does not exist.
```

Most of the time, the data generating nonunique infinite solutions will not be this simple.

8.7.2   Exact Methods in Logistic Regression

Until recently, there was no convenient alternative in situations where maximum likelihood estimation failed or small cell counts made the resulting maximum likelihood estimates inappropriate. However, it is now possible to compute parameter estimates, confidence intervals, and p-values for statistical tests using methodology based on exact permutation distributions. The key is to condition on the appropriate sufficient statistic. The idea is not a new one, having been suggested by Cox (1970), but recent algorithmic advances in computing the exact distributions have made the methodology computationally feasible. Refer to Tritchler (1984) and Hirji, Mehta, and Patel (1987) for more details regarding these algorithms.

While the SAS System does not presently provide this methodology, it is useful to demonstrate its benefit. Consider the following data in Table 8.9 from a study on liver function outcomes for high risk overdose patients in which antidote and historical control groups are compared. The data are stratified by time to hospital admission (Koch, Gillings, and Stokes 1980).

Table 8.9   Liver Function Outcomes

Time	Antidote		Control	
to Hospital	Severe	Not Severe	Severe	Not Severe
Early	6	12	6	2
Delayed	3	4	3	0
Late	5	1	6	0

The small counts in many cells—seven of the twelve cells have values less than 5—make the applicability of large sample theory somewhat questionable. The following PROC LOGISTIC statements request a logistic regression analysis of the severity of the outcome with explanatory variables based on time to admission and treatment group.

```
data liver;
    input time $ group $ status $ count @@;
    dtime=(time='delayed');
    ltime=(time='late');
    agroup=(group='antidote');
    cards;
early    antidote severe 6 early    antidote not 12
early    control  severe 6 early    control  not  2
delayed antidote severe 3 delayed antidote not 4
delayed control  severe 3 delayed control  not 0
late     antidote severe 5 late     antidote not 1
late     control  severe 6 late     control  not 0
;
run;
proc logistic descending;
    freq count;
    model status = dtime ltime agroup / scale=none aggregate;
run;
```

Output 8.30 contains the goodness-of-fit statistics, and Output 8.31 contains the resulting maximum likelihood parameter estimates.

Output 8.30   Goodness-of-Fit Statistics

```
        Deviance and Pearson Goodness-of-Fit Statistics

                                               Pr >
    Criterion      DF      Value    Value/DF   Chi-Square

    Deviance        2     1.1728    0.5864     0.5563
    Pearson         2     0.7501    0.3751     0.6872
```

Output 8.31   MLE Estimates

```
┌──────────────────────────────────────────────────────────────────────┐
│         Analysis of Maximum Likelihood Estimates                       │
│                                                                        │
│           Parameter Standard    Wald       Pr >     Standardized       │
│  Variable DF Estimate  Error  Chi-Square Chi-Square   Estimate         │
│                                                                        │
│  INTERCPT 1   1.4133  0.7970    3.1440     0.0762          .           │
│  DTIME    1   0.7024  0.8344    0.7087     0.3999      0.158944        │
│  LTIME    1   2.5535  1.1667    4.7902     0.0286      0.616060        │
│  AGROUP   1  -2.2171  0.8799    6.3482     0.0118     -0.590782        │
└──────────────────────────────────────────────────────────────────────┘
```

Exact estimates and confidence intervals are available from the software LogXact©, available from CYTEL Software Corporation (Mehta and Patel 1992). Table 8.10 contains the estimates it produces:

Table 8.10   Exact and Asymptotic Estimates

Variable	Inference Type	Estimate	Lower 95% CI bound	Upper 95% CI bound	p-value
Intercept	Asymptotic	1.4133	---	---	---
	Exact	---	---	---	---
Dtime	Asymptotic	0.7024	−0.9330	2.3378	0.3999
	Exact	0.6676	−1.2075	2.6438	0.6667
Ltime	Asymptotic	2.5535	0.2666	4.8404	0.0286
	Exact	2.4388	0.1375	6.4078	0.0331
GroupA	Asymptotic	−2.2171	−3.9418	−0.4924	0.0118
	Exact	−2.0992	−4.5204	−0.3119	0.0154

For exact methods, the p-value listed is twice the one-sided p-value. Note that the exact methods do not produce a standard error for the estimate. Also, you are essentially conditioning away the intercept parameter, so you do not produce an estimate for that either. For these data, you can see that exact logistic regression produces estimates that are different, although not substantially, from the maximum likelihood estimates. For each parameter, the p-values listed for the exact estimates are larger than those for the asymptotic estimates. In general, the exact methods lead to more conservative results than the approximate methods. As a general rule, when the sample sizes are small and the approximate p-values are less than 0.10, it is a good idea to look at the exact results. If the approximate p-values are larger than 0.15, then the approximate methods are probably satisfactory.

Besides being appropriate for data sets with small cell counts, exact methods often can produce estimates and corresponding confidence bounds for data sets for which maximum likelihood methods fail to converge.

It is likely that the SAS System will include such methods in a future release.

8.8   Using the CATMOD Procedure

PROC CATMOD is an alternative way in which to fit the logistic regression model for some analyses. The main advantage is that you do not have to create indicator variables in order to handle qualitative explanatory variables. Assuming that data set SENTENCE from Section 8.3 has been created, the following PROC CATMOD statements fit a main effects model.

```
proc catmod order=data;
    weight count;
    model sentence = type prior;
run;
```

The following output is produced.

Output 8.32   PROC CATMOD

```
                         CATMOD PROCEDURE

Response: SENTENCE                Response Levels (R)=      2
Weight Variable: COUNT            Populations     (S)=      4
Data Set: SENTENCE                Total Frequency (N)=    863
Frequency Missing: 0              Observations   (Obs)=      8




                    POPULATION PROFILES
                                   Sample
          Sample  TYPE   PRIOR      Size
          ------------------------------------
             1    nrb    some        151
             2    nrb    none         92
             3    other  some        208
             4    other  none        412




                    RESPONSE PROFILES

          Response   SENTENCE
          ------------------
             1          y
             2          n
```

The CATMOD procedure determines the model matrix structure from the explanatory variables listed on the MODEL statement. It forms a separate group, or 'sample,' for each combination of explanatory variable values. These groups are displayed in the "POPULATION PROFILES" table. The four different rows, or profiles, correspond to rows in Table 8.5. The sample sizes correspond to the row totals listed in that table. The "RESPONSE PROFILES" table in the PROC CATMOD output lists the response variable and its values. The ORDER=DATA option was used to put the response value 'y' first, so that the model fit would be based on Pr{prison}. It is always important to check these tables in the PROC CATMOD output to make sure that you understand the internal order of the response variable values and the classification of explanatory effects.

After the iteration history is printed (not shown here), PROC CATMOD prints the
ANOVA table and the table of maximum likelihood estimates, as displayed in
Output 8.33. The ANOVA table contains Wald statistics for the model effects; the entry
labeled "LIKELIHOOD RATIO" is the likelihood ratio goodness-of-fit test. Note that
the likelihood ratio statistic and the Wald statistics are identical to those computed for the
main effects model fit with PROC LOGISTIC, as displayed in Section 8.3.

Output 8.33   PROC CATMOD

```
             MAXIMUM-LIKELIHOOD ANALYSIS-OF-VARIANCE TABLE

        Source                   DF    Chi-Square      Prob
        -------------------------------------------------------
        INTERCEPT                 1       243.25      0.0000
        TYPE                      1         9.05      0.0026
        PRIOR                     1         3.31      0.0687


        LIKELIHOOD RATIO          1         0.51      0.4762

             ANALYSIS OF MAXIMUM-LIKELIHOOD ESTIMATES

                                         Standard    Chi-
    Effect            Parameter  Estimate   Error    Square   Prob
    ----------------------------------------------------------------
    INTERCEPT             1       -1.4828   0.0951   243.25   0.0000
    TYPE                  2        0.2960   0.0984     9.05   0.0026
    PRIOR                 3        0.1735   0.0953     3.31   0.0687
```

However, if you compare the parameter estimates in this PROC CATMOD output to those
for PROC LOGISTIC, you will find that they are different. This is because the model fit
with PROC CATMOD uses a different parameterization than that used by PROC
LOGISTIC. The models fit with the LOGISTIC procedure were incremental effects
models, sometimes called *reference cell models*. The intercept parameter corresponds to a
reference or baseline group, and the other parameters correspond to incremental effects
over that baseline group for the other groups.

The default parameterization in PROC CATMOD is called a *deviation from the mean*
model. The effects are differential rather than incremental. This model is written as
follows:

$$\begin{bmatrix} \mathrm{logit}(\theta_{11}) \\ \mathrm{logit}(\theta_{12}) \\ \mathrm{logit}(\theta_{21}) \\ \mathrm{logit}(\theta_{22}) \end{bmatrix} = \begin{bmatrix} \alpha + \beta_1 + \beta_2 \\ \alpha + \beta_1 - \beta_2 \\ \alpha - \beta_1 + \beta_2 \\ \alpha - \beta_1 - \beta_2 \end{bmatrix} = \begin{bmatrix} 1 & 1 & 1 \\ 1 & 1 & -1 \\ 1 & -1 & 1 \\ 1 & -1 & -1 \end{bmatrix} \begin{bmatrix} \alpha \\ \beta_1 \\ \beta_2 \end{bmatrix}$$

Here, α is the average log odds (across the four populations) of a prison sentence, β_1 is the
differential change in log odds for whether a nonresidential burglary was committed, and
β_2 is the differential change in log odds for having a prior arrest record. β_1 is an added
amount for a nonresidential burglary and subtracted amount for other burglary. β_2 is an
added amount for a prior arrest record and subtracted amount for no previous arrest
record. The formulas for the model-predicted probabilities and odds for this
parameterization are listed in Table 8.11.

Table 8.11   Model-Predicted Probabilities and Odds

Type	Prior Arrest	Pr{Prison}	Odds of Prison
Nonresidential	Some	$e^{\alpha+\beta_1+\beta_2}/(1+e^{\alpha+\beta_1+\beta_2})$	$e^{\alpha+\beta_1+\beta_2}$
Nonresidential	None	$e^{\alpha+\beta_1-\beta_2}/(1+e^{\alpha+\beta_1-\beta_2})$	$e^{\alpha+\beta_1-\beta_2}$
Other	Some	$e^{\alpha-\beta_1+\beta_2}/(1+e^{\alpha-\beta_1+\beta_2})$	$e^{\alpha-\beta_1+\beta_2}$
Other	None	$e^{\alpha-\beta_1-\beta_2}/(1+e^{\alpha-\beta_1-\beta_2})$	$e^{\alpha-\beta_1-\beta_2}$

The odds of a prison sentence for nonresidential burglary (nrb) versus other is obtained by forming the ratio of the odds for nrb versus other for either prior arrest level. Using some prior arrest, this is computed as

$$\frac{e^{\alpha+\beta_1+\beta_2}}{e^{\alpha-\beta_1+\beta_2}} = e^{2\beta_1}$$

The odds of a prison sentence for some arrest record versus none is obtained by forming the ratio of the odds for some prior arrest versus no prior arrest for either level of burglary type. Using nrb, this is computed as

$$\frac{e^{\alpha+\beta_1+\beta_2}}{e^{\alpha+\beta_1-\beta_2}} = e^{2\beta_2}$$

Thus, with this parameterization, you need to exponentiate twice the parameter estimates to calculate the odds ratios, instead of simply exponentiating them, as was true for the reference cell model used with PROC LOGISTIC. You also have to do this yourself, as PROC CATMOD does not print odds ratios. However, the CATMOD procedure is a convenient way to perform logistic regression when you have qualitative explanatory variables. It can also handle continuous variables that have a relatively limited number of unique values. You just specify the variable in the DIRECT statement, and PROC CATMOD inserts its values directly into the model matrix. This feature is discussed in Chapter 12, "Weighted Least Squares," which discusses the CATMOD procedure comprehensively for weighted least squares applications.

However, PROC CATMOD is not an appropriate procedure for logistic regression when you have continuous explanatory variables with many distinct values. The internal CATMOD machinery always creates a separate group for each distinct combination of explanatory variable values. Computationally, this is not an efficient way to set up logistic regression estimation, and the procedure can run out of memory if requested to do logistic regression for certain data sets.

8.9 Using the GENMOD Procedure

8.9.1 Generalized Linear Models

The GENMOD procedure fits generalized linear models. Such models are a generalization of the general linear model that is fit by the GLM procedure. Generalized linear models include not only classical linear models but logistic and probit models for binary data, loglinear models for multinomial data, and Poisson regression models for Poisson data. You can generate many other statistical models by the appropriate selection of a *link function* and the probability distribution of the response.

A generalized linear model has three components:

- a response variable $\{y_i\}$ with some probability distribution, $i = 1, 2, \ldots, n$

- a set of explanatory variables $\mathbf{x}_i$ and parameter vector $\boldsymbol{\beta}$

- a monotonic link function g that describes how the expected value of y_i, μ_i, is related to $\mathbf{x}_i'\boldsymbol{\beta}$:

$$g(\mu_i) = \mathbf{x}_i'\boldsymbol{\beta}$$

You thus construct a generalized linear model by choosing the appropriate link function and response probability distribution. In the classical linear model, the probability distribution is the normal and the link function is the identity: $g(\mu) = \mu$. For logistic regression, the distribution is the binomial and the link function is the logit:

$$g(\mu) = \log\left(\frac{\mu}{1-\mu}\right)$$

For Poisson regression, the distribution is Poisson and the link function is $g(\mu) = \log(\mu)$.

In the SAS System, the GENMOD procedure fits the generalized linear model and thus provides another mechanism for performing logistic regression analysis (SAS/INSIGHT software also fits generalized linear models). The following section describes how to perform logistic regression using PROC GENMOD. Sections 15.3 and 15.4 discuss fitting Poisson regression models with the GENMOD procedure. For a comprehensive discussion of the generalized linear model, refer to McCullagh and Nelder (1989). For an introduction to the topic, refer to Dobson (1990) or Agresti (1995).

8.9.2 Fitting Logistic Regression Models with PROC GENMOD

There are several advantages to using the GENMOD procedure to perform logistic regression. The major advantage is that qualitative variables are easily handled because PROC GENMOD includes a CLASS statement that is identical in use to the CLASS statement in PROC GLM. You list your qualitative explanatory variables in this statement, and the correct model matrix is generated. The parameterization it produces is equivalent to the incremental effects parameterization implemented for most of the analyses performed in this chapter. In PROC GENMOD, the reference cell is the combination of the last sorted levels of the effects listed in the CLASS statement. Incremental effects parameters are estimated for the remaining levels.

Consider the urinary tract infection data analyzed in Section 8.4. If you sorted the values of TREAT and DIAGNOSS, those observations that had an uncomplicated diagnosis and treatment C would become the reference cell. This is actually the parameterization that was created in Section 8.4 using dummy variables.

Currently, for binomial data, the GENMOD procedure only handles data that come in the *events/trials* data form. This style of response input is an alternative style for the LOGISTIC and PROBIT procedures as well. Instead of using a variable that contains the response variable value for each observation or each count observation, you input a ratio of variables for each combination of explanatory variable values. This ratio includes a variable for the *events*, or number of observations with the outcome of interest or the response level you wish to model, and another variable for the *trials* or the total number of observations for that particular combination of explanatory variable values.

The following statements illustrate a DATA step that inputs the urinary tract data now transformed to an events/trials form. Note that the column for cured responses is kept, and a column containing the sum of the cured and uncured responses is created. The first variable is named EVENTS, and the second is named TRIALS. These names are not required; the events variable is the ratio numerator, and the trials variable is the ratio denominator. That's all you have to do if your data are in count form. Such an input style is not an arbitrary convention; bioassay data are often collected this way.

```
data uti2;
   input diagnoss : $13. treat $ events trials;
   cards;
complicated     A    78    106
complicated     B   101    112
complicated     C    68    114
uncomplicated   A    40    45
uncomplicated   B    54    59
uncomplicated   C    34    40
;
run;
```

The following statements produce an analysis using PROC GENMOD. You need to specify LINK=LOGIT and DIST=BINOMIAL to request logistic regression with PROC GENMOD.

```
proc genmod;
   class diagnoss treat;
   model events/trials = diagnoss treat /
   link=logit dist=binomial type3;
run;
```

The output is displayed in Output 8.34.

Output 8.34   Goodness of Fit

```
                    The GENMOD Procedure

                Class Level Information

        Class     Levels  Values

        DIAGNOSS     2   complicated uncomplicated
        TREAT        3   A B C

           Criteria For Assessing Goodness Of Fit

        Criterion            DF      Value      Value/DF

        Deviance              2      2.5147      1.2573
        Scaled Deviance       2      2.5147      1.2573
        Pearson Chi-Square    2      2.7574      1.3787
        Scaled Pearson X2     2      2.7574      1.3787
        Log Likelihood        .   -225.0355         .
```

The table labeled "Criteria for Assessing Goodness of Fit" includes the Log Likelihood statistic, with a value of -225.0355. Note that if you multiply this value by two and reverse the sign, you get the same value as -2LOG L displayed in the output for the same model in the PROC LOGISTIC output. Other criteria displayed are approximate chi-square statistics. The Deviance is the log likelihood statistic for the difference between this main effects model and the saturated model, the same as computed by PROC LOGISTIC.

The estimates displayed in Output 8.35 are identical to those produced with PROC LOGISTIC for the same model. However, those levels that become the reference levels under incremental effects coding, uncomplicated diagnosis and treatment C, are assigned 0s for the parameter estimate and related statistics.

The table labeled "LR Statistics For Type 3 Analysis" can be viewed as serving a similar role to that of an ANOVA table. It includes likelihood ratio tests for each of the effects. The effect for treatment, which has three levels, has 2 df. The effect for diagnosis, with two levels, has 1 df. Both tests are clearly significant, with values of 28.11 and 11.72, respectively.

Output 8.35   Parameter Estimates

```
                    Analysis Of Parameter Estimates

    Parameter                   DF Estimate  Std Err   ChiSquare   Pr>Chi

    INTERCEPT                     1   1.4184  0.2987    22.5505    0.0000
    DIAGNOSS   complicated        1  -0.9616  0.2998    10.2885    0.0013
    DIAGNOSS   uncomplicated      0   0.0000  0.0000       .          .
    TREAT      A                  1   0.5847  0.2641     4.9020    0.0268
    TREAT      B                  1   1.5608  0.3160    24.4010    0.0000
    TREAT      C                  0   0.0000  0.0000       .
    SCALE                         0   1.0000  0.0000       .

NOTE:   The scale parameter was held fixed.

              LR Statistics For Type 3 Analysis

           Source       DF    ChiSquare   Pr>Chi

           DIAGNOSS      1     11.7183    0.0006
           TREAT         2     28.1137    0.0000
```

To assess whether any of the treatments are similar, linear combinations of the parameters are tested to see if they are significantly different from zero.

$$H_0: \mathbf{L}\beta = \mathbf{0}$$

By choosing the right elements of $\mathbf{L}$, you can construct linear combinations of the parameters that will produce the appropriate test. By default, PROC GENMOD computes a likelihood ratio test; on request, it can produce the corresponding Wald test. The likelihood ratio test for a contrast is twice the difference between the log likelihood of the current fitted model and the log likelihood of the model fitted under the constraint that the linear function of the parameters defined by the contrast is equal to zero.

The test for whether treatment A is equivalent to treatment B is expressed as

$$H_0: \beta_A = \beta_B$$

and the test for whether treatment A is equivalent to treatment C is expressed as

$$H_0: \beta_A = \beta_C$$

You request these tests with the CONTRAST statement in PROC GENMOD. The following CONTRAST statement is required to produce the first test. You place an identifying name for the test in quotes, name the effect variable, and then list the appropriate coefficients for $\mathbf{L}$. These coefficients are listed according to the order in which the levels of the variable are known to PROC GENMOD. When you use a CONTRAST statement, or specify the ITPRINT, COVB, CORRB, WALDCI, or LRCI options in the MODEL statement, the GENMOD output includes information on what levels of effects the parameters represent.

The CONTRAST statement is very similar to the CONTRAST statement in PROC GLM.

```
contrast 'A-B' treat 1 -1  0;
```

The following SAS code produces the tests of interest.

```
proc genmod;
   class diagnoss treat;
   model events/trials = diagnoss treat /
   link=logit dist=binomial;
   contrast 'treatment' treat 1 0 -1 ,
                        treat 0 1 -1;
   contrast 'A-B' treat 1 -1  0;
   contrast 'A-C' treat 1  0 -1;
run;
```

Output 8.36 contains the information about what the parameters represent.

Output 8.36   Contrasts

```
                    Parameter Information

        Parameter  Effect      DIAGNOSS        TREAT

               1   INTERCEPT
               2   DIAGNOSS    complicated
               3   DIAGNOSS    uncomplicated
               4   TREAT                       A
               5   TREAT                       B
               6   TREAT                       C
```

Output 8.37 contains the results of the hypothesis tests.

Output 8.37   Contrasts

```
                CONTRAST Statement Results

        Contrast     DF   ChiSquare  Pr>Chi  Type

        treatment    2     28.1137   0.0000  LR
        A-B          1      9.2218   0.0024  LR
        A-C          1      4.9883   0.0255  LR
```

$Q_L = 9.22$ for the test of whether treatment A and treatment B are the same; $Q_L = 4.99$ for the test of whether treatment A and treatment C are the same; both of these are clearly significant at the $\alpha = 0.05$ level of significance. Note that these tests are similar to those displayed in the analysis performed in Section 8.4. If you execute these same statements using the WALD option, you will obtain identical results to the Wald tests obtained from PROC LOGISTIC in Section 8.4.

8.10   Statistical Methodology for Dichotomous Logistic Regression

Consider the relationship of a dichotomous outcome variable to a set of explanatory variables. Such situations can arise from clinical trials where the explanatory variables are treatment, stratification variables, and background covariables; another common source of such analyses are observational studies where the explanatory variables represent factors for evaluation and background variables.

The model for θ, the probability of the event, can be specified as follows:

$$\theta = \frac{\exp(\alpha + \sum_{k=1}^{t} \beta_k x_k)}{1 + \exp(\alpha + \sum_{k=1}^{t} \beta_k x_k)}$$

It follows that the odds are written

$$\frac{\theta}{1 - \theta} = \exp(\alpha + \sum_{k=1}^{t} \beta_k x_k)$$

so the model for the logit is linear:

$$\log\left\{\frac{\theta}{1 - \theta}\right\} = \alpha + \sum_{k=1}^{t} \beta_k x_k$$

The $\exp(\beta_k)$ are the odds ratios for unit changes in x_k, that is, the amount by which $\theta/(1 - \theta)$ is multiplied per unit change in x_k.

You can apply the product binomial distribution when the data for the dichotomous outcome are from a sampling process equivalent to stratified simple random sampling from subpopulations according to the explanatory variables. Relative to this structure, the maximum likelihood estimates are obtained by iteratively solving the equations:

$$\sum_{i=1}^{s} n_{i+} \hat{\theta}_i(1, x_{i1}, \ldots, x_{it}) = \sum_{i=1}^{s} n_{i1}(1, x_{i1}, \ldots, x_{it})$$

where n_{i1} is the number of subjects who have the event corresponding to θ among n_i subjects with $(x_{i1}, \ldots, x_{it})$ status.

The quantity

$$\hat{\theta}_i = \frac{\exp\{\hat{\alpha} + \sum_{k=1}^{t} \hat{\beta}_k x_{ik}\}}{1 + \exp\{\hat{\alpha} + \sum_{k=1}^{t} \hat{\beta}_k x_{ik}\}}$$

is the model-predicted value for θ_i.

The quantities $\hat{\alpha}$ and $\hat{\beta}_k$ have approximate multivariate normal distributions for which a consistent estimate of the covariance structure is available.

You can assess goodness of fit of the model with Pearson chi-square statistics when sample sizes are sufficiently large (80% of the $\{n_{i1}\}$ and the $\{n_i - n_{i1}\}$ are ≥ 5 and all others are ≥ 2).

$$Q_P = \sum_{i=1}^{s} \frac{(n_{i1} - n_{i+}\hat{\theta}_i)^2}{n_{i+}\hat{\theta}_i(1 - \hat{\theta}_i)}$$

is approximately chi-square with $(s - 1 - t)$ degrees of freedom.

You can also use log-likelihood ratio statistics to evaluate goodness of fit by evaluating the need for a model to include additional explanatory variables.

In the setting where you have continuous explanatory variables, you cannot use Q_P to assess goodness of fit because you no longer have sufficient sample sizes n_{i+}. However, you can still apply the strategy of fitting an expanded model and then verifying that the effects not in the original model are nonsignificant. If the model matrix for the original model X has rank t, then the expanded model $[X, W]$ has rank $t + w$, where w is the rank of W. You can evaluate the significance of W with the difference of the log-likelihood statistics for the models X and $[X, W]$.

$$Q_{LR} = \sum_{i=1}^{2} \sum_{j=1}^{2} 2n_{ij}\log\left(\frac{m_{ij,w}}{m_{ij}}\right)$$

where s is the total number of groups with at least one subject, m_{ij} is the predicted value of n_{ij} for model X ($m_{i1} = n_i\hat{\theta}_i$ and $m_{i2} = n_i(1 - \hat{\theta}_i)$), and $m_{ij,w}$ is the predicted value of n_{ij} for model $[X, W]$. Q_{LR} has an approximate chi-square distribution with w degrees of freedom.

Another approach that doesn't involve fitting an expanded model is the score statistic for assessing the association of the residuals $(n_{*1} - m_{*1})$ with W via the linear functions $g = W'(n_{*1} - m_{*1})$. The score statistic is written

$$Q_S = g'\{W'[D_v^{-1} - D_v^{-1}X_A(X_A'D_v^{-1}X_A)^{-1}X_A'D_v^{-1}]W\}^{-1}g$$

where $n_{*1} = (n_{11}, n_{21}, \ldots, n_{s1})'$, $X_A = [1, X]$, $m_{*1} = (m_{11}, m_{21}, \ldots, m_{s1})'$, and D_v is a diagonal matrix with diagonal elements $v_i = [n_{i+}\hat{\theta}_i(1 - \hat{\theta}_i)]^{-1}$. Q_S approximately has a chi-square distribution with w degrees of freedom when the total sample size is large enough to support an approximately multivariate normal distribution for the linear functions $[X_A', W']n_{*1}$.

Chapter 9
Logistic Regression II: Polytomous Response

Chapter Table of Contents

Chapter 9
Logistic Regression II: Polytomous Response

9.1 Introduction

While the typical logistic regression analysis models a dichotomous response as discussed in Chapter 8, "Logistic Regression I: Dichotomous Response," logistic regression is also applicable to multi-level responses. The response may be ordinal (no pain, slight pain, substantial pain) or nominal (Democrats, Republicans, Independents). For ordinal response outcomes, you can model functions called *cumulative logits* by performing ordered logistic regression using the proportional odds model (McCullagh 1980). For nominal response outcomes, you form *generalized logits* and perform a logistic analysis similar to those described in the previous chapter, except that you model multiple logits per subpopulation. The analysis of generalized logits is a form of the log-linear model, discussed in Chapter 14, "Loglinear Models." The LOGISTIC procedure is used to model cumulative logits, and the CATMOD procedure is used to model generalized logits.

9.2 Ordinal Response: Proportional Odds Model

9.2.1 Methodology

Consider the arthritis pain data in Table 9.1. Male and female subjects received an active or placebo treatment for their arthritis pain, and the subsequent extent of improvement was recorded as marked, some, or none (Koch and Edwards 1988).

Table 9.1   Arthritis Data

Sex	Treatment	Improvement			Total
		Marked	Some	None	
Female	Active	16	5	6	27
Female	Placebo	6	7	19	32
Male	Active	5	2	7	14
Male	Placebo	1	0	10	11

One possible analysis strategy is to create a dichotomous response variable by combining two of the response categories, basing a model on either Pr{marked improvement} versus Pr{some or no improvement} or Pr{marked or some improvement} versus

Pr{no improvement}. However, since there is a natural ordering to these response levels, it makes sense to consider a strategy that takes advantage of this ordering.

Consider the quantities

$$\theta_{hi1} = \pi_{hi1}, \quad \theta_{hi2} = \pi_{hi1} + \pi_{hi2}$$

where π_{hi1} denotes the probability of marked improvement, π_{hi2} denotes the probability of some improvement, and π_{hi3} denotes the probability of no improvement. The $\{\theta_{hij}\}$ represent cumulative probabilities: θ_{hi1} is the probability of marked improvement, and θ_{hi2} is the probability of marked or some improvement ($h=1$ for females, $h = 2$ for males; $i = 1$ for active treatment, $i = 2$ for placebo).

For a dichotomous response, you compute a logit function for each subpopulation. For a multi-level response, you create more than one logit function for each subpopulation. With ordinal data, you can compute *cumulative logits*, which are based on the cumulative probabilities. For three response levels, you compute two cumulative logits:

$$\text{logit}(\theta_{hi1}) = \log\left[\frac{\pi_{hi1}}{\pi_{hi2} + \pi_{hi3}}\right], \; \text{logit}(\theta_{hi2}) = \log\left[\frac{\pi_{hi1} + \pi_{hi2}}{\pi_{hi3}}\right]$$

These cumulative logits are the log odds of marked improvement to none or some improvement and the log odds of marked or some improvement to no improvement, respectively. Both log odds focus on more favorable to less favorable response. The proportional odds model takes both of these odds into account.

Assuming that the data arise from a stratified simple random sample or are at least conceptually representative of a stratified population, they have the following likelihood:

$$\Pr\{n_{hij}\} = \prod_{h=1}^{2} \prod_{i=1}^{2} n_{hi+}! \prod_{j=1}^{3} \frac{\pi_{hij}^{n_{hij}}}{n_{hij}!}$$

where

$$\sum_{j=1}^{3} \pi_{hij} = 1$$

You could write a model that applies to both logits simultaneously for each combination of gender and treatment.

$$\text{logit}(\theta_{hik}) = \alpha_k + \mathbf{x}_{hi}'\boldsymbol{\beta}_k$$

where k indexes the two logits. This says that there are separate intercept parameters (α_k) and different sets of regression parameters ($\boldsymbol{\beta}_k$) for each logit.

If you take the difference in logits between two subpopulations for this model, you get

$$\text{logit}(\theta_{hik}) - \text{logit}(\theta_{hi'k}) = (\mathbf{x}_{hi} - \mathbf{x}_{hi'})'\boldsymbol{\beta}_k \text{ for } k = 1, 2$$

Thus, you would need to look at two differences in logits simultaneously to compare the response between two subpopulations. This is the same number of comparisons you would need to compare two subpopulations for a three-level nominal response, for example, in a test for association in a contingency table (that is, $r - 1$ where r is the number of response outcomes). Therefore, this model doesn't take the ordinality of the data into account.

The proportional odds assumption is that $\beta_k = \beta$ for all k, simplifying the model to

$$\text{logit}(\theta_{hik}) = \alpha_k + \mathbf{x}'_{hi}\boldsymbol{\beta}$$

If you take the difference in logits for this model, you obtain the equations

$$\text{logit}(\theta_{hi1}) - \text{logit}(\theta_{hi'1}) = \log\left[\frac{\pi_{hi1}/(\pi_{hi2} + \pi_{hi3})}{\pi_{hi'1}/(\pi_{hi'2} + \pi_{hi'3})}\right] = (\mathbf{x}_{hi} - \mathbf{x}_{hi'})'\boldsymbol{\beta}$$

$$\text{logit}(\theta_{hi2}) - \text{logit}(\theta_{hi'2}) = \log\left[\frac{(\pi_{hi1} + \pi_{hi2})/\pi_{hi3}}{(\pi_{hi'1} + \pi_{hi'2})/\pi_{hi'3}}\right] = (\mathbf{x}_{hi} - \mathbf{x}_{hi'})'\boldsymbol{\beta}$$

This says that the log cumulative odds are proportional to the distance between the explanatory variable values and that the influence of the explanatory variables is independent of the cutpoint for the cumulative logit. In this case, there is a "cut" at marked improvement to form $\text{logit}(\theta_{hi1})$ and a cut at some improvement to form $\text{logit}(\theta_{hi2})$. This proportionality is what gives the proportional odds model its name. The regression lines for the different cumulative log odds are parallel to each other, for a single continuous explanatory variable, differing only by the difference between the values of the intercept parameter.

This model can also be stated as

$$\theta_{hik} = \frac{\exp(\alpha_k + \mathbf{x}'_{hi}\boldsymbol{\beta})}{1 + \exp(\alpha_k + \mathbf{x}'_{hi}\boldsymbol{\beta})}$$

and is written in summation notation as

$$\theta_{hik} = \frac{\exp\{\alpha_k + \sum_{g=1}^{t} \beta_g x_{hig}\}}{1 + \exp\{\alpha_k + \sum_{g=1}^{t} \beta_g x_{hig}\}}$$

where $g = (1, 2, \ldots, t)$ references the explanatory variables. This model is similar to the previous logistic regression models and is also fit with maximum likelihood methods. You can determine the values for π_{hij} from this model by performing the appropriate subtractions of the θ_{hik}.

$$\pi_{hi1} = \theta_{hi1}$$
$$\pi_{hi2} = \theta_{hi2} - \theta_{hi1}$$
$$\pi_{hi3} = 1 - \theta_{hi2}$$

The main effects model is an appropriate starting point for the analysis of the arthritis data. You can write this model in matrix notation as

$$
\begin{bmatrix}
\text{logit}(\theta_{111}) \\
\text{logit}(\theta_{112}) \\
\text{logit}(\theta_{121}) \\
\text{logit}(\theta_{122}) \\
\text{logit}(\theta_{211}) \\
\text{logit}(\theta_{212}) \\
\text{logit}(\theta_{221}) \\
\text{logit}(\theta_{222})
\end{bmatrix}
=
\begin{bmatrix}
\alpha_1 \quad\ \ + \beta_1 + \beta_2 \\
\alpha_2 + \beta_1 + \beta_2 \\
\alpha_1 \quad\ \ + \beta_1 \\
\alpha_2 + \beta_1 \\
\alpha_1 \qquad\quad\ + \beta_2 \\
\alpha_2 \qquad\ + \beta_2 \\
\alpha_1 \\
\alpha_2
\end{bmatrix}
=
\begin{bmatrix}
1 & 0 & 1 & 1 \\
0 & 1 & 1 & 1 \\
1 & 0 & 1 & 0 \\
0 & 1 & 1 & 0 \\
1 & 0 & 0 & 1 \\
0 & 1 & 0 & 1 \\
1 & 0 & 0 & 0 \\
0 & 1 & 0 & 0
\end{bmatrix}
\begin{bmatrix}
\alpha_1 \\
\alpha_2 \\
\beta_1 \\
\beta_2
\end{bmatrix}
$$

This is very similar to the models described in Chapter 8 except that there are two intercept parameters corresponding to the two cumulative logit functions being modeled for each group. The parameter α_1 is the intercept for the first cumulative logit, α_2 is the intercept for the second cumulative logit, β_1 is an incremental effect for females, and β_2 is an incremental effect for active. Males on placebo comprise the reference cell.

Table 9.2 contains the cell probabilities for marked improvement and no improvement based on this model. Table 9.3 contains the odds. The cell probabilities for marked improvement are based on the model for the first logit function, and the probabilities for no improvement are based on the model for the second logit function (these probabilities are computed from $1 - \theta_{hi2}$). Since the probabilities for all three levels sum to 1, you can determine the cell probabilities for some improvement through subtraction.

The odds ratio for females versus males is e^{β_1}, and the odds ratio for active treatment versus placebo is e^{β_2}. The odds ratios are computed in the same manner as for the logistic regression analysis for a dichotomous response—you form the ratio of the appropriate odds.

Table 9.2   Formulas for Cell Probabilities

Sex	Treatment	Improvement	
		Marked	None
Female	Active	$e^{\alpha_1+\beta_1+\beta_2}/(1 + e^{\alpha_1+\beta_1+\beta_2})$	$1/(1 + e^{\alpha_2+\beta_1+\beta_2})$
Female	Placebo	$e^{\alpha_1+\beta_1}/(1 + e^{\alpha_1+\beta_1})$	$1/(1 + e^{\alpha_2+\beta_1})$
Male	Active	$e^{\alpha_1+\beta_2}/(1 + e^{\alpha_1+\beta_2})$	$1/(1 + e^{\alpha_2+\beta_2})$
Male	Placebo	$e^{\alpha_1}/(1 + e^{\alpha_1})$	$1/(1 + e^{\alpha_2})$

For example, the odds of marked improvement versus some or no improvement for females compared to males is

$$
\frac{e^{\alpha_1+\beta_1+\beta_2}}{e^{\alpha_1+\beta_2}} = e^{\beta_1}
$$

As constrained by the proportional odds model, this is also the odds ratio for marked or some improvement versus no improvement.

Table 9.3 Formulas for Model Odds

		Improvement	
		Marked Versus	Marked or Some
Sex	Treatment	Some or None	Versus None
Female	Active	$e^{\alpha_1+\beta_1+\beta_2}$	$e^{\alpha_2+\beta_1+\beta_2}$
Female	Placebo	$e^{\alpha_1+\beta_1}$	$e^{\alpha_2+\beta_1}$
Male	Active	$e^{\alpha_1+\beta_2}$	$e^{\alpha_2+\beta_2}$
Male	Placebo	e^{α_1}	e^{α_2}

9.2.2 Fitting the Proportional Odds Model with PROC LOGISTIC

PROC LOGISTIC fits the proportional odds model whenever the response variable has more than two levels. While several other procedures in the SAS System fit logistic regression models, only the LOGISTIC procedure fits the proportional odds model with maximum likelihood estimation.

The following SAS statements create the data set ARTHRIT, which includes the appropriate indicator variables _SEX_, which takes the value 1 if female and 0 if male, _TREAT_, which takes the value 1 for active treatment and 0 otherwise; and SEXTRT, a variable for the interaction term that is 1 if both _SEX_ and _TREAT_ are 1 and is 0 otherwise. Note that these data are in the form of count data, so a variable named COUNT is created to contain the frequencies for each table cell. The variable IMPROVE is a character variable that takes the values marked, some, or none to indicate the subject's extent of improvement of arthritic pain.

```
data arthrit;
   length treat $7. sex $6.;
   input sex $ treat $ improve $ count @@;
   _treat_ = (treat ='active');
   _sex_   = (sex = 'female');
   sextrt  = _sex_*_treat_;
   cards;
female active   marked 16 female active   some 5 female active   none  6
female placebo marked  6 female placebo some 7 female placebo none 19
male    active   marked  5 male    active   some 2 male    active   none  7
male    placebo marked  1 male    placebo some 0 male    placebo none 10
;
run;
```

The use of PROC LOGISTIC is identical to previous invocations for dichotomous response logistic regression. The response variable is listed on the left-hand side of the equal sign and the explanatory variables are listed on the right-hand side. Since ORDER=DATA is specified in the PROC statement, the values for IMPROVE are ordered in the sequence in which PROC LOGISTIC encounters them, which is marked, some, and none. (Another legitimate ordering would be none, some, and marked). It is very important to ensure that the ordering is correct when you are using ordinal data strategies. The procedure still performs an analysis if the response values are ordered incorrectly, but the results will be erroneous. The burden is on the user to specifiy the correct order and then to check the results.

The following code requests that PROC LOGISTIC fit a proportional odds model.

```
proc logistic order=data;
   freq count;
   model  improve = _sex_  _treat_ /scale=none aggregate;
run;
```

The "Response Profile" table in Output 9.1 shows that the response variable values are ordered correctly in terms of decreasing improvement. The procedure also prints out a note that a zero count observation has been encountered. For these data, this is not a problem since the total row counts are acceptably large. Computationally, zero counts are discarded. The model still produces predicted values for the cell that corresponds to the zero cell, males on placebo who showed some improvement.

Output 9.1   Response Profiles

```
                    Response Profile

            Ordered
             Value   IMPROVE        Count

               1     marked           28
               2     some             14
               3     none             42

NOTE: 1 observation(s) having zero frequencies or weights were
      excluded since they do not contribute to the analysis.
```

Next, PROC LOGISTIC prints out a test for the appropriateness of the proportional odds assumption. The test performed is a score test that determines whether, if you fit a different set of explanatory variable parameters β_k for each logit function, those sets of parameters are equivalent. Thus, the model considered is

$$\text{logit}(\theta_{hik}) = \alpha_k + \mathbf{x}'_{hi}\beta_k$$

The hypothesis tested is that there is a common parameter vector β instead of distinct β_k. The hypothesis can be stated as $\beta_k = \beta$ for all k. Thus, if you reject the null hypothesis, you reject the assumption of proportional odds and you need to consider a different approach, such as modeling generalized logits, discussed in Section 9.3. If the null hypothesis is not rejected, then the test supports the assumption of proportional odds. Since the test is comparing t parameters for the t explanatory variables across $(r-1)$ logits, where r is the number of response levels, it has $t * (r-2)$ degrees of freedom.

The sample size requirements for this test are moderately demanding; you need approximately five observations at each outcome at each level of each main effect, or roughly the same sample size if you were fitting a generalized logit model. Small samples may artificially make the statistic large, meaning that any resulting significance needs to be interpreted cautiously. However, nonsignificant results are always informative.

The partial proportional odds model is an alternative model that can be fit when the proportionality assumption does not hold for all levels of the response variable, but there is proportionality across sets of levels. Refer to Koch, Amara, and Singer (1985) for a discussion of this model.

Output 9.2 displays this score test.

Output 9.2   Proportional Odds Test

```
     Score Test for the Proportional Odds Assumption

       Chi-Square = 1.8833 with 2 DF (p=0.3900)
```

Q_{RS} takes the value 1.8833 with 2 df. This is clearly nonsignificant, and so the assumption of proportional odds is a reasonable one for these data.

The evaluation of goodness of fit for the proportional odds model is similar to the evaluation of goodness of fit for the dichotomous response logistic regression model. If you have sufficient sample size, with eighty percent of the observed cell counts at least 5, then you can use counterparts of Q_P and Q_L. Q_P is distributed as chi-square with df = $\{(r-1)(s-1) - t\}$, where t is the number of explanatory variables, r is the number of response levels, and s is the number of subpopulations. Output 9.3 contains these statistics. With values of 2.7121 and 1.91, respectively, and 4 df, Q_L and Q_P support the adequacy of the model. The 4 df come from $(3-1)(4-1) - 2 = 4$.

Output 9.3   Goodness of Fit Statistics

```
          Deviance and Pearson Goodness-of-Fit Statistics

                                                Pr >
        Criterion         DF       Value    Value/DF    Chi-Square

        Deviance           4       2.7121     0.6780       0.6071
        Pearson            4       1.9100     0.4775       0.7523

             Number of unique profiles: 4

        Testing Global Null Hypothesis: BETA=0

                            Intercept
                 Intercept     and
Criterion          Only     Covariates   Chi-Square for Covariates

AIC              173.916     158.029          .
SC               178.778     167.753          .
-2 LOG L         169.916     150.029       19.887 with 2 DF  (p=0.0001)
Score               .           .          17.868 with 2 DF  (p=0.0001)
```

The tests for assessing model fit through explanatory capability are also supportive of the model; the likelihood ratio test has a value of 19.887 with 2 df and the score test has a value of 17.868 with 2 df.

You can also investigate goodness of fit by performing the score test for a set of additional terms not in the model. In this case, this effect would simply be the treatment × sex interaction. The following code requests that PROC LOGISTIC fit a main effects model and then perform a score test for the other effect listed in the MODEL statement, which is the interaction.

```
proc logistic order=data;
   freq count;
   model  improve = _sex_  _treat_  sextrt /
                    selection=forward start=2;
run;
```

The score test of interest is labeled "Residual Chi-Square" and is printed after the "Testing Global Null Hypothesis: BETA=0" table, as displayed in Output 9.4. The value is 0.2801 (1 df since you are testing the addition of one term to the model) with $p = 0.5967$. This indicates that the main effects model is adequate.

An alternative goodness-of-fit test is the difference in the likelihood ratios for the main effects model and the saturated model. Although the output is not displayed here, the difference in these statistics is $(150.029 - 149.721) = 0.308$. This is also clearly nonsignificant, compared to a chi-square distribution with 1 df. (Again, note that whenever you form a test statistic based on the difference in likelihoods, then the corresponding degrees of freedom are equal to the difference in the number of parameters for the two models.)

Output 9.4   Score Statistic to Evaluate Goodness of Fit

```
              Testing Global Null Hypothesis: BETA=0

                             Intercept
               Intercept        and
Criterion        Only        Covariates   Chi-Square for Covariates

AIC             173.916       158.029           .
SC              178.778       167.753           .
-2 LOG L        169.916       150.029      19.887 with 2 DF (p=0.0001)
Score              .             .         17.868 with 2 DF (p=0.0001)

         Residual Chi-Square = 0.2801 with 1 DF (p=0.5967)
```

Output 9.5 contains the parameter estimates from PROC LOGISTIC; Table 9.4 displays their interpretation.

Output 9.5   Parameter Estimates

```
            Analysis of Maximum Likelihood Estimates

              Parameter Standard    Wald       Pr >     Standardized
Variable DF   Estimate   Error   Chi-Square Chi-Square   Estimate

INTERCP1 1     -2.6672   0.5997   19.7809    0.0001          .
INTERCP2 1     -1.8128   0.5566   10.6072    0.0011          .
_SEX_    1      1.3187   0.5292    6.2102    0.0127       0.334418
_TREAT_  1      1.7973   0.4728   14.4493    0.0001       0.498287

    Analysis of
     Maximum
   Likelihood
    Estimates

                  Odds
Variable         Ratio

INTERCP1           .
INTERCP2           .
_SEX_            3.739
_TREAT_          6.033
```

Table 9.4   Parameter Estimates

Parameter	Estimate(SE)	Interpretation
α_1	$-2.667(0.600)$	log odds of marked improvement versus some or no improvement for males receiving placebo
α_2	$-1.813(0.557)$	log odds of marked or some improvement versus no improvement for males receiving placebo
β_1	$1.319(0.529)$	increment for both types of log odds due to female sex
β_2	$1.797(0.473)$	increment for both types of log odds due to active drug

Females have $e^{1.319}$=3.7 times higher odds of showing improvement as males, both for marked improvement versus some or no improvement and for marked or some improvement versus no improvement. Those subjects receiving the active drug have $e^{1.8} = 6$ times higher odds of showing improvement as those on placebo, both for marked improvement versus some or no improvement and for some or marked improvement versus no improvement.

9.2.3 Multiple Qualitative Explanatory Variables

The inclusion of multiple explanatory variables in a proportional odds model produces no additional problems. The data in Table 9.5 are from an epidemiological study of chronic respiratory disease analyzed in Semenya and Koch (1980). Researchers collected information on subjects' exposure to general air pollution, exposure to pollution in their jobs, and whether they smoked. The response measured was chronic respiratory disease status. Subjects were assigned to one of four possible categories.

- Level I: no symptoms
- Level II: cough or phlegm less than three months a year
- Level III: cough or phlegm more than three months a year
- Level IV: cough and phlegm plus shortness of breath more than three months a year

Table 9.5 Chronic Respiratory Disease Data

Air Pollution	Job Exposure	Smoking Status	I	II	III	IV	Total
Low	No	Non	158	9	5	0	172
Low	No	Ex	167	19	5	3	194
Low	No	Current	307	102	83	68	560
Low	Yes	Non	26	5	5	1	37
Low	Yes	Ex	38	12	4	4	58
Low	Yes	Current	94	48	46	60	248
High	No	Non	94	7	5	1	107
High	No	Ex	67	8	4	3	82
High	No	Current	184	65	33	36	318
High	Yes	Non	32	3	6	1	42
High	Yes	Ex	39	11	4	2	56
High	Yes	Current	77	48	39	51	215

The outcome is clearly ordinal, although there is no obvious distance between adjacent levels. You could combine response categories and fit the set of models that compared Level I versus Level II, III, and IV; Levels I and II versus Levels III and IV; and Levels I, II, and III versus Level IV. Note that if you did this, you would be computing models for the individual cumulative logits. The proportional odds model addresses these cumulative logits simultaneously by assuming that the slope parameters for the explanatory variables are the same regardless of the cumulative logit cutpoints.

From these data, you form three cumulative logits:

$$\text{logit}(\theta_{i1}) = \log\left[\frac{\pi_{i1}}{\pi_{i2} + \pi_{i3} + \pi_{i4}}\right]$$

$$\text{logit}(\theta_{i2}) = \log\left[\frac{\pi_{i1} + \pi_{i2}}{\pi_{i3} + \pi_{i4}}\right]$$

$$\text{logit}(\theta_{i3}) = \log\left[\frac{\pi_{i1} + \pi_{i2} + \pi_{i3}}{\pi_{i4}}\right]$$

where $i = 1, 2, \ldots, 12$ references the 12 populations determined by the levels of air pollution, job exposure, and smoking status, as ordered in Table 9.5. These cumulative logits are the log odds of a Level I response to a Level II, III, or IV response, the log odds of a Level I or II response to a Level III or IV response, and the log odds of a Level I, II, or III response to a Level IV response, respectively.

However, if you are more interested in the odds of more severe responses to less severe responses, you may want to order the cumulative logits in the opposite direction.

$$\text{logit}(\theta_{i1}) = \log\left[\frac{\pi_{i4}}{\pi_{i3} + \pi_{i2} + \pi_{i1}}\right]$$

$$\text{logit}(\theta_{i2}) = \log\left[\frac{\pi_{i4} + \pi_{i3}}{\pi_{i2} + \pi_{i1}}\right]$$

$$\text{logit}(\theta_{i3}) = \log\left[\frac{\pi_{i4} + \pi_{i3} + \pi_{i2}}{\pi_{i1}}\right]$$

You can generate this ordering in PROC LOGISTIC by using the DESCENDING option in the PROC statement, as shown in the following analysis.

The primary model of interest for these data is a main effects model. Besides three intercept terms α_1, α_2, and α_3 for the three cumulative logits, the main effects model includes the parameters β_1, β_2, β_3, and β_4 for incremental effects for air pollution exposure, job pollution exposure, ex-smoker status, and current smoking status, respectively.

The following SAS statements create the data set RESPIRE and compute the appropriate indicator variables for use with PROC LOGISTIC.

```
data respire;
   input air $ exposure $ smoking $ level count @@;
   iair=(air='high');
   iexp=(exposure='yes');
   ismkex=(smoking='ex');
   ismkcur=(smoking='cur');
   iairexp=iair*iexp;
   iairex=iair*ismkex;
   iaircur=iair*ismkcur;
   iexpex=iexp*ismkex;
   iexpcur=iexp*ismkcur;
   cards;
   low no non   1 158 low  no   non 2    9
   low no ex    1 167 low  no   ex  2   19
   low no cur   1 307 low  no   cur 2  102
   low yes non  1  26 low  yes  non 2    5
   low yes ex   1  38 low  yes  ex  2   12
```

```
      low  yes cur 1  94 low  yes cur 2  48
      high no  non 1  94 high no  non 2   7
      high no  ex  1  67 high no  ex  2   8
      high no  cur 1 184 high no  cur 2  65
      high yes non 1  32 high yes non 2   3
      high yes ex  1  39 high yes ex  2  11
      high yes cur 1  77 high yes cur 2  48
      low  no  non 3   5 low  no  non 4   0
      low  no  ex  3   5 low  no  ex  4   3
      low  no  cur 3  83 low  no  cur 4  68
      low  yes non 3   5 low  yes non 4   1
      low  yes ex  3   4 low  yes ex  4   4
      low  yes cur 3  46 low  yes cur 4  60
      high no  non 3   5 high no  non 4   1
      high no  ex  3   4 high no  ex  4   3
      high no  cur 3  33 high no  cur 4  36
      high yes non 3   6 high yes non 4   1
      high yes ex  3   4 high yes ex  4   2
      high yes cur 3  39 high yes cur 4  51
      ;
  run;
```

Note that since air pollution and job exposure are dichotomous effects, they are represented by the single indicator variables IAIR and IEXP, respectively. Since smoking has three levels, it is represented by two indicator variables. ISMKEX has the value 1 if the subject is an ex-smoker and 0 otherwise. ISMKCUR has the value 1 if the subject is a current smoker and 0 otherwise. Indicator variables are also created to represent pairwise interactions of the explanatory effects. Since two indicator variables are needed for smoking status, the interactions including smoking also consist of two indicator variables.

The following PROC LOGISTIC code requests a main effects proportional odds model. The statements are set up to specify a score statistic for the goodness of fit of the expanded model containing all pairwise interaction terms. The SCALE=NONE and AGGREGATE=(IAIR IEXP ISMKEX ISMKCUR) options request the goodness-of-fit tests based on the 12 subpopulations.

```
  proc logistic descending;
     freq count;
     model level = iair iexp ismkex ismkcur
            iairexp iairex iaircur iexpex iexpcur /
            selection=forward include=4 scale=none
            aggregate=(iair iexp ismkex ismkcur);
  run;
```

Output 9.6 shows the internal ordered values that PROC LOGISTIC uses. Since the response variable LEVEL has numeric values, the DESCENDING option causes PROC LOGISTIC to sort the values numerically, then reverses them to form the ordered values. The score test for the proportional odds assumption takes the value $Q_{RS} = 12.07$ ($p = 0.1479$) with 8 df ($4(4 - 2)$). Thus, the proportional odds assumption is not contradicted.

Output 9.6   Response Profile

```
                    Response Profile

               Ordered
                Value    LEVEL      Count

                  1        4         230
                  2        3         239
                  3        2         337
                  4        1        1283

NOTE: 1 observation(s) having zero frequencies or weights were
      excluded since they do not contribute to the analysis.



                 Forward Selection Procedure

The following variables will be included in each model:

       INTERCP1  INTERCP2  INTERCP3  IAIR      IEXP        ISMKEX
       ISMKCUR


Step  0. The INCLUDE variables were entered.


       Score Test for the Proportional Odds Assumption

          Chi-Square = 12.0745 with 8 DF (p=0.1479)
```

The three intercepts and four indicator variables representing the main effects are first entered into the model. The Residual Chi-Square has a value of 2.722 with 5 df and $p = 0.7428$, so this measure of goodness of fit suggests that model-predicted cell proportions are acceptably close to the observed proportions.

Output 9.7   Assessment of Fit

```
            Testing Global Null Hypothesis: BETA=0

                              Intercept
                   Intercept     and
Criterion            Only     Covariates   Chi-Square for Covariates

AIC                4537.722    4192.511        .
SC                 4554.655    4232.022        .
-2 LOG L           4531.722    4178.511     353.211 with 4 DF (p=0.0001)
Score                 .           .         318.720 with 4 DF (p=0.0001)

         Residual Chi-Square = 2.7220 with 5 DF (p=0.7428)
```

Output 9.8 displays the goodness-of-fit statistics. $Q_L = 29.9969$ and $Q_P = 28.0796$, both with $(r-1)(s-1) - t = 29$ df ($r = 4$, $s = 12$, $t = 4$). Model adequacy is again supported.

Output 9.8   Goodness-of-Fit Statistics

```
              Goodness of Fit Statistics

                                              Pr >
   Criterion      DF      Value    Value/DF   Chi-Square

   Deviance       29     29.9969    1.0344    0.4142
   Pearson        29     28.0796    0.9683    0.5137
```

Output 9.9   Parameter Estimates

```
         Analysis of Maximum Likelihood Estimates

              Parameter Standard    Wald        Pr >     Standardized
   Variable DF Estimate  Error   Chi-Square Chi-Square    Estimate

   INTERCP1 1   -3.8938  0.1779   479.2836    0.0001         .
   INTERCP2 1   -2.9696  0.1693   307.7926    0.0001         .
   INTERCP3 1   -2.0884  0.1633   163.5858    0.0001         .
   IAIR     1   -0.0393  0.0937     0.1758    0.6750     -0.010581
   IEXP     1    0.8648  0.0955    82.0601    0.0001      0.221334
   ISMKEX   1    0.4000  0.2019     3.9267    0.0475      0.085960
   ISMKCUR  1    1.8527  0.1650   126.0384    0.0001      0.489834

    Analysis of
      Maximum
    Likelihood
     Estimates

                 Odds
   Variable      Ratio

   INTERCP1        .
   INTERCP2        .
   INTERCP3        .
   IAIR          0.961
   IEXP          2.374
   ISMKEX        1.492
   ISMKCUR       6.377
```

The "Analysis of Maximum Likelihood Estimates" table displayed in Output 9.9
suggests a strong effect for job pollution exposure but no significant effect for outside air
pollution ($p = 0.675$). The term for current smoking is highly significant ($p = 0.0001$),
while the term for ex-smoking is significant at the $\alpha = 0.05$ level of significance.

The following PROC LOGISTIC statements request a joint test for the effect of smoking.

```
proc logistic data=respire descending;
    freq count;
    model level = iair iexp ismkex ismkcur;
    smoking: test ismkex=ismkcur=0;
run;
```

Output 9.10 contains the results from the TEST statement. The Wald statistic has a value
of 209.8514 with 2 df. The joint smoking effect is clearly significant.

Output 9.10   Joint Test for Smoking

```
                    Linear Hypotheses Testing

                        Wald                      Pr >
         Label        Chi-Square       DF      Chi-Square

         SMOKING       209.8514         2        0.0001
```

The predicted odds ratios illustrate this model's conclusions. Those exposed to air pollution on the job have $e^{0.86} = 2.37$ times higher odds of having serious problems to less serious problems compared with those not exposed on the job. Current smokers have $e^{1.85} = 6.377$ times higher odds of having serious problems to less serious problems compared to nonsmokers. Both of these odds ratios have been adjusted for the other variables in the model.

Note that if you fit the same model without reversing the order of the cumulative logits with the DESCENDING option, you fit an equivalent model. The intercepts will be in the opposite order and have opposite signs; that is, INTERCEP3 will have the value of this model's INTERCEP1 with the opposite sign. The parameters for the effects will have opposite signs and the odds ratios will be inverted since they would represent the odds of less serious response to more serious response.

9.2.4   Optional: Constructing Wald Tests Using SAS/IML Software

While Release 6.10 of PROC LOGISTIC includes the TEST statement, some readers may be using earlier releases that do not include this feature. In that case, you can still construct tests for the types of hypotheses tested with the TEST statement by using the output capabilities of PROC LOGISTIC in combination with SAS/IML software. In addition, it is useful to see how to construct tests yourself by using the facilities of SAS/IML software.

Wald statistics are easily computed as functions of the estimated parameter vector and the covariance matrix. The parameter vector for the final respiratory data model is

$$
\begin{bmatrix}
\alpha_1 \\
\alpha_2 \\
\alpha_3 \\
\beta_1 \\
\beta_2 \\
\beta_3 \\
\beta_4
\end{bmatrix}
$$

You construct your hypothesis in terms of linear combinations of the parameters.

$$H_0: \mathbf{L}\boldsymbol{\beta} = \mathbf{0}$$

The Wald statistic for a given linear combination $\mathbf{L}$ is

$$Q_W = (\mathbf{Lb})'(\mathbf{L Cov(b) L'})^{-1}(\mathbf{Lb})$$

where $\mathbf{b}$ is the vector of estimated parameters. Q_W follows the chi-square distribution with degrees of freedom equal to the number of linearly independent rows of $\mathbf{L}$. The test for the joint effect of smoking in the model in the previous section is whether β_3 and β_4 are simultaneously equal to zero.

$$H_0: \beta_3 = \beta_4 = 0$$

The test for whether the effects for current smoking and previous smoking are the same is

$$H_0: \beta_3 = \beta_4$$

The respective Ls for these hypotheses are

$$L_1 = \begin{bmatrix} 0 & 0 & 0 & 0 & 0 & 1 & 0 \\ 0 & 0 & 0 & 0 & 0 & 0 & 1 \end{bmatrix}$$

and

$$L_2 = \begin{bmatrix} 0 & 0 & 0 & 0 & 0 & 1 & -1 \end{bmatrix}$$

To compute these statistics with the SAS System, you output the parameter estimates and estimated covariance matrix into a SAS data set. This is done with the OUTEST= and COVOUT options in the PROC LOGISTIC statement. The following statements produce an output data set named ESTIMATE. Variables _LINK_ and _LNLIKE_ are dropped.

```
proc logistic data=respire descending outest=estimate
             (drop= _link_ _lnlike_) covout;
    freq count;
    model level = iair iexp ismkex ismkcur;
run;
```

The following PROC IML code uses the estimates in the data set ESTIMATE and computes the appropriate Wald statistics. Note that the third test statistic is for the effect of air pollution exposure. This test should match the statistic for IAIR presented in the "Analysis of Maximum Likelihood Estimates" table in the PROC LOGISTIC output displayed in Output 9.9.

```
proc iml;
    title 'Wald tests';
    use estimate;
    read all into beta where (_type_='PARMS');
    read all into cov  where (_type_='COV');
    start waldtest (L,beta,cov,label);
       DF=nrow(L);
       wald=(L*beta')'*inv(L*cov*L')*(L*beta');
       prob=1-probchi(wald,DF);
```

```
      print label wald[format=8.4] DF prob [format=6.4];
   finish;
L1 ={ 0 0 0 0 0 1 0 , 0 0 0 0 0 0 1};
label1={'smoking              '};
L2 ={ 0 0 0 0 0 1 -1};
label2={'current vs. predicted'};
L3 ={0 0 0 1 0 0 0 };
label3={'exposure             '};
reset noname;
run waldtest(L1,beta,cov,label1);
run waldtest(L2,beta,cov,label2);
run waldtest(L3,beta,cov,label3);
```

Output 9.11   Results for Hypothesis Tests

	Wald tests		
smoking	209.8514	2	0.0000
current vs. predicted	109.8459	1	0.0000
exposure	0.1758	1	0.6750

The joint test for smoking has a $Q_W - 209.8514$ with 2 df, the same result obtained with the TEST statement in PROC LOGISTIC. The test to see if current smoking and previous smoking effects are similar is also significant; $Q_W = 109.8459$ with 1 df, indicating that these effects are not the same. Current smoking is a much bigger effect.

9.3   Nominal Response: Generalized Logits Model

9.3.1   Methodology

When you have nominal response variables, you can also use logistic regression to model your data. Instead of fitting a model to cumulative logits, you fit a model to generalized logits. Table 9.6 redisplays the data analyzed in Section 6.3.3. Recall that schoolchildren in experimental learning settings were surveyed to determine which program they preferred. Investigators were interested in whether their response was associated with their school and their school day, which could be a standard school day or include afterschool care.

Table 9.6   School Program Data

School	Program	Learning Style Preference		
		Self	Team	Class
1	Regular	10	17	26
1	After	5	12	50
2	Regular	21	17	26
2	After	16	12	36
3	Regular	15	15	16
3	After	12	12	20

Since the levels of the response variable (self, team, and class) have no inherent ordering, the proportional odds model is not an appropriate mechanism for their analysis. You could form logits comparing self to (team or class) or (self or team) to class, but that collapses the original structure of the response levels, which you may want to keep in your analysis. You can model a nominal response variable with more than two levels by performing a logistic analysis on the generalized logits.

The generalized logit is defined as

$$\text{logit}_{hij} = \log\left[\frac{\pi_{hij}}{\pi_{hir}}\right]$$

for $j = 1, 2, \ldots, (r-1)$. A logit is formed for the probability of each succeeding category over the last response category.

Thus, the generalized logits for a three-level response like that displayed in Table 9.6 is

$$\text{logit}_{hi1} = \log\left[\frac{\pi_{hi1}}{\pi_{hi3}}\right], \quad \text{logit}_{hi2} = \log\left[\frac{\pi_{hi2}}{\pi_{hi3}}\right]$$

for $h = 1, 2, 3$ for the schools, $i = 1$ for regular program, and $i = 2$ for after school program.

The model you fit for generalized logits is the model discussed in Section 9.2.1.

$$\text{logit}_{hik} = \alpha_k + \mathbf{x}'_{hi}\boldsymbol{\beta}_k$$

where k indexes the two logits. This says that there are separate intercept parameters (α_k) and different sets of regression parameters $(\boldsymbol{\beta}_k)$ for each logit. The matrix $\mathbf{x}_{hi}$ is the set of explanatory variable values for the hith group. Instead of estimating one set of parameters for one logit function, as in logistic regression for a dichotomous response variable, you are estimating sets of parameters for multiple logit functions. Whereas for the proportional odds model you estimated multiple intercept parameters for the cumulative logit functions but only one set of parameters corresponding to the explanatory variables, for the generalized logits model you are estimating multiple sets of parameters for both the intercept terms and the explanatory variables.

This poses no particular problems. Since there are multiple response functions being modeled per group, there are more degrees of freedom associated with each effect. Since the model matrix needs to account for multiple response functions, it takes a more complicated form. However, the modeling proceeds as usual; you fit your specified model, examine goodness-of-fit statistics, and possibly perform model reduction. Note that since you are predicting more than one response function per group, the sample size needs to be large enough to support the number of functions you are predicting.

9.3.2 Fitting Models to Generalized Logits with PROC CATMOD

The CATMOD procedure is used to perform an analysis of generalized logits; the LOGISTIC procedure currently does not perform this analysis. You should read Section 8.8, ''Using the CATMOD Procedure,'' before continuing with this section.

The following SAS statements request the desired analysis. First, the data set SCHOOL is created, then the CATMOD procedure is invoked. Since the generalized logit is the default response for PROC CATMOD, and maximum likelihood is the default estimation method for generalized logit functions, all you have to specify is the WEIGHT statement and the MODEL statement. PROC CATMOD constructs two generalized logits per group from the levels of the variable STYLE; it composes six groups based on the unique values of the explanatory variables, SCHOOL and PROGRAM.

```
data school;
   input school program $ style $ count @@;
   cards;
   1 regular  self 10  1 regular  team 17  1 regular class  26
   1 after    self  5  1 after    team 12  1 after   class  50
   2 regular  self 21  2 regular  team 17  2 regular class  26
   2 after    self 16  2 after    team 12  2 after   class  36
   3 regular  self 15  3 regular  team 15  3 regular class  16
   3 after    self 12  3 after    team 12  3 after   class  20
   ;
proc catmod order=data;
   weight count;
   model style=school program school*program;
run;
```

Output 9.12 contains the population profiles for the data. There are six groups formed based on the values of SCHOOL and PROGRAM. This table also contains the sample sizes for each group. They are all moderately-sized.

Output 9.12   Population Profiles

```
                   POPULATION PROFILES
                                        Sample
         Sample   SCHOOL   PROGRAM       Size
         ---------------------------------------
            1        1     regular        53
            2        1     after          67
            3        2     regular        64
            4        2     after          64
            5        3     regular        46
            6        3     after          44
```

Output 9.13 contains the response profiles. While the analysis does not require the response values to be ordered in any particular way, unlike the proportional odds model analyses, it is often useful to order the levels in a manner that facilitates interpretation. Since the ORDER=DATA option was specified, the response variable levels are in the order self, team, and class. This means that generalized logits are formed for the probability of self with respect to class, and for the probability of team with respect to class.

Output 9.13   Response Profiles

```
              RESPONSE PROFILES

           Response   STYLE
           -----------------
              1        self
              2        team
              3        class
```

The iteration history follows in the output, but it is not displayed here. Convergence took four iterations, which is not unusual for these types of applications.

The analysis of variance table is displayed in Output 9.14.

Output 9.14   ANOVA Table

```
        MAXIMUM-LIKELIHOOD ANALYSIS-OF-VARIANCE TABLE

     Source                DF    Chi-Square     Prob
     ----------------------------------------------------
     INTERCEPT              2       40.05       0.0000
     SCHOOL                4       14.55       0.0057
     PROGRAM               2       10.48       0.0053
     SCHOOL*PROGRAM        4        1.74       0.7827

     LIKELIHOOD RATIO      0         .           .
```

Since the model is saturated, with as many response functions being modeled as there are groups or subpopulations, the likelihood ratio test does not apply. PROC CATMOD prints missing values and 0 df when the model is saturated. The school $\times$ program interaction is nonsignificant, with a Wald chi-square of 1.74 with 4 df. Note that the degrees of freedom for modeling two generalized logits are twice what you would expect for modeling one logit: instead of 1 df for the intercept you have 2 df; instead of 2 df for SCHOOL, which has three levels, you have 4. This is because you are modeling two response functions instead of one; you are doubling the number of parameters being estimated since you have to estimate parameters for both logits. To determine the correct number of degrees of freedom for effects in models using generalized logits, multiply the number you would expect for modeling one logit (the usual logistic regression for a dichotomous outcome) by $r - 1$, where r is the number of response levels.

Since the interaction is nonsignificant, the main effects model is fit.

$$
\begin{bmatrix}
\text{logit}_{111} \\
\text{logit}_{112} \\
\text{logit}_{121} \\
\text{logit}_{122} \\
\text{logit}_{211} \\
\text{logit}_{212} \\
\text{logit}_{221} \\
\text{logit}_{222} \\
\text{logit}_{311} \\
\text{logit}_{312} \\
\text{logit}_{321} \\
\text{logit}_{322}
\end{bmatrix}
=
\begin{bmatrix}
1 & 0 & 1 & 0 & 0 & 0 & 1 & 0 \\
0 & 1 & 0 & 1 & 0 & 0 & 0 & 1 \\
1 & 0 & 1 & 0 & 0 & 0 & -1 & 0 \\
0 & 1 & 0 & 1 & 0 & 0 & 0 & -1 \\
1 & 0 & 0 & 0 & 1 & 0 & 1 & 0 \\
0 & 1 & 0 & 0 & 0 & 1 & 0 & 1 \\
1 & 0 & 0 & 0 & 1 & 0 & -1 & 0 \\
0 & 1 & 0 & 0 & 0 & 1 & 0 & -1 \\
1 & 0 & -1 & 0 & -1 & 0 & 1 & 0 \\
0 & 1 & 0 & -1 & 0 & -1 & 0 & 1 \\
1 & 0 & -1 & 0 & -1 & 0 & -1 & 0 \\
0 & 1 & 0 & -1 & 0 & -1 & 0 & -1
\end{bmatrix}
\begin{bmatrix}
\alpha_1 \\
\alpha_2 \\
\beta_1 \\
\beta_2 \\
\beta_3 \\
\beta_4 \\
\beta_5 \\
\beta_6
\end{bmatrix}
$$

Essentially, this model matrix has the same structure as one for modeling a single response function, except that it models two response functions. Thus, the odd rows are for the first logit, and the even rows are for the second logit. Similarly, the odd columns correspond to parameters for the first logit, and the even columns correspond to parameters for the second logit. Note that PROC CATMOD uses differential effects by default, as opposed to the incremental effects fit with PROC LOGISTIC for the proportional odds model discussed in the previous sections (see Section 8.8 for further discussion). See Table 9.7 for the interpretation of these parameters.

The following statements produce the main effects model.

```
proc catmod order=data;
    weight count;
    model style=school program;
run;
```

Output 9.15 contains the ANOVA table for the main effects model.

Output 9.15   ANOVA Table

```
        MAXIMUM-LIKELIHOOD ANALYSIS-OF-VARIANCE TABLE

    Source              DF      Chi-Square      Prob
    -------------------------------------------------
    INTERCEPT            2        39.88        0.0000
    SCHOOL               4        14.84        0.0050
    PROGRAM              2        10.92        0.0043

    LIKELIHOOD RATIO     4         1.78        0.7766
```

The likelihood ratio statistic has a value of 1.78 with 4 df, which is indicative of a good fit. The tests for the school and program effects are also significant; SCHOOL has a Wald chi-square value of 14.84 with 4 df, and PROGRAM has a Wald chi-square value of 10.92 with 2 df.

The parameter estimates and tests for individual parameters are displayed in Output 9.16. The order of these parameters corresponds to the order in which the response variable and explanatory variable levels are listed in the response profiles table and the population profiles table.

Output 9.16   Parameter Estimates

```
            ANALYSIS OF MAXIMUM-LIKELIHOOD ESTIMATES

                                   Standard   Chi-
Effect          Parameter  Estimate  Error   Square   Prob
------------------------------------------------------------
INTERCEPT           1      -0.7979   0.1465   29.65   0.0000
                    2      -0.6589   0.1367   23.23   0.0000
SCHOOL              3      -0.7992   0.2198   13.22   0.0003
                    4      -0.2786   0.1867    2.23   0.1356
                    5       0.2836   0.1899    2.23   0.1352
                    6      -0.0985   0.1892    0.27   0.6028
PROGRAM             7       0.3737   0.1410    7.03   0.0080
                    8       0.3713   0.1353    7.53   0.0061
```

For example, since the order of the response values is self, team, and class, Parameter 1 is the intercept for logit_{hi1} and Parameter 2 is the intercept for logit_{hi2}. For the SCHOOL effect, Parameter 3 is the parameter for School 1 for the first logit and Parameter 4 is the parameter for School 1 for the second logit. Parameters 5 and 6 are the corresponding parameters for School 2, and parameters 7 and 8 are the parameters for logit_{hi1} and logit_{hi2}, respectively, for the regular school program. If you go down the list of parameters in order, the response function varies most quickly, and the groups vary the same way that they vary in the population profiles table. Table 9.7 summarizes the correspondence between the PROC CATMOD numbered parameters in the output and the model parameters.

Table 9.7   Parameter Interpretations

CATMOD Parameter	Model Parameter	Interpretation
1	α_1	Intercept for logit_{hi1}
2	α_2	Intercept for logit_{hi2}
3	β_1	Differential Effect for School 1 for logit_{hi1}
4	β_2	Differential Effect for School 1 for logit_{hi2}
5	β_3	Differential Effect for School 2 for logit_{hi1}
6	β_4	Differential Effect for School 2 for logit_{hi2}
7	β_5	Differential Effect for Regular School for logit_{hi1}
8	β_6	Differential Effect for Regular School for logit_{hi2}

Table 9.8 contains the parameter estimates arranged according to the logits they reference. This is often a useful way to display the results from an analysis of generalized logits.

Table 9.8   Coefficients from Final Model

Variable	logit(self/class) Coefficient	Standard Error	logit(team/class) Coefficient	Standard Error
Intercept	-0.798 ($\hat{\alpha}_1$)	0.146	-0.659 ($\hat{\alpha}_2$)	0.137
School 1	-0.799 ($\hat{\beta}_1$)	0.220	-0.279 ($\hat{\beta}_2$)	0.187
School 2	0.284 ($\hat{\beta}_3$)	0.190	-0.099 ($\hat{\beta}_4$)	0.189
Program	0.374 ($\hat{\beta}_5$)	0.141	0.371 ($\hat{\beta}_6$)	0.135

School 1 has the largest effect of the schools, particularly for the logit comparing self to class. Program has a nearly similar effect on both logits.

Odds ratios can also be used in models for generalized logits to facilitate model interpretation. Table 9.9 contains the odds corresponding to each logit function for each subpopulation in the data. However, unlike the proportional odds model where the form of the odds ratio was the same regardless of the cumulative logit being considered, the formulas for the odds ratio for the generalized logits model depend on which generalized logit is being considered.

Table 9.9   Model-Predicted Odds

School	Program	Odds Self/Class	Team/Class
1	Regular	$e^{\alpha_1+\beta_1+\beta_5}$	$e^{\alpha_2+\beta_2+\beta_6}$
1	After	$e^{\alpha_1+\beta_1-\beta_5}$	$e^{\alpha_2-\beta_2-\beta_6}$
2	Regular	$e^{\alpha_1+\beta_3+\beta_5}$	$e^{\alpha_2+\beta_4+\beta_6}$
2	After	$e^{\alpha_1+\beta_3-\beta_5}$	$e^{\alpha_2+\beta_4-\beta_6}$
3	Regular	$e^{\alpha_1-\beta_1-\beta_3+\beta_5}$	$e^{\alpha_2-\beta_2-\beta_4+\beta_6}$
3	After	$e^{\alpha_1-\beta_1-\beta_3-\beta_5}$	$e^{\alpha_2-\beta_2-\beta_4-\beta_6}$

To determine the odds ratio of self to class for school program, you compute

$$\frac{e^{\alpha_1+\beta_1+\beta_5}}{e^{\alpha_1+\beta_1-\beta_5}} = e^{2\beta_5}$$

Thus, the odds were $e^{(2)(0.374)} = 2.11$ times higher of choosing the self-learning style over the class learning style if students attended the regular school program versus the after school program. If you work through the same exercise for the odds ratio of team to class, you find that the odds were $e^{(2)(0.371)} = 2.10$ times higher of choosing the team learning style as the class learning style if students attended the regular school program versus the after school program.

Comparing the odds ratio for School 1 to School 2 produces a slightly more complicated form for the odds ratio. You form the ratio of the odds for School 1, regular school program to School 2, regular school program (after school program would also work) to obtain (for self/class logit)

$$\frac{e^{\alpha_1+\beta_1+\beta_5}}{e^{\alpha_1+\beta_3+\beta_5}} = e^{\beta_1-\beta_3}$$

Thus, the subjects from School 1 were $e^{-0.799-0.284} = 0.33$ times as likely to choose the self-learning style over the class learning style as those students from School 2.

9.3.3 Activity Limitation Data Example

The data in Table 9.10 are derived from an analysis of activity limitation data that were obtained in the 1989 National Health Interview Study (Lafata, Koch, and Weissert 1994). Researchers were interested in generating estimates of activity limitation for the civilian population of the United States for small areas such as individual states. The original data included children, adults, and the elderly; a possible consequence of providing such estimates is better health care resources to assist such persons. The data in Table 9.10 are those corresponding to the older children's age groups.

The counts are weighted because the data were collected as part of a complex survey design and various sampling-related adjustments were performed. Normally, you would use methods that account for the sample design in your analysis of such data, such as those provided by SUDAAN Software (Shah, Barnwell, Hunt, and LaVange 1991); but for illustrative purposes, stratified simple random sampling is assumed here.

Since there is some kind of order to the levels of the response variable (major limitation is more than other limitation is more than no limitation), it may seem that activity limitation could be treated as an ordinal response. However, the necessary proportional odds assumption is not met by these data, so ordered regression is not a potential analysis strategy. Thus, analyzing the generalized logits is the strategy of choice.

The logits of interest are

$$\text{logit}_{hijk1} = \log\left[\frac{\pi_{hijk1}}{\pi_{hijk3}}\right], \quad \text{logit}_{hijk2} = \log\left[\frac{\pi_{hijk2}}{\pi_{hijk3}}\right]$$

where π_{hijk1} is the Pr{major limitation}, π_{hijk2} is the Pr{other limitation}, and π_{hijk3} is the Pr{no limitation} for the $hijk$th group ($h = 1$ for ages 10–14, $h = 2$ for ages 15–19; $i = 1$ for males and $i = 2$ for females; $j = 1$ for whites and $j = 2$ for other; $k = 1$ for low poverty, $k = 2$ for medium poverty, and $k = 3$ for high poverty). The logits are comparing major activity limitation to no activity limitation and other activity limitation to no activity limitation.

Table 9.10   Activity Limitation Study

				Activity Limitation		
Age	Sex	Race	Poverty	Major	Other	None
10–14	males	whites	low	5.361	1.329	102.228
10–14	males	whites	medium	20.565	13.952	336.160
10–14	males	whites	high	21.299	5.884	284.931
10–14	males	other	low	53.314	16.402	827.900
10–14	males	other	medium	102.076	36.551	1518.796
10–14	males	other	high	52.338	21.105	666.909
10–14	females	whites	low	1.172	1.199	87.292
10–14	females	whites	medium	11.169	2.945	304.234
10–14	females	whites	high	15.286	3.665	302.511
10–14	females	other	low	21.882	16.979	846.270
10–14	females	other	medium	52.354	33.106	1452.895
10–14	females	other	high	28.203	11.455	687.109
15–19	males	whites	low	0.915	1.711	91.071
15–19	males	whites	medium	12.591	8.066	326.930
15–19	males	whites	high	21.059	6.993	313.633
15–19	males	other	low	36.384	27.558	888.833
15–19	males	other	medium	85.974	42.755	1509.087
15–19	males	other	high	40.112	23.493	725.004
15–19	females	whites	low	5.876	2.550	115.968
15–19	females	whites	medium	8.772	6.922	344.076
15–19	females	whites	high	17.385	2.354	286.068
15–19	females	other	low	42.741	31.025	817.478
15–19	females	other	medium	72.688	35.979	1499.816
15–19	females	other	high	26.296	29.321	716.860

The first model fit is the model with all pairwise interactions. The following SAS statements input the data.

```
data survey;
   input age sex race poverty function $ count @@;
   cards;
1 0 0 0 major 5.361    1 0 0 0 other    1.329    1 0 0 0 not 102.228
1 0 0 1 major 20.565   1 0 0 1 other   13.952    1 0 0 1 not  336.160
1 0 0 2 major 21.299   1 0 0 2 other    5.884    1 0 0 2 not  284.931
1 0 1 0 major 53.314   1 0 1 0 other   16.402    1 0 1 0 not 827.900
1 0 1 1 major 102.076  1 0 1 1 other   36.551    1 0 1 1 not 1518.796
1 0 1 2 major 52.338   1 0 1 2 other   21.105    1 0 1 2 not 666.909
1 1 0 0 major 1.172    1 1 0 0 other    1.199    1 1 0 0 not  87.292
1 1 0 1 major 11.169   1 1 0 1 other    2.945    1 1 0 1 not 304.234
1 1 0 2 major 15.286   1 1 0 2 other    3.665    1 1 0 2 not 302.511
1 1 1 0 major 21.882   1 1 1 0 other   16.979    1 1 1 0 not 846.270
1 1 1 1 major 52.354   1 1 1 1 other   33.106    1 1 1 1 not 1452.895
1 1 1 2 major 28.203   1 1 1 2 other   11.455    1 1 1 2 not 687.109
2 0 0 0 major .915     2 0 0 0 other    1.711    2 0 0 0 not  91.071
2 0 0 1 major 12.591   2 0 0 1 other    8.026    2 0 0 1 not 326.930
2 0 0 2 major 21.059   2 0 0 2 other    6.993    2 0 0 2 not 313.633
```

```
2 0 1 0 major 36.384   2 0 1 0 other  27.558   2 0 1 0 not 888.833
2 0 1 1 major 85.974   2 0 1 1 other  42.755   2 0 1 1 not 1509.87
2 0 1 2 major 40.112   2 0 1 2 other  23.493   2 0 1 2 not 725.004
2 1 0 0 major  5.876   2 1 0 0 other   2.550   2 1 0 0 not 115.968
2 1 0 1 major  8.772   2 1 0 1 other   6.922   2 1 0 1 not 344.076
2 1 0 2 major 17.385   2 1 0 2 other   2.354   2 1 0 2 not 286.68
2 1 1 0 major 42.741   2 1 1 0 other  31.025   2 1 1 0 not 817.478
2 1 1 1 major 72.688   2 1 1 1 other  35.979   2 1 1 1 not 1499.816
2 1 1 2 major 26.296   2 1 1 2 other  29.321   2 1 1 2 not 716.860
;
run;
```

The following PROC CATMOD invocation requests the model with all pairwise interactions. Note the use of the @2 notation to request all pairwise interactions. The fact that the counts are not integers is not a problem for the CATMOD procedure; it accepts all counts that are nonnegative. It does not truncate the values.

```
proc catmod order=data;
   direct poverty;
   weight count;
   model function=age|sex|race|poverty@2;
run;
```

Output 9.17 contains the population profiles for these data. With two levels each for AGE, SEX, and RACE, and three categories for POVERTY, 24 groups are formed. The counts have been preserved in their noninteger form.

Output 9.17   Population Profiles

```
                  POPULATION PROFILES
                                         Sample
        Sample   AGE   SEX   RACE   POVERTY   Size
        ------------------------------------------------
           1      1     0     0       0      108.918
           2      1     0     0       1      370.677
           3      1     0     0       2      312.114
           4      1     0     1       0      897.616
           5      1     0     1       1     1657.423
           6      1     0     1       2      740.352
           7      1     1     0       0       89.663
           8      1     1     0       1      318.348
           9      1     1     0       2      321.462
          10      1     1     1       0      885.131
          11      1     1     1       1     1538.355
          12      1     1     1       2      726.767
          13      2     0     0       0       93.697
          14      2     0     0       1      347.547
          15      2     0     0       2      341.685
          16      2     0     1       0      952.775
          17      2     0     1       1     1638.599
          18      2     0     1       2      788.609
          19      2     1     0       0      124.394
          20      2     1     0       1      359.77
          21      2     1     0       2      306.419
          22      2     1     1       0      891.244
          23      2     1     1       1     1608.483
          24      2     1     1       2      772.477
```

Output 9.18 contains the response profiles. Since the ORDER=DATA option is specified, the values of FUNCTION are ordered internally as major, other, and none. This means that the desired generalized logit functions are formed, since PROC CATMOD forms the logit for the first level compared to the third level and the second level compared to the third level.

Output 9.18   Response Profiles

```
                RESPONSE PROFILES

        Response   FUNCTION
        ------------------
            1      major
            2      other
            3      none
```

The ANOVA table and likelihood ratio goodness-of-fit statistic are displayed in Output 9.19. $Q_L = 25.66$ with 26 df and $p = 0.4818$, which is supportive of model fit. Note the degrees of freedom associated with each of the effects in the table. Since AGE, SEX, and RACE would be associated with 1 df in the dichotomous outcome case, they are associated with 2 df since two logits are being modeled. Similarly, POVERTY is associated with 2 df, since it is entered on the DIRECT statement and its values are used directly in a column of the model matrix. If you have interactions, you determine their df by multiplying the df of each constituent effect that would be associated with a dichotomous outcome, then multiplying that by the number of functions being modeled.

A look at the p-values associated with these effects shows that the model could be simplified by eliminating terms.

Output 9.19   ANOVA Table

```
    MAXIMUM-LIKELIHOOD ANALYSIS-OF-VARIANCE TABLE

    Source          DF   Chi-Square    Prob
    ----------------------------------------------
    INTERCEPT        2     1518.29    0.0000
    AGE              2        1.21    0.5467
    SEX              2        2.89    0.2357
    AGE*SEX          2       14.72    0.0006
    RACE             2        4.53    0.1037
    AGE*RACE         2        1.27    0.5296
    SEX*RACE         2        4.00    0.1355
    POVERTY          2        8.95    0.0114
    POVERTY*AGE      2        0.72    0.6979
    POVERTY*SEX      2        1.53    0.4650
    POVERTY*RACE     2        5.52    0.0632

    LIKELIHOOD RATIO 26       25.66    0.4818
```

A reduced model is then fit, with only the AGE*SEX, SEX*RACE, and RACE*POVERTY interactions being retained.

```
proc catmod order=data;
    direct poverty;
    weight count;
```

```
    model function=age sex race poverty
       age*sex sex*race race*poverty;
  run;
```

The ANOVA table pertaining to this model is displayed in Output 9.20.

Output 9.20   ANOVA Table for Reduced Model

```
    MAXIMUM-LIKELIHOOD ANALYSIS-OF-VARIANCE TABLE

    Source              DF    Chi-Square     Prob
    ------------------------------------------------
    INTERCEPT            2       1527.92    0.0000
    AGE                  2          6.61    0.0367
    SEX                  2         18.47    0.0001
    RACE                 2          4.62    0.0991
    POVERTY              2          9.64    0.0081
    AGE*SEX              2         15.10    0.0005
    SEX*RACE             2          4.44    0.1088
    POVERTY*RACE         2          5.28    0.0713

    LIKELIHOOD RATIO    32         29.67    0.5848
```

Since the model has been reduced by 6 parameters, the df for the likelihood ratio test is increased by 10 df. However, since $Q_L = 29.67$ with 32 df, the reduced model has an adequate fit. The only further model reduction that seems warranted at this point is the removal of the SEX*RACE term. It would appear that RACE*POVERTY is marginally influential, and that may change once the SEX*RACE effect is removed.

```
proc catmod order=data;
    direct poverty;
    weight count;
    model function=age sex race poverty
       age*sex race*poverty /pred=freq;
  run;
```

Output 9.21 displays the results when the SEX*RACE term is removed.

Output 9.21   ANOVA Table for Final Reduced Model

```
    MAXIMUM-LIKELIHOOD ANALYSIS-OF-VARIANCE TABLE

    Source              DF    Chi-Square     Prob
    ------------------------------------------------
    INTERCEPT            2       1536.94    0.0000
    AGE                  2          6.51    0.0385
    SEX                  2         26.44    0.0000
    RACE                 2          4.71    0.0950
    POVERTY              2          9.59    0.0083
    AGE*SEX              2         15.09    0.0005
    POVERTY*RACE         2          5.22    0.0736

    LIKELIHOOD RATIO    34         34.27    0.4548
```

The goodness of fit is adequate for this model ($Q_L = 34.27$ with 34 df and $p = 0.4548$). Since RACE*POVERTY remains marginally influential, it is kept in the model. Thus, this model includes main effects for age, sex, race, and poverty, along with interactions for age and sex and poverty and race. You could compute odds ratios to aid in model interpretation.

The PRED=FREQ option in PROC CATMOD requests the computation of model-predicted frequencies for this model (you can also generate model-predicted probabilities with the PRED=PROB option). Output 9.22 contains a partial listing of these predicted frequencies from the PROC CATMOD output. Table 9.11 contains the complete set of predicted values. You can compare these to the original frequencies to see how well the model works.

Output 9.22   Partial Listing of Predicted Frequencies

```
        ML PREDICTED VALUES FOR RESPONSE FUNCTIONS AND FREQUENCIES

                    -----Observed-----    -----Predicted----
        Function              Standard              Standard
Sample  Number  Function      Error     Function    Error     Residual
-----------------------------------------------------------------------
   1       1    -2.94806    0.443074    -3.22367    0.216401   0.275611
           2    -4.34278    0.873056     -3.7639    0.280956   -0.57888

          F1       5.361    2.257682     4.07892    0.849289    1.28208
          F2       1.329    1.145768    2.376429    0.652845   -1.04743
          F3     102.228     2.50581    102.4627    1.055218   -0.23465

   2       1      -2.794    0.227159     -2.8465     0.11613   0.052508
           2    -3.18196     0.27322    -3.88864    0.165319   0.708679

          F1      20.565    4.407274    19.95014    2.191072   0.614855
          F2      13.952    3.664268    7.036412    1.140648   6.915588
          F3      336.16    5.594892    343.6904    2.433505   -7.53044

   3       1    -2.59359    0.224633    -2.46934    0.127302   -0.12424
           2    -3.88001    0.416488    -4.01339    0.220373   0.133377

          F1      21.299    4.454833    23.95679    2.814102   -2.65779
          F2       5.884    2.402722     5.11516    1.108229    0.76884
          F3     284.931     4.98152    283.0421    2.980315   1.888946

   4       1    -2.74269    0.141296    -2.74572    0.088292   0.003023
           2    -3.92149    0.249351    -3.67036    0.131124   -0.25113

          F1      53.314    7.081484    52.88666    4.391243   0.427342
          F2      16.402    4.012766    20.97862    2.684635   -4.57662
          F3       827.9    8.018809    823.7507    5.054315   4.149279

   5       1    -2.69996     0.10225    -2.67402    0.067223   -0.02593
           2    -3.72696    0.167384    -3.61625    0.106153   -0.11071

          F1     102.076    9.787207    104.3194    6.566059   -2.24344
          F2      36.551    5.978708    40.65949    4.206884   -4.10849
          F3    1518.796    11.27086    1512.444    7.647375   6.351926

   6       1    -2.54493    0.143548    -2.60233    0.089565   0.057401
           2    -3.45314    0.221092    -3.56214    0.133379   0.108992

          F1      52.338    6.974098    49.76105    4.154098   2.576947
          F2      21.105    4.528064    19.05689    2.474509   2.048109
          F3     666.909    8.133723    671.5341    4.731773   -4.62506
```

Table 9.11   Activity Limitation Study

Age	Sex	Race	Poverty	Predicted % Limitation		
				Major	Other	None
10-14	males	whites	low	4.0789	2.376	102.463
10-14	males	whites	medium	19.950	7.0364	343.690
10-14	males	whites	high	23.957	5.115	283.042
10-14	males	other	low	52.887	20.979	823.751
10-14	males	other	medium	104.319	40.659	1512.444
10-14	males	other	high	49.761	19.057	671.534
10-14	females	whites	low	1.774	1.481	86.408
10-14	females	whites	medium	9.117	4.610	304.621
10-14	females	whites	high	13.272	4.063	304.127
10-14	females	other	low	27.854	15.839	841.438
10-14	females	other	medium	51.835	28.963	1457.557
10-14	females	other	high	26.215	14.393	686.159
15-19	males	whites	low	2.635	2.315	88.747
15-19	males	whites	medium	14.109	7.505	325.933
15-19	males	whites	high	19.907	6.410	315.368
15-19	males	other	low	42.376	25.351	885.048
15-19	males	other	medium	77.923	45.803	1514.873
15-19	males	other	high	40.085	23.152	725.372
15-19	females	whites	low	3.170	3.0737	118.15
15-19	females	whites	medium	13.254	7.779	338.738
15-19	females	whites	high	16.227	5.766	284.426
15-19	females	other	low	35.984	23.753	831.508
15-19	females	other	medium	69.457	45.050	1493.976
15-19	females	other	high	35.666	22.730	714.081

Chapter 10
Conditional Logistic Regression

Chapter Table of Contents

Chapter 10
Conditional Logistic Regression

10.1   Introduction

Sometimes, the usual maximum likelihood approach to estimation in logistic regression is not appropriate. As discussed in Chapter 8, "Logistic Regression I: Dichotomous Response," there may be insufficient sample size for logistic regression, particularly if the data are highly stratified and there are a small number of subjects in each stratum. In these situations, you have a small sample size relative to the number of parameters being estimated since you will be estimating parameters for the stratification effects. For the maximum likelihood estimates to be valid, you need a large sample size relative to the number of parameters.

Often, highly stratified data come from a design with cluster sampling, that is, designs with two or more observations for each primary sampling unit or cluster. Common examples of such data are paired observations, such as fraternal twins (or litter mates), right and left sides of the body in a dermatology study, or two occasions for an expression of an opinion. Ordinary logistic regression may be inappropriate for such data, since you have insufficient sample size to estimate the pair effect (family, litter, patient, respondent) without bias. However, by using conditioning arguments, you can eliminate the pair effect and estimate the other effects in which you are interested.

Matched case control studies in epidemiology also produce highly stratified data. In these studies, you match cases (those persons with a disease or condition) to controls (those persons without the disease or condition) on the basis of variables thought to be potential confounders such as age, race, and sex. Other types of matching are by neighborhoods and families.

- In a 1:1 matched study, the matched set consists of one case and one control from each stratum. This is the most common situation.

- In a 1:m matched study, the matched set consists of one case and m controls. Usually, m ranges between 2 and 5.

- In the m:n matched study, the matched set consists of n cases with m controls, where usually both m and n are between 1 and 5.

The appropriate form of logistic regression for these types of data is called *conditional logistic regression*. It takes the stratification into account by basing the maximum likelihood estimation of the model parameters on a conditional likelihood. In the following sections, the conditional likelihood for paired observations from small clusters is derived, and the methodology is illustrated for a randomized clinical trial and a crossover design study using the LOGISTIC procedure. Next, the conditional likelihood for the 1:1 matched study is discussed, along with an example using both the LOGISTIC procedure and the PHREG procedure. Finally, data from a 1:m matched study are analyzed with the PHREG procedure.

10.2   Paired Observations from a Highly Stratified Cohort Study

Consider a randomized clinical trial where $i = 1, 2, \ldots, q$ centers are randomly selected, and, at each center, one randomly selected patient is placed on treatment, and another randomly selected patient is placed on placebo. Interest lies in whether the patients improve; thus, improvement is the event of interest. Since there are only two observations per center, it is not possible to estimate a center effect (pair effect) without bias. As a general rule, you need each possible outcome to have five observations per explanatory variable in the model for valid estimation to proceed.

Suppose $y_{ij} = 1$ for the event and $y_{ij} = 0$ for not having the event ($j = 1$ for treatment and $j = 2$ for the placebo; $i = 1, 2, \ldots, q$). Suppose $x_{ij} = 1$ for treatment and $x_{ij} = 0$ for placebo, and $\mathbf{z}_{ij} = (z_{ij1}, z_{ij2}, \ldots, z_{ijt})'$ represents the t explanatory variables.

The usual logistic likelihood for $\{y_{ij}\}$ is written

$$\Pr\{y_{ij}\} = \pi_{ij} = \frac{\exp\{\alpha_i + \beta x_{ij} + \boldsymbol{\gamma}' \mathbf{z}_{ij}\}}{1 + \exp\{\alpha_i + \beta x_{ij} + \boldsymbol{\gamma}' \mathbf{z}_{ij}\}}$$

where α_i is the effect of the ith center, β is the treatment parameter, and $\boldsymbol{\gamma}' = (\gamma_1, \gamma_2, \ldots, \gamma_t)$ is the parameter vector for the covariates $\mathbf{z}$. Since there are only two observations per center, you can't estimate the α_i without bias. However, you can fit a model based on conditional probabilities that condition away the center effects and thus results in a model that contains substantially fewer parameters. In this context, the α_i are known as *nuisance parameters*. It is of interest to describe these data with a model that considers the probability of a pair's treatment patient improving and the pair's placebo patient not improving, compared to the probability that one of them improved.

You can write a conditional probability for $\{y_{ij}\}$ as the ratio of the joint probability of a pair's treatment patient having the event and the pair's placebo patient not having the event to the joint probability that either the treatment patient or the placebo patient has the event.

$$\Pr\left\{y_{i1}{=}1, y_{i2}{=}0 \middle| y_{i1}{=}1, y_{i2}{=}0 \text{ or } y_{i1}{=}0, y_{i2}{=}1\right\} =$$

$$\frac{\Pr\{y_{i1}{=}1\}\Pr\{y_{i2}{=}0\}}{\Pr\{y_{i1}{=}1\}\Pr\{y_{i2}{=}0\} + \Pr\{y_{i1}{=}0\}\Pr\{y_{i2}{=}1\}}$$

If you write the probabilities in terms of the logistic model,

$$\Pr\{y_{i1}{=}1\}\Pr\{y_{i2}{=}0\} = \frac{\exp\{\alpha_i + \beta + \gamma'\mathbf{z}_{i1}\}}{1 + \exp\{\alpha_i + \beta + \gamma'\mathbf{z}_{i1}\}} \cdot \frac{1}{1 + \exp\{\alpha_i + \gamma'\mathbf{z}_{i2}\}}$$

and

$$\Pr\{y_{i1}{=}1\}\Pr\{y_{i2}{=}0\} + \Pr\{y_{i1}{=}0\}\Pr\{y_{i2}{=}1\} =$$

$$\frac{\exp\{\alpha_i + \beta + \gamma'\mathbf{z}_{i1}\}}{1 + \exp\{\alpha_i + \beta + \gamma'\mathbf{z}_{i1}\}} \cdot \frac{1}{1 + \exp\{\alpha_i + \gamma'\mathbf{z}_{i2}\}} + \frac{1}{1 + \exp\{\alpha_i + \beta + \gamma'\mathbf{z}_{i1}\}} \cdot \frac{\exp\{\alpha_i + \gamma'\mathbf{z}_{i2}\}}{1 + \exp\{\alpha_i + \gamma'\mathbf{z}_{i2}\}}$$

If you form their ratio, you obtain

$$\frac{\exp\{\alpha_i + \beta + \gamma'\mathbf{z}_{i1}\}}{\exp\{\alpha_i + \beta + \gamma'\mathbf{z}_{i1}\} + \exp\{\alpha_i + \gamma'\mathbf{z}_{i2}\}}$$

since the denominators cancel out. This expression reduces to

$$\frac{\exp\{\beta + \gamma'(\mathbf{z}_{i1} - \mathbf{z}_{i2})\}}{1 + \exp\{\beta + \gamma'(\mathbf{z}_{i1} - \mathbf{z}_{i2})\}}$$

which no longer contains the α_i. Thus, by focusing on modeling a meaningful conditional probability, you can develop a model with a number of parameters that can be estimated without bias.

The conditional likelihood for the entire data is written

$$\prod_{i=1}^{q} \frac{\exp\{\beta + \gamma'(\mathbf{z}_{i1} - \mathbf{z}_{i2})\}}{1 + \exp\{\beta + \gamma'(\mathbf{z}_{i1} - \mathbf{z}_{i2})\}}$$

This is the unconditional likelihood for the usual logistic model, except that the intercept is now β, the effect for treatment, and each observation represents a pair of observations from a center where the response is 1 if the pair represents the combination $\{y_{i1}{=}1$ and $y_{i2}{=}0\}$ and 0 if the pair has the combination $\{y_{i1}{=}0$ and $y_{i2}{=}1\}$. The explanatory variables are the differences in values of the explanatory variables for the treatment patient and the placebo patient. Since the likelihood conditioned on the discordant pairs, the concordant pairs (the observations where $\{y_{i1}{=}1$ and $y_{i2}{=}1\}$ and $\{y_{i1}{=}0$ and $y_{i2}{=}0\}$) are noninformative and thus can be ignored.

If there are no covariates for such a study, so that the data represent a 2×2 table where the responses for treatment are crossclassified with the responses for placebo, then testing $\beta = 0$ is equivalent to McNemar's test. Also, it can be shown that e^{β} is estimated by n_{12}/n_{21}, where n_{12} and n_{21} are the off-diagonal counts from this table.

10.2.1   Clinical Trials Study Analysis

Researchers studying the effect of a new treatment on a skin condition collected
information from 79 clinics. In each clinic, one patient received the treatment, and another
patient received a placebo. Variables collected included age, sex, and an initial grade for
the skin condition, which ranged from 1 to 4 for mild to severe. The response variable was
whether the skin condition improved. Using conditional logistic regression is suitable for
the analysis of such data.

Each data line in the following input data includes two observations from each clinic: one
for the patient receiving the treatment and one for the patient receiving the placebo. The
DATA step creates indicator variables for sex and treatment and then creates the desired
interaction terms. These include treatment $\times$ sex, treatment $\times$ initial score, treatment $\times$
age, sex $\times$ age, sex $\times$ initial score, and age $\times$ initial score effects. Then, it combines the
paired observations and creates variables whose values are the differences in their
respective values. Note that all the interaction terms are computed before the observations
are combined. Since observations where the response variable IMPROVE had the same
value for both treatment and placebo do not affect the analysis, only those observations
with discordant responses are output to the data set TRIAL.

```
data trial;
   drop center1 i_sex1 age1 initial1 improve1 trtsex1 trtinit1
        trtage1 isexage1 isexint1 iageint1;
   retain center1 i_sex1 age1 initial1 improve1 trtsex1 trtinit1
          trtage1 isexage1 isexint1 iageint1 0;
   input center treat $ sex $ age improve initial @@;
   /* compute model terms for each observation */
   i_sex=(sex='m');        i_trt=(treat='t');
   trtsex=i_sex*i_trt;     trtinit=i_trt*initial;
   trtage=i_trt*age;       isexage=i_sex*age;
   isexinit=i_sex*initial;iageinit=age*initial;
   /* compute differences for paired observations */
   if (center=center1) then do;
      pair=10*improve + improve1;
         i_sex=i_sex1-i_sex;
         age=age1-age;
         initial=initial1-initial;
         trtsex=trtsex1-trtsex;
         trtinit=trtinit1-trtinit;
         trtage=trtage1-trtage;
         isexage=isexage1-isexage;
         isexint=isexint1-isexinit;
         iageinit=iageint1-iageinit;
         if (pair=10 or pair=1) then do;
                 /* output discordant pair observations */
               improve=(pair=1); output trial; end;
      end;
   else do;
       center1=center; age1=age;
       initial1=initial; i_sex1=i_sex; improve1=improve;
       trtsex1=trtsex; trtinit1=trtinit; trtage1=trtage;
       isexage1=isexage; isexint1=isexinit; iageint1=iageinit;
       end;
```

```
    cards;
 1   t f 27 0 1    1 p f 32 0 2
 2   t f 41 1 3    2 p f 47 0 1
 3   t m 19 1 4    3 p m 31 0 4
 4   t m 55 1 1    4 p m 24 1 3
 5   t f 51 1 4    5 p f 44 0 2
 6   t m 23 0 1    6 p f 44 1 3
 7   t m 31 1 2    7 p f 39 0 2
 8   t m 22 0 1    8 p m 54 1 4
 9   t m 37 1 3    9 p m 63 0 2
10   t m 33 0 3   10 p f 43 0 3
11   t f 32 1 1   11 p m 33 0 3
12   t m 47 1 4   12 p m 24 0 4
13   t m 55 1 3   13 p f 38 1 1
14   t f 33 0 1   14 p f 28 1 2
15   t f 48 1 1   15 p f 42 0 1
16   t m 55 1 3   16 p m 52 0 1
17   t m 30 0 4   17 p m 48 1 4
18   t f 31 1 2   18 p m 27 1 3
19   t m 66 1 3   19 p f 54 0 1
20   t f 45 0 2   20 p f 66 1 2
21   t m 19 1 4   21 p f 20 1 4
22   t m 34 1 4   22 p f 31 0 1
23   t f 46 0 1   23 p m 30 1 2
24   t m 48 1 3   24 p f 62 0 4
25   t m 50 1 4   25 p m 45 1 4
26   t m 57 1 3   26 p f 43 0 3
27   t f 13 0 2   27 p m 22 1 3
28   t m 31 1 1   28 p f 21 0 1
29   t m 35 1 3   29 p m 35 1 3
30   t f 36 1 3   30 p f 37 0 3
31   t f 45 0 1   31 p f 41 1 1
32   t m 13 1 2   32 p m 42 0 1
33   t m 14 0 4   33 p f 22 1 2
34   t f 15 1 2   34 p m 24 0 1
35   t f 19 1 3   35 p f 31 0 1
36   t m 20 0 2   36 p m 32 1 3
37   t m 23 1 3   37 p f 35 0 1
38   t f 23 0 1   38 p m 21 1 1
39   t m 24 1 4   39 p m 30 1 3
40   t m 57 1 3   40 p f 43 1 3
41   t f 13 1 2   41 p m 22 0 3
42   t m 31 1 1   42 p f 21 1 3
43   t f 19 1 3   43 p m 35 1 3
44   t m 31 1 3   44 p f 37 0 2
45   t f 44 0 1   45 p f 41 1 1
46   t m 41 1 2   46 p m 41 0 1
47   t m 41 1 2   47 p f 21 0 4
48   t f 51 1 2   48 p m 22 1 1
49   t f 62 1 3   49 p f 32 0 3
50   t m 21 0 1   50 p m 34 0 1
51   t m 55 1 3   51 p f 35 1 2
52   t f 61 0 1   52 p m 19 0 1
53   t m 43 1 2   53 p m 31 0 2
```

```
54 t f 44 1 1 54 p f 41 1 1
55 t m 67 1 2 55 p m 41 0 1
56 t m 41 0 2 56 p m 21 1 4
57 t f 51 1 3 57 p m 51 0 2
58 t m 62 1 3 58 p m 54 1 3
59 t m 22 0 1 59 p f 22 0 1
60 t m 42 1 2 60 p f 29 1 2
61 t f 51 1 1 61 p f 31 0 1
62 t m 27 0 2 62 p m 32 1 2
63 t m 31 1 1 63 p f 21 0 1
64 t m 35 0 3 64 p m 33 1 3
65 t m 67 1 2 65 p m 19 0 1
66 t m 41 0 2 66 p m 62 1 4
67 t f 31 1 2 67 p m 45 1 3
68 t m 34 1 1 68 p f 54 0 1
69 t f 21 0 1 69 p m 34 1 4
70 t m 64 1 3 70 p m 51 0 1
71 t f 61 1 3 71 p m 34 1 3
72 t m 33 0 1 72 p f 43 0 1
73 t f 36 0 2 73 p m 37 0 3
74 t m 21 1 1 74 p m 55 0 1
75 t f 47 0 2 75 p f 42 1 3
76 t f 51 1 4 76 p m 44 0 2
77 t f 23 1 1 77 p m 41 1 3
78 t m 31 0 2 78 p f 23 1 4
79 t m 22 0 1 79 p m 19 1 4
;
```

The following PROC LOGISTIC invocation requests forward selection, forcing all the
main effects in the model with the INCLUDE=3 option and making all interaction terms
available for consideration.

```
proc logistic data=trial descending;
    model improve = initial age i_sex
        isexage isexinit iageinit
        trtsex trtinit trtage /
        selection=forward include=3 details;
run;
```

The response profiles indicate that 34 pairs of observations had the (1,0) profile (treatment
improved, placebo did not) and 20 pairs had the (0,1) profile (treatment didn't improve,
placebo did).

Output 10.1   Response Profiles

Response Profile		
Ordered Value	IMPROVE	Count
1	1	34
2	0	20

Output 10.2 shows the residual score statistic ($Q_{RS} = 4.9937$ with 6 df and $p = 0.5446$) as well as the score statistics for the addition of the individual terms into the model. Since there are 20 observations with the less prevalent response, this model can support about $20/5 = 4$ terms. Thus, there are possibly too many terms to rely entirely on the residual score statistic to assess goodness of fit. However, considering the residual test as well as the individual tests provides reasonable confidence that the model fits adequately. All of the individual tests have p values greater than 0.08, and most of them have p-values greater than 0.5. This model doesn't require the addition of any interaction terms. (Note that you could have assessed goodness of fit by taking the difference of -2 LOG L for this model and for one that included all the interaction terms.)

Output 10.2   Score Statistics

```
        Residual Chi-Square = 4.9937 with 6 DF (p=0.5446)

            Analysis of Variables Not in the Model

                              Score          Pr >
            Variable       Chi-Square     Chi-Square

            ISEXAGE          0.6593         0.4168
            ISEXINIT         0.0074         0.9312
            IAGEINIT         2.9195         0.0875
            TRTSEX           0.2681         0.6046
            TRTINIT          0.0121         0.9125
            TRTAGE           0.4336         0.5102
```

Output 10.3 contains the maximum likelihood estimates of the parameters. Recall that, in this model, the treatment effect is represented by the intercept. It takes the value 0.7025, which is nearly significant with $p = 0.0511$. Neither age nor sex appear to be very influential but are left in the model as covariates. The effect for initial score is highly significant ($p = 0.0011$).

Output 10.3   Maximum Likelihood Estimates

```
            Analysis of Maximum Likelihood Estimates

            Parameter Standard     Wald      Pr >     Standardized   Odds
   Variable DF Estimate  Error  Chi-Square Chi-Square   Estimate    Ratio

   INTERCPT 1   0.7025  0.3601   3.8054    0.0511         .           .
   INITIAL  1   1.0915  0.3351  10.6109    0.0011      0.870834    2.979
   AGE      1   0.0248  0.0224   1.2253    0.2683      0.223839    1.025
   I_SEX    1   0.5312  0.5545   0.9176    0.3381      0.190972    1.701
```

Note that the LOGISTIC procedure does not print the odds ratio for the INTERCEPT, as usually it is of no interest. However, since the intercept represents the treatment effect in this model, it is appropriate to determine the odds ratio. The odds of improving for those patients receiving the treatment is $e^{0.7025} = 2.019$ times higher than for those patients receiving the placebo. The odds of improvement also increase by a factor of 2.979 for each unit increase in the initial grade. Thus, even adjusting for the effect of initial grade, treatment has a nearly significant effect. And, performing this stratified analysis has taken into account the effect of center.

Consider the model where the intercept is the only term.

```
proc logistic data=trial descending;
   model improve =;
run;
```

Output 10.4 contains the parameter estimates.

```
            Analysis of Maximum Likelihood Estimates


            Parameter Standard    Wald      Pr >    Standardized
  Variable DF Estimate  Error  Chi-Square Chi-Square  Estimate

  INTERCPT 1   0.5306  0.2818    3.5457    0.0597          .
```

Note that $e^\beta = e^{0.5306} = 1.70$. In addition, the Wald test for the intercept takes the value 3.5457 with $p = 0.0597$, which is nearly significant.

Table 10.1 displays the crosstabulation of pairs by treatment and response.

Table 10.1   Pairs Breakdown

	Improvement	
Treatment	No	Yes
No	7	34
Yes	20	18

Thus, McNemar's test statistic is computed as

$$\frac{(34-20)^2}{(34+20)} = 3.63$$

which is also nearly significant. As the sample size grows, the Wald statistic for the intercept and McNemar's test statistic become asymptotically equivalent. In addition, note that $n_{12}/n_{21} = 1.7$, which is the same as $e^{\hat\beta} = e^{0.5306}$.

10.2.2   Crossover Design Study

Another application for conditional logistic regression for paired data is the *crossover design study*, also called the *changeover study*. In these designs, often used in clinical trials, the study is divided into periods and patients receive a different treatment during each period. Thus, the patients act as their own controls. Interest lies in comparing the efficacy of the treatments, adjusting for period effects and carryover effects.

Table 10.2 contains data from a two-period crossover design clinical trial (Koch et al. 1977). Patients were stratified according to two age groups and then assigned to one of three treatment sequences. Responses were measured as favorable (F) or unfavorable (U); thus, (FF) indicates a favorable response in both Period 1 and Period 2.

Table 10.2   Two Period Crossover Study

Age	Sequence	Response Profiles				Total
		FF	FU	UF	UU	
older	A:B	12	12	6	20	50
older	B:P	8	5	6	31	50
older	P:A	5	3	22	20	50
younger	B:A	19	3	25	3	50
younger	A:P	25	6	6	13	50
younger	P:B	13	5	21	11	50

Sequence A:B means that Drug A was administered during the first period and Drug B was administered during the second period. P indicates Placebo. There are six possible sequences over the two age groups; each sequence occurs once.

These data can be considered paired data in the sense that there is a response for both Period 1 and Period 2. One strategy for analyzing these data is to model the probability of improvement for each patient in the first period (and not the second) versus the probability of improvement in either the first or second period. This can be expressed as the conditional probability

$$\frac{\Pr\{Period1=F\} \; \Pr\{Period2=U\}}{\Pr\{Period1=F\} \; \Pr\{Period2=U\} + \Pr\{Period1=U\} \; \Pr\{Period2=F\}}$$

Thus, the analysis strategy can proceed in the same manner as for the highly stratified paired data discussed above. In that example, the analysis adjusted out center-to-center variability (intercenter variability) and concentrated on intracenter variability. In this example, you are conditioning away, or adjusting out, patient to patient variability (interpatient variability) and concentrating on intrapatient information. This allows you to perform analyses that may not be possible with population-averaging methods (such as ordinary logistic regression) because of small sample size, although the resulting strategy may not be as efficient. These conditioning methods also lead to results with different interpretation; for example, the resulting odds ratios apply to each patient individually in the study rather than to patients on average.

The effects of interest are the period effect, effects for drugs A and B, and a carryover effect for drugs A and B from Period 1 to Period 2. Table 10.3 and Table 10.4 display the effects for Period 1 and Period 2, using incremental effects parameterization.

Table 10.3   Period 1 Data

Age	Treatment	Period1	Period × Age	Drug A	Drug B	CarryA	CarryB
older	A	1	1	1	0	0	0
older	B	1	1	0	1	0	0
older	P	1	1	0	0	0	0
younger	B	1	0	0	1	0	0
younger	A	1	0	1	0	0	0
younger	P	1	0	0	0	0	0

Table 10.4   Period 2 Data

Age	Treatment	Period1	Period × Age	Drug A	Drug B	CarryA	CarryB
older	B	0	0	0	1	1	0
older	P	0	0	0	0	0	1
older	A	0	0	1	0	0	0
younger	A	0	0	1	0	0	1
younger	P	0	0	0	0	1	0
younger	B	0	0	0	1	0	0

To fit the paired observations paradigm, you subtract the values for the variables for Period 1 and Period 2. Recall that the effect that distinguishes the paired observations, the period effect in this case, is represented by the intercept in this model. Table 10.5 displays the results. It includes the counts for FU and UF, since they are the informative response profiles in this model, as well as the values of the difference variables for the effects for period, drug effects, and carryover.

Table 10.5   Two Period Crossover Study

Age	Sequence	Response Profiles		Drug A	Drug B	CarryA	CarryB	Period × Age
		FU	UF					
older	A:B	12	6	1	−1	−1	0	1
older	B:P	5	6	0	1	0	−1	1
older	P:A	3	22	−1	0	0	0	1
younger	B:A	3	25	−1	1	0	−1	0
younger	A:P	6	6	1	0	−1	0	0
younger	P:B	5	21	0	−1	0	0	0

Note that there are six response functions, logits based on FU, and thus six degrees of freedom with which to work. If you include the two effects for drugs A and B, the age × period effect, and the period effect, then there are two degrees of freedom left over. These can be used to explore the carryover effects or the age × drug effects. The two degree-of-freedom tests for both sets of effects are identical.

The model employed includes the carryover effects. You can write this model as

$$\Pr\{FU|FU \text{ or } UF\} = \frac{\exp\{\beta + \tau'z\}}{1 + \exp\{\beta + \tau'z\}}$$

where z consists of the difference values for period $\times$ age, Drug A, Drug B, CarryA, and CarryB. The parameter β is the effect for period, τ_0 is the effect for period $\times$ age, τ_1 and τ_2 are the effects for Drug A and Drug B, respectively, and τ_3 and τ_4 are the effects for CarryA and CarryB, respectively.

The following DATA step inputs the values of Table 10.5. The variable OUTCOME contains the response profile; the profile FU will be modeled by default.

```
data cross;
    input outcome $ per_age DrugA DrugB CarryA CarryB count;
    cards;
FU 1  1 -1 -1  0 12
UF 1  1 -1 -1  0  6
FU 1  0  1  0 -1  5
UF 1  0  1  0 -1  6
FU 1 -1  0  0  0  3
UF 1 -1  0  0  0 22
FU 0 -1  1  0 -1  3
UF 0 -1  1  0 -1 25
FU 0  1  0 -1  0  6
UF 0  1  0 -1  0  6
FU 0  0 -1  0  0  5
UF 0  0 -1  0  0 21
;
proc logistic;
    freq count;
    model outcome=per_age DrugA DrugB CarryA CarryB;
run;
```

The response profiles displayed in Output 10.5 show that 34 patients had the (FU) profile, and 86 patients had the (UF) profile.

Output 10.5   Response Profiles

```
                        Response Profile

               Ordered
                 Value    OUTCOME        Count

                    1     FU               34
                    2     UF               86
```

Output 10.6 displays the log likelihood statistic. Since the model is a saturated one, goodness-of-fit statistics take the value zero and thus were not specified.

Output 10.6   Joint Tests

```
               Testing Global Null Hypothesis: BETA=0

                                 Intercept
                    Intercept       and
Criterion             Only       Covariates   Chi-Square for Covariates

AIC                 145.058       129.579           .
SC                  147.845       146.304           .
-2 LOG L            143.058       117.579       25.479 with 5 DF (p=0.0001)
Score                  .             .          26.014 with 5 DF (p=0.0001)
```

The table of maximum likelihood estimates in Output 10.7 indicates that neither carryover effect is influential. There appears to be a significant period effect and a significant Drug A effect.

Output 10.7   Maximum Likelihood Estimates for Reduced Model

```
             Analysis of Maximum Likelihood Estimates

             Parameter Standard    Wald        Pr >     Standardized
  Variable DF Estimate  Error   Chi-Square  Chi-Square    Estimate

  INTERCPT 1  -1.4370   0.7026    4.1832      0.0408          .
  PER_AGE  1   0.6912   0.4654    2.2056      0.1375       0.190392
  DRUGA    1   1.2467   0.6807    3.3547      0.0670       0.558580
  DRUGB    1  -0.00190  0.6412    0.0000      0.9976      -0.000873
  CARRYA   1  -0.1903   1.1125    0.0293      0.8642      -0.045619
  CARRYB   1  -0.5653   1.1556    0.2393      0.6247      -0.146592
```

The reduced model that excludes the carryover effects is fit next. Since the period × age effect is modestly suggestive, it is kept in the model. The following PROC LOGISTIC invocation fits this model and includes a request for goodness-of-fit statistics with the SCALE=NONE and AGGREGATE=(DrugA DrugB) options so that goodness-of-fit statistics are based on the six groups determined by the six drug sequences. It also includes a test for whether Drug A and Drug B have similar effects.

```
proc logistic;
   freq count;
   model outcome=per_age DrugA DrugB /
   scale=none aggregate=(DrugA DrugB);
   ab: test DrugA - DrugB =0;
run;
```

Output 10.8 displays model assessment statistics. $Q_P = 0.2459$ ($p = 0.8843$) indicates a satisfactory goodness of fit. In addition, if you take the difference in -2 LOG L for the full and reduced models, $25.479 - 25.232 = 0.247$, you get the log likelihood ratio test for the carryover effects. Since $Q_L = 0.247$ with 2 df, this test is nonsignificant. (If you fit the model with age and drug interactions and perform a similar model reduction, this test would have the same value.)

Output 10.8   Model Assessment Statistics

```
           Deviance and Pearson Goodness-of-Fit Statistics

                                                    Pr >
      Criterion        DF     Value    Value/DF   Chi-Square

      Deviance          2     0.2465    0.1232      0.8840
      Pearson           2     0.2459    0.1230      0.8843

                 Number of unique profiles: 6

            Testing Global Null Hypothesis: BETA=0

                            Intercept
                 Intercept      and
   Criterion       Only      Covariates   Chi-Square for Covariates

   AIC            145.058     125.826           .
   SC             147.845     136.976           .
   -2 LOG L       143.058     117.826       25.232 with 3 DF (p=0.0001)
   Score             .           .          25.369 with 3 DF (p=0.0001)
```

The maximum likelihood estimates are displayed in Output 10.9. The period effect remains clearly significant ($Q_W = 12.9542$, $p = 0.0003$). Drug A appears to be strongly significant relative to placebo, while Drug B appears to be nonsignificant.

Output 10.9   Maximum Likelihood Estimates

```
            Analysis of Maximum Likelihood Estimates

              Parameter Standard    Wald       Pr >    Standardized
   Variable DF Estimate   Error  Chi-Square Chi-Square   Estimate

   INTERCPT 1  -1.1905   0.3308   12.9542     0.0003        .
   PER_AGE  1   0.7102   0.4576    2.4089     0.1206     0.195604
   DRUGA    1   1.3462   0.3289   16.7505     0.0001     0.603174
   DRUGB    1   0.2662   0.3233    0.6777     0.4104     0.122408
```

The period × age effect is still suggestive. Whether you remove this effect from the model depends on your approach to the analysis. If you think of the study as two separate studies of older and younger people, then you probably will want to keep this effect in the model. If your general structural purpose did not include the distinction of older and younger groups, then you will probably want to remove this effect.

Output 10.10 contains the results of the test comparing the Drug B effect and the Drug A effect. The test is clearly significant; the drugs have different effects.

Output 10.10   Drug A versus Drug B

```
             Linear Hypotheses Testing

                        Wald                Pr >
       Label         Chi-Square    DF     Chi-Square

        AB            10.9228       1       0.0009
```

10.3   Paired Observations in a Retrospective Matched Study

In a retrospective study, a person known to have the event of interest (case) is paired, or matched, with a person that doesn't have the event (control). Then, data are collected to determine whether the case and control were exposed to certain risk factors, as measured by the explanatory variables. Through the use of a conditional likelihood, you can define a model that allows you to predict the event given the explanatory variables. This involves setting up the probabilities for having the exposure given the event and then using Bayes theorem to determine a relevant conditional probability concerning the event.

Suppose that you have q matched pairs, $h = 1, 2, \ldots, q$, and θ_{hi} is the probability of the ith subject in the hth matched pair having the event ($i = 1, 2$). Suppose that x_{hi} represents the set of explanatory variables for the ith subject in the hth matched pair.

You derive the conditional likelihood by first focusing on the conditional probability of observing the explanatory variables given the outcome (event or not). The likelihood for the vector of explanatory variables being x_{h1} given that subject $h1$ is the case (e) and being x_{h2} given that subject $h2$ is the control ($\bar{e}$) is

$$\Pr\{x_{h1}|e\} \Pr\{x_{h2}|\bar{e}\}$$

The sum of this likelihood and that for its reverse counterpart, the likelihood for the vector of explanatory variables being x_{h1} given the control and being x_{h2} given the case, is

$$\Pr\{x_{h1}|e\} \Pr\{x_{h2}|\bar{e}\} + \Pr\{x_{h1}|\bar{e}\} \Pr\{x_{h2}|e\}$$

and thus the conditional likelihood for a particular matched pair having the observed pairing of explanatory variables x_{h1} with the case e and the explanatory variables x_{h2} with the control $\bar{e}$ is

$$\frac{\Pr\{x_{h1}|e\} \Pr\{x_{h2}|\bar{e}\}}{\Pr\{x_{h1}|e\} \Pr\{x_{h2}|\bar{e}\} + \Pr\{x_{h1}|\bar{e}\} \Pr\{x_{h2}|e\}}$$

Applying Bayes Theorem, $(P(A|B) = P(B|A)P(A)/P(B))$, to each of these six terms, you can rewrite the preceding as

$$\frac{\Pr\{e|x_{h1}\} \Pr\{\bar{e}|x_{h2}\}}{\Pr\{e|x_{h1}\} \Pr\{\bar{e}|x_{h2}\} + \Pr\{\bar{e}|x_{h1}\} \Pr\{e|x_{h2}\}}$$

Thus, the conditional probabilities have been reversed so that they are the probabilities of the event given the explanatory variables.

If you assume a logistic model for θ_{hi}, the probability of the ith subject in the hth matched pair having the event, then you can make the appropriate substitutions into the conditional likelihood. The following is the logistic model for θ_{hi}.

$$\theta_{hi} = \frac{\exp\{\alpha_h + \beta' x_{hi}\}}{1 + \exp\{\alpha_h + \beta' x_{hi}\}}$$

where α_h is an effect for the hth stratum, or pair, the x_{hik} are the $k = 1, 2, \ldots, t$ explanatory variables for the ith subject in the hth matched pair, and the β_k are the corresponding parameters.

Substituting θ_{hi} for $\Pr\{e|\mathbf{x}_{hi}\}$ and $(1 - \theta_{hi})$ for $\Pr\{\bar{e}|\mathbf{x}_{hi}\}$ produces

$$\frac{\exp\{\alpha_h + \beta'\mathbf{x}_{h1}\}}{\exp\{\alpha_h + \beta'\mathbf{x}_{h1}\} + \exp\{\alpha_h + \beta'\mathbf{x}_{h2}\}}$$

which is equivalent to

$$\frac{\exp\{\beta'(\mathbf{x}_{h1} - \mathbf{x}_{h2})\}}{1 + \exp\{\beta'(\mathbf{x}_{h1} - \mathbf{x}_{h2})\}}$$

Note that the α_h have dropped out and thus you have eliminated the stratum-specific parameters.

The conditional likelihood for the entire data is the product of the likelihoods for the individual strata.

$$\prod_{h=1}^{q} \frac{\exp\{\beta'(\mathbf{x}_{h1} - \mathbf{x}_{h2})\}}{1 + \exp\{\beta'(\mathbf{x}_{h1} - \mathbf{x}_{h2})\}}$$

This likelihood is similar to that seen in the preceding sections for highly stratified data. Note that the conditional likelihood for the matched pairs data is the unconditional likelihood for a logistic regression model where the response is always equal to 1, the covariate values are equal to the differences between the values for the case and the control, and there is no intercept. This means that you can use standard logistic regression computer programs by configuring your data appropriately and eliminating the intercept term. You need to do the following:

- Make the sampling unit the matched pair by creating one record per matched set and making the explanatory variables the differences between the case values and the control values.

- Set the response variable equal to 1 (or any constant value).

- Set the model intercept equal to zero.

For this conditional likelihood, matched pairs with $x_{h1k} = x_{h2k}$ for all k are noninformative (that is, their contribution to the likelihood is the constant 0.5), and so these matched pairs can be excluded from the analysis.

Through a similar process, you can show that the conditional likelihood for the 1:m matched setting is

$$\prod_{h=1}^{q} \left[1 + \sum_{i=1}^{m} \exp\left\{ \beta'(\mathbf{x}_{hi} - \mathbf{x}_{h0}) \right\} \right]^{-1}$$

where $i = 1, 2, \ldots, m$ indexes the controls and $i = 0$ corresponds to the case. However, this is not equivalent to any unconditional form, so you have to use special computer programs to fit models for the cases of $1{:}m$ as well as $m{:}n$ matched data.

Similar to the previous examples, the LOGISTIC procedure can be used to fit conditional logistic models for 1:1 matching. In addition, the PHREG procedure fits conditional logistic models and must be used for the case of $1{:}m$ and $m{:}n$ matching. The following sections illustrate the use of PROC LOGISTIC and PROC PHREG in applications of conditional logistic regression. Refer to Breslow and Day (1980) and Collett (1991) for more detail on conditional logistic regression.

10.4   1:1 Conditional Logistic Regression

Researchers studied women in a retirement community in the 1970s to determine if there was an association between the use of estrogen and the incidence of endometrial cancer (Mack et al. 1976)*. Cases were matched to controls who were within a year of the same age, had the same marital status, and were living in the same community at the time of the diagnosis of the case. Information was also collected on obesity, hypertension, gallbladder disease history, and non-estrogen drug use. The data used here is a subset of the actual data. There are 63 matched pairs, with the variable CASE=1 indicating a case and CASE=0 indicating a control. The goal of the analysis is to determine whether the presence of endometrial disease is associated with any of the explanatory variables.

Each matched pair is transformed into a single observation, where the explanatory variable value is the difference between the corresponding values for the case and the control. The outcome variable CASE has the value 0 for all paired observations; the value does not matter as long as it is constant.

```
data match1;
    drop   id1 gall1 hyper1 age1 est1 nonest1 gallest1;
    retain id1 gall1 hyper1 age1 est1 nonest1 gallest1 0;
    input id case age est gall hyper nonest @@;
    gallest=est*gall;
    if (id = id1) then do;
        gall=gall1-gall; hyper=hyper1-hyper; age=age1-age;
        est=est1-est;   nonest=nonest1-nonest;
        gallest=gallest1-gallest;
        output;
    end;
    else do;
        id1=id;    gall1=gall;         hyper1=hyper; age1=age;
        est1=est; nonest1=nonest; gallest1=gallest;
    end;
    cards;
1 1 74 1 0 0  1  1 0 75 0 0 0  0
2 1 67 1 0 0  1  2 0 67 0 0 1  1
3 1 76 1 0 1  1  3 0 76 1 0 1  1
```

*Data provided by Norman Breslow

4	1	71	1	0	0	0	4	0	70	1	1	0	1
5	1	69	1	1	0	1	5	0	69	1	0	1	1
6	1	70	1	0	1	1	6	0	71	0	0	0	0
7	1	65	1	1	0	1	7	0	65	0	0	0	0
8	1	68	1	1	1	1	8	0	68	0	0	1	1
9	1	61	0	0	0	1	9	0	61	0	0	0	1
10	1	64	1	0	0	1	10	0	65	0	0	0	0
11	1	68	1	1	0	1	11	0	69	1	1	0	0
12	1	74	1	0	0	1	12	0	74	1	0	0	0
13	1	67	1	1	0	1	13	0	68	1	0	1	1
14	1	62	1	1	0	1	14	0	62	0	1	0	0
15	1	71	1	1	0	1	15	0	71	1	0	1	1
16	1	83	1	0	1	1	16	0	82	0	0	0	0
17	1	70	0	0	0	1	17	0	70	0	0	1	1
18	1	74	1	0	0	1	18	0	75	0	0	0	0
19	1	70	1	0	0	1	19	0	70	0	0	0	0
20	1	66	1	0	1	1	20	0	66	1	0	0	1
21	1	77	1	0	0	1	21	0	77	1	1	1	1
22	1	66	1	0	1	1	22	0	67	0	0	1	1
23	1	71	1	0	1	0	23	0	72	0	0	0	0
24	1	80	1	0	0	1	24	0	79	0	0	0	0
25	1	64	1	0	0	1	25	0	64	1	0	0	1
26	1	63	1	0	0	1	26	0	63	1	0	1	1
27	1	72	0	1	0	1	27	0	72	0	0	1	0
28	1	57	1	0	0	0	28	0	57	1	0	1	1
29	1	74	0	1	0	1	29	0	74	0	0	0	1
30	1	62	1	0	1	1	30	0	62	1	0	0	1
31	1	73	1	0	1	1	31	0	72	1	0	0	1
32	1	71	1	0	1	1	32	0	71	1	0	1	1
33	1	64	0	0	1	1	33	0	65	1	0	0	1
34	1	63	1	0	0	1	34	0	64	0	0	0	1
35	1	79	1	1	1	1	35	0	78	1	1	1	1
36	1	80	1	0	0	1	36	0	81	0	0	1	1
37	1	82	1	0	1	1	37	0	82	0	0	0	1
38	1	71	1	0	1	1	38	0	71	0	0	1	1
39	1	83	1	0	1	1	39	0	83	0	0	0	1
40	1	61	1	0	1	1	40	0	60	0	0	0	1
41	1	71	1	0	0	1	41	0	71	0	0	0	0
42	1	69	1	0	1	1	42	0	69	0	1	0	1
43	1	77	1	0	0	1	43	0	76	1	0	1	1
44	1	64	1	0	0	0	44	0	64	1	0	0	0
45	1	79	0	1	0	0	45	0	82	1	0	0	1
46	1	72	1	0	0	1	46	0	72	1	0	0	1
47	1	82	1	1	1	1	47	0	81	0	0	0	0
48	1	73	1	0	1	1	48	0	74	1	0	0	1
49	1	69	1	0	0	1	49	0	68	0	0	0	1
50	1	79	1	0	1	1	50	0	79	0	0	0	1
51	1	72	1	0	0	0	51	0	71	1	0	1	1
52	1	72	1	0	1	1	52	0	72	1	0	1	1
53	1	65	1	0	1	1	53	0	67	0	0	0	0
54	1	67	1	0	1	1	54	0	66	1	0	0	1
55	1	64	1	1	0	1	55	0	63	0	0	0	1
56	1	62	1	0	0	0	56	0	63	0	0	0	0
57	1	83	0	1	1	1	57	0	83	0	1	0	0

```
58 1 81 1 0 0   1 58 0 79 0 0 0   0
59 1 67 1 0 0   1 59 0 66 1 0 1   1
60 1 73 1 1 1   1 60 0 72 1 0 0   1
61 1 67 1 1 0   1 61 0 67 1 1 0   1
62 1 74 1 0 1   1 62 0 75 0 0 0   1
63 1 68 1 1 0   1 63 0 69 1 0 0   1
;
```

The following PROC LOGISTIC invocation requests forward model selection; in
addition, the NOINT option is specified so that no intercept term is included.

```
proc logistic;
   model case = gall hyper age est nonest /
                 noint selection=forward details;
run;
```

Output 10.11 contains the response profiles. Note that since all responses have been
assigned the value 0, there is effectively one profile.

Output 10.11   Response Profile

```
                         Response Profile

               Ordered
                Value      CASE        Count

                  1         0            63
```

In the model selection process, only EST and GALL are entered into the model.
Output 10.12 displays the residual score statistic, which has a value of 0.2077 with 3 df,
indicating an adequate fit. Output 10.12 also displays the score statistic for each variable's
entry into the model; since all of these are strongly nonsignificant, the model goodness of
fit is supported.

Output 10.12   Model Selection Results

```
        Residual Chi-Square = 0.2077 with 3 DF (p=0.9763)

            Analysis of Variables Not in the Model

                           Score          Pr >
            Variable    Chi-Square     Chi-Square

            HYPER          0.0186        0.8915
            AGE            0.1432        0.7051
            NONEST         0.0370        0.8474
```

Output 10.13 displays the statistics that assess the model's explanatory capacity.

Output 10.13   Explanatory Capacity

```
                  Testing Global Null Hypothesis: BETA=0

                    Without        With
         Criterion  Covariates    Covariates   Chi-Square for Covariates

         AIC          87.337        57.691          .
         SC           87.337        61.977          .
         -2 LOG L     87.337        53.691       33.646 with 2 DF (p=0.0001)
         Score          .             .          27.059 with 2 DF (p=0.0001)
```

Output 10.14 contains the parameter estimates for the model containing main effects EST and GALL.

Output 10.14   Parameter Estimates and Odds Ratios

```
                  Analysis of Maximum Likelihood Estimates

                 Parameter Standard    Wald      Pr >   Standardized   Odds
     Variable DF Estimate   Error   Chi-Square Chi-Square  Estimate    Ratio

     GALL     1   1.6551    0.7980    4.3017    0.0381    0.429163     5.234
     EST      1   2.7786    0.7605   13.3492    0.0003    0.857543    16.096
```

Parameter estimates for both GALL and EST are significant. The odds ratio for GALL indicates that those persons with gallbladder disease history are 5.234 times as likely to contract endometrial cancer as those persons without it, adjusting for estrogen use. The odds ratio for EST indicates that those women who used estrogen are 16.096 times as likely to contract endometrial cancer as those women who don't use estrogen, adjusting for gall bladder disease history.

10.5   Conditional Logistic Regression Using PROC PHREG

The PHREG procedure is designed to model survival data with the Cox proportional hazards model. It turns out that there are computional equivalences so that you can use this procedure to perform conditional logistic analyses. You can use it to analyze data from 1:1 matched designs without first having to create a data set with difference variables; it also allows you to analyze data from $1:m$ and $m:n$ matched studies. You do not have to be familiar with survival analysis methods to use PROC PHREG for this purpose. You specify a model similar to how you would specify a model with the LOGISTIC procedure, and you can use model-building features that work the same as they do for PROC LOGISTIC. You must specify the TIES=DISCRETE option in the MODEL statement (for the 1:1 case, all TIES= options are equivalent, so using the default is adequate).

In this section, the same analysis of the endometrial cancer data is performed using PROC PHREG. The following statements create the data set MATCH2. The variable CASE is redefined so it has the value 1 if the observation is a case and the value 2 if the observation is a control. This is required so that the probability of being a case is modeled.

```
    data match2;
        input id case age est gall hyper nonest @@;
        case=2-case;
        cards;
  1 1 74 1 0 0   1   1 0 75 0 0 0   0
  2 1 67 1 0 0   1   2 0 67 0 0 1   1
  3 1 76 1 0 1   1   3 0 76 1 0 1   1
  4 1 71 1 0 0   0   4 0 70 1 1 0   1
  5 1 69 1 1 0   1   5 0 69 1 0 1   1
  6 1 70 1 0 1   1   6 0 71 0 0 0   0
  7 1 65 1 1 0   1   7 0 65 0 0 0   0
  8 1 68 1 1 1   1   8 0 68 0 0 1   1
  9 1 61 0 0 0   1   9 0 61 0 0 0   1
 10 1 64 1 0 0   1  10 0 65 0 0 0   0
 11 1 68 1 1 0   1  11 0 69 1 1 0   0
 12 1 74 1 0 0   1  12 0 74 1 0 0   0
 13 1 67 1 1 0   1  13 0 68 1 0 1   1
 14 1 62 1 1 0   1  14 0 62 0 1 0   0
 15 1 71 1 1 0   1  15 0 71 1 0 1   1
 16 1 83 1 0 1   1  16 0 82 0 0 0   0
 17 1 70 0 0 0   1  17 0 70 0 0 1   1
 18 1 74 1 0 0   1  18 0 75 0 0 0   0
 19 1 70 1 0 0   1  19 0 70 0 0 0   0
 20 1 66 1 0 1   1  20 0 66 1 0 0   1
 21 1 77 1 0 0   1  21 0 77 1 1 1   1
 22 1 66 1 0 1   1  22 0 67 0 0 1   1
 23 1 71 1 0 1   0  23 0 72 0 0 0   0
 24 1 80 1 0 0   1  24 0 79 0 0 0   0
 25 1 64 1 0 0   1  25 0 64 1 0 0   1
 26 1 63 1 0 0   1  26 0 63 1 0 1   1
 27 1 72 0 1 0   1  27 0 72 0 0 1   0
 28 1 57 1 0 0   0  28 0 57 1 0 1   1
 29 1 74 0 1 0   1  29 0 74 0 0 0   1
 30 1 62 1 0 1   1  30 0 62 1 0 0   1
 31 1 73 1 0 1   1  31 0 72 1 0 0   1
 32 1 71 1 0 1   1  32 0 71 1 0 1   1
 33 1 64 0 0 1   1  33 0 65 1 0 0   1
 34 1 63 1 0 0   1  34 0 64 0 0 0   1
 35 1 79 1 1 1   1  35 0 78 1 1 1   1
 36 1 80 1 0 0   1  36 0 81 0 0 1   1
 37 1 82 1 0 1   1  37 0 82 0 0 0   1
 38 1 71 1 0 1   1  38 0 71 0 0 1   1
 39 1 83 1 0 1   1  39 0 83 0 0 0   1
 40 1 61 1 0 1   1  40 0 60 0 0 0   1
 41 1 71 1 0 0   1  41 0 71 0 0 0   0
 42 1 69 1 0 1   1  42 0 69 0 1 0   1
 43 1 77 1 0 0   1  43 0 76 1 0 1   1
 44 1 64 1 0 0   0  44 0 64 1 0 0   0
 45 1 79 0 1 0   0  45 0 82 1 0 0   1
 46 1 72 1 0 0   1  46 0 72 1 0 0   1
 47 1 82 1 1 1   1  47 0 81 0 0 0   0
 48 1 73 1 0 1   1  48 0 74 1 0 0   1
 49 1 69 1 0 0   1  49 0 68 0 0 0   1
 50 1 79 1 0 1   1  50 0 79 0 0 0   1
```

```
51 1 72 1 0 0   0 51 0 71 1 0 1   1
52 1 72 1 0 1   1 52 0 72 1 0 1   1
53 1 65 1 0 1   1 53 0 67 0 0 0   0
54 1 67 1 0 1   1 54 0 66 1 0 0   1
55 1 64 1 1 0   1 55 0 63 0 0 0   1
56 1 62 1 0 0   0 56 0 63 0 0 0   0
57 1 83 0 1 1   1 57 0 83 0 1 0   0
58 1 81 1 0 0   1 58 0 79 0 0 0   0
59 1 67 1 0 0   1 59 0 66 1 0 1   1
60 1 73 1 1 1   1 60 0 72 1 0 0   1
61 1 67 1 1 0   1 61 0 67 1 1 0   1
62 1 74 1 0 1   1 62 0 75 0 0 0   1
63 1 68 1 1 0   1 63 0 69 1 0 0   1
;
```

The following statements request the PHREG procedure to perform the conditional logistic analysis. You use the name of the variable identifying the matched set as the STRATA variable.

```
proc phreg;
   strata id;
   model case = gall est / selection=forward details;
run;
```

Output 10.15 contains a partial listing of the data. For 1:1 matching, each stratum contains two observations, the case and the control. You should check this table to see that the strata have been set up correctly and contain the correct number of subjects.

Output 10.15   Summary Table

Summary of the Number of Event and Censored Values					
Stratum	ID	Total	Event	Censored	Percent Censored
1	1	2	2	0	0.00
2	2	2	2	0	0.00
3	3	2	2	0	0.00
4	4	2	2	0	0.00
5	5	2	2	0	0.00
6	6	2	2	0	0.00
7	7	2	2	0	0.00
8	8	2	2	0	0.00
9	9	2	2	0	0.00
10	10	2	2	0	0.00
11	11	2	2	0	0.00
12	12	2	2	0	0.00
13	13	2	2	0	0.00
14	14	2	2	0	0.00
15	15	2	2	0	0.00
16	16	2	2	0	0.00
17	17	2	2	0	0.00
18	18	2	2	0	0.00
19	19	2	2	0	0.00
20	20	2	2	0	0.00

Output 10.16 contains the model-fitting results. Variables EST and GALL were entered into the model, and HYPER, AGE, and NONEST were not. The residual score statistic has the value 0.2077, with 3 df, and $p = 0.9763$. These are the same results as produced with the PROC LOGISTIC analysis.

Output 10.16   Residual Score Statistic

```
        Residual Chi-Square = 0.2077 with 3 DF (p=0.9763)

            Analysis of Variables Not in the Model

                             Score          Pr >
             Variable      Chi-Square     Chi-Square

             HYPER           0.0186         0.8915
             AGE             0.1432         0.7051
             NONEST          0.0370         0.8474
```

Output 10.17 contains the table of statistics that assess the explanatory capability of the model; note that the score test, with a value of 27.059 and 2 df, is the same as the score test printed in the PROC LOGISTIC output.

Output 10.17   Explanatory Capacity

```
           Testing Global Null Hypothesis: BETA=0

                Without      With
Criterion      Covariates  Covariates   Model Chi-Square

-2 LOG L         87.337      53.691      33.646 with 2 DF (p=0.0001)
Score              .           .         27.059 with 2 DF (p=0.0001)
Wald               .           .         15.329 with 2 DF (p=0.0005)
```

The parameter estimates table is identical to the one printed by the PROC LOGISTIC analysis as well. The "Risk Ratio" column contains the odds ratio estimates.

Output 10.18   Parameter Estimates

```
           Analysis of Maximum Likelihood Estimates

                  Parameter   Standard    Wald       Pr >      Risk
  Variable DF      Estimate     Error   Chi-Square Chi-Square  Ratio

  GALL     1       1.655085    0.79799   4.30174    0.0381     5.234
  EST      1       2.778564    0.76049  13.34920    0.0003    16.096
```

The PHREG procedure also performs $1:m$ and $m:n$ matching; you follow the same steps as that illustrated previously. For both these cases, you must request TIES=DISCRETE in the MODEL statement to obtain the correct results.

10.6   1:*m* **Conditional Logistic Regression**

Researchers in a midwestern county tracked flu cases requiring hospitalization in those residents aged 65 and older during a two month period in one winter. They then matched each case with two controls according to sex and age and also determined whether the cases and controls had a flu vaccine shot and whether they had lung disease. Vaccines were then verified by county health and individual medical practice records. Researchers were interested in whether vaccination had a protective influence on the odds of getting a severe case of flu.

This study is an example of a 1:2 matched study since two controls were chosen for each case. Thus, in order to analyze these data with the SAS System, you need to use the PHREG procedure. The following DATA step reads the data and computes the frequency of vaccine and lung disease for both cases and non-cases. The variable LUNG_VAC is the interaction of lung and vaccination. The variable OUTCOME is redefined so that the probability of being a case is modeled.

```
data matched;
   input id outcome lung vaccine @@;
   outcome=2-outcome;
   lung_vac=lung*vaccine;
   cards;
 1 1 0 0    1 0 1 0    1 0 0 0    2 1 0 0    2 0 0 0    2 0 1 0
 3 1 0 1    3 0 0 1    3 0 0 0    4 1 1 0    4 0 0 0    4 0 1 0
 5 1 1 0    5 0 0 1    5 0 0 1    6 1 0 0    6 0 0 0    6 0 0 1
 7 1 0 0    7 0 0 0    7 0 0 1    8 1 1 1    8 0 0 0    8 0 0 1
 9 1 0 0    9 0 0 1    9 0 0 0   10 1 0 0   10 0 1 0   10 0 0 0
11 1 1 0   11 0 0 1   11 0 0 0   12 1 1 1   12 0 0 1   12 0 0 0
13 1 0 0   13 0 0 1   13 0 1 0   14 1 0 0   14 0 0 0   14 0 0 1
15 1 1 0   15 0 0 0   15 0 0 1   16 1 0 1   16 0 0 1   16 0 0 1
17 1 0 0   17 0 1 0   17 0 0 0   18 1 1 0   18 0 0 1   18 0 0 1
19 1 1 0   19 0 0 1   19 0 0 1   20 1 0 0   20 0 0 0   20 0 0 0
21 1 0 0   21 0 0 1   21 0 0 1   22 1 0 1   22 0 0 0   22 0 1 0
23 1 1 1   23 0 0 0   23 0 0 0   24 1 0 0   24 0 0 1   24 0 0 1
25 1 1 0   25 0 1 0   25 0 0 0   26 1 1 1   26 0 0 0   26 0 0 0
27 1 1 0   27 0 0 1   27 0 0 0   28 1 0 1   28 0 1 0   28 0 0 0
29 1 0 0   29 0 0 0   29 0 1 1   30 1 0 0   30 0 0 0   30 0 0 0
31 1 0 0   31 0 0 0   31 0 0 1   32 1 1 0   32 0 0 0   32 0 0 0
33 1 0 1   33 0 0 0   33 0 0 0   34 1 0 0   34 0 1 0   34 0 0 0
35 1 1 0   35 0 1 1   35 0 0 0   36 1 0 1   36 0 0 0   36 0 0 1
37 1 0 1   37 0 0 0   37 0 0 1   38 1 1 1   38 0 0 1   38 0 0 0
39 1 0 0   39 0 0 1   39 0 0 1   40 1 0 0   40 0 0 0   40 0 1 1
41 1 1 0   41 0 0 0   41 0 0 1   42 1 1 0   42 0 0 0   42 0 0 0
43 1 0 0   43 0 0 1   43 0 0 0   44 1 1 0   44 0 0 0   44 0 0 0
45 1 1 0   45 0 0 0   45 0 0 0   46 1 1 0   46 0 1 1   46 0 0 0
47 1 0 1   47 0 0 0   47 0 0 1   48 1 0 0   48 0 0 0   48 0 0 0
49 1 1 0   49 0 1 0   49 0 1 1   50 1 1 1   50 0 0 0   50 0 0 1
51 1 1 0   51 0 0 1   51 0 0 1   52 1 0 1   52 0 0 0   52 0 0 0
53 1 0 1   53 0 0 1   53 0 0 1   54 1 1 0   54 0 0 0   54 0 0 0
55 1 0 0   55 0 0 1   55 0 0 0   56 1 0 0   56 0 0 0   56 0 1 0
57 1 1 1   57 0 1 0   57 0 0 0   58 1 1 0   58 0 0 1   58 0 0 1
59 1 0 0   59 0 0 0   59 0 1 1   60 1 0 0   60 0 0 0   60 0 0 1
61 1 0 1   61 0 0 0   61 0 0 1   62 1 0 0   62 0 0 0   62 0 0 1
```

```
63 1 0 0 63 0 0 1 63 0 0 0 64 1 0 0 64 0 1 0 64 0 0 0
65 1 1 1 65 0 0 0 65 0 1 0 66 1 1 1 66 0 0 1 66 0 1 0
67 1 0 0 67 0 0 0 67 0 0 1 68 1 0 0 68 0 0 1 68 0 0 1
69 1 1 1 69 0 0 1 69 0 0 1 70 1 0 0 70 0 0 1 70 0 1 1
71 1 0 0 71 0 0 0 71 0 0 1 72 1 1 0 72 0 0 0 72 0 0 0
73 1 1 0 73 0 0 1 73 0 0 0 74 1 0 0 74 0 0 0 74 0 0 1
75 1 0 0 75 0 0 1 75 0 0 0 76 1 0 0 76 0 0 0 76 0 0 0
77 1 0 1 77 0 0 0 77 0 0 1 78 1 0 0 78 0 0 1 78 0 0 0
79 1 1 0 79 0 0 1 79 0 0 1 80 1 0 1 80 0 0 0 80 0 0 0
81 1 0 0 81 0 1 1 81 0 0 1 82 1 1 1 82 0 1 0 82 0 0 0
83 1 0 1 83 0 0 0 83 0 0 1 84 1 0 0 84 0 0 0 84 0 0 1
85 1 1 0 85 0 0 0 85 0 0 0 86 1 0 0 86 0 1 1 86 0 1 0
87 1 1 1 87 0 0 0 87 0 0 0 88 1 0 0 88 0 0 0 88 0 0 0
89 1 0 0 89 0 0 1 89 0 1 1 90 1 0 0 90 0 0 0 90 0 0 0
91 1 0 1 91 0 0 0 91 0 0 1  92 1 0 0  92 0 1 1  92 0 0 0
93 1 0 1 93 0 0 0 93 0 1 0  94 1 1 0  94 0 0 0  94 0 0 0
95 1 1 1 95 0 0 1 95 0 0 0  96 1 1 0  96 0 0 1  96 0 0 1
97 1 1 1 97 0 0 0 97 0 0 1  98 1 0 0  98 0 0 0  98 0 1 1
99 1 0 1 99 0 1 1 99 0 0 1 100 1 1 0 100 0 0 0 100 0 0 0
101 1 0 0 101 0 0 0 101 0 0 0 102 1 0 1 102 0 0 0 102 0 0 0
103 1 0 1 103 0 0 0 103 0 0 0 104 1 1 0 104 0 0 1 104 0 1 0
105 1 1 0 105 0 1 0 105 0 0 0 106 1 0 0 106 0 0 0 106 0 0 1
107 1 0 0 107 0 0 1 107 0 0 1 108 1 1 1 108 0 0 0 108 0 0 1
109 1 0 1 109 0 0 0 109 0 0 0 110 1 0 0 110 0 0 0 110 0 0 0
111 1 1 0 111 0 0 1 111 0 0 1 112 1 0 0 112 0 0 1 112 0 0 0
113 1 0 1 113 0 0 0 113 0 1 0 114 1 1 1 114 0 0 1 114 0 0 1
115 1 1 1 115 0 0 1 115 0 0 1 116 1 0 0 116 0 0 1 116 0 1 0
117 1 0 1 117 0 0 0 117 0 0 0 118 1 1 0 118 0 1 0 118 0 0 0
119 1 1 0 119 0 0 0 119 0 0 0 120 1 1 0 120 0 0 0 120 0 0 1
121 1 0 0 121 0 0 1 121 0 0 0 122 1 0 1 122 0 0 0 122 0 0 0
123 1 1 0 123 0 0 0 123 0 1 1 124 1 0 0 124 0 0 1 124 0 0 0
125 1 1 0 125 0 1 0 125 0 0 0 126 1 1 1 126 0 0 0 126 0 0 0
127 1 1 0 127 0 0 1 127 0 0 0 128 1 0 1 128 0 1 0 128 0 0 0
129 1 0 0 129 0 0 0 129 0 1 1 130 1 0 0 130 0 0 0 130 0 0 0
131 1 0 0 131 0 0 0 131 0 0 1 132 1 1 0 132 0 0 0 132 0 0 1
133 1 0 1 133 0 0 0 133 0 0 0 134 1 0 0 134 0 1 0 134 0 0 1
135 1 1 0 135 0 1 1 135 0 0 0 136 1 0 0 136 0 0 0 136 0 0 0
137 1 0 0 137 0 0 0 137 0 0 1 138 1 1 0 138 0 0 0 138 0 0 0
139 1 0 0 139 0 0 0 139 0 0 0 140 1 0 0 140 0 0 1 140 0 1 1
141 1 1 1 141 0 0 0 141 0 0 1 142 1 1 0 142 0 0 0 142 0 0 0
143 1 0 0 143 0 0 1 143 0 1 1 144 1 1 1 144 0 0 1 144 0 0 1
145 1 1 0 145 0 0 1 145 0 0 0 146 1 1 0 146 0 1 0 146 0 0 0
147 1 0 1 147 0 0 0 147 0 0 1 148 1 0 0 148 0 0 1 148 0 0 0
149 1 1 0 149 0 1 0 149 0 1 0 150 1 1 1 150 0 0 0 150 0 0 1
;
```

The following PROC FREQ statements request crossclassifications of vaccine by outcome status and lung disease by outcome status.

```
proc freq;
   tables outcome*lung outcome*vaccine / nocol nopct;
run;
```

Output 10.19 contains the frequencies of vaccine and lung disease for both cases and controls. Sixteen percent of the controls had lung disease. and forty-two percent of the cases had lung disease. Thirty-nine percent of the controls and thirty-one percent of the cases had been vaccinated.

Output 10.19   Frequencies of Vaccine and Smoking by Cases and Controls

```
                    TABLE OF OUTCOME BY LUNG

             OUTCOME     LUNG

             Frequency|
             Row Pct  |       0|       1| Total
             ---------+--------+--------+
                  1 |      87 |     63 |    150
                    |   58.00 |  42.00 |
             ---------+--------+--------+
                  2 |     252 |     48 |    300
                    |   84.00 |  16.00 |
             ---------+--------+--------+
             Total          339      111      450

                  TABLE OF OUTCOME BY VACCINE

             OUTCOME     VACCINE

             Frequency|
             Row Pct  |       0|       1| Total
             ---------+--------+--------+
                  1 |     103 |     47 |    150
                    |   68.67 |  31.33 |
             ---------+--------+--------+
                  2 |     183 |    117 |    300
                    |   61.00 |  39.00 |
             ---------+--------+--------+
             Total          286      164      450
```

The following statements request the conditional logistic regression analysis. The SELECTION=FORWARD option is specified to request forward selection model building.

```
proc phreg;
   strata id;
   model outcome = lung vaccine lung_vac /
   selection=forward details ties=discrete;
run;
```

Output 10.20   Model Building Results

```
Step  1: Variable LUNG is entered.  The model contains the following
         explanatory variables.

         LUNG

               Testing Global Null Hypothesis: BETA=0

              Without      With
Criterion    Covariates   Covariates   Model Chi-Square

-2 LOG L      329.584       296.613      32.971 with 1 DF (p=0.0001)
Score            .             .         34.180 with 1 DF (p=0.0001)
Wald             .             .         30.357 with 1 DF (p=0.0001)

               Analysis of Maximum Likelihood Estimates

              Parameter   Standard    Wald        Pr >       Risk
  Variable DF  Estimate    Error    Chi-Square  Chi-Square   Ratio

  LUNG     1   1.282160   0.23271    30.35690     0.0001     3.604

               Analysis of Variables Not in the Model

                            Score        Pr >
             Variable     Chi-Square   Chi-Square

             VACCINE        3.2529       0.0713
             LUNG_VAC       0.5916       0.4418

        Residual Chi-square = 3.2982  with 2 DF (p=0.1922)

NOTE: No (additional) variables met the 0.05 level for entry into the model.
```

The variable LUNG is entered into the model, but variables VACCINE and LUNG_VAC
are not. However, the *p*-value of 0.0713 for VACCINE is suggestive, so the model
including LUNG and VACCINE is fit next. The interaction LUNG_VAC is included to
obtain the residual score test as a measure of goodness of fit.

```
proc phreg;
   strata id;
   model outcome = lung vaccine lung_vac /
         selection=forward include=2 details ties=discrete;
run;
```

Output 10.21 displays the residual score statistic. With a value of 0.0573 and $p = 0.8107$,
this statistic supports goodness of fit. Since there is only one variable, LUNG_VAC, being
considered by this test, it has the same value as the individual test for LUNG_VAC that is
displayed in the table "Analysis of Variables Not in the Model."

Output 10.21   Residual Score Statistic

```
           Analysis of Variables Not in the Model

                        Score          Pr >
           Variable   Chi-Square     Chi-Square

           LUNG_VAC     0.0573         0.8107

    Residual Chi-square = 0.0573   with 1 DF (p=0.8107)
```

Output 10.22 includes the parameter estimates.

Output 10.22   Parameter Estimates

```
         Analysis of Maximum Likelihood Estimates

              Parameter  Standard    Wald       Pr >      Risk
Variable DF    Estimate    Error  Chi-Square Chi-Square  Ratio

LUNG      1    1.305336   0.23484  30.89672    0.0001    3.689
VACCINE   1   -0.400803   0.22328   3.22227    0.0726    0.670
```

The odds ratio for getting a case of flu resulting in hospitalization is $e^{-0.4008} = 0.67$ for those with vaccine versus those without vaccine. Thus, study participants with vaccination reduced their odds of getting hospitalizable flu by 33 percent compared to their nonvaccinated matched counterparts. This means that vaccination had a protective effect, controlling for lung disease status (and age and sex, via matching).

Note: The usage of the PHREG procedure described in these sections is correct but computationally inefficient, although the inefficiency is unlikely to produce noticeable differences in time requirements. The usage described is the most straightforward for most users and that is why it is illustrated here. If you are familiar with the PHREG procedure for survival analysis, you may want to proceed more efficiently. If an outcome variable named OUTCOME takes the value 1 for case and 0 for control, create a variable TIME that is 2 – OUTCOME. Then use the syntax

```
TIME*OUTCOME(0)
```

as your response in the MODEL statement, remembering to use the TIES=DISCRETE option for m:n matching. The computations are more efficient, and the results are identical.

Chapter 11
Quantal Bioassay Analysis

Chapter Table of Contents

Chapter 11
Quantal Bioassay Analysis

11.1   Introduction

Bioassay is the process of determining the potency or strength of a reagent or stimuli based on the response it elicits in biological organisms. Often, the reagent is a new drug and the subjects are experimental animals. Other possible stimuli include radiation and environmental exposures, and other possible subjects include humans and bacteria. Researchers are interested in the tolerance of the subjects to the stimulus or drug, where tolerance is defined as the amount of the stimulus required to produce a response. They are also interested in the relative potency of a new drug to a standard drug. In a direct assay, you steadily increase the doses until you generate the desired reaction. In an indirect assay, you observe the reaction of groups of subjects to specified sets of doses.

The measured response to the drug in an indirect assay can be either quantitative or quantal. An example of a quantitative response is red blood cells per milliliter of blood, and an example of a quantal response is death or survival. This chapter is concerned with quantal responses, which are analyzed with categorical data analysis strategies. Refer to Tsutakawa (1982) for an overview of general bioassay methods, and refer to Finney (1978) and Govindarajulu (1988) for textbook discussion of these areas.

11.2   Estimating Tolerance Distributions

Table 11.1 displays data from an experiment in which animals were exposed to bacterial challenges after having one-quarter of their spleen removed (splenectomy). After 96 hours, their survival status was assessed. The stimulus is the bacterial challenge, and interest lies in assessing the tolerances of the animals' immune systems to the bacterial challenge after they have had partial splenectomies (Koch and Edwards 1985).

In bioassay analysis, you make the assumption that responses of subjects are determined through a tolerance distribution. This means that at certain levels of the dose (bacterial challenge in this case) the animals will die; that is, death will occur if dose exceeds the tolerance, and survival will occur when dose is below tolerance. Historically, the tolerances have been assumed to follow a normal distribution. This allows you to write the probability of death at a level x_i of the bacterial challenge as

$$p_i = \Phi\left(\frac{x_i - \mu}{\sigma}\right)$$

Table 11.1   Status 96 Hours After Bacterial Challenge

	Status	
Bacterial Dose	Dead	Alive
1.2×10^3	0	5
1.2×10^4	0	5
1.2×10^5	2	3
1.2×10^6	4	2
1.2×10^7	5	1
1.2×10^8	5	0

where Φ is the cumulative distribution function for the standard normal distribution with mean 0 and variance 1; the parameter μ is the mean (or median) of the tolerance distribution, and σ is the standard deviation.

If $\alpha = -\mu/\sigma$ and $\beta = 1/\sigma$, then

$$p_i = \Phi(\alpha + \beta x_i)$$

and

$$\Phi^{-1}(p_i) = \alpha + \beta x_i$$

The function $\Phi^{-1}(p_i)$ is called the *probit* (or *normit*), and its analysis is called probit analysis. Sometimes the value 5 is added to $\Phi^{-1}(p_i)$ in order to have positive values for all p_i.

Berkson (1951) pointed out that the logistic distribution also works well as a tolerance distribution, generating essentially the same results as the normal distribution. This is particularly true for values of p_i in the middle of the (0, 1) range and when the median μ of the tolerance distribution is the primary parameter. While sometimes a probit analysis of a data set is of more interest to researchers in some disciplines (for example, growth and development) because of the correspondence of its parameters to the mean and standard deviation of the underlying tolerance distribution, the focus in this chapter is on logistic analysis. Note that the measures discussed are also relevant to a model based on the probit.

If you assume the logistic distribution for the tolerances,

$$p_i = \frac{\exp\{\alpha + \beta x_i\}}{1 + \exp\{\alpha + \beta x_i\}}$$

and

$$\log\left\{\frac{p_i}{1 - p_i}\right\} = \alpha + \beta x_i$$

The parameters α and β are estimated with maximum likelihood estimation. Usually, the log of the tolerances is most likely to have a logistic distribution, so frequently you work with the log of the drug or concentration under investigation as the x_i.

One parameter of interest for estimation is the median of the tolerance distribution, or the dose at which 50 percent of the subjects produce a response. When the response is death, this estimate is called the LD50, for lethal dose. Otherwise, this measure is called the ED50, for effective dose. If you are working with log dose levels, you compute the log LD50 and then exponentiate it if you are also interested in the actual LD50.

Suppose x_{50} represents the log LD50 and p_{50} represents the probability of response at the median of the tolerance distribution.

$$\log\left\{\frac{p_{50}}{1-p_{50}}\right\} = \log\left\{\frac{.5}{.5}\right\}$$
$$= 0$$

Thus, the logistic parameters $\hat{\alpha}$ and $\hat{\beta}x_{50}$ can be set to zero to obtain

$$\hat{x}_{50} = \frac{-\hat{\alpha}}{\hat{\beta}}$$

An approximate form of the variance of $\hat{x}_{50}$ for situations where β is clearly different from 0 is written

$$\text{var}\{\hat{x}_{50}\} = \{\hat{x}_{50}\}^2 \left\{\frac{V(\hat{\alpha})}{\hat{\alpha}^2} - \frac{2V(\hat{\alpha},\hat{\beta})}{\hat{\alpha}\hat{\beta}} + \frac{V(\hat{\beta})}{\hat{\beta}^2}\right\}$$

where $V(\hat{\alpha})$, $V(\hat{\alpha},\hat{\beta})$, and $V(\hat{\beta})$ represent the variance of $\hat{\alpha}$, the covariance of $\hat{\alpha}$ and $\hat{\beta}$, and the variance of $\hat{\beta}$, respectively. (Refer to page 286 for references on using Fieller's theorem to compute confidence intervals for these measures.)

This allows you to express the confidence interval for log LD50 as

$$\hat{x}_{50} \pm z_{1-\alpha/2}\sqrt{\text{var}\{\hat{x}_{50}\}}$$

In order to compute the LD50, the actual dosage at which 50 percent of the subjects die, you exponentiate $\hat{x}_{50}$ (and its confidence limits). Sometimes analysts work on the log log scale for LD50 to produce more stable computations. In that case, you would use

$$\frac{\text{var}(\hat{x}_{50})}{\hat{x}_{50}^2}$$

as the applicable variance for log $\hat{x}_{50}$, and you would double exponentiate the results to generate the estimate of the actual LD50 and its confidence interval.

The LOGISTIC procedure is used to fit these bioassay models. In the following section, a logistic model is fit to the data in Table 11.1, and the log LD50 is computed.

11.2.1   Analyzing the Bacterial Challenge Data

The following SAS statements input the data from Table 11.1 and compute two additional variables: LDOSE is the log dose (natural log), and SQ_LDOSE is the square of LDOSE. Using the log scale results in more evenly spaced dose levels. The variable SQ_LDOSE is used as a quadratic term in the model to help assess goodness of fit.

```
data bacteria;
   input dose status $ count @@;
   ldose=log(dose);
   sq_ldose=ldose*ldose;
   cards;
1200        dead   0    1200       alive 5
12000       dead   0    12000      alive 5
120000      dead   2    120000     alive 3
1200000     dead   4    1200000    alive 2
12000000    dead   5    12000000   alive 1
120000000   dead   5    120000000  alive 0
;
proc print;
run;
```

In the PROC LOGISTIC specification, both LDOSE and SQ_LDOSE are listed in the MODEL statement. The SELECTION=FORWARD option is specified so that a score statistic for the quadratic term is computed. The COVB option requests that PROC LOGISTIC print the covariance matrix for the parameter estimates, quantities necessary to compute the confidence interval for the log LD50.

```
proc logistic data=bacteria descending;
   freq count;
   model status = ldose sq_ldose / scale=none aggregate
         selection=forward start=1 details covb;
run;
```

Output 11.1 displays the data, including values for the created variables LDOSE and SQ_LDOSE.

Output 11.1   Data Listing

OBS	DOSE	STATUS	COUNT	LDOSE	SQ_LDOSE
1	1200	dead	0	7.0901	50.269
2	1200	alive	5	7.0901	50.269
3	12000	dead	0	9.3927	88.222
4	12000	alive	5	9.3927	88.222
5	120000	dead	2	11.6952	136.779
6	120000	alive	3	11.6952	136.779
7	1200000	dead	4	13.9978	195.939
8	1200000	alive	2	13.9978	195.939
9	12000000	dead	5	16.3004	265.704
10	12000000	alive	1	16.3004	265.704
11	120000000	dead	5	18.6030	346.072
12	120000000	alive	0	18.6030	346.072

Since the option START=1 is specified, the first model fit includes the intercept and the LDOSE term. The residual score statistic for the SQ_LDOSE term is not significant with $Q_S = 0.2580$ and $p = 0.6115$, so clearly this term makes no contribution to the model. This result supports the satisfactory fit of the intercept and slope model; the residual score test serves as a goodness-of-fit test for this model.

Output 11.2   Residual Score Statistic

	Analysis of Variables Not in the Model		
Variable		Score Chi-Square	Pr > Chi-Square
SQ_LDOSE		0.2580	0.6115

The Pearson and deviance goodness-of-fit statistics also indicate that the model provides an adequate fit, as displayed in Output 11.3. However, note that the sampling requirements for these statistics are minimally met; certainly the expected values for all cell counts are not greater than 4 for several cells. In such cases, it is better to support assessment of fit with methods such as the residual score statistic for the addition of the quadratic term.

Output 11.3   Goodness of Fit Statistics

Goodness of Fit Statistics				
Criterion	DF	Value	Value/DF	Pr > Chi-Square
Deviance	4	1.7508	0.4377	0.7815
Pearson	4	1.3379	0.3345	0.8549
Number of unique profiles: 6				

Output 11.4 contains the maximum likelihood estimates for α and β. The estimate $\hat{\beta} = 0.7071$ has $p = 0.0027$ for the test of its significance. The level of bacterial challenge has a significant effect on survival. The intercept $\hat{\alpha} = -9.2680$.

Output 11.4   Maximum Likelihood Estimates

		Analysis of Maximum Likelihood Estimates				
Variable	DF	Parameter Estimate	Standard Error	Wald Chi-Square	Pr > Chi-Square	Standardized Estimate
INTERCPT	1	-9.2680	3.1630	8.5857	0.0034	.
LDOSE	1	0.7071	0.2354	9.0223	0.0027	1.528441

Output 11.5 contains the estimated covariance matrix for the parameter estimates. The variance of $\hat{\alpha}$ is 10.0046, the variance of $\hat{\beta}$ is 0.05542, and the covariance of $\hat{\alpha}$ and $\hat{\beta}$ is -0.7334. Taking the square root of the variances produces the standard errors displayed in Output 11.4.

Output 11.5   Estimated Covariance Matrix

```
              Estimated Covariance Matrix

     Variable          INTERCPT              LDOSE

     INTERCPT        10.004575447        -0.733376897
     LDOSE           -0.733376897         0.0554177125
```

To compute the log LD50, use the estimated values of $\hat{\alpha}$ and $\hat{\beta}$.

$$\log \text{LD50} = \frac{-\hat{\alpha}}{\hat{\beta}} = \frac{9.2680}{0.7071} = 13.1070$$

Using the covariances from Output 11.5 in the formula for $\text{var}\{x_{50}\}$ yields the value 0.6005. Thus, a confidence interval for the log LD50 is written

$$13.1070 \pm 1.96\sqrt{0.6005}$$

so that the confidence interval is (11.588, 14.626). To determine the LD50 on the actual dose scale, you exponentiate the LD50 for the log scale.

$$\text{actual LD50} = e^{13.1070} = 4.9238 \times 10^5$$

To determine its confidence interval, exponentiate both bounds of the confidence interval to obtain $(1.0780 \times 10^5, 2.2490 \times 10^6)$. This confidence interval describes the location of the median bacterial challenge for the death of animals with one-fourth of the spleen removed.

11.3   Comparing Two Drugs

Bioassay often involves the comparison of two drugs, usually a new drug versus a standard drug. Consider the data in Table 11.2. Researchers studied the effects of the peptides neurotensin and somatostatin in potentiating nonlethal doses of the barbiturate pentobarbital. Groups of mice were administered various dose levels of either neurotensin or somatostatin (Nemeroff, et al. 1977; analyzed in Imrey, Koch, and Stokes 1982).

Many times, one drug acts as a dilution of another drug. If this is the case, then the dose response relationship is parallel on the logit scale. Assays that are designed for the dilution assumption are called *parallel lines assays*. The quantity that describes the relationship of such drugs to one another through the ratio of doses of the two drugs that produce the same response is called the *relative potency*.

Table 11.2   N and S Comparison

Dose	Drug	Status Dead	Status Alive	Total
0.01	N	0	30	30
0.03	N	1	29	30
0.10	N	1	9	10
0.30	N	1	9	10
0.30	S	0	10	10
1.00	N	4	6	10
1.00	S	0	10	10
3.00	N	4	6	10
3.00	S	1	9	10
10.00	N	5	5	10
10.00	S	4	6	10
30.00	S	5	5	10
30.00	N	7	3	10
100.00	S	8	2	10

The dilution assumption for doses z_s of somatostatin and z_n of neurotensin can be stated as

$$z_s = \rho z_n$$

which means that the doses with comparable response for the two drugs are related by the constant ρ, the relative potency; that is, ρ units of neurotensin produce the same behavior as one unit of somatostatin. If x_n and x_s represent log doses, then the dilution assumption also implies that

$$x_s = \log \rho + x_n$$

Thus, assuming the logistic model structure for somatostatin is

$$p_s(x_{si}) = \{1 + \exp(-\alpha_s - \beta x_{si})\}^{-1}$$

where x_{si} denotes log dose levels of somatostatin, you can write the implied structure for log dose levels x_{ni} of neurotensin as

$$p_n(x_{ni}) = p_s(\log \rho + x_{ni}) = \{1 + \exp(-\alpha_s - \beta \log \rho - \beta x_{ni})\}^{-1}$$

$$= \{1 + \exp(-\alpha_n - \beta x_{ni})\}^{-1}$$

where $\alpha_n = \alpha_s + \beta \log \rho$.

By forming

$$\frac{p_n(x_{ni})}{1 - p_n(x_{ni})}$$

you obtain the result

$$\log\left\{\frac{p_n(x_{ni})}{1 - p_n(x_{ni})}\right\} = \{\alpha_s + \beta \log \rho\} + \beta x_{ni}$$
$$= \alpha_n + \beta x_{ni}$$

and

$$\log\left\{\frac{p_s(x_{si})}{1 - p_s(x_{si})}\right\} = \alpha_s + \beta x_{si}$$

Thus, the dilution assumption can be tested by fitting a model with separate intercepts and slopes and then testing for a common slope.

The constant ρ is the relative potency, and since

$$\alpha_n = \alpha_s + \beta \log \rho$$

then

$$\rho = \exp\left\{\frac{\alpha_n - \alpha_s}{\beta}\right\}$$

This means that ρ units of somatostatin produce the same reaction as one unit of neurotensin.

Fieller's theorem can be used to produce confidence intervals for the relative potency. This theorem is a general result that enables confidence intervals to be computed for the ratio of two normally distributed random variables. Fieller's theorem can also be used to produce confidence intervals for the LD50. Refer to Read (1983) for a description of Fieller's formula, and refer to Collett (1991) for a discussion of how to apply it to LD50s and relative potency. Zerbe (1978) describes a matrix implementation of Fieller's formula for use with the general linear model as illustrated in the following analysis.

11.3.1   Analysis of the Peptide Data

The following DATA step creates data set ASSAY for use with PROC LOGISTIC. Indicator variables INT_S and INT_N are created to form the intercepts for each drug, and indicator variables LDOSE_N and LDOSE_S are created to form separate dose columns (slopes) for each drug. LDOSE is dose on the log scale. Since the cell counts in Table 11.2 are small, the squared terms SQLDOS_S and SQLDOS_N are created so that a test of quadratic terms can be performed to help assess goodness of fit.

```
data assay;
   input drug $ dose status $ count;
   int_n=(drug='n');
   int_s=(drug='s');
   ldose=log(dose);
   ldose_n=int_n*ldose;
   ldose_s=int_s*ldose;
   sqdose_n=int_n*ldose*ldose;
   sqdose_s=int_s*ldose*ldose;
   cards;
n 0.01    dead   0
n 0.01    alive 30
n  .03    dead   1
n  .03    alive 29
n  .10    dead   1
n  .10    alive  9
n  .30    dead   1
n  .30    alive  9
n 1.00    dead   4
n 1.00    alive  6
n 3.00    dead   4
n 3.00    alive  6
n 10.00   dead   5
n 10.00   alive  5
n 30.00   dead   7
n 30.00   alive  3
s   .30   dead   0
s   .30   alive 10
s  1.00   dead   0
s  1.00   alive 10
s 3.00    dead   1
s 3.00    alive  9
s 10.00   dead   4
s 10.00   alive  6
s 30.00   dead   5
s 30.00   alive  5
s 100.00  dead   8
s 100.00  alive  2
;
```

The following PROC LOGISTIC statements request the two intercepts and two slopes model. The NOINT option must be specified to suppress the default intercept. The TEST statement requests a test for equality of the two slope parameters β_n and β_s.

```
proc logistic data=assay descending;
   freq count;
   model status = int_n int_s ldose_n ldose_s
                  sqdose_n sqdose_s / noint
                  scale=none aggregate
                  start=4 selection=forward details;
   eq_slope: test ldose_n=ldose_s;
run;
```

Output 11.6 contains a listing of the response profile. There are 14 groups based on the drug and dose level combinations, and the model is estimating the probability of death.

Output 11.6   Response Profiles

```
                   Response Profile

              Ordered
               Value   STATUS        Count

                  1    dead           41
                  2    alive         139
```

Output 11.7 displays the goodness-of-fit statistics. With values of 4.4144 and 3.6352 for Q_L and Q_P, respectively, these statistics support an adequate model fit.

Output 11.7   Goodness-of-Fit Statistics

```
             Goodness of Fit Statistics

                                             Pr >
   Criterion      DF      Value   Value/DF   Chi-Square

   Deviance       10     4.4144    0.4414    0.9267
   Pearson        10     3.6352    0.3635    0.9623

             Number of unique profiles: 14
```

Output 11.8 contains the results for the residual score test for the two quadratic terms. It is nonsignificant, as are each of the individual tests. These results support the goodness of fit of the model.

Output 11.8   Tests for Quadratic Terms

```
   Residual Chi-Square = 1.4817 with 2 DF (p=0.4767)

      Analysis of Variables Not in the Model

                          Score        Pr >
          Variable      Chi-Square    Chi-Square

          SQDOSE_N        0.9311       0.3346
          SQDOSE_S        0.5506       0.4581
```

The parameter estimates are all significant, as seen in the ''Analysis of Maximum Likelihood Estimates'' table displayed in Output 11.9. However, if you examine the slope estimates (labeled LDOSE_N and LDOSE_S) and their standard errors, you see that it is possible that these two slopes can be represented by one slope. The Wald statistic for the hypothesis test H_0: $\beta_n = \beta_s$ bears this out with a nonsignificant $p = 0.149$.

Output 11.9   Maximum Likelihood Estimates

```
            Analysis of Maximum Likelihood Estimates

              Parameter Standard    Wald       Pr >    Standardized
Variable DF   Estimate   Error   Chi-Square Chi-Square   Estimate

INT_N    1    -1.1302    0.2948   14.6984    0.0001    -0.294545
INT_S    1    -3.3782    0.8797   14.7479    0.0001    -0.880435
LDOSE_N  1     0.6199    0.1240   24.9909    0.0001     0.810773
LDOSE_S  1     1.0615    0.2798   14.3915    0.0001     0.817738
```

Output 11.10   Equal Slopes Hypothesis Test Results

```
                Linear Hypotheses Testing

                    Wald                    Pr >
    Label        Chi-Square      DF       Chi-Square

    EQ_SLOPE       2.0820         1         0.1490
```

Thus, it appears that a parallel lines model fits these data, and the following PROC LOGISTIC statements request this model. The COVB option in the MODEL statement requests that the covariances of the parameters be printed, and the OUTEST=ESTIMATE and COVOUT options request that they be placed into a SAS data set for further processing. Without the specification of the COVOUT option, only the parameter estimates are placed in the OUTEST data set. For convenience, the _LINK_ and _LNLIKE_ variables placed in the OUTEST data set by default are dropped.

```
proc logistic data=assay descending outest=estimate
          (drop= _link_ _lnlike_) covout;
   freq count;
   model status = int_n int_s ldose /
              noint scale=none aggregate covb;
run;
```

Output 11.11 contains the goodness-of-fit statistics for this model, and they indicate that the model is adequate.

Output 11.11   Goodness-of-Fit Results

```
            Goodness of Fit Statistics

                                              Pr >
    Criterion     DF     Value    Value/DF  Chi-Square

    Deviance      11    6.8461    0.6224     0.8114
    Pearson       11    5.6481    0.5135     0.8958
```

Output 11.12 contains the parameter estimates; all of them are clearly significant.

Output 11.12   Maximum Likelihood Estimates

```
           Analysis of Maximum Likelihood Estimates

            Parameter Standard    Wald      Pr >    Standardized
 Variable DF Estimate   Error  Chi-Square Chi-Square  Estimate

 INT_N   1   -1.1931   0.3158   14.2784    0.0002    -0.310962
 INT_S   1   -2.4476   0.4532   29.1637    0.0001    -0.637906
 LDOSE   1    0.7234   0.1177   37.7687    0.0001     1.190735
```

Output 11.13 contains the estimated covariance matrix.

Output 11.13   Covariance Matrix

```
                Estimated Covariance Matrix

 Variable        INT_N            INT_S            LDOSE

 INT_N       0.099702221      0.0259072114     -0.009840945
 INT_S       0.0259072114     0.205420033      -0.036476727
 LDOSE      -0.009840945     -0.036476727       0.013855813
```

The estimated log LD50s from this model are

$$\log \text{LD50}_n = \frac{-\hat{\alpha}_n}{\hat{\beta}} = \frac{1.1931}{0.7234} = 1.65$$

and

$$\log \text{LD50}_s = \frac{-\hat{\alpha}_s}{\hat{\beta}} = \frac{2.44476}{0.7234} = 3.38$$

The relative potency is estimated as

$$\hat{\rho} = \frac{\hat{\alpha}_n - \hat{\alpha}_s}{\hat{\beta}} = \frac{-1.1931 - (-2.4476)}{0.7234} = 1.73$$

You can compute approximate confidence intervals for these quantities using the linearized Taylor series, as in the previous section for the log LD50, or you can produce confidence intervals based on Fieller's theorem. The following SAS/IML code produces confidence intervals based on Fieller's theorem for ratios of estimates from a general linear model (Zerbe 1978).

```
proc iml;
  use estimate;
  start fieller;
  title 'Confidence Intervals';
  use estimate;
```

```
read all into beta where (_type_='PARMS');
beta=beta';
read all into cov where (_type_='COV');
ratio=(k'*beta) / (h'*beta);
a=(h'*beta)**2-(3.84)*(h'*cov*h);
b=2*(3.84*(k'*cov*h)-(k'*beta)*(h'*beta));
c=(k'*beta)**2 -(3.84)*(k'*cov*k);
 disc=((b**2)-4*a*c);
if (disc<=0 | a<=0) then do;
print "confidence interval can't be computed", ratio;
stop; end;
sroot=sqrt(disc);
 l_b=((-b)-sroot)/(2*a);
 u_b=((-b)+sroot)/(2*a);
interval=l_b||u_b;
lname={"l_bound", "u_bound"};
print "95 % ci for ratio based on fieller", ratio interval[colname=lname];
finish fieller;
k={ 1 -1 0 }';
h={ 0  0 1 }';
 run fieller;
k={-1 0 0 }';
h={ 0 0 1 }';
 run fieller;
k={ 0 -1 0 }';
h={ 0 0 1 }';
 run fieller;
```

You specify coefficients for vectors **k** and **h** that premultiply the parameter vector to form the numerator and the denominator of the ratio of interest. For example, if $\boldsymbol{\beta} = \{\alpha_n, \alpha_s, \beta\}$, $\mathbf{k} = \{1, -1, 0\}$, and $\mathbf{h} = \{0, 0, 1\}$, then

$$\frac{\mathbf{k}'\boldsymbol{\beta}}{\mathbf{h}'\boldsymbol{\beta}} = \frac{\alpha_n - \alpha_s}{\beta}$$

which is the relative potency. Other choices of coefficients produce $\log LD50_n$ and $\log LD50_s$. The program inputs the covariance matrix for the parameters and applies the appropriate manipulations to produce the corresponding 95 percent confidence intervals for the ratios that are specified. Executing the SAS/IML code produces the output in Output 11.14.

The ratio estimates for the log potency, $\log LD50_n$, and $\log LD50_s$ are displayed, and the lower and upper bounds of their confidence intervals appear under "l_bound" and "u_bound," respectively.

Output 11.14   Confidence Intervals Based on Fieller's Theorem

```
         95 % ci for ratio based on fieller

        RATIO INTERVAL    l_bound    u_bound

     1.7341139           0.4262191 2.9993993

         95 % ci for ratio based on fieller

        RATIO INTERVAL    l_bound    u_bound

     1.6493414           0.823739 2.6875161

         95 % ci for ratio based on fieller

        RATIO INTERVAL    l_bound    u_bound

     3.3834554           2.486309 4.4505644
```

Table 11.3 contains these results. Thus, a dose of somatostatin must be 5.64 times higher than a dose of neurotensin to have the same effect, with a 95 percent confidence interval of (1.53, 20.06).

Table 11.3   Estimated Measures from Parallel Assay

Estimate	Value	95 Percent Confidence Interval	Exponentiated Value	Exponentiated Confidence Interval
$\log(\text{Potency})$	1.73	(0.4262, 2.9993)	5.64	(1.53, 20.07)
$\log \text{LD50}_n$	1.65	(0.8237, 2.6875)	5.21	(2.28, 14.69)
$\log \text{LD50}_s$	3.38	(2.4863, 4.4506)	29.37	(12.02, 85.68)

11.4   Analysis of Pain Study

Researchers investigated a new drug for pain relief by studying its effect on groups of subjects with two different diagnoses. The drug was administered at five dosages, and the outcome measured was whether the subjects reported adverse effects. Table 11.4 contains the data. Interest lies in investigating the association of adverse effects with dose and diagnosis; in addition, there is interest in describing the influence of dose and diagnosis on whether there are adverse effects with a statistical model.

Table 11.4   Pain Study

Dose	Diagnosis I Adverse	Not	Diagnosis II Adverse	Not
1	3	26	6	26
5	7	26	20	12
10	10	22	26	6
12	14	18	28	4
15	18	14	31	1

Unlike the previous bioassay analysis, this study does not compare the tolerance distributions of two drugs and is not strictly concerned with estimating the tolerance distribution for either drug. But even though the study does not completely fall into the usual realm of bioassay, it has a bioassay flavor. Its analysis also serves to illustrate the blend of hypothesis testing and model fitting that is often desired in a statistical analysis of categorical data.

Mantel-Haenzsel statistics are computed to determine if there is an an association between adverse effects and dose, adverse effects and diagnosis, and adverse effects and dose, controlling for diagnosis. A logistic model is then fit to describe the influence of dose and diagnosis on adverse effects, and ED50s are estimated for both diagnosis groups.

The following DATA step statements input the data and create indicator variables to be used later for the PROC LOGISTIC runs.

```
data adverse;
   input diagnos $ dose status $ count @@;
   i_diagII=(diagnos='II');
   i_diagI= (diagnos='I');
   doseI=i_diagI*dose;
   doseII=i_diagII*dose;
   diagdose=i_diagII*dose;
   if doseI > 0 then ldoseI=log(doseI); else ldoseI=0;
   if doseII > 0 then ldoseII=log(doseII); else ldoseII=0;
   cards;
I    1     adverse  3 I     1 no 26
I    5     adverse  7 I     5 no 26
I    10    adverse 10 I    10 no 22
I    12    adverse 14 I    12 no 18
I    15    adverse 18 I    15 no 14
II   1     adverse  6 II    1 no 26
II   5     adverse 20 II    5 no 12
II   10    adverse 26 II   10 no  6
II   12    adverse 28 II   12 no  4
II   15    adverse 31 II   15 no  1
;

proc freq data=adverse;
   weight count;
   tables dose*status diagnos*status diagnos*dose*status /
          nopct nocol cmh;
run;
```

Output 11.15 contains the crosstabulation for DOSE × STATUS. There is a positive association between dose level and proportion of adverse effects.

Output 11.15   Table of DOSE × STATUS

```
              TABLE OF DOSE BY STATUS

    DOSE        STATUS

    Frequency|
    Row Pct   |adverse |no       |   Total
    ---------+--------+--------+
          1 |      9 |     52 |     61
            |  14.75 |  85.25 |
    ---------+--------+--------+
          5 |     27 |     38 |     65
            |  41.54 |  58.46 |
    ---------+--------+--------+
         10 |     36 |     28 |     64
            |  56.25 |  43.75 |
    ---------+--------+--------+
         12 |     42 |     22 |     64
            |  65.63 |  34.38 |
    ---------+--------+--------+
         15 |     49 |     15 |     64
            |  76.56 |  23.44 |
    ---------+--------+--------+
    Total         163      155       318
```

Output 11.16 contains the Mantel-Haenszel statistics. Since the dose levels are numeric, the 1 df correlation statistic is appropriate. $Q_{CS} = 55.798$, which is strongly significant. As the dose increases, the proportion of subjects who experienced adverse effects also increases.

Output 11.16   Mantel-Haenszel Statistics

```
           SUMMARY STATISTICS FOR DOSE BY STATUS


    Cochran-Mantel-Haenszel Statistics (Based on Table Scores)

    Statistic   Alternative Hypothesis    DF      Value      Prob
    -----------------------------------------------------------------
        1       Nonzero Correlation        1      55.798     0.001
        2       Row Mean Scores Differ     4      57.140     0.001
        3       General Association        4      57.140     0.001
```

Output 11.17 displays the crosstabulation for DIAGNOS × STATUS.

Output 11.17   DIAGNOS × STATUS Table

```
                TABLE OF DIAGNOS BY STATUS

        DIAGNOS       STATUS

        Frequency|
        Row Pct   |adverse |no      |  Total
        ---------+--------+--------+
        I        |     52 |    106 |    158
                 |  32.91 |  67.09 |
        ---------+--------+--------+
        II       |    111 |     49 |    160
                 |  69.38 |  30.63 |
        ---------+--------+--------+
        Total          163      155      318
```

Output 11.18 contains the Mantel-Haenszel statistics. $Q_{MH} = 42.173$ with 1 df, which is also strongly significant. Subjects with diagnosis II were more likely to experience adverse effects.

Output 11.18   Mantel-Haenszel Statistics

```
        SUMMARY STATISTICS FOR DIAGNOS BY STATUS


    Cochran-Mantel-Haenszel Statistics (Based on Table Scores)

    Statistic   Alternative Hypothesis    DF      Value     Prob
    ------------------------------------------------------------------
        1       Nonzero Correlation        1     42.173    0.001
        2       Row Mean Scores Differ     1     42.173    0.001
        3       General Association        1     42.173    0.001
```

Output 11.19 contains the extended Mantel-Haenszel statistics for the association of dose and status after adjusting for diagnosis. The correlation statistic is appropriate, and $Q_{CS} = 65.557$ with 1 df, which is clearly significant.

Output 11.19   DIAGNOS*DRUG*STATUS

```
                CONTROLLING FOR DIAGNOS

    Cochran-Mantel-Haenszel Statistics (Based on Table Scores)

    Statistic   Alternative Hypothesis    DF      Value     Prob
    ------------------------------------------------------------
        1       Nonzero Correlation        1     65.557    0.001
        2       Row Mean Scores Differ     4     67.436    0.001
        3       General Association        4     67.436    0.001
```

The following PROC LOGISTIC statements fit a model that contains separate intercepts and slopes for the two diagnoses. First, the actual dose is used.

```
proc logistic data=adverse outest=estimate
              (drop= _link_ _lnlike_) covout;
    freq count;
```

```
model status = i_diagI i_diagII doseI doseII  /
              noint scale=none aggregate;
   eq_slope: test doseI=doseII;
run;
```

Output 11.20 contains the response profiles and goodness-of-fit statistics. The model fit appears to be quite good.

Output 11.20   Response Profiles and Goodness of Fit

```
                        Response Profile

                  Ordered
                  Value  STATUS      Count

                     1   adverse       163
                     2   no            155

           Goodness of Fit Statistics

                                            Pr >
        Criterion    DF    Value   Value/DF  Chi-Square

        Deviance      6   2.7345   0.4557    0.8414
        Pearson       6   2.7046   0.4508    0.8449

           Number of unique profiles: 10
```

Output 11.21 contains the model parameters, and Output 11.22 contains the test for a common slope. The hypothesis of a common slope is rejected at the $\alpha = 0.05$ level of significance.

Output 11.21   Parameter Estimates

```
           Analysis of Maximum Likelihood Estimates

                 Parameter Standard    Wald      Pr >     Standardized
        Variable DF Estimate  Error  Chi-Square Chi-Square  Estimate

        I_DIAGI  1   -2.2735  0.4573   24.7197    0.0001    -0.627686
        I_DIAGII 1   -1.4341  0.3742   14.6891    0.0001    -0.395944
        DOSEI    1    0.1654  0.0414   15.9478    0.0001     0.509490
        DOSEII   1    0.3064  0.0486   39.8201    0.0001     0.943473
```

Output 11.22   Hypothesis Test

```
              Linear Hypotheses Testing

                         Wald                 Pr >
        Label         Chi-Square      DF    Chi-Square

        EQ_SLOPE        4.8791         1      0.0272
```

Next, the model based on log doses is fit.

```
proc logistic data=adverse;
   freq count;
   model status = i_diagI i_diagII ldoseI ldoseII   /
                  noint scale=none aggregate;
   eq_slope: test ldoseI=ldoseII;
run;
```

Output 11.23 contains the goodness-of-fit tests, which are not as supportive of this model as they are for the model based on actual dose; however, they are still entirely satisfactory.

Output 11.23   Goodness-of-Fit Tests

Goodness of Fit Statistics				
Criterion	DF	Value	Value/DF	Pr > Chi-Square
Deviance	6	4.8774	0.8129	0.5596
Pearson	6	4.4884	0.7481	0.6109

Output 11.24 contains the results for the test that the slopes are equal.

Output 11.24   Hypothesis Test Results

Linear Hypotheses Testing			
Label	Wald Chi-Square	DF	Pr > Chi-Square
EQ_SLOPE	2.4034	1	0.1211

With $p = 0.1211$, you would not usually reject the hypothesis that the slopes are equal.

Thus, both models do fit the data, and one model offers the possibility of a parallel lines model. Frequently, you do encounter different model choices in your analyses and need to make a decision about which model to present. Since this is not a true bioassay, in the sense of a study comparing two drugs, the fact that you can fit a model with a common slope has less motivation. Potency in this setting means only that the shape of the tolerance distribution of the analgesic is similar for the two diagnoses, which may not be as important as simply determining that the drug works differently for the two diagnoses.

The model with the actual dose is used, since it fits very well and since there is no *a priori* reason to need to use log doses. (One very good reason might be to compare results with other studies if they worked with dose on the log scale.) It is of interest to compute ED50s for both diagnoses, to help describe the median impact on adverse effects for the two diagnoses. The SAS/IML routine is again used to compute the ED50s and to produce a confidence interval based on Fieller's formula. (The entire module is not displayed again.)

The required coefficients are

```
k={ -1 0 0 0}`;
h={  0 0 1 0}`;
```

and

```
k={ 0 -1 0 0}`;
h={ 0  0 0 1}`;
 run fieller;
```

Output 11.25 contains the results. You need 13.74 units of the analgesic to produce adverse effects in 50 percent of the subjects with Diagnosis I; you only need 4.68 units of the drug to produce adverse effects in 50 percent of the subjects with Diagnosis II. The respective confidence intervals are $(11.5095, 18.2537)$ and $(2.9652, 6.0377)$.

Output 11.25   ED50s

```
          Confidence Intervals

     95 % ci for ratio based on fieller

     RATIO INTERVAL   l_bound   u_bound

   13.741832         11.509478 18.253682

      95 ci for ratio based on fieller

     RATIO INTERVAL   l_bound   u_bound

    4.6799313         2.9651591 6.0376683
```

This example illustrates that bioassay methods can be used for the analysis of data that are not strictly bioassay data but are concerned with the investigation of drug responses. Bioassay methods can also be extended to other application areas as well, such as child development studies. For example, concepts like ED50 can be applied to describe the median ages at which certain physical developments occur. Understanding the strategies that are designed for certain specialty areas can lead to useful applications in nonrelated areas. Refer to Bock and Jones (1968) and Bock (1975) for some statistical methodology related to child development and behavioral areas. Refer to Landis and Koch (1979) for examples of categorical analysis of behavioral data.

Chapter 12
Weighted Least Squares

Chapter Table of Contents

Chapter 12
Weighted Least Squares

12.1   Introduction

Previous chapters discussed statistical modeling of categorical data with logistic regression. Maximum likelihood estimation (ML) was used to estimate parameters for models based on logits and cumulative logits. Logistic regression is suitable for many situations, particularly for dichotomous response outcomes. However, there are situations where modeling techniques other than logistic regression are of interest. You may be interested in modeling functions besides logits, such as mean scores, proportions, or more complicated functions of the responses. In addition, the analysis framework may dictate a different modeling approach, such as in the case of repeated measurements studies.

Weighted least squares (WLS) estimation provides a methodology for modeling a wide range of categorical data outcomes. This chapter focuses on the application of weighted least squares for the modeling of mean scores and proportions in the stratified simple random sampling framework, as well as for the modeling of estimates produced by more complex sampling mechanisms, such as those required for complex sample surveys. The methodology is explained in the context of a basic example.

The CATMOD procedure is a general procedure for modeling categorical data. It performs logistic regression analysis using maximum likelihood estimation when the response functions are generalized logits, and it performs weighted least squares estimation for a variety of other response functions. This chapter discusses the use of PROC CATMOD for numerous applications of weighted least squares analyses. Chapter 13, ''Modeling Repeated Measurements Data,'' discusses the use of weighted least squares for the advanced topic of repeated measurements analysis.

You should be familiar with the material in Chapter 8, ''Logistic Regression I: Dichotomous Response,'' and Chapter 9, ''Logistic Regression II: Polytomous Response,'' before proceeding with this chapter.

12.2   Weighted Least Squares Methodology

To motivate the discussion of weighted least squares methodology, consider the following example. Epidemiologists investigating air pollution effects conducted a study of childhood respiratory disease (Stokes 1986). Investigators visited groups of children two times and recorded whether they were exhibiting symptoms of colds. The children were recorded as having no periods with a cold, one period with a cold, or two periods with a cold. Investigators were interested in determining whether sex or residence affected the distribution of colds. These data are displayed in Table 12.1.

Table 12.1   Colds in Children

Sex	Residence	Periods with Colds 0	1	2	Total
Female	Rural	45	64	71	180
Female	Urban	80	104	116	300
Male	Rural	84	124	82	290
Male	Urban	106	117	87	310

As previously discussed, statistical modeling addresses the question of how a response outcome is distributed across the various levels of the explanatory variables. In the standard linear model, this is done by fitting a model to the response mean. In logistic regression, the function modeled is the logit or cumulative logit. For these data, a response measure of interest is the mean number of periods with colds. However, because there are a small, discrete number of response values, it is unlikely that the normality assumptions usually required for the standard linear model are met. However, weighted least squares methodology provides a useful strategy for analyzing these data.

12.2.1   Weighted Least Squares Framework

Underlying most types of weighted least squares methods for categorical data analysis is a contingency table. The general idea is to model the distribution of the response variable, represented in the columns of the table, across the levels of the explanatory variables, represented by the rows of the table. These rows are determined by the crossclassification of the levels, or values, of the explanatory variables. The contingency table for the colds data has four rows and three columns. There are four rows since there are four combinations of sex and residence; there are three columns because the response variable has three possible outcomes: 0, 1, and 2.

The general contingency table is displayed in Table 12.2, where s represents the number of rows, or groups, in the table and r represents the number of responses. The rows of the table are also referred to as subpopulations.

Table 12.2   Underlying Contingency Table

Group	Response 1	2	$\cdots$	r	Total
1	n_{11}	n_{12}	$\cdots$	n_{1r}	n_{1+}
2	n_{21}	n_{22}	$\cdots$	n_{2r}	n_{2+}
$\cdots$	$\cdots$	$\cdots$	$\cdots$	$\cdots$	$\cdots$
s	n_{s1}	n_{s2}	$\cdots$	n_{sr}	n_{s+}

The proportion of subjects in each group who have each response is written

$$p_{ij} = n_{ij}/n_{i+}$$

where n_{ij} is the number of subjects in the ith group who have the jth response. For example, $p_{11} = 45/180$ in Table 12.1. You can put the proportions for one group together in a proportion vector that describes the response distribution for that group. For the colds data, it looks like the following:

$$\mathbf{p}_i = (p_{i1}, p_{i2}, p_{i3})'$$

You can then form a proportion vector for each group in the contingency table. The proportions for each group add up to 1. All the functions that can be modeled with weighted least squares methodology are generated from these proportion vectors.

The rows of the contingency table are considered to be simple random samples from the multinomial distribution; since the rows are independent, the entire table is distributed as product multinomial. You can write the covariance matrix for the proportions in the ith row as

$$\mathbf{V}_i = \frac{1}{n_{i+}} \begin{bmatrix} p_{i1}(1 - p_{i1}) & -p_{i1}p_{i2} & \cdots & -p_{i1}p_{ir} \\ -p_{i2}p_{i1} & p_{i2}(1 - p_{i2}) & \cdots & -p_{i2}p_{ir} \\ \vdots & \vdots & \vdots & \vdots \\ -p_{ir}p_{i1} & -p_{ir}p_{i2} & \cdots & p_{ir}(1 - p_{ir}) \end{bmatrix}$$

and then write the covariance matrix for the entire table as

$$\mathbf{V_p} = \begin{bmatrix} \mathbf{V}_1 & \mathbf{0} & \cdots & \mathbf{0} \\ \mathbf{0} & \mathbf{V}_2 & \cdots & \mathbf{0} \\ \vdots & \vdots & \vdots & \vdots \\ \mathbf{0} & \mathbf{0} & \cdots & \mathbf{V}_s \end{bmatrix}$$

where $\mathbf{V}_i$ is the covariance matrix for the ith row.

12.2.2   Weighted Least Squares Estimation

Once the proportion vector and covariance matrix are computed, the modeling phase begins with the choice of a response function. You can model the proportions themselves; mean scores, which are simple linear functions of the proportions; logits, which are constructed by taking a linear function (difference) of the log proportions; and a number of more complicated functions that are created by combinations of various transformations of the proportions, such as the kappa statistic for observer agreement (refer to Landis and Koch 1977) or rank measures of association (refer to Koch and Edwards 1988).

For the colds data, the response function is the mean number of periods with a cold. You construct these means from the proportions of responses in each row of Table 12.1 and then apply a statistical model that determines the effect of sex and residence on their distribution. Table 12.3 displays the row proportions.

Table 12.3   Colds in Children

Sex	Residence	Periods with Colds 0	1	2	Total
Female	Rural	0.25	0.36	0.39	1.00
Female	Urban	0.27	0.35	0.39	1.00
Male	Rural	0.29	0.43	0.28	1.00
Male	Urban	0.34	0.38	0.28	1.00

For example, to compute the mean number of periods of colds for females in a rural residence, you would perform the following computation.

$$\text{mean colds} = 0 * p_{11} + 1 * p_{12} + 2 * p_{13}$$
$$= 0 * (0.25) + 1 * (0.36) + 2 * (0.39)$$
$$= 1.14$$

In matrix terms, you have multiplied the proportion vector by a linear transformation matrix **A**.

$$\mathbf{A}\mathbf{p}_1 = \begin{bmatrix} 0 & 1 & 2 \end{bmatrix} \begin{bmatrix} 0.25 \\ 0.36 \\ 0.39 \end{bmatrix} = 1.14$$

Means are generated for each sex $\times$ residence group to produce a total of four functions for the table. The ith function is denoted $F(\mathbf{p}_i)$. The following expression shows how you generate a function vector by applying a linear transformation matrix to the total proportion vector $\mathbf{p} = (\mathbf{p}_1', \mathbf{p}_2', \mathbf{p}_3', \mathbf{p}_4')'$ to produce the four means of interest.

$$F(\mathbf{p}) = \mathbf{A}\mathbf{p} = \begin{bmatrix} 0 & 1 & 2 & 0 & 0 & 0 & 0 & 0 & 0 & 0 & 0 & 0 \\ 0 & 0 & 0 & 0 & 1 & 2 & 0 & 0 & 0 & 0 & 0 & 0 \\ 0 & 0 & 0 & 0 & 0 & 0 & 0 & 1 & 2 & 0 & 0 & 0 \\ 0 & 0 & 0 & 0 & 0 & 0 & 0 & 0 & 0 & 0 & 1 & 2 \end{bmatrix} \mathbf{p} = \begin{bmatrix} 1.14 \\ 1.12 \\ 0.99 \\ 0.94 \end{bmatrix}$$

If the groups have sufficient sample size, usually $n_{i+} \geq 25$, then the variation among the response functions can be investigated by fitting linear regression models with weighted least squares.

$$E_A\{\mathbf{F}(\mathbf{p})\} = \mathbf{F}(\boldsymbol{\pi}) = \mathbf{X}\boldsymbol{\beta}$$

E_A denotes asymptotic expectation, and $\boldsymbol{\pi} = E\{\mathbf{p}\}$ denotes the vector of population probabilities for all the populations together. The vector $\boldsymbol{\beta}$ contains the parameters that describe the variation among the response functions, and $\mathbf{X}$ is the model specification matrix. The equations for WLS estimation are similar to those for least squares estimation.

$$\mathbf{b} = (\mathbf{X}'\mathbf{V}_\mathbf{F}^{-1}\mathbf{X})^{-1}\mathbf{X}'\mathbf{V}_\mathbf{F}^{-1}\mathbf{F}$$

$\mathbf{V}_\mathbf{F}$ is the covariance matrix for the vector of response functions and is usually nonsingular when the sample sizes n_{i+} are sufficiently large (for example, $n_{i+} \geq 25$ and at least two $n_{ij} \geq 1$ in each row). This is the weight matrix component of weighted least squares estimation. Its form depends on the nature of the response functions. In the case of the colds data, where the response functions are means computed as $\mathbf{Ap}$, the covariance matrix is computed as

$$\mathbf{V}_\mathbf{F} = \mathbf{A}\mathbf{V}_\mathbf{p}\mathbf{A}'$$

The covariance matrix for $\mathbf{b}$ is written

$$V(\mathbf{b}) = (\mathbf{X}'\mathbf{V}_\mathbf{F}^{-1}\mathbf{X})^{-1}$$

Model adequacy is assessed with Wald goodness-of-fit statistics. They are computed as

$$Q_W = (\mathbf{F} - \mathbf{X}\mathbf{b})'\mathbf{V}_\mathbf{F}^{-1}(\mathbf{F} - \mathbf{X}\mathbf{b})$$

Q_W is distributed as chi-square for moderately large sample sizes (for example, all $n_{i+} \geq 25$), and its degrees of freedom are equal to the difference between the number of rows of $F(\mathbf{p})$ and the number of parameters. If only one response function is created per row of the contingency table, then this is the number of table rows minus the number of estimated parameters.

You can address questions about the parameters with the use of hypothesis tests. Each hypothesis is written in the form

$$H_0\colon \mathbf{C}\boldsymbol{\beta} = \mathbf{0}$$

and can investigate whether specified linear combinations of the parameters are equal to zero. The test statistic employed is a Wald statistic that is expressed as

$$Q_C = (\mathbf{C}\mathbf{b})'[\mathbf{C}(\mathbf{X}'\mathbf{V}_\mathbf{F}^{-1}\mathbf{X})^{-1}\mathbf{C}']^{-1}(\mathbf{C}\mathbf{b})$$

Q_C is distributed as chi-square with degrees of freedom equal to the number of linearly independent rows in $\mathbf{C}$.

You can also generate predicted values $\hat{\mathbf{F}} = \mathbf{X}\mathbf{b}$ of the response functions and their covariance matrix $\mathbf{V}_{\hat{\mathbf{F}}} = \mathbf{X}V(\mathbf{b})\mathbf{X}'$. See Section 12.10 for more statistical theory concerning weighted least squares estimation.

12.2.3 Model Parameterization

The preliminary model of interest for a WLS analysis is often the *saturated* model, in which all the variation is explained by the parameters. In a saturated model, there are as many parameters in the model as there are response functions. For these data, the saturated model is written

$$
\begin{bmatrix} F(\mathbf{p}_1) \\ F(\mathbf{p}_2) \\ F(\mathbf{p}_3) \\ F(\mathbf{p}_4) \end{bmatrix} = \begin{bmatrix} \alpha + \beta_1 + \beta_2 + \beta_3 \\ \alpha + \beta_1 - \beta_2 - \beta_3 \\ \alpha - \beta_1 + \beta_2 - \beta_3 \\ \alpha - \beta_1 - \beta_2 + \beta_3 \end{bmatrix} = \begin{bmatrix} 1 & 1 & 1 & 1 \\ 1 & 1 & -1 & -1 \\ 1 & -1 & 1 & -1 \\ 1 & -1 & -1 & 1 \end{bmatrix} \begin{bmatrix} \alpha \\ \beta_1 \\ \beta_2 \\ \beta_3 \end{bmatrix}
$$

Here, α is a centered intercept, β_1 is the differential effect for sex, β_2 is the differential effect for residence, and β_3 represents their interaction. The intercept is the mean number of colds averaged over all the groups. The differential effects represent average deviations from the mean; β_1 is the amount you need to add to the average of the mean periods with colds to compute the mean number of colds for females (averaged over residence); it is also the amount you need to subtract from the average of the mean periods with colds to compute the mean number of colds for males (averaged over residence).

As discussed in Section 8.8, this type of parameterization is the default for the CATMOD procedure and is called deviation from the mean parameterization; it is a *fullrank* parameterization. This imposes restrictions on the parameters, unlike the GLM procedure, which uses an overparameterized model that does not place restrictions on the parameters. In PROC CATMOD, if an effect such as sex or residence has s levels, then it is represented by $s - 1$ parameters. The same effect would be represented by s parameters in PROC GLM. To understand the restrictions imposed by PROC CATMOD, consider the sex effect for the colds data and consider a model that contains only the intercept and the sex effect. You could write such a model as

$$
E\{F(\mathbf{p}_i)\} = \alpha + \tau_i
$$

where α represents the overall mean, and τ_i represents the ith level of the main effect.

$$
E\{F(\mathbf{p}_1)\} = \alpha + \tau_1, \quad E\{F(\mathbf{p}_2)\} = \alpha + \tau_1
$$

and

$$
E\{F(\mathbf{p}_3)\} = \alpha + \tau_2, \quad E\{F(\mathbf{p}_4)\} = \alpha + \tau_2
$$

In matrix terms, this model would be written

$$
\begin{bmatrix} F(\mathbf{p}_1) \\ F(\mathbf{p}_2) \\ F(\mathbf{p}_3) \\ F(\mathbf{p}_4) \end{bmatrix} = \begin{bmatrix} \alpha + \tau_1 \\ \alpha + \tau_1 \\ \alpha \quad + \tau_2 \\ \alpha \quad + \tau_2 \end{bmatrix} = \begin{bmatrix} 1 & 1 & 0 \\ 1 & 1 & 0 \\ 1 & 0 & 1 \\ 1 & 0 & 1 \end{bmatrix} \begin{bmatrix} \alpha \\ \tau_1 \\ \tau_2 \end{bmatrix}
$$

If you add these equations, you obtain

$$E\left\{\sum_{i=1}^{4} F(\mathbf{p}_i)\right\} = 4\alpha + 2(\tau_1 + \tau_2)$$

or

$$E\{\bar{F}\} = \alpha + (\tau_1 + \tau_2)/2$$

Since

$$E\{\bar{F}\} = \alpha$$

and α is the overall mean, there is an implied restriction that

$$\tau_1 + \tau_2 = 0$$

or that $\tau_1 = -\tau_2$. Thus, τ_2 would be redundant in the model since it is a linear combination of other model parameters, and it can be eliminated. If you have an effect with two levels, it is represented in PROC CATMOD with one parameter. Similarly, if you have an effect that has s levels, then that effect is represented with $s - 1$ parameters. Understanding the parameterization is important in understanding what the model coefficients represent, how the degrees of freedom are determined, and how to construct contrast tests.

12.3   Using PROC CATMOD for Weighted Least Squares Analysis

Since the CATMOD procedure is very general, it offers great flexibility in its input. Standard uses that take advantage of defaults may require no more than three or four statements. More statements are required if you take advantage of the facilities for repeated measurements analysis or loglinear model analysis. And the input can be quite rich if you choose to create your own response functions through the specification of the appropriate matrix operations or create your own parameterization by directly inputting your model matrix.

The analysis for the colds data requires minimal input. You need to specify the input data set, the WEIGHT variable if the data are in count form, the response function, and the desired model in a MODEL statement. The MODEL statement is the only required statement for PROC CATMOD.

First, a SAS data set is created for the colds data.

```
data colds;
   input sex $ residnce $ periods count @@;
   cards;
female rural 0 45 female rural 1 64   female rural 2 71
female urban 0 80 female urban 1 104 female urban 2 116
male rural   0 84 male    rural 1 124 male    rural 2 82
male urban   0 106 male   urban 1 117 male    urban 2 87
;
run;
```

The following set of SAS statements request that a weighted least squares analysis be performed for the mean response, using the saturated model.

```
proc catmod;
   weight count;
   response means;
   model periods = sex residnce sex*residnce /freq prob;
run;
```

The WEIGHT statement works the same as it does for the FREQ procedure; the WEIGHT variable contains the count of observations that have the values listed on the data line. As with PROC FREQ, you can supply input data in raw form, one observation per data line, or in count form. The RESPONSE statement specifies the response functions. If you leave out this statement, PROC CATMOD models generalized logits with maximum likelihood estimation. Specifying the MEANS keyword requests that mean response functions be constructed for each subpopulation; the default estimation method for functions other than generalized logits is weighted least squares.

The MODEL statement requests that PROC CATMOD fit a model that includes main effects for sex and residence as well as their interaction. The effects specification is similar to that used in the GLM procedure. The effects for sex and residence each have 1 df, and their interaction also has 1 df. Since the model also includes an intercept by default, this model is saturated. There are four parameters for the four response functions.

PROC CATMOD uses the explanatory variables listed on the right-hand side of the MODEL statement to determine the rows of the underlying contingency table. Since the variable SEX has two levels and the variable RESIDNCE has two levels, PROC CATMOD forms a contingency table that has four rows. The columns of the underlying contingency table are determined by the number of values for the response variable on the left-hand side of the MODEL statement. Since there can be 0, 1, or 2 periods with colds, there are three columns in this table.

The FREQ and PROB options in the MODEL statement cause the frequencies and proportions from the underlying contingency table to be printed.

Output 12.1 displays the population and response profiles, which represent the rows and columns of the underlying table, respectively. Output 12.2 displays the underlying frequency table and the corresponding table of proportions. PROC CATMOD labels each group or subpopulation ''Sample n''; you often need to refer back to the ''POPULATION PROFILES'' table to interpret other parts of the PROC CATMOD output. You should always check the population and response profiles to ensure that you have defined the underlying frequency table as you intended.

Output 12.1   Population and Response Profiles

```
                 POPULATION PROFILES
                                     Sample
        Sample   SEX      RESIDNCE    Size
        -----------------------------------
           1     female   rural       180
           2     female   urban       300
           3     male     rural       290
           4     male     urban       310


                 RESPONSE PROFILES

           Response  PERIODS
           ----------------
              1         0
              2         1
              3         2
```

Output 12.2   Table Frequencies and Proportions

```
               RESPONSE FREQUENCIES

                       Response Number
        Sample      1          2          3
        ----------------------------------------
          1        45         64         71
          2        80        104        116
          3        84        124         82
          4       106        117         87


               RESPONSE PROBABILITIES

                       Response Number
        Sample      1          2          3
        ----------------------------------------
          1       0.25     0.35556    0.39444
          2    0.26667     0.34667    0.38667
          3    0.28966     0.42759    0.28276
          4    0.34194     0.37742    0.28065
```

PROC CATMOD output includes a table of response function values and the model matrix, labeled "DESIGN MATRIX" in Output 12.3. The response functions are the mean number of periods with colds for each of the populations.

Output 12.3   Observed Response Functions and Model Matrix

```
                Response        DESIGN MATRIX
        Sample  Function    1      2      3      4
        ----------------------------------------------
          1     1.14444     1      1      1      1
          2     1.12000     1      1     -1     -1
          3     0.99310     1     -1      1     -1
          4     0.93871     1     -1     -1      1
```

Model-fitting results are displayed in Output 12.4 in a table labeled "ANALYSIS-OF-VARIANCE TABLE" for its similarity in function to an ANOVA table.

Output 12.4   ANOVA Table

```
            ANALYSIS-OF-VARIANCE TABLE

Source              DF    Chi-Square    Prob
--------------------------------------------------
INTERCEPT            1      1841.13    0.0000
SEX                  1        11.57    0.0007
RESIDNCE             1         0.65    0.4202
SEX*RESIDNCE         1         0.09    0.7594

RESIDUAL             0          .         .
```

The effects listed on the right-hand side of the MODEL statement are listed under
"Source." Unless otherwise specified, an intercept is included in the model. If there is
one response function per subpopulation, the intercept has 1 df. The statistics printed
under "Chi-Square" are Wald statistics. Also provided are the degrees of freedom for
each effect and corresponding p-value.

The last row contains information labeled "RESIDUAL." Normally, this line contains a
chi-square value that serves as a goodness-of-fit test for the specified model. However, in
this case, the model uses four parameters to fit four response functions. The fit must
necessarily be perfect, and thus the model explains all the variation among the response
functions. The degrees of freedom are zero since the degrees of freedom for Q_W are equal
to the difference in the number of response functions and the number of parameters. The
SAS System prints out missing values under "Chi-Square" and "Prob" for zero degrees
of freedom.

Since the model fits, it is appropriate to examine the chi-square statistics for the individual
effects. With a chi-square value of 0.09 and $p = 0.7594$, the SEX*RESIDNCE interaction
is clearly nonsignificant. SEX appears to be a strong effect and RESIDNCE a negligible
effect, but these are better assessed in the context of the main effects model that remains
after the interaction term is deleted, since the estimation of these main effects is better in
the absence of the interaction.

The following statements request the main effects model and produce the analysis of
variance table displayed in Output 12.5.

```
proc catmod;
   weight count;
   response means;
   model periods = sex residnce;
run;
```

Output 12.5   Preliminary Colds Output

```
                  ANALYSIS-OF-VARIANCE TABLE

        Source              DF    Chi-Square     Prob
        ----------------------------------------------------
        INTERCEPT            1      1882.77      0.0000
        SEX                  1        12.08      0.0005
        RESIDNCE             1         0.76      0.3839

        RESIDUAL             1         0.09      0.7594
```

Look at the goodness-of-fit statistic. $Q_W = 0.09$ with 1 df and $p = 0.7594$. The main effects model adequately fits the data. The smaller the goodness-of-fit chi-square value, and correspondingly the larger the p value, the better the fit. This is different from the model F statistic in the usual linear model setting, where the F value is high for a model that fits the data well in the sense of explaining a large amount of the variation. Strictly speaking, using the usual significance level of $\alpha = 0.05$, any p-value greater than 0.05 supports an adequate model fit. However, many analysts are more comfortable with goodness-of-fit p-values that are greater than 0.15.

The effect for sex is highly significant, $p < 0.001$. However, the effect for residence remains nonsignificant when the interaction is removed from the model, $p = 0.3839$. These results suggest that a model with a single main effect for SEX is appropriate.

Consider the following statements to perform this task. The MODEL statement contains the response variable PERIODS and a single explanatory variable, SEX. This should produce the desired model. However, recall that the variables listed on the right-hand side of the MODEL statement are also used to determine the underlying contingency table structure. This table has its rows determined by both SEX and RESIDNCE. If RESIDNCE is *not* included in the MODEL statement, as shown in the following statements, then PROC CATMOD would create two groups based on SEX instead of four groups based on SEX and RESIDNCE.

```
proc catmod;
   weight count;
   response means;
   model periods = sex;
run;
```

However, you need to maintain the sampling structure of the underlying table. The solution is the addition of the POPULATION statement. When a POPULATION statement is included, the variables listed in it determine the populations, not the variables listed in the MODEL statement. So, you can let the right-hand variables on the MODEL statement determine the populations so long as all the necessary variables are included; if not, you need to use a POPULATION statement. Some analysts use the POPULATION statement for all PROC CATMOD invocations as a precautionary measure.

The following code requests the single main effect model.

```
proc catmod;
   population sex residnce;
```

```
       weight count;
       response means;
       model periods = sex;
   run;
```

The table of population profiles for the invocation using the POPULATION statement is identical to those produced by previous invocations without it, but including both SEX and RESIDNCE as explanatory variables.

Output 12.6   POPULATION Statement Results

```
                    POPULATION PROFILES
                                        Sample
           Sample   SEX      RESIDNCE    Size
           ------------------------------------
              1     female   rural       180
              2     female   urban       300
              3     male     rural       290
              4     male     urban       310
```

The analysis of variance table now includes only one main effect, SEX. The residual goodness-of-fit $Q_W = 0.85$, with 2 df and $p = 0.6531$, indicating an adequate fit.

Output 12.7   Single Main Effect ANOVA Table

```
                    ANALYSIS-OF-VARIANCE TABLE

           Source           DF   Chi-Square   Prob
           ------------------------------------------------
           INTERCEPT         1     1899.55    0.0000
           SEX               1       11.53    0.0007

           RESIDUAL          2        0.85    0.6531
```

Compare this analysis of variance table with that displayed in Output 12.5.

Note that Q_W for the reduced model (0.85) is the sum of Q_W for the two effects model ($Q_W = 0.09$) plus the value of the Wald statistic for the effect for residence (0.76). This is a property of weighted least squares. When you delete a term from a model, the residual chi-square for the goodness of fit for the new model is equal to the old model's residual chi-square value plus the chi-square value for the particular effect. This is also true for maximum likelihood estimation when likelihood ratio tests are used for goodness of fit and for particular effects, but not when the Wald statistic is used with maximum likelihood estimation. Similarly, note that the $Q_W = 0.09$ for the two main effects model of Output 12.5 is equal to the chi-square for the interaction term in the saturated model (Output 12.4).

When an effect is deleted, any variation attributed to that effect is put into the residual variation, which is the variation that the model does not explain; this variation is essentially random for well-fitting models. If the residual variation is low, the residual chi-square will be small, indicating that the model explains the variation in the response fairly well. If the residual variation is high, the residual chi-square will be large, with a correspondingly low p-value, indicating that the residual variation is significantly different from zero. The implication is that the model lacks necessary terms.

Finally, note that the degrees of freedom for the goodness of fit for the reduced model are increased by the number of degrees of freedom for the deleted effect, in this case from 1 to 2, since residence had one degree of freedom.

PROC CATMOD also prints out a table containing the parameter estimates. Since the model fits, it is appropriate to examine this table, displayed in Output 12.8.

Output 12.8   Single Main Effect Model

```
           ANALYSIS OF WEIGHTED-LEAST-SQUARES ESTIMATES

                                      Standard   Chi-
Effect             Parameter  Estimate  Error   Square   Prob
------------------------------------------------------------
INTERCEPT              1       1.0477   0.0240  1899.55  0.0000
SEX                   2       0.0816   0.0240    11.53  0.0007
```

Listed under ''Effect'' are the parameters estimated for the model. Since sex is represented by one parameter, only one estimate is listed. Since females are listed first under SEX in the population profile of Output 12.6, the effect for sex is the differential effect for females. If an effect has more than one parameter, each of them is listed, as well as the associated standard error, Wald statistic, and p-value. Since sex is represented by only one parameter, the chi-square value listed in the table of WLS estimates is identical to that listed in the analysis of variance table. This won't happen for those effects comprised of more than one parameter, since the effect test listed in the analysis of variance table is the test of whether all the effect's parameters are jointly zero, and the chi-square tests listed in the parameter estimates table are always one degree of freedom tests for each of the individual parameters.

To summarize, the model that most effectively describes these data is a single main effect model where sex is the main effect. Its goodness of fit is satisfactory and the model is parsimonious in the sense of not including factors with essentially no association with the response. Girls reported more colds than boys; the model-predicted mean number of periods with colds for girls is

$$\bar{F}_{\text{girls}} = \alpha + \beta_1 = 1.0477 + 0.0816 = 1.1293$$

and the model-predicted mean number of periods with colds for boys is

$$\bar{F}_{\text{boys}} = \alpha - \beta_1 = 1.0477 - 0.0816 = 0.9661$$

12.4   Analysis of Means: Performing Contrast Tests

Frequently, the underlying contingency table is based on more than two factors. This section discusses how to build models in a multi-factor framework, how to specify scores for the response variable, and how to construct contrast tests with the CATMOD procedure. In addition, the interactive use of PROC CATMOD is explained.

Model building for more complicated crossclassification structures follows a similar strategy to that illustrated in the analysis of the colds data set. Consider the following data from a randomized clinical trial of chronic pain. Investigators were interested in comparing an active treatment with a placebo for an aspect of the condition of patients in the study. These patients were obtained from two investigators whose research design included stratified randomization relative to four diagnostic classes.

Table 12.4   Chronic Pain Clinical Trial

Diagnostic			Patient Status				
Class	Investigator	Treatment	Poor	Fair	Moderate	Good	Excellent
I	A	Active	3	2	2	1	0
I	A	Placebo	7	0	1	1	1
I	B	Active	1	6	1	5	3
I	B	Placebo	5	4	2	3	3
II	A	Active	1	0	1	2	2
II	A	Placebo	1	1	0	1	1
II	B	Active	0	1	1	1	6
II	B	Placebo	3	1	1	5	0
III	A	Active	2	0	3	3	2
III	A	Placebo	5	0	0	8	1
III	B	Active	2	4	1	10	3
III	B	Placebo	2	5	1	4	2
IV	A	Active	8	1	3	4	0
IV	A	Placebo	5	0	3	3	0
IV	B	Active	1	5	2	3	1
IV	B	Placebo	3	4	3	4	2

If you look at the cell sizes in this table, you will see that they are small, ranging from 0 to 10. Such small sample sizes rule out the possibility of modeling multiple response functions per group, such as generalized logits or cumulative logits, as was discussed in previous chapters. However, there is marginally adequate sample size to model one function per group, such as a mean score. If you assign scores to the categories of patient status, such as the integers 1–5 to poor–excellent, respectively, then you can model the mean patient response score with weighted least squares.

The following SAS statements input the data.

```
data cpain;
   input dstatus $ invest $ treat $ status $ count @@;
   cards;
I  A active poor  3 I   A active   fair 2 I A active moderate 2
I  A active good  1 I   A active   excel 0
I  A placebo poor 7 I   A placebo  fair 0 I A placebo moderate 1
I  A placebo good 1 I   A placebo  excel 1
I  B active poor  1 I   B active   fair 6 I B active moderate 1
I  B active good  5 I   B active   excel 3
I  B placebo poor 5 I   B placebo  fair 4 I B placebo moderate 2
```

```
  I   B placebo good  3 I    B placebo excel 3
 II   A active  poor  1 II   A active  fair 0 II A active moderate 1
 II   A active  good  2 II   A active  excel 2
 II   A placebo poor  1 II   A placebo fair 1 II A placebo moderate 0
 II   A placebo good  1 II   A placebo excel 1
 II   B active  poor  0 II   B active  fair  1 II B active moderate 1
 II   B active  good  1 II   B active  excel 6
 II   B placebo poor  3 II   B placebo fair 1 II B placebo moderate 1
 II   B placebo good  5 II   B placebo excel 0
III   A active  poor  2 III  A active  fair 0 III A active moderate 3
III   A active  good  3 III  A active  excel 2
III   A placebo poor  5 III  A placebo fair 0 III A placebo moderate 0
III   A placebo good  8 III  A placebo excel 1
III   B active  poor  2 III  B active  fair 4 III B active moderate 1
III   B active  good 10 III  B active  excel 3
III   B placebo poor  2 III  B placebo fair 5 III B placebo moderate 1
III   B placebo good  4 III  B placebo excel 2
 IV   A active  poor  8 IV   A active  fair 1 IV A active moderate 3
 IV   A active  good  4 IV   A active  excel 0
 IV   A placebo poor  5 IV   A placebo fair 0 IV A placebo moderate 3
 IV   A placebo good  3 IV   A placebo excel 0
 IV   B active  poor  1 IV   B active  fair 5 IV B active moderate 2
 IV   B active  good  3 IV   B active  excel 1
 IV   B placebo poor  3 IV   B placebo fair 4 IV B placebo moderate 3
 IV   B placebo good  4 IV   B placebo excel 2
;
```

The saturated model is fit as the preliminary model. The following PROC CATMOD statements request this analysis. Note the use of the bar notation in the MODEL statement to specify that the model includes all interactions of the specified factors in addition to their main effects.

```
proc catmod order=data;
  weight count;
  response 1 2 3 4 5;
  model status=dstatus|invest|treat;
run;
```

Since the response variable STATUS is character valued, you need to specify scores for its levels. You can do this by specifying numeric values in the RESPONSE statement. This RESPONSE statement causes a mean score to be created based on scoring the first response variable level as 1, the second response variable level as 2, and so on. Specifying the ORDER=DATA option in the PROC CATMOD statement forces the levels of the response variable to be the same as the order in which they appear in the data, that is, poor, fair, moderate, good, and excellent.

Output 12.9 contains the population profiles, and Output 12.10 contains the response profiles.

Output 12.9   Population Profiles

```
                    POPULATION PROFILES
                                          Sample
   Sample  DSTATUS  INVEST    TREAT       Size
   ------------------------------------------------
      1       I        A       active       8
      2       I        A       placebo     10
      3       I        B       active      16
      4       I        B       placebo     17
      5       II       A       active       6
      6       II       A       placebo      4
      7       II       B       active       9
      8       II       B       placebo     10
      9       III      A       active      10
     10       III      A       placebo     14
     11       III      B       active      20
     12       III      B       placebo     14
     13       IV       A       active      16
     14       IV       A       placebo     11
     15       IV       B       active      12
     16       IV       B       placebo     16
```

Output 12.10   Response Profiles

```
            RESPONSE PROFILES

         Response    STATUS
         ------------------
            1        poor
            2        fair
            3        moderate
            4        good
            5        excel
```

Output 12.11 contains just the Response Function column of the "DESIGN MATRIX" table. These are the mean patient status scores based on integer scoring.

Output 12.11   Response Functions

```
                 Response
        Sample   Function
        ------------------
           1     2.12500
           2     1.90000
           3     3.18750
           4     2.70588
           5     3.66667
           6     3.00000
           7     4.33333
           8     2.80000
           9     3.30000
          10     3.00000
          11     3.40000
          12     2.92857
          13     2.18750
          14     2.36364
          15     2.83333
          16     2.87500
```

The saturated model results are displayed in Output 12.12.

Output 12.12   ANOVA Table for Saturated Model

```
                     ANALYSIS-OF-VARIANCE TABLE

          Source                DF   Chi-Square    Prob
          -------------------------------------------------
          INTERCEPT              1      764.24    0.0000
          DSTATUS                3       13.83    0.0031
          INVEST                 1        4.36    0.0368
          DSTATUS*INVEST         3        3.28    0.3506
          TREAT                  1        4.21    0.0401
          DSTATUS*TREAT          3        3.55    0.3143
          INVEST*TREAT           1        0.72    0.3966
          DSTATUS*INVEST*TREAT   3        0.34    0.9515

          RESIDUAL               0          .        .
```

Since the model is saturated, there is no residual variation and the fit is perfect. The interaction DSTATUS*INVEST*TREAT has a chi-square of 0.34 with 3 df ($p = 0.9515$), which is clearly nonsignificant. Thus, the next stage of modeling is to remove this interaction and examine the two-way interactions to see if they change. Since the reduced model is reduced by this one term, its goodness-of-fit chi-square will be equal to 0.34. With PROC CATMOD, you can enter statements interactively. For example, you can specify that the pairwise interactions model be fit by submitting the following MODEL statement.

```
model status=dstatus|invest|treat@2; run;
```

The procedure will be invoked using the previously submitted statements (from page 315) and substituting the new MODEL statement for the previous one. PROC CATMOD remains in this interactive mode until it encounters a QUIT, PROC, or DATA statement. (Most of the examples in this book contain the full code for completeness).

Output 12.13 contains the ANOVA table for this reduced model.

Output 12.13   ANOVA Table for Pairwise Interactions Model

```
                     ANALYSIS-OF-VARIANCE TABLE

          Source              DF   Chi-Square    Prob
          ----------------------------------------------
          INTERCEPT            1      776.58    0.0000
          DSTATUS              3       13.50    0.0037
          INVEST               1        4.87    0.0274
          DSTATUS*INVEST       3        3.22    0.3589
          TREAT                1        5.31    0.0212
          DSTATUS*TREAT        3        5.33    0.1494
          INVEST*TREAT         1        0.47    0.4943

          RESIDUAL             3        0.34    0.9515
```

Since the pairwise interactions DSTATUS*INVEST, DSTATUS*TREAT, and INVEST*TREAT are all nonsignificant, with p-values of 0.3589, 0.1494, and 0.4943, respectively, the model excluding these terms is fit next.

```
model status=dstatus invest treat; run;
```

Output 12.14 contains the ANOVA table for the main effects model.

Output 12.14   ANOVA Table for Main Effects Model

```
          ANALYSIS-OF-VARIANCE TABLE

    Source          DF    Chi-Square      Prob
    ---------------------------------------------------
    INTERCEPT         1       843.00      0.0000
    DSTATUS           3        15.41      0.0015
    INVEST            1         6.74      0.0094
    TREAT             1         3.71      0.0540

    RESIDUAL         10        10.20      0.4229
```

$Q_W = 10.20$, with 10 df and $p = 0.4229$, and is indicative of a satisfactory fit. All of the main effects are significant, although TREAT is on the border for the $\alpha = 0.05$ significance level criterion with $p = 0.0540$. It is kept in the model.

The model matrix for this model is displayed in Output 12.15, and the parameter estimates are displayed in Output 12.16.

Output 12.15   Model Matrix

```
          Response              DESIGN MATRIX
    Sample  Function    1    2    3    4    5    6
    ------------------------------------------------------
      1     2.12500     1    1    0    0    1    1
      2     1.90000     1    1    0    0    1   -1
      3     3.18750     1    1    0    0   -1    1
      4     2.70588     1    1    0    0   -1   -1
      5     3.66667     1    0    1    0    1    1
      6     3.00000     1    0    1    0    1   -1
      7     4.33333     1    0    1    0   -1    1
      8     2.80000     1    0    1    0   -1   -1
      9     3.30000     1    0    0    1    1    1
     10     3.00000     1    0    0    1    1   -1
     11     3.40000     1    0    0    1   -1    1
     12     2.92857     1    0    0    1   -1   -1
     13     2.18750     1   -1   -1   -1    1    1
     14     2.36364     1   -1   -1   -1    1   -1
     15     2.83333     1   -1   -1   -1   -1    1
     16     2.87500     1   -1   -1   -1   -1   -1
```

Output 12.16   Parameter Estimates

```
        ANALYSIS OF WEIGHTED-LEAST-SQUARES ESTIMATES

                                  Standard   Chi-
    Effect        Parameter  Estimate  Error    Square   Prob
    ------------------------------------------------------------------
    INTERCEPT         1       2.9079   0.1002   843.00   0.0000
    DSTATUS           2      -0.3904   0.1621     5.80   0.0161
                      3       0.5660   0.1916     8.73   0.0031
                      4       0.1893   0.1569     1.46   0.2275
    INVEST            5      -0.2511   0.0967     6.74   0.0094
    TREAT             6       0.1816   0.0942     3.71   0.0540
```

DSTATUS is represented by three parameters, and both INVEST and TREAT are represented by one parameter. Table 12.5 contains the parameter interpretations and illustrates how they relate to the numbered parameters in the PROC CATMOD output. Referring to the order of the variable values in the population profiles of Output 12.9 enables you to determine that the three DSTATUS effects are for diagnostic classes I, II, and III, respectively (the first three levels listed), and that the TREAT effect is for active treatment.

Table 12.5   Parameter Interpretations

CATMOD Parameter	Model Parameter	Interpretation
1	α	intercept
2	β_1	differential effect for diagnosis I
3	β_2	differential effect for diagnosis II
4	β_3	differential effect for diagnosis III
5	β_4	differential effect for investigator A
6	β_5	differential effect for active treatment

12.4.1 Constructing Contrast Tests

Researchers were interested in whether there were differences between the diagnostic classes. If you look at the values for these effects and their standard errors, $\hat{\beta}_1 = -0.3904(0.1621)$, $\hat{\beta}_2 = 0.5660(0.1916)$, $\hat{\beta}_3 = 0.1893(0.1569)$, and the implied effect for diagnostic class IV, which is $(-\hat{\beta}_1 - \hat{\beta}_2 - \hat{\beta}_3) = -0.365$, it seems like there are probably several individual differences. You can formally address questions about the parameters with the use of contrast tests.

The tests of interest, barring a priori considerations, are whether diagnostic class I is different from classes II, III, and IV; whether diagnostic class II is different from classes III and IV; and whether diagnostic class III is different from class IV. You perform the hypothesis test

$$H_0: \beta_1 - \beta_2 = 0$$

to determine whether the differential effect for diagnostic class I is equal to the differential effect for diagnostic class II, and you construct similar hypotheses to test for the differences between classes I and III and classes II and III.

Since the effect for diagnostic class IV is equal to $(-\hat{\beta}_1 - \hat{\beta}_2 - \hat{\beta}_3)$, you test whether there is a difference between diagnostic class I and class IV with the hypothesis:

$$H_0: \beta_1 - (-\beta_1 - \beta_2 - \beta_3) = 2\beta_1 + \beta_2 + \beta_3 = 0$$

You construct similar hypotheses to test whether there is a difference between the other diagnostic classes and class IV.

In Chapter 8, the TEST statement in PROC LOGISTIC and the CONTRAST statement in PROC GENMOD were discussed. These statements serve the same purpose as the

CONTRAST statement in PROC CATMOD, testing linear combinations of the parameters, but they all function somewhat differently. With PROC CATMOD you specify the following CONTRAST statement to request the test of the first hypothesis listed:

```
contrast 'Diag I versus II' dstatus 1 -1 0;
```

You list a character string that labels the contrast, list the effect whose parameters you are interested in, and then supply a coefficient for each of the effect parameters that PROC CATMOD estimates. Remember that since PROC CATMOD uses fullrank parameterization, it produces $s - 1$ estimated parameters for an effect that has s levels. Thus, since DSTATUS is represented by parameters β_1, β_2, and β_3, you need to specify three coefficients when you name the variable DSTATUS in the CONTRAST statement. Since the hypothesis being tested is $H_0: \beta_1 - \beta_2 = 0$, you supply the coefficient 1 for β_1, -1 for β_2, and 0 for β_3. The other contrast statements are specified similarly, inserting the coefficients corresponding to the hypothesis being tested.

The following statements produced the desired results. You can specify as many CONTRASTS as you want; the results are placed into a single table.

```
contrast 'I versus II'      dstatus 1 -1  0;
contrast 'I versus III'     dstatus 1  0 -1;
contrast 'I versus IV'      dstatus 2  1  1;
contrast 'II versus III'    dstatus 0  1 -1;
contrast 'II versus IV'     dstatus 1  2  1;
contrast 'III versus IV'    dstatus 1  1  2;
contrast 'dstatus'  dstatus 1 0 0 ,
                    dstatus 0 1 0 ,
                    dstatus 0 0 1 ;
run;
```

The last contrast specified is included to demonstrate that the results in the ANOVA table can be generated with contrast tests. This contrast is testing the hypothesis

$$H_0: \beta_1 = \beta_2 = \beta_3 = 0$$

and is performed with the contrast matrix

$$C = \begin{bmatrix} 1 & 0 & 0 \\ 0 & 1 & 0 \\ 0 & 0 & 1 \end{bmatrix}$$

The test has 3 df, one for each linearly independent row of the contrast matrix. It requires 3 sets of coefficients in the CONTRAST statement, each separated by a comma. The variable name DSTATUS needs to be listed on each of the 3 lines. All of the results are displayed in Output 12.17.

Output 12.17   Contrast Results

```
                   ANALYSIS OF CONTRASTS

     Contrast              DF   Chi-Square     Prob
     ------------------------------------------------
     I versus II            1       10.30     0.0013
     I versus III           1        5.18     0.0229
     I versus IV            1        0.01     0.9194
     II versus III          1        1.67     0.1966
     II versus IV           1       10.25     0.0014
     III versus IV          1        5.11     0.0238
     dstatus                3       15.41     0.0015
```

First, note that $Q_C = 15.41$ for dstatus, with 3 df, which is the same as the chi-square value listed for DSTATUS in Output 12.14 in the ANOVA table. This contrast test is the same as the test automatically produced for the DSTATUS effect in the model.

The contrast test results indicate that diagnostic class I is different from both II and III but not IV; both II and III are different from IV. There are substantial differences in how diagnostic class influences patient response score; diagnostic classes I and IV decrease patient scores and diagnostic classes II and III increase patient scores. The influences of classes I and IV are not significantly different from each other, and the influences of classes II and III are not significantly different from each other.

12.5   Analysis of Proportions: Occupational Data

The previous section focused on the analysis of means with weighted least squares. Weighted least squares analysis can be performed for many different types of response functions composed from the proportions in a contingency table. The simplest of these is the response proportions themselves, which are analyzed in this section. In addition, the capability of the CATMOD procedure to fit *nested* models is demonstrated.

12.5.1   Occupational Data Example

The data displayed in Table 12.6 are from a cross-sectional prevalence study done in 1973 to investigate textile worker complaints about respiratory symptoms experienced while working in the mills (Higgins and Koch 1977). Investigators were interested in whether occupational environment was related to the prevalence of respiratory ailments associated with the disease byssinosis.

Since this was a cross-sectional study rather than a prospective one, you cannot make inferences to a more general population without making some rather restrictive assumptions. If such assumptions can be made—that the symptoms remained for the duration of a worker's presence in the same work environment, that worker departures were not related to the presence or absence of symptoms, and so on—then you may be able to make inferences to all workers employed in those mills or possibly even to workers engaged in similar work in similar mills. If not, then the results of the analysis apply only to the observed population and serve only to describe the variation found for that observed population. It is always important to clarify the inferential implications of an analysis based on the relevant sampling framework.

Table 12.6   Byssinosis Complaints

Workplace Condition	Years Employment	Smoking	Complaints Yes	Complaints No
Dusty	<10	Yes	30	203
Dusty	<10	No	7	119
Dusty	≥ 10	Yes	57	161
Dusty	≥ 10	No	11	81
Not Dusty	<10	Yes	14	1340
Not Dusty	<10	No	12	1004
Not Dusty	≥ 10	Yes	24	1360
Not Dusty	≥ 10	No	10	986

If you can assume that there is a justifiable target population, then it becomes reasonable to think of these frequencies as coming from some stratified simple random sampling scheme, so that the table is distributed as product multinomial. A logical response function to model for these dichotomous responses is the logit, and logits are usually analyzed with the maximum likelihood estimation of logistic regression. However, you may be interested in modeling the proportion of byssinosis complaints in each classification group. Using the proportion has the interpretative advantage that model parameters have a direct effect on the size of the proportions. Fitting a model to proportions is not so easily performed with maximum likelihood methods; however, it is easily done with weighted least squares methods.

Since there are eight groups in the contingency table formed from the different combinations of workplace condition, years of employment, and smoking status, and two possible responses, respiratory complaints or not, there are sixteen elements in the overall proportion vector. Consider the elements p_{ij} where $i = 1, \ldots, 8$ represents the groups, and $j = 1, 2$ represents yes and no, respectively. Since the proportions in each row add up to 1, only one response per group needs to be included in the analysis. Otherwise, the responses would be linearly dependent and the computations would fail.

The transformation matrix that generates the yes proportions from the proportion vector is straightforward: each row of the matrix picks up the yes proportion from the corresponding row of the underlying contingency table. The matrix formulation required to construct the response functions is

$$F(\mathbf{p}) = \mathbf{A}\mathbf{p} = \begin{bmatrix} 1 & 0 & 0 & 0 & 0 & 0 & 0 & 0 & 0 & 0 & 0 & 0 & 0 & 0 & 0 & 0 \\ 0 & 0 & 1 & 0 & 0 & 0 & 0 & 0 & 0 & 0 & 0 & 0 & 0 & 0 & 0 & 0 \\ 0 & 0 & 0 & 0 & 1 & 0 & 0 & 0 & 0 & 0 & 0 & 0 & 0 & 0 & 0 & 0 \\ 0 & 0 & 0 & 0 & 0 & 0 & 1 & 0 & 0 & 0 & 0 & 0 & 0 & 0 & 0 & 0 \\ 0 & 0 & 0 & 0 & 0 & 0 & 0 & 0 & 1 & 0 & 0 & 0 & 0 & 0 & 0 & 0 \\ 0 & 0 & 0 & 0 & 0 & 0 & 0 & 0 & 0 & 0 & 1 & 0 & 0 & 0 & 0 & 0 \\ 0 & 0 & 0 & 0 & 0 & 0 & 0 & 0 & 0 & 0 & 0 & 0 & 1 & 0 & 0 & 0 \\ 0 & 0 & 0 & 0 & 0 & 0 & 0 & 0 & 0 & 0 & 0 & 0 & 0 & 0 & 1 & 0 \end{bmatrix} \mathbf{p} = \begin{bmatrix} 0.129 \\ 0.056 \\ 0.261 \\ 0.120 \\ 0.010 \\ 0.012 \\ 0.017 \\ 0.010 \end{bmatrix}$$

This is a linear transformation, just as the transformation required to compute means from the previous section's proportion vector was a linear transformation. Thus, the covariance matrix for $F(\mathbf{p})$ is $\mathbf{V_F} = \mathbf{A V_p A'}$.

12.5.2 Fitting a Preliminary Model

The preliminary model for this analysis is the saturated model that includes all interactions. This includes pairwise and three-way interactions.

$$
\begin{bmatrix} F(\mathbf{p}_{11}) \\ F(\mathbf{p}_{21}) \\ F(\mathbf{p}_{31}) \\ F(\mathbf{p}_{41}) \\ F(\mathbf{p}_{51}) \\ F(\mathbf{p}_{61}) \\ F(\mathbf{p}_{71}) \\ F(\mathbf{p}_{81}) \end{bmatrix} =
\begin{bmatrix}
1 & 1 & 1 & 1 & 1 & 1 & 1 & 1 \\
1 & 1 & 1 & 1 & -1 & -1 & -1 & -1 \\
1 & 1 & -1 & -1 & 1 & 1 & -1 & -1 \\
1 & 1 & -1 & -1 & -1 & -1 & 1 & 1 \\
1 & -1 & 1 & -1 & 1 & -1 & 1 & -1 \\
1 & -1 & 1 & -1 & -1 & 1 & -1 & 1 \\
1 & -1 & -1 & 1 & 1 & -1 & -1 & 1 \\
1 & -1 & -1 & 1 & -1 & 1 & 1 & -1
\end{bmatrix}
\begin{bmatrix} \alpha \\ \beta_1 \\ \beta_2 \\ \beta_3 \\ \beta_4 \\ \beta_5 \\ \beta_6 \\ \beta_7 \end{bmatrix}
$$

In this model, α is the intercept term, and β_1, β_2, and β_4 are parameters for workplace, years employment, and smoking behavior, respectively. β_3 is the parameter for interaction between workplace and years employment, β_5 is the parameter for interaction between workplace and smoking behavior, and β_6 is the parameter for interaction between years of employment and smoking behavior. Finally, β_7 is the parameter for the three-way interaction.

The following statements fit this model with PROC CATMOD. Instead of using the keyword MEANS in the RESPONSE statement to generate the mean of the responses, you use the keyword MARGINALS. This specifies that the response functions are marginal proportions defined across the population profiles. For a dichotomous response outcome, this generates the proportions corresponding to the first response level. For response variables with r outcome levels, the keyword MARGINALS generates proportions for the first $r - 1$ response levels. In Chapter 13, "Modeling Repeated Measurements Data," you learn about analyses where multiple response variables are used. In these cases, *marginal distributions* are of interest.

The following DATA step creates the data set BYSS.

```
data byss;
   input workplce $ em_years $ smoking $ status $ count @@;
   cards ;
dusty         <10   yes  yes 30   dusty      <10   yes no  203
dusty         <10   no   yes 7    dusty      <10   no  no  119
dusty         >=10  yes  yes 57   dusty      >=10  yes no  161
dusty         >=10  no   yes 11   dusty      >=10  no  no   81
notdusty      <10   yes  yes 14   notdusty   <10   yes no 1340
notdusty      <10   no   yes 12   notdusty   <10   no  no 1004
notdusty      >=10  yes  yes 24   notdusty   >=10  yes no 1360
notdusty      >=10  no   yes 10   notdusty   >=10  no  no  986
;
run;
```

The CATMOD procedure invocation is very similar to those seen before; the keyword MARGINALS in the RESPONSE statement is the only difference. Note the use of the ORDER=DATA option in the PROC CATMOD statement. This maintains the response variable levels in the order in which they occur in the input data set. Thus, "yes" is the first ordered value, as desired, and the response functions will be Pr{STATUS=yes}. PROC CATMOD by default orders its response levels alphanumerically. Since the response function is not the default logit, you get weighted least squares estimation.

```
proc catmod order=data;
   weight count;
   response marginals;
   model status = workplce|em_years|smoking;
run;
```

Output 12.18 displays the population and response profiles as well as the response functions and model matrix.

Output 12.18   Populations, Response Profiles, and Response Functions

```
                    POPULATION PROFILES
                                         Sample
          Sample  WORKPLCE  EM_YEARS  SMOKING   Size
          ------------------------------------------------
            1     dusty      <10       yes       233
            2     dusty      <10       no        126
            3     dusty      >=10      yes       218
            4     dusty      >=10      no         92
            5     notdusty   <10       yes      1354
            6     notdusty   <10       no       1016
            7     notdusty   >=10      yes      1384
            8     notdusty   >=10      no        996


                    RESPONSE PROFILES

                Response   STATUS
                ------------------
                   1       yes
                   2       no

         Response               DESIGN MATRIX
 Sample   Function   1    2    3    4    5    6    7    8
 -------------------------------------------------------------
    1     0.12876    1    1    1    1    1    1    1    1
    2     0.05556    1    1    1    1   -1   -1   -1   -1
    3     0.26147    1    1   -1   -1    1    1   -1   -1
    4     0.11957    1    1   -1   -1   -1   -1    1    1
    5     0.01034    1   -1    1   -1    1   -1    1   -1
    6     0.01181    1   -1    1   -1   -1    1   -1    1
    7     0.01734    1   -1   -1    1    1   -1   -1    1
    8     0.01004    1   -1   -1    1   -1    1    1   -1
```

The ANOVA table displayed in Output 12.19 indicates a nonsignificant three-way interaction, with a Wald statistic of $Q_W = 1.21$ and a corresponding $p = 0.2714$. Based on this result, the model including all two-way interactions is fit. Recall that since the only effect being eliminated is the three-way interaction, the residual goodness-of-fit statistic for the reduced model will have the same value as the three-way interaction in the full model. Note that the label for the three-way interaction includes the truncation WORKPLC for WORKPLCE.

Output 12.19   ANOVA Table for Saturated Model

```
                    ANALYSIS-OF-VARIANCE TABLE

     Source                    DF   Chi-Square    Prob
     ---------------------------------------------------
     INTERCEPT                  1      127.33     0.0000
     WORKPLCE                   1       89.61     0.0000
     EM_YEARS                   1       13.74     0.0002
     WORKPLCE*EM_YEARS          1       12.35     0.0004
     SMOKING                    1       16.44     0.0001
     WORKPLCE*SMOKING           1       14.75     0.0001
     EM_YEARS*SMOKING           1        2.02     0.1551
     WORKPLC*EM_YEARS*SMOKING   1        1.21     0.2714

     RESIDUAL                   0        .          .
```

The following code requests the model with all pairwise interactions.

```
proc catmod order=data;
   weight count ;
   response marginals;
   model status = workplce|em_years workplce|smoking
                  em_years|smoking;
run;
```

The resulting ANOVA table is displayed in Output 12.20.

Output 12.20   ANOVA Table for All Pairwise Interactions

```
                    ANALYSIS-OF-VARIANCE TABLE

     Source                DF   Chi-Square    Prob
     ---------------------------------------------------
     INTERCEPT              1      131.73     0.0000
     WORKPLCE              1       92.90     0.0000
     EM_YEARS             1       14.33     0.0002
     WORKPLCE*EM_YEARS     1       12.92     0.0003
     SMOKING              1       15.46     0.0001
     WORKPLCE*SMOKING     1       13.70     0.0002
     EM_YEARS*SMOKING     1        2.26     0.1324

     RESIDUAL             1        1.21     0.2714
```

Note that the residual $Q_W = 1.21$ for this model is the same as the Q_W for the three-way interaction in the saturated model (Output 12.19). Thus, you could eliminate the step of fitting the saturated model and assess the three-way interaction from the analysis results for the model with all pairwise interactions.

This model fits adequately; however, the years of employment and smoking behavior interaction appears to be an unimportant source of variation, with $Q_W = 2.26$ and $p = 0.1324$. Thus, a further reduced model is fit that includes all main effects and only the workplace × smoking behavior and workplace × years of employment interactions. The code required for this PROC CATMOD invocation is not reproduced here; the results are displayed in Output 12.21.

Output 12.21   ANOVA Table for Reduced Model

```
               ANALYSIS-OF-VARIANCE TABLE

    Source              DF    Chi-Square     Prob
    -------------------------------------------------
    INTERCEPT            1       131.56      0.0000
    WORKPLCE            1        93.89      0.0000
    EM_YEARS            1        14.47      0.0001
    WORKPLCE*EM_YEARS   1        12.95      0.0003
    SMOKING             1        14.82      0.0001
    WORKPLCE*SMOKING    1        13.29      0.0003

    RESIDUAL            2         3.47      0.1761
```

This model fits the data with a residual goodness-of-fit statistic of $Q_W = 3.47$ with 2 df. It includes the main effects workplace, years of employment, and smoking, as well as the interactions workplace × years of employment and workplace × smoking. Often it is useful to examine the nature of the interactions to determine exactly where the differences are occurring.

12.5.3   Reduced Models Using Nested-By-Value Effects

Pairwise interactions occur when one variable's effect depends on the level of a second variable. A main effect in the absence of an interaction means that the variable's effect has roughly the same influence at all levels of the second variable. One explanation for the occurrence of an interaction is when one variable has a measurable effect at one level of a second variable but virtually no effect at a different level of that variable. Nested-by-value effects coding enables you to determine whether this behavior is occurring and also allows you to fit a reduced model that incorporates this behavior.

To investigate both the workplace × smoking behavior interaction and the workplace × years of employment interaction with nested-by-value effects, you replace the interaction term and the main effect for the term that you want nested with the corresponding nested-by-value terms. For example,

`workplce|em_years` and `em_years`

in the MODEL statement are replaced with

`em_years(workplce='dusty')` and `em_years(workplce='notdusty')`

You can see what happens by examining the model matrices that are produced by the two different models in Table 12.7 and Table 12.8. In the first model matrix, the second column corresponds to workplace, the third column to years of employment, and the fourth column represents their interaction. In the second model matrix, the third and fourth columns represent the effect of employment years nested in the dusty workplace and the not dusty workplace, respectively. For each, there are nonzero coefficients only in the rows that correspond to that particular value for workplace. You can think of this as splitting the main effect for employment into two components: one for dusty workplace and one for not dusty workplace. The same principle applies to splitting the main effect for smoking into two such components.

Table 12.7   Model Matrix for Interactions Model

Group			1	2	3	4	5	6
dusty	<10	yes	1	1	1	1	1	1
dusty	<10	no	1	1	1	1	-1	-1
dusty	>=10	yes	1	1	-1	-1	1	1
dusty	>=10	no	1	1	-1	-1	-1	-1
notdusty	<10	yes	1	-1	1	-1	1	-1
notdusty	<10	no	1	-1	1	-1	-1	1
notdusty	>=10	yes	1	-1	-1	1	1	-1
notdusty	>=10	no	1	-1	-1	1	-1	1

Columns span 1–6.

Table 12.8   Model Matrix for Nested-by-Value Model

Group			1	2	3	4	5	6
dusty	<10	yes	1	1	1	0	1	0
dusty	<10	no	1	1	1	0	-1	0
dusty	>=10	yes	1	1	-1	0	1	0
dusty	>=10	no	1	1	-1	0	-1	0
notdusty	<10	yes	1	-1	0	1	0	1
notdusty	<10	no	1	-1	0	1	0	-1
notdusty	>=10	yes	1	-1	0	-1	0	1
notdusty	>=10	no	1	-1	0	-1	0	-1

Columns span 1–6.

The following statements fit the nested-by-value model.

```
proc catmod order=data;
    weight count;
    response marginals;
    model status = workplce
                em_years(workplce='dusty')
                em_years(workplce='notdusty')
                smoking(workplce='dusty')
                smoking(workplce='notdusty') ;
run;
```

The model matrix in Output 12.22 is the same as that displayed in Table 12.8.

Output 12.22   Model Matrix for Nested-By-Value Effects Model

Sample	Response Function	DESIGN MATRIX 1	2	3	4	5	6
1	0.12876	1	1	1	0	1	0
2	0.05556	1	1	1	0	-1	0
3	0.26147	1	1	-1	0	1	0
4	0.11957	1	1	-1	0	-1	0
5	0.01034	1	-1	0	1	0	1
6	0.01181	1	-1	0	1	0	-1
7	0.01734	1	-1	0	-1	0	1
8	0.01004	1	-1	0	-1	0	-1

The ANOVA table displayed in Output 12.23 lists the nested-by-value effects.

Output 12.23   ANOVA Table for Nested-By-Value Effects Model

ANALYSIS-OF-VARIANCE TABLE

Source	DF	Chi-Square	Prob
INTERCEPT	1	131.56	0.0000
WORKPLCE	1	93.89	0.0000
EM_YEARS(WORKPLCE=dusty)	1	13.90	0.0002
EM_YEA(WORKPLC=notdusty)	1	0.75	0.3860
SMOKING(WORKPLCE=dusty)	1	14.27	0.0002
SMOKIN(WORKPLC=notdusty)	1	0.64	0.4225
RESIDUAL	2	3.47	0.1761

The residual goodness-of-fit test is the same as for the previous reduced model with interactions. The degrees of freedom have not decreased with the nested-by-value model, but they have been used differently with the new parameterization. The statistic for WORKPLCE has also remained the same, since the new coding does not change the meaning of the parameter for WORKPLCE. Neither years of employment nor smoking behavior are significant effects for the notdusty level of WORKPLCE, $p = 0.3860$ and $p = 0.4225$, respectively, while they both appear to be strongly significant for the dusty level of WORKPLCE, $p = 0.0002$ for both effects. Thus, it appears that both interactions can be explained by the interplay of years of employment and smoking behavior in the dusty workplace.

The model excluding the nonsignificant nested-by-value effects is fit next.

```
proc catmod order=data;
   weight count ;
   response marginals;
   model status = workplce
                  em_years(workplce='dusty')
                  smoking(workplce='dusty') / pred;
run;
```

Output 12.24 contains the ANOVA table for the final model, and Output 12.25 contains the parameter estimates.

Output 12.24   ANOVA Table for Final Model

```
             ANALYSIS-OF-VARIANCE TABLE

   Source                      DF   Chi-Square    Prob
   --------------------------------------------------------
   INTERCEPT                    1      131.50    0.0000
   WORKPLCE                     1       93.98    0.0000
   EM_YEARS(WORKPLCE=dusty)     1       13.90    0.0002
   SMOKING(WORKPLCE=dusty)      1       14.27    0.0002

   RESIDUAL                     4        4.68    0.3215
```

Output 12.25   Parameter Estimates

```
        ANALYSIS OF WEIGHTED-LEAST-SQUARES ESTIMATES

                                    Standard    Chi-
   Effect              Parameter  Estimate    Error    Square    Prob
   ----------------------------------------------------------------------
   INTERCEPT                1      0.0776   0.00677   131.50   0.0000
   WORKPLCE                 2      0.0656   0.00677    93.98   0.0000
   EM_YEARS(WORKPLCE=dusty) 3     -0.0503   0.0135     13.90   0.0002
   SMOKING(WORKPLCE=dusty)  4      0.0471   0.0125     14.27   0.0002
```

The model goodness of fit chi-square is 4.68 with 4 df, clearly an adequate fit. This model contains a main effect for workplace and effects for years of employment and smoking only in the dusty workplace. See Table 12.9 for a display of parameter interpretations.

Table 12.9   Parameter Interpretations

CATMOD Parameter	Model Parameter	Interpretation
1	α	intercept
2	β_1	differential effect for dusty workplace
3	β_2	differential effect for < 10 years employment within a dusty workplace
4	β_3	differential effect for smoking within a dusty workplace

A dusty workplace increases the proportion of subjects in this study who had byssinosis complaints. Having less than 10 years employment lessens the proportion with byssinosis complaints within a dusty workplace, $\hat{\beta}_2 = -0.0503$, which means that having 10 or more years of employment increases the proportion with byssinosis complaints in a dusty workplace. Smoking increases the proportion with byssinosis complaints if the workplace is dusty.

The PRED option in the MODEL statement produces predicted values for the proportions with byssinosis symptoms for each group. In order to interpret this table, compare the "Sample" values with those listed in the "POPULATION PROFILES" of Output 12.18. For example, the model-predicted proportion with byssinosis complaints for smokers with less than ten years employment who also worked in a dusty workplace (sample 1) is 0.140

$\pm$ 0.020. For smokers with at least ten years employment who worked in a dusty workplace (sample 3), the predicted proportion with byssinosis symptoms is 0.241 $\pm$ 0.025.

Output 12.26   Predicted Values for Final Model

```
            PREDICTED VALUES FOR RESPONSE FUNCTIONS

                 -----Observed-----    -----Predicted----
           Function          Standard           Standard
  Sample    Number   Function   Error   Function   Error    Residual
  -------------------------------------------------------------------
    1         1      0.128755  0.021942  0.140053  0.020057  -0.0113
    2         1      0.055556  0.020406  0.045784   0.0189    0.009771
    3         1      0.261468  0.029762  0.240683  0.024856   0.020785
    4         1      0.119565  0.033827  0.146415  0.026402  -0.02685
    5         1       0.01034  0.002749  0.012003   0.00158  -0.00166
    6         1      0.011811  0.003389  0.012003   0.00158  -0.00019
    7         1      0.017341  0.003509  0.012003   0.00158   0.005338
    8         1       0.01004  0.003159  0.012003   0.00158  -0.00196
```

12.6   Highway Safety Data Analysis

This section examines the analysis of proportions with WLS for highway safety data. Table 12.10 contains information collected in the late 1960s concerning driver injury in multiple vehicle accidents in North Carolina. Investigators were interested in looking at the relationship between the severity of injury and the age, size, and model year of the car. In addition to being multiple vehicle accidents, these accidents involved left side or front impact for sober drivers traveling at relatively high speeds (Koch, Gillings, and Stokes 1980).

Table 12.10   Driver Status in N.C. Multiple Vehicle Accidents

Vehicle Size	Vehicle Age In Years	Model Year	Serious Injury ?		Percentage	
			No	Yes	Estimate	SE
Small	0-2	$\leq$ 66	119	31	20.7	3.3
Small	0-2	67-69	262	61	18.9	2.2
Small	3-5	$\leq$ 66	255	66	20.6	2.3
Small	3-5	67-69	171	42	19.7	2.7
Middle	0-2	$\leq$ 66	143	29	16.9	2.9
Middle	0-2	67-69	405	67	14.2	1.6
Middle	3-5	$\leq$ 66	297	69	18.9	2.0
Middle	3-5	67-69	223	49	18.0	2.3
Standard	0-2	$\leq$ 66	137	31	18.5	3.0
Standard	0-2	67-69	624	87	12.2	1.2
Standard	3-5	$\leq$ 66	470	82	14.9	1.5
Standard	3-5	67-69	407	50	10.9	1.5

These data are historical: they were not a random sample, they are all the accidents occurring in North Carolina that met the criteria. Thus, you can think of the analysis as a strictly local one. The results simply describe what happened; the frequencies can be considered to be fixed constants. However, if you can consider these data to be in some sense equivalent to simple stratified random sampling, you could make inferences to highway accidents in other North Carolina years or perhaps to other states with relevant characteristics similar to those in North Carolina. This perspective is adopted here.

The analysis begins with the saturated model. The following statements create the SAS data set HIGHWAY. The variable SIZE is the size of the car (small, mid-sized, or standard), the variable AGE is the age of the car (0–2 or 3–5 years), and the variable MODELYR is the model year of the car (before 1967 or made in 1967–1969). The outcome variable STATUS takes the values yes and no for whether the accident resulted in serious injury. The variable LINSIZE is described later in this section.

```
data highway ;
   input size $ age $ modelyr $ status $ count @@ ;
   linsize = (size='middle') + 2*(size='small') ;
   cards;
small      0-2 <67    yes 31   small      0-2 <67    no   119
small      0-2 67-69 yes 61   small      0-2 67-69 no   262
small      3-5 <67    yes 66   small      3-5 <67    no   255
small      3-5 67-69 yes 42   small      3-5 67-69 no   171
middle     0-2 <67    yes 29   middle     0-2 <67    no   143
middle     0-2 67-69 yes 67   middle     0-2 67-69 no   405
middle     3-5 <67    yes 69   middle     3-5 <67    no   297
middle     3-5 67-69 yes 49   middle     3-5 67-69 no   223
standard   0-2 <67    yes 31   standard 0-2 <67    no   137
standard   0-2 67-69 yes 87   standard 0-2 67-69 no   624
standard   3-5 <67    yes 82   standard 3-5 <67    no   470
standard   3-5 67-69 yes 50   standard 3-5 67-69 no   407
;
proc catmod order=data;
   weight count;
   response marginals;
   model status = size|age|modelyr ;
run ;
```

The population profiles are displayed in Output 12.27, and the response profiles are displayed in Output 12.28. Note the large sample sizes in each size × age × model year group.

Since the MARGINALS keyword was used on the RESPONSE statement, and since the first ordered value in the RESPONSE PROFILES table is yes, the response function is simply the proportion of serious accidents in each group. These response functions are listed in the "DESIGN MATRIX" table in Output 12.29. The model matrix has 12 rows and 12 columns since it represents a saturated model.

Output 12.27   Population Profiles

```
                      POPULATION PROFILES
                                                   Sample
            Sample    SIZE      AGE   MODELYR       Size
            ------------------------------------------------
              1     small     0-2    <67           150
              2     small     0-2    67-69         323
              3     small     3-5    <67           321
              4     small     3-5    67-69         213
              5     middle    0-2    <67           172
              6     middle    0-2    67-69         472
              7     middle    3-5    <67           366
              8     middle    3-5    67-69         272
              9     standard  0-2    <67           168
             10     standard  0-2    67-69         711
             11     standard  3-5    <67           552
             12     standard  3-5    67-69         457
```

Output 12.28   Response Profiles

```
            RESPONSE PROFILES

            Response   STATUS
            ----------------
               1       yes
               2       no
```

Output 12.29   Response Functions and Model Matrix

```
          Response            DESIGN MATRIX
  Sample  Function    1       2       3       4       5
  --------------------------------------------------------
     1    0.20667     1       1       0       1       1
     2    0.18885     1       1       0       1       1
     3    0.20561     1       1       0      -1      -1
     4    0.19718     1       1       0      -1      -1
     5    0.16860     1       0       1       1       0
     6    0.14195     1       0       1       1       0
     7    0.18852     1       0       1      -1       0
     8    0.18015     1       0       1      -1       0
     9    0.18452     1      -1      -1       1      -1
    10    0.12236     1      -1      -1       1      -1
    11    0.14855     1      -1      -1      -1       1
    12    0.10941     1      -1      -1      -1       1


                        DESIGN MATRIX
  Sample    6       7       8       9      10      11      12
  ------------------------------------------------------------
     1      0       1       1       0       1       1       0
     2      0      -1      -1       0      -1      -1       0
     3      0       1       1       0      -1      -1       0
     4      0      -1      -1       0       1       1       0
     5      1       1       0       1       1       0       1
     6      1      -1       0      -1      -1       0      -1
     7     -1       1       0       1      -1       0      -1
     8     -1      -1       0      -1       1       0       1
     9     -1       1      -1      -1       1      -1      -1
    10     -1      -1       1       1      -1       1       1
    11      1       1      -1      -1      -1       1       1
    12      1      -1       1       1       1      -1      -1
```

The analysis of variance table displayed in Output 12.30 suggests that neither the three-way interaction nor the two-way interactions are very influential. The three-way interaction SIZE*AGE*MODELYR has a chi-square of 0.04, with 2 df, and $p = 0.979$.

Output 12.30   Analysis of Variance Table

```
              ANALYSIS-OF-VARIANCE TABLE

    Source              DF    Chi-Square    Prob
    ---------------------------------------------------
    INTERCEPT            1      657.69      0.0000
    SIZE                 2       13.03      0.0015
    AGE                  1        0.04      0.8363
    SIZE*AGE             2        3.29      0.1935
    MODELYR              1        4.17      0.0412
    SIZE*MODELYR         2        1.85      0.3968
    AGE*MODELYR          1        0.41      0.5245
    SIZE*AGE*MODELYR     2        0.04      0.9787

    RESIDUAL             0         .          .
```

In the next stage, both the three-way and two-way interactions are dropped. Some analysts may feel that this strategy is too aggressive, and they may wish to examine the two-way interactions in the absence of the three-way interaction and then fit further models that eliminated the two-way interactions.

Even though the main effect AGE has a chi-square value of 0.04, which would be very nonsignificant at the $\alpha = 0.05$ level of significance, the main effects model fit includes all main effects. The interpretation of a main effect is different in the presence of interactions, so it's more appropriate to include all main effects in an additive model and then do further model reduction, if it is indicated.

The MODEL statement that specifies the main effects model follows.

```
model status = size age modelyr; run;
```

The resulting analysis of variance table shows that this model fits well ($Q_W = 4.52$, 7 df, $p = 0.718$). The main effect AGE is nonsignificant in this model, with $p = 0.953$, and MODELYR is significant with $p = 0.015$.

Output 12.31   ANOVA Table

```
              ANALYSIS-OF-VARIANCE TABLE

    Source          DF    Chi-Square    Prob
    ---------------------------------------------
    INTERCEPT        1      740.41      0.0000
    SIZE             2       20.67      0.0000
    AGE              1        0.00      0.9526
    MODELYR          1        5.97      0.0146

    RESIDUAL         7        4.52      0.7179
```

Consider the parameter estimates for the SIZE effect in the "ANALYSIS OF WEIGHTED-LEAST-SQUARES ESTIMATES" table.

Output 12.32   Parameter Estimates

```
           ANALYSIS OF WEIGHTED-LEAST-SQUARES ESTIMATES

                                    Standard   Chi-
Effect          Parameter  Estimate   Error   Square   Prob
----------------------------------------------------------------
INTERCEPT           1       0.1676   0.00616  740.41  0.0000
SIZE                2       0.0321   0.00945   11.54  0.0007
                    3      0.000682  0.00849    0.01  0.9360
AGE                 4      -0.00035  0.00591    0.00  0.9526
MODELYR             5       0.0150   0.00614    5.97  0.0146
```

Since SIZE has three levels, it is represented in PROC CATMOD's fullrank parameterization with two parameters. To determine the levels of SIZE to which each parameter refers, see Output 12.27; the order of the parameters listed in the parameter estimates table is the same as the order of the effect variable's values listed in the "POPULATION PROFILES" table. Thus, if you represent Parameter 2 as β_1 and Parameter 3 as β_2, β_1 is the differential effect for small cars and β_2 is the differential effect for mid-sized cars. (Recall that due to the sum-to-zero restrictions, the effect for standard-sized cars is $-\beta_1 - \beta_2$.)

Since β_1 is larger than β_2, smaller cars contribute to a higher proportion of serious injuries than larger cars. Since one might consider this effect to lie on an ordinal scale, it is of interest to determine whether the effect can be treated as a linear one. If the effect is essentially linear, then the effect for small cars would be twice as great as the effect for midsized cars.

You test this by determining whether the differences between the first and second levels and the second and third levels are equal. If so, then the effect is a linear one. If not, the effect contains a nonlinear component. Using β_3 to represent the effect for the standard cars,

$$H_0: \beta_1 - \beta_2 = \beta_2 - \beta_3$$

or, since $\beta_3 = -\beta_1 - \beta_2$,

$$H_0: \beta_1 - 2\beta_2 - \beta_1 - \beta_2 = -3\beta_2 = \beta_2 = 0$$

The following PROC CATMOD invocation fits the model containing only effects for size and model year and performs this hypothesis test. Note that since the variable AGE is removed from the MODEL statement, the POPULATION statement is necessary in order to create the correct crossclassification. If it is omitted, then PROC CATMOD would produce six populations based on the levels of variables SIZE and MODELYR. Since the sampling framework consists of the 12 subpopulations, and the distributional assumptions are based on that framework, the analysis must continue in this context.

```
proc catmod order=data;
   population size age modelyr;
   weight count;
```

```
      response marginals;
      model status = size modelyr;
      contrast 'linearity' size 0 1;
   run ;
```

Since AGE is so unimportant in the main effects model, the Q_W is virtually unchanged for the reduced model, from a chi-square value of 4.52 to a value of 4.53.

Output 12.33   Two Effects Model

```
              ANALYSIS-OF-VARIANCE TABLE

        Source            DF    Chi-Square    Prob
        --------------------------------------------
        INTERCEPT          1       745.96     0.0000
        SIZE               2        20.73     0.0000
        MODELYR            1         6.85     0.0089

        RESIDUAL           8         4.53     0.8068
```

The results of the contrast test displayed in Output 12.34 indicate that automobile size can be represented by a linear effect ($Q_C = 0.01$, $p = 0.9392$), which reduces the number of parameters required for size from 2 to 1.

Output 12.34   Test for Linearity

```
                ANALYSIS OF CONTRASTS

        Contrast          DF    Chi-Square    Prob
        --------------------------------------------
        linear effect      1         0.01     0.9392
```

This is done in the final model, where the variable LINSIZE, constructed previously in the DATA step creating SAS data set HIGHWAY, is substituted for the variable SIZE. It takes the value 0 for standard cars, 1 for midsized cars, and 2 for small cars.

In order to specify that these values be used as the values in a column in the model matrix, you need to list LINSIZE in the DIRECT statement. The DIRECT statement allows you to specify variables whose values are to be placed directly into the model matrix; otherwise, every variable on the right-hand side of the MODEL statement is considered a classification variable. The following statements fit the model with the linear automobile size effect and produce model-predicted values for the proportions with serious injury. The DIRECT statement must appear before the MODEL statement.

```
   proc catmod order=data;
      population size age modelyr;
      direct linsize ;
      weight count;
      response marginal;
      model status = linsize modelyr / pred;
   run ;
```

The "DESIGN MATRIX" table includes the three column model matrix. The values for LINSIZE are inserted as the second column, so this effect has one parameter.

Output 12.35   Model Matrix

```
                    Response       DESIGN MATRIX
            Sample  Function       1     2     3
            --------------------------------------
               1    0.20667        1     2     1
               2    0.18885        1     2    -1
               3    0.20561        1     2     1
               4    0.19718        1     2    -1
               5    0.16860        1     1     1
               6    0.14195        1     1    -1
               7    0.18852        1     1     1
               8    0.18015        1     1    -1
               9    0.18452        1     0     1
              10    0.12236        1     0    -1
              11    0.14855        1     0     1
              12    0.10941        1     0    -1
```

The model fits well ($Q_W = 4.53$, 9 df, $p = 0.873$), as seen in Output 12.36.

Output 12.36   ANOVA Table and Parameter Estimates

```
              ANALYSIS-OF-VARIANCE TABLE

        Source          DF    Chi-Square    Prob
        ----------------------------------------------
        INTERCEPT        1       314.13    0.0000
        LINSIZE          1        20.73    0.0000
        MODELYR          1         6.85    0.0089

        RESIDUAL         9         4.53    0.8730


        ANALYSIS OF WEIGHTED-LEAST-SQUARES ESTIMATES

                                        Standard    Chi-
        Effect      Parameter  Estimate    Error   Square   Prob
        -----------------------------------------------------------
        INTERCEPT        1      0.1351   0.00762   314.13  0.0000
        LINSIZE          2      0.0326   0.00715    20.73  0.0000
        MODELYR          3      0.0151   0.00578     6.85  0.0089
```

Both MODELYR and LINSIZE are very significant. The estimated parameters are listed in Output 12.36. You can write the prediction equation for proportion with serious injury as

$$\hat{\mathbf{F}}\{\mathbf{p}\} = \hat{\mathbf{p}} = 0.1351 + 0.0326 * \begin{Bmatrix} 2 & \text{if small car} \\ 1 & \text{if midsized} \\ 0 & \text{if standard} \end{Bmatrix} + .0151 * \begin{Bmatrix} 1 & \text{if before 1967} \\ -1 & \text{if after 1966} \end{Bmatrix}$$

Drivers of small cars with model years prior to 1967 have higher proportions of serious injury when involved in multiple vehicle accidents. Model-predicted proportions of serious injury are displayed in Output 12.37.

Output 12.37   Predicted Values

```
              PREDICTED VALUES FOR RESPONSE FUNCTIONS

                     -----Observed-----  -----Predicted----
          Function             Standard             Standard
Sample    Number   Function     Error    Function    Error    Residual
-----------------------------------------------------------------------
   1        1      0.206667   0.033061   0.215367   0.012619   -0.0087
   2        1      0.188854   0.021778   0.185111   0.012114    0.003744
   3        1      0.205607   0.022557   0.215367   0.012619   -0.00976
   4        1      0.197183   0.027262   0.185111   0.012114    0.012072
   5        1      0.168605   0.028548   0.182806   0.009267   -0.0142
   6        1      0.141949   0.016064   0.152549   0.007507   -0.0106
   7        1      0.188525   0.020445   0.182806   0.009267    0.005719
   8        1      0.180147   0.023302   0.152549   0.007507    0.027598
   9        1      0.184524   0.029928   0.150244   0.010716    0.03428
  10        1      0.122363    0.01229   0.119987   0.008262    0.002375
  11        1      0.148551   0.015137   0.150244   0.010716   -0.00169
  12        1      0.109409   0.014602   0.119987   0.008262   -0.01058
```

12.6.1   Other Models

Another useful response function is the logit function. For these data, using the logit as the response leads to the same final model as using the proportion as the response. Using the proportion has the advantage that it leads to a more easily interpretable model, since the coefficient values have a direct effect on the size of the proportions. Using the logit has the advantage that it always restricts predicted values for the proportions to be between 0 and 1. Fitting the logit function also has the advantage of being estimated with maximum likelihood estimation. This is more appropriate in situations where many of the cell counts are small, that is, less than or equal to 5, even though the overall sample size is moderate or large.

The following PROC CATMOD statements fit the same final model, except that it is applied to the logit response function. The logit is the default response function in PROC CATMOD, so the RESPONSE statement is not required. All other statements are unchanged from the previous PROC CATMOD invocation.

```
proc catmod order=data;
   population size age modelyr;
   direct linsize;
   weight count;
   model status = linsize modelyr / pred;
run;
```

This produces the results in Output 12.38. The goodness-of-fit statistic $Q_L = 5.53$ with 9 df, which compares favorably with the previous Q_W of 4.53 for the linear model for the marginal proportion with severe injury. Recall that the goodness-of-fit statistic printed for maximum likelihood estimation is the likelihood ratio statistic, which is also distributed as chi-square. This model fits the logit function very well.

Output 12.38   Logit: ML Estimation

```
          MAXIMUM-LIKELIHOOD ANALYSIS-OF-VARIANCE TABLE

          Source                 DF    Chi-Square      Prob
          -----------------------------------------------------
          INTERCEPT               1       853.16      0.0000
          LINSIZE                 1        20.49      0.0000
          MODELYR                 1         6.37      0.0116

          LIKELIHOOD RATIO        9         5.53      0.7854

          ANALYSIS OF MAXIMUM-LIKELIHOOD ESTIMATES

                                           Standard   Chi-
          Effect          Parameter  Estimate   Error    Square   Prob
          ---------------------------------------------------------------
          INTERCEPT            1      -1.8498   0.0633   853.16   0.0000
          LINSIZE              2       0.2349   0.0519    20.49   0.0000
          MODELYR              3       0.1078   0.0427     6.37   0.0116
```

For the sake of illustration, the same model for the logit function is fitted with weighted least squares estimation. Note that since maximum likelihood estimation is the default method for the logit function, you have to explicitly specify the WLS option on the MODEL statement if you want PROC CATMOD to use weighted least squares estimation for the logit function. Output 12.39 contains the results of this analysis.

```
proc catmod order=data;
    population size age modelyr;
    direct linsize;
    weight count;
    model status = linsize modelyr / pred wls;
run;
```

Output 12.39   Logit: WLS Estimation

```
              ANALYSIS-OF-VARIANCE TABLE

          Source                 DF    Chi-Square      Prob
          -----------------------------------------------------
          INTERCEPT               1       847.91      0.0000
          LINSIZE                 1        20.21      0.0000
          MODELYR                 1         6.35      0.0118

          RESIDUAL                9         5.65      0.7746

          ANALYSIS OF WEIGHTED-LEAST-SQUARES ESTIMATES

                                           Standard   Chi-
          Effect          Parameter  Estimate   Error    Square   Prob
          ---------------------------------------------------------------
          INTERCEPT            1      -1.8453   0.0634   847.91   0.0000
          LINSIZE              2       0.2336   0.0520    20.21   0.0000
          MODELYR              3       0.1075   0.0427     6.35   0.0118
```

The WLS goodness of fit for the same model is $Q_W = 5.65$, which is fairly close to the value of 5.53 for Q_L. These two statistics are asymptotically equivalent. As the sample sizes increase, you would expect the values of these statistics to converge for good fitting models. Compare the estimates from ML estimation and WLS estimation. They are nearly identical to three decimal places. Thus, WLS estimation for the logit response function can yield nearly identical results to ML estimation for adequate sample sizes. Since ML estimation is available, you should use it, and that is why it is the default estimation method in the PROC CATMOD procedure for the logit function. However, this example does serve to show that WLS estimates can be very close to ML estimates for sufficient sample sizes.

12.7   Obstetrical Pain Data: Advanced Modeling of Means

Sections 12.3 and 12.4 discussed analyses of means. This section is concerned with an advanced application of modeling means, and it includes a lengthy analysis of contrasts to fully investigate various effects and interactions.

The data displayed in Table 12.11 are from a multi-center randomized study of obstetrical-related pain for women who had recently delivered a baby (Koch, Imrey, et al 1985). Investigators were interested in comparing four treatments: placebo, drug a, drug b, and a combined treatment of drug a and drug b. Each patient was classified as initially having some pain or a lot of pain. Then, a randomly assigned treatment was administered at the beginning of the study period and again at 4 hours. Each patient was observed at hourly intervals for 8 hours and pain status was recorded as little or no pain or some or more pain. The response measure of interest is the average proportion of hours for which the patient reported little or no pain.

The patients for each center × initial status × treatment group can be considered to be representative of some corresponding large target population in a manner that is consistent with stratified simple random sampling. Each of the patient's responses can also be assumed to be independent of other patient responses. Thus, the data in Table 12.11 are distributed as product multinomial. There are many small cell frequencies (less than 5) in this table. This means that the asymptotic requirements necessary for modeling functions such as multiple cell proportions or generalized logits are not met. However, the average proportion of hours with little or no pain is a reasonable response measure, and there is sufficient sample size for modeling means.

Table 12.11   Number of Hours with Little or No Pain for Women Who Recently Delivered a Baby

Center	Initial Pain Status	Treatment	Hours With Little or No Pain									Total
			0	1	2	3	4	5	6	7	8	
1	lot	placebo	6	1	2	2	2	3	7	3	0	26
1	lot	a	6	3	1	2	4	4	7	1	0	28
1	lot	b	3	1	0	4	2	3	11	4	0	28
1	lot	ba	0	0	0	1	1	7	9	6	2	26
1	some	placebo	1	0	3	0	2	2	4	4	2	18
1	some	a	2	1	0	2	1	2	4	5	1	18
1	some	b	0	0	0	1	0	3	7	6	2	19
1	some	ba	0	0	0	0	1	3	5	4	6	19
2	lot	placebo	7	2	3	2	3	2	3	2	2	26
2	lot	a	3	1	0	0	3	2	9	7	1	26
2	lot	b	0	0	0	1	1	5	8	7	4	26
2	lot	ba	0	1	0	0	1	2	8	9	5	26
2	some	placebo	2	0	2	1	3	1	2	5	4	20
2	some	a	0	0	0	1	1	1	8	1	7	19
2	some	b	0	2	0	1	0	1	4	6	6	20
2	some	ba	0	0	0	1	3	0	4	7	5	20
3	lot	placebo	6	0	2	2	2	6	1	2	1	22
3	lot	a	4	2	1	5	1	1	3	2	3	22
3	lot	b	5	0	2	3	1	0	2	6	7	26
3	lot	ba	3	2	1	0	0	2	5	9	4	26
3	some	placebo	5	0	0	1	3	1	4	4	5	23
3	some	a	1	0	0	1	3	5	3	3	6	22
3	some	b	3	0	1	1	0	0	3	7	11	26
3	some	ba	0	0	0	1	1	4	2	4	13	25
4	lot	placebo	4	0	1	3	2	1	1	2	2	16
4	lot	a	0	1	3	1	1	6	1	3	6	22
4	lot	b	0	0	0	0	2	7	2	2	9	22
4	lot	ba	1	0	3	0	1	2	3	4	8	22
4	some	placebo	1	0	1	1	4	1	1	0	10	19
4	some	a	0	0	0	1	0	2	2	1	13	19
4	some	b	0	0	0	1	1	1	1	5	11	20
4	some	ba	1	0	0	0	0	2	2	2	14	21

The proportion vector for each group i is written

$$\mathbf{p} = (p_{i0}, p_{i1}, p_{i2}, p_{i3}, p_{i4}, p_{i5}, p_{i6}, p_{i7}, p_{i8})'$$

where p_{ij} is the proportion of patients with j hours of pain for the ith group, and $i = 1, \ldots, 32$ is the group corresponding to the ith row of Table 12.11. You compute the average proportion response function by applying the following matrix operation to the proportion vector for each group.

$$\mathbf{F}_i = \mathbf{F}(\mathbf{p}_i) = \mathbf{A}\mathbf{p} = \left[\frac{0}{8}, \frac{1}{8}, \frac{2}{8}, \frac{3}{8}, \frac{4}{8}, \frac{5}{8}, \frac{6}{8}, \frac{7}{8}, \frac{8}{8} \right] \mathbf{p}_i$$

A useful preliminary model is one that includes effects for center, initial pain, treatment, and initial pain × treatment interaction; initial pain and treatment are believed to be similar across centers, so their interactions with center are not included.

12.7.1   Performing the Analysis with PROC CATMOD

The following DATA step creates the SAS data set PAIN. The raw data contains an observation for each line of Table 12.11, although they are in a different order. The ARRAY and OUTPUT statements in the DATA step modify the input data by creating an individual observation for each different response value, or number of hours with little or no pain. It creates the variables NO_HOURS and COUNT. The CATMOD procedure requires that each response value be represented on a different observation. This data set contains 288 observations, or 9 observations for each of the 32 original data lines. The values for the variable INITIAL are 'some' for some pain and 'lot' for a lot of pain.

```
data pain (drop=h0-h8);
   input center initial $ treat $ h0-h8;
   array hours h0-h8;
   do i=1 to 9;
       no_hours=i-1; count=hours(i); output;
   end;
   cards;
1 some placebo  1 0 3 0 2 2 4 4 2
1 some treat_a  2 1 0 2 1 2 4 5 1
1 some treat_b  0 0 0 1 0 3 7 6 2
1 some treat_ba 0 0 0 0 1 3 5 4 6
1 lot  placebo  6 1 2 2 2 3 7 3 0
1 lot  treat_a  6 3 1 2 4 4 7 1 0
1 lot  treat_b  3 1 0 4 2 3 11 4 0
1 lot  treat_ba 0 0 0 1 1 7 9 6 2
2 some placebo  2 0 2 1 3 1 2 5 4
2 some treat_a  0 0 0 1 1 1 8 1 7
2 some treat_b  0 2 0 1 0 1 4 6 6
2 some treat_ba 0 0 0 1 3 0 4 7 5
2 lot  placebo  7 2 3 2 3 2 3 2 2
2 lot  treat_a  3 1 0 0 3 2 9 7 1
2 lot  treat_b  0 0 0 1 1 5 8 7 4
2 lot  treat_ba 0 1 0 0 1 2 8 9 5
3 some placebo  5 0 0 1 3 1 4 4 5
3 some treat_a  1 0 0 1 3 5 3 3 6
3 some treat_b  3 0 1 1 0 0 3 7 11
3 some treat_ba 0 0 0 1 1 4 2 4 13
3 lot  placebo  6 0 2 2 2 6 1 2 1
3 lot  treat_a  4 2 1 5 1 1 3 2 3
3 lot  treat_b  5 0 2 3 1 0 2 6 7
3 lot  treat_ba 3 2 1 0 0 2 5 9 4
4 some placebo  1 0 1 1 4 1 1 0 10
4 some treat_a  0 0 0 1 0 2 2 1 13
4 some treat_b  0 0 0 1 1 1 1 5 11
4 some treat_ba 1 0 0 0 0 2 2 2 14
4 lot  placebo  4 0 1 3 2 1 1 2 2
4 lot  treat_a  0 1 3 1 1 6 1 3 6
```

```
4 lot   treat_b   0 0 0 0 2 7 2 2 9
4 lot   treat_ba 1 0 3 0 1 2 3 4 8
;
proc print;
run;
```

Output 12.40 displays the observations for the group from center 1 who had some initial pain and received the placebo.

Output 12.40   Partial Listing of Data Set PAIN

OBS	CENTER	INITIAL	TREAT	NO_HOURS	COUNT
1	1	some	placebo	0	1
2	1	some	placebo	1	0
3	1	some	placebo	2	3
4	1	some	placebo	3	0
5	1	some	placebo	4	2
6	1	some	placebo	5	2
7	1	some	placebo	6	4
8	1	some	placebo	7	4
9	1	some	placebo	8	2

The following SAS statements invoke the CATMOD procedure and fit the preliminary model. Note that the RESPONSE statement includes the coefficients required to compute the average proportions per group. Using the MEANS keyword on the RESPONSE statement would compute the mean number of hours with little or no pain, not the average proportion of hours with little or no pain, which is desired here. Actually the results will be the same; the decision is whether you want the parameter estimates to apply to proportions or means.

```
proc catmod;
   weight count;
   response 0 .125 .25 .375 .5 .625 .75 .875 1;
   model no_hours =  center initial treat
                     treat*initial;
run;
```

The population profiles and the response profiles are displayed in Output 12.41 and Output 12.42, respectively.

Output 12.41   Population Profiles

```
                    POPULATION PROFILES
                                           Sample
      Sample  CENTER  INITIAL   TREAT        Size
      ----------------------------------------------
           1      1      lot     placebo       26
           2      1      lot     treat_a       28
           3      1      lot     treat_b       28
           4      1      lot     treat_ba      26
           5      1      some    placebo       18
           6      1      some    treat_a       18
           7      1      some    treat_b       19
           8      1      some    treat_ba      19
           9      2      lot     placebo       26
          10      2      lot     treat_a       26
          11      2      lot     treat_b       26
          12      2      lot     treat_ba      26
          13      2      some    placebo       20
          14      2      some    treat_a       19
          15      2      some    treat_b       20
          16      2      some    treat_ba      20
          17      3      lot     placebo       22
          18      3      lot     treat_a       22
          19      3      lot     treat_b       26
          20      3      lot     treat_ba      26
          21      3      some    placebo       23
          22      3      some    treat_a       22
          23      3      some    treat_b       26
          24      3      some    treat_ba      25
          25      4      lot     placebo       16
          26      4      lot     treat_a       22
          27      4      lot     treat_b       22
          28      4      lot     treat_ba      22
          29      4      some    placebo       19
          30      4      some    treat_a       19
          31      4      some    treat_b       20
          32      4      some    treat_ba      21
```

Output 12.42   Response Profiles

```
              RESPONSE PROFILES

          Response   NO_HOURS
          ------------------
               1         0
               2         1
               3         2
               4         3
               5         4
               6         5
               7         6
               8         7
               9         8
```

The response functions listed as part of the "DESIGN MATRIX" table in Output 12.43 are the average proportions of hours with little or no pain.

Output 12.43   Model Matrix

Sample	Response Function	DESIGN MATRIX 1	2	3	4	5
1	0.46635	1	1	0	0	1
2	0.42857	1	1	0	0	1
3	0.58036	1	1	0	0	1
4	0.74038	1	1	0	0	1
5	0.63889	1	1	0	0	-1
6	0.61111	1	1	0	0	-1
7	0.77632	1	1	0	0	-1
8	0.82237	1	1	0	0	-1
9	0.40385	1	0	1	0	1
10	0.64423	1	0	1	0	1
11	0.77404	1	0	1	0	1
12	0.79808	1	0	1	0	1
13	0.64375	1	0	1	0	-1
14	0.80921	1	0	1	0	-1
15	0.77500	1	0	1	0	-1
16	0.80000	1	0	1	0	-1
17	0.43182	1	0	0	1	1
18	0.47727	1	0	0	1	1
19	0.61058	1	0	0	1	1
20	0.66827	1	0	0	1	1
21	0.60870	1	0	0	1	-1
22	0.72159	1	0	0	1	-1
23	0.76923	1	0	0	1	-1
24	0.85500	1	0	0	1	-1
25	0.46875	1	-1	-1	-1	1
26	0.67614	1	-1	-1	-1	1
27	0.80114	1	-1	-1	-1	1
28	0.73864	1	-1	-1	-1	1
29	0.73684	1	-1	-1	-1	-1
30	0.89474	1	-1	-1	-1	-1
31	0.88125	1	-1	-1	-1	-1
32	0.88095	1	-1	-1	-1	-1

Output 12.44   Model Matrix (continued)

```
                         DESIGN MATRIX
    Sample      6       7       8       9      10      11
    ------------------------------------------------------
       1        1       0       0       1       0       0
       2        0       1       0       0       1       0
       3        0       0       1       0       0       1
       4       -1      -1      -1      -1      -1      -1
       5        1       0       0      -1       0       0
       6        0       1       0       0      -1       0
       7        0       0       1       0       0      -1
       8       -1      -1      -1       1       1       1
       9        1       0       0       1       0       0
      10        0       1       0       0       1       0
      11        0       0       1       0       0       1
      12       -1      -1      -1      -1      -1      -1
      13        1       0       0      -1       0       0
      14        0       1       0       0      -1       0
      15        0       0       1       0       0      -1
      16       -1      -1      -1       1       1       1
      17        1       0       0       1       0       0
      18        0       1       0       0       1       0
      19        0       0       1       0       0       1
      20       -1      -1      -1      -1      -1      -1
      21        1       0       0      -1       0       0
      22        0       1       0       0      -1       0
      23        0       0       1       0       0      -1
      24       -1      -1      -1       1       1       1
      25        1       0       0       1       0       0
      26        0       1       0       0       1       0
      27        0       0       1       0       0       1
      28       -1      -1      -1      -1      -1      -1
      29        1       0       0      -1       0       0
      30        0       1       0       0      -1       0
      31        0       0       1       0       0      -1
      32       -1      -1      -1       1       1       1
```

The goodness-of-fit statistic for this preliminary model is $Q_W = 26.90$ with 21 df, as displayed in Output 12.45. With $p = 0.1743$, this indicates that the model fits the data adequately. All the constituent effects are highly significant, $p < 0.01$.

Output 12.45   Preliminary ANOVA Table

```
                  ANALYSIS-OF-VARIANCE TABLE

        Source             DF    Chi-Square     Prob
        ----------------------------------------------
        INTERCEPT           1      5271.98     0.0000
        CENTER              3        29.02     0.0000
        INITIAL             1        62.65     0.0000
        TREAT               3        92.15     0.0000
        INITIAL*TREAT       3        12.63     0.0055

        RESIDUAL           21        26.90     0.1743
```

It is useful to examine further the interaction between the treatments and initial pain status. The significant interaction means that some of the treatment effects depend on the level of initial pain status.

Some questions of interest are:

- Which treatment effects depend on the level of initial pain status ? Where exactly is the interaction occurring ?

- In which levels of initial pain do treatments differ ?

To address these questions, it is helpful to fit a differently parameterized model. If you nest the effects of treatment within levels of initial pain, then these questions can be addressed with the use of contrasts. By using the nested effects model, you are trading the three df for TREAT and three df for TREAT*INITIAL for six df for the nested effect TREAT(INITIAL). Accordingly, the TREAT(INITIAL) effect is associated with six parameters, three of which pertain to the effects of treatment within some initial pain and three of which pertain to the effects of treatment within a lot of initial pain.

The following PROC CATMOD statements fit the nested model. The difference between specifying the nested effect TREAT(INITIAL) and the nested-by-values effects (see page 326) TREAT(INITIAL=some) and TREAT(INITIAL=lot) is that the former yields the 6 df test in the ANOVA table that tests whether the six parameters for treatment effects within both some and a lot of initial pain levels are essentially zero; the latter results in two separate 3 df tests in the ANOVA table, one for whether the three treatment parameters for some pain are essentially zero and one for whether the three treatment parameters for a lot of pain are essentially zero.

```
proc catmod;
   weight count;
   response 0 .125 .25 .375 .5 .625 .75 .875 1;
   model no_hours = center initial
                    treat(initial);
run;
```

Submitting these statements produces the results contained in Output 12.46.

Output 12.46   Nested Value ANOVA Table

```
             ANALYSIS-OF-VARIANCE TABLE

    Source              DF   Chi-Square     Prob
    -------------------------------------------------
    INTERCEPT            1     5271.98    0.0000
    CENTER               3       29.02    0.0000
    INITIAL              1       62.65    0.0000
    TREAT(INITIAL)       6      102.70    0.0000

    RESIDUAL            21       26.90    0.1743
```

The model goodness-of-fit test is the same, $Q_W = 26.90$ with 21 df, since no model reduction was performed. The current model simply redistributes the variation over different degrees of freedom. Geometrically, you can think of the model space as being spanned by a different, but equivalent, vector set. The tests for CENTER effect and INITIAL effect remain the same as well. However, now there is the six df nested effect TREAT(INITIAL) in place of a TREAT effect and a TREAT*INITIAL interaction.

The next table that PROC CATMOD produces is the table of parameter estimates. These are listed in the same order as the corresponding explanatory variables in the MODEL statement. Besides the intercept, there are three parameters corresponding to CENTER for the effects of center 1, center 2, and center 3, respectively. As discussed previously, for the fullrank parameterization that PROC CATMOD uses, you can determine the estimate of the effect for center 4 by taking the negative of the sum of these three displayed center effect parameters. Since INITIAL has two levels, it is represented by one parameter; this is the effect for a lot of initial pain.

Output 12.47   Nested Value ANOVA Table

			Standard	Chi-	
Effect	Parameter	Estimate	Error	Square	Prob
INTERCEPT	1	0.6991	0.00963	5271.98	0.0000
CENTER	2	-0.0484	0.0145	11.24	0.0008
	3	0.0187	0.0145	1.66	0.1982
	4	-0.0415	0.0176	5.56	0.0184
INITIAL	5	-0.0753	0.00951	62.65	0.0000
TREAT(INITIAL)	6	-0.1739	0.0283	37.81	0.0000
	7	-0.0644	0.0255	6.39	0.0115
	8	0.0952	0.0206	21.45	0.0000
	9	-0.1159	0.0284	16.68	0.0000
	10	0.00740	0.0217	0.12	0.7331
	11	0.0347	0.0206	2.84	0.0921

ANALYSIS OF WEIGHTED-LEAST-SQUARES ESTIMATES

The last six parameters are those for the nested effect TREAT(INITIAL). It is useful to examine the model matrix to understand what these parameters mean. The model matrix is displayed in Output 12.48.

The first column of the model matrix corresponds to the intercept, columns 2–4 correspond to the parameters for CENTER, and column 5 corresponds to the parameter for INITIAL. Notice the structure of the next six columns, 6–11. There are nonzero entries in columns 6–8 for those rows that correspond to groups that are from the same initial pain level. You can compare the "Sample" column value to the same values in the "POPULATION PROFILES" table previously displayed to determine exactly which group is represented by each row of the model matrix. Columns 6–8 are the effects for placebo, treatment a, and treatment b, nested within the 'a lot of pain' level. This ordering is also determined by the order in which the TREAT values are listed in the "POPULATION PROFILES" table. You see a similar pattern in the final three columns of the model matrix, columns 9–11. Effects for placebo, treatment a, and treatment b are nested within the 'some pain' level.

Output 12.48   Model Matrix for Nested Model

```
            Response                              DESIGN MATRIX
  Sample    Function   1   2   3   4   5   6   7   8   9  10  11
  ------------------------------------------------------------------
     1       0.46635   1   1   0   0   1   1   0   0   0   0   0
     2       0.42857   1   1   0   0   1   0   1   0   0   0   0
     3       0.58036   1   1   0   0   1   0   0   1   0   0   0
     4       0.74038   1   1   0   0   1  -1  -1  -1   0   0   0
     5       0.63889   1   1   0   0  -1   0   0   0   1   0   0
     6       0.61111   1   1   0   0  -1   0   0   0   0   1   0
     7       0.77632   1   1   0   0  -1   0   0   0   0   0   1
     8       0.82237   1   1   0   0  -1   0   0   0  -1  -1  -1
     9       0.40385   1   0   1   0   1   1   0   0   0   0   0
    10       0.64423   1   0   1   0   1   0   1   0   0   0   0
    11       0.77404   1   0   1   0   1   0   0   1   0   0   0
    12       0.79808   1   0   1   0   1  -1  -1  -1   0   0   0
    13       0.64375   1   0   1   0  -1   0   0   0   1   0   0
    14       0.80921   1   0   1   0  -1   0   0   0   0   1   0
    15       0.77500   1   0   1   0  -1   0   0   0   0   0   1
    16       0.80000   1   0   1   0  -1   0   0   0  -1  -1  -1
    17       0.43182   1   0   0   1   1   1   0   0   0   0   0
    18       0.47727   1   0   0   1   1   0   1   0   0   0   0
    19       0.61058   1   0   0   1   1   0   0   1   0   0   0
    20       0.66827   1   0   0   1   1  -1  -1  -1   0   0   0
    21       0.60870   1   0   0   1  -1   0   0   0   1   0   0
    22       0.72159   1   0   0   1  -1   0   0   0   0   1   0
    23       0.76923   1   0   0   1  -1   0   0   0   0   0   1
    24       0.85500   1   0   0   1  -1   0   0   0  -1  -1  -1
    25       0.46875   1  -1  -1  -1   1   1   0   0   0   0   0
    26       0.67614   1  -1  -1  -1   1   0   1   0   0   0   0
    27       0.80114   1  -1  -1  -1   1   0   0   1   0   0   0
    28       0.73864   1  -1  -1  -1   1  -1  -1  -1   0   0   0
    29       0.73684   1  -1  -1  -1  -1   0   0   0   1   0   0
    30       0.89474   1  -1  -1  -1  -1   0   0   0   0   1   0
    31       0.88125   1  -1  -1  -1  -1   0   0   0   0   0   1
    32       0.88095   1  -1  -1  -1  -1   0   0   0  -1  -1  -1
```

Table 12.12 describes each parameter.

Table 12.12   Parameter Interpretations

CATMOD Parameter	Model Parameter	Interpretation
1	α	intercept
2	β_1	differential effect for center 1
3	β_2	differential effect for center 2
4	β_3	differential effect for center 3
5	β_4	differential effect for a lot of initial pain
6	β_5	differential effect for placebo for a lot of pain
7	β_6	differential effect for treatment a for a lot of pain
8	β_7	differential effect for treatment b for a lot of pain
9	β_8	differential effect for placebo for some pain
10	β_9	differential effect for treatment a for some pain
11	β_{10}	differential effect for treatment b for some pain

Consider testing to see if the effect for treatment a is the same as the effect for placebo for those patients with some pain. The appropriate hypothesis is stated

$$H_0: \beta_9 - \beta_8 = 0$$

Since the implicit effect for treatment ba is written in terms of the other treatment parameters,

$$\beta_{\text{treatment ba}} = -\beta_8 - \beta_9 - \beta_{10}$$

the hypothesis test to see if the effect for treatment ba is the same as the effect for placebo is written

$$H_0: -2\beta_8 - \beta_9 - \beta_{10} = 0$$

The hypotheses of interest and their corresponding contrasts and coefficients are displayed in Table 12.13. The coefficients are required in the CONTRAST statement in PROC CATMOD to perform a particular contrast test.

Table 12.13 Hypothesis Tests

Hypothesis	Initial Pain	Contrast	Coefficients					
			β_5	β_6	β_7	β_8	β_9	β_{10}
treatment a vs. placebo	a lot	$-\beta_5 + \beta_6$	-1	1	0	0	0	0
treatment b vs. placebo	a lot	$-\beta_5 + \beta_7$	-1	0	1	0	0	0
treatment ba vs. placebo	a lot	$-2\beta_5 - \beta_6 - \beta_7$	-2	-1	-1	0	0	0
treatment ba vs. a	a lot	$-\beta_5 - 2\beta_6 - \beta_7$	-1	-2	-1	0	0	0
treatment ba vs. b	a lot	$-\beta_5 - \beta_6 - 2\beta_7$	-1	-1	-2	0	0	0
treatment a vs. placebo	some	$-\beta_8 + \beta_9$	0	0	0	-1	1	0
treatment b vs. placebo	some	$-\beta_8 + \beta_{10}$	0	0	0	-1	0	1
treatment ba vs. placebo	some	$-2\beta_8 - \beta_9 - \beta_{10}$	0	0	0	-2	-1	-1
treatment ba vs. a	some	$-\beta_8 - 2\beta_9 - \beta_{10}$	0	0	0	-1	-2	-1
treatment ba vs. b	some	$-\beta_8 - \beta_9 - 2\beta_{10}$	0	0	0	-1	-1	-2

The following CONTRAST statements request that the CATMOD procedure perform the appropriate tests. The statements can be submitted interactively, following the previous nested model invocation, or in batch, included at the end of the nested model invocation. Since you are only interested in the parameters corresponding to the TREAT(INITIAL) effect, you list that effect on the CONTRAST statement and then specify the appropriate six coefficients that pertain to the contrast involving the parameters β_5–β_{10}.

```
contrast 'lot: a-placebo'  treat(initial) -1  1  0  0  0  0 ;
contrast 'lot: b-placebo'  treat(initial) -1  0  1  0  0  0 ;
contrast 'lot: ba-placebo' treat(initial) -2 -1 -1  0  0  0 ;
contrast 'lot: ba-a'       treat(initial) -1 -2 -1  0  0  0 ;
contrast 'lot: ba-b'       treat(initial) -1 -1 -2  0  0  0 ;
contrast 'some:a-placebo'  treat(initial)  0  0  0 -1  1  0 ;
contrast 'some:b-placebo'  treat(initial)  0  0  0 -1  0  1 ;
```

```
contrast 'some:ba-placebo' treat(initial)  0  0  0 -2 -1 -1 ;
contrast 'some:ba-a'        treat(initial)  0  0  0 -1 -2 -1 ;
contrast 'some:ba-b'        treat(initial)  0  0  0 -1 -1 -2 ;
run;
```

These statements produce the following "ANALYSIS OF CONTRASTS" table. It includes the results for all the individual hypothesis tests.

Output 12.49   Contrast Results

```
                    ANALYSIS OF CONTRASTS

Contrast                 DF    Chi-Square     Prob
----------------------------------------------------
lot: a-placebo            1         5.59     0.0180
lot: b-placebo            1        42.81     0.0000
lot: ba-placebo           1        61.48     0.0000
lot: ba-a                 1        32.06     0.0000
lot: ba-b                 1         2.59     0.1076
some:a-placebo            1         8.19     0.0042
some:b-placebo            1        12.83     0.0003
some:ba-placebo           1        21.45     0.0000
some:ba-a                 1         4.37     0.0365
some:ba-b                 1         1.67     0.1964
```

Most of these contrasts are significant, using the $\alpha = 0.05$ criterion; however, it appears that the difference between the ba treatment and the b treatment is marginal for both some initial pain and a lot of initial pain.

Additional contrasts of interest are the individual components of the treatment $\times$ initial pain status interaction, detailed in the first three rows of Table 12.14, as well as the individual components of the overall treatment effect. The interaction components are constructed by taking the difference of the pertinent contrasts for the some pain and a lot of pain contrasts, that is, taking the differences of rows 1 and 6, 2 and 7, and 3 and 8, in Table 12.13. The treatment effect is the joint effect of the various treatments averaged over the some initial pain and a lot of initial pain domains, so the individual components are the sum of the following rows from Table 12.13: 1 and 6, 2 and 7, 3 and 8. (You naturally think of averaging as summing and dividing by the number of summands; however, multiplying the contrast equations by a constant yields equivalent results, and so summing is all you really have to do.)

Table 12.14 Hypothesis Tests

Hypothesis	Coefficients					
	β_5	β_6	β_7	β_8	β_9	β_{10}
treatment a vs. placebo, some vs. a lot	1	1	0	1	−1	0
treatment b vs. placebo, some vs. a lot	−1	0	1	1	0	−1
treatment ba vs. placebo, some vs. a lot	−2	−1	−1	2	1	1
treatment ba vs. a, some vs. a lot	−1	−2	−1	1	2	1
treatment ba vs. b, some vs. a lot	−1	−1	−2	1	1	2
average treatment a effect	−1	1	0	−1	1	0
average treatment b effect	−1	0	1	−1	0	1
average treatment ba effect	−2	−1	−1	−2	−1	−1
average ba vs. a	−1	−2	−1	−1	−2	−1
average ba vs. b	−1	−1	−2	−1	−1	−2

The next block of CONTRAST statements performs these tests. The last two CONTRAST statements request the three df TREAT*INITIAL interaction and the three df TREAT effect, respectively. The output is displayed in Output 12.50.

```
contrast 'interact:a-placebo'    treat(initial) -1  1  0  1 -1  0 ;
contrast 'interact:b-placebo'    treat(initial) -1  0  1  1  0 -1 ;
contrast 'interact:ba-placebo'   treat(initial) -2 -1 -1  2  1  1 ;
contrast 'average:a-placebo'     treat(initial) -1  1  0 -1  1  0 ;
contrast 'average:b-placebo'     treat(initial) -1  0  1 -1  0  1 ;
contrast 'average:ba-placebo'    treat(initial) -2 -1 -1 -2 -1 -1 ;
contrast 'average:ba-a'          treat(initial) -1 -2 -1 -1 -2 -1 ;
contrast 'average:ba-b'          treat(initial) -1 -1 -2 -1 -1 -2 ;
contrast 'interaction'           treat(initial) -1  1  0  1 -1  0 ,
                                 treat(initial) -1  0  1  1  0 -1 ,
                                 treat(initial) -2 -1 -1  2  1  1 ;
contrast 'treatment effect'      treat(initial) -1  1  0 -1  1  0 ,
                                 treat(initial) -1  0  1 -1  0  1 ,
                                 treat(initial) -2 -1 -1 -2 -1 -1 ;
```

Output 12.50 Contrast Results

```
                    ANALYSIS OF CONTRASTS

     Contrast            DF   Chi-Square    Prob
     -------------------------------------------------
     interact:a-placebo   1       0.05     0.8266
     interact:b-placebo   1       4.05     0.0441
     interact:ab-placebo  1       4.89     0.0271
     interact:ba-a        1       8.61     0.0033
     interact:ba-b        1       0.04     0.8344
     average:a-placebo    1      13.51     0.0002
     average:b-placebo    1      50.93     0.0000
     average:ab-placebo   1      77.60     0.0000
     average:ba-a         1      31.42     0.0000
     average:ba-b         1       4.22     0.0399
     interaction          3      12.63     0.0055
     treatment effect     3      92.15     0.0000
```

These contrasts indicate that the interaction component corresponding to the comparison of treatment a and placebo is nonsignificant; therefore, treatment a has similar effects for an initial pain status of some or a lot. Treatments b and ba do appear to have different effects at the different levels of initial pain when compared to placebo; however these effects may be quite similar. The interaction component corresponding to the comparison of treatment a and treatment ba is significant; their difference depends on the level of initial pain. This is not the case for treatment b compared to treatment ba; their interaction component is nonsignificant.

All the components of the treatment effect, those tests marked average, are significant.

The 'interaction' and the 'treatment effect' are testing the same thing as the TREAT effect and the TREAT*INITIAL effects listed in the ANOVA table for the preliminary model. Compare the Q_W values, 12.63 and 92.15, to those listed in that table. They are identical.

These results address the pertinent questions of this analysis. Other approaches may include fitting a reduced model that incorporates the results of these hypothesis tests. This is not pursued in this example.

12.8   Analysis of Survey Sample Data

In addition to analyzing data based on an underlying contingency table, the CATMOD procedure provides a convenient way to analyze data that come in the form of a function vector and covariance matrix. Often, such data come from complex surveys, and the covariance matrix has been computed using other software that takes the sampling design into account. If the number of response function estimates and the corresponding covariance matrix is large, then software designed for survey data analysis may be more appropriate.

12.8.1   HANES Data

The following data are from the Health and Nutrition Examination Survey (HANES) that was conducted in the United States from 1971–1974. This survey obtained various information concerning health from over 10,000 households in the United States. One of the measures constructed for analysis of these data was a well-being index, a composite index comprised from the answers to a questionnaire on general well-being. Table 12.15 contains the well-being ordered categorical estimates and standard errors for a crossclassification based on sex and age. The covariance matrix was computed using other software that used balanced repeated replication and took into account the sampling framework of the survey (Koch and Stokes 1979).

Table 12.15   Well-being Index

Sex	Age	Estimate	S.E.
Female	25–34	7.250	0.105
Female	35–44	7.190	0.153
Female	45–54	7.360	0.103
Female	55–64	7.319	0.152
Female	65–74	7.552	0.139
Male	25–34	7.937	0.086
Male	35–44	7.925	0.108
Male	45–54	7.828	0.102
Male	55–64	7.737	0.116
Male	65–74	8.168	0.120

12.8.2   Direct Input of Response Functions

In the typical PROC CATMOD analysis, you input a contingency table or raw data and specify the response functions, and PROC CATMOD computes the appropriate covariance matrix based on the product multinomial distribution. In this case, your data are the vector of response functions and its covariance matrix. Thus, in order to describe the variation of these functions across various groups, you need to inform the procedure of the structure of your underlying crossclassification. Ordinarily, you would do this with the explanatory variables that define the contingency table. For this case, you need to rely on the FACTOR statement to express the crossclassification relationships.

The following is the DATA step that inputs the response functions and their covariance matrix into the SAS data set WBEING. The first two data lines are the well-being estimates, listed in the same order as they appear in Table 12.15. The following data lines contain the 10×10 covariance matrix corresponding to the estimates, each row takes two lines. The variable _TYPE_ identifies whether each data line corresponds to parameter estimates or covariance estimates. The value 'parms' identifies the lines with parameter estimates and the value 'cov' identifies the lines with the covariance estimates. The variable _NAME_ identifies the name of the variable that has its covariance elements stored in that data line. Note that the diagonal element in the ith row of the covariance matrix is the variance for the ith well-being estimate. (The square root of the element is the standard error for the estimate.)

```
data wbeing;
    input #1 b1-b5 _type_ $ _name_ $8. #2 b6-b10;
    cards;
 7.24978    7.18991    7.35960    7.31937    7.55184 parms
 7.93726    7.92509    7.82815    7.73696    8.16791
 0.01110    0.00101    0.00177   -0.00018   -0.00082 cov        b1
 0.00189   -0.00123    0.00434    0.00158   -0.00050
 0.00101    0.02342    0.00144    0.00369    0.25300 cov        b2
 0.00118   -0.00629   -0.00059    0.00212   -0.00098
 0.00177    0.00144    0.01060    0.00157    0.00226 cov        b3
 0.00140   -0.00088   -0.00055    0.00211    0.00239
```

```
   -0.00018     0.00369     0.00157     0.02298     0.00918 cov         b4
   -0.00140    -0.00232     0.00023     0.00066    -0.00010
   -0.00082     0.00253     0.00226     0.00918     0.01921 cov         b5
    0.00039     0.00034    -0.00013     0.00240     0.00213
    0.00189     0.00118     0.00140    -0.00140     0.00039 cov         b6
    0.00739     0.00019     0.00146    -0.00082     0.00076
   -0.00123    -0.00629    -0.00088    -0.00232     0.00034 cov         b7
    0.00019     0.01172     0.00183     0.00029     0.00083
    0.00434    -0.00059    -0.00055     0.00023    -0.00013 cov         b8
    0.00146     0.00183     0.01050    -0.00173     0.00011
    0.00158     0.00212     0.00211     0.00066     0.00240 cov         b9
   -0.00082     0.00029    -0.00173     0.01335     0.00140
   -0.00050    -0.00098     0.00239    -0.00010     0.00213 cov         b10
    0.00076     0.00083     0.00011     0.00140     0.01430
;
```

12.8.3 The FACTOR Statement

The FACTOR statement is where you define the crossclassification structure of the estimates. You need to specify names for the CATMOD procedure to use internally that correspond to grouping variables. You specify the number of levels for each and whether their values are character. This is done in the first part of the FACTOR statement. The internal variable SEX has two levels, and its values are character, as denoted by the dollar sign; the internal variable AGE has five levels, and its values are also character. The values for these internal variables are listed under the PROFILE option after a slash (/) in the FACTOR statement. The values are listed according to the order of the estimates; thus, they are listed in the same order as they appear in Table 12.15.

Since SEX and AGE are internal variables, not part of the input data set, you cannot refer to them in the MODEL statement. Thus, you use the keyword _RESPONSE_ to specify the desired model effects. In the following code, the saturated model is assigned to the keyword _RESPONSE_ in the FACTOR statement. This keyword is later used on the right-hand side of the MODEL statement. The _RESPONSE_ construction is also used to perform repeated measurements analyses and loglinear model analyses with the CATMOD procedure. Since the response functions are input directly, the keyword _F_ is used to represent them on the left-hand side of the MODEL statement.

The following PROC CATMOD statements invoke the procedure _RESPONSE_ specifies that the variation among the dependent variables is

and specify that a saturated model be fit to the data. The keyword READ on the RESPONSE statement tells PROC CATMOD that the response functions and covariance matrix are to be directly input. The variables B1-B10 after the keyword READ specify that ten response functions are involved and thus that the covariance matrix is 10×10.

```
proc catmod data=wbeing;
     response read b1-b10;
     factors sex $ 2, age $  5 /
          _response_ = sex|age
     profile = (female '25-34',
               female '35-44',
```

```
                              female  '45-54',
                              female  '55-64',
                              female  '65-74',
                              male    '25-34',
                              male    '35-44',
                              male    '45-54',
                              male    '55-64',
                              male    '65-74');
              model _f_ = _response_; run;
```

12.8.4 Preliminary Analysis

Since populations and responses are not determined by input data variables, the population profiles and response profiles are not printed as usual at the beginning of the PROC CATMOD output. Instead, the first table displayed contains the response functions and the model matrix, as shown in Output 12.51.

Output 12.51   Directly Input Response Functions

```
                       CATMOD PROCEDURE

        Response Functions Directly Input from Data Set WBEING

            Function    Response          DESIGN MATRIX
  Sample    Number      Function     1        2       3       4
  ------------------------------------------------------------------
     1         1        7.24978      1        1       1       0
               2        7.18991      1        1       0       1
               3        7.35960      1        1       0       0
               4        7.31937      1        1       0       0
               5        7.55184      1        1      -1      -1
               6        7.93726      1       -1       1       0
               7        7.92509      1       -1       0       1
               8        7.82815      1       -1       0       0
               9        7.73696      1       -1       0       0
              10        8.16791      1       -1      -1      -1


            Function                DESIGN MATRIX
  Sample    Number      5       6       7       8       9      10
  ------------------------------------------------------------------
     1         1        0       0       1       0       0       0
               2        0       0       0       1       0       0
               3        1       0       0       0       1       0
               4        0       1       0       0       0       1
               5       -1      -1      -1      -1      -1      -1
               6        0       0      -1       0       0       0
               7        0       0       0      -1       0       0
               8        1       0       0       0      -1       0
               9        0       1       0       0       0      -1
              10       -1      -1       1       1       1       1
```

Next is the analysis of variance table. The internal variables SEX and AGE are listed under "Source" just as if they were explanatory variables on the input data set. The SEX*AGE interaction is clearly nonsignificant, with $p = 0.5713$. Thus, the additive model with effects SEX and AGE has an adequate goodness of fit with $Q_W = 2.92$ and 4 df.

Output 12.52   Saturated Model

```
                  ANALYSIS-OF-VARIANCE TABLE

        Source              DF    Chi-Square      Prob
        ----------------------------------------------------
        INTERCEPT            1     27117.73      0.0000
        SEX                  1        47.07      0.0000
        AGE                  4        10.87      0.0281
        SEX*AGE              4         2.92      0.5713

        RESIDUAL             0          .           .
```

The additive model is fit next, with contrasts requested to determine whether any of the parameters for age are essentially the same. The following statements fit the additive model.

```
proc catmod data=wbeing;
   response read b1-b10;
   factors sex $ 2, age $ 5 /
      _response_ = sex age
      profile = (male '25-34' ,
                 male '35-44',
                 male '45-54' ,
                 male '55-64',
                 male '65-74' ,
                 female '25-34',
                 female '35-44',
                 female '45-54',
                 female '55-64' ,
                 female '65-74');
   model _f_ = _response_;
```

The contrasts are set up to compare the first parameter for the age effect with each of the others. Recall that the implicit parameter for the last level age effect (ages 65–74) is the negative of the sum of the other parameters. Since the response functions are input directly, coefficients must be supplied for all the effects, including the intercept. Thus, the ALL_PARMS keyword is required. When you specify this keyword, you must supply coefficients for all the model parameters. Here, 0s are supplied on all contrasts for the intercept term and the sex effect term, and the final four coefficients apply to the age effect.

```
contrast '25-34 vs. 35-44' all_parms 0 0 1 -1  0  0;
contrast '25-34 vs. 45,54' all_parms 0 0 1  0 -1  0;
contrast '25-34 vs. 55,64' all_parms 0 0 1  0  0 -1;
contrast '25-34 vs. 65,74' all_parms 0 0 2  1  1  1;
run;
```

When all these statements are submitted, they produce the results displayed in Output 12.53 and Output 12.54. There are six parameters, one for the intercept, one for the sex effect, and four for the age effect. None of the age effect parameters listed appears to be of much importance. However, there does appear to be suggestive variation among age groups, with the *p*-value for the age effect at 0.0561.

Output 12.53   Additive Model

```
              ANALYSIS-OF-VARIANCE TABLE

    Source                DF    Chi-Square     Prob
    ------------------------------------------------
    INTERCEPT              1      28089.07    0.0000
    SEX                   1         65.84    0.0000
    AGE                   4          9.21    0.0561


    RESIDUAL              4          2.92    0.5713


        ANALYSIS OF WEIGHTED-LEAST-SQUARES ESTIMATES

                                    Standard   Chi-
    Effect      Parameter  Estimate  Error    Square   Prob
    -----------------------------------------------------------
    INTERCEPT       1       7.6319   0.0455  28089.07  0.0000
    SEX             2      -0.2900   0.0357     65.84  0.0000
    AGE             3      -0.00780  0.0645      0.01  0.9037
                    4      -0.0465   0.0636      0.54  0.4642
                    5      -0.0343   0.0557      0.38  0.5387
                    6      -0.1098   0.0764      2.07  0.1506
```

The contrasts indicate that the first four age groups act essentially the same and that the oldest age group is responsible for the age effect, $p = 0.0744$; note that its estimate is $-\{-0.008 - 0.046 - 0.034 - 0.110\} = 0.198$.

Output 12.54   Contrasts for Age Effect

```
              ANALYSIS OF CONTRASTS

    Contrast            DF    Chi-Square     Prob
    ------------------------------------------------
    25,34 vs. 35-44      1        0.16      0.6937
    25,34 vs. 45,54      1        0.12      0.7288
    25,34 vs. 55,64      1        0.72      0.3954
    25,34 vs. 65,74      1        3.18      0.0744
```

One more contrast is specified to test the joint hypothesis that the lower four age groups are essentially the same. The following CONTRAST statement is submitted. Note that these three sets of coefficients, separated by commas, result in a 3 df test.

```
contrast '25-64 the same'    all_parms  0 0 1 -1  0  0,
                             all_parms  0 0 1  0 -1  0,
                             all_parms  0 0 1  0  0 -1;
run;
```

The result of this test is nonsignificant, $p = 0.868$.

Output 12.55   Joint Test for Ages 25-64

```
                    ANALYSIS OF CONTRASTS

       Contrast                    DF   Chi-Square    Prob
       ---------------------------------------------------
       25-64 the same               3       0.72     0.8678
```

12.8.5   Inputting the Model Matrix Directly

These results suggest that an appropriate model for these data is one that includes the sex effect and an effect for the oldest age group. Since the response functions and their covariance matrix are inputted directly, it isn't possible to create a new explanatory variable in a DATA step that takes the value 0 for ages 25-64 and the value 1 for ages 65–74 and then use it in a DIRECT statement.

However, PROC CATMOD does allow you to specify your model matrix directly, instead of building one based on the explanatory variables or the effects represented by the _RESPONSE_ keyword. This means that you can fit the desired model with a sex effect and an older age effect. The MODEL statement containing such a model matrix specification follows. You write in the coefficients for the model matrix row-wise, separating each row with a comma. The entire matrix is enclosed by parentheses. This is similar to how you would input a matrix in the SAS/IML matrix programming language.

```
model _f_ = ( 1 0 0 ,
              1 0 0 ,
              1 0 0 ,
              1 0 0 ,
              1 0 1 ,
              1 1 0 ,
              1 1 0 ,
              1 1 0 ,
              1 1 0 ,
              1 1 1 );
```

This matrix represents an incremental effects model. The first column of 1s is for the intercept, the second column is for the incremental effect of sex, where the reference level is for females and the incremental effect is for males, and the third column is an incremental effect for age, where the increment is for those aged 65–74.

Note that model matrices can be inputted directly for all applications of the CATMOD procedure, if desired.

The PROC CATMOD statements required to fit this model follow. After the model matrix is listed a set of labels for the effects; the numbers correspond to the columns of the model matrix. Without the _RESPONSE_ keyword in the MODEL statement, the CATMOD procedure has no way of knowing how to divide the model variability into various components. You can request that various column parameters be tested jointly, or singly, as specified here. Refer to the CATMOD procedure chapter in the *SAS/STAT User's Guide, Version 6, Fourth Edition, Volume I* for more detail. If you don't specify information concerning the columns, PROC CATMOD performs a joint test for the significance of the model beyond an overall mean, labeling this effect MODEL|MEAN in the ANOVA table.

```
proc catmod data=wbeing;
    response read b1-b10;
    factors sex $ 2, age $  5 /
         _response_ = sex age
    profile = (female '25-34',
              female '35-44',
              female '45-54',
              female '55-64',
              female '65-74',
              male   '25-34',
              male   '35-44',
              male   '45-54',
              male   '55-64',
              male   '65-74');
    model _f_ = ( 1 0 0 ,
                  1 0 0 ,
                  1 0 0 ,
                  1 0 0 ,
                  1 0 1 ,
                  1 1 0 ,
                  1 1 0 ,
                  1 1 0 ,
                  1 1 0 ,
                  1 1 1 ) (1='Intercept', 2='Sex', 3='65-74')
                          / pred;
```

The resulting tables for the analysis of variance and the parameter estimates are displayed in Output 12.56. The model fits very well, with a Q_W of 3.64 and 7 df, which results in $p = 0.820$. The effects are listed as specified in the MODEL statement, and each is significant.

Output 12.56   Reduced Model

ANALYSIS-OF-VARIANCE TABLE

Source	DF	Chi-Square	Prob
Intercept	1	14432.10	0.0000
Sex	1	72.64	0.0000
65-74	1	8.49	0.0036
RESIDUAL	7	3.64	0.8198

ANALYSIS OF WEIGHTED-LEAST-SQUARES ESTIMATES

Effect	Parameter	Estimate	Standard Error	Chi-Square	Prob
MODEL	1	7.3079	0.0608	14432.10	0.0000
	2	0.5601	0.0657	72.64	0.0000
	3	0.2607	0.0895	8.49	0.0036

Finally, the predicted values are displayed in Output 12.57. Fitting this model has resulted in estimates of the standard error that are on the order of twice as small as the standard errors for the original data.

Output 12.57   Reduced Model

```
                  PREDICTED VALUES FOR RESPONSE FUNCTIONS

                 -------Observed-------   -------Predicted------
         Function              Standard              Standard
 Sample  Number   Function      Error      Function    Error      Residual
 ------------------------------------------------------------------------------
    1       1      7.24978    0.10535654   7.30786049  0.06083107  -0.0580805
            2      7.18991    0.15303594   7.30786049  0.06083107  -0.1179505
            3      7.3596     0.1029563    7.30786049  0.06083107   0.05173951
            4      7.31937    0.15159156   7.30786049  0.06083107   0.01150951
            5      7.55184    0.13860014   7.56860832  0.09814674  -0.0167683
            6      7.93726    0.08596511   7.86795492  0.04773703   0.06930508
            7      7.92509    0.10825895   7.86795492  0.04773703   0.05713508
            8      7.82815    0.10246951   7.86795492  0.04773703  -0.0398049
            9      7.73696    0.1155422    7.86795492  0.04773703  -0.1309949
           10      8.16791    0.11958261   8.12870275  0.09592879   0.03920725
```

12.9   Optional: Cell Mean Model Approach to Model Fitting

Sometimes you want to assess the sources of variation in your data by investigating specific hypothesis tests. The *cell mean model* allows you to do that. The results help to determine what reduced model will fit the data appropriately; this approach is often useful when no *a priori* model is available.

Table 12.16 presents data from a study on sheep litter sizes (Koch, Imrey, et al. 1985). Investigators were interested in whether two types of treatments could affect the litter sizes and whether their effects were additive. FSH-LH is a hormone that tends to increase the number of births per litter, and pessary is a device that tends to reduce the conception rate while regulating the estrous cycle.

Table 12.16   Sheep Litter Births

Treatment	Single	Twin	Triplet	Total	Mean Size	S.E.
Control	11	32	9	52	1.962	0.086
Pessary	24	27	3	54	1.611	0.080
FSH-LH	12	31	15	58	2.052	0.089
Both	14	32	9	55	1.909	0.086

The sheep receiving each of the four treatments can be considered conceptually representative of corresponding large subpopulations in a manner that is equivalent to stratified simple random sampling. Thus, the likelihood for these data can be written

$$\Pr\{y_{ij}\} = \prod_{i=1}^{4}\left\{ n_{i+}! \prod_{j=1}^{3}\left(\pi_{ij}^{y_{ij}}/y_{ij}! \right) \right\}$$

where y_{ij} is the number of sheep litters for the ith treatment and jth type of birth. Weighted least squares analysis is an appropriate strategy for examining location shifts for the mean litter sizes across the four treatment groups.

The model matrix for a cell mean model is just the identity matrix. If $\mathbf{F}(\mathbf{p})$ represents the four mean litter sizes, the model equation can be written

$$E\{\mathbf{F}(\mathbf{p})\} = A\boldsymbol{\pi} = \begin{bmatrix} 1 & 0 & 0 & 0 \\ 0 & 1 & 0 & 0 \\ 0 & 0 & 1 & 0 \\ 0 & 0 & 0 & 1 \end{bmatrix} \boldsymbol{\beta}$$

For the cell mean model, $\mathbf{b} = \mathbf{F}$, $\mathbf{V_b} = \mathbf{V_F}$, and $Q_\mathbf{W} = 0$ with zero df.

In other words, the cell mean model is a special kind of saturated model where the parameters correspond to the response functions themselves. You can then test hypotheses that address the following questions:

- Is there any variation among the treatments ?

- Do the mean litter sizes show a difference between the presence and absence of FSH-LH ?

- Is there any difference between the presence and absence of pessary ?

- Is there an interaction between FSH-LH and pessary ?

The results of these tests determine the model-fitting direction.

12.9.1   Using the DIRECT Statement to Fit the Cell Mean Model

The CATMOD procedure fits a cell mean model, but only if you perform certain manipulations on the input data and use a DIRECT statement or if you input the model matrix directly, as demonstrated in Section 12.8.5. In this section, the DIRECT statement approach is used.

The DIRECT statement allows you to specify variables whose values are placed directly into the model matrix. To fit the cell mean model, you have to create dummy variables that indicate whether or not each observation corresponds to a particular treatment group and then list them in the DIRECT statement.

The following DATA step creates the SAS data set SHEEP and computes the dummy variables IC, IP, IF, and IB, which take the value 1 if the treatment group is control, pessary, FSH-LH, or both, respectively. Otherwise, these variables take the value 0. Two additional variables, IPB and IFP, are also created and are described later in this section.

```
data sheep;
    input treatmnt $ size count @@;
    ic=(treatmnt='control');
    ip=(treatmnt='pessary');
```

```
        if=(treatmnt='FSH-LH');
        ib=(treatmnt='both');
        ipb = (treatmnt='pessary' or treatmnt='both');
        ifb = (treatmnt='FSH-LH' or treatmnt='both');
        cards;
        control 1 11 control 2 32 control 3  9
        pessary 1 24 pessary 2 27 pessary 3  3
        FSH-LH  1 12 FSH-LH  2 31 FSH-LH  3 15
        both    1 14 both    2 32 both    3  9
        ;
   run;
```

The PROC CATMOD step for the cell mean model analysis includes a DIRECT statement in which the dummy variables are listed. The values of these variables are placed directly into the model matrix, which becomes the 4×4 identity matrix. The DIRECT statement must precede the MODEL statement. The NOINT option is used to suppress the intercept term, which would be redundant in the cell mean model. The POPULATION statement is not required; leaving it out would result in the same populations being formed, since PROC CATMOD would form them on the basis of the unique combinations of values for the explanatory variables. The advantage of using the POPULATION statement is that the population profiles will be listed in terms of the TREATMNT values and not the more esoteric profiles of the dummy variables.

```
   proc catmod data=sheep order=data;
      population treatmnt;
      direct ic ip if ib;
      weight count;
      response means;
      model size  = ic ip if ib / noint;
   run;
```

The population and response profiles follow.

Output 12.58   Population and Response Profiles

```
              POPULATION PROFILES
                            Sample
       Sample  TREATMNT     Size
       --------------------------
          1    control        52
          2    pessary        54
          3    FSH-LH         58
          4    both           55

          RESPONSE PROFILES

          Response  SIZE
          ---------------
             1       1
             2       2
             3       3
```

The response functions listed in Output 12.59 are the mean sheep litter sizes for each treatment group. The model matrix is the identity matrix. The first column takes the value

1 for the control treatment since IC was set to 1 for controls, the second column takes the value 1 in the second row since IP was set to 1 for the pessary group, and so on.

Output 12.59   Model Matrix

Sample	Response Function	DESIGN MATRIX 1	2	3	4
1	1.96154	1	0	0	0
2	1.61111	0	1	0	0
3	2.05172	0	0	1	0
4	1.90909	0	0	0	1

Output 12.60 contains the results of the model-fitting process. The residual chi-square df are 0 since the cell mean model is a saturated one. Since the response functions are the mean sheep litter sizes themselves, the effects listed in the ANOVA table and the parameters listed in the table of estimates are the same. Thus, the Wald statistics printed in each table are identical; however, these statistics are not informative here because they test that mean litter size is 0 (which is impossible since liter sizes are 1, 2, 3).

Output 12.60   ANOVA Table and Parameter Estimates

ANALYSIS-OF-VARIANCE TABLE

Source	DF	Chi Square	Prob
IC	1	522.21	0.0000
IP	1	401.89	0.0000
IF	1	527.51	0.0000
IB	1	489.01	0.0000
RESIDUAL	0	.	.

ANALYSIS OF WEIGHTED-LEAST-SQUARES ESTIMATES

Effect	Parameter	Estimate	Standard Error	Chi-Square	Prob
IC	1	1.9615	0.0858	522.21	0.0000
IP	2	1.6111	0.0804	401.89	0.0000
IF	3	2.0517	0.0893	527.51	0.0000
IB	4	1.9091	0.0863	489.01	0.0000

12.9.2   Contrasts

Once a cell mean model is fit, you can apply contrasts to investigate the differences among the group means. The following are the C matrices required to test each of the hypotheses previously proposed.

- no variation among the treatments

$$C = \begin{bmatrix} 1 & 0 & 0 & -1 \\ 0 & 1 & 0 & -1 \\ 0 & 0 & 1 & -1 \end{bmatrix}$$

- no difference between absence/presence of FSH-LH

$$C = \begin{bmatrix} 1 & 1 & -1 & -1 \end{bmatrix}$$

- no difference between absence/presence of pessary

$$C = \begin{bmatrix} 1 & -1 & 1 & -1 \end{bmatrix}$$

- no interaction between FSH-LH and pessary

$$C = \begin{bmatrix} 1 & -1 & -1 & 1 \end{bmatrix}$$

The following CONTRAST statements request the CATMOD procedure to perform these tests.

```
contrast 'treatments'  all_parms 1  0  0 -1,
                       all_parms 0  1  0 -1,
                       all_parms 0  0  1 -1;
contrast 'FHS-LH'      all_parms 1  1 -1 -1;
contrast 'pessary'     all_parms 1 -1  1 -1;
contrast 'interaction' all_parms 1 -1 -1  1;
run;
```

The following is the table of contrasts. These results indicate that there is a substantial treatment effect and that both FHS-LH and pessary are significant. However, there is no evidence of an interaction, since that test has a Q_C of 1.48 and 1 df ($p = 0.2244$).

Output 12.61   Contrast Test Results

```
                  ANALYSIS OF CONTRASTS

     Contrast              DF   Chi-Square    Prob
     ---------------------------------------------------
     treatments            3       15.86     0.0012
     FHS-LH                1        5.15     0.0233
     pessary               1        8.31     0.0039
     interaction           1        1.48     0.2244
```

These results suggest that a main effects model fits the data. The following model is fit next:

$$E\{\mathbf{F}(\mathbf{p})\} = \mathbf{X}_R \boldsymbol{\beta}_R = \begin{bmatrix} 1 & 0 & 0 \\ 1 & 0 & 1 \\ 1 & 1 & 0 \\ 1 & 1 & 1 \end{bmatrix} \begin{bmatrix} \beta_1 \\ \beta_2 \\ \beta_3 \end{bmatrix}$$

In this model, which reduces the number of model parameters from 4 to 3, β_1 is the predicted mean value for the control, β_2 is the incremental effect for presence of FSH-LH, and β_3 is the incremental effect for presence of pessary. Since this model uses incremental effects parameterization, it cannot be fit with the default PROC CATMOD model matrix. However, you can continue to use the DIRECT statement to fit this model. In the DATA step creating the SHEEP data set, two additional dummy variables are created with the following statements.

```
ipb = (treatmnt='pessary' or treatmnt='both');
ifb = (treatmnt='FSH-LH' or treatmnt='both');
```

IPB is equal to 1 if a treatment group receives pessary either singly or in combination with FSH-LH. IFB is equal to 1 if a treatment group receives FSH-LH either singly or in combination with pessary. The following statements fit the model with explanatory variables IPB and IFB, which are listed in both the MODEL and DIRECT statements.

```
direct ipb ifb;
model size = ifb ipb / pred; run;
```

These statements are entered interactively. The keyword PRED requests the procedure to produce model-predicted response functions. Output 12.62 contains the ANOVA tables for the reduced model as well as the parameter estimates. Note that the residual chi-square goodness-of-fit statistic has the value $Q_W = 1.48$, which is the same value as Q_C for the interaction in the cell mean model. This makes sense because the only variation left over from that explained by the model is the interaction.

Output 12.62   Reduced Model ANOVA Table and Parameter Estimates

```
                       ANALYSIS-OF-VARIANCE TABLE

        Source                 DF   Chi-Square      Prob
        ---------------------------------------------------
        INTERCEPT               1      661.23      0.0000
        IFB                     1        5.44      0.0197
        IPB                     1        8.72      0.0031

        RESIDUAL                1        1.48      0.2244


           ANALYSIS OF WEIGHTED-LEAST-SQUARES ESTIMATES

                                       Standard    Chi-
        Effect       Parameter  Estimate   Error   Square   Prob
        ----------------------------------------------------------
        INTERCEPT        1       1.9092   0.0742   661.23  0.0000
        IFB              2       0.1992   0.0854     5.44  0.0197
        IPB              3      -0.2522   0.0854     8.72  0.0031
```

Output 12.63 contains the observed and predicted mean litter sizes from the model, as well as their standard errors. Note that the model fitting has produced predicted values with smaller standard errors than those for the observed values; eliminating the interaction effect has removed extraneous variation. Pessary lowers the predicted litter size from 1.91 for the control to 1.66; the difference is the value of the parameter estimate for IPB, which is -0.252. FSH-LH alone raises the predicted mean value to 2.11. The predicted mean litter size for the treatment of both FSH-LH and pessary is 1.86 and additively corresponds to the sum of the predicted control mean, the FSH-LH effect, and the pessary effect (that is, $1.86 = 1.91 + 0.20 - 0.25$).

Output 12.63   Reduced Model Predicted Values

```
            PREDICTED VALUES FOR RESPONSE FUNCTIONS

                   -----Observed-----   -----Predicted----
            Function            Standard            Standard
   Sample   Number   Function    Error    Function    Error    Residual
   --------------------------------------------------------------------
      1        1     1.961538  0.085837   1.909213  0.074247   0.052325
      2        1     1.611111  0.080366   1.656978  0.070944  -0.04587
      3        1     2.051724  0.089331   2.108396  0.076182  -0.05667
      4        1     1.909091  0.086331   1.856161  0.074529   0.052929
```

12.9.3   Comments on the Cell Mean Model Approach

The cell mean approach followed in this example can be pursued for many analyses without actually fitting the cell mean model. It turns out that many of the tests you would generate from the cell mean model are equivalent to the tests of effects that are generated when you fit a saturated model with all possible interactions.

As you recall, IPB takes the value 1 if the treatment includes pessary, and IFB takes the value 1 if the treatment includes FSH-LH. Thus, the crossclassification creates four groups: control, FSH-LH, pessary, and both, like before. You can fit a model that includes IPB, IFB, and their interaction. This is a saturated model.

```
proc catmod data=sheep order=data;
   weight count;
   response means;
   model size= ipb ifb ipb*ifb;
run;
```

Output 12.64 displays the model matrix. Compare the second, third, and fourth columns of the model matrix to the contrasts tested for the cell mean model; the second column corresponds to the contrast for FHS-LH, the third column corresponds to the contrast for pessary, and the fourth column corresponds to the contrast for their interaction.

Output 12.64   Model Matrix

```
           Response        DESIGN MATRIX
   Sample  Function    1      2      3      4
   ----------------------------------------------
      1     1.96154     1      1      1      1
      2     2.05172     1      1     -1     -1
      3     1.61111     1     -1      1     -1
      4     1.90909     1     -1     -1      1
```

Compare the tests in the ANOVA table in Output 12.65 with the results of the contrasts performed on the parameters from the cell mean model.

Output 12.65   Main Effects Model

```
                  ANALYSIS-OF-VARIANCE TABLE

       Source              DF   Chi-Square      Prob
       ----------------------------------------------------
       INTERCEPT            1     1939.63      0.0000
       IPB                  1        8.31      0.0039
       IFB                  1        5.15      0.0233
       IPB*IFB              1        1.48      0.2244

       RESIDUAL             0         .           .
```

The test for the parameter for IPB (pessary) is identical to the test performed on the cell mean parameters for pessary. The test for the parameter for IFB (FSH-LH) is identical to the test performed on the cell mean parameters for FSH-LH. Finally, the test for their interaction in this saturated model is the same as the test for interaction in the cell mean model. The agreement among these tests occurs because the same (or equivalent) mutually orthogonal sets of vectors are both the rows of the contrasts for the cell mean model and the columns of the default model specification matrix in this situation.

Thus, if your model is set up in the typical main effects and interactions fashion, you can fit the saturated model in PROC CATMOD by specifying all main effects and interactions. The tests listed in the ANOVA table for that model will be the same as those you would usually construct to assess the variation in a cell mean model.

12.10   Statistical Methodology for Weighted Least Squares

Consider the general contingency table displayed in Table 12.17, where s represents the number of rows, or groups, in the table, and r represents the number of responses.

Table 12.17   Underlying Contingency Table

Group	Response 1	2	$\cdots$	r	Total
1	n_{11}	n_{12}	$\cdots$	n_{1r}	n_{1+}
2	n_{21}	n_{22}	$\cdots$	n_{2r}	n_{2+}
$\cdots$	$\cdots$	$\cdots$	$\cdots$	$\cdots$	$\cdots$
s	n_{s1}	n_{s2}	$\cdots$	n_{sr}	n_{s+}

The proportion of subjects in the ith group who have the jth response is written

$$p_{ij} = n_{ij}/n_{i+}$$

Suppose $\mathbf{n}'_i=(n_{i1}, n_{i2}, \ldots, n_{ir})$ represents the vector of responses for the ith subpopulation. If $\mathbf{n}' = (\mathbf{n}'_1, \mathbf{n}'_2, \ldots, \mathbf{n}'_r)$, then n follows the product multinomial distribution, given that each group has an independent sample. You can write the likelihood of n as

$$\Pr\{\mathbf{n}\} = \prod_{i=1}^{s} n_{i+}! \prod_{j=1}^{r} \pi_{ij}{}^{n_{ij}}/n_{ij}!$$

where π_{ij} is the probability that a randomly selected subject from the ith group has the jth response profile. The π_{ij} satisfy the natural restrictions

$$\sum_{j=1}^{r} \pi_{ij} = 1 \text{ for } i = 1, 2, \ldots, s$$

Suppose $\mathbf{p}_i = \mathbf{n}_i/n_{i+}$ is the $r \times 1$ vector of observed proportions associated with the ith group and suppose $\mathbf{p}' = (\mathbf{p}'_1, \mathbf{p}'_2, \ldots, \mathbf{p}'_s)$ is the $(sr \times 1)$ compound vector of proportions.

A consistent estimator of the covariance matrix for the proportions in the ith row is

$$\mathbf{V}(\mathbf{p}_i) = \frac{1}{n_i} \begin{bmatrix} p_{i1}(1 - p_{i1}) & -p_{i1}p_{i2} & \cdots & -p_{i1}p_{ir} \\ -p_{i2}p_1 & p_{i2}(1 - p_{i2}) & \cdots & -p_{i2}p_{ir} \\ \vdots & \vdots & \vdots & \vdots \\ -p_{ir}p_{i1} & -p_{ir}p_{i2} & \cdots & p_{ir}(1 - p_{ir}) \end{bmatrix}$$

and the covariance matrix for the vector $\mathbf{p}$ is

$$\mathbf{V_p} = \begin{bmatrix} \mathbf{V}_1 & \mathbf{0} & \cdots & \mathbf{0} \\ \mathbf{0} & \mathbf{V}_2 & \cdots & \mathbf{0} \\ \vdots & \vdots & \vdots & \vdots \\ \mathbf{0} & \mathbf{0} & \cdots & \mathbf{V}_s \end{bmatrix}$$

where $\mathbf{V}_i$ is the covariance matrix for $\mathbf{p}_i$.

Suppose $\mathbf{F}_1(\mathbf{p}), \mathbf{F}_2(\mathbf{p}), \ldots, \mathbf{F}_u(\mathbf{p})$ is a set of u functions of $\mathbf{p}$. Each of the functions is required to have continuous partial derivatives through order two, and $\mathbf{F}$ must have a nonsingular covariance matrix, which can be written

$$\mathbf{V_F}(\boldsymbol{\pi}) = [\mathbf{H}(\boldsymbol{\pi})][\mathbf{V}(\boldsymbol{\pi})][\mathbf{H}(\boldsymbol{\pi})]'$$

where $\mathbf{H}(\boldsymbol{\pi}) = [\partial \mathbf{F}/\partial \mathbf{z}|\mathbf{z} = \boldsymbol{\pi}]$ is the first derivative matrix of $\mathbf{F}(\mathbf{z})$.

$\mathbf{F}$ is a consistent estimator of $\mathbf{F}(\boldsymbol{\pi})$, so you can investigate the variation among the elements of $\mathbf{F}(\boldsymbol{\pi})$ with the linear model

$$E_A\{\mathbf{F}(\mathbf{p})\} = \mathbf{F}(\boldsymbol{\pi}) = \mathbf{X}\boldsymbol{\beta}$$

where $\mathbf{X}$ is a known model matrix with rank $t \leq u$, $\boldsymbol{\beta}$ is a $t \times 1$ vector of unknown parameters, and E_{As} means asymptotic expectation.

The goodness of fit of the model is assessed with

$$Q(\mathbf{X}, \mathbf{F}) = (\mathbf{WF})'[\mathbf{WV_F W}']^{-1}\mathbf{WF}$$

where $\mathbf{W}$ is any fullrank $[(u - t) \times u]$ matrix orthogonal to $\mathbf{X}$. The quantity $Q(\mathbf{X}, \mathbf{F})$ is approximately distributed as chi-square with $(u - t)$ degrees of freedom when the sample sizes n_{i+} are large enough so that the elements of $\mathbf{F}$ have an approximate multivariate normal distribution. Such statistics are known as Wald statistics (Wald 1943).

The following statistic

$$Q_W = (\mathbf{F} - \mathbf{Xb})'\mathbf{V_F^{-1}}(\mathbf{F} - \mathbf{Xb})$$

is identical to $Q(\mathbf{X}, \mathbf{F})$ and is obtained by using weighted least squares to produce an estimate for β.

$$\mathbf{b} = (\mathbf{X}'\mathbf{V_F^{-1}}\mathbf{X})^{-1}\mathbf{X}'\mathbf{V_F^{-1}}\mathbf{F}$$

which is the minimum modified chi-square estimator (Neyman 1949).

A consistent estimator for the covariance matrix of b is given by

$$V(\mathbf{b}) = (\mathbf{X}'\mathbf{V_F^{-1}}\mathbf{X})^{-1}$$

If the model adequately characterizes the data as indicated by the goodness-of-fit criterion, then linear hypotheses of the form $\mathbf{C}\beta = 0$, where $\mathbf{C}$ is a known $c \times t$ matrix of constants of rank c, can be tested with the Wald statistic

$$Q_C = (\mathbf{Cb})'[\mathbf{C}(\mathbf{X}'\mathbf{V_F^{-1}}\mathbf{X})^{-1}\mathbf{C}']^{-1}(\mathbf{Cb})$$

Q_C is distributed as chi-square with degrees of freedom equal to c.

Predicted values for $\mathbf{F}(\pi)$ can be calculated from

$$\hat{\mathbf{F}} = \mathbf{Xb} = \mathbf{X}(\mathbf{X}'\mathbf{V_F}^{-1}\mathbf{X})^{-1}\mathbf{X}'\mathbf{V_F}^{-1}\mathbf{F}$$

and consistent estimators for the variances of $\hat{\mathbf{F}}$ can be obtained from the diagonal elements of

$$\mathbf{V_{\hat{F}}} = \mathbf{X}(\mathbf{X}'\mathbf{V_F}^{-1}\mathbf{X})^{-1}\mathbf{X}'$$

While the functions $\mathbf{F}(\mathbf{p})$ can take on a wide range of forms, a few functions are commonly used. In particular, you can fit a strictly linear model

$$\mathbf{F}(\mathbf{p}) = \mathbf{Ap}$$

where $\mathbf{A}$ is a matrix of known constants. The covariance matrix of $\mathbf{F}$ is written

$$\mathbf{V_F} = \mathbf{A}\mathbf{V_p}\mathbf{A}'$$

Another common model is loglinear:

$$\mathbf{F(p)} = \mathbf{A}\log\mathbf{p}$$

where log transforms a vector to the corresponding vector of natural logarithms and $\mathbf{A}$ is orthogonal to $\mathbf{1}$ (vector of 1s), that is, $\mathbf{A}\mathbf{1} = \mathbf{0}$. In this case,

$$\mathbf{V_F} = \mathbf{A}\mathbf{D_p}^{-1}\mathbf{A}'$$

where $\mathbf{D_p}$ is a diagonal matrix with the elements of $\mathbf{p}$ on the diagonal.

Many other useful functions can be generated as a sequence of linear, logarithmic, and exponential operations on the vector $\mathbf{p}$.

- linear transformations: $\mathbf{F}_1(\mathbf{p}) = \mathbf{A}_1\mathbf{p} = \mathbf{a}_1$

- logarithmic: $\mathbf{F}_2(\mathbf{p}) = \log(\mathbf{p}) = \mathbf{a}_2$

- exponential: $\mathbf{F}_3(\mathbf{p}) = \exp(\mathbf{p}) = \mathbf{a}_3$

The corresponding $\mathbf{H}_k$ matrix operators needed to produce the covariance matrix for $\mathbf{F}$ are

- $\mathbf{H}_1 = \mathbf{A}_1$

- $\mathbf{H}_2 = \mathbf{D_p}^{-1}$

- $\mathbf{H}_3 = \mathbf{D_{a_3}}$

$\mathbf{V_F}$ is estimated by $\mathbf{V_F} = [\mathbf{H(p)}]\mathbf{V_p}[\mathbf{H(p)}]'$ where $\mathbf{H(p)}$ is a product of the first derivative matrices $\mathbf{H}_k(\mathbf{p})$ where k indicates the ith operation in accordance with the chain rule.

Chapter 13
Modeling Repeated Measurements Data

Chapter Table of Contents

Chapter 13
Modeling Repeated Measurements Data

13.1 Introduction

Many types of studies have research designs that involve multiple measurements of a response variable. Longitudinal studies, in which repeated measures are obtained over time from each subject, are one important and commonly used type of repeated measures study. In other applications, the response from each experimental unit is measured under multiple conditions rather than at multiple time points. In some settings in which repeated measures data are obtained, the independent experimental units are not individual subjects. For example, in a toxicological study the experimental units might be litters; responses are then obtained from the multiple newborns in each litter. In a genetic study, experimental units might be defined by families; responses are then obtained from the members of each family.

There are two main difficulties in the analysis of data from repeated measures studies. First, the analysis is complicated by the dependence among repeated observations made on the same experimental unit. Second, the investigator often cannot control the circumstances for obtaining measurements, so that the data may be unbalanced or partially incomplete. For example, in a longitudinal study the response from a subject may be missing at one or more of the time points due to factors that are unrelated to the outcome of interest. In toxicology or genetic studies, litter or family sizes are variable rather than fixed; hence, the number of repeated measures is not constant across experimental units.

While many approaches to the analysis of repeated measures data have been studied, most are restricted to the setting in which the response variable is normally distributed and the data are balanced and complete. Although the development of methods for the analysis of repeated measures categorical data has received substantially less attention in the past, this has recently become an important and active area of research. Still, the methodology is not nearly as well developed as for continuous, normally distributed outcomes. The practical application of methods for repeated categorical outcomes also lags behind that for normal theory methods due to the lack of readily accessible software.

The SAS System provides two useful methodologies for analyzing repeated measures categorical data. Both are applicable when a univariate response variable is measured repeatedly for each independent experimental unit.

One of these approaches, based on Mantel-Haenszel (MH) test statistics, is described as an advanced topic in Chapter 6, "Sets of s × r Tables." The MH methodology is useful for testing the null hypothesis of no association between the response variable and the repeated time points or conditions within each subject (that is, interchangeability). Although these randomization model methods require minimal assumptions and the sample size requirements are less stringent than for other methods, they have important limitations. First, the MH methods are restricted to the analysis of data from a single sample; thus, the effects of additional factors (for example, treatment group) cannot be incorporated. In addition, the methods are oriented primarily to hypothesis testing rather than to parameter estimation.

Another approach is to model categorical repeated measurements in terms of a parsimonious number of parameters. Chapter 8, "Logistic Regression I: Dichotomous Response," introduces statistical modeling of categorical data using maximum likelihood to estimate parameters of models for logits, and Chapter 12, "Weighted Least Squares," describes weighted least squares (WLS) methodology for modeling a wide range of types of categorical data outcomes. Both of these chapters, however, focus on statistical modeling of the relationship between a single dependent categorical variable and one or more explanatory variables. When you model repeated measurements data, you are dealing with multiple dependent variables that reflect different times or conditions under which the outcome of interest was measured.

Sections 13.2 and 13.3 describe basic and advanced WLS analyses of repeated categorical outcomes. These techniques are a direct extension of the general approach introduced and described in Chapter 12. The WLS methodology is an extremely versatile modeling approach that can be used efficiently for parameter estimation and hypothesis testing. However, the price of this versatility is that large sample sizes are required.

The MH and WLS methodologies are very useful in analyzing repeated measures categorical data. Still, these two approaches have certain practical shortcomings. Perhaps the most important limitation is that neither method accommodates continuous explanatory variables. In contrast, the generalized estimating equation (GEE) approach (Liang and Zeger 1986; Zeger and Liang 1986) is a recent methodology for the regression analysis of repeated measurements that can be used with continuous and discrete explanatory variables. While this methodology is not yet implemented in a SAS procedure, Karim and Zeger (1988) have written a SAS/IML macro that implements it. Section 13.4 describes and demonstrates this approach.

13.2   Weighted Least Squares

13.2.1   Introduction

Chapter 12 discusses the use of weighted least squares in modeling categorical data. The first step of this methodology is to arrange the data from the experiment or study as an $s \times r$ contingency table. In this general WLS framework, there are s groups defined by the crossclassification of the factors of interest (explanatory variables) and r response profiles. Chapter 12 considers situations in which there is a single outcome (dependent) variable, so that the response profiles are defined by the r possible levels of the dependent variable. In each group, at most $r - 1$ linearly independent response functions can be analyzed. Thus, in the applications in which the response variable is dichotomous, there is one response function per group. In other applications, the response is polytomous but a single response function, such as a mean score, is computed for each group. In both of these situations, there are s independent response functions (one for each row of the table) and their estimated covariance matrix $\mathbf{V_F}$ is diagonal.

However, the methodology can also be used when there are multiple response functions per group. In these situations, the response functions from the same group are correlated and their covariance matrix $\mathbf{V_F}$ is block diagonal. Since the usual covariance structure based on the multinomial distribution accounts for correlated proportions, it is a natural candidate for handling the correlation structure of repeated measurements.

In repeated measures applications, interest generally focuses on the analysis of the marginal distributions of the response at each time point, that is, regardless of the responses at the other time points. Thus, there are multiple response functions per group, and the correlation structure induced by the repeated measures must be taken into consideration. In the general situation in which a c-category response variable is measured at t time points, the crossclassification of the possible outcomes results in $r = c^t$ response profiles. You will generally consider $t(c - 1)$ correlated marginal proportions, generalized logits, or cumulative logits, or t correlated mean scores (if the response is ordinal), in the analysis.

Provided that the appropriate covariance matrix is computed for these correlated response functions, the WLS computations are no different than those described in Chapter 12. Koch and Reinfurt (1971) and Koch et al. (1977) first described the application of WLS to repeated measures categorical data. Further work is described in Stanish, Gillings, and Koch (1978), Koch et al (1985), and Koch et al (1989). Stanish (1986), Landis et al. (1988), Agresti (1988, 1989), and Davis (1992) further developed this methodology and also illustrated various aspects of the use of the CATMOD procedure in analyzing categorical repeated measures.

The following sections illustrate several basic types of WLS analyses of repeated measurements data when the outcome is categorical. The examples progress in difficulty and gradually introduce more sophisticated analyses. Section 13.2.2 illustrates the methodology with a basic example.

13.2.2   One Population, Dichotomous Response

Grizzle, Starmer, and Koch (1969) analyze data in which 46 subjects were treated with three drugs (A, B, and C). The response to each drug was recorded as favorable or unfavorable. The null hypothesis of interest is that the marginal probability of a favorable response is the same for all three drugs, that is, the hypothesis of marginal homogeneity (see 6.4.1). Since the same 46 subjects were used in testing each of the three drugs, the estimates for the three marginal probabilities are correlated. In Section 6.4, this null hypothesis was tested using the Mantel-Haenszel general association statistic. The conclusion of this analysis was that there was a statistically significant difference among the three marginal probabilities.

Table 13.1 displays the data from Section 6.4 in the general WLS framework. There is one subpopulation (since there is a single group of subjects) and $r = 2^3 = 8$ response profiles, corresponding to the possible combinations of favorable and unfavorable response for the three drugs. For example, there are 6 subjects who had a favorable response to all three drugs (FFF) and 16 subjects who responded favorably to drugs A and B and unfavorably to drug C (FFU). In the notation of Section 13.2.1, $s = 1$, $c = 2$, $t = 3$, and $r = 2^3 = 8$.

Based on the underlying multinomial distribution of the cell counts, computation of response functions of interest and subsequent analysis using the WLS approach follows the same principles described in Chapter 12. However, the eight response profiles are not defined by the eight levels of a single response but rather by the response combinations resulting from the measurement of three dichotomous variables. From the proportions of these eight profiles, you can construct three correlated marginal proportions that correspond to those subjects who responded favorably to Drug A, Drug B, and Drug C, respectively.

Table 13.1   Drug Response Data

	F=favorable, U=unfavorable								
Drug A response	F	F	F	F	U	U	U	U	
Drug B response	F	F	U	U	F	F	U	U	
Drug C response	F	U	F	U	F	U	F	U	Total
Number of subjects	6	16	2	4	2	4	6	6	46

Suppose that p_i denotes the observed proportion of subjects in the ith response profile (ordered from left to right as displayed in Table 13.1) and let $\mathbf{p} = (p_1, \ldots, p_8)'$. For example, $p_1 = \Pr\{\text{FFF}\}$ is the probability of a favorable response to all three drugs. Now let p_A, p_B, and p_C denote the marginal proportions with a favorable response to drugs A, B, and C, respectively. For example, $p_A = \Pr\{\text{FFF or FFU or FUF or FUU}\}$. The vector of response functions $\mathbf{F}(\mathbf{p}) = (p_A, p_B, p_C)'$ can be computed by the linear transformation $\mathbf{F}(\mathbf{p}) = \mathbf{A}\mathbf{p}$, where

$$\mathbf{A} = \begin{bmatrix} 1 & 1 & 1 & 1 & 0 & 0 & 0 & 0 \\ 1 & 1 & 0 & 0 & 1 & 1 & 0 & 0 \\ 1 & 0 & 1 & 0 & 1 & 0 & 1 & 0 \end{bmatrix}$$

The first row of $\mathbf{A}$ sums p_1, p_2, p_3, and p_4 to compute the proportion of subjects with a favorable response to drug A. Similarly, the second row of $\mathbf{A}$ sums p_1, p_2, p_5, and p_6 to yield the proportion with a favorable response to drug B. Finally, the corresponding proportion for drug C is computed by summing p_1, p_3, p_5, and p_7. The hypothesis of marginal homogeneity specifies that the marginal proportions with a favorable response to drugs A, B, and C are equal. This hypothesis can be tested by fitting a model of the form $\mathbf{F}(\boldsymbol{\pi}) = \mathbf{X}\boldsymbol{\beta}$, where $\boldsymbol{\pi}$ is the vector of population probabilities estimated by $\mathbf{p}$, $\mathbf{X}$ is a known model matrix, and $\boldsymbol{\beta}$ is a vector of unknown parameters. If the drug effect is significant, then the hypothesis of marginal homogeneity can be rejected.

This analysis is performed with the CATMOD procedure. The following statements create the SAS data set DRUG. The variables DRUGA, DRUGB, and DRUGC contain the responses for drugs, A, B, and C, respectively.

```
data drug;
   input druga $ drugb $ drugc $ count;
   cards;
F F F  6
F F U 16
F U F  2
F U U  4
U F F  2
U F U  4
U U F  6
U U U  6
;
```

The next group of statements requests a repeated measurements analysis that tests the hypothesis of marginal homogeneity.

```
proc catmod;
   weight count;
   response marginals;
   model druga*drugb*drugc=_response_ / oneway cov;
   repeated drug 3 / _response_=drug;
run;
```

A major difference between this PROC CATMOD invocation and those discussed in Chapter 12 is the syntax of the MODEL statement. One function of the MODEL statement is to specify the underlying $s \times r$ contingency table; that is, it defines the r response profiles by the values of the response variable and the s population profiles by the crossclassification of the levels of the explanatory variables. The fundamental distinction of repeated measures analyses is that there are now multiple response variables and they determine both the response functions and the variation to be modeled.

The response variables are crossed (separated by asterisks) on the left-hand side of the MODEL statement, and the r response profiles are defined by the crossclassification of their levels.

```
   model druga*drugb*drugc=_response_ / oneway cov;
```

The response profiles are ordered so that the rightmost variable on the left-hand side of the MODEL statement varies fastest and the leftmost variable varies slowest. In this example, the drug C response changes from favorable to unfavorable most rapidly, followed by drug B, with drug A changing the slowest. Look ahead to Output 13.2 to see these response profiles listed in the resulting PROC CATMOD output. Since MARGINALS is specified in the RESPONSE statement, the marginal proportions for Drug A, Drug B, and Drug C are computed as the three response functions, as seen in Output 13.3.

Since the right-hand side of the MODEL statement does not include any explanatory variables, the data are correctly structured as a single population with $r = 8$ response profiles. The keyword _RESPONSE_ specifies that the variation among the dependent variables is to be modeled; by default, PROC CATMOD builds a full factorial _RESPONSE_ effect with respect to the repeated measurement factors. In this case, there is only one repeated factor, drug, so the full factorial includes only the drug main effect.

However, you can specify a different model matrix in the REPEATED statement, which is usually used in repeated measurements analysis. The general purpose of the REPEATED statement is to specify how to incorporate repeated measurement factors into the model. You can specify a name for each repeated measurement factor in the REPEATED statement, as well as specify the type (numeric or character), number of levels, and the label or value of each level. You can also define the model matrix in terms of the repeated measurement factors.

```
repeated drug 3 / _response_=drug;
```

In this example, the REPEATED statement specifies that there is a single repeated measurement factor that has three levels (Drugs A, B, C). Although it is convenient to name this factor DRUG, any valid SAS variable name can be used, with the restriction that it cannot be the same as the name of an existing variable in the data set. If there is only one repeated measurements factor and the number of levels is omitted, then the CATMOD procedure assumes that the number of levels is equal to the number of response functions per group. So, in this case, the number 3 could have been omitted from the REPEATED statement.

The _RESPONSE_= option in the REPEATED statement specifies the effects to be included in the model matrix as a result of using the _RESPONSE_ keyword in the MODEL statement. The variables named in the effects must be listed in the REPEATED statement. If this option is omitted, then PROC CATMOD builds a full factorial _RESPONSE_ effect with respect to the repeated measurement factors. In this example, the _RESPONSE_ option specifies that the model matrix include a DRUG main effect. Note that since there is only one repeated measurement factor, you could replace the preceding REPEATED statement with

```
repeated drug;
```

Note that the ONEWAY option in the MODEL statement prints one-way marginal frequency distributions for each response variable in the MODEL statement. This is very useful in verifying that your model is set up as intended. The COV option in the MODEL statement prints the covariance matrix of the vector of response functions $F(p)$.

Output 13.1 displays the one-way frequency distributions of the variables DRUGA, DRUGB, and DRUGC; they are useful for checking that the response functions are defined as desired. The variables DRUGA, DRUGB, and DRUGC have two levels, so the marginal proportion of subjects with the first level (F) is computed for each variable.

Output 13.1   One-Way Frequency Distributions

```
              ONE-WAY FREQUENCIES

        Variable  Value  Frequency
        -----------------------------
        DRUGA     F         28
                  U         18

        DRUGB     F         28
                  U         18

        DRUGC     F         16
                  U         30
```

Output 13.2 displays the population and response profiles.

Output 13.2   Population and Response Profiles

```
                              Sample
                 Sample       Size
                 ----------------------
                    1          46


                   RESPONSE PROFILES

          Response   DRUGA   DRUGB   DRUGC
          -----------------------------------
              1        F       F       F
              2        F       F       U
              3        F       U       F
              4        F       U       U
              5        U       F       F
              6        U       F       U
              7        U       U       F
              8        U       U       U
```

Output 13.3 displays the vector of response functions, its covariance matrix, and the model matrix. Compare these three response functions with the one-way distributions in Output 13.1 and verify that they are equal to the marginal proportions with a favorable response to drugs A, B, and C, respectively; for example, $28/(28 + 18) = 0.6087$ for drugs A and B, $16/(16 + 30) = 0.34783$ for drug C. The covariance matrix $V_F = AV_pA'$ of the response function vector F is printed because the COV option was specified in the MODEL statement. While V_p is the 8×8 covariance matrix of the proportions in the eight response categories, V_F is the 3×3 covariance matrix of F. Note that the off-diagonal elements of V_F are nonzero, since the three marginal proportions are correlated. The model matrix has three columns, and the corresponding parameters are an overall intercept, an effect for drug A, and an effect for drug B.

Output 13.3   Response Functions and Model Matrix

```
          Function   Response          COVARIANCE MATRIX
 Sample    Number    Function      1          2          3
 ------------------------------------------------------------------
    1         1        0.6087    0.005178   0.002342  -0.000822
              2        0.6087    0.002342   0.005178  -0.000822
              3        0.3478   -0.000822  -0.000822   0.004931


                     Function       DESIGN MATRIX
          Sample      Number      1      2      3
          -------------------------------------------
             1           1        1      1      0
                         2        1      0      1
                         3        1     -1     -1
```

Output 13.4 displays the analysis of variance (ANOVA) table. The source of variation labeled "DRUG" tests the null hypothesis that the probability of a favorable response is the same for all three drugs. Since the observed value of the 2 df test statistic is 6.58, the hypothesis of marginal homogeneity is rejected at the 0.05 level of significance ($p = 0.0372$).

Output 13.4   ANOVA Table

```
                     ANALYSIS-OF-VARIANCE TABLE

        Source              DF    Chi-Square      Prob
        --------------------------------------------------
        INTERCEPT            1       146.84      0.0000
        DRUG                 2         6.58      0.0372

        RESIDUAL             0          .          .
```

From inspection of the marginal proportions of favorable response, it is clear that drug C is inferior to drugs A and B. You can test the equality of drugs A and C using a contrast statement. Since β_2 and β_3 are the parameters for drugs A and B (corresponding to the second and third columns of the model matrix in Output 13.3), the null hypothesis is

$$H_0: \beta_2 = -\beta_2 - \beta_3$$

or, equivalently,

$$H_0: 2\beta_2 + \beta_3 = 0$$

The corresponding CONTRAST statement is

```
contrast 'A versus C' _response_ 2 1;
```

Note that the keyword _RESPONSE_ is specified in the CONTRAST statement. You could also test this hypothesis using the ALL_PARMS keyword. The CONTRAST statement would be

```
contrast 'A versus C' all_parms 0 2 1;
```

The results in Output 13.5 indicate a significant difference between drugs A and C ($Q_W = 5.79$, 1 df, $p = 0.0161$).

Output 13.5   Contrast Results

```
                     ANALYSIS OF CONTRASTS

        Contrast            DF    Chi-Square      Prob
        --------------------------------------------------
        A versus C           1         5.79      0.0161
```

13.2.3   Two Populations, Dichotomous Response

The previous example involved the analysis of three responses from a single population. This section extends the methodology to situations in which there are multiple groups of subjects.

The Iowa 65+ Rural Health Study (Cornoni-Huntley et al. 1986) followed a cohort of elderly males and females over a six-year period. At each of three surveys, the response to one of the variables of interest, church attendance, was classified as yes if the subject was a regular church attender, and no if the subject was not a regular church attender. Table 13.2 displays the data from the 1311 females and 662 males who responded to all three surveys. Interest focuses on determining if church attendance rates change over time, if the attendance rates differ between females and males, and if the observed patterns of change over time are the same for females and males.

Table 13.2   Church Attendance Data

Gender	Year 0	Year 3	Year 6	Count
		Regular Church Attender at:		
Female	Yes	Yes	Yes	904
	Yes	Yes	No	88
	Yes	No	Yes	25
	Yes	No	No	51
	No	Yes	Yes	33
	No	Yes	No	22
	No	No	Yes	30
	No	No	No	158
Male	Yes	Yes	Yes	391
	Yes	Yes	No	36
	Yes	No	Yes	12
	Yes	No	No	26
	No	Yes	Yes	15
	No	Yes	No	21
	No	No	Yes	18
	No	No	No	143

When you obtain repeated measures data from multiple populations, you are interested not only in the effect of the repeated measures factor but also in the effect of the explanatory variables defining the multiple populations. In fact, when there are explanatory variables (factors) in a study involving repeated measures, there are three types of variation:

- main effects and interactions of the repeated measurement factors (within subjects variation)

- main effects and interactions of the explanatory variables (between subjects variation)

- interactions between the explanatory variables and the repeated measurement factors

In this example, there are two populations (females, males). Since a dichotomous response variable is measured at each of three time points (the repeated measurement factor), there are $r = 2^3 = 8$ response profiles. The between subjects variation is due to differences between females and males, and the within subjects variation is due to differences among time points. The analysis investigates both sources of variation, as well as the variation due to their interaction.

The following SAS statements read in the counts displayed in Table 13.2 and fit a saturated model with effects due to gender, time, and their interaction.

```
data church;
   input gender $ attend0 $ attend3 $ attend6 $ count;
cards;
F Y Y Y 904
F Y Y N  88
F Y N Y  25
F Y N N  51
F N Y Y  33
F N Y N  22
F N N Y  30
F N N N 158
M Y Y Y 391
M Y Y N  36
M Y N Y  12
M Y N N  26
M N Y Y  15
M N Y N  21
M N N Y  18
M N N N 143
;
proc catmod order=data;
   weight count;
   response marginals;
   model attend0*attend3*attend6=gender|_response_ / oneway;
   repeated year;
run;
```

The ORDER=DATA option in the PROC CATMOD statement keeps the levels of the explanatory and response variables in the same order as in Table 13.2 and ensures that the response functions are the marginal probabilities of attendance, rather than nonattendance. The MODEL statement specifies a saturated model with all potential sources of variation for the marginal probabilities of regular church attendance using the usual vertical bar (|) notation. The REPEATED statement is not necessary here, but it makes the output a little clearer by naming the repeated effect YEAR instead of _RESPONSE_. The populations are determined by the effects listed in the right-hand side of the MODEL statement since a POPULATION statement is not used. Here, two populations based on the values of GENDER will be formed.

Output 13.6 displays the one-way frequency distributions of the variables ATTEND0, ATTEND3, ATTEND6, and GENDER.

Output 13.6   One-Way Frequency Distributions

```
                  ONE-WAY FREQUENCIES

         Variable  Value  Frequency
         --------------------------------
         ATTEND0     Y       1533
                     N        440

         ATTEND3     Y       1510
                     N        463

         ATTEND6     Y       1428
                     N        545

         GENDER      F       1311
                     M        662
```

When a repeated measures analysis contains explanatory variables, the ONEWAY option of the MODEL statement produces the marginal distributions of the response variables for the total sample of observations. Thus, this option does not provide the marginal distributions of females and males regularly attending church at each of the three surveys. You can obtain the marginal distributions for females and males by using the FREQ procedure as follows:

```
proc freq;
   weight count;
   by gender;
   tables attend0 attend3 attend6;
run;
```

Output 13.7 shows that the proportions of females who regularly attend church at years 0, 3, and 6 are 0.815, 0.799, and 0.757, respectively.

Output 13.7   One-Way Frequency Distributions for Females

```
---------------------------------- GENDER=F ------------------------------------

                                      Cumulative  Cumulative
        ATTEND0  Frequency   Percent  Frequency    Percent
        --------------------------------------------------------
        N            243      18.5       243         18.5
        Y           1068      81.5      1311        100.0


                                      Cumulative  Cumulative
        ATTEND3  Frequency   Percent  Frequency    Percent
        --------------------------------------------------------
        N            264      20.1       264         20.1
        Y           1047      79.9      1311        100.0


                                      Cumulative  Cumulative
        ATTEND6  Frequency   Percent  Frequency    Percent
        --------------------------------------------------------
        N            319      24.3       319         24.3
        Y            992      75.7      1311        100.0
```

The corresponding proportions of males regularly attending church are 0.702, 0.699, and 0.659.

Output 13.8 displays the population and response profiles produced by the CATMOD procedure. These results verify that there are two groups (populations) and eight response profiles.

Output 13.8   Population and Response Profiles

```
                        POPULATION PROFILES
                                       Sample
                  Sample   GENDER       Size
                  -----------------------------
                     1       F          1311
                     2       M           662


                        RESPONSE PROFILES

         Response   ATTEND0   ATTEND3   ATTEND6
         ------------------------------------------
             1         Y         Y         Y
             2         Y         Y         N
             3         Y         N         Y
             4         Y         N         N
             5         N         Y         Y
             6         N         Y         N
             7         N         N         Y
             8         N         N         N
```

The response functions displayed in Output 13.9 agree with those from the FREQ procedure. Refer to the population profiles (Output 13.8) to determine that sample 1 corresponds to females and sample 2 to males. The model has six parameters: an overall intercept for the probability of regular church attendance, a gender effect, two survey year effects (corresponding to columns 3 and 4 of the model matrix) and two differential survey year effects for females and males, that is, the gender $\times$ year interaction (corresponding to columns 5 and 6 of the model matrix).

Output 13.9   Response Functions and Model Matrix

```
          Function   Response                  DESIGN MATRIX
 Sample    Number     Function      1     2      3      4      5      6
 ---------------------------------------------------------------------------
    1         1        0.81465       1     1      1      0      1      0
              2        0.79863       1     1      0      1      0      1
              3        0.75667       1     1     -1     -1     -1     -1

    2         1        0.70242       1    -1      1      0     -1      0
              2        0.69940       1    -1      0      1      0     -1
              3        0.65861       1    -1     -1     -1      1      1
```

Output 13.10 displays the ANOVA table. There are clearly significant effects due to gender ($Q_W = 30.04$, 1 df, $p < 0.001$) and survey year ($Q_W = 34.83$, 2 df, $p < 0.001$), but the gender $\times$ year interaction is not significant ($Q_W = 0.87$, 2 df, $p = 0.6476$).

Output 13.10   ANOVA Table

```
            ANALYSIS-OF-VARIANCE TABLE

    Source              DF    Chi-Square      Prob
    ---------------------------------------------------
    INTERCEPT            1      6154.13      0.0000
    GENDER              1        30.04      0.0000
    YEAR                2        34.83      0.0000
    GENDER*YEAR         2         0.87      0.6476

    RESIDUAL            0          .           .
```

The following statements fit the model with main effects for gender and survey year.

```
proc catmod order=data;
    weight count;
    response marginals;
    model attend0*attend3*attend6=gender _response_ / noprofile;
    repeated year;
run;
```

The NOPROFILE option of the MODEL statement suppresses the listing of the population and response profiles. You may want to use this option when fitting multiple models to the same data.

Output 13.11 displays the resulting ANOVA table. Note that the residual chi-square statistic from this model is identical to the chi-square statistic for the gender × survey year interaction from the saturated model (Output 13.10).

Output 13.11   ANOVA Table for Main Effects Model

```
            ANALYSIS-OF-VARIANCE TABLE

    Source              DF    Chi-Square      Prob
    ---------------------------------------------------
    INTERCEPT            1      6156.36      0.0000
    GENDER              1        30.63      0.0000
    YEAR                2        40.58      0.0000

    RESIDUAL            2         0.87      0.6476
```

The results of this model indicate that the gender effect and the survey year effect are both clearly significant. Moreover, since the interaction was not significant, the observed patterns of change over time are not significantly different for males and females. You may also want to test if the survey year effect departs from linearity. In terms of the default parameterization, the effects at years 0, 3, and 6 are given by β_3, β_4, and $-\beta_3 - \beta_4$, respectively. The null hypothesis of no departure from linearity is thus equivalent to

$$H_0: \beta_4 - \beta_3 = (-\beta_3 - \beta_4) - \beta_4$$

which simplifies to $H_0: \beta_4 = 0$. Although this hypothesis could be tested using a CONTRAST statement, it is also provided in the table of parameter estimates, which are displayed in Output 13.12.

Output 13.12   Parameter Estimates for Main Effects Model

```
             ANALYSIS OF WEIGHTED-LEAST-SQUARES ESTIMATES

                                        Standard    Chi-
   Effect              Parameter   Estimate   Error    Square   Prob
   ---------------------------------------------------------------------
   INTERCEPT               1        0.7385   0.00941   6156.36  0.0000
   GENDER                  2        0.0520   0.00940     30.63  0.0000
   YEAR                    3        0.0216   0.00460     22.13  0.0000
                           4        0.00978  0.00418      5.47  0.0193
```

In this example, there is significant departure from linearity ($Q_W = 5.47$, 1 df, $p = 0.0193$); the difference between year 6 and year 3 is significantly larger than that between year 3 and baseline.

13.2.4   Two Populations, Polytomous Response

The previous two sections describe repeated measures analyses when the response variable is dichotomous. In these situations, there is a single response function at each time point (level of the repeated measurement factor). This section describes the application of the WLS methodology when the response variable has more than two levels and the repeated measurement factor isn't time.

Table 13.3 * displays unaided distance vision data from 30–39 year old employees of United Kingdom Royal Ordnance factories during the years 1943–1946 (Kendall and Stuart 1961, p. 564 and p. 586). Vision was graded in both the right eye and the left eye on a four-point ordinal categorical scale where 1=highest grade and 4=lowest grade. Interest focuses on determining if the marginal vision grade distributions are the same in the right eye as in the left eye, if the marginal distributions differ between females and males, and if differences between right eye and left eye vision are the same for females and males.

Table 13.3   Unaided Distance Vision Data

Gender	Right Eye Grade	Left Eye Grade				Total
		1	2	3	4	
Female	1	1520	266	124	66	1976
	2	234	1512	432	78	2256
	3	117	362	1772	205	2456
	4	36	82	179	492	789
	Total	1907	2222	2507	841	7477
Male	1	821	112	85	35	1053
	2	116	494	145	27	782
	3	72	151	583	87	893
	4	43	34	106	331	514
	Total	1952	791	919	480	3242

---

*Reprinted by permission of Edward Arnold.

In this example, there are two populations (females, males). Two measurements of an ordered four-category response variable were obtained from each subject. Thus, there are $r = 4^2 = 16$ response profiles defined by the possible combinations of right eye and left eye vision grade. The between subjects variation is due to differences between females and males and the within subjects variation is due to differences between the right eye and the left eye.

The following SAS statements read in the counts displayed in Table 13.3 and create the SAS data set VISION.

```
data vision;
    input gender $ right left count;
cards;
F 1 1 1520
F 1 2  266
F 1 3  124
F 1 4   66
F 2 1  234
F 2 2 1512
F 2 3  432
F 2 4   78
F 3 1  117
F 3 2  362
F 3 3 1772
F 3 4  205
F 4 1   36
F 4 2   82
F 4 3  179
F 4 4  492
M 1 1  821
M 1 2  112
M 1 3   85
M 1 4   35
M 2 1  116
M 2 2  494
M 2 3  145
M 2 4   27
M 3 1   72
M 3 2  151
M 3 3  583
M 3 4   87
M 4 1   43
M 4 2   34
M 4 3  106
M 4 4  331
;
```

Since there are two populations, the null hypothesis of marginal homogeneity can be tested separately for females and males. The marginal distribution of vision grade in each eye involves three linearly independent proportions, since the proportions in the four categories sum to one. Thus, the null hypothesis of marginal homogeneity has 3 df for each gender. The following statements produce the analysis.

```
proc catmod;
   weight count;
   response marginals;
   model right*left=gender _response_(gender='F')
                          _response_(gender='M');
   repeated eye 2;
run;
```

The RESPONSE statement computes six correlated marginal proportions in each of the two populations. The first three response functions in each population are the proportions of subjects with right eye vision grades of 1, 2, and 3, while the next three are the proportions with left eye vision grades of 1, 2, and 3. For example, the response function for sample 1 (females), function number 1 (right eye vision grade of 1) is the marginal proportion of subjects in this category

$$\frac{\text{number of females with right eye grade 1}}{\text{total number of females}} = \frac{1976}{7477} = 0.26428$$

In this example, you must specify that the repeated measures factor labeled EYE has two levels. If this specification is omitted, PROC CATMOD constructs a model matrix to test the 5 df null hypothesis that the six response functions from each population are equal. It is, however, not necessary to include the option _RESPONSE_=EYE in the REPEATED statement, since there is only one repeated measures factor and the default factorial _RESPONSE_ effect is desired.

Output 13.13 displays the population and response profiles, and Output 13.14 displays the response functions and model matrix.

Output 13.13   Population and Response Profiles

```
                  POPULATION PROFILES
                                  Sample
             Sample   GENDER       Size
             ----------------------------
                1       F          7477
                2       M          3242


             RESPONSE PROFILES

        Response   RIGHT   LEFT
        ---------------------
             1       1       1
             2       1       2
             3       1       3
             4       1       4
             5       2       1
             6       2       2
             7       2       3
             8       2       4
             9       3       1
            10       3       2
            11       3       3
            12       3       4
            13       4       1
            14       4       2
            15       4       3
            16       4       4
```

Output 13.14   Response Functions and Model Matrix

Sample	Function Number	Response Function	1	2	3	4	5
1	1	0.26428	1	0	0	1	0
	2	0.30173	0	1	0	0	1
	3	0.32847	0	0	1	0	0
	4	0.25505	1	0	0	1	0
	5	0.29718	0	1	0	0	1
	6	0.33529	0	0	1	0	0
2	1	0.32480	1	0	0	-1	0
	2	0.24121	0	1	0	0	-1
	3	0.27545	0	0	1	0	0
	4	0.32449	1	0	0	-1	0
	5	0.24399	0	1	0	0	-1
	6	0.28347	0	0	1	0	0

Sample	Function Number	6	7	8	9	10	11	12
1	1	0	1	0	0	0	0	0
	2	0	0	1	0	0	0	0
	3	1	0	0	1	0	0	0
	4	0	-1	0	0	0	0	0
	5	0	0	-1	0	0	0	0
	6	1	0	0	-1	0	0	0
2	1	0	0	0	0	1	0	0
	2	0	0	0	0	0	1	0
	3	-1	0	0	0	0	0	1
	4	0	0	0	0	-1	0	0
	5	0	0	0	0	0	-1	0
	6	-1	0	0	0	0	0	-1

The first three parameters, which correspond to the first three columns of the model matrix, are overall intercepts for the probability of vision grades 1, 2, and 3. Recall that with a dichotomous response, the first column of the model matrix is an overall intercept for the probability of the first level of response. Likewise, with a polytomous response with r levels, there are $r - 1$ columns in the model matrix corresponding to overall intercepts for the probability of the first $r - 1$ levels of response, respectively. The next three parameters compare females to males at vision grades 1, 2, and 3, respectively. Parameters 7–9 (10–12) compare the right eye to the left eye at grades 1, 2, and 3 for females (males).

Output 13.15 displays the resulting ANOVA table. The test of marginal homogeneity is clearly significant in females ($Q_W = 11.98$, 3 df, $p = 0.0075$), but the differences between the right and left eye vision grade distributions in males are not statistically significant ($Q_W = 3.68$, 3 df, $p = 0.2984$).

Output 13.15   ANOVA Table for Gender-Specific Tests of Marginal Homogeneity

```
                      ANALYSIS-OF-VARIANCE TABLE

        Source              DF    Chi-Square      Prob
        ------------------------------------------------------
        INTERCEPT            3     71753.50      0.0000
        GENDER              3       142.07      0.0000
        EYE(GENDER=F)       3        11.98      0.0075
        EYE(GENDER=M)       3         3.68      0.2984


        RESIDUAL            0          .           .
```

If the differences between right eye and left eye vision are the same for females and males, there is no interaction between gender and eye. This hypothesis is tested using the following CONTRAST statement to compare parameters within the EYE(GENDER=F) and EYE(GENDER=M) effects.

```
contrast 'Interaction' all_parms 0 0 0 0 0 0 1 0 0 -1  0  0,
                        all_parms 0 0 0 0 0 0 0 1 0  0 -1  0,
                        all_parms 0 0 0 0 0 0 0 0 1  0  0 -1;
run;
```

The results in Output 13.16 indicate that there is evidence of interaction ($Q_W = 8.27$, 3 df, $p = 0.0407$).

Output 13.16   Test of Interaction

```
                  ANALYSIS OF CONTRASTS

        Contrast            DF    Chi-Square      Prob
        ------------------------------------------------------
        Interaction         3        8.27        0.0407
```

You could also test the hypothesis of no interaction between gender and eye by fitting the model

```
model right*left=gender|_response_;
repeated eye 2;
run;
```

and looking at the GENDER*EYE effect in the ANOVA table. Although this model would provide a more straightforward test of no interaction, it would not provide tests of marginal homogeneity in females and males.

Since vision grade is an ordinal dependent variable, an alternative approach is to assign scores to its four levels and test the hypothesis that the average vision scores in the right and left eyes are the same. Using the scores 1, 2, 3, and 4 (the actual vision grades recorded), you can test the hypothesis of homogeneity for females and males by requesting that mean scores be computed as follows:

```
proc catmod;
   weight count;
   response means;
   model right*left=gender _response_(gender='F')
         _response_(gender='M') / noprofile;
   repeated eye;
run;
```

You do not need to specify the number of levels of the repeated measures factor in the REPEATED statement since there are only two response functions per group and, by default, the model matrix will be constructed to test their equality.

Output 13.17 displays the response functions and model matrix. Response function 1 in sample 1 is the average right eye vision grade for females. This is computed as follows:

$$\frac{1 \times 1976 + 2 \times 2256 + 3 \times 2456 + 4 \times 789}{7477} = 2.27524$$

The model matrix now includes an overall intercept, a gender effect, and two eye effects (one for females and one for males).

Output 13.17   Response Functions and Model Matrix for Mean Score Model

	Function	Response	DESIGN MATRIX			
Sample	Number	Function	1	2	3	4
1	1	2.27524	1	1	1	0
	2	2.30520	1	1	-1	0
2	1	2.26774	1	-1	0	1
	2	2.25509	1	-1	0	-1

Output 13.18 displays the resulting ANOVA table. The test of homogeneity is again clearly significant in females ($Q_W = 11.97$, 1 df, $p = 0.0005$), and the difference between the right and left average vision scores in males is not statistically significant ($Q_W = 0.73$, 1 df, $p = 0.3916$).

Output 13.18   ANOVA Table for Mean Score Model

ANALYSIS-OF-VARIANCE TABLE

Source	DF	Chi-Square	Prob
INTERCEPT	1	50866.50	0.0000
GENDER	1	2.04	0.1534
EYE(GENDER=F)	1	11.97	0.0005
EYE(GENDER=M)	1	0.73	0.3916
RESIDUAL	0	.	.

The following CONTRAST statement tests the null hypothesis that the mean score differences between right eye and left eye are equal for females and males.

```
contrast 'Interaction' all_parms 0 0 1 -1;
run;
```

The results in Output 13.19 again indicate that there is evidence of interaction
($Q_W = 6.20$, 1 df, $p = 0.0128$).

Output 13.19   Test of Interaction for Mean Score Model

```
                   ANALYSIS OF CONTRASTS

     Contrast                  DF    Chi-Square    Prob
     -------------------------------------------------------
     Interaction               1        6.20       0.0128
```

Note that the values of the test statistics are affected only by the spacing between scores,
not by their values. Thus, the same test statistics would have been obtained using any set
of equally spaced scores, for example, vision scores of (1 3 5 7) instead of (1 2 3 4). If it is
not reasonable to assume that the vision grades levels are equally-spaced, you may
redefine the values of the RIGHT and LEFT variables to a different set of scores in a
DATA step prior to invoking PROC CATMOD.

13.2.5   Multiple Repeated Measurement Factors

In each of the previous examples, a single categorical outcome variable was measured on
multiple occasions or under multiple conditions. The multiple measurements were defined
by the values of a single repeated measures factor, such as time, drug, and so on. In some
applications, there may be more than one repeated measurement factor. For example, an
outcome variable might be measured at four time points under each of two conditions,
resulting in a total of eight repeated measures.

MacMillan et al. (1981) analyze data from a one-population ($s = 1$) observational study
involving 793 subjects. For each subject, two diagnostic procedures (standard and test)
were carried out at each of two times. The results of the four evaluations were classified as
positive or negative. Since a dichotomous response ($c = 2$) was measured at $t = 4$
occasions, there are $r = 2^4 = 16$ response profiles. Table 13.4 displays the resulting data.

In this example, the four repeated measures are obtained from a factorial design involving
two factors, each with two levels. Although the hypothesis of marginal homogeneity (with
3 df) could be tested, it is of greater interest to investigate the effects of time and treatment
on the probability of a positive test result.

Table 13.4 Diagnostic Test Results for 793 Subjects

Time 1		Time 2		No. of
Standard	Test	Standard	Test	Subjects
Negative	Negative	Negative	Negative	509
Negative	Negative	Negative	Positive	4
Negative	Negative	Positive	Negative	17
Negative	Negative	Positive	Positive	3
Negative	Positive	Negative	Negative	13
Negative	Positive	Negative	Positive	8
Negative	Positive	Positive	Negative	0
Negative	Positive	Positive	Positive	8
Positive	Negative	Negative	Negative	14
Positive	Negative	Negative	Positive	1
Positive	Negative	Positive	Negative	17
Positive	Negative	Positive	Positive	9
Positive	Positive	Negative	Negative	7
Positive	Positive	Negative	Positive	4
Positive	Positive	Positive	Negative	9
Positive	Positive	Positive	Positive	170

The following statements read in the data and fit a model incorporating main effects for time and treatment, as well as the time $\times$ treatment interaction.

```
data diagnos;
   input std1 $ test1 $ std2 $ test2 $ count;
   cards;
Neg Neg Neg Neg 509
Neg Neg Neg Pos   4
Neg Neg Pos Neg  17
Neg Neg Pos Pos   3
Neg Pos Neg Neg  13
Neg Pos Neg Pos   8
Neg Pos Pos Neg   0
Neg Pos Pos Pos   8
Pos Neg Neg Neg  14
Pos Neg Neg Pos   1
Pos Neg Pos Neg  17
Pos Neg Pos Pos   9
Pos Pos Neg Neg   7
Pos Pos Neg Pos   4
Pos Pos Pos Neg   9
Pos Pos Pos Pos 170
;
proc catmod;
   weight count;
   response marginals;
   model std1*test1*std2*test2=_response_ / oneway;
   repeated time 2, trtment 2 / _response_=time|trtment;
run;
```

Output 13.20 displays the one-way frequency distributions for each of the four response variables. Since this is a single population example, these distributions are useful for checking that the response functions are defined as desired.

Output 13.20   One-Way Frequency Distributions

```
                        ONE-WAY FREQUENCIES

                  Variable   Value   Frequency
                  -------------------------------
                  STD1       Neg         562
                             Pos         231

                  TEST1      Neg         574
                             Pos         219

                  STD2       Neg         560
                             Pos         233

                  TEST2      Neg         586
                             Pos         207
```

The population and response profiles are displayed in Output 13.21. Note that only 15 of the 16 potential response profiles occur in the data. There were no subjects who were negative for standard at time 1, positive for test at time 1, positive for standard at time 2, and negative for test at time 2.

Output 13.21   Population and Response Profiles

```
                                Sample
                   Sample        Size
                   ----------------
                      1          793


                     RESPONSE PROFILES

        Response  STD1   TEST1   STD2   TEST2
        ------------------------------------
              1    Neg    Neg    Neg    Neg
              2    Neg    Neg    Neg    Pos
              3    Neg    Neg    Pos    Neg
              4    Neg    Neg    Pos    Pos
              5    Neg    Pos    Neg    Neg
              6    Neg    Pos    Neg    Pos
              7    Neg    Pos    Pos    Pos
              8    Pos    Neg    Neg    Neg
              9    Pos    Neg    Neg    Pos
             10    Pos    Neg    Pos    Neg
             11    Pos    Neg    Pos    Pos
             12    Pos    Pos    Neg    Neg
             13    Pos    Pos    Neg    Pos
             14    Pos    Pos    Pos    Neg
             15    Pos    Pos    Pos    Pos
```

Output 13.22 displays the response functions and the model matrix. Since the MODEL statement lists the four dependent variables in the order standard at time 1, test at time 1, standard at time 2, and test at time 2, the response functions computed by the keyword MARGINALS on the RESPONSE statement are the corresponding four marginal proportions with a negative response. The marginal probability of a negative response is used since 'Neg' is the first level for each response variable. The REPEATED statement specifies that there are two repeated measures factors, each with two levels, and that the model matrix includes the main effects and interaction of these two factors. Since the MODEL statement groups the results from time 1 together, followed by the results from time 2, the repeated measures factor for time is listed first in the REPEATED statement. Recall that the factor that changes most slowly is listed first.

Output 13.22   Response Functions and Model Matrix

	Function	Response	DESIGN MATRIX			
Sample	Number	Function	1	2	3	4
1	1	0.70870	1	1	1	1
	2	0.72383	1	-1	1	-1
	3	0.70618	1	1	-1	-1
	4	0.73897	1	-1	-1	1

The results of fitting this model (Output 13.23) indicate that the main effect of time ($Q_W = 0.85$, 1 df, $p = 0.357$) and the time $\times$ treatment interaction ($Q_W = 2.40$, 1 df, $p = 0.1215$) are not significantly different from zero.

Output 13.23   ANOVA Table

ANALYSIS-OF-VARIANCE TABLE

Source	DF	Chi-Square	Prob
INTERCEPT	1	2385.34	0.0000
TIME	1	0.85	0.3570
TRTMENT	1	8.20	0.0042
TIME*TRTMENT	1	2.40	0.1215
RESIDUAL	0	.	.

The preceding results could also have been produced using a different ordering of the response variables and repeated measurement factors on the MODEL and REPEATED statements:

```
model std1*std2*test1*test2=_response_ / oneway;
repeated trtment 2, time 2 / _response_=time|trtment;
```

In this case, the responses from the standard treatment precede those from the test treatment.

A reduced model including only the treatment main effect can be fit by modifying the _RESPONSE_= option of the REPEATED statement, as shown below.

```
proc catmod;
   weight count;
   response marginals;
   model std1*test1*std2*test2=_response_ / noprofile;
   repeated time 2, trtment 2 / _response_=trtment;
run;
```

The results in Output 13.24 indicate that this model provides a good fit to the observed data ($Q_W = 3.51$, 2 df, $p = 0.17$) and that the treatment effect is clearly significant ($Q_W = 9.55$, 1 df, $p = 0.002$). Since the parameter for the first treatment (standard) is -0.0128, the parameter estimate for the test treatment is 0.0128. Consequently, it is estimated that the marginal probability of a negative response is $2 \times 0.0128 = 0.0256$ higher for the test treatment than for the standard treatment.

Output 13.24   Results from the Reduced Model

```
                                               DESIGN
                    Function   Response        MATRIX
          Sample    Number     Function        1       2
          -------------------------------------------------
            1         1        0.70870          1       1
                      2        0.72383          1      -1
                      3        0.70618          1       1
                      4        0.73897          1      -1


                 ANALYSIS-OF-VARIANCE TABLE

          Source             DF    Chi-Square    Prob
          -------------------------------------------------
          INTERCEPT           1      2386.97     0.0000
          TRTMENT             1         9.55     0.0020

          RESIDUAL            2         3.51     0.1731


              ANALYSIS OF WEIGHTED-LEAST-SQUARES ESTIMATES

                                        Standard   Chi-
          Effect       Parameter  Estimate  Error    Square    Prob
          -------------------------------------------------------------
          INTERCEPT        1       0.7196   0.0147   2386.97   0.0000
          TRTMENT          2      -0.0128   0.00416     9.55   0.0020
```

13.3 Advanced Topic: Further Weighted Least Squares Applications

13.3.1 One Population Regression Analysis of Marginal Proportions and Logits

In a longitudinal study of the health effects of air pollution (Ware, Lipsitz, and Speizer 1988), children were examined annually at ages 9, 10, 11, and 12. At each examination, the response measured was the presence of wheezing. Two questions of interest are

- Does the prevalence of wheezing change with age?
- Is there a quantifiable trend in the age-specific prevalence rates?

Table 13.5 [†], from Agresti (1990, p. 408), displays data from 1019 children included in this study. In this single population example, the crossclassification of a dichotomous outcome at four time points defines $r = 2^4 = 16$ response profiles.

[†]Reprinted by permission of John Wiley & Sons, Inc. Copyright © John Wiley & Sons.

Table 13.5   Breath Test Results at Four Ages for 1019 Children

| Wheeze | | | | No. of |
Age 9	Age 10	Age 11	Age 12	Children
Present	Present	Present	Present	94
Present	Present	Present	Absent	30
Present	Present	Absent	Present	15
Present	Present	Absent	Absent	28
Present	Absent	Present	Present	14
Present	Absent	Present	Absent	9
Present	Absent	Absent	Present	12
Present	Absent	Absent	Absent	63
Absent	Present	Present	Present	19
Absent	Present	Present	Absent	15
Absent	Present	Absent	Present	10
Absent	Present	Absent	Absent	44
Absent	Absent	Present	Present	17
Absent	Absent	Present	Absent	42
Absent	Absent	Absent	Present	35
Absent	Absent	Absent	Absent	572

The following SAS statements read the observed counts for each of the 16 response profiles and test the hypothesis of marginal homogeneity using PROC CATMOD. The RESPONSE, MODEL, and REPEATED statements are used in the same way as was described in Section 13.2.

```
data wheeze;
    input wheeze9 $ wheeze10 $ wheeze11 $ wheeze12 $ count;
    cards;
Present Present Present Present   94
Present Present Present Absent    30
Present Present Absent  Present   15
Present Present Absent  Absent    28
Present Absent  Present Present   14
Present Absent  Present Absent     9
Present Absent  Absent  Present   12
Present Absent  Absent  Absent    63
Absent  Present Present Present   19
Absent  Present Present Absent    15
Absent  Present Absent  Present   10
Absent  Present Absent  Absent    44
Absent  Absent  Present Present   17
Absent  Absent  Present Absent    42
Absent  Absent  Absent  Present   35
Absent  Absent  Absent  Absent   572
;
proc catmod order=data;
    weight count;
    response marginals;
    model wheeze9*wheeze10*wheeze11*wheeze12=_response_ / oneway;
```

```
        repeated age;
    run;
```

Since this is a single population example, the one-way frequency distributions for each of the four response variables (Output 13.25) are useful in checking that the response functions are defined as desired.

Output 13.25   One-Way Frequency Distributions

```
                    ONE-WAY FREQUENCIES

              Variable    Value    Frequency
              -----------------------------------
              WHEEZE9    Present        265
                         Absent         754

              WHEEZE10   Present        255
                         Absent         764

              WHEEZE11   Present        240
                         Absent         779

              WHEEZE12   Present        216
                         Absent         803
```

The response profile listing in Output 13.26 verifies that all 16 possible response profiles occur in the data.

Output 13.26   Population and Response Profiles

```
                        RESPONSE PROFILES

      Response  WHEEZE9   WHEEZE10  WHEEZE11  WHEEZE12
      -------------------------------------------------------
          1     Present   Present   Present   Present
          2     Present   Present   Present   Absent
          3     Present   Present   Absent    Present
          4     Present   Present   Absent    Absent
          5     Present   Absent    Present   Present
          6     Present   Absent    Present   Absent
          7     Present   Absent    Absent    Present
          8     Present   Absent    Absent    Absent
          9     Absent    Present   Present   Present
         10     Absent    Present   Present   Absent
         11     Absent    Present   Absent    Present
         12     Absent    Present   Absent    Absent
         13     Absent    Absent    Present   Present
         14     Absent    Absent    Present   Absent
         15     Absent    Absent    Absent    Present
         16     Absent    Absent    Absent    Absent
```

Output 13.27 displays the response functions and the model matrix. The results of the ANOVA table in Output 13.28 indicate that the hypothesis of marginal homogeneity is rejected ($Q_W = 12.85$, 3 df, $p = 0.005$). Thus, the prevalence of wheezing changes with age.

Output 13.27   Response Functions and Model Matrix

```
               Function   Response        DESIGN MATRIX
      Sample   Number     Function     1    2    3    4
      -----------------------------------------------------
         1        1        0.26006     1    1    0    0
                  2        0.25025     1    0    1    0
                  3        0.23553     1    0    0    1
                  4        0.21197     1   -1   -1   -1
```

Output 13.28   ANOVA Table

```
               ANALYSIS-OF-VARIANCE TABLE

      Source              DF    Chi-Square    Prob
      -----------------------------------------------
      INTERCEPT            1       523.63     0.0000
      AGE                 3        12.85     0.0050

      RESIDUAL            0          .          .
```

In order to quantify the trend in the age-specific prevalence rates, the proportion of
children with wheezing present is modeled as a linear function of age. In this case, it is not
possible to use the _RESPONSE_ keyword of the MODEL statement in conjunction with
the REPEATED statement, since a repeated measurement factor cannot be specified in a
DIRECT statement. Therefore, the model matrix must be specified explicitly, as described
in Section 12.8.5 The SAS statements are as follows:

```
proc catmod order=data;
   weight count;
   response marginals;
   model wheeze9*wheeze10*wheeze11*wheeze12=(1   9,
                                             1 10,
                                             1 11,
                                             1 12)
                                            (1='Intercept',
                                             2='Linear Age')
                                            / noprofile;
run;
```

When you input the model matrix directly, you have the option of testing the significance
of selected parameters or subsets of parameters. The specification enclosed in parentheses
after the model matrix stipulates that the ANOVA table include tests that the first
(intercept) and second (linear age) parameters are equal to zero. Note that the label
describing the parameter or subset to be tested must be 24 characters or less. The results of
this model statement are displayed in Output 13.29 and Output 13.30.

Output 13.29   Response Functions and Model Matrix

Sample	Function Number	Response Function	DESIGN MATRIX 1	2
1	1	0.26006	1	9
	2	0.25025	1	10
	3	0.23553	1	11
	4	0.21197	1	12

Output 13.30   ANOVA Table

ANALYSIS-OF-VARIANCE TABLE

Source	DF	Chi-Square	Prob
Intercept	1	66.70	0.0000
Linear Age	1	12.31	0.0005
RESIDUAL	2	0.54	0.7620

The residual chi-square tests the null hypothesis that the nonlinear (quadratic, cubic) components of the age effect are not significantly different from zero. These data provide little evidence of nonlinearity ($Q_W = 0.54$, 2 df, $p = 0.76$). If this test had been statistically significant, the quadratic and, if necessary, cubic terms could also have been specified in the model matrix. The test of the linear age effect is clearly significant ($Q_W = 12.31$, 1 df, $p < 0.001$).

With reference to the estimated parameters displayed in Output 13.31, the resulting model for predicting the effect of age on the prevalence of wheezing is

$$\Pr\{\text{wheezing}\} = 0.4083 - 0.0161 \times \text{age in years}$$

Thus, the prevalence is estimated to decrease by 0.0161 per year of age.

Output 13.31   Parameter Estimates

ANALYSIS OF WEIGHTED-LEAST-SQUARES ESTIMATES

Effect	Parameter	Estimate	Standard Error	Chi-Square	Prob
MODEL	1	0.4083	0.0500	66.70	0.0000
	2	-0.0161	0.00460	12.31	0.0005

Chapter 8 describes logistic models for dichotomous response variables. As an alternative to modeling the probability of wheezing as a linear function of age, you could choose to model the marginal logit of the probability of wheezing. In this case, the logarithm of the odds is modeled as a linear function of age. Even if there are no substantive grounds for preferring a logit analysis over the analysis on the proportion scale, you may decide to consider both types of models and select the model that provides the simplest interpretation.

Since it is not possible to analyze repeated measurements using the LOGISTIC procedure, maximum likelihood parameter estimates can not be obtained. However, PROC CATMOD can be used to estimate model parameters using weighted least squares.

Suppose L_x denotes the observed log odds of wheezing at age x, for $x = 9, 10, 11, 12$, respectively, that is,

$$L_x = \log\left(\frac{p_x}{1 - p_x}\right)$$

where p_x denotes the marginal probability of wheezing at age x. The following statements fit the regression model

$$L_x = \alpha + \beta x$$

The only change from the previous model is that the keyword MARGINALS on the RESPONSE statement is replaced by the keyword LOGITS.

```
proc catmod order=data;
   weight count;
   response logits;
   model wheeze9*wheeze10*wheeze11*wheeze12=(1   9,
                                             1  10,
                                             1  11,
                                             1  12)
                                   (1='Intercept',
                                    2='Linear Age') / noprofile;
run;
```

Output 13.32 displays the marginal logit response functions and the model matrix. The ANOVA table in Output 13.33 indicates that the regression model for marginal logits also provides a good fit to the observed data ($Q_W = 0.67$, 2 df, $p = 0.72$) and that the linear effect of age is clearly significant ($Q_W = 11.77$, 1 df, $p < 0.001$).

Output 13.32   Response Functions and Model Matrix

Sample	Function Number	Response Function	DESIGN MATRIX 1	2
1	1	-1.04566	1	9
	2	-1.09730	1	10
	3	-1.17737	1	11
	4	-1.31308	1	12

Output 13.33   ANOVA Table

ANALYSIS-OF-VARIANCE TABLE			
Source	DF	Chi-Square	Prob
Intercept	1	0.76	0.3824
Linear Age	1	11.77	0.0006
RESIDUAL	2	0.67	0.7167

The model for predicting the log odds of wheezing (Output 13.34) is

$$\text{logit}[\Pr\{\text{wheezing}\}] = -0.2367 - 0.0879 \times \text{age in years}$$

The parameter estimates are interpreted in the same manner as was described in Chapter 8. For example, the odds of wheezing are estimated to decrease by $e^{-0.0879} = 0.916$ for each one-year increase in age.

Output 13.34   Parameter Estimates

```
            ANALYSIS OF WEIGHTED-LEAST-SQUARES ESTIMATES

                                     Standard    Chi-
    Effect          Parameter  Estimate  Error   Square   Prob
    -------------------------------------------------------------
    MODEL               1      -0.2367   0.2710   0.76    0.3824
                        2      -0.0879   0.0256  11.77    0.0006
```

As described in Section 12.6.1, the logit function is the default response function for the CATMOD procedure, and maximum likelihood is the default estimation method. However, Output 13.34 displays weighted least squares parameter estimates. In a repeated measures analysis, the specification

```
    response logits;
```

analyzes marginal logits using weighted least squares. If the RESPONSE statement is omitted in this example, 15 generalized logits would be computed, comparing each of the first 15 response profiles with the last one. Since the model matrix has only four rows, an error message would then be printed.

13.3.2   Logistic Analysis with Multiple Explanatory Variables

In a randomized experiment designed to determine if driver education

reduces the number of collisions among teenage drivers (Stock et al. 1983), eligible students were randomized to one of three groups:

- Safe Performance Curriculum (SPC)
- Pre-Driver Licensing Curriculum (PDL)
- Control

At the time of the study, the 70-hour SPC was considered to be the most advanced and thorough high school driver education program in the nation. The PDL was a 30-hour course containing only the minimum training required to pass a license test. Students assigned to the Control group received no formal driver education coursework through the school system and were expected to be taught to drive by their parents or private driver training schools. Follow-up data concerning the occurrence of collisions involving study participants were obtained from the state department of motor vehicles. The primary question of interest was whether driver education affects the occurrence of collisions, and if so, how long after licensing do any effects persist.

Table 13.6 displays data from the first three years of the study for 14,127 individuals with complete follow-up data. Since subjects were stratified by gender prior to randomization, there are $s = 6$ subpopulations (three groups $\times$ two genders). For each of the three years of follow-up ($t = 3$), the response variable is dichotomous ($c = 2$); thus, there are $r = 2^3 = 8$ response profiles.

Table 13.6   Occurrence of Collisions for 14,127 Teenage Drivers during Three Years of Follow-up

		Year 1								
		No				Yes				
		Year 2				Year 2				
		No		Yes		No		Yes		
		Year 3		Year 3		Year 3		Year 3		
Program	Gender	No	Yes	No	Yes	No	Yes	No	Yes	Total
SPC	Male	1467	295	305	79	190	68	60	19	2483
	Female	1659	218	217	28	120	30	17	4	2293
PDL	Male	1495	264	278	80	206	52	46	25	2446
	Female	1618	228	191	24	122	12	17	3	2215
Control	Male	1552	288	271	94	167	47	55	23	2497
	Female	1640	217	185	24	96	13	16	2	2193

The following SAS statements read in the frequencies displayed in Table 13.6. The response variables COLL1, COLL2, and COLL3 denote the occurrence (Yes) or nonoccurrence (No) of a collision in which a study participant was a driver during years 1, 2, and 3 of follow-up. It should be noted that the starting date for each subject was the date that driver education began (or would have begun).

```
data collisn;
   input program $ gender $ coll1 $ coll2 $ coll3 $ count;
   cards;
SPC      Male   Yes Yes Yes    19
SPC      Male   No  No  No   1467
SPC      Male   No  No  Yes   295
SPC      Male   No  Yes No    305
SPC      Male   No  Yes Yes    79
SPC      Male   Yes No  No    190
SPC      Male   Yes No  Yes    68
SPC      Male   Yes Yes No     60
SPC      Female No  No  No   1659
SPC      Female No  No  Yes   218
SPC      Female No  Yes No    217
SPC      Female No  Yes Yes    28
SPC      Female Yes No  No    120
SPC      Female Yes No  Yes    30
SPC      Female Yes Yes No     17
SPC      Female Yes Yes Yes     4
PDL      Male   No  No  No   1495
```

```
PDL      Male   No  No  Yes   264
PDL      Male   No  Yes No    278
PDL      Male   No  Yes Yes    80
PDL      Male   Yes No  No    206
PDL      Male   Yes No  Yes    52
PDL      Male   Yes Yes No     46
PDL      Male   Yes Yes Yes    25
PDL      Female No  No  No   1618
PDL      Female No  No  Yes   228
PDL      Female No  Yes No    191
PDL      Female No  Yes Yes    24
PDL      Female Yes No  No    122
PDL      Female Yes No  Yes    12
PDL      Female Yes Yes No     17
PDL      Female Yes Yes Yes     3
Control  Male   No  No  No   1552
Control  Male   No  No  Yes   288
Control  Male   No  Yes No    271
Control  Male   No  Yes Yes    94
Control  Male   Yes No  No    167
Control  Male   Yes No  Yes    47
Control  Male   Yes Yes No     55
Control  Male   Yes Yes Yes    23
Control  Female No  No  No   1640
Control  Female No  No  Yes   217
Control  Female No  Yes No    185
Control  Female No  Yes Yes    24
Control  Female Yes No  No     96
Control  Female Yes No  Yes    13
Control  Female Yes Yes No     16
Control  Female Yes Yes Yes     2
;
run;
```

The goal of the analysis is to model the logit of the probability of a collision as a function of driver education program, gender, and time. Since there are six groups of subjects and three response functions from each group, the model matrices for models of interest have 18 rows. Although the primary focus is not on trends over time but rather on differences among groups during each of the three years of follow-up, it is convenient to first consider factorial models that can be specified by using the MODEL statement. You can then specify reduced models in terms of parameters that are more easily interpreted.

The first PROC CATMOD invocation fits a model that includes main effects for program (2 df), gender (1 df), and year (2 df), and all of the two-factor interactions. The keyword LOGITS is used on the RESPONSE statement to request marginal logits at years 1, 2, and 3 in each of the six groups. The ORDER=DATA option ensures that the logit of the probability of a collision is analyzed (since the value 'Yes' occurs before 'No' in the data lines).

```
proc catmod order=data;
   weight count;
   response logits;
   model col11*col12*col13=program|gender program|_response_
```

```
        gender|_response_ / oneway nodesign noparm;
    repeated year;
  run;
```

Output 13.35 displays the one-way frequency distributions. While just under 10% of the students were involved in a collision during the first year of follow-up, the corresponding proportions during years 2 and 3 increased to 14.6% and 15.1%, respectively. The one-way distributions also show that there were roughly equal numbers of students in each of the three groups and that there were more males than females in the study.

Output 13.35   One-Way Frequency Distributions

```
                    ONE-WAY FREQUENCIES

           Variable   Value    Frequency
           --------------------------------
           COLL1      Yes           1410
                      No           12717

           COLL2      Yes           2063
                      No           12064

           COLL3      Yes           2137
                      No           11990

           PROGRAM    SPC           4776
                      PDL           4661
                      Control       4690

           GENDER     Male          7426
                      Female        6701
```

Output 13.36 displays the population and response profiles. The populations are ordered as shown in Table 13.6, and all eight of the possible response profiles occur.

Output 13.36   Population and Response Profiles

```
                POPULATION PROFILES
                                    Sample
            Sample  PROGRAM  GENDER   Size
            -----------------------------------
              1     SPC      Male     2483
              2     SPC      Female   2293
              3     PDL      Male     2446
              4     PDL      Female   2215
              5     Control  Male     2497
              6     Control  Female   2193

                RESPONSE PROFILES

            Response  COLL1  COLL2  COLL3
            -----------------------------------
              1       Yes    Yes    Yes
              2       Yes    Yes    No
              3       Yes    No     Yes
              4       Yes    No     No
              5       No     Yes    Yes
              6       No     Yes    No
              7       No     No     Yes
              8       No     No     No
```

Output 13.37 displays the ANOVA table. The source of variation labeled RESIDUAL tests the null hypothesis that the three-factor interaction between PROGRAM, GENDER, and YEAR is not significantly different from zero. The chi-square value of 0.72 with 4 df is nonsignificant. In addition, the test of the 2 df PROGRAM $\times$ GENDER interaction is nonsignificant.

Output 13.37   ANOVA Table

```
                ANALYSIS-OF-VARIANCE TABLE

     Source            DF   Chi-Square      Prob
     ---------------------------------------------------
     INTERCEPT          1     15321.92     0.0000
     PROGRAM            2         9.35     0.0093
     GENDER             1       358.01     0.0000
     PROGRAM*GENDER     2         0.80     0.6709
     YEAR               2       208.22     0.0000
     PROGRAM*YEAR       4         6.23     0.1829
     GENDER*YEAR        2        10.48     0.0053

     RESIDUAL           4         0.72     0.9486
```

Based on these results, the next model includes main effects and the two-factor interactions with the repeated measurements factor.

```
model col11*col12*col13=program|_response_ gender|_response_
                    / noprofile nodesign noparm;
run;
```

The 6 df residual chi-square in the ANOVA table (Output 13.38) now includes the three-factor interaction and the PROGRAM $\times$ GENDER interaction. There is no evidence to reject the null hypothesis that these effects are jointly significantly different from zero.

Output 13.38   ANOVA Table for Reduced Factorial Model

```
                ANALYSIS-OF-VARIANCE TABLE

     Source            DF   Chi-Square      Prob
     ---------------------------------------------------
     INTERCEPT          1     15325.66     0.0000
     PROGRAM            2         8.79     0.0123
     YEAR               2       207.93     0.0000
     PROGRAM*YEAR       4         6.02     0.1974
     GENDER             1       357.41     0.0000
     GENDER*YEAR        2        10.32     0.0057

     RESIDUAL           6         1.52     0.9581
```

There are only two interaction terms in this model, both of which involve the repeated measurements factor YEAR. The GENDER $\times$ YEAR interaction is clearly significant. Since the p value for the PROGRAM $\times$ YEAR interaction is 0.2, you might choose to delete this effect. However, the chi-square statistic is relatively large (6.02) and the main effects of both PROGRAM and YEAR are significant. Therefore, for purposes of illustration, the next model includes separate PROGRAM and GENDER effects for each of the three years of follow-up. Since nested effects such as PROGRAM(_RESPONSE_) are not permitted in the MODEL statement, the model matrix must be specified explicitly. In such situations, the POPULATION statement is required to define the groups. The statement

```
population program gender;
```

defines six groups in the same order as in the first two models (that is, SPC male, SPC female, PDL male, PDL female, Control male, Control female). (Note that the statement

```
population gender program;
```

would alternatively order the populations as male SPC, male PDL, male Control, female SPC, female PDL, female Control.) The SAS statements follow.

```
proc catmod order=data;
    weight count;
    population program gender;
    response logits;
    model col11*col12*col13=(1  0  0  1  1  0  0  0  0  1  0  0,
                             1  1  0  0  0  1  1  0  0  0  1  0,
                             1  1  1  0  0  0  0  1  1  0  0  1,
                             1  0  0  1  1  0  0  0  0  0  0  0,
                             1  1  0  0  0  1  1  0  0  0  0  0,
                             1  1  1  0  0  0  0  1  1  0  0  0,
                             1  0  0  1 -1  0  0  0  0  1  0  0,
                             1  1  0  0  0  1 -1  0  0  0  1  0,
                             1  1  1  0  0  0  0  1 -1  0  0  1,
                             1  0  0  1 -1  0  0  0  0  0  0  0,
                             1  1  0  0  0  1 -1  0  0  0  0  0,
                             1  1  1  0  0  0  0  1 -1  0  0  0,
                             1  0  0 -2  0  0  0  0  0  1  0  0,
                             1  1  0  0  0 -2  0  0  0  0  1  0,
                             1  1  1  0  0  0  0 -2  0  0  0  1,
                             1  0  0 -2  0  0  0  0  0  0  0  0,
                             1  1  0  0  0 -2  0  0  0  0  0  0,
                             1  1  1  0  0  0  0 -2  0  0  0  0)
                         (1='Intercept',
                        2 3='Year',
                          2='  Year 2 Increment',
                          3='  Year 3 Increment',
                4 5 6 7 8 9='Program',
                        4 5='  Year 1',
                          4='    Education',
                          5='    Method',
                        6 7='  Year 2',
                          6='    Education',
                          7='    Method',
                        8 9='  Year 3',
                          8='    Education',
                          9='    Method',
                  10 11 12='Gender',
```

```
                                         10='  Year 1',
                                         11='  Year 2',
                                         12='  Year 3') / noprofile;
      run;
```

For ease of interpretation, Table 13.7 displays the model matrix with row identifiers corresponding to each population and response function. The first three columns of the model matrix correspond to an overall intercept and incremental threshold effects for year 1 to year 2 and year 2 to year 3. Columns 4–5, 6–7, and 8–9 correspond to separate PROGRAM effects for years 1, 2, and 3, respectively. Since the PROGRAM effect has 2 df at each year, the first parameter compares the two driver education groups (SPC, PDL) to the control group and thus assesses the effect of driver education. In the rows pertaining to the appropriate year, the model matrix has a 1 if PROGRAM is SPC or PDL and a −2 in the control group. The second parameter, which compares SPC to PDL, contrasts the two methods of driver education. The values 1 for SPC and −1 for PDL are used in the appropriate rows. The final three columns (10–12) correspond to separate GENDER effects for each of the three years; each is parameterized as an incremental effect for males (1 for males, 0 for females).

Table 13.7   Model Matrix with Separate PROGRAM and GENDER Effects for Each Year

Program	Gender	Year	Column of Model Matrix											
			1	2	3	4	5	6	7	8	9	10	11	12
SPC	Male	1	1	0	0	1	1	0	0	0	0	1	0	0
		2	1	1	0	0	0	1	1	0	0	0	1	0
		3	1	1	1	0	0	0	0	1	1	0	0	1
	Female	1	1	0	0	1	1	0	0	0	0	0	0	0
		2	1	1	0	0	0	1	1	0	0	0	0	0
		3	1	1	1	0	0	0	0	1	1	0	0	0
PDL	Male	1	1	0	0	1	-1	0	0	0	0	1	0	0
		2	1	1	0	0	0	1	-1	0	0	0	1	0
		3	1	1	1	0	0	0	0	1	-1	0	0	1
	Female	1	1	0	0	1	-1	0	0	0	0	0	0	0
		2	1	1	0	0	0	1	-1	0	0	0	0	0
		3	1	1	1	0	0	0	0	1	-1	0	0	0
Control	Male	1	1	0	0	-2	0	0	0	0	0	1	0	0
		2	1	1	0	0	0	-2	0	0	0	0	1	0
		3	1	1	1	0	0	0	0	-2	0	0	0	1
	Female	1	1	0	0	-2	0	0	0	0	0	0	0	0
		2	1	1	0	0	0	-2	0	0	0	0	0	0
		3	1	1	1	0	0	0	0	-2	0	0	0	0

In the MODEL statement, the specification in parentheses following the model matrix requests tests of significance of individual parameters. In addition, joint tests of parameter subsets are also requested. These results are included in the ANOVA table in Output 13.39.

Output 13.39   ANOVA Table for Nested Model

```
                    ANALYSIS-OF-VARIANCE TABLE

        Source              DF    Chi-Square      Prob
        ---------------------------------------------------
        Intercept            1      2903.33      0.0000
        Year                 2       115.07      0.0000
          Year 2 Increment   1        71.36      0.0000
          Year 3 Increment   1         4.12      0.0423
        Program              6        13.28      0.0388
          Year 1             2         9.75      0.0076
            Education        1         9.48      0.0021
            Method           1         0.22      0.6364
          Year 2             2         2.90      0.2342
            Education        1         0.79      0.3734
            Method           1         2.05      0.1520
          Year 3             2         1.18      0.5537
            Education        1         0.03      0.8575
            Method           1         1.14      0.2850
        Gender               3       359.75      0.0000
          Year 1             1       144.14      0.0000
          Year 2             1       140.45      0.0000
          Year 3             1        97.27      0.0000

        RESIDUAL             6         1.52      0.9581
```

Although parameterized differently, this model contains exactly the same effects as the previous factorial model. Thus, the lack-of-fit tests are identical. While the 2 df PROGRAM effect at year 1 is clearly significant, the 1 df component comparing the two driver education methods (SPC, PDL) is not significantly different from zero. In addition, the 2 df PROGRAM effects at both year 2 and year 3 are nonsignificant.

The following CONTRAST statements test that there is no EDUCATION × YEAR interaction and no METHOD × YEAR interaction. Note that EDUCATION assesses the effect of driver education by comparing the SPC and PDL groups to the control group, while METHOD contrasts the two driver education methods (SPC versus PDL).

```
contrast 'Education x Year' all_parms 0 0 0 1 0 0 0 -1  0 0 0 0,
                            all_parms 0 0 0 0 0 1 0 -1  0 0 0 0;
contrast 'Method x Year'    all_parms 0 0 0 0 1 0 0  0 -1 0 0 0,
                            all_parms 0 0 0 0 0 0 1  0 -1 0 0 0;
run;
```

Output 13.40 indicates there is no METHOD × YEAR interaction ($Q_W = 0.35$, 2 df, $p = 0.8408$), while the EDUCATION × YEAR interaction is nearly significant at the 0.05 level ($Q_W = 5.73$, 2 df, $p = 0.0571$). Recall that in the reduced factorial model, the chi-square statistic from the four df test of the PROGRAM × YEAR interaction was 6.02.

Output 13.40   Tests of EDUCATION × YEAR and METHOD × YEAR Interactions

```
                  ANALYSIS OF CONTRASTS

        Contrast           DF    Chi-Square      Prob
        ---------------------------------------------------
        Education x Year    2         5.73      0.0571
        Method x Year       2         0.35      0.8408
```

Since the METHOD effects at years 1, 2, and 3 are individually nonsignificant in Output 13.39, a CONTRAST statement can be used to test the joint significance of these three parameters. Similarly, while the EDUCATION effect at year 1 is clearly significant, the effects at years 2 and 3 are nonsignificant. Thus, you may wish to test the joint significance of the EDUCATION effects at years 2 and 3. The CONTRAST statements are as follows:

```
contrast 'Method Effects'     all_parms 0 0 0 0 1 0 0  0  0 0 0 0,
                              all_parms 0 0 0 0 0 0 1  0  0 0 0 0,
                              all_parms 0 0 0 0 0 0 0  0  1 0 0 0;
contrast 'Educ. (yrs. 2 & 3)' all_parms 0 0 0 0 0 1 0  0  0 0 0 0,
                              all_parms 0 0 0 0 0 0 0  1  0 0 0 0;
run;
```

Output 13.41 indicates that the METHOD effects are jointly nonsignificant, as are the EDUCATION effects at years 2 and 3.

Output 13.41   Tests of METHOD and EDUCATION Effects

```
                   ANALYSIS OF CONTRASTS

Contrast                   DF   Chi-Square    Prob
-------------------------------------------------------
Method Effects              3       3.23      0.3574
Educ. (yrs. 2 & 3)         2       0.81      0.6671
```

These results motivate a reduced model with an overall intercept, incremental YEAR effects for years 2 and 3, an incremental effect comparing driver education (SPC, PDL) to control at year 1, and separate incremental GENDER effects for each of the three years. The MODEL statement is

```
model coll1*coll2*coll3=(1 0 0 1 1 0 0,
                         1 1 0 0 0 1 0,
                         1 1 1 0 0 0 1,
                         1 0 0 1 0 0 0,
                         1 1 0 0 0 0 0,
                         1 1 1 0 0 0 0,
                         1 0 0 1 1 0 0,
                         1 1 0 0 0 1 0,
                         1 1 1 0 0 0 1,
                         1 0 0 1 0 0 0,
                         1 1 0 0 0 0 0,
                         1 1 1 0 0 0 0,
                         1 0 0 0 1 0 0,
                         1 1 0 0 0 1 0,
                         1 1 1 0 0 0 1,
                         1 0 0 0 0 0 0,
                         1 1 0 0 0 0 0,
                         1 1 1 0 0 0 0)
                        (1='Intercept',
                       2 3='Year',
                         2=' Year 2 Increment',
```

```
                              3='  Year 3 Increment',
                              4='Year 1 Education',
                        5 6 7='Gender',
                              5='  Year 1',
                              6='  Year 2',
                              7='  Year 3') / noprofile;
        run;
```

Output 13.42 displays the response functions and model matrix and Output 13.43 displays the ANOVA table. This model provides a very good fit to the observed data ($Q_W = 5.64$, 11 df, $p = 0.896$).

Output 13.42   Response Functions and Model Matrix for Reduced Model

Sample	Function Number	Response Function	1	2	3	4	5	6	7
1	1	-1.85128	1	0	0	1	1	0	0
	2	-1.47313	1	1	0	0	0	1	0
	3	-1.47844	1	1	1	0	0	0	1
2	1	-2.51845	1	0	0	1	0	0	0
	2	-2.03082	1	1	0	0	0	0	0
	3	-1.97259	1	1	1	0	0	0	0
3	1	-1.86170	1	0	0	1	1	0	0
	2	-1.54791	1	1	0	0	0	1	0
	3	-1.57069	1	1	1	0	0	0	1
4	1	-2.59399	1	0	0	1	0	0	0
	2	-2.13127	1	1	0	0	0	0	0
	3	-1.98731	1	1	1	0	0	0	0
5	1	-2.02173	1	0	0	0	1	0	0
	2	-1.53397	1	1	0	0	0	1	0
	3	-1.50947	1	1	1	0	0	0	1
6	1	-2.78918	1	0	0	0	0	0	0
	2	-2.15881	1	1	0	0	0	0	0
	3	-2.02372	1	1	1	0	0	0	0

(DESIGN MATRIX columns are labeled 1 through 7)

Output 13.43   ANOVA Table for Reduced Model

ANALYSIS-OF-VARIANCE TABLE

Source	DF	Chi-Square	Prob
Intercept	1	1762.08	0.0000
Year	2	104.31	0.0000
Year 2 Increment	1	73.55	0.0000
Year 3 Increment	1	3.96	0.0467
Year 1 Education	1	9.15	0.0025
Gender	3	360.23	0.0000
Year 1	1	144.40	0.0000
Year 2	1	140.04	0.0000
Year 3	1	98.02	0.0000
RESIDUAL	11	5.64	0.8960

With reference to the estimated parameters displayed in Output 13.44, the odds of collision involvement during the first year are estimated to be $e^{0.1857} = 1.2$ times higher for students randomized to driver education than for control students. During years 2 and 3, there appears to be no effect due to driver education. These somewhat surprising results agree with other analyses of the entire data set (Stock et al. 1983; Lund, Williams, and Zador 1986). One possible explanation is that the only effect of driver education is that students obtain their licenses earlier.

Output 13.44   Parameter Estimates from Reduced Model

```
            ANALYSIS OF WEIGHTED-LEAST-SQUARES ESTIMATES

                                    Standard   Chi-
    Effect            Parameter  Estimate   Error    Square   Prob
    -------------------------------------------------------------
    MODEL                 1      -2.7539    0.0656  1762.08   0.0000
                          2       0.6507    0.0759    73.55   0.0000
                          3       0.1083    0.0544     3.96   0.0467
                          4       0.1857    0.0614     9.15   0.0025
                          5       0.7182    0.0598   144.40   0.0000
                          6       0.5862    0.0495   140.04   0.0000
                          7       0.4775    0.0482    98.02   0.0000
```

The parameters for the gender effect at years 1, 2, and 3 indicate that the odds of accident involvement are higher for males than for females at all three years but that the magnitude of the difference decreases over time. The following CONTRAST statements test various hypotheses concerning the gender parameters.

```
contrast 'Equal. of Gender Effects' all_parms 0 0 0 0 1 -1  0,
                                    all_parms 0 0 0 0 1  0 -1;
contrast '   Year 1=Year 2'         all_parms 0 0 0 0 1 -1  0;
contrast '   Year 1=Year 3'         all_parms 0 0 0 0 1  0 -1;
contrast '   Year 2=Year 3'         all_parms 0 0 0 0 0  1 -1;
contrast 'Gender Nonlinearity'      all_parms 0 0 0 0 1 -2  1;
run;
```

As displayed in Output 13.45, the two df test of the null hypothesis of equality of the gender effects is clearly significant ($Q_W = 10.21$, $p = 0.006$). The separate pairwise comparisons indicate that the effect at year 1 differs significantly from the effect at year 3 but that the comparisons between year 1 and year 2, and between year 2 and year 3, are not statistically significant. The test of nonlinearity of the gender effects across time is also not statistically significant ($Q_W = 0.04$, $p = 0.8503$). Based on these results, you could now fit a final model in which the three separate gender effects are replaced by two parameters (a common incremental effect for males and a linear year effect in males).

Output 13.45   Tests of Hypotheses Concerning Gender Effects

```
                    ANALYSIS OF CONTRASTS

    Contrast                   DF   Chi-Square    Prob
    -------------------------------------------------------
    Equal. of Gender Effects    2      10.21     0.0061
        Year 1=Year 2           1       2.99     0.0839
        Year 1=Year 3           1      10.17     0.0014
        Year 2=Year 3           1       2.54     0.1112
    Gender Nonlinearity         1       0.04     0.8503
```

13.4 Advanced Topic: The Generalized Estimating Equation (GEE) Method

13.4.1 Introduction

The WLS methodology described in Section 13.2 is a useful approach to the analysis of repeated binary and ordered categorical outcome variables. However, it can only accommodate categorical explanatory variables. In addition, the WLS methodology requires sufficient sample size for the marginal response functions at each time point within each subpopulation from the multi-way crossclassification of the explanatory variables to have an approximately multivariate normal distribution.

Recently, several authors have proposed extensions of generalized linear models (McCullagh and Nelder 1989) for the analysis of repeated measurements, for example, Liang and Zeger (1986), Zeger and Liang (1986), Wei and Stram (1988), Stram, Wei, and Ware (1988), Moulton and Zeger (1989), and Zhao and Prentice (1990). These semi-parametric approaches are useful in longitudinal data analyses with univariate outcomes for which the quasi-likelihood formulation is sensible, for example, normal, Poisson, binomial, and gamma response variables. The methods allow for missing observations and continuous covariates that may even be time dependent.

In this section, the generalized estimating equation (GEE) approach (Liang and Zeger 1986; Zeger and Liang 1986) for regression analysis of repeated measurements is discussed. The primary reasons for considering the GEE approach are that it can be used for repeated categorical outcomes (specifically, binary and Poisson response variables) and that the methodology has been implemented in the SAS/IML macro GEE1 (Karim and Zeger 1988).

13.4.2 Methodology

The GEE methodology models a known function of the marginal expectation of the dependent variable as a linear function of one or more explanatory variables. As in the generalized linear models framework, the variance is assumed to be a known function of the mean. In addition, a *working correlation matrix* for the observations from each subject is required. The GEE methodology provides consistent estimators of the regression coefficients and of their variances under weak assumptions about the actual correlation among a subject's observations. This approach avoids the need for multivariate distributions by assuming only a functional form for the marginal distribution at each time point. The covariance structure across time is treated as a nuisance. The method relies on the independence across subjects to consistently estimate the variance of the proposed estimators even when the assumed working correlation structure is incorrect. Zeger (1988), Zeger, Liang, and Albert (1988), and Liang, Zeger, and Qaqish (1992) provide further background on the GEE methodology.

For ease of notation, consider the situation in which repeated measurements are obtained at t time points from each of n subjects. (Note that if the number and spacing of the repeated measurements vary among subjects, t can be set equal to the total number of distinct measurement times.) Although this notation is most natural for longitudinal studies, it will also be used for the general case of correlated responses. For example, t might instead denote the number of conditions under which dependent measurements are obtained from each subject, or there might be n clusters with at most t experimental units per cluster.

Now let y_{ij} denote the response from subject i at time j, for $i = 1, \ldots, n$ and $j = 1, \ldots, t$. Although the GEE methodology can be used for normally distributed outcomes, attention is restricted to situations in which each y_{ij} is a binary $(0, 1)$ outcome or a Poisson count $(0, 1, 2, \ldots)$. Also let $x_{ij} = (x_{ij1}, \ldots, x_{ijp})'$ denote a $p \times 1$ vector of explanatory variables (covariates) associated with y_{ij}. If all covariates are time independent, then $x_{i1} = x_{i2} = \cdots = x_{it}$. Note that y_{ij} and x_{ij} are missing if observations are not obtained at time j.

The first step of the GEE approach is to relate the marginal response $\mu_{ij} = \text{E}(y_{ij})$ to a linear combination of the covariates: $g(\mu_{ij}) = x'_{ij}\beta$, where $\beta = (\beta_1, \ldots, \beta_p)'$ is a $p \times 1$ vector of unknown parameters and g is a known link function. Common link functions are the logit function $g(x) = \log(x/(1 - x))$ for binary responses and the log function $g(x) = \log(x)$ for Poisson counts. The $p \times 1$ parameter vector β characterizes how the cross-sectional response distribution depends on the explanatory variables.

The second step is to describe the variance of y_{ij} as a function of the mean: $\text{Var}(y_{ij}) = v(\mu_{ij})\,\phi$, where v is a known variance function and ϕ is a possibly unknown scale parameter. For binary responses, $v(\mu_{ij}) = \mu_{ij}(1 - \mu_{ij})$; and for Poisson responses, $v(\mu_{ij}) = \mu_{ij}$. For these two types of response variables, $\phi = 1$.

The third step is to choose the form of a $t \times t$ working correlation matrix $R_i(\alpha)$ for each $y_i = (y_{i1}, \ldots, y_{it})'$. The (j, j') element of $R_i(\alpha)$ is the known, hypothesized, or estimated correlation between y_{ij} and $y_{ij'}$. This working correlation matrix may depend on a vector of unknown parameters α, which is the same for all subjects. You assume that $R_i(\alpha)$ is known except for a fixed number of parameters α that must be estimated from the data. Although this correlation matrix can differ from subject to subject, you commonly use a working correlation matrix $R(\alpha)$ that approximates the average dependence among repeated observations over subjects.

R is called a working correlation matrix because with non-normal responses, the actual correlation among a subject's outcomes may depend on the mean values and, hence, on $x'_{ij}\beta$. The GEE method yields consistent estimates of the regression coefficients and their variances, even with misspecification of the structure of the covariance matrix. In addition, the loss of efficiency from an incorrect choice of R is usually not consequential when the number of subjects is large.

Several possibilities for the working correlation structure have been suggested (Liang and Zeger 1986). First, when the number of subjects is large relative to the number of observations per subject, the influence of correlation is often small enough so that the ordinary least-squares regression coefficients are nearly efficient. The correlations among repeated measures, however, may have a substantial effect on the estimated variances of the parameters and hence must be taken into account to make correct inferences. This suggests the *independence* working model with R equal to the identity matrix. The independence model adopts the working assumption that repeated observations for a subject are independent. In this case, solving the GEE is the same as fitting the usual regression models for independent data and can be accomplished using standard software packages. However, standard software packages do not provide the correct variances and covariances for repeated measures data. This working model leads to consistent estimates of the parameter vector and its covariance matrix given only that the regression model is specified correctly.

The *exchangeable* working correlation model assumes that the correlation is constant between any two observation times, that is, $R_{jj'} = \alpha$, for $j \neq j'$. This is the correlation structure assumed in a random effects model. Although the assumption of constant correlation between any two repeated measurements may not be justified in a longitudinal study, it is often reasonable in situations in which the repeated measures are not obtained over time. An arbitrary number of observations per subject are permissible with both the independence and exchangeable working correlation structures.

Finally, when the correlation matrix is completely unspecified, there are $t(t-1)/2$ parameters to be estimated. This provides the most efficient estimator but is useful only when there are relatively few observation times. In addition, when there are missing data and/or varying numbers of observations per subject, estimation of the complete correlation structure may result in a nonpositive definite matrix. The SAS/IML macro GEE1 permits the use of the unspecified correlation structure only when there are no missing data and every subject has the same number of observations. Liang and Zeger (1986) also discuss other possibilities for the working correlation matrix.

The fourth step of the GEE approach is to estimate the parameter vector β and its covariance matrix. First, let A_i be the $t \times t$ diagonal matrix with $v(\mu_{ij})$ as the jth diagonal element. The working covariance matrix for y_i is $V_i(\alpha) = \phi\, A_i^{1/2}\, R_i(\alpha)\, A_i^{1/2}$. The GEE estimate of β is the solution of the estimating equation

$$U(\beta) = \sum_{i=1}^{n} \left(\frac{\partial \mu_i}{\partial \beta}\right)' [V_i(\widehat{\alpha})]^{-1} (y_i - \mu_i) = 0_p$$

where $\mu_i = (\mu_{i1}, \ldots, \mu_{it})'$, 0_p is the $p \times 1$ vector $(0, \ldots, 0)'$, and $\widehat{\alpha}$ is a consistent estimate of α.

This estimating equation is solved by iterating between quasi-likelihood methods for estimating β and a robust method for estimating α as a function of β, as follows:

1. Given current estimates of $R_i(\alpha)$ and ϕ, calculate an updated estimate of β using iteratively reweighted least squares.

2. Given the estimate $\widehat{\beta}$ of β, calculate standardized residuals

$$g_{ij} = \frac{y_{ij} - \widehat{\mu}_{ij}}{\sqrt{\left[[V_i(\widehat{\alpha})]^{-1}\right]_{jj}}}$$

3. Use the residuals g_{ij} to consistently estimate α and ϕ.

4. Repeat steps 1–3 until convergence.

The variance of $\widehat{\beta}$ is then estimated by $\widehat{\mathrm{Var}}(\widehat{\beta}) = M_0^{-1} M_1 M_0^{-1}$, where

$$M_0 = \sum_{i=1}^{n} \left(\frac{\partial \mu_i}{\partial \beta}\right)' [V_i(\widehat{\alpha})]^{-1} \left(\frac{\partial \mu_i}{\partial \beta}\right)$$

and

$$M_1 = \sum_{i=1}^{n} \left(\frac{\partial \mu_i}{\partial \beta}\right)' [V_i(\hat{\alpha})]^{-1} (y_i - \mu_i)(y_i - \mu_i)' [V_i(\hat{\alpha})]^{-1} \left(\frac{\partial \mu_i}{\partial \beta}\right)$$

This is a consistent estimator of $\mathrm{Var}(\hat{\beta})$ even when $\mathrm{Var}(y_{ij}) \neq \phi\, v(\mu_{ij})$ or when $R_i(\alpha)$ is not the correlation matrix of y_i.

13.4.3   Example

Tables 13.8 and 13.9 display data from a clinical trial comparing two treatments for a respiratory illness (Koch et al. 1990). In each of two centers, eligible patients were randomly assigned to active treatment or placebo. During treatment, respiratory status (categorized here as 0=poor, 1=good) was determined at four visits. Potential explanatory variables were center, sex, and baseline respiratory status (all dichotomous), as well as age (in years) at the time of study entry. There were 111 patients (54 active, 57 placebo) with no missing data for responses or covariates.

Since age is a continuous covariate, it is not possible to analyze these data using the CATMOD procedure. Even without considering age as a covariate, the four dichotomous covariates define $2^4 = 16$ subpopulations. Since there are four response functions, the total sample size of 111 patients is not large enough to support a weighted least squares repeated measures analysis. However, the GEE marginal modeling approach is applicable.

Suppose y_{ij} denotes the respiratory status (0=poor, 1=good) at visit $j = 1, \ldots, 4$ for subject $i = 1, \ldots, 111$ and let $\mu_{ij} = \mathrm{E}(y_{ij})$. In addition to the intercept ($x_{ij1} \equiv 1$), the covariates of interest are treatment (x_{ij2}), center (x_{ij3}), sex (x_{ij4}), age (x_{ij5}), and baseline respiratory status (x_{ij6}). In this example, the covariates for each subject are time-independent (constant over j). The four dichotomous covariates are coded as

$$x_{ij2} = \begin{cases} 0 & \text{placebo} \\ 1 & \text{active} \end{cases} \qquad x_{ij3} = \begin{cases} 0 & \text{center 1} \\ 1 & \text{center 2} \end{cases}$$

$$x_{ij4} = \begin{cases} 0 & \text{male} \\ 1 & \text{female} \end{cases} \qquad x_{ij6} = \begin{cases} 0 & \text{poor} \\ 1 & \text{good} \end{cases}$$

Using the logit link function $h(x) = \log(x/(1-x))$ and the variance function $g(\mu_{ij}) = \mu_{ij}(1 - \mu_{ij})$, the model is $h(\mu_{ij}) = x_{ij}' \beta$, where $x_{ij}' = (x_{ij1}, \ldots, x_{ij6})$. Since there are only four time points and no missing data, the unspecified working correlation structure should be most efficient.

The following statements create a SAS data set from input data lines structured as shown in Tables 13.8 and 13.9. Since the input data are organized with one observation per subject, the DATA step outputs four observations for each subject (one for each of the four time points). Note also that the intercept term and the indicator covariates for treatment group, center, and sex are created in the DATA step.

Table 13.8   Respiratory Disorder Data for 56 Subjects from Center 1

Patient	Treatment	Sex	Age	Respiratory Status (0=poor, 1=good)				
				Baseline	Visit 1	Visit 2	Visit 3	Visit 4
1	P	M	46	0	0	0	0	0
2	P	M	28	0	0	0	0	0
3	A	M	23	1	1	1	1	1
4	P	M	44	1	1	1	1	0
5	P	F	13	1	1	1	1	1
6	A	M	34	0	0	0	0	0
7	P	M	43	0	1	0	1	1
8	A	M	28	0	0	0	0	0
9	A	M	31	1	1	1	1	1
10	P	M	37	1	0	1	1	0
11	A	M	30	1	1	1	1	1
12	A	M	14	0	1	1	1	0
13	P	M	23	1	1	0	0	0
14	P	M	30	0	0	0	0	0
15	P	M	20	1	1	1	1	1
16	A	M	22	0	0	0	0	1
17	P	M	25	0	0	0	0	0
18	A	F	47	0	0	1	1	1
19	P	F	31	0	0	0	0	0
20	A	M	20	1	1	0	1	0
21	A	M	26	0	1	0	1	0
22	A	M	46	1	1	1	1	1
23	A	M	32	1	1	1	1	1
24	A	M	48	0	1	0	0	0
25	P	F	35	0	0	0	0	0
26	A	M	26	0	0	0	0	0
27	P	M	23	1	1	0	1	1
28	P	F	36	0	1	1	0	0
29	P	M	19	0	1	1	0	0
30	A	M	28	0	0	0	0	0
31	P	M	37	0	0	0	0	0
32	A	M	23	0	1	1	1	1
33	A	M	30	1	1	1	1	0
34	P	M	15	0	0	1	1	0
35	A	M	26	0	0	0	1	0
36	P	F	45	0	0	0	0	0
37	A	M	31	0	0	1	0	0
38	A	M	50	0	0	0	0	0
39	P	M	28	0	0	0	0	0
40	P	M	26	0	0	0	0	0
41	P	M	14	0	0	0	0	1
42	A	M	31	0	0	1	0	0
43	P	M	13	1	1	1	1	1
44	P	M	27	0	0	0	0	0
45	P	M	26	0	1	0	1	1
46	P	M	49	0	0	0	0	0
47	P	M	63	0	0	0	0	0
48	A	M	57	1	1	1	1	1
49	P	M	27	1	1	1	1	1
50	A	M	22	0	0	1	1	1
51	A	M	15	0	0	1	1	1
52	P	M	43	0	0	0	1	0
53	A	F	32	0	0	0	1	0
54	A	M	11	1	1	1	1	0
55	P	M	24	1	1	1	1	1
56	A	M	25	0	1	1	0	1

Table 13.9   Respiratory Disorder Data for 55 Subjects from Center 2

Patient	Treatment	Sex	Age	Respiratory Status (0=poor, 1=good)				
				Baseline	Visit 1	Visit 2	Visit 3	Visit 4
1	P	F	39	0	0	0	0	0
2	A	M	25	0	0	1	1	1
3	A	M	58	1	1	1	1	1
4	P	F	51	1	1	0	1	1
5	P	F	32	1	0	0	1	1
6	P	M	45	1	1	0	0	0
7	P	F	44	1	1	1	1	1
8	P	F	48	0	0	0	0	0
9	A	M	26	0	1	1	1	1
10	A	M	14	0	1	1	1	1
11	P	F	48	0	0	0	0	0
12	A	M	13	1	1	1	1	1
13	P	M	20	0	1	1	1	1
14	A	M	37	1	1	0	0	1
15	A	M	25	1	1	1	1	1
16	A	M	20	0	0	0	0	0
17	P	F	58	0	1	0	0	0
18	P	M	38	1	1	0	0	0
19	A	M	55	1	1	1	1	1
20	A	M	24	1	1	1	1	1
21	P	F	36	1	1	0	0	1
22	P	M	36	0	1	1	1	1
23	A	F	60	1	1	1	1	1
24	P	M	15	1	0	0	1	1
25	A	M	25	1	1	1	1	0
26	A	M	35	1	1	1	1	1
27	A	M	19	1	1	0	1	1
28	P	F	31	1	1	1	1	1
29	A	M	21	1	1	1	1	1
30	A	F	37	0	1	1	1	1
31	P	M	52	0	1	1	1	1
32	A	M	55	0	0	1	1	0
33	P	M	19	1	0	0	1	1
34	P	M	20	1	0	1	1	1
35	P	M	42	1	0	0	0	0
36	A	M	41	1	1	1	1	1
37	A	M	52	0	0	0	0	0
38	P	F	47	0	1	1	0	1
39	P	M	11	1	1	1	1	1
40	P	M	14	0	0	0	1	0
41	P	M	15	1	1	1	1	1
42	P	M	66	1	1	1	1	1
43	A	M	34	0	1	1	0	1
44	P	M	43	0	0	0	0	0
45	P	M	33	1	1	1	0	1
46	P	M	48	1	1	0	0	0
47	A	M	20	0	1	1	1	1
48	P	F	39	1	0	1	0	0
49	A	M	28	0	1	0	0	0
50	P	F	38	0	0	0	0	0
51	A	M	43	1	1	1	1	0
52	A	F	39	0	1	1	1	1
53	A	M	68	0	1	1	1	1
54	A	F	63	1	1	1	1	1
55	A	M	31	1	1	1	1	1

```
data resp;
   keep id intercpt active center2 female age baseline visit outcome;
   input center id treatmnt $ sex $ age baseline visit1-visit4;
   intercpt=1;
   active=(treatmnt='A');
   center2=(center=2);
   female=(sex='F');
   visit=1;   outcome=visit1;   output;
   visit=2;   outcome=visit2;   output;
   visit=3;   outcome=visit3;   output;
   visit=4;   outcome=visit4;   output;
   cards;
1  1 P M 46 0 0 0 0 0
1  2 P M 28 0 0 0 0 0
1  3 A M 23 1 1 1 1 1
      .   .   .
2 53 A M 68 0 1 1 1 1
2 54 A F 63 1 1 1 1 1
2 55 A M 31 1 1 1 1 1
;
run;
```

The SAS/IML macro GEE1 [‡] is then used to estimate the vector of regression parameters
and its covariance matrix. This macro, which requires SAS/IML software, allocates
memory dynamically. Thus, there is no constraint within GEE1 regarding the number of
explanatory variables or number of observations. It is only limited by the amount of
memory available. The statements are as follows:

```
%GEE1(DATA=resp,
      YVAR=outcome,
      XVAR=intercpt active center2 female age baseline,
      LINK=3,
      VARI=3,
      CORR=6);
run;
```

The DATA= option of GEE1 specifies the input SAS data set. The YVAR= option
specifies the name of the response variable, and the XVAR= option lists the covariates to
be included in the model. A covariate for the overall intercept must be defined and
explicitly specified, if desired, and categorical covariates must be coded using indicator
variables in the DATA step.

The permissible values of the LINK= option, which specifies the choice of link function,
are 1=identity, 2=log, 3=logit, and 4=reciprocal. In analyzing repeated categorical data,
the log (for Poisson counts) and logit (for dichotomous responses) are most useful.
Similarly, the VARI=option specifies the relationship between the variance and the mean;
permissible values of this option are 1 (variance=1), 2 (variance=mean), 3
(variance=mean(1−mean)), and 4 (variance=mean squared). In most applications, the
VARI= option will be set equal to the same value as the LINK= option.

[‡]If you do not have access to this macro, the Technical Support Division at SAS Institute can provide
current information on how to obtain it.

The macro GEE1 implements a wide variety of working correlation structures using the CORR=, M=, and R= options. The simplest three choices are the identity, exchangeable, and unspecified structures, which are specified by CORR=1, CORR=4, and CORR=6, respectively. The unspecified correlation structure (CORR=6) can only be used if measurements are obtained at the same time points for all subjects and there are no missing data. The exchangeable (CORR=4) working correlation structure requires a minimum of two repeated measurements for every subject.

The working correlation matrix can be set equal to a specified matrix using the R= option, in which case the entire matrix is given. Each row must begin on a new line and each column must be separated by a space. The R= option must be used in conjunction with CORR=1. The other types of permissible working correlation structures are stationary M-dependent (CORR=2), nonstationary M-dependent (CORR=3), and autoregressive of order M (CORR=5); these are discussed by Liang and Zeger (1986). For each of these three choices of the CORR= option, the order is specified using the M= option. The value of the M= option must be less than the minimum number of repeated measurements per subject.

Since the unspecified correlation structure was used in this example, the R= and M= options are unnecessary. Four other options of GEE1 are also not used in this example. The ID= option specifies the name of the subject identifier variable. Since the default variable name (ID) was used, it was not necessary to specify this option. The OUT= option creates an output SAS data set containing fitted values and residuals, the ITER= option specifies the maximum number of iterations (default=20), and the CRIT= option defines the convergence criterion. The default value for the convergence criterion (the maximum absolute relative change in the estimate of the vector of regression parameters) is 0.001.

Output 13.46   Results from the GEE1 Macro

```
Regression analysis using GEE:                           ( GEE1 - Ver 1.00 )
==============================
Outcome variable: OUTCOME

Covariates: INTERCPT ACTIVE    CENTER2  FEMALE    AGE       BASELINE

Link:  3 (Logit)

Variance:  3 (Binomial)

Correlation:  6 (Unspecified)

Total number of records read:        444

Total number of clusters:    111

Maximum and minimum cluster size      4 and       4

Averages of Outcome variable and Covariates (over all)

               OUTCOME  INTERCPT   ACTIVE   CENTER2    FEMALE       AGE
:              BASELINE

Observations:  0.5585586        1 0.4864865 0.4954955 0.2072072 33.279279
:              0.4504505

Cluster Means: 0.5585586        1 0.4864865 0.4954955 0.2072072 33.279279
:              0.4504505
```

The output of the GEE1 macro first summarizes the data set and analysis options (Output 13.46). Descriptive statistics concerning the outcome variable and covariates and initial estimates of the regression parameters are also provided.

Output 13.47 contains the initial estimates of the regression parameters.

Output 13.47   Results from the GEE1 Macro (continued)

```
Initial estimate of regression coefficients:
INTERCPT  0.321798
ACTIVE    0.2436191
CENTER2   0.1238693
FEMALE    0.0290492
AGE       -0.003622
BASELINE 0.3805003
```

Output 13.48 and Output 13.49 display the parameter estimates at each iteration. In this example, the estimation procedure converged after five iterations.

Output 13.48   Results from the GEE1 Macro (continued)

```
===> Iteration:    1

           Estimate

INTERCPT  -0.780868
ACTIVE    1.0379366
CENTER2   0.5227862
FEMALE     0.085526
AGE       -0.014006
BASELINE  1.7045106

===> Iteration:    2

           Estimate

INTERCPT  -0.881353
ACTIVE    1.2326007
CENTER2   0.6442539
FEMALE     0.110505
AGE       -0.017256
BASELINE  1.8843409

===> Iteration:    3

           Estimate

INTERCPT  -0.887007
ACTIVE    1.2454388
CENTER2   0.6552745
FEMALE    0.1140933
AGE        -0.01758
BASELINE  1.8948548
```

Output 13.49   Results from the GEE1 Macro (continued)

```
===> Iteration:    4

           Estimate

INTERCPT  -0.886879
ACTIVE     1.2454673
CENTER2    0.6555169
FEMALE     0.114341
AGE       -0.01759
BASELINE   1.8944705

===> Iteration:    5

           Estimate

INTERCPT  -0.886875
ACTIVE     1.2454763
CENTER2    0.6555148
FEMALE     0.1143511
AGE       -0.01759
BASELINE   1.894446

Convergence after    5 iteration(s).
```

Output 13.50 displays the estimated working correlation matrix and the vector of
estimated parameters and their variances and covariances.

Output 13.50   Results from the GEE1 Macro (continued)

```
Working Correlation:
        1 0.3214887 0.2056208 0.2836194
0.3214887         1 0.4244621 0.3433206
0.2056208 0.4244621         1 0.3802176
0.2836194 0.3433206 0.3802176         1

Scale parameter: 1.0121199

Mean Squared Error: 0.1843533

Standardized (scaled) MSE:        1

Variance estimate (robust):

          INTERCPT    ACTIVE   CENTER2    FEMALE       AGE  BASELINE

INTERCPT 0.2086207 -0.059055 0.0001147 -0.004262 -0.004051 -0.051889
ACTIVE   -0.374201 0.1193859 -0.015771 0.0575328 -0.000837 0.0326604
CENTER2  0.0007152 -0.129935 0.1233972 -0.044456 -0.000394 -0.035571
FEMALE    -0.02117 0.3777992 -0.287144  0.194248 -0.002242 0.0396068
AGE      -0.689496 -0.188274 -0.087116 -0.395388 0.0001655 -0.000398
BASELINE -0.330134 0.2746851  -0.29426 0.2611446 -0.090009 0.1184187

NOTE: Covariances are above diagonal and correlations are below diagonal.
```

Table 13.10 displays the estimated regression coefficients, standard errors and
standardized statistics (estimate/s.e.) for the intercept, treatment, center, sex, age, and
baseline respiratory status effects. The results from the independence working correlation
model are also shown. There are clearly significant effects of treatment and baseline status

and some evidence of a difference between centers. There is little difference between the results of the unspecified and independence working correlation models. Adjusting for the main effects of center and baseline respiratory status, estimates of the odds of a good response versus a poor response are approximately $e^{1.25} = 3.5$ times higher for the standard treatment than for the placebo treatment. The corresponding adjusted odds ratios for center and baseline respiratory status are approximately equal to $e^{0.65} = 1.9$ (center 2 versus center 1) and $e^{1.9} = 6.7$ (good versus poor baseline status). A more detailed analysis would also investigate the existence of interactions between the explanatory variables.

In this analysis, the marginal relationship between the outcome variable and the covariates was modeled. You could also assess the effect of the repeated measures variable by including one or more covariates involving the VISIT variable and its interactions with the other covariates. For example, if you wanted to investigate whether the effect of treatment changed over time, covariates for the visit $\times$ treatment interaction could be included.

Table 13.10   GEE Analyses of Respiratory Disorder Data

Covariate	Correlation Structure	Regression coefficients		
		Estimate	Standard Error	Est./S.E.
Intercept	Unspecified	−0.887	0.457	−1.94
	Independence	−0.856	0.456	−1.88
Treatment	Unspecified	1.245	0.346	3.60
	Independence	1.265	0.347	3.65
Center	Unspecified	0.656	0.351	1.87
	Independence	0.649	0.353	1.84
Sex	Unspecified	0.114	0.441	0.26
	Independence	0.137	0.440	0.31
Age	Unspecified	−0.018	0.013	−1.37
	Independence	−0.019	0.013	−1.45
Baseline	Unspecified	1.894	0.344	5.51
Status	Independence	1.846	0.346	5.33

Chapter 14
Loglinear Models

Chapter Table of Contents

Chapter 14
Loglinear Models

14.1   Introduction

Chapters 2–6 discuss methods for testing hypotheses of no association in two-way and stratified two-way contingency tables. These approaches focus on hypothesis testing rather than on model fitting and parameter estimation. In contrast, Chapters 8–12 describe logistic regression and weighted least squares methods for modeling a categorical response variable as a function of one or more categorical and/or continuous explanatory variables. These methods, which are analogous to ANOVA and regression techniques for normally distributed response variables, are appropriate when there is a clearly defined response variable of interest and you want to model how the response is affected by a set of explanatory variables or design factors. In such situations, you are most interested in estimating the parameters of a statistical model and in testing hypotheses concerning model parameters.

Loglinear models are another important tool for the analysis of categorical data. This methodology was primarily developed during the 1960s. Although many investigators made significant contributions, Leo Goodman was a particularly influential researcher in the social sciences. Two of his key papers (Goodman 1968, 1970) summarize much of his earlier work. Bishop, Fienberg, and Holland (1975) first comprehensively described the methodology for the general statistical community.

Loglinear model methodology is most appropriate when there is no clear distinction between response and explanatory variables, for example, when all of the variables are observed simultaneously. The loglinear model point of view treats all variables as response variables, and the focus is on statistical independence and dependence. Loglinear modeling of categorical data is analogous to correlation analysis for normally distributed response variables and is useful in assessing patterns of statistical dependence among subsets of variables.

You perform loglinear model analysis in the SAS System by using the CATMOD procedure, even though the structure and syntax of PROC CATMOD was designed originally for regression analyses of categorical response variables. Other programs designed specifically for loglinear modeling may be more convenient to use than PROC CATMOD in carrying out certain routine analyses, such as fitting all possible hierarchical loglinear models to a given data set. On the other hand, the CATMOD procedure permits the fitting of complicated types of loglinear models, some of which can not be fit conveniently using other programs.

Section 14.2 describes the loglinear model for a two-way contingency table and introduces the use of PROC CATMOD for loglinear modeling. Although the simplest application of loglinear models is in testing statistical independence between two categorical variables, the methodology is most useful in situations in which there are several variables. Section 14.3 considers the loglinear model for three-way contingency tables. Section 14.4 demonstrates loglinear modeling for higher-order tables, and Section 14.5 describes the correspondence between logistic models and loglinear models.

14.2 Two-Way Contingency Tables

14.2.1 Loglinear Model for the 2×2 Table

Table 14.1 displays the 2×2 table of frequencies resulting from the crossclassification of a row variable X and a column variable Y, each with two levels. Chapter 2 discusses tests and estimators of association for 2×2 contingency tables arising from several different sampling frameworks described in Section 2.1. In this chapter, attention focuses on tables representing a simple random sample from one population. Therefore, the crossclassification of the two binary responses X and Y yields a single multinomial distribution with total sample size n and cell probabilities π_{ij} displayed in Table 14.2.

Table 14.1   Cell Counts in a 2×2 Contingency Table

	Level of Y		
Level of X	1	2	Total
1	n_{11}	n_{12}	n_{1+}
2	n_{21}	n_{22}	n_{2+}
Total	n_{+1}	n_{+2}	n

Table 14.2   Cell Probabilities in a 2×2 Contingency Table

	Level of Y		
Level of X	1	2	Total
1	π_{11}	π_{12}	π_{1+}
2	π_{21}	π_{22}	π_{2+}
Total	π_{+1}	π_{+2}	1

The motivation for the use of loglinear models is that statistical independence can be expressed in terms of a linear combination of the logarithms of the cell probabilities. In particular, if the variables X and Y in a 2×2 table are statistically independent, then the probability of individuals being in the first row (level 1 of X) among those in the first column (level 1 of Y) would be the same as the probability for the first row among those in the second column (level 2 of Y). Therefore,

$$\frac{\pi_{11}}{\pi_{+1}} = \frac{\pi_{12}}{\pi_{+2}} = \pi_{1+}$$

and $\pi_{11} = \pi_{1+}\pi_{+1}$. Similar arguments lead to the general result that if the row and column variables are independent, then $\pi_{ij} = \pi_{i+}\pi_{+j}$, for $i, j = 1, 2$.

You can then express independence as a general relation involving all four cell probabilities. First, if X and Y are statistically independent

$$\frac{\pi_{11}}{\pi_{+1}} = \frac{\pi_{12}}{\pi_{+2}}$$

Since $\pi_{+1} = \pi_{11} + \pi_{21}$ and $\pi_{+2} = \pi_{12} + \pi_{22}$, the relationship is

$$\frac{\pi_{11}}{\pi_{11} + \pi_{21}} = \frac{\pi_{12}}{\pi_{12} + \pi_{22}}$$

so that $\pi_{11}(\pi_{12} + \pi_{22}) = \pi_{12}(\pi_{11} + \pi_{21})$. This simplifies to $\pi_{11}\pi_{22} = \pi_{12}\pi_{21}$. Therefore, the row and column variables are independent if

$$\Psi = \frac{\pi_{11}\pi_{22}}{\pi_{12}\pi_{21}} = 1$$

where Ψ is called the *cross-product ratio*, or the odds ratio. Taking logarithms of both sides expresses statistical independence as a linear combination of the logarithms of the cell probabilities:

$$\log \Psi = \log \pi_{11} - \log \pi_{12} - \log \pi_{21} + \log \pi_{22} = 0$$

Loglinear models for 2×2 contingency tables involve the logarithm of the cross-product ratio in a special way. The *saturated loglinear model* for a 2×2 table is

$$\log(m_{ij}) = \mu + \lambda_i^X + \lambda_j^Y + \lambda_{ij}^{XY} \qquad i, j = 1, 2$$

where $m_{ij} = n\pi_{ij}$ is the expected frequency in the (i, j) cell. This model is similar to the two-way analysis of variance model for a continuous response y:

$$E(y_{ij}) = \mu + \alpha_i + \beta_j + (\alpha\beta)_{ij}$$

with overall mean μ, main effects α_i and β_j, and interaction effects $(\alpha\beta)_{ij}$. The use of the terms λ_i^X, λ_j^Y, and λ_{ij}^{XY} instead of α_i, β_j, and $(\alpha\beta)_{ij}$ is common loglinear model notation and is especially convenient when considering tables of higher dimensions.

Since there are $1 + 2 + 2 + 4 = 9$ parameters in the saturated loglinear model, but only four observations, the model is overparameterized. Imposing the usual sum-to-zero constraints

$$\sum_{i=1}^{2} \lambda_i^X = 0 \qquad \sum_{j=1}^{2} \lambda_j^Y = 0 \qquad \sum_{i=1}^{2} \lambda_{ij}^{XY} = \sum_{j=1}^{2} \lambda_{ij}^{XY} = 0$$

yields three nonredundant λ parameters (λ_1^X, λ_1^Y, λ_{11}^{XY}). The fourth parameter, μ, is fixed by the total sample size n. Table 14.3 displays the expected cell frequencies m_{ij} in terms of the model parameters μ, λ_1^X, λ_1^Y, and λ_{11}^{XY}.

The odds ratio can also be expressed as a function of the expected frequencies:

$$\Psi = \frac{m_{11}m_{22}}{m_{12}m_{21}}$$

Table 14.3 Loglinear Model Expected Cell Counts

	Level of Y	
Level of X	1	2
1	$\exp(\mu + \lambda_1^X + \lambda_1^Y + \lambda_{11}^{XY})$	$\exp(\mu + \lambda_1^X - \lambda_1^Y - \lambda_{11}^{XY})$
2	$\exp(\mu - \lambda_1^X + \lambda_1^Y - \lambda_{11}^{XY})$	$\exp(\mu - \lambda_1^X - \lambda_1^Y + \lambda_{11}^{XY})$

so that

$$\log \Psi = \log m_{11} - \log m_{12} - \log m_{21} + \log m_{22} = 4\lambda_{11}^{XY}$$

Therefore, the hypothesis of independence of X and Y is equivalent to $H_0\colon \lambda_{11}^{XY} = 0$. The corresponding *independence loglinear model* is given by

$$\log(m_{ij}) = \mu + \lambda_i^X + \lambda_j^Y \qquad i, j = 1, 2$$

This model has one degree of freedom for testing lack of fit.

Chapter 2 discusses the Pearson chi-square test of independence for a 2×2 contingency table. An alternative approach is to test $H_0\colon \lambda_{11}^{XY} = 0$ using the likelihood ratio test to compare the fit of the independence and saturated loglinear models.

The likelihood ratio test of independence can be derived directly from the multinomial likelihood

$$f(n_{11}, n_{12}, n_{21}, n_{22}) = \frac{n!}{n_{11}!\, n_{12}!\, n_{21}!\, n_{22}!}\, \pi_{11}^{n_{11}}\, \pi_{12}^{n_{12}}\, \pi_{21}^{n_{21}}\, \pi_{22}^{n_{22}}$$

The unrestricted maximum likelihood estimates (MLEs) of the π_{ij} values are given by $p_{ij} = n_{ij}/n$. The maximized likelihood is then

$$\max L = \frac{n!}{n_{11}!\, n_{12}!\, n_{21}!\, n_{22}!} \prod_{i=1}^{2} \prod_{j=1}^{2} \left(\frac{n_{ij}}{n}\right)^{n_{ij}}$$

Under the independence hypothesis $H_0\colon \pi_{ij} = \pi_{i+}\pi_{+j}$, the likelihood is

$$L_0 = \frac{n!}{n_{11}!\, n_{12}!\, n_{21}!\, n_{22}!}\, \pi_{1+}^{n_{1+}}\, \pi_{2+}^{n_{2+}}\, \pi_{+1}^{n_{+1}}\, \pi_{+2}^{n_{+2}}$$

The MLEs for the π_{ij} under this model are $p_{ij} = n_{i+}n_{+j}/n^2$ and the maximized log-likelihood is

$$\max L_0 = \frac{n!}{n_{11}!\, n_{12}!\, n_{21}!\, n_{22}!} \prod_{i=1}^{2} \prod_{j=1}^{2} \left(\frac{n_{i+}n_{+j}}{n^2}\right)^{n_{ij}}$$

The likelihood ratio is

$$\lambda = \frac{\max L_0}{\max L} = \prod_{i=1}^{2} \prod_{j=1}^{2} \left(\frac{\widehat{m}_{ij}}{n_{ij}}\right)^{n_{ij}}$$

where $\widehat{m}_{ij} = n_{i+}n_{+j}/n$, and the likelihood ratio statistic is

$$G^2 = -2\log\lambda = 2\sum_{i=1}^{2}\sum_{j=1}^{2} n_{ij}\log\left(\frac{n_{ij}}{\widehat{m}_{ij}}\right)$$

The statistic G^2 has an asymptotic chi-square distribution with 1 df if H_0 is true, and it is asymptotically equivalent to the Pearson chi-square statistic Q_P discussed in Chapter 2.

14.2.2 Bicycle Example

Table 14.4 displays the crossclassification of type of bicycle (categorized as mountain or other) and safety helmet usage for a sample of 100 bicycle riders. Under the assumption that the variables bicycle type and helmet usage are observed for a sample of 100 riders, both are response variables.

Table 14.4 Bicycle Data

Bicycle Type	Wearing Helmet		Total
	Yes	No	
Mountain	34	32	66
Other	10	24	34
Total	44	56	100

The following statements create a SAS data set containing the cell counts.

```
data bicycle;
    input type $ helmet $ count;
    cards;
Mountain Yes  34
Mountain No   32
Other    Yes  10
Other    No   24
;
run;
```

Suppose X denotes the row variable (bicycle type) and Y denotes the column variable (helmet usage). The saturated model

$$\log(m_{ij}) = \mu + \lambda_i^X + \lambda_j^Y + \lambda_{ij}^{XY} \qquad i,j = 1,2$$

is requested by the following PROC CATMOD invocation.

```
proc catmod;
    weight count;
    model type*helmet=_response_ / noresponse noiter noparm;
    loglin type|helmet;
run;
```

The response variables TYPE and HELMET are both listed on the left-hand side of the MODEL statement (separated by an asterisk). This usage of the MODEL statement is similar to that for repeated measures analyses (Chapter 13). Since PROC CATMOD allows only independent variables on the right-hand side of the MODEL statement, you can't specify a loglinear model directly in the MODEL statement. Instead, you use the special keyword _RESPONSE_ on the right-hand side and specify the loglinear model effects in the LOGLIN statement. In this example, the saturated model includes the TYPE and HELMET main effects, as well as the TYPE × HELMET interaction through the TYPE|HELMET specification.

The three options specified in the MODEL statement suppress printed output that may not always be necessary in loglinear model analysis. The NORESPONSE option suppresses printing of the loglinear model design matrix, the NOITER option suppresses printing of the parameter estimates and other information at each iteration of the maximum likelihood procedure, and the NOPARM option suppresses printing of the estimated parameters.

Output 14.1 displays the population and response profiles. There is one population, and the four response profiles are defined by the crossclassification of the response variables TYPE and HELMET.

Output 14.1   Population and Response Profiles

```
                          Sample
                  Sample   Size
                  ----------------
                     1      100




                  RESPONSE PROFILES

          Response    TYPE     HELMET
          --------------------------
             1      Mountain   No
             2      Mountain   Yes
             3      Other      No
             4      Other      Yes
```

Output 14.2 displays the analysis of variance table. Since the four multinomial cell probabilities sum to one, there are three linearly independent expected frequencies m_{ij}. Since there are also three parameters, the model is saturated and the expected counts m_{ij} are equal to the observed counts n_{ij}. Thus, the likelihood ratio statistic G^2 is equal to zero. Although the model was fit using maximum likelihood, the test statistics in the analysis of variance table are Wald tests.

Output 14.2   Analysis of Variance Table for Saturated Loglinear Model

```
         MAXIMUM-LIKELIHOOD ANALYSIS-OF-VARIANCE TABLE

    Source              DF    Chi-Square      Prob
    ------------------------------------------------------
    TYPE                 1       11.29       0.0008
    HELMET               1        3.28       0.0700
    TYPE*HELMET          1        4.33       0.0374

    LIKELIHOOD RATIO     0          .           .
```

The next PROC CATMOD invocation fits the independence loglinear model

$$\log(m_{ij}) = \mu + \lambda_i^X + \lambda_j^Y \qquad i,j = 1,2$$

which is specified by excluding the TYPE $\times$ HELMET term from the LOGLIN statement.

```
proc catmod;
   weight count;
   model type*helmet=_response_ /  noprofile noresponse noiter noparm;
   loglin type helmet;
run;
```

As shown in Output 14.3, the likelihood ratio statistic for testing the null hypothesis of independence of HELMET and TYPE is $G^2 = 4.56$. Therefore, there is clear evidence that the two variables are not independent. Helmet usage is more associated with mountain bikes than other bikes. The main effect TYPE tests the null hypothesis that the subjects are distributed evenly over the two levels of this variable. The strongly significant results of this test ($Q_W = 9.87$, 1 df, $p = 0.0017$) reflect the fact that 66% of the cyclists were riding mountain bikes and only 34% were riding other types of bicycles (Table 14.4). The subjects were relatively evenly distributed over the levels of the HELMET variable (44% wore helmets, 56% did not); this is reflected in the nonsignificant HELMET main effect ($Q_W = 1.43$). However, since there is evidence of interaction between HELMET and TYPE, the main effects should be interpreted with caution.

Output 14.3   Analysis of Variance Table for Independence Loglinear Model

```
         MAXIMUM-LIKELIHOOD ANALYSIS-OF-VARIANCE TABLE

    Source              DF    Chi-Square      Prob
    ------------------------------------------------------
    TYPE                 1        9.87       0.0017
    HELMET               1        1.43       0.2313

    LIKELIHOOD RATIO     1        4.56       0.0328
```

For comparison, the FREQ procedure can also be used to compute the likelihood ratio test of independence. The statements

```
proc freq order=data;
   weight count;
   tables type*helmet / nopercent norow chisq;
run;
```

produce the results shown in Output 14.4. The statistic G^2 is labeled "Likelihood Ratio Chi-Square."

Output 14.4   Likelihood Ratio Test of Independence Using PROC FREQ

```
                     TABLE OF TYPE BY HELMET

          TYPE       HELMET

          Frequency|
          Col Pct  |Yes     |No      |  Total
          ---------+--------+--------+
          Mountain |     34 |     32 |     66
                   |  77.27 |  57.14 |
          ---------+--------+--------+
          Other    |     10 |     24 |     34
                   |  22.73 |  42.86 |
          ---------+--------+--------+
          Total         44        56       100


          STATISTICS FOR TABLE OF TYPE BY HELMET

          Statistic                  DF    Value      Prob
          ------------------------------------------------------
          Chi-Square                  1    4.449      0.035
          Likelihood Ratio Chi-Square 1    4.557      0.033
          Continuity Adj. Chi-Square  1    3.598      0.058
          Mantel-Haenszel Chi-Square  1    4.405      0.036
          Fisher's Exact Test (Left)                  0.991
                              (Right)                 0.028
                              (2-Tail)                0.055
          Phi Coefficient                  0.211
          Contingency Coefficient          0.206
          Cramer's V                       0.211

          Sample Size = 100
```

14.2.3   Loglinear Model for the $s \times r$ Table

When a sample of n observations is classified with respect to two categorical variables, one having s levels and the other having r levels, the resulting frequencies can be displayed in an $s \times r$ contingency table, as shown in Table 14.5. The corresponding cell probabilities are π_{ij}, with row and column marginal probabilities $\{\pi_{i+}\}$ and $\{\pi_{+j}\}$, respectively.

The generalization of the loglinear model from the 2×2 table to the $s \times r$ table is straightforward. The saturated model is

$$\log(m_{ij}) = \mu + \lambda_i^X + \lambda_j^Y + \lambda_{ij}^{XY} \qquad i = 1, \ldots, s, j = 1, \ldots, r$$

where $m_{ij} = n\pi_{ij}$ is the expected frequency in the (i, j) cell. The parameter μ is fixed by the sample size n and the model has $s + r + sr$ parameters λ_i^X, λ_j^Y, and λ_{ij}^{XY}. The sum-to-zero constraints

$$\sum_{i=1}^{s} \lambda_i^X = 0 \qquad \sum_{j=1}^{r} \lambda_j^Y = 0 \qquad \sum_{i=1}^{s} \lambda_{ij}^{XY} = \sum_{j=1}^{r} \lambda_{ij}^{XY} = 0$$

Table 14.5   Cell Counts in an $s \times r$ Contingency Table

Level of X	Level of Y				Total
	1	2	$\cdots$	r	
1	n_{11}	n_{12}	$\cdots$	n_{1r}	n_{1+}
2	n_{21}	n_{22}	$\cdots$	n_{2r}	n_{2+}
$\vdots$	$\vdots$	$\vdots$		$\vdots$	$\vdots$
s	n_{s1}	n_{s2}	$\cdots$	n_{sr}	n_{s+}
Total	n_{+1}	n_{+2}	$\cdots$	n_{+r}	n

implies $(s-1) + (r-1) + (s-1)(r-1) = sr - 1$ parameters and zero df for testing lack of fit. Letting $\widehat{m}_{ij} = n_{i+} n_{+j}/n$, the likelihood ratio statistic

$$G^2 = 2 \sum_{i=1}^{s} \sum_{j=1}^{r} n_{ij} \log \left(n_{ij}/\widehat{m}_{ij} \right)$$

tests the null hypothesis $H_0: \lambda_{ij}^{XY} = 0$, for $i = 1, \ldots, s-1$, $j = 1, \ldots, r-1$. Under the null hypothesis of independence, G^2 has an approximate chi-square distribution with $(s-1)(r-1)$ df.

If H_0 is true, the reduced model $\log(m_{ij}) = \mu + \lambda_i^X + \lambda_j^Y$ is the model of independence of X and Y. This model has $(s-1) + (r-1)$ linearly independent λ parameters and $(s-1)(r-1)$ df for testing lack of fit.

14.2.4   Malignant Melanoma Example

Table 14.6 displays data from a cross-sectional study of 400 patients with malignant melanoma (Roberts et al. 1981). For each patient, the site of the tumor and its histological type were recorded. The following statements create a SAS data set containing the cell frequencies for this 4×3 contingency table.

Table 14.6   Malignant Melanoma Data

Tumor Type	Tumor Site			Total
	Head and Neck	Trunk	Extremities	
Hutchinson's melanotic freckle	22	2	10	34
Superficial spreading melanoma	16	54	115	185
Nodular	19	33	73	125
Indeterminate	11	17	28	56
Total	68	106	226	400

```
data melanoma;
   input type $ site $ count;
   cards;
Hutchinson's  Head&Neck    22
Hutchinson's  Trunk         2
```

```
Hutchinson's   Extremities  10
Superficial    Head&Neck    16
Superficial    Trunk        54
Superficial    Extremities 115
Nodular        Head&Neck    19
Nodular        Trunk        33
Nodular        Extremities  73
Indeterminate  Head&Neck    11
Indeterminate  Trunk        17
Indeterminate  Extremities  28
;
run;
```

The following PROC CATMOD invocation fits the independence loglinear model

$$\log(m_{ij}) = \mu + \lambda_i^X + \lambda_j^Y \qquad i = 1,\ldots,4;, j = 1,\ldots,3$$

```
proc catmod;
   weight count;
   model type*site=_response_ / noresponse noiter noparm;
   loglin type site;
run;
```

The analysis of variance table in Output 14.5 provides strong evidence that tumor type and tumor site are not independent ($G^2 = 51.80$, 6 df, $p < 0.0001$). Hutchinson's tumor type is more associated with head and neck, and other types are more associated with extremities.

Output 14.5   Analysis of Variance Table for Independence Loglinear Model

```
        MAXIMUM-LIKELIHOOD ANALYSIS-OF-VARIANCE TABLE

        Source            DF      Chi-Square       Prob
        ----------------------------------------------------
        TYPE              3         121.48        0.0000
        SITE              2          93.30        0.0000

        LIKELIHOOD RATIO  6          51.80        0.0000
```

14.2.5   Hierarchical and Nonhierarchical Loglinear Models

Hierarchical loglinear models are defined to be members of the family of models such that if any λ-term is set equal to zero, all higher-order effects containing the subscripted λ-terms are also set equal to zero (Bishop, Fienberg, and Holland 1975, p. 34). Thus, whenever a model contains higher-order effects, it also must contain the corresponding lower-order effects. For two-way tables, the saturated model

$$\log(m_{ij}) = \mu + \lambda_i^X + \lambda_j^Y + \lambda_{ij}^{XY} \qquad i = 1,\ldots,s, j = 1,\ldots,r$$

and the independence model

$$\log(m_{ij}) = \mu + \lambda_i^X + \lambda_j^Y \qquad i = 1,\ldots,s, j = 1,\ldots,r$$

are the only hierarchical loglinear models that involve both variables. The other possible hierarchical models are

$$\log(m_{ij}) = \mu + \lambda_i^X$$
$$\log(m_{ij}) = \mu + \lambda_j^Y$$
$$\log(m_{ij}) = \mu$$

An example of a nonhierarchical model would be

$$\log(m_{ij}) = \mu + \lambda_i^X + \lambda_{ij}^{XY}$$

This model is nonhierarchical since it contains the higher-order term λ_{ij}^{XY} but not the lower-order effect λ_j^Y.

For two-way tables, closed form estimates of the cell frequencies can be obtained for hierarchical models: $\widehat{m}_{ij} = n_{ij}$ for the saturated model and $\widehat{m}_{ij} = n_{i+}n_{+j}/n$ for the independence model. In multi-way tables, explicit estimates are not usually available. Historically, the restriction to consideration of hierarchical loglinear models was at least partially due to the fact that the more readily accessible methods of obtaining MLEs of the cell frequencies were primarily applicable to hierarchical models.

14.3 Three-Way Contingency Tables

14.3.1 Mutual, Joint, Marginal, and Conditional Independence

Consider a three-dimensional table containing the crossclassification of variables X, Y, and Z. The distributions of X, Y cell counts at different levels of Z can be displayed using cross-sections of the three-way table. These cross-sections are called *partial tables*. In the partial tables, the value of Z is held constant.

For example, Section 3.2.2 of Chapter 3 discusses health policy opinion data with variables X=stress, Y=opinion, and Z=residence. Table 14.7 displays the two partial tables of the stress × opinion crossclassification for subjects from urban and rural residences.

Table 14.7 Partial Tables for Health Policy Opinion Data

| Residence | Stress | Opinion | | Total |
		Favorable	Unfavorable	
Urban	Low	48	12	60
	High	96	94	190
	Total	144	106	250
Rural	Low	55	135	190
	High	7	53	60
	Total	62	188	250

Alternatively, the two-way contingency table obtained by adding the cell counts in the partial tables is called the X, Y *marginal table*. This table ignores the variable Z. Table 14.8 displays the marginal stress × opinion crossclassification ignoring the variable residence.

Table 14.8 Marginal Table for Health Policy Opinion Data

Stress	Opinion		Total
	Favorable	Unfavorable	
Low	103	147	250
High	103	147	250
Total	206	294	500

Partial tables can exhibit quite different associations than marginal tables, as was described in Section 3.2.2 for the health policy opinion data. In fact, it can be quite misleading to analyze only the marginal tables of a multi-way contingency table. Simpson's Paradox, the result that a pair of variables can have marginal association of different direction from their partial associations, is discussed in Section 3.2.2.

Before describing some of the various types of loglinear models, it is important to consider the four types of independence for cell probabilities in the three-way crossclassification of variables X, Y, and Z. Denote the cell probabilities by π_{ijk}, for $i = 1, \ldots, I, j = 1, \ldots, J$, and $k = 1, \ldots, K$, where I, J, and K denote the number of levels of variables X, Y, and Z, respectively.

The three variables are *mutually independent* when

$$\pi_{ijk} = \pi_{i++}\, \pi_{+j+}\, \pi_{++k} \qquad i = 1, \ldots, I, j = 1, \ldots, J, k = 1, \ldots, K$$

Variable Y is *jointly independent* of X and Z when

$$\pi_{ijk} = \pi_{i+k}\, \pi_{+j+} \qquad i = 1, \ldots, I, j = 1, \ldots, J, k = 1, \ldots, K$$

This is ordinary two-way independence between Y and a new variable composed of the IK combinations of the levels of X and Z. Similar definitions apply for X to be jointly independent of Y and Z, and for Z to be jointly independent of X and Y. Note that mutual independence implies joint independence of any one variable from the others.

Variables X and Y are *marginally independent* if

$$\pi_{ij+} = \pi_{i++}\, \pi_{+j+} \qquad i = 1, \ldots, I, \ j = 1, \ldots, J$$

In general, two variables are marginally independent if they are independent in the two-way table obtained by collapsing over the levels of the remaining variables. If Y is jointly independent of X and Z, then X and Y, as well as Y and Z, are marginally independent. Thus, joint independence implies marginal independence.

Next consider the relationship between any pair of variables, controlling for the levels of the third variable. For example, if X and Y are independent in the partial table for the kth category of Z, then X and Y are said to be *conditionally independent at level k of Z*. Suppose

$$\pi_{ij|k} = \pi_{ijk}/\pi_{++k} \qquad i = 1, \ldots, I, j = 1, \ldots, J$$

denotes the joint distribution of X and Y at level k of Z. Then conditional independence at level k of Z is

$$\pi_{ijk} = \pi_{i+|k}\,\pi_{+j|k} \qquad i = 1,\ldots,I, j = 1,\ldots,J$$

More generally, the variables X and Y are *conditionally independent given* Z when they are conditionally independent at every level of Z, or when

$$\pi_{ijk} = \pi_{i+k}\,\pi_{+jk}/\pi_{++k} \qquad i = 1,\ldots,I, j = 1,\ldots,J, k = 1,\ldots,K$$

Suppose that Y is jointly independent of X and Z. Then X and Y are conditionally independent, as are Y and Z.

In summary, two variables (say X and Y) are conditionally independent and marginally independent when X, Y, and Z are mutually independent, or when Y is jointly independent of X and Z. However, conditional independence of X and Y, given Z, does not imply that X and Y are marginally independent.

14.3.2 Hierarchical Loglinear Models

The saturated loglinear model for a three-way table is

$$\log(m_{ijk}) = \mu + \lambda_i^X + \lambda_j^Y + \lambda_k^Z + \lambda_{ij}^{XY} + \lambda_{ik}^{XZ} + \lambda_{jk}^{YZ} + \lambda_{ijk}^{XYZ}$$

This model has

$$1 + (I-1) + (J-1) + (K-1) + (I-1)(J-1) + (I-1)(K-1)$$
$$+ (J-1)(K-1) + (I-1)(J-1)(K-1) = IJK$$

parameters and zero df for testing lack of fit. The saturated model allows for three-way interaction, that is, each pair of variables may be conditionally dependent, and an odds ratio for any pair of variables may vary across levels of the third variable.

The reduced model

$$\log(m_{ijk}) = \mu + \lambda_i^X + \lambda_j^Y + \lambda_k^Z + \lambda_{ij}^{XY} + \lambda_{ik}^{XZ} + \lambda_{jk}^{YZ}$$

is called the loglinear model of *no three-factor interaction*. In this model, no pair of variables is conditionally independent. Thus, for each pair of variables, marginal odds ratios may differ from partial odds ratios. The "no three-factor interaction" model implies that the conditional odds ratios between any two variables are identical at each level of the third variable. Except in special cases, closed form expressions for the expected cell frequencies do not exist.

There are three hierarchical models in which only one pair of variables is conditionally independent. For example, if X and Y are conditionally independent, given Z, the corresponding loglinear model is

$$\log(m_{ijk}) = \mu + \lambda_i^X + \lambda_j^Y + \lambda_k^Z + \lambda_{ik}^{XZ} + \lambda_{jk}^{YZ}$$

The parameters $\{\lambda_{ik}^{XZ}\}$ and $\{\lambda_{jk}^{YZ}\}$ pertain to the X, Z and Y, Z partial associations. There are also three models in which only one pair of variables is conditionally dependent. For example, if Y is jointly independent of X and Z, the corresponding model is

$$\log(m_{ijk}) = \mu + \lambda_i^X + \lambda_j^Y + \lambda_k^Z + \lambda_{ik}^{XZ}$$

In this model, the parameters $\{\lambda_{ik}^{XZ}\}$ pertain to the dependence between X and Z.

Finally, the loglinear model corresponding to mutual independence is

$$\log(m_{ijk}) = \mu + \lambda_i^X + \lambda_j^Y + \lambda_k^Z$$

In this model, each pair of variables is also conditionally and marginally independent.

14.3.3 Fitting Loglinear Models

After selecting a loglinear model, the observed data are used to estimate model parameters, cell probabilities, and expected frequencies. Although alternative methods of estimation are sometimes useful, the maximum likelihood (ML) method offers several advantages. First of all, the MLEs for hierarchical loglinear models are relatively easy to compute, since the estimates satisfy certain intuitive marginal constraints. In addition, the ML method can be used when data are sparse, that is, when there are several observed cell counts of zero. (Note that marginal totals, however, cannot be equal to zero.) Although beyond the scope of this book, the ML method also has some theoretical advantages over other approaches (Rao 1961, 1962).

Birch (1963) showed that the MLEs are the same for simple multinomial sampling, independent Poisson sampling, and product multinomial sampling. For hierarchical loglinear models, Birch's (1963) results also enable the derivation of estimates of the expected cell counts without first going through the intermediate step of estimating the λ-terms. For some models, the cell estimates are explicit closed-form functions of the marginal totals. For example, the expected cell frequencies for the independence loglinear model in a two-way table are functions of the row and column marginal totals; specifically $\hat{m}_{ij} = n_{i+}n_{+j}/n$ (Section 14.2.3). However, many loglinear models do not have direct ML estimates. As one example, direct estimates do not exist for unsaturated models containing all two-factor interactions. When direct estimates do not exist, iterative procedures must be used.

The iterative proportional fitting (IPF) algorithm, originally presented by Deming and Stephan (1940), is a simple method for calculating MLEs of cell frequencies for hierarchical loglinear models. Since the estimated cell counts depend only on the marginal totals, no special provision need be made for sporadic cells with no observations. Any set of starting values may be chosen that conforms to the model being fit; for example, all expected cell counts can initially be set equal to one. If direct estimates exist, the procedure yields these estimates in one cycle. IPF is used by many computer programs, since it is a simple method not requiring matrix inversion or complicated calculations.

The Newton-Raphson method can also be used to fit loglinear models. This method is more complex, since each step requires solving a system of equations. When the contingency table has several dimensions and the parameter vector is large, the

Newton-Raphson method may not be feasible. However, since Newton-Raphson is a general purpose method that can solve more complex systems of likelihood equations, restriction to the class of hierarchical loglinear models is not necessary. In addition, Newton-Raphson is more efficient numerically, since the rate of convergence is quadratic (compared to linear for IPF). Of course, this is partially counterbalanced by the fact that each cycle takes less time with IPF. Another advantage of the Newton-Raphson method is that the estimated covariance matrix of the parameter estimates is automatically produced as a by-product. The CATMOD procedure uses the Newton-Raphson method to fit loglinear models.

14.3.4   Testing Goodness of Fit

The goodness of fit of a loglinear model can be assessed by comparing the fitted cell counts to the observed cell counts. The general form of the likelihood ratio chi-square statistic is $G^2 = 2 \sum n \log(n/\hat{m})$, where n and $\hat{m}$ denote the observed and fitted cell frequencies. The corresponding Pearson chi-square statistic is equal to $Q_P = \sum (n - \hat{m})^2/\hat{m}$. When the model holds, both statistics have asymptotic chi-square distributions with degrees of freedom equal to the number of cells in the table minus the number of linearly independent parameters.

The likelihood ratio statistic G^2 has two important properties not possessed by Q_P. First, it is the statistic that is minimized by the MLEs. In addition, suppose you want to compare two models M_1 and M_2, where M_2 is a special case of M_1. In terms of loglinear model parameters, M_2 contains only a subset of the λ-terms contained in M_1. In this case, the simpler model M_2 is said to be nested within M_1.

Suppose $G^2(M_1)$ and $G^2(M_2)$ denote the goodness-of-fit statistics for models M_1 and M_2, and suppose v_1 and v_2 denote the corresponding df. Since M_2 is simpler than M_1, $v_1 < v_2$ and $G^2(M_1) \le G^2(M_2)$. Assuming model M_1 holds, the likelihood ratio approach for testing that M_2 holds uses the statistic

$$G^2(M_2 \mid M_1) = G^2(M_2) - G^2(M_1)$$

which has an asymptotic chi-square distribution with $(v_2 - v_1)$ df when model M_2 holds. A comparable decomposition for the Pearson chi-square statistic Q_P does not correspondingly apply.

14.3.5   Job Satisfaction Example

Table 14.9 displays the three-way crossclassification of quality of management, supervisor's job satisfaction, and worker's job satisfaction for a random sample of 715 workers selected from Danish industry (Andersen 1991, p. 155).* Quality of management was categorized from an external evaluation of each factory, while the job satisfaction ratings were based on questionnaires completed by each worker and his or her supervisor. Since all three variables are response variables, the use of loglinear models to investigate the patterns of association among management quality, supervisor's job satisfaction, and worker's job satisfaction seems appropriate.

---

*Reprinted by permission of Springer-Verlag.

Table 14.9   Job Satisfaction Data

Quality of Management	Supervisor's Job Satisfaction	Worker's Job Satisfaction		Total
		Low	High	
Bad	Low	103	87	190
	High	32	42	74
Good	Low	59	109	168
	High	78	205	283

Let X, Y, and Z denote quality of management, supervisor's job satisfaction, and worker's job satisfaction, respectively, and let π_{ijk} denote the corresponding multinomial cell probabilities for $i = 1, 2$, $j = 1, 2$, and $k = 1, 2$. The following statements read in the cell counts and fit the saturated loglinear model

$$\log(m_{ijk}) = \mu + \lambda_i^X + \lambda_j^Y + \lambda_k^Z + \lambda_{ij}^{XY} + \lambda_{ik}^{XZ} + \lambda_{jk}^{YZ} + \lambda_{ijk}^{XYZ}$$

which is expressed using the vertical bar (|) notation in the LOGLIN statement.

```
data satisfac;
   input managmnt $ supervis $ worker $ count;
   cards;
Bad  Low  Low  103
Bad  Low  High  87
Bad  High Low   32
Bad  High High  42
Good Low  Low   59
Good Low  High 109
Good High Low   78
Good High High 205
;
proc catmod order=data;
   weight count;
   model managmnt*supervis*worker=_response_
         / noresponse noiter noparm;
   loglin managmnt|supervis|worker;
run;
```

Output 14.6 displays the population and response profiles. There is a single multinomial sample with eight categories of response. Since the model is saturated, the likelihood ratio test of fit is equal to zero (see Output 14.7). The Wald test of the three-factor interaction is nonsignificant ($Q_W = 0.06$, 1 df, $p = 0.7989$).

Output 14.6   Population and Response Profiles

```
                          Sample
                 Sample    Size
                 ----------------
                   1       715



                 RESPONSE PROFILES

   Response  MANAGMNT  SUPERVIS  WORKER
   ------------------------------------
       1       Bad       Low      Low
       2       Bad       Low      High
       3       Bad       High     Low
       4       Bad       High     High
       5       Good      Low      Low
       6       Good      Low      High
       7       Good      High     Low
       8       Good      High     High
```

Output 14.7   Analysis of Variance Table for Saturated Model

```
         MAXIMUM-LIKELIHOOD ANALYSIS-OF-VARIANCE TABLE

      Source                   DF   Chi-Square     Prob
      -----------------------------------------------------
      MANAGMNT                  1      38.30      0.0000
      SUPERVIS                  1       8.10      0.0044
      MANAGMNT*SUPERVIS         1      65.67      0.0000
      WORKER                    1      23.59      0.0000
      MANAGMNT*WORKER           1      18.17      0.0000
      SUPERVIS*WORKER           1       5.24      0.0221
      MANAGMNT*SUPERVIS*WORKER  1       0.06      0.7989


      LIKELIHOOD RATIO          0        .          .
```

The second model includes only the main effects and two-factor interactions.

```
proc catmod order=data;
   weight count;
   model managmnt*supervis*worker=_response_
         / noprofile noresponse noiter p=freq;
   loglin managmnt|supervis managmnt|worker supervis|worker;
run;
```

The likelihood ratio test in the analysis of variance table (Output 14.8) compares this model to the saturated model and thus tests the null hypothesis of no three-factor interaction. In this example, the G^2 statistic of 0.06 is the same as the Wald statistic from the saturated model. Although the two statistics are asymptotically equivalent, they are not identical in general.

Output 14.8   Analysis of Variance Table for Model with No Three-Factor Interaction

```
        MAXIMUM-LIKELIHOOD ANALYSIS-OF-VARIANCE TABLE

        Source                 DF    Chi-Square      Prob
        --------------------------------------------------
        MANAGMNT                1       38.37       0.0000
        SUPERVIS                1        8.32       0.0039
        MANAGMNT*SUPERVIS       1       67.06       0.0000
        WORKER                  1       25.96       0.0000
        MANAGMNT*WORKER         1       19.57       0.0000
        SUPERVIS*WORKER         1        5.33       0.0210

        LIKELIHOOD RATIO        1        0.06       0.7989
```

The Wald tests of the two-factor interactions and main effects are all significant. This indicates that a more parsimonious model for the data may not be justified. However, you may wish to fit each of the three models containing only two of the two-factor interactions and compare these models to the model with no three-factor interaction using likelihood ratio tests. The SAS statements are as follows:

```
proc catmod order=data;
    weight count;
    model managmnt*supervis*worker=_response_
          / noprofile noresponse noiter noparm;
    loglin managmnt|supervis managmnt|worker;
proc catmod order=data;
    weight count;
    model managmnt*supervis*worker=_response_
          / noprofile noresponse noiter noparm;
    loglin managmnt|supervis supervis|worker;
proc catmod order=data;
    weight count;
    model managmnt*supervis*worker=_response_
          / noprofile noresponse noiter noparm;
    loglin managmnt|worker supervis|worker;
run;
```

The corresponding likelihood ratio statistics for goodness of fit (output not shown) are $G^2 = 5.39$, 19.71, and 71.90, all with 2 df. The 1 df likelihood ratio statistics comparing each of these three models to the model with no three-factor interaction are $5.39 - 0.06 = 5.33$, $19.71 - 0.06 = 19.65$, and $71.90 - 0.06 = 71.84$, respectively. Relative to the chi-square distribution with 1 df, all indicate a significant lack of fit.

The model with no three-factor interaction provides a good fit to the observed data. Thus, no pair of variables is conditionally independent. In this model, the conditional odds ratios between any two variables are identical at each level of the third variable. For example, the odds ratio for the association between the employee's job satisfaction and the supervisor's job satisfaction is the same at each level of management quality. You can compute the estimated odds ratios from the table of maximum likelihood estimates (Output 14.9).

Output 14.9   Parameter Estimates from Model with No Three-Factor Interaction

```
            ANALYSIS OF MAXIMUM-LIKELIHOOD ESTIMATES

                                      Standard   Chi-
    Effect              Parameter  Estimate  Error   Square   Prob
    ------------------------------------------------------------------
    MANAGMNT                1      -0.2672   0.0431   38.37   0.0000
    SUPERVIS                2       0.1243   0.0431    8.32   0.0039
    MANAGMNT*SUPERVIS       3       0.3491   0.0426   67.06   0.0000
    WORKER                  4      -0.2065   0.0405   25.96   0.0000
    MANAGMNT*WORKER         5       0.1870   0.0423   19.57   0.0000
    SUPERVIS*WORKER         6       0.0962   0.0417    5.33   0.0210
```

From the model with no three-factor interaction, the log odds of low job satisfaction for employees, at fixed levels of management quality and supervisor's job satisfaction, is

$$\log(m_{ij1}/m_{ij2}) = \log(m_{ij1}) - \log(m_{ij2})$$
$$= \lambda_1^Z + \lambda_{i1}^{XZ} + \lambda_{j1}^{YZ} - (\lambda_2^Z + \lambda_{i2}^{XZ} + \lambda_{j2}^{YZ})$$
$$= 2\lambda_1^Z + 2\lambda_{i1}^{XZ} + 2\lambda_{j1}^{YZ}$$

since $\lambda_1^Z + \lambda_2^Z = 0$, $\lambda_{i1}^{XZ} + \lambda_{i2}^{XZ} = 0$, and $\lambda_{j1}^{YZ} + \lambda_{j2}^{YZ} = 0$. Thus, at a fixed level of management quality, the logarithm of the odds ratio at low and high levels of supervisor satisfaction is

$$\log(m_{i11}/m_{i12}) - \log(m_{i21}/m_{i22}) = (2\lambda_1^Z + 2\lambda_{i1}^{XZ} + 2\lambda_{11}^{YZ}) - (2\lambda_1^Z + 2\lambda_{i1}^{XZ} + 2\lambda_{21}^{YZ})$$
$$= 2\lambda_{11}^{YZ} - 2\lambda_{21}^{YZ}$$
$$= 4\lambda_{11}^{YZ}$$

Since the estimate of λ_{11}^{YZ} from Output 14.9 is 0.0962, the odds of low worker job satisfaction are estimated to be $\exp(4 \times 0.0962) = 1.47$ times higher when the supervisor's job satisfaction is low than when the supervisor's job satisfaction is high. Note that this estimate of the odds ratio is the same for factories with bad and good management quality. Using the observed counts from Table 14.9, the observed odds ratios are

$$\frac{103 \times 42}{87 \times 32} = 1.55$$

in factories where the external evaluation of management quality was bad and

$$\frac{59 \times 205}{109 \times 78} = 1.42$$

in factories where the quality of management was good.

You can estimate additional odds ratios using the parameter estimates listed in Output 14.9. For a fixed level of supervisor job satisfaction, the odds of low worker satisfaction are estimated to be $\exp(4 \times 0.1870) = 2.1$ times higher when the quality of management is bad than when the management quality is good. This value is in between the corresponding observed odds ratios of

$$\frac{103 \times 109}{87 \times 59} = 2.19$$

when supervisor job satisfaction is low and

$$\frac{32 \times 205}{42 \times 78} = 2.00$$

when supervisor job satisfaction is high. Similarly, for a fixed level of worker job satisfaction, the odds of low supervisor job satisfaction are estimated to be $\exp(4 \times 0.3491) = 4.0$ times higher when the quality of management is bad than when the management quality is good. This value is in between the corresponding observed odds ratios of

$$\frac{103 \times 78}{32 \times 59} = 4.26$$

when worker job satisfaction is low and

$$\frac{87 \times 205}{42 \times 109} = 3.90$$

when worker job satisfaction is high.

These results show that the odds of low worker job satisfaction are somewhat more affected by the quality of management than by the supervisor's job satisfaction. In addition, bad quality management has a greater effect on the job satisfaction of supervisors than on worker job satisfaction.

The P=FREQ option of the MODEL statement prints predicted cell frequencies. Output 14.10 displays the resulting output from the model with no three-factor interaction. The first seven rows are the observed and predicted response functions, given by $\log(m_{ijk}) - \log(m_{222})$. The next eight rows, labeled F1–F8, are the observed and predicted cell counts. Instead of using the parameter estimates from Output 14.9, you could compute the estimated odds ratios using the predicted cell frequencies.

Output 14.10   Predicted Cell Counts

```
MAXIMUM-LIKELIHOOD PREDICTED VALUES FOR RESPONSE FUNCTIONS AND FREQUENCIES

               -------Observed-------  -------Predicted------
        Function          Standard              Standard
Sample  Number  Function   Error     Function    Error      Residual
------------------------------------------------------------------------
   1       1   -0.688281  0.12077577 -0.6990376 0.11335559  0.01075664
           2   -0.8571019 0.1279543  -0.8522608 0.12609959 -0.0048411
           3   -1.8572741 0.1900738  -1.8381157 0.17290271 -0.0191584
           4   -1.5853404 0.16937406 -1.6066064 0.14840625  0.02126605
           5   -1.2454725 0.14774032 -1.2366577 0.14291076 -0.0088148
           6   -0.6316621 0.11854265 -0.6420226 0.11152395  0.01036049
           7   -0.9663012 0.13303594 -0.9793675 0.12311034  0.01306639

          F1      103     9.38947484  102.263895 8.90423148  0.73610549
          F2       87     8.74150937  87.7361054 8.2834328  -0.7361054
          F3       32     5.52881833  32.7361056 4.78369542 -0.7361056
          F4       42     6.28751677  41.2638946 5.52536429  0.73610537
          F5       59     7.35740909  59.7361055 6.81145736 -0.7361055
          F6      109     9.61161884  108.263895 9.13883891  0.7361055
          F7       78     8.33612075  77.2638945 7.78218591  0.73610546
          F8      205    12.0923024   205.736105 11.7553532 -0.7361053
```

14.4   Higher-Order Contingency Tables

14.4.1   Dyke-Patterson Cancer Knowledge Data

As the number of dimensions of a contingency table increases, there are some complicating factors. One difficulty is the tremendous increase in the number of possible interaction parameters. Another problem is caused by the dramatic increase in the number of cells. Unless the sample size is very large, there may be many observed cell counts equal to zero. There may even be marginal totals equal to zero.

Table 14.10 displays data obtained from a sample of 1729 individuals crossclassified according to five dichotomous variables (Dyke and Patterson 1952). The purpose of the study was to investigate the relationship between cancer knowledge (good, poor) and four media exposure variables.

- Do you read newspapers?
- Do you listen to the radio?
- Do you read books and magazines? (solid reading)
- Do you attend lectures?

Since this was a cross-sectional study, it is reasonable to treat all five variables as response variables and to investigate the patterns of dependence using loglinear models.

14.4.2   Hierarchical Loglinear Models

There are a large number of possible hierarchical models that can be considered for the cancer knowledge data of Table 14.10. The possible terms to be included in a model are

Table 14.10   Cancer Knowledge Data

Read Newspapers	Listen to Radio	Solid Reading	Attend Lectures	Cancer Knowledge Good	Cancer Knowledge Poor
Yes	Yes	Yes	Yes	23	8
Yes	Yes	Yes	No	102	67
Yes	Yes	No	Yes	8	4
Yes	Yes	No	No	35	59
Yes	No	Yes	Yes	27	18
Yes	No	Yes	No	201	177
Yes	No	No	Yes	7	6
Yes	No	No	No	75	156
No	Yes	Yes	Yes	1	3
No	Yes	Yes	No	16	16
No	Yes	No	Yes	4	3
No	Yes	No	No	13	50
No	No	Yes	Yes	3	8
No	No	Yes	No	67	83
No	No	No	Yes	2	10
No	No	No	No	84	393

the intercept μ, 5 main effects, 10 two-factor interaction terms, 10 three-factor interactions, 5 four-factor interactions, and the five-factor interaction.

The following statements read in the observed cell frequencies and fit the loglinear model of no five-factor interaction.

```
data cancer;
    input news $ radio $ reading $ lectures $ knowledg $ count;
    cards;
Yes Yes Yes Yes  Good  23
Yes Yes Yes Yes  Poor   8
Yes Yes Yes No   Good 102
Yes Yes Yes No   Poor  67
Yes Yes No  Yes  Good   8
Yes Yes No  Yes  Poor   4
Yes Yes No  No   Good  35
Yes Yes No  No   Poor  59
Yes No  Yes Yes  Good  27
Yes No  Yes Yes  Poor  18
Yes No  Yes No   Good 201
Yes No  Yes No   Poor 177
Yes No  No  Yes  Good   7
Yes No  No  Yes  Poor   6
Yes No  No  No   Good  75
Yes No  No  No   Poor 156
No  Yes Yes Yes  Good   1
No  Yes Yes Yes  Poor   3
No  Yes Yes No   Good  16
No  Yes Yes No   Poor  16
```

```
      No  Yes  No  Yes  Good   4
      No  Yes  No  Yes  Poor   3
      No  Yes  No  No   Good  13
      No  Yes  No  No   Poor  50
      No  No  Yes  Yes  Good   3
      No  No  Yes  Yes  Poor   8
      No  No  Yes  No   Good  67
      No  No  Yes  No   Poor  83
      No  No  No  Yes   Good   2
      No  No  No  Yes   Poor  10
      No  No  No  No    Good  84
      No  No  No  No    Poor 393
   ;
   proc catmod order=data;
      weight count;
      model news*radio*reading*lectures*knowledg=_response_
            / noresponse noiter noparm;
      loglin news|radio|reading|lectures     news|radio|reading|knowledg
             news|radio|lectures|knowledg    news|reading|lectures|knowledg
             radio|reading|lectures|knowledg;
   run;
```

Although the model could be specified by listing the $5 + 10 + 10 + 5 = 30$ main effect and interaction terms, it is simpler to use the vertical bar notation to specify the five four-factor interactions.

Output 14.11 displays the population and response profiles. There is a single multinomial population and $2^5 = 32$ response profiles. The likelihood ratio goodness-of-fit statistic from this model is $G^2 = 1.02$ (see Output 14.12). This statistic, with 1 df, tests the null hypothesis of no five-factor interaction and is not significant ($p = 0.3116$). Note that it is not necessary to fit the saturated model first in order to test this hypothesis.

Output 14.11   Population and Response Profiles

```
                            Sample
                  Sample     Size
                  ----------------
                    1        1729


              RESPONSE PROFILES

Response  NEWS   RADIO   READING   LECTURES   KNOWLEDG
----------------------------------------------------
    1     Yes    Yes     Yes       Yes        Good
    2     Yes    Yes     Yes       Yes        Poor
    3     Yes    Yes     Yes       No         Good
    4     Yes    Yes     Yes       No         Poor
    5     Yes    Yes     No        Yes        Good
    6     Yes    Yes     No        Yes        Poor
    7     Yes    Yes     No        No         Good
    8     Yes    Yes     No        No         Poor
    9     Yes    No      Yes       Yes        Good
   10     Yes    No      Yes       Yes        Poor
   11     Yes    No      Yes       No         Good
   12     Yes    No      Yes       No         Poor
   13     Yes    No      No        Yes        Good
   14     Yes    No      No        Yes        Poor
   15     Yes    No      No        No         Good
   16     Yes    No      No        No         Poor
   17     No     Yes     Yes       Yes        Good
   18     No     Yes     Yes       Yes        Poor
   19     No     Yes     Yes       No         Good
   20     No     Yes     Yes       No         Poor
   21     No     Yes     No        Yes        Good
   22     No     Yes     No        Yes        Poor
   23     No     Yes     No        No         Good
   24     No     Yes     No        No         Poor
   25     No     No      Yes       Yes        Good
   26     No     No      Yes       Yes        Poor
   27     No     No      Yes       No         Good
   28     No     No      Yes       No         Poor
   29     No     No      No        Yes        Good
   30     No     No      No        Yes        Poor
   31     No     No      No        No         Good
   32     No     No      No        No         Poor
```

Output 14.12   Analysis of Variance Table from Model with No Five-Factor Interaction

```
        MAXIMUM-LIKELIHOOD ANALYSIS-OF-VARIANCE TABLE

     Source                      DF    Chi-Square      Prob
     -----------------------------------------------------------
     NEWS                         1       47.96       0.0000
     RADIO                        1       49.57       0.0000
     NEWS*RADIO                   1        5.60       0.0180
     READING                      1        1.66       0.1976
     NEWS*READING                 1       28.96       0.0000
     RADIO*READING                1        0.15       0.7024
     NEWS*RADIO*READING           1        0.01       0.9099
     LECTURES                     1      377.03       0.0000
     NEWS*LECTURES                1        2.72       0.0989
     RADIO*LECTURES               1       11.28       0.0008
     NEWS*RADIO*LECTURES          1        1.52       0.2177
     READING*LECTURES             1        2.94       0.0864
     NEWS*READING*LECTURES        1        0.08       0.7833
     RADIO*READING*LECTURES       1        1.78       0.1825
     NEWS*RADIO*READIN*LECTUR     1        0.39       0.5348
     KNOWLEDG                     1        5.34       0.0209
     NEWS*KNOWLEDG                1       15.37       0.0001
     RADIO*KNOWLEDG               1        4.96       0.0259
     NEWS*RADIO*KNOWLEDG          1        0.07       0.7868
     READING*KNOWLEDG             1        5.22       0.0224
     NEWS*READING*KNOWLEDG        1        0.01       0.9307
     RADIO*READING*KNOWLEDG       1        0.27       0.6013
     NEWS*RADIO*READIN*KNOWLE     1        0.19       0.6667
     LECTURES*KNOWLEDG            1        2.41       0.1208
     NEWS*LECTURES*KNOWLEDG       1        2.26       0.1329
     RADIO*LECTURES*KNOWLEDG      1        1.79       0.1806
     NEWS*RADIO*LECTUR*KNOWLE     1        0.14       0.7115
     READING*LECTURE*KNOWLEDG     1        4.67       0.0307
     NEWS*READI*LECTUR*KNOWLE     1        0.77       0.3795
     RADIO*READI*LECTU*KNOWLE     1        0.32       0.5703


     LIKELIHOOD RATIO             1        1.02       0.3116
```

In Output 14.12, none of the Wald statistics for the four-factor interaction terms is larger than 0.77. Thus, the next statements fit the loglinear model with no four-way and five-way interaction terms. Again, the vertical bar notation is used to specify the 10 three-factor interactions. This is simpler than explicitly listing the 5 main effects, 10 two-factor interactions, and 10 three-factor interactions.

```
proc catmod order=data;
   weight count;
   model news*radio*reading*lectures*knowledg=_response_
         / noprofile noresponse noiter noparm;
   loglin news|radio|reading      news|radio|lectures
          news|radio|knowledg      news|reading|lectures
          news|reading|knowledg    news|lectures|knowledg
          radio|reading|lectures   radio|reading|knowledg
          radio|lectures|knowledg  reading|lectures|knowledg;
run;
```

In the analysis of variance table displayed in Output 14.13, the likelihood ratio goodness-of-fit statistic tests the null hypothesis that the four-factor and five-factor interactions are jointly equal to zero. You would not reject this hypothesis ($G^2 = 3.23$,

6 df, $p = 0.7791$). You can also compare this model to the model with no five-way interaction. The value of the test statistic is $3.23 - 1.02 = 2.21$ with 5 df, which is clearly nonsignificant.

Output 14.13   Analysis of Variance Table from Model with No Four-Factor Interactions

```
              MAXIMUM-LIKELIHOOD ANALYSIS-OF-VARIANCE TABLE

         Source                    DF    Chi-Square    Prob
         ------------------------------------------------------
         NEWS                       1       47.86      0.0000
         RADIO                      1       57.25      0.0000
         NEWS*RADIO                 1        6.36      0.0117
         READING                    1        2.96      0.0855
         NEWS*READING               1       28.47      0.0000
         RADIO*READING              1        0.04      0.8408
         NEWS*RADIO*READING         1        1.26      0.2616
         LECTURES                   1      391.77      0.0000
         NEWS*LECTURES              1        2.37      0.1236
         RADIO*LECTURES             1       13.84      0.0002
         NEWS*RADIO*LECTURES        1        1.51      0.2187
         KNOWLEDG                   1        4.70      0.0302
         NEWS*KNOWLEDG              1       16.85      0.0000
         RADIO*KNOWLEDG             1        5.20      0.0226
         NEWS*RADIO*KNOWLEDG        1        0.00      0.9528
         READING*LECTURES           1        5.24      0.0221
         NEWS*READING*LECTURES      1        0.01      0.9418
         READING*KNOWLEDG           1        9.29      0.0023
         NEWS*READING*KNOWLEDG      1        2.76      0.0969
         LECTURES*KNOWLEDG          1        3.10      0.0782
         NEWS*LECTURES*KNOWLEDG     1        3.03      0.0818
         RADIO*READING*LECTURES     1        1.50      0.2213
         RADIO*READING*KNOWLEDG     1        0.01      0.9434
         RADIO*LECTURES*KNOWLEDG    1        1.38      0.2409
         READING*LECTURE*KNOWLEDG   1        3.84      0.0500

         LIKELIHOOD RATIO           6        3.23      0.7791
```

Output 14.13 also displays Wald statistics for the 10 three-factor interactions. The one df Wald statistics for seven of these interactions are relatively small (1.5 or less). However, the statistics for the NEWS $\times$ READING $\times$ KNOWLEDG, NEWS $\times$ LECTURES $\times$ KNOWLEDG, and READING $\times$ LECTURES $\times$ KNOWLEDG interactions range from 2.76 to 3.84. The next statements fit the model that includes these three interaction terms, as well as all main effects and two-factor interactions.

```
proc catmod order=data;
   weight count;
   model news*radio*reading*lectures*knowledg=_response_
        / noprofile noresponse noiter noparm;
   loglin news|radio              radio|reading
          radio|lectures          radio|knowledg
          news|reading|knowledg   news|lectures|knowledg
          reading|lectures|knowledg;
run;
```

As shown in Output 14.14, this model provides a good fit relative to the saturated model ($G^2 = 9.50$, 13 df, $p = 0.7341$). In comparison to the previous model with no four-factor and higher interactions, the likelihood ratio test that the seven excluded three-factor interactions are jointly equal to zero is $G^2 = 9.50 - 3.23 = 6.27$ with $13 - 6 = 7$ df ($p = 0.39$). Thus, you would not reject the null hypothesis that the excluded three-factor interactions are jointly equal to zero.

Output 14.14 Analysis of Variance Table from Model with 3 Three-Factor Interactions

```
              MAXIMUM-LIKELIHOOD ANALYSIS-OF-VARIANCE TABLE

       Source                      DF    Chi-Square      Prob
       ---------------------------------------------------------
       NEWS                         1        53.36      0.0000
       RADIO                        1       100.01      0.0000
       NEWS*RADIO                   1        43.62      0.0000
       READING                      1         2.88      0.0899
       RADIO*READING                1         0.48      0.4864
       LECTURES                     1       434.50      0.0000
       RADIO*LECTURES               1        10.60      0.0011
       KNOWLEDG                     1         5.22      0.0224
       RADIO*KNOWLEDG               1         6.28      0.0122
       NEWS*READING                 1       142.56      0.0000
       NEWS*KNOWLEDG                1        17.99      0.0000
       READING*KNOWLEDG             1         9.17      0.0025
       NEWS*READING*KNOWLEDG        1         3.03      0.0818
       NEWS*LECTURES                1         4.29      0.0384
       LECTURES*KNOWLEDG            1         2.80      0.0941
       NEWS*LECTURES*KNOWLEDG       1         3.09      0.0787
       READING*LECTURES             1         7.90      0.0049
       READING*LECTURE*KNOWLEDG     1         5.49      0.0191

       LIKELIHOOD RATIO            13         9.50      0.7341
```

With five exceptions, all of the Wald tests in Output 14.14 are statistically significant ($p < 0.05$). One of these nonsignificant effects is the main effect for READING. Since the main effect terms in a loglinear model fix the marginal totals, these are generally included in the model regardless of statistical significance. In addition, since READING is a lower-order effect for interactions included in the model, its removal would complicate interpretation of the retained interaction terms involving READING. This principle also motivates retention of the nonsignificant LECTURES $\times$ KNOWLEDG interaction; its removal would make it difficult to interpret the statistically significant READING $\times$ LECTURES $\times$ KNOWLEDG interaction.

Both of the nonsignificant three-factor interactions are suggestive with $p < 0.10$: NEWS $\times$ READING $\times$ KNOWLEDG ($Q_W = 3.03$, $p = 0.0818$) and NEWS $\times$ LECTURES $\times$ KNOWLEDG ($Q_W = 3.09$, $p = 0.0787$). Higher-order interactions like these are often retained to avoid oversimplification of the model. Finally, the RADIO $\times$ READING interaction has the smallest chi-square statistic of the effects in Output 14.14 ($Q_W = 0.48$, $p = 0.4864$). In addition, none of the higher-order interactions involves this effect. Therefore, the following statements fit a reduced model that excludes the RADIO $\times$ READING interaction.

```
proc catmod order=data;
   weight count;
   model news*radio*reading*lectures*knowledg=_response_
         / noprofile noresponse noiter noparm;
   loglin news|radio radio|lectures
          radio|knowledg news|reading|knowledg
```

```
          news|lectures|knowledg reading|lectures|knowledg; run;
```

Output 14.15 indicates that this model provides a good fit to the observed cell counts ($G^2 = 9.99$, 14 df, $p = 0.7632$). The likelihood ratio statistic for testing the RADIO $\times$ READING effect is $G^2 = 9.99 - 9.50 = 0.49$ with 1 df ($p = 0.48$).

Output 14.15   Analysis of Variance Table from Reduced Hierarchical Model

```
          MAXIMUM-LIKELIHOOD ANALYSIS-OF-VARIANCE TABLE

     Source                       DF    Chi-Square      Prob
     ---------------------------------------------------------
     NEWS                          1        54.21      0.0000
     RADIO                         1        99.63      0.0000
     NEWS*RADIO                    1        50.94      0.0000
     LECTURES                      1       434.52      0.0000
     RADIO*LECTURES                1        10.97      0.0009
     KNOWLEDG                      1         5.09      0.0240
     RADIO*KNOWLEDG                1         7.35      0.0067
     READING                       1         2.47      0.1160
     NEWS*READING                  1       149.31      0.0000
     NEWS*KNOWLEDG                 1        17.82      0.0000
     READING*KNOWLEDG              1         9.35      0.0022
     NEWS*READING*KNOWLEDG         1         3.00      0.0835
     NEWS*LECTURES                 1         4.20      0.0404
     LECTURES*KNOWLEDG             1         2.76      0.0968
     NEWS*LECTURES*KNOWLEDG        1         3.08      0.0792
     READING*LECTURES              1         8.27      0.0040
     READING*LECTURE*KNOWLEDG      1         5.47      0.0194

     LIKELIHOOD RATIO             14         9.99      0.7632
```

The three-factor interaction between READING, LECTURES, and KNOWLEDG is significant at the $\alpha = 0.05$ level. Thus, the dependence between any pair of these variables is affected by the third variable. The two other three-factor interactions included in this model are NEWS $\times$ READING $\times$ KNOWLEDG and NEWS $\times$ LECTURES $\times$ KNOWLEDG. Both are suggestive at the $\alpha = 0.10$ level of significance. In addition, all three two-factor interactions involving NEWS, READING, and KNOWLEDG, as well as two of the three NEWS, LECTURES, and KNOWLEDG two-way interactions, are significant at $\alpha = 0.05$.

Thus, the model indicates that all four media exposure variables (NEWS, RADIO, READING, LECTURES) are associated with cancer knowledge. In addition, there are significant associations between NEWS and RADIO, NEWS and READING, NEWS and LECTURES, RADIO and LECTURES, and READING and LECTURES.

14.4.3   Loglinear Models with Nested Effects

The hierarchical model displayed in Output 14.15 contains 3 three-factor interaction terms. Each of these three-way interactions represents heterogeneity of the association between two of the variables across the levels of the third variable. A useful way to interpret these patterns of association more fully is to fit a model that specifically incorporates separate two-factor interactions across the levels of the third factor.

Since all three of the three-way interactions in Output 14.15 include the KNOWLEDG variable, the next statements use nested-by-value effects in the LOGLIN statement to fit a model with separate two-factor interactions for each level of KNOWLEDG.

```
proc catmod order=data;
   weight count;
   model news*radio*reading*lectures*knowledg=_response_
         / noprofile noresponse noiter noparm;
   loglin news|radio              radio|lectures
          radio|knowledg          reading|knowledg
          news|knowledg           lectures|knowledg
          news*reading(knowledg='Good')
          news*reading(knowledg='Poor')
          news*lectures(knowledg='Good')
          news*lectures(knowledg='Poor')
          reading*lectures(knowledg='Good')
          reading*lectures(knowledg='Poor');
run;
```

Output 14.16 displays the analysis of variance table for this model. Note that the likelihood ratio statistic is identical to that in Output 14.15. The two models are equivalent, even though they are parameterized differently. For example, Output 14.15 includes the NEWS $\times$ READING and NEWS $\times$ READING $\times$ KNOWLEDG interactions. These two effects are replaced in Output 14.16 by two NEWS $\times$ READING interactions, one for subjects with good cancer knowledge and one for subjects with poor cancer knowledge. Since the two models are equivalent, the hierarchical principle is actually still maintained, but the structure of the model is modified through nesting.

Output 14.16   Analysis of Variance Table from Model with Nested Effects

```
        MAXIMUM-LIKELIHOOD ANALYSIS-OF-VARIANCE TABLE

        Source                    DF    Chi-Square      Prob
        -------------------------------------------------------
        NEWS                       1        54.21      0.0000
        RADIO                      1        99.63      0.0000
        NEWS*RADIO                 1        50.94      0.0000
        LECTURES                   1       434.52      0.0000
        RADIO*LECTURES             1        10.97      0.0009
        KNOWLEDG                   1         5.09      0.0240
        RADIO*KNOWLEDG             1         7.35      0.0067
        READING                    1         2.47      0.1160
        READING*KNOWLEDG           1         9.35      0.0022
        NEWS*KNOWLEDG              1        17.82      0.0000
        LECTURES*KNOWLEDG          1         2.76      0.0968
        NEWS*READIN(KNOWLE=Good)   1        44.17      0.0000
        NEWS*READIN(KNOWLE=Poor)   1       128.92      0.0000
        NEWS*LECTUR(KNOWLE=Good)   1         6.05      0.0139
        NEWS*LECTUR(KNOWLE=Poor)   1         0.06      0.8001
        READI*LECTU(KNOWLE=Good)   1         0.15      0.6962
        READI*LECTU(KNOWLE=Poor)   1        12.91      0.0003

        LIKELIHOOD RATIO          14         9.99      0.7632
```

The nested effects for NEWS $\times$ LECTURES in individuals with poor cancer knowledge and for READING $\times$ LECTURES in individuals with good cancer knowledge are clearly nonsignificant. The next CATMOD invocation excludes these two effects.

```
proc catmod order=data;
   weight count;
   model news*radio*reading*lectures*knowledg=_response_
         / noprofile noresponse noiter;
   loglin news|radio              radio|lectures
          radio|knowledg          reading|knowledg
          news|knowledg           lectures|knowledg
          news*reading(knowledg='Good')
          news*reading(knowledg='Poor')
          news*lectures(knowledg='Good')
          reading*lectures(knowledg='Poor');
run;
```

The analysis of variance table displayed in Output 14.17 indicates that this model provides a good fit to the observed data ($G^2 = 10.20$, 16 df, $p = 0.8557$). In addition, it has two fewer parameters than the final model in Section 14.4.2 (Output 14.15). The READING main effect and the LECTURES $\times$ KNOWLEDG interaction are the only nonsignificant effects at the $\alpha = 0.05$ level of significance; both of these terms are retained in the model to preserve hierarchy.

Output 14.17   Analysis of Variance Table from Reduced Model with Nested Effects

```
        MAXIMUM-LIKELIHOOD ANALYSIS-OF-VARIANCE TABLE

        Source                    DF   Chi-Square    Prob
        ------------------------------------------------------
        NEWS                       1       74.74    0.0000
        RADIO                      1      100.03    0.0000
        NEWS*RADIO                 1       51.18    0.0000
        LECTURES                   1      444.55    0.0000
        RADIO*LECTURES             1       11.32    0.0008
        KNOWLEDG                   1        5.07    0.0244
        RADIO*KNOWLEDG             1        7.32    0.0068
        READING                    1        3.11    0.0778
        READING*KNOWLEDG           1       12.06    0.0005
        NEWS*KNOWLEDG              1       28.40    0.0000
        LECTURES*KNOWLEDG          1        2.96    0.0856
        NEWS*READIN(KNOWLE=Good)   1       45.47    0.0000
        NEWS*READIN(KNOWLE=Poor)   1      131.33    0.0000
        NEWS*LECTUR(KNOWLE=Good)   1        6.75    0.0094
        READI*LECTU(KNOWLE=Poor)   1       15.71    0.0001

        LIKELIHOOD RATIO          16       10.20    0.8557
```

You interpret the results of this model in the same manner as was described in Section 14.3.5. Output 14.18 displays the parameter estimates, from which you can compute estimated odds ratios.

Output 14.18   Parameter Estimates from Reduced Model with Nested Effects

```
              ANALYSIS OF MAXIMUM-LIKELIHOOD ESTIMATES

                                      Standard    Chi-
  Effect                Parameter  Estimate  Error   Square   Prob
  ----------------------------------------------------------------
  NEWS                      1      0.4443   0.0514    74.74  0.0000
  RADIO                     2     -0.4979   0.0498   100.03  0.0000
  NEWS*RADIO                3      0.2308   0.0323    51.18  0.0000
  LECTURES                  4     -1.2210   0.0579   444.55  0.0000
  RADIO*LECTURES            5      0.1597   0.0475    11.32  0.0008
  KNOWLEDG                  6     -0.1305   0.0580     5.07  0.0244
  RADIO*KNOWLEDG            7      0.0808   0.0299     7.32  0.0068
  READING                   8      0.0732   0.0415     3.11  0.0778
  READING*KNOWLEDG          9      0.1441   0.0415    12.06  0.0005
  NEWS*KNOWLEDG            10      0.2564   0.0481    28.40  0.0000
  LECTURES*KNOWLEDG        11      0.0960   0.0559     2.96  0.0856
  NEWS*READIN(KNOWLE=Good) 12      0.3017   0.0447    45.47  0.0000
  NEWS*READIN(KNOWLE=Poor) 13      0.3995   0.0349   131.33  0.0000
  NEWS*LECTUR(KNOWLE=Good) 14      0.2296   0.0884     6.75  0.0094
  READI*LECTU(KNOWLE=Poor) 15      0.2716   0.0685    15.71  0.0001
```

For example, the model includes two parameters pertaining to the NEWS × READING association. The estimate for individuals with good cancer knowledge is 0.3017, from which the odds of reading newspapers are estimated to be $\exp(4 \times 0.3017) = 3.3$ times higher in individuals who do solid reading than in individuals who do not. The corresponding parameter estimate in individuals with poor cancer knowledge is 0.3995, with an associated estimated odds ratio of $\exp(4 \times 0.3995) = 4.9$. Similarly, in individuals with good cancer knowledge, the odds of reading newspapers are estimated to be $\exp(4 \times 0.2296) = 2.5$ times higher in those who attend lectures than in individuals who do not, and in individuals with poor cancer knowledge, the odds of reading books and magazines are estimated to be $\exp(4 \times 0.2716) = 3.0$ times higher in those who attend lectures than in individuals who do not.

When higher-order interactions are included in a model, either directly or through the use of nested effects, you should be cautious in interpreting lower-order main effects or interactions. Since the NEWS × READING × KNOWLEDG interaction is included through the two nested effects, the NEWS × KNOWLEDG effect is difficult to interpret in light of the interaction with the READING effect. Similarly, the READING × KNOWLEDG and LECTURES × KNOWLEDG effects are difficult to interpret due to the three-factor interactions containing these effects.

You can, however, interpret the NEWS × RADIO, RADIO × LECTURES, and RADIO × KNOWLEDG effects. For example, the odds of good cancer knowledge are estimated to be $\exp(4 \times 0.0808) = 1.4$ times higher for individuals who listen to the radio than for individuals who do not listen to the radio.

14.5   Correspondence Between Logistic Models and Loglinear Models

In Section 14.3.5, loglinear models were used to investigate the patterns of association in the three-way crossclassification of quality of management, supervisor's job satisfaction, and worker's job satisfaction for a random sample of 715 workers selected from Danish industry. The final model included main effects for MANAGMNT, SUPERVIS, and WORKER, as well as the three two-factor interactions.

Now suppose that the data displayed in Table 14.9 had instead been obtained from the four subpopulations defined by the crossclassification of quality of management and supervisor job satisfaction. In this case, you would be interested in modeling the probability of worker job satisfaction as a function of management quality and supervisor's job satisfaction. In practice, for situations where all of the variables are technically response variables, interest often focuses on modeling one of the variables as a function of the remaining ones.

The following statements model the logit of the probability of low worker job satisfaction as a function of management quality and supervisor job satisfaction.

```
proc catmod order=data;
   weight count;
   model worker=managmnt supervis
         / noprofile noresponse noiter p=freq;
run;
```

Output 14.19 displays the resulting analysis of variance table. For comparison, examine Output 14.20 for the corresponding analysis of variance table from the loglinear model with no three-factor interaction (Output 14.8 from Section 14.3.5).

Output 14.19   Analysis of Variance Table from Logistic Model

```
        MAXIMUM-LIKELIHOOD ANALYSIS-OF-VARIANCE TABLE

        Source              DF    Chi-Square     Prob
        ---------------------------------------------------
        INTERCEPT            1       25.96      0.0000
        MANAGMNT             1       19.57      0.0000
        SUPERVIS             1        5.33      0.0210

        LIKELIHOOD RATIO     1        0.06      0.7989
```

Output 14.20   Analysis of Variance Table from Loglinear Model

```
           MAXIMUM-LIKELIHOOD ANALYSIS-OF-VARIANCE TABLE

      Source                DF    Chi-Square      Prob
      -----------------------------------------------------
      MANAGMNT               1       38.37      0.0000
      SUPERVIS               1        8.32      0.0039
      MANAGMNT*SUPERVIS      1       67.06      0.0000
      WORKER                 1       25.96      0.0000
      MANAGMNT*WORKER        1       19.57      0.0000
      SUPERVIS*WORKER        1        5.33      0.0210

      LIKELIHOOD RATIO       1        0.06      0.7989
```

The likelihood ratio goodness of fit statistics for the two models are identical. In addition, the logistic model Wald chi-square statistics for the MANAGMNT and SUPERVIS main effects are identical to the loglinear model Wald statistics for the MANAGMNT $\times$ WORKER and SUPERVIS $\times$ WORKER interactions, and the logistic model INTERCEPT chi-square statistic is identical to the loglinear model Wald statistic for the WORKER main effect.

Output 14.21 displays the parameter estimates from the logistic model. The log odds of low worker satisfaction are estimated to be $\exp(2 \times 0.3739) = 2.1$ times higher when the quality of management is bad than when the management quality is good and $\exp(2 \times 0.1924) = 1.47$ times higher when the supervisor's job satisfaction is low than when the supervisor's job satisfaction is high. These estimates are the same as those computed in Section 14.3.5.

Output 14.21   Parameter Estimates from Logistic Model

```
             ANALYSIS OF MAXIMUM-LIKELIHOOD ESTIMATES

                                     Standard    Chi-
      Effect         Parameter  Estimate  Error  Square   Prob
      ----------------------------------------------------------
      INTERCEPT          1      -0.4131   0.0811  25.96  0.0000
      MANAGMNT           2       0.3739   0.0845  19.57  0.0000
      SUPERVIS           3       0.1924   0.0833   5.33  0.0210
```

Finally, Output 14.22 displays the observed and predicted response functions and frequencies from the logistic model. The predicted cell counts in each of the four logistic model subpopulations are the same as the predicted loglinear model frequencies in the $2 \times 2 \times 2$ contingency table, as displayed in Output 14.23 (Output 14.10 from Section 14.3.5).

Output 14.22   Predicted Response Functions and Cell Frequencies from Logistic Model

```
MAXIMUM-LIKELIHOOD PREDICTED VALUES FOR RESPONSE FUNCTIONS AND FREQUENCIES

                 -------Observed-------   -------Predicted------
        Function              Standard                 Standard
Sample  Number   Function     Error       Function     Error       Residual
-----------------------------------------------------------------------------
   1       1     0.16882087  0.14561247   0.15322317  0.13202748    0.0155977
          F1          103    6.8675438   102.263895   6.23464059   0.73610548
          F2           87    6.8675438    87.7361055  6.23464059  -0.7361055

   2       1    -0.2719337   0.23464766  -0.2315093   0.17239025   -0.0404244
          F1           32    4.26170883   32.7361055  3.14686559   -0.7361055
          F2           42    4.26170883   41.2638945  3.14686559   0.73610548

   3       1    -0.6138104   0.16162755  -0.5946351   0.14262302   -0.0191753
          F1           59    6.18706408   59.7361055  5.49036109   -0.7361055
          F2          109    6.18706408  108.263895   5.49036109   0.73610548

   4       1    -0.9663012   0.13303594  -0.9793675   0.12311043    0.01306639
          F1           78    7.51676571   77.2638945  6.91505331   0.73610548
          F2          205    7.51676571  205.736105   6.91505331  -0.7361055
```

Output 14.23   Predicted Cell Counts from Loglinear Model

```
MAXIMUM-LIKELIHOOD PREDICTED VALUES FOR RESPONSE FUNCTIONS AND FREQUENCIES

                 -------Observed-------   -------Predicted------
        Function              Standard                 Standard
Sample  Number   Function     Error       Function     Error       Residual
-----------------------------------------------------------------------------
   1       1    -0.688281    0.12077577  -0.6990376   0.11335559    0.01075664
           2    -0.8571019   0.1279543   -0.8522608   0.12609959   -0.0048411
           3    -1.8572741   0.1900738   -1.8381157   0.17290271   -0.0191584
           4    -1.5853404   0.16937406  -1.6066064   0.14840625    0.02126605
           5    -1.2454725   0.14774032  -1.2366577   0.14291076   -0.0088148
           6    -0.6316621   0.11854265  -0.6420226   0.11152395    0.01036049
           7    -0.9663012   0.13303594  -0.9793675   0.12311034    0.01306639

          F1          103    9.38947484  102.263895   8.90423148   0.73610549
          F2           87    8.74150937   87.7361054  8.2834328    -0.7361054
          F3           32    5.52881833   32.7361056  4.78369542   -0.7361056
          F4           42    6.28751677   41.2638946  5.52536429   0.73610537
          F5           59    7.35740909   59.7361055  6.81145736   -0.7361055
          F6          109    9.61161884  108.263895   9.13883891   0.7361055
          F7           78    8.33612075   77.2638945  7.78218591   0.73610546
          F8          205   12.0923024   205.736105  11.7553532   -0.7361053
```

In summary, the crossclassification of the explanatory variables is fixed for logistic models and the effects of the factors are specified explicitly in the model statement. The loglinear model counterpart has the effects of factors specified through interactions with the response. In addition, the crossclassification of the explanatory variables is incorporated as a further component of the structure of the model.

The general result is that you can always rewrite a logistic analysis with one response variable as a loglinear model. First, move the explanatory variables to the left-hand side of the MODEL statement and use _RESPONSE_ as the only effect on the right-hand side of the MODEL statement. In addition, use a LOGLIN statement that includes all the main effects and interactions of the explanatory variables, as well as each effect from the logistic analysis crossed with the response variable.

Chapter 15
Categorized Time-to-Event Data

Chapter Table of Contents

Chapter 15
Categorized Time-to-Event Data

15.1 Introduction

Categorical data often are generated from studies that have time from treatment or exposure until some event as their outcome. Such data are known as *time-to-event* data. The event may be death, the recurrence of some condition, or the emergence of a developmental characteristic. Often, the outcome is the actual lifetime (or waiting time), which is the response analyzed in typical survival analyses. However, due to resource constraints or the need to perform a diagnostic procedure, you sometimes can determine only the interval of time during which an event occurs. Examples include examining dental patients for caries at six month periods, evaluating animals every four hours after their exposure to bacteria, and examining patients every six weeks for the recurrence of a medical condition for which they've been treated. Such data are often referred to as *grouped survival data* or as *categorized survival data*.

Since the study is conducted over a period of time, some subjects may leave before the study ends. This is called *withdrawal*. There may be protocol violations, subjects may join the study in progress and not complete the desired number of evaluations, or the subjects may drop out for other reasons. Thus, not only is status determined for each interval between successive evaluations, but the number of withdrawals for that interval is also determined. Most analysis strategies assume that withdrawal is independent of the condition being studied and that multiple withdrawals occur uniformly throughout the interval.

Frequently, interest lies in computing the survival rates. Section 15.2 discusses life table methods for computing these results. In addition, you generally want to compare survival rates for treatment groups and determine whether there is a treatment effect. Section 15.3 discusses the Mantel-Cox test, one strategy for addressing this question. It is similar to the log rank test used in traditional survival analysis.

In addition to hypothesis testing, you may be interested in describing the variation in survival rates. Sections 15.4 and 15.5 are concerned with statistical modeling. Since Poisson regression techniques are utilized in statistical modeling of survival data, Section 15.4 provides an overview of Poisson regression. Section 15.5 discusses the piecewise exponential model, one that is commonly used to model grouped survival data, as well as how to implement it using a Poisson regression strategy.

For an overview on grouped survival data analysis, refer to Deddens and Koch (1988).

15.2   Life Table Estimation of Survival Rates

Consider Table 15.1. Investigators were interested in comparing an active and control treatment to prevent the recurrence of a medical condition that had been healed. They applied a diagnostic procedure at the end of the first, second, and third years to determine whether there was a recurrence (based on Johnson and Koch 1978).

Table 15.1   Recurrences of Medical Condition

	Withdrawals			Recurrences				
Treatment	Year 1	Year 2	Year 3	Year 1	Year 2	Year 3	No Recurrence	Total
Control	9	7	6	15	13	7	17	74
Active	9	3	4	12	7	10	45	90

The survival rate, or the waiting time rate, is a key measure in the analysis of time-to-event data. It is written

$$S(y) = 1 - F(y) = \Pr\{Y \geq y\}$$

where Y denotes the continuous lifetime of a subject and $F(y) = \Pr\{Y \leq y\}$ is the cumulative probability distribution function. The exact form of $S(y)$ depends on the nature of $F(y)$, the probability distribution. The Weibull distribution and the exponential distribution are commonly used.

One way of estimating survival rates is with the *life table*, or *actuarial* method. Table 15.2 displays the life table format for the data displayed in Table 15.1. You determine the number of subjects at risk for each interval (the sum of those with no recurrence, those with recurrences, and those who withdrew). By knowing the number who survived all three intervals with no recurrence, you can determine the number with no recurrence for each interval.

Table 15.2   Life Table Format for Medical Condition Data

	Controls			
Interval	No Recurrences	Recurrences	Withdrawals	At Risk
0–1 Years	50	15	9	74
1–2 Years	30	13	7	50
2–3 Years	17	7	6	30
	Active			
Interval	No Recurrences	Recurrences	Withdrawals	At Risk
0–1 Years	69	12	9	90
1–2 Years	59	7	3	69
2–3 Years	45	10	4	59

Define n_{ijk} to be the number of patients in the ith group with the jth status for the kth time interval where $j = 0$ corresponds to no recurrence during the time interval, and $j = 1, 2$ corresponds to those with recurrence and those withdrawn during the kth interval, respectively; $i = 1, 2$ for the control and active groups and $k = 1, 2, \ldots, t$. The n_{i0k} are determined from

$$n_{i0k} = \sum_{j=1}^{2} \sum_{g=k+1}^{t} n_{ijg} + n_{i0t}$$

The life table estimates for the probability of surviving at least k intervals are computed as

$$G_{ik} = \prod_{g=1}^{k} \frac{n_{i0g} + 0.5n_{i2g}}{n_{i0g} + n_{i1g} + 0.5n_{i2g}} = \prod_{g=1}^{k} p_{ig}$$

where p_{ig} denotes the estimated conditional probability for surviving the gth interval given that survival of all preceding intervals has occurred.

The standard error of G_{ik} is estimated as

$$\text{s.e.}(G_{ik}) = G_{ik} \left\{ \sum_{g=1}^{k} \frac{(1 - p_{ig})}{(n_{i0g} + n_{i1g} + 0.5n_{i2g})p_{ig}} \right\}^{1/2}$$

$$= G_{ik} \left\{ \sum_{g=1}^{k} \frac{(1 - p_{ig})}{(n_{i0g} + 0.5n_{i2g})} \right\}^{1/2}$$

where $(n_{i0g} + n_{i1g} + 0.5n_{i2g})$ is the effective number at risk during the gth interval. Since

$$p_{ig} = \frac{n_{i0g} + 0.5n_{i2g}}{n_{i0g} + n_{i1g} + 0.5n_{i2g}}$$

then

$$1 - p_{ig} = \frac{n_{i1g}}{n_{i0g} + n_{i1g} + 0.5n_{i2g}}$$

The quantity $0.5 \times n_{i2g}$ is used in the numerator and denominator of p_{ig} since uniform withdrawals throughout the interval are assumed; the average exposure to risk for the withdrawing subjects is assumed to be one-half the interval.

For the active treatment, the life table estimates of surviving the kth interval are

$$G_{21} = \frac{69 + 0.5(9)}{69 + 12 + 0.5(9)} = 0.8596$$

$$G_{22} = 0.8596 \times \frac{59 + 0.5(3)}{59 + 7 + 0.5(3)} = 0.7705$$

$$G_{23} = 0.7705 \times \frac{45 + 0.5(4)}{45 + 10 + 0.5(4)} = 0.6353$$

Their standard errors are computed as follows:

$$\text{s.e.}(G_{21}) = 0.8596 \times \left\{ \frac{12/85.5}{69 + 0.5(9)} \right\}^{1/2} = 0.0376$$

$$\text{s.e.}(G_{22}) = 0.7705 \times \left\{ \frac{12/85.5}{69 + 0.5(9)} + \frac{7/67.5}{59 + 0.5(3)} \right\}^{1/2} = 0.0464$$

$$\text{s.e.}(G_{23}) = 0.6352 \times \left\{ \frac{12/85.5}{69 + 0.5(9)} + \frac{7/67.5}{59 + 0.5(3)} + \frac{10/57}{45 + 0.5(4)} \right\}^{1/2} = 0.0545$$

Table 15.3 contains the estimated survival rates and their standard errors for both active treatment and controls. The estimated survival rates for the active treatment are higher than for the controls for each of the intervals.

Table 15.3   Life Table Format for Medical Condition Data

	Estimated Survival Rates	Standard Errors
Controls		
0–1 Years	0.7842	0.0493
1–2 Years	0.5650	0.0627
2–3 Years	0.4185	0.0665
Active		
0–1 Years	0.8596	0.0376
1–2 Years	0.7705	0.0463
2–3 Years	0.6353	0.0545

Section 15.3 discusses the Mantel-Cox test, which tests the null hypothesis that the survival rates are the same.

15.3   Mantel-Cox Test

You are often interested in comparing survival curves to determine which treatment had the more favorable outcome. Mantel (1966) and later Cox (1972) suggested an extension of the Mantel-Haenszel methodology that applies to survival data. You restructure the usual frequency table format of the data to a set of 2×2 tables, each with a life table format, and perform the Mantel-Haenszel computations on that set of tables.

The tables are generated by regarding treatment as the row variable, the numbers recurred and not recurred as the column variable, and the intervals as the strata. You are thus proceeding as though the time interval results are uncorrelated; methodological results for survival analysis establish that you can consider the respective time intervals to be essentially uncorrelated risk sets for survival information. It turns out that the Mantel-Cox test for grouped data is equivalent to the log rank test for comparing survival curves for ungrouped data (refer to Koch, Sen, and Amara 1985). Withdrawals are handled by either grouping them with the no recurrences or eliminating them entirely (this is the more conservative approach).

Table 15.4 contains the life table format for the study of the medical condition recurrence with the data grouped together by intervals and with the withdrawals excluded.

Table 15.4   Medical Condition Data

Years	Treatment	Recurrences	No Recurrences
0–1	Control	15	50
	Active	12	69
1–2	Control	13	30
	Active	7	59
2–3	Control	7	17
	Active	10	45

The following DATA step inputs these data, and the PROC FREQ statements specify that the MH test be computed. Recall that for sets of 2×2 tables, all scores are equivalent, so no scores need to be specified.

```
data clinical;
   input time $ treatmnt $ status $ count @@;
   cards;
   0-1 control recur 15 0-1 control not 50
   0-1 active  recur 12 0-1 active  not 69
   1-2 control recur 13 1-2 control not 30
   1-2 active  recur  7 1-2 active  not 59
   2-3 control recur  7 2-3 control not 17
   2-3 active  recur 10 2-3 active  not 45
;
proc freq order=data;
   weight count;
   tables time*treatmnt*status / cmh;
run;
```

Output 15.1 contains the PROC FREQ output (the individual printed tables are not displayed). $Q_{MC} = 8.029$ with 1 df, $p = 0.005$. There is a significant treatment effect on survival.

Output 15.1   Results for Mantel-Cox Test

```
        Cochran-Mantel-Haenszel Statistics (Based on Table Scores)

    Statistic   Alternative Hypothesis    DF      Value      Prob
    ---------------------------------------------------------------
        1        Nonzero Correlation       1      8.029      0.005
        2        Row Mean Scores Differ    1      8.029      0.005
        3        General Association       1      8.029      0.005
```

You can also apply the Mantel-Cox test when you have additional explanatory variables. Table 15.5 contains data from a study on gastrointestinal patients being treated for ulcers. Investigations conducted in three medical centers compared an active treatment to a placebo.

Table 15.5   Healing for Gastrointestinal Patients

Center	Treatment	Healed at Two Weeks	Healed at Four Weeks	Not Healed at 4 Weeks	Total
1	A	15	17	2	34
1	P	15	17	7	39
2	A	17	17	10	44
2	P	12	13	15	40
3	A	7	17	16	40
3	P	3	17	18	38

Table 15.6 contains the life table format for the same data.

Table 15.6   Healing for Gastrointestinal Patients

Center	Weeks	Treatment	Number Healed	Number Not Healed	Total
1	0–2	A	15	19	34
		P	15	24	39
	2–4	A	17	2	19
		P	17	7	24
2	0–2	A	17	27	44
		P	12	28	40
	2–4	A	17	10	27
		P	13	15	28
3	0–2	A	7	33	40
		P	3	35	38
	2–4	A	17	16	33
		P	17	18	35

The following DATA step inputs these data, and the PROC FREQ statements specify that the MH test be computed. For these data, both TIME and CENTER are used as stratification variables.

```
data duodenal;
   input center time $ treat $ status $ count @@;
   cards;
1 0-2 A healed 15 1 0-2 A not 19
1 0-2 P healed 15 1 0-2 P not 24
1 2-4 A healed 17 1 2-4 A not  2
1 2-4 P healed 17 1 2-4 P not  7
2 0-2 A healed 17 2 0-2 A not 27
2 0-2 P healed 12 2 0-2 P not 28
2 2-4 A healed 17 2 2-4 A not 10
2 2-4 P healed 13 2 2-4 P not 15
```

```
3 0-2 A healed  7 3 0-2 A not 33
3 0-2 P healed  3 3 0-2 P not 35
3 2-4 A healed 17 3 2-4 A not 16
3 2-4 P healed 17 3 2-4 P not 18
;
proc freq;
   weight count;
   tables center*time*treat*status / cmh;
run;
```

Output 15.2 contains the results.

Output 15.2   Results for Mantel-Cox Test

```
          SUMMARY STATISTICS FOR TREAT BY STATUS
              CONTROLLING FOR CENTER AND TIME


    Cochran-Mantel-Haenszel Statistics (Based on Table Scores)

    Statistic   Alternative Hypothesis    DF    Value    Prob
    -----------------------------------------------------------
        1       Nonzero Correlation        1    4.253    0.039
        2       Row Mean Soores Differ     1    4.253    0.039
        3       General Association        1    4.253    0.039
```

The null hypothesis is that within each center, the distribution of time to healing is the same for placebo and active treatment. $Q_{MC} = 4.253$ with 1 df ($p = 0.039$), so that there is a significant effect of active treatment on time to healing after adjusting for center.

15.4   Poisson Regression

Categorical data sometimes have the Poisson distribution. Examples include colony counts for bacteria or viruses, accidents or equipment failures, and incidence for diseases. You are generally interested in estimating a rate or incidence (bacteria counts per unit volume or cancer deaths per person-months of exposure to a carcinogen) and determining the relationship of the rate to a set of explanatory variables.

For such data, you can write a Poisson regression model as

$$\mu(\mathbf{x}) = \{N(\mathbf{x})\}\{g(\boldsymbol{\beta}|\mathbf{x})\}$$

where $\mu(\mathbf{x})$ is the expected value of the number of events $n(\mathbf{x})$, $\mathbf{x}$ is the vector of explanatory variables, $\mathbf{x} = (x_1, x_2, \ldots, x_t)'$, and $N(\mathbf{x})$ is the known total exposure to risk in the units in which the events occur (subject-days, for example). The rate for incidence is written

$$\lambda(\mathbf{x}) = \mu(\mathbf{x})/N(\mathbf{x})$$

The most common model for Poisson regression is the loglinear model. This is written

$$\log\left\{\frac{\mu(\mathbf{x})}{N(\mathbf{x})}\right\} = \mathbf{x}'\boldsymbol{\beta}$$

for counts n with independent Poisson distributions. An equivalent form is

$$\mu(\mathbf{x}) = \{N(\mathbf{x})\}\{\exp(\mathbf{x}'\boldsymbol{\beta})\}$$

If you have s independent groups referenced by $i = 1, 2, \ldots, s$, each with a vector $\mathbf{x}_i = (x_{i1}, x_{i2}, \ldots, x_{it})$ of t explanatory variables, you can write a likelihood function for the data as

$$\Phi(\mathbf{n}|\boldsymbol{\mu}) = \prod_{i=1}^{s} \mu_i^{n_i}\{\exp(-\mu_i)\}/n_i!$$

where $\mathbf{n} = (n_1, n_2, \ldots, n_s)'$ and $\boldsymbol{\mu} = (\mu_1, \mu_2, \ldots, \mu_s)'$.

The Poisson loglinear model belongs to a class of models known as generalized linear models. These models extend the traditional linear model to encompass responses such as counts and proportions. See Section 8.9.1 for an introduction to the generalized linear model. For the loglinear Poisson regression model, the probability distribution is the Poisson distribution, and the link function is the log. Maximum likelihood estimators are obtained through iterative reweighted least squares algorithms.

The loglinear Poisson model is often written as

$$\log\{n_i\} = \log\{N_i\} + \mathbf{x}_i'\boldsymbol{\beta}$$

in the generalized linear models framework. The quantity $\log\{N_i\}$ is generally known as an *offset*, which means that it is a quantitative variable whose regression coefficient is known to be 1.

For more information on Poisson regression, refer to Koch, Atkinson, and Stokes (1986).

15.4.1   An Application of Poisson Regression

Consider Table 15.7. The counts n_{hi} are the number of new melanoma cases reported in 1969–1971 for white males in two areas (Gail 1978 and Koch, Imrey, et al. 1985). The totals N_{hi} are the sizes of the estimated populations at risk; they may represent counts of people or counts of exposure units. Researchers were interested in whether the rates n_{hi}/N_{hi}, which are incidence densities, varied across age groups or region ($h = 1$ for Northern region, $h = 2$ for Southern region; $i = 1, 2, 3, 4, 5, 6$ for ascending age groups).

Table 15.7   New Melanoma Cases Among White Males: 1969-1971

Region	Age Group	Cases	Total
Northern	< 35	61	2880262
Northern	35–44	76	564535
Northern	45–54	98	592983
Northern	55–64	104	450740
Northern	65–74	63	270908
Northern	> 75	80	161850
Southern	< 35	64	1074246
Southern	35–44	75	220407
Southern	45–54	68	198119
Southern	55–64	63	134084
Southern	65–74	45	70708
Southern	> 75	27	34233

As illustrated in Section 8.9.2, the GENMOD procedure fits generalized linear models in the SAS System. See this section for a discussion of using PROC GENMOD to fit the logistic model. For this application of Poisson regression, the model of interest includes incremental effects for age levels and region. The following DATA step inputs the melanoma data.

```
data melanoma;
   input age $ region $ cases total;
   ltotal=log(total);
   cards;
35-44 south 75   220407
45-54 south 68   198119
55-64 south 63   134084
65-74 south 45    70708
75+   south 27    34233
<35   south 64 1074246
35-44 north 76   564535
45-54 north 98   592983
55-64 north 104 450740
65-74 north 63   270908
75+   north 80   161850
<35   north 61 2880262
;
proc genmod data=melanoma order=data;
   class age region;
   model cases = age region
      / dist=poisson link=log offset=ltotal;
run;
```

In PROC GENMOD, the last sorted value of the CLASS variable determines the reference cell. In order for the reference cell to be those subjects from the north who are less than 35 years old, the data are entered so that those less than 35 appear last for each region, and the data for the south appear before the data for the north. Then, the ORDER=DATA option is specified in the PROC GENMOD statement.

The MODEL statement specifies that a main effects model be fit; CASES is the response variable, and AGE and REGION are the effects. The option DIST=POISSON specifies the Poisson distribution, and the option LINK=LOG specifies that the link function is the log function. The variable LTOTAL is to be treated as the offset. If you look in the preceding DATA step, you see that LTOTAL is the log of TOTAL. Thus, you are fitting a loglinear model to the ratio of cancer incidences to exposure.

Output 15.3 contains model specification information, and Output 15.4 contains information about the sort levels of the CLASS variables. This confirms that the reference level for the parameterization are those persons from the northern region who are younger than 35.

Output 15.3   Model Information

```
                     Model Information

          Description                   Value

          Data Set                      WORK.MELANOMA
          Distribution                  POISSON
          Link Function                 LOG
          Dependent Variable            CASES
          Offset Variable               LTOTAL
```

Output 15.4   Class Variable Information

```
                  Class Level Information

          Class     Levels  Values

          AGE            6  35-44 45-54 55-64 65-74 75+
                            <35
          REGION         2  south north
```

Output 15.5 contains information on assessment of fit. Since $Q_P = 6.12$ and the deviance has the value 6.21, each with 5 df for their approximately chi-square distributions, the fit is satisfactory.

Output 15.5   Assessment of Fit

```
             Criteria For Assessing Goodness Of Fit

          Criterion          DF       Value      Value/DF

          Deviance            5      6.2149        1.2430
          Scaled Deviance     5      6.2149        1.2430
          Pearson Chi-Square  5      6.1151        1.2230
          Scaled Pearson X2   5      6.1151        1.2230
          Log Likelihood      .   2694.9262             .
```

Output 15.6 contains the table of estimated model parameters. The log incidence density increases over each of the age intervals and also increases for the southern region.

Output 15.6   Estimated Model Parameters

```
                 Analysis Of Parameter Estimates

    Parameter              DF    Estimate    Std Err   ChiSquare   Pr>Chi

    INTERCEPT              1     -10.6583    0.0952   12538.4289   0.0001
    AGE        35-44       1       1.7974    0.1209     220.9204   0.0001
    AGE        45-54       1       1.9131    0.1184     260.9033   0.0001
    AGE        55-64       1       2.2418    0.1183     358.8872   0.0001
    AGE        65-74       1       2.3657    0.1315     323.5631   0.0001
    AGE        75-84       1       2.9447    0.1320     497.2981   0.0001
    AGE        <35         0       0.0000    0.0000         .         .
    REGION     1           1       0.8195    0.0710     133.1138   0.0001
    REGION     2           0       0.0000    0.0000         .         .
    SCALE                  0       1.0000    0.0000         .         .
```

You can exponentiate these parameters to express incidence density ratios in a similar manner to exponentiating parameters in logistic regression to obtain odds ratios. For example, exponentiating the parameter estimate for the increment for ages 45–54, $e^{1.9131} = 6.774$, gives you the ratio of the incidence of melanoma for those aged 45–54 relative to those less than 35. Similarly, $e^{0.8195} = 2.269$ is the ratio of the incidence of melanoma for those from the southern region relative to those in the northern region.

15.5   Piecewise Exponential Models

Statistical models can extend the analysis of grouped survival data by providing a description of the pattern of event rates. They can describe this pattern over time as well as describe the variation due to the influence of treatment and other explanatory variables. One particularly useful model is the piecewise exponential model.

Consider Table 15.8, which contains information pertaining to the experience of patients undergoing treatment for duodenal ulcers (based on Johnson and Koch 1978). One of two types of surgeries was randomly assigned: vagotomy and drainage or antrectomy, or vagotomy and hemigastrectomy. The patients were evaluated at 6 months, 24 months, and 60 months. Death and recurrence are considered failure events, and reoperation and loss to follow-up are considered withdrawal events.

Table 15.8   Comparison of Two Surgeries for Duodenal Ulcer

Operation	Time (months)	Death or Recurrence	Reoperation or Lost	Satisfactory	Exposure (months)
V + D/A	0–6	23	15	630	3894
	7–24	32	20	578	10872
	25–60	45	71	462	18720
V + H	0–6	9	5	329	2016
	7–24	5	17	307	5724
	25–60	10	24	273	10440

In this study there are two treatment groups: $i = 1$ for V and D/A, $i = 2$ for V + H and three time intervals: $k = 1$ for 0–6 months, $k = 2$ for 7–24 months, and $k = 3$ for 25–60 months.

If you can make the following assumptions, then you can fit the piecewise exponential model to these data.

- The withdrawals are uniformly distributed during the time intervals in which they occur and are unrelated to treatment failures.

- The within-interval probabilities of the treatment failures are small. The time-to-failure events have independent exponential distributions.

The piecewise exponential likelihood is written

$$\Phi_{PE} = \prod_{i=1}^{2} \prod_{k=1}^{3} \lambda_{ik}^{n_{i1k}} \left\{ \exp[-\lambda_{ik} N_{ik}] \right\}$$

where n_{i1k} is the number of failures for the ith group during the kth interval, N_{ik} is the total person-months of exposure, and λ_{ik} is the hazard parameter. The piecewise exponential model assumes that there are independent exponential distributions with hazard parameters λ_{ik} for the respective time periods.

The N_{ik} are computed as

$$N_{ik} = a_k(n_{i0k} + 0.5 n_{i1k} + 0.5 n_{i2k})$$

where $a_k = 6, 18, 36$ is the length of the kth interval, n_{i0k} is the number of patients completing the kth interval without failure or withdrawal, and n_{i2k} denotes the number of withdrawals. The quantity n_{i1k} is the number of failures during the interval.

If you think of the number of deaths n_{i1k}, conditional on the exposures N_{ik}, as having independent Poisson distributions, then you can write a Poisson likelihood for these data.

$$\Phi_{PO} = \prod_{i=1}^{2} \prod_{k=1}^{3} (N_{ik}\lambda_{ik})^{n_{i1k}} \left\{ \frac{\exp[-N_{ik}\lambda_{ik}]}{n_{i1k}!} \right\}$$

$$= \Phi_{PE} \left\{ \prod_{i=1}^{2} \prod_{k=1}^{3} \frac{N_{ik}^{n_{i1k}}}{n_{i1k}!} \right\}$$

Since these likelihoods are proportional, whatever maximizes Φ_{PO} also maximizes Φ_{PE}. Thus, you can still assume the piecewise exponential model but obtain the estimates from Poisson regression computations, which are more accessible, regardless of whether you want to make the conditional arguments necessary to assume a Poisson distribution.

The relationship of the failure events to the explanatory variables is specified through models for the λ_{ik}. One class of models has the structure

$$\lambda_{ik} = \exp(\mathbf{x}'_{ik}\boldsymbol{\beta})$$

A useful subset of these models has the specification

$$\lambda_{ik} = \exp(\alpha + \eta_k + \mathbf{x}'_i\boldsymbol{\beta})$$

This latter model has the proportional hazards structure, where $\{\eta_k\}$ is the constant value of the hazard function within the kth interval when $\mathbf{x}_i = 0$. The parameter vector $\boldsymbol{\beta}$ relates the hazard function for the ith population to the explanatory variables $\mathbf{x}_i$.

Those familiar with survival analysis may recognize the general form of the proportional hazards model as

$$h(y, \mathbf{x}) = h_0(y)\{\exp(\mathbf{x}'\boldsymbol{\beta})\}$$

where y denotes continuous time and $h_0(y)$ is the hazard function for the reference population. In reference to this general form, $\exp(\alpha + \eta_k)$ corresponds to $h_0(y)$ for y in the kth interval.

15.5.1 An Application of the Proportional Hazards Piecewise Exponential Model

Since the GENMOD procedure fits Poisson regression models in the SAS System, you also use it to fit piecewise exponential models. The DATA step inputs the duodenal ulcer data and computes the variable NMONTHS as the log of MONTHS. The following PROC GENMOD statements request that the main effects model consisting of time and treatment be fit. The variable TREAT has the value vda for V and D/A and the value vh for V + H. Note that the value for 0–6 months for the variable TIME is _0-6 so that it will sort last and thus become the reference value in the PROC GENMOD parameterization.

```
data vda;
    input treat $ time $ failure months;
    nmonths=log(months);
    cards;
vda  _0-6    23   3894
vda  7-24    32  10872
vda 25-60    45  18720
vh   _0-6     9   2016
vh   7-24     5   5724
vh  25-60    10  10440
;
proc genmod data=vda;
   class treat time;
   model failure = time treat
       / dist=poisson link=log offset=nmonths;
run;
```

Both TIME and TREAT are defined as class variables. The LINK=LOG option is specified so that the model is in loglinear form, and the OFFSET=NMONTHS is specified since the quantity n_{ik}/N_{ik} is being modeled.

Information about the model specification and the sort levels of the CLASS variables are displayed in Output 15.7.

Output 15.7   Model Information

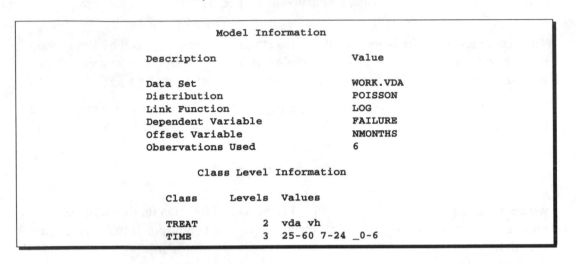

```
                    Model Information

        Description                      Value

        Data Set                         WORK.VDA
        Distribution                     POISSON
        Link Function                    LOG
        Dependent Variable               FAILURE
        Offset Variable                  NMONTHS
        Observations Used                6

             Class Level Information

        Class      Levels  Values

        TREAT         2     vda vh
        TIME          3     25-60 7-24 _0-6
```

Statistics for assessing fit are displayed in Output 15.8. Q_P and the deviance both indicate an adequate fit, with values of 2.6730 and 2.5529, respectively, and 2 df for their approximately chi-square distributions.

Output 15.8   Goodness-of-Fit Criteria

```
          Criteria For Assessing Goodness Of Fit

          Criterion            DF       Value       Value/DF

          Deviance              2       2.5529       1.2764
          Scaled Deviance       2       2.5529       1.2764
          Pearson Chi-Square    2       2.6730       1.3365
          Scaled Pearson X2     2       2.6730       1.3365
          Log Likelihood        .     279.8914          .
```

The "Analysis of Parameter Estimates" table includes an intercept parameter, incremental effects for 7–24 months and 25–60 months, and an incremental effect for the V + D/A treatment. The 0–6 months time interval and the V + H treatment are the reference cell. See Output 15.9.

Output 15.9   Parameter Estimates

```
              Analysis Of Parameter Estimates

  Parameter            DF    Estimate    Std Err    ChiSquare    Pr>Chi

  INTERCEPT             1     -5.8164     0.2556     517.6601    0.0001
  TIME       25-60      1     -1.0429     0.2223      22.0015    0.0001
  TIME       7-24       1     -0.8847     0.2414      13.4319    0.0002
  TIME       _0-6       0      0.0000     0.0000         .          .
  TREAT      vda        1      0.8071     0.2273      12.6067    0.0004
  TREAT      vh         0      0.0000     0.0000         .          .
  SCALE                 0      1.0000     0.0000         .          .
```

All of these effects are significant. Table 15.9 contains the parameter interpretations.

Table 15.9   Parameter Interpretations

GENMOD Parameter	Model Parameter	Value	Interpretation
INTERCEPT	α	-5.8164	log incidence density for V + H, 0-6 months (reference)
TIME 25-60	η_2	-1.0429	increment for 25-60 interval
TIME 7-24	η_1	-0.8847	increment for 7-25 interval
TREAT vda	β	0.8071	increment for treatment V + D/A

Log incidence density decreases with the 7–24 interval and further decreases with the 25–60 interval. The V + D/A treatment increases log incidence density. What this means is that the failure rate is highest for the first interval and lower for the other two intervals; the failure rate is higher for V + D/A than for V + H. Table 15.10 displays the estimated failure rates (incidence densities) per person-month for each group and interval.

The survival rates can be calculated as follows:

$$\Pr\{\text{survival for } k \text{ intervals}\} = \Pr\{\text{survival for } k - 1 \text{ intervals}\} \times e^{-\lambda_{ik} a_k}$$

where a_k is the length of the kth interval, $k = 1, 2, \ldots, t$. Table 15.10 contains the survival estimates for each interval for each treatment group.

Table 15.10   Model-Estimated Failure Rates

Group	Interval	Failure Rate Formula	Estimated Failure Rate	Estimated Survival Rate
V + H	0–6	$e^{\hat{\alpha}}$	0.002978	0.9823
V + H	7–24	$e^{\hat{\alpha}+\hat{\eta}_1}$	0.001230	0.9608
V + H	25–60	$e^{\hat{\alpha}+\hat{\eta}_2}$	0.001050	0.9252
V + D/A	0–6	$e^{\hat{\alpha}+\hat{\beta}}$	0.006676	0.9607
V + D/A	7–24	$e^{\hat{\alpha}+\hat{\beta}+\hat{\eta}_1}$	0.002756	0.9142
V + D/A	25–60	$e^{\hat{\alpha}+\hat{\beta}+\hat{\eta}_2}$	0.002353	0.8399

15.5.2   Performing Poisson Regression with PROC LOGISTIC

When the incidence rates $\{\lambda_{ik}\}$ are small (less than 0.05) and the exposures N_{ik} are very large, then you can approximate Poisson regression with logistic regression (Vine et al. 1990). Thus, you can take advantage of the features of the LOGISTIC procedure, such as its model-building facilities, to fit models such as the piecewise exponential model. You can facilitate the approximation by rescaling the exposure factor by multiplying it by a number such as 10,000; the only adjustment you need to make after parameter estimation is to add to the resulting intercept estimate the log of the multiplier you choose.

The following SAS statements fit a piecewise exponential model to the duodenal ulcer data using the LOGISTIC procedure. TIME1 and TIME2 are variables representing incremental effects for the 7–24 months and 25–60 months intervals, respectively. The variable TREAT takes the value 1 for the V + D/A treatment and 0 for the V + H treatment. The terms TRTTIME1 and TRTTIME2 are interaction terms for treatment with the 7–24 and 25–60 months intervals, respectively. The variable SMONTHS is the exposure in months multiplied by a factor of 100,000.

The events/trials syntax is employed in the MODEL statement, with FAILURE in the numerator and SMONTHS in the denominator. The SELECTION=FORWARD option specifies forward model selection, and INCLUDE=3 specifies that the first three variables listed in the MODEL statement, TIME1, TIME2, and TREAT, be forced into the first model so that a score test is produced for the contribution of the remaining variables to the model (interactions). This serves as a goodness-of-fit test.

```
data vda;
   input treat time $ failure months;
   time1=(time='7-24');
   time2=(time='25-60');
   smonths=100000*months;
   trttime1=treat*time1;
   trttime2=treat*time2;
   cards;
1   _0-6    23   3894
1   7-24    32   10872
1   25-60   45   18720
0   _0-6    9    2016
0   7-24    5    5724
0   25-60   10   10440
;
proc logistic;
   model failure/smonths = time1 time2 treat trttime1 trttime2 /
                           scale=none include=3 selection=forward;
run;
```

Output 15.10 contains the resulting statistics for explanatory variable contribution and the score statistic (Residual Chi-Square) for the contribution of variables not in the model. Q_S has a value of 2.6730 and is nonsignificant with 2 df and $p = 0.2628$. The model fits adequately and the proportional hazards assumption is reasonable (no time $\times$ treatment interaction).

Output 15.10   Score Statistic

```
Step  0. The INCLUDE variables were entered.

                    Testing Global Null Hypothesis: BETA=0

                                    Intercept
                        Intercept      and
        Criterion         Only      Covariates    Chi-Square for Covariates

        AIC             4601.209     4572.439          .
        SC              4621.575     4653.901          .
        -2 LOG L        4599.209     4564.439      34.770 with 3 DF  (p=0.0001)
        Score              .            .          39.055 with 3 DF  (p=0.0001)

                Residual Chi-Square = 2.6730 with 2 DF  (p=0.2628)
```

Output 15.11 displays the goodness-of-fit statistics, which are adequate.

Output 15.11   Goodness-of-Fit Statistics

```
            Deviance and Pearson Goodness-of-Fit Statistics

                                                       Pr >
        Criterion       DF      Value    Value/DF    Chi-Square

        Deviance         2      2.5529    1.2764       0.2790
        Pearson          2      2.6730    1.3365       0.2628

                Number of events/trials observations: 6
```

The resulting parameter estimates are displayed in Output 15.12. The estimates for
TIME1, TIME2, and TREAT are identical to the estimates resulting from the PROC
GENMOD analysis in the previous section, and if you add log(100000) to the intercept,
−17.3293, you obtain −5.8164, which is identical to the intercept estimate obtained from
PROC GENMOD. This approximation is usually very good.

Output 15.12   Parameter Estimates

```
                Analysis of Maximum Likelihood Estimates

                Parameter Standard    Wald       Pr >     Standardized   Odds
        Variable DF Estimate  Error  Chi-Square Chi-Square  Estimate     Ratio

        INTERCPT 1  -17.3293  0.2556 4595.1968    0.0001        .           .
        TIME1    1   -0.8847  0.2414   13.4320    0.0002    -0.227769     0.413
        TIME2    1   -1.0429  0.2223   22.0017    0.0001    -0.285108     0.352
        TREAT    1    0.8071  0.2273   12.6068    0.0004     0.212510     2.241
```

At this point, you would proceed to produce survival rates and survival estimates as
computed in the previous section.

References

Agresti, A. (1988). Logit models for repeated ordered categorical response data, *Proceedings of the 13th Annual SAS Users Group International Conference*, Cary, NC: SAS Institute Inc., 997–1005.

Agresti, A. (1989). A survey of models for repeated ordered categorical response data, *Statistics in Medicine*, 8, 1209–1224.

Agresti, A. (1990). *Categorical Data Analysis*, New York: John Wiley & Sons, Inc.

Agresti, A. (1995). *An Introduction to Categorical Data Analysis*, New York: John Wiley & Sons, Inc. (Upcoming)

Albert, A. and Anderson, J. A. (1984). On the existence of maximum likelihood estimates in logistic regression models, *Biometrika*, 71, 1–10.

Andersen, E. B. (1991). *The Statistical Analysis of Categorical Data, Second Edition*, Berlin: Springer-Verlag.

Armitage, P. (1955). Tests for linear trends in proportions and frequencies, *Biometrics*, 11, 375–386.

Baglivo, J., Olivier, D., and Pagano, M. (1988). Methods for the analysis of contingency tables with large and small cell counts, *Journal of the American Statistical Society*, 83, 1006–1013.

Bauman, K. E., Koch, G. G., and Lentz, M. (1989). Parent characteristics, perceived health risk, and smokeless tobacco use among white adolescent males, *NI Monographs 8*, 43–48.

Benard, A. and van Elteren, P. (1953). A generalization of the method of m rankings, *Proceedings Koninklijke Nederlands Akademie van Wetenschappen (A)*, 56, 358–369.

Berkson, J. (1951). Why I prefer logits to probits. *Biometrics*, 7, 327–339.

Berry, D. A. (1987). Logarithmic transformations in ANOVA, *Biometrics*, 43, 439–456.

Birch, M. W. (1963). Maximum likelihood in three-way contingency tables, *Journal of the Royal Statistical Society, Series B*, 25, 220–233.

Bishop, Y. M. M., Fienberg, S. E., and Holland, P. W. (1975). *Discrete Multivariate Analysis*, Cambridge, MA: MIT Press.

Bock, R. D. (1975). *Multivariate Statistical Methods in Behavioral Research*, New York: McGraw-Hill, Inc.

Bock, R. D. and Jones, L.V. (1968). *The Measurement and Prediction of Judgement and Choice*, San Francisco: Holden-Day.

Bowker, A. H. (1948). Bowker's test for symmetry, *Journal of the American Statistical Association*, 43, 572–574.

Breslow, N. E. and Day, N. E. (1980). *Statistical Methods in Cancer Research, Volume 1: The Analysis of Case-Control Studies*, Lyon, International Agency for Research on Cancer.

Bruce, R. A., Kusumi, F., and Hosmer, D. (1973). Maximal oxygen intake and nomographic assessment of functional aerobic impairment in cardiovascular disease, *American Heart Journal*, 65, 546–562.

Cartwright, H. V., Lindahl, R. L., and Bawden, J. W. (1968). Clinical findings on the effectiveness of stannous fluoride and acid phosphate fluoride as caries reducing agents in children, *Journal of Dentistry for Children*, 35, 36–40.

Cawson M. J., Anderson, A. B. M., Turnbull, A. C., and Lampe, L. (1974). Cortisol, cortisone, and 11-deoxycortisol levels in human umbilical and maternal plasma in relation to the onset of labour, *Journal of Obstetrics and Gynaecology of the British Commonwealth*, 81, 737–745.

Cochran, W. G. (1950). The comparison of percentages in matched samples, *Biometrika*, 37, 256–266.

Cochran, W. G. (1954). Some methods of strengthening the common χ^2 tests, *Biometrics*, 10, 417–451.

Cohen, J. (1960). A coefficient of agreement for nominal data, *Educational and Psychological Measurement*, 20, 37–46.

Collett, D. (1991). *Modelling Binary Data*, London: Chapman and Hall.

Cook, R. D. and Weisberg, S. (1982). *Residuals and Influence in Regression*, London: Chapman and Hall.

Cornoni-Huntley, J., Brock, D. B., Ostfeld, A., Taylor, J. O., and Wallace, R. B. (1986). *Established Populations for Epidemiologic Studies of the Elderly, Resource Data Book*, Bethesda, MD: National Institutes of Health (NIH Pub. No. 86–2443).

Cox, D. R. (1970). *Analysis of Binary Data*, London: Chapman and Hall.

Cox, D. R. (1972). Regression models and life tables, *Journal of the Royal Statistical Society, Series B*, 34, 187–220.

Cox, M. A. A. and Plackett, R. L. (1980). Small samples in contingency tables, *Biometrika* 67, 1–13.

Davis, C. S. (1992). Analysis of incomplete categorical repeated measures, *Proceedings of the 17th Annual SAS Users Group International Conference*, Cary, NC: SAS Institute Inc., 1374–1379.

Deddens, J. A. and Koch, G. G. (1988). Survival analysis, grouped data, in *Encyclopedia of Statistical Sciences*, 9, eds. Kotz, S. and Johnson, N. L, New York: John Wiley & Sons, Inc., 129–134.

Deming, W. E. and Stephan, F. F. (1940). On a least squares adjustment of a sample frequency table when the expected marginal totals are known, *Annals of Mathematical Statistics*, 11, 427–444.

Dobson, A. J. (1990). *An Introduction to Generalized Linear Models*, London: Chapman and Hall.

Draper, N. R. and Smith, H. (1981). *Applied Regression Analysis*, New York: John Wiley & Sons, Inc.

Durbin, J. (1951). Incomplete blocks in ranking experiments, *British Journal of Mathematical and Statistical Psychology*, 4, 85–90.

Dyke, G. V. and Patterson, H. D. (1952). Analysis of factorial arrangements when the data are proportions, *Biometrics*, 8, 1–12.

Finney, D. J. (1978). *Statistical Methods in Biological Assay, Third edition*, New York: MacMillan Publishing Company, Inc.

Fisher, L. D. and van Belle, G. (1993). *Biostatistics: A Methodology for the Health Sciences*, New York: John Wiley & Sons, Inc.

Fleiss, J. L. (1975). Measuring agreement between two judges on the presence or absence of a trait, *Biometrics*, 31, 651–659.

Fleiss, J. L. (1981). *Statistical Methods for Rates and Proportions*, New York: John Wiley & Sons, Inc.

Fleiss, J. L. (1986). *The Design and Analysis of Clinical Experiments*, New York: John Wiley & Sons, Inc.

Fleiss, J. L. and Cohen, J. (1973). The equivalence of weighted kappa and the intraclass correlation coefficient as measures of reliability, *Educational and Psychological Measurement*, 33, 613–619.

Friedman, M. (1937). The use of ranks to avoid the assumption of normality implicit in the analysis of variance, *Journal of the American Statistical Association*, 32, 675–701.

Gail, M. (1978). The analysis of heterogeneity for indirect standardized mortality ratios, *Journal of the Royal Statistical Society A*, 141, Part 2, 224–234.

Goodman, L. A. (1968). The analysis of cross-classified data: independence, quasi-independence, and interactions in contingency tables with or without missing entries, *Journal of the American Statistical Association*, 63, 1091–1131.

Goodman, L. A. (1970). The multivariate analysis of qualitative data: interaction among multiple classifications, *Journal of the American Statistical Association*, 65, 226–256.

Govindarajulu, Z. (1988). *Statistical Methods in Bioassay*, Basel: Karger.

Graubard, B. I. and Korn, E. L. (1987). Choice of column scores for testing independence in ordered $2 \times k$ contingency tables, *Biometrics*, 43, 471–476.

Grizzle, J. E., Starmer, C. F., and Koch, G. G. (1969). Analysis of categorical data by linear models, *Biometrics*, 25, 489–504.

Harrell, F. E. (1989). Analysis of repeated measurements, Unpublished course notes.

Higgins, J. E. and Koch, G. G. (1977). Variable selection and generalized chi-square analysis of categorical data applied to a large cross-sectional occupational health survey, *International Statistical Review*, 45, 51–62.

Hirji, K. F., Mehta, C. R., and Patel, N. R. (1987). Computing distributions for exact logistic regression, *Journal of the American Statistical Association*, 82, 1110–1117.

Hochberg, Y., Stutts, J. C., and Reinfurt, D. W. (1977). Observed shoulder belt usage of drivers in North Carolina: a follow-up, *University of North Carolina Highway Safety Research Center Report, May 1977*.

Hodges, J. L. and Lehmann, E. L. (1962). Rank methods for combination of independent experiments in analysis of variance, *Annals of Mathematical Statistics*, 33, 482–497.

Hosmer, D. W. and Lemeshow, S. (1989). *Applied Logistic Regression*, New York: John Wiley & Sons, Inc.

Imrey, P. B., Koch, G. G., and Stokes, M. E. (1982). Categorical data analysis: some reflections on the log linear model and logistic regression, part II, *International Statistical Review*, 50, 35–64.

Johnson, W. D. and Koch, G. G. (1978). Linear models analysis of competing risks for grouped survival times, *International Statistical Review*, 46, 21–51.

Karim, M. R. and Zeger, S. L. (1988). GEE: A SAS macro for longitudinal data analysis, Technical Report No. 674, Department of Biostatistics, The Johns Hopkins University.

Kendall, M. G. and Stuart, A. (1961). *The Advanced Theory of Statistics, Volume 2: Inference and Relationship*, London: Charles Griffin and Company.

Koch, G. G., Amara, I. A., Davis, G. W., and Gillings, D. B. (1982). A review of some statistical methods for covariance analysis of categorical data, *Biometrics*, 38, 563–595.

Koch, G. G., Amara, I. A., and Singer, J. M. (1985). A two-stage procedure for the analysis of ordinal categorical data, in *Statistics in Biomedical, Public Health and Environmental Sciences*, ed. P.K. Sen, Amsterdam: North-Holland, 357–387.

Koch, G. G., Atkinson, S. S., and Stokes, M. E. (1986). Poisson regression, in *Encyclopedia of Statistical Sciences*, 7, eds. Kotz, S. and Johnson, N. L., New York: John Wiley & Sons, Inc, 32–41.

Koch, G. G., Carr, G. J., Amara, I. A., Stokes, M. E., and Uryniak, T. J. (1990). Categorical data analysis, in *Statistical Methodology in the Pharmaceutical Sciences*, ed. D.A. Berry, New York: Marcel Dekker Inc., 391–475.

Koch, G. G. and Edwards, S. (1985). Logistic regression, in *Encyclopedia of Statistics*, 5, New York: John Wiley & Sons, Inc, 128-133.

Koch, G. G. and Edwards, S. (1988). Clinical efficacy trials with categorical data, in *Biopharmaceutical Statistics for Drug Development*, ed. K.E. Peace, New York: Marcel Dekker, 403–451.

Koch, G. G., Gillings, D. B., and Stokes, M. E. (1980). Biostatistical implications of design, sampling, and measurement to health science data, in *Annual Review of Public Health*, 1, 163–225.

Koch, G. G., Imrey, P. B, Singer, J. M., Atkinson, S. S., and Stokes, M. E. (1985). *Analysis of Categorical Data*, Montreal, Canada: *Les Presses De L'Universite' de Montreal*.

Koch, G. G., Landis, J. R., Freeman, J. L., Freeman, D. H., and Lehnen, R. G. (1977). A general methodology for the analysis of experiments with repeated measurement of categorical data, *Biometrics*, 33, 133–158.

Koch, G. G. and Reinfurt, D. W. (1971). The analysis of categorical data from mixed models, *Biometrics*, 27, 157–173.

Koch, G. G. and Sen, P. K. (1968). Some aspects of the statistical analysis of the mixed model, *Biometrics*, 24, 27–48.

Koch, G. G., Sen, P. K., and Amara, I. A. (1985). Log-rank scores, statistics, and tests, in *Encyclopedia of Statistics*, 5, New York: John Wiley & Sons, Inc, 136–141.

Koch, G. G., Singer, J. M., Stokes, M. E., Carr, G. J., Cohen, S. B., and Forthofer, R. N. (1989). Some aspects of weighted least squares analysis for longitudinal categorical data, in *Statistical Models for Longitudinal Studies of Health,* ed. J.H. Dywer, Oxford: Oxford University Press, Inc., 215-258.

Koch, G. G. and Stokes, M. E. (1979). Annotated computer applications of weighted least squares methods for illustrative analyses of examples involving health survey data, Technical Report prepared for the U.S. National Center for Health Statistics.

Kruskal, W. H. and Wallis, W. A. (1952). Use of ranks in one-criterion variance analysis, *Journal of the American Statistical Association*, 47, 583–621.

Kuritz, S. J., Landis, J. R., and Koch, G. G. (1988). A general overview of Mantel-Haenszel methods: applications and recent developments, *Annual Review of Public Health*, 1988, 123–160.

Lafata, J. E., Koch, G. G., and Weissert, W. G. (1994). Estimating activity limitation in the noninstitutionalized population: a method for small areas, *American Journal of Public Health*, 84, 1813–1817.

Landis, J. R. and Koch, G. G. (1977). The measurement of observer agreement for categorical data, *Biometrics*, 33, 159–174.

Landis, J. R. and Koch, G. G. (1979). The analysis of categorical data on longitudinal studies of behavioral development, in *Longitudinal Research in the Study of Behavior and Development*, ed. J.R. Nesselroade and P. B. Bates, New York: Academic Press, Inc., 231–261.

Landis, J. R., Heyman, E. R., and Koch, G. G. (1978). Average partial association in three-way contingency tables: a review and discussion of alternative tests, *International Statistical Review*, 46, 237–254.

Landis, J. R., Stanish, W. M., and Koch, G. G. (1976). A computer program for the generalized chi-square analysis of categorical data using weighted least squares, (GENCAT), *Computer Programs in Biomedicine*, 6, 196–231.

Landis, J. R., Miller, M. E., Davis, C. S., and Koch, G. G. (1988). Some general methods for the analysis of categorical data in longitudinal studies, *Statistics in Medicine*, 7, 233–261.

Lehmann, E. L. (1975). *Nonparametrics: Statistical Methods Based on Ranks*, San Francisco: Holden-Day.

Lemeshow, S. and Hosmer, D. (1989). *Applied Logistic Regression Analysis*, New York: John Wiley & Sons, Inc.

Liang, K. Y. and Zeger, S. L. (1986). Longitudinal data analysis using generalized linear models, *Biometrika*, 73, 13–22.

Liang, K. Y., Zeger, S. L., and Qaqish, B. (1992). Multivariate regression analyses for categorical data (with discussion), *Journal of the Royal Statistical Society, Series B*, 54, 3–40.

Lund, A. K., Williams, A. F., and Zador, P. (1986). High school driver education: further evaluation of the Dekalb County study, *Accident Analysis and Prevention*, 18, 349–357.

Mack, T. M., Pike, M. C., Henderson, B. E., Pfeffer, R. I., Gerkins, V. R., Arthur, M., and Brown, S. E. (1976). Estrogens and endometrial cancer in a retirement community, *New England Journal of Medicine*, 294, 23, 1262–1267.

Macknin, M.L., Mathew, S., and Medendorp, S.V. (1990). Effect of inhaling heated vapor on symptoms of the common cold, *Journal of the American Medical Association*, 264, 989–991.

MacMillan, J., Becker, C., Koch, G. G., Stokes, M. E., and Vandivire, H. M. (1981). An Application of weighted least squares methods to the analysis of measurement process components of variability in an observational study, *American Statistical Association Proceedings of Survey Research Methods*, 680–685.

Madansky, A. (1963). Test of homogeneity for correlated samples, *Journal of the American Statistical Association*, 58, 97–119.

Mann, H. B. and Whitney, D. R. (1947). On a test of whether one of two random variables is stochastically larger than the other, *Annals of Mathematical Statistics,* 18, 50–60.

Mantel, N. (1963). Chi-square tests with one degree of freedom; extensions of the Mantel-Haenszel procedure, *Journal of the American Statistical Association*, 58, 690–700.

Mantel, N. (1966). Evaluation of survival data and two new rank order statistics arising in its consideration, *Cancer Chemotherapy Report*, 50, 163–170.

Mantel, N. and Fleiss, J. (1980). Minimum expected cell size requirements for the Mantel-Haenszel one-degree of freedom chi-square test and a related rapid procedure, *American Journal of Epidemiology*, 112, 129–143.

Mantel, N. and Haenszel, W. (1959). Statistical aspects of the analysis of data from retrospective studies of disease, *Journal of the National Cancer Institute* 22, 719–748.

McCullagh, P. (1980). Regression models for ordinal data (with discussion), *Journal of the Royal Statistical Society, Series B*, 42, 109–142.

McCullagh, P. and Nelder, J. A. (1989). *Generalized Linear Models, Second Edition*, London: Chapman and Hall.

McNemar, Q. (1947). Note on the sampling error of the difference between correlated proportions or precentages, *Psychometrika*, 12, 153–157.

Mehta, C. R. and Patel, N. R. (1983). A network algorithm for performing Fisher's exact test in r by c contingency tables, *Journal of the American Statistical Association*, 427–434.

Mehta, C. R. and Patel N. R. (1991). *StatXact: Statistical Software for Exact Nonparametric Inference,* Cambridge, MA: CYTEL Software Corporation.

Mehta, C. R. and Patel, N. R. (1992). *LogXact-Turbo User Manual*, Cambridge, MA: CYTEL Software Corporation.

Mehta, C. R., Patel, N. R., and Tsiatis, A. A. (1984). Exact significance testing to establish treatment equivalence with ordered categorical data, *Biometrics*, 40: 427–434.

Moulton, L. H. and Zeger, S. L. (1989). Analyzing repeated measures on generalized linear models via the bootstrap, *Biometrics*, 45, 381–394.

Nemeroff, C. B., Bissette, G., Prange, A. J., Loosen, P. Y., Barlow, F. S. and Lipton, M. A. (1977). Neurotensin: central nervous system effects of a hypothalamic peptide, *Brain Research*, 128, 485–496.

Neyman, J. (1949). in *Proceedings of the Berkeley Symposium of Mathematical Statistics and Probability*, Berkeley: University of California Press, 239–273.

Odeh, R. E., Owen, D. B., Birnbaum, Z. W., and Fisher, L. D. (1977). *Pocket Book of Statistical Tables,* New York: Marcel Dekker, Inc.

Ogilvie, J. C. (1965). Paired comparison models with tests for interaction, *Biometrics*, 21, 651–654.

Pagano, M. and Halvorsen, K. T. (1981). An algorithm for finding the exact significance levels of r × c contingency tables, *Journal of the American Statistical Society*, 76, 931–934.

Pitman, E. J. G. (1948). *Lecture Notes on Nonparametric Statistics,* New York: Columbia University.

Pregibon, D. (1981). Logistic regression diagnostics, *Annals of Statistics*, 9: 705–724.

Quade, D. (1967). Rank analysis of covariance, *Journal of the American Statistical Association*, 62, 1187–1200.

Quade, D. (1982). Nonparametric analysis of covariance by matching, *Biometrics*, 38, 597–611.

Rao, C. R. (1961). Asymptotic efficiency and limiting information, *Proceedings of the 4th Berkeley Symposium on Mathematical Statistics and Probability*, 1, 531–545.

Rao, C. R. (1962). Efficient estimates and optimum inference procedures in large samples (with discussion), *Journal of the Royal Statistical Society, Series B*, 24, 46–72.

Read, C. B. (1983). Fieller's theorem, in *Encyclopedia of Statistical Sciences*, 3, eds. Kotz, S. and Johnson, N. L., New York: John Wiley & Sons, Inc., 86–88.

Roberts, G., Martyn, A. L., Dobson, A. J., and McCarthy, W. H. (1981). Tumour thickness and histological type in malignant melanoma in New South Wales, Australia, *Pathology*, 13, 763–770.

Robins, J., Breslow, N., and Greenland, S. (1986). Estimators of the Mantel-Haenszel variance consistent in both sparse data and large-strata limiting models, *Biometrics*, 42, 311–323.

Schechter, P. J., Horwitz, D., and Henkin, R. I. (1973). Sodium chloride preference in essential hypertension, *Journal of the American Medical Association*, 225, 1311–1315.

Semenya, K. A. and Koch, G. G. (1979). Linear models analysis for rank functions of ordinal categorical data, *Proceedings of the Statistical Computing Section of the American Statistical Association*, 271–276.

Semenya, K. A. and Koch, G. G. (1980). Compound function and linear model methods for the multivariate analysis of ordinal categorical data, *Institute of Statistics Mimeo Series No. 1323*, Chapel Hill: University of North Carolina.

Shah, B. V., Barnwell, B. G., Hunt, P. N., and LaVange, L. M. (1991). *SUDAAN User's Manual, Release 5.50*, Research Triangle Institute, RTP, NC.

Silvapulle, M. J. (1981). On the existence of maximum likelihood estimators for the binomial response models, *Journal of the Royal Statistics Society*, 43, 310–313.

Simpson, E. H. (1951). The interpretation of interaction in contingency tables, *Journal of the Royal Statistical Society*, B13, 238–241.

Stanish, W. M., Gillings, D. B., and Koch, G. G., (1978). An application of multivariate ratio methods for the analysis of a longitudinal clinical trial with missing data, *Biometrics*, 34, 305–317.

Stanish, W. M. (1986). Categorical data analysis strategies using SAS software, in *Computer Science and Statistics: Proceedings of the 17th Symposium on the Interface*, ed. D.M. Allen, New York: Elsevier Science Publishing Company.

Stanish, W. M. and Koch, G. G. (1984). The use of CATMOD for repeated measurement analysis of categorical data, *Proceedings of the 9th Annual SAS Users Group International Conference*, Cary, NC: SAS Institute Inc., 761–770.

Stewart, J. R. (1975). An analysis of automobile accidents to determine which variables are most strongly associated with driver injury: relationships between driver injury and vehicle model year, *University of North Carolina Highway Safety Research Center Technical Report*.

Stock, J. R., Weaver, J. K., Ray, H. W., Brink, J. R., and Sadof, M. G. (1983). *Evaluation of Safe Performance Secondary School Driver Education Curriculum Demonstration Project*, Washington, D.C.: U.S. Department of Transportation, National Highway Traffic Safety Administration.

Stokes, M. E. (1986). An application of categorical data analysis to a large environmental data set with repeated measurements and missing values, *Institute of Statistics Mimeo Series No. 1807T*, Chapel Hill: University of North Carolina.

Stram, D.O., Wei, L.J., and Ware, J.H. (1988). Analysis of repeated ordered categorical outcomes with possibly missing observations and time-dependent covariates, *Journal of the American Statistical Association*, 83, 631–637.

Tardif, S. (1980). On the asymptotic distribution of a class of aligned rank order test statistics in randomized block designs, *Canadian Journal of Statistics*, 8, 7–25.

Tardif, S. (1981). On the almost sure convergence of the permutation distribution for aligned rank test statistics in randomized block designs, *Annals of Statistics*, 9, 190–193.

Tardif, S. (1985). On the asymptotic efficiency of aligned-rank tests in randomized block designs, *Canadian Journal of Statistics*, 13, 217–232.

Tritchler, D. (1984). An algorithm for exact logistic regression, *Journal of the American Statistical Association*, 79, 709–711.

Tsutakawa, R. K. (1982). Statistical methods in bioassay, in *Encyclopedia of Statistical Sciences*, 1, eds. Kotz, S. and Johnson, N. L., New York: John Wiley & Sons, Inc., 237–243.

van Elteren, P. H. (1960). On the combination of independent two-sample tests of Wilcoxon, *Bulletin of the International Statistical Institute*, 37, 351–361.

Vine, M.F., Schoenbach, V., Hulka, B. S., Koch, G. G., and Samsa, G. (1990). Atypical metaplasia as a risk factor for bronchogenic carcinoma, *American Journal of Epidemiology*, 131, 781–793.

Wald, A. (1943). Tests of statistical hypotheses concerning general parameters when the number of observations is large, *Transactions of the American Mathematical Society*, 54, 426–482.

Ware, J. H., Lipsitz, S. and Speizer, F. E. (1988). Issues in the analysis of repeated categorical outcomes, *Statistics in Medicine*, 7, 95–107.

Wei, L. J. and Stram, D. O. (1988). Analyzing repeated measurements with possibly missing observations by modelling marginal distributions, *Statistics in Medicine*, 7, 139–148.

Wilcoxon, F. (1945). Individual comparison by ranking methods, *Biometrics*, 1, 80–83.

Yule, G. U. (1903). Notes on the theory of association of attributes in statistics, *Biometrika*, 2, 121–134.

Zeger, S. L. (1988). Commentary, *Statistics in Medicine*, 7, 161–168.

Zeger, S. L. and Liang, K. Y. (1986). Longitudinal data analysis for discrete and continuous outcomes, *Biometrics*, 42, 121–130.

Zeger, S. L., Liang, K. Y., and Albert, P. S. (1988). Models for longitudinal data: a generalized estimating equation approach, *Biometrics*, 44, 1049–1060.

Zerbe, G. O. (1978). On Fieller's theorem and the general linear model, *The American Statistician*, 32 (3).

Zhao, L. P. and Prentice, R. L. (1990). Correlated binary regression using a quadratic exponential model, *Biometrika*, 77, 642–648.

Index

Call your local SAS® office to order these other books and tapes available through the Books by Users℠ program:

Applied Multivariate Statistics with SAS® Software
by **Ravindra Khattree**
and **Dayanand N. Naik** ....Order #A55234

Applied Statistics and the SAS® Programming Language, Third Edition
by **Ronald P. Cody**
and **Jeffrey K. Smith** ....Order #A56191

Beyond the Obvious with SAS® Screen Control Language
by **Don Stanley**....................................Order #A55073

The Cartoon Guide to Statistics
by **Larry Gonick**
and **Woollcott Smith** ....Order #A55153

Essential Client/Server Survival Guide
by **Robert Orfali, Dan Harkey,**
and **Jeri Edwards** ....Order #A55305

The How-To Book for SAS/GRAPH® Software
by **Thomas Miron** ....Order #A55203

Learning SAS® in the Computer Lab
by **Rebecca J. Elliott** ....Order #A55273

The Little SAS® Book: A Primer
by **Lora D. Delwiche**
and **Susan J. Slaughter** ....Order #A55200

Mastering the SAS® System, Second Edition
by **Jay A. Jaffe** ....Order #A55123

Professional SAS® Programmer's Pocket Reference
by **Rick Aster**......................................Order #A56198

Professional SAS® Programming Secrets
by **Rick Aster**
and **Rhena Seidman** ....Order #A56192

Professional SAS® User Interfaces
by **Rick Aster**......................................Order #A56197

Quick Results with SAS/GRAPH® Software
by **Arthur L. Carpenter**
and **Charles E. Shipp**..........................Order #A55127

Reporting from the Field: SAS® Software Experts Present Real-World Report-Writing Applications ....Order #A55135

SAS® Applications Programming: A Gentle Introduction
by **Frank C. DiIorio** ....Order #A56193

SAS® Foundations: From Installation to Operation
by **Rick Aster** ....Order #A55093

SAS® Programming by Example
by **Ron Cody**
and **Ray Pass** ....Order #A55126

SAS® Programming for Researchers and Social Scientists
by **Paul E. Spector** ....Order #A56199

SAS® Software Roadmaps: Your Guide to Discovering the SAS® System
by **Laurie Burch**
and **SherriJoyce King**..........................Order #A56195

SAS® Software Solutions
by **Thomas Miron** ....Order #A56196

SAS® System for Elementary Statistical Analysis
by **Sandra D. Schlotzhauer**
and **Ramon C. Littell** ....Order #A5619

SAS® System for Forecasting Time Series, 1986 Edition
by **John C. Brocklebank**
and **David A. Dickey** ....Order #A5612

SAS® System for Linear Models, Third Edition
by **Ramon C. Littell, Rudolf J. Freund,**
and **Philip C. Spector**...........................Order #A56140

*SAS® System for Regression,
Second Edition*
by **Rudolf J. Freund**
and **Ramon C. Littell** ....Order #A56141

*SAS® System for Statistical Graphics,
First Edition*
by **Michael Friendly** ....Order #A56143

*A Step-by-Step Approach to Using the SAS®
System for Factor Analysis and Structural
Equation Modeling*
by **Larry Hatcher** ....Order #A55129

*A Step-by-Step Approach to Using the SAS®
System for Univariate and Multivariate Statistics*
by **Larry Hatcher**
and **Edward Stepanski** ....Order #A55072

*Table-Driven Strategies for Rapid SAS®
Applications Development*
by **Tanya Kolosova**
and **Samuel Berestizhevsky** ....Order #A55198

Working with the SAS® System
by **Erik W. Tilanus**..............................Order #A55190

Audio Tapes

100 Essential SAS® Software Concepts (set of two)
by **Rick Aster** ....Order #A55309

A Look At SAS® Files (set of two)
by **Rick Aster** ....Order #A55207